FOR KING AND COUNTRY

This is a groundbreaking history of the British monarchy in the First World War and of the social and cultural functions of monarchism in the British war effort. Heather Jones examines how the conflict changed British cultural attitudes to the monarchy, arguing that the conflict ultimately helped to consolidate the crown's sacralised status. She looks at how the monarchy engaged with war recruitment, bereavement and gender norms, as well as at its political and military powers and its relationship with Ireland and the empire. She considers the role that monarchism played in military culture and examines royal visits to the front, as well as the monarchy's role in home front morale and in interwar war commemoration. Her findings suggest that the rise of republicanism in wartime Britain has been overestimated and that war commemoration was central to the monarchy's revered interwar status up to the abdication crisis.

HEATHER JONES is Professor of Modern and Contemporary European History at University College London. An expert on the First World War, her previous publications include *Violence against Prisoners of War in the First World War: Britain, France and Germany, 1914–1920* (2011). She is a former Max Weber Fellow of the European University Institute and is a director of the International Research Centre of the Historial de la Grande Guerre, Péronne. She has been awarded the Irish Research Council's Eda Sagarra Gold Medal.

Studies in the Social and Cultural History of Modern Warfare

General Editors
Robert Gerwarth, *University College Dublin*
Jay Winter, *Yale University*

Advisory Editors
Heather Jones, *University College London*
Rana Mitter, *University of Oxford*
Michelle Moyd, *Indiana University Bloomington*
Martin Thomas, *University of Exeter*

In recent years the field of modern history has been enriched by the exploration of two parallel histories. These are the social and cultural history of armed conflict, and the impact of military events on social and cultural history.

Studies in the Social and Cultural History of Modern Warfare presents the fruits of this growing area of research, reflecting both the colonisation of military history by cultural historians and the reciprocal interest of military historians in social and cultural history, to the benefit of both. The series offers the latest scholarship in European and non-European events from the 1850s to the present day.

A full list of titles in the series can be found at:
www.cambridge.org/modernwarfare

FOR KING AND COUNTRY

The British Monarchy and the First World War

HEATHER JONES

University College London

CAMBRIDGE
UNIVERSITY PRESS

CAMBRIDGE
UNIVERSITY PRESS

University Printing House, Cambridge CB2 8BS, United Kingdom

One Liberty Plaza, 20th Floor, New York, NY 10006, USA

477 Williamstown Road, Port Melbourne, VIC 3207, Australia

314–321, 3rd Floor, Plot 3, Splendor Forum, Jasola District Centre,
New Delhi – 110025, India

103 Penang Road, #05–06/07, Visioncrest Commercial, Singapore 238467

Cambridge University Press is part of the University of Cambridge.

It furthers the University's mission by disseminating knowledge in the pursuit of
education, learning, and research at the highest international levels of excellence.

www.cambridge.org
Information on this title: www.cambridge.org/9781108429368
DOI: 10.1017/9781108554619

© Heather Jones 2021

First published 2021

Printed in the United Kingdom by TJ Books Limited, Padstow Cornwall

A catalogue record for this publication is available from the British Library.

Library of Congress Cataloging-in-Publication Data
Names: Jones, Heather, 1978– author.
Title: For king and country : the British monarchy and the First World War / Heather Jones,
University College London.
Description: First edition. | New York : Cambridge University Press, 2021. | Series: Studies in
the social and cultural history of modern warfare | Includes bibliographical references and
index.
Identifiers: LCCN 2021006787 (print) | LCCN 2021006788 (ebook) | ISBN 9781108429368
(hardback) | ISBN 9781108554619 (ebook)
Subjects: LCSH: Windsor, House of. | World War, 1914–1918 – Great Britain. | Monarchy –
Great Britain – History – 20th century. | Great Britain–Kings and rulers – History – 20th
century. | Great Britain – Politics and government – 20th century. | BISAC: HISTORY /
Europe / Great Britain / General | HISTORY / Europe / Great Britain / General
Classification: LCC DA28.35.W54 J66 2021 (print) | LCC DA28.35.W54 (ebook) | DDC
940.3/410922–dc23
LC record available at https://lccn.loc.gov/2021006787
LC ebook record available at https://lccn.loc.gov/2021006788

ISBN 978-1-108-42936-8 Hardback

CONTENTS

FIGURES

TABLE

ACKNOWLEDGEMENTS

In researching and writing this book, I have been helped by the generosity and knowledge of many archivists, librarians, fellow historians and students. It has been my good fortune to work with some of the leading cultural historians of the First World War – John Horne, Jay Winter, Annette Becker, Alan Kramer and Stéphane Audoin-Rouzeau – who have encouraged me in this project and inspired with their own work in equal measure. John and Alan deserve a special note of gratitude as they mentored my undergraduate and doctoral studies and have been my teachers and colleagues for over twenty years. Laurence Van Ypersele kindly shared her own expertise on the Belgian monarchy in the First World War. Others helped by offering the chance to test out some of the ideas of this book. Hew Strachan provided a crucial opportunity to develop some of the ideas in this study through a conference invitation in 2018 and subsequent paper publication. Sophie de Schaepdrijver helped me to crystallise my thoughts on monarchy and gender by inviting me to present at the University of Kent while Mathilde von Bulow invited me to the University of Glasgow. James McConnel allowed me to trial my arguments on wartime monarchy at Northumbria University; Christoph Mick enabled me to present parts of this book to the Modern European Research Seminar at Warwick University; Philip Mansell kindly invited me to present my ideas to the Society for Court Studies; Christopher Clark and Tim Rogan helpfully invited me to present at Cambridge University and discussed ideas for the book in detail. Gary Sheffield, Matthew Stibbe, Claire Shaw, Mark Connelly, Brian Walker, Jonathan Boff, Dennis Wardleworth, Judith Rowbotham, Ana Carden-Coyne, Frédéric Hadley, Alan Fidler and Jenny Macleod offered invaluable source advice, support, sources or suggestions at key moments. Jonathan Lewis kindly allowed me to cite his unpublished thesis. Among those historians whose conversations have advanced and encouraged this study, I would particularly like to thank Alison Fell, Catriona Pennell, Max Jones, Richard Grayson, Santanu Das, Aimée Fox, Adrian Gregory, John Röhl, Annika Mombauer, Alexander Watson, Edward Madigan, Sven Oliver Müller, Daniel Steinbach, Nicolas Beaupré, Franziska Heimburger, Arndt Weinrich, Pierre Purseigle, William Philpott, Dominic Lieven, George

Morton-Jack and the late, much missed, Clare Makepeace. This book was greatly improved by enjoyable conversations with a number of fellow monarchy historians – Edward Owens, Heidi Mehrkens, Matthew Glencross, Frank Lorenz Müller, Frank Mort and Axel Körner. Philip Williamson and Frank Mort both kindly read extracts and suggested a number of important amendments; John Horne and Mark Jones generously read final drafts. I am immensely grateful for their suggestions.

Earlier extracts from Chapters 1 and 2 appeared as Heather Jones, 'The Nature of Kingship in First World War Britain' in Matthew Glencross, Judith Rowbotham and Michael Kandiah, eds., *The Windsor Dynasty, 1910 to the Present: 'Long to Reign over Us?'* (London, 2016), pp. 195–216; Heather Jones, 'A Prince in the Trenches? Edward VIII and the First World War' in Heidi Merkhens and Frank Lorenz Müller, eds., *Sons and Heirs: Succession and Political Culture in 19th Century Europe* (Basingstoke, 2015), pp. 229–46. This book also benefited from the opportunity in 2017 to script and present a BBC Radio 4 documentary on the First World War experiences of the future Edward VIII; producer Mark Burman provided many helpful sources and suggestions. My fellow convenors of the War, Society and Culture Seminar at the Institute of Historical Research have offered a welcome forum for debate and discussion. The two anonymous readers for Cambridge University Press provided crucial comments; this book is all the better for them. My editor at CUP, Michael Watson, has safely steered this project to publication; my sincere thanks to him, Jane Burkowski, Tanya Izzard Melissa Ward, Jayavel Radhakrishnan and Emily Sharp for all their help. The usual disclaimer applies that any errors that may remain are my own responsibility.

The British Library has proved a wonderful haven in which to research and write. The Royal Archives very kindly fielded my many queries and helpfully allowed me access to consult a number of key documents, including the wartime diaries of King George V, Queen Mary and the Prince of Wales, the later Edward VIII. In particular, I would like to thank Pamela Clark, Julie Crocker and Laura Hobbs for their painstaking work in locating documents and their generosity with their time and support. All extracts from the Royal Archives are reproduced here by gracious permission of Her Majesty Queen Elizabeth II. The staff of the following archives and libraries also assisted this book either in person or by email; I am extremely grateful to them: The Churchill Archives Centre, Churchill College, Cambridge; the Imperial War Museum and, in particular, Suzanne Bardgett and Alan Wakefield; the Lincolnshire Archives; the Commonwealth War Graves Commission Archive and, in particular, former CWGC historian Glyn Prysor; the Bodleian Libraries, Oxford; Cambridge University Library; the Lambeth Palace Library; Dublin City Library and Archive; the National Library of Ireland and, in particular, Glenn Dunne and Berni Metcalfe; the Essex Record Office; the National Archives at Kew; the Liddle Collection at Leeds

University Library; Southampton University Library; St Bartholomew's Hospital Museum and Archives, London and, in particular, Dan Heather; the Liddell Hart Centre for Military Archives at King's College London; Newcastle University Library Special Collections and Archives; the Parliamentary Archives; the Templer Study Centre at the National Army Museum; Trinity College Library, University of Dublin; the Mary Evans Picture Library and, in particular, Jessica Talmage and Lucinda Gosling; the UK Government Art Collection (GACS); and the staff of The Keep at Sussex University Library. Bette Baldwin and Phil Curme of Clevedon Pier and Heritage Trust Archives and Michael Pegum of www .irishwarmemorials.ie were fantastic in helping me to include images from their collections here. I would also like to thank Jasper Olivier and the Estate of Herbert Arnould Olivier. The Historial de la Grande Guerre at Péronne provided a number of sources, and my fellow directors of its International Centre for the Research of the First World War continue to inspire; Caroline Fontaine merits a special word of thanks for her deft management support, as well as Marie-Pascale Prévost-Bault and Christine Cazé. Every effort has been made to trace copyright holders and to obtain their permission for the use of copyright material. The author apologises for any omissions and correction and acknowledgement will be made in any future reprints or editions of this book.

Much of this book was researched during my time at the Department of International History at the London School of Economics and Political Science, where I benefited from the outstanding First World War knowledge of David Stevenson and Alan Sked and from collegial support from all of the department. It is not possible to list everyone here, but Matthew Jones, Janet Hartley, Nigel Ashton, Tanya Harmer, Paul Keenan, David Motadel, Taylor Sherman, Paul Stock, Kristina Spohr, Demetra Frini, Nayna Bhatti and Milada Fomina merit a special mention of thanks. This book was completed in the congenial surroundings of the History Department at University College London. I would like to thank UCL for supporting this project to completion and, in particular, Nicola Miller, Eleanor Robson, Margot Finn, Johanna Dale, Iain Stewart and Michael Collins. My students, at undergraduate, taught Masters and doctoral levels, at both the LSE and at UCL, have provided constant intellectual stimulation and ideas; they continue to make me a better historian. I would particularly like to thank my current and former doctoral students Alex Mayhew, Ian Stewart, Tommaso Milani, Mahon Murphy, Giovanni Graglia, Chloe Pieters, Nick Sorrie, Yorai Linenberg, Artemis Photiadou, Chris Batten and my MA student Nicole Souders for valuable discussions.

I owe my brother, the historian Mark Jones, a debt of gratitude that goes well beyond our history discussions. To Ulrike Ruemer, Luke and Ben Jones, my thanks for the many blessings of family. My grateful thanks also to Louie and

Constantina Loizou for all their help. This book was produced against a background of very significant personal events. My wonderful parents Valerie and Stuart Jones did not live to see its completion; their loss is keenly felt and this book owes much to their lifetime of love and care. While working on this book, my life was immeasurably enriched by the birth of two beautiful, beloved children, Evelyn and Patrick. This book is dedicated to my husband Nicholas, without whose tireless support, love and true partnership neither it, nor so much else, would have ever been possible.

Introduction

On 4 August 2014, the United Kingdom marked the centenary of the outbreak of the First World War with three major ceremonies – a service at Glasgow Cathedral to commemorate the Commonwealth contribution to the war effort, a vigil at Westminster Abbey and a moving twilight ceremony at St Symphorien Military Cemetery near Mons in Belgium. At each of these solemn events, the British monarchy was prominently represented: Prince Charles attended in Glasgow; the Duchess of Cornwall was at Westminster Abbey; and the younger generation of royals, Prince William, his wife Catherine, the Duchess of Cambridge, and Prince Harry, took part in the St Symphorien commemoration. The three younger royals, together with Prince Charles and his wife, performed a similar role at the centenary ceremony at Thiepval, marking the start of the Battle of the Somme, on 1 July 2016. One hundred years on from the start of the war, the British monarchy took the central part in representing the nations of the United Kingdom and the Commonwealth in honouring the war dead.

Yet, while the monarchy remains visibly at the heart of British First World War commemoration, it is largely absent from the historiography of the conflict. This study is the first academic monograph on the British monarchy's role during the First World War and the first to explore the social and cultural functions of monarchism in the British war effort.[1] Historians of monarchy have largely focused upon either the 'long' nineteenth century, ending with the outbreak of the war in 1914, or upon individual reigns in which the war receives cursory treatment as only a background context for royal biography.[2] Notably David Cannadine's seminal essay on the British monarchy and the 'invention of tradition' skips the war in its focus upon four phases: 1820–70; 1877–1914; 1918–53; and the period between Queen Elizabeth II's coronation and her jubilee.[3] Historians studying popular opposition to the British monarchy and its response, such as Antony Taylor, do discuss the conflict, but almost entirely focus on 1917 and the impact of the Russian Revolution upon the monarchy, especially the question of asylum for the Russian Tsar and his family, and the name change to Windsor.[4] Frank Prochaska's key article on 'republicanism' in Britain likewise focuses on 1917.[5]

These works generally ask the same question – why did the British monarchy survive the First World War? – and concur in their answer: that the British monarchy was already in a process of long-term modernisation and democratisation from the nineteenth century into which the war fitted. Frank Prochaska, for example, argues that Britain was already effectively a 'crowned republic' by 1914 due to the stripping away of royal power that had previously taken place and that, from the late Victorian period, the monarchy turned to philanthropy to sustain its popularity, becoming a 'welfare' monarchy.[6] He argues the war further catalysed modernisation processes and emphasises the successful strategies of royal political impartiality that George V and his advisors chose and the monarchy's increasing visibility and democratisation during the conflict.[7] Frank Mort suggests that George V profoundly modernised the monarchy before the First World War by investing in 'new styles of royal accessibility' to combat the challenge of labour militancy and the rise of mass politics to project, through successful media management, 'a different relationship between sovereign and people'.[8] He also highlights how George V pioneered royal political impartiality and his 1912 and 1913 tours, with Queen Mary, of Welsh and northern English industrial areas. Edward Owens looks at how the monarchy modernised its relationship with modern media, while Vernon Bogdanor focuses on a modernising narrative in which the Crown ceded 'power and partisanship' for more neutral, detached influence.[9] All of this important work on the monarchy's modernisation has profoundly inspired this book. Yet, it also triggered questions: how did the clearly delineated, long-term modernisation of the monarchy that these studies show interact with older ideas about royalty? And what was the impact of cataclysmic 'total war' in 1914–18 upon this process?[10]

The emphasis on the long-term history of modernisation of the monarchy means that the First World War generally only appears – if at all – as another historical accelerator among many factors or subsumed into a broader biographical narrative about George V's reign.[11] Even in those few cases where historians of monarchy have examined the war more closely, they have continued to focus on modernisation. The recent volume *Monarchies and the Great War*, edited by Matthew Glencross and Judith Rowbotham, has two chapters dedicated to the British monarchy: one a diplomatic history of King George V's visits to the Western Front, the other a social history of Queen Mary's charitable war work; both put forward the modernisation of monarchy paradigm outlined above.[12] In 2018, Alexandra Churchill published a popular history of King George V at war which emphasises his importance in modernising the monarchy. While it is not an academic work, it contains many useful and important revelations of new primary source material on aspects of the king's role that have not been documented in the existing historiography, thanks to the access she was granted by the Royal Archives.[13]

However, it is a fair assertion that the British monarchy and British monarchism during the First World War is still a largely unresearched academic subject, and its cultural history virtually non-existent.[14] As Frank Mort has argued, 'the issue of cultural expression has been a significant focus for recent historians of the Great War, but until recently it has been largely absent from studies of popular responses to the modern British monarchy'.[15] Mort's 2020 article on public responses to the wartime monarchy is a rare attempt to redress this. It looks at monarchy 'as part of the routines and emotional fabric of ordinary lives', and argues that 'the outpouring of opinions about George V and his family during the Great War' allow us to map responses to the monarchy and achieve a 'clearer assessment of the effectiveness of royal experiments in accessibility and democratization'.[16] Mort finds that the war promoted a more modern royal 'accessibility'.[17] Yet as Andrzej Olechnowicz has argued, historians have focused more readily on how the British monarchy modernised rather than on popular perceptions of it: '"the assimilation of the monarchy into individual subjectivities" is still unexplored'.[18] If, as Benedict Anderson has convincingly argued, the rise of modern nationalism saw nations function as 'imagined communities', it seems pertinent to consider the role that the British monarchy and monarchism played in the collective wartime imagination of British identity.[19]

Overall, the war itself has never been studied in detail in its own terms as an exceptional, specific, four-and-a-half-year-long episode of national and imperial crisis and totalising warfare which set up particular dynamics with regard to the British monarchy and saw it operate in very different ways to peacetime. This book argues that the war not only accelerated powerful, nascent modernising languages about the British monarchy – as democratic and accessible – but also reconfigured traditional representations of the king and queen, and led to the reconstruction of the popular image of the monarchy in freshly mythologised, sacralised ways that contributed to its meaning and purpose, and its survival, which were embedded with older concepts of honour, duty, religion and service. Moreover, in wartime in 1914–18, the king had greater powers than in peacetime – cultural, but also military and political – as this study shows. It argues that in wartime, modernisation processes *coexisted*, often symbiotically, with much more archaic cultures of honour codes, dynastic leadership, royal myth and romanticisation which the war rejuvenated; the conflict does not fit seamlessly into a modernisation narrative. This reflects the findings of studies on other aspects of the conflict, such as war mourning.[20] Generation was a factor here: by 1914 George V and his Queen were middle-aged. They had been socialised in nineteenth-century values regarding monarchy and were steeped in older belief systems concerning tradition, the religious role of the king and class cultures, as well as duty, honour and other leadership virtues.

This is a book about the sacralisation discourses built around the British monarchy in the Great War, how they operated and were perceived and to what extent they were challenged. Its primary purpose is to explore what the role of the British monarchy during the war tells us about the *cultural meanings* of the monarchy at the time and how the war affected them. It asks if the monarchy and monarchism did indeed matter in wartime, then in what ways – cultural, social, political, military – did this significance manifest itself? And what does this tell us about the nature of the First World War United Kingdom and British identity? These are largely new questions. As Frank Mort has argued, 'research on British patriotism has tended to infer, rather than demonstrate, the effectiveness of monarchy's appeal as a symbol of national unity'.[21]

This study thus differs to the existing historiography in a number of regards. Not only does it adopt a cultural history methodology, but it also gives full weight to all the war years, as without covering the conflict in full, the 1917 moment lacks context.[22] It also analyses the war's aftermath and its legacy for the monarchy into the interwar period, as well as integrating the transnational historiography: it is difficult to assert why the British monarchy survived without incorporating the broader European wartime context. Victory mattered – defeated monarchies were much more likely to collapse – but so too did royal behaviour: perceptions of personal conduct played key roles in popular hostility to the ill-fated Tsarina Alexandra of Russia, Kaiser Wilhelm II of Germany and his son Crown Prince Wilhelm and King Constantine of Greece. Individual royal personal sensitivity to wartime public expectations was an important factor in a monarchy's outcome. Unusually for studies of the British monarchy, this book also reintegrates the history of Ireland, which is often treated separately.[23]

Interwar British attitudes of reverence to the monarchy which lasted until the 1936 abdication crisis are inexplicable without understanding its First World War role. This book suggests that the modernisation narrative in historiography on the British monarchy, while very important, has its limits: it sets out to explore the relationship between older sacralising languages and cultures of monarchy and the ways in which these survived into, or were even revived by the First World War, in tandem with modernisation. It also considers how new challenges due to the war led to the creation of innovative sacralising royal rituals. Moreover, it suggests that many of the changes historians have pointed to as signs of the monarchy's increasing 'modernity' – its greater visibility, through visits to war factories and shipyards, hospitals and troop inspections and through photography and film – were intended to promote archaic ideas about the direct, personal subject–sovereign relationship of loyalty and duty as drivers of war service, belief systems which were also widespread among those populations the royals visited. The means adopted for publicising royal visits may have been more modern, but their purpose was frequently about sustaining much older monarchist value systems and ensuring they were at the heart of the war effort and society. This also accounts for their success: the wartime monarchy presented itself as a monarchy built on a specific kind of royal leadership – with strong Protestant overtones – that promoted the values of honour, duty, humility, religion, dynastic loyalty and service. These were recognisably familiar, older norms, and this proved very popular with a wartime public, disorientated and often frightened by the scale and rapidity of the social changes the conflict was bringing.

In many respects, the monarchy projected itself as representing reassuring continuity during the war. Even the royal wartime acceptance of the need for greater democracy, and promotion of the narrative of a 'democratic' British monarchy, was based upon an ideal of the king treating all his loyal subjects equally and a concomitant promotion of the monarchy as the core foundation of empire. None of this was particularly 'modern'. The monarchy's most important role by the end of the conflict was honouring the war dead who had died in its name; the scale of this role was new and the means used often innovative, such as the burial of the Unknown Soldier, but the concept behind it, the royal recognition of war service by loyal subjects, was not. It was the processes of royal 'sacralisation' that the war unleashed that ultimately explain why, as Edward Owens has shown, by the mid-1930s, 'the crown occupied a near-sacred place in national life'.[24] David Starkey has argued its supporters rendered it virtually a secular religion, while Philip Murphy refers to the cult of the interwar monarchy as 'British Shintoism'.[25] Jay Winter has argued that the conflict led to a resurgence in traditional cultural motifs for understanding conflict and loss; in Britain, the royal role in mourning the war dead was a central part of this process.[26]

If historians of monarchy have only very partially addressed the war, academic historians of the conflict have generally ignored the British monarchy completely.[27] This is partly because the focus since the social and cultural turns of the 1960s and 1980s respectively has been away from political history – the subfield of history which, until the 1960s, had been considered most relevant to the wartime monarchy – and partly because the history of elites has declined in prominence as a focus for war historians more generally during the past forty years.[28] These factors help to explain why the British monarchy has been largely ignored in the new wave of cultural historiography of the First World War.[29] This gap also applies to the history of the British monarchy and twentieth-century conflict as a whole, which, as historian David Cannadine has highlighted, has so far 'gone largely unexplored'.[30]

However, changes in historiographical trends alone do not entirely explain the gap: after all, the historiography of British wartime generals, another elite, has not suffered from similar academic neglect by First World War historians, nor has the German monarchy.[31] In fact, Kaiser Wilhelm II, the Prussian court and wartime German royal dynasties in general have been subjected to detailed academic scrutiny.[32] Other factors have clearly contributed, such as the ongoing association of royal biography in Britain with non-academic, popular history, the inaccurate image of George V as a staid, stamp-collecting figure less interesting than his predecessors, Queen Victoria and King Edward VII, or successor Edward VIII, and problems of access to sources.[33] The history of the Royal Archives at Windsor Castle and the Great War merits its own study.[34] Royal papers have an obvious sensitivity: one of the roles of King George V's Private Secretary Lord Stamfordham was to ensure that when one of the royal family's close correspondents died, the fate of the royal letters they had received was carefully managed, because, as he wrote in 1919 to the family of the late Bishop of Ripon, 'unfortunately from time to time Their Majesties have painful experiences of family letters being exposed for sale'.[35] Such letters were to be destroyed or returned to the Royal Archives; in cases where they were retained by descendants, the Royal Archives were often consulted regarding who had access to them, even after they were donated to other archive repositories. This was the case for some of Prime Minister Stanley Baldwin's correspondence held at Cambridge University Library relating to the 1936 abdication, and remains so for certain of Alan 'Tommy' Lascelles's papers at the Churchill Archives Centre, Cambridge.[36] As with any letters, legally copyright rests with the author. In other words, the Royal Archives at Windsor are a private archive and follow the norms governing granting access to private family papers, not official state archival material; several other European monarchies follow similar practices, while others are now part of state archives.[37] Until very recently the Royal Archives' policy was to grant access on a case-by-case basis and only archivists – not researchers – have access to the inventories. The Royal Archives is now reviewing its access policy, the principles of which can be viewed at www.royal.uk/archives.[38] In previous generations, figures such as Lascelles, a former Keeper of the Royal Archives, also destroyed 'documents that reflected badly' on royal figures or the monarchy.[39] This particular archival history may also be a factor in the major historiographical gaps in the academic study of the twentieth-century British monarchy which are only now beginning to be addressed by historians.[40]

Another important factor was the monarchy's own desire to play up certain aspects of its war role and marginalise others as public opinion towards the conflict changed. By 1919, it was much more prudent to emphasise the monarchy's wartime charitable aid than how monarchism had been utilised to promote voluntary recruitment in 1914–16, for example. After the war George V was not keen for his political and military influence during the conflict to be known, according to historian Ian Beckett: 'Understandably, it was also certainly the King's wish that much of his own role in events should remain concealed. Thus, George V appears, if at all, in the major postwar memoirs very much on the periphery, visiting munitions factories, making an occasional national appeal, or setting an example by his pledge of wartime abstinence.'[41]

There has also been a lack of engagement with innovations in the historiography of Continental European monarchies, where a cultural, and indeed a transnational approach has emerged, rejuvenating monarchy history, which has not yet fed into new work on twentieth-century British monarchy.[42] Moreover, while Wilhelm II has received enormous attention from academic historians, his cousin, George V, and the role of the British monarchy, has remained remarkably overlooked.[43] This greater historiographical profile has ensured cultural history approaches have been applied to studying the German 'court' and royal social and gender roles, issues that this book is the first to explore for the British 1914–18 case.[44] In the European context, this greater academic attention is also due to the fact that monarchism was a very live, legitimised and visible *political* creed in the years leading up to 1914, which existed alongside the other 'isms' of the period, such as socialism and liberalism, as the question of to how to organise a modern state became increasingly debated. Britain at the time was aware of these questions in other countries, and figures such as Reginald Brett, Lord Esher, Deputy Constable and Lieutenant Governor of Windsor Castle, a long-term key court advisor, were influenced by them.[45] There was also discussion in the public sphere as to whether Prussian-German 'direct' monarchical government was more modern than Britain's more constitutionally limited version.[46] At a European level, monarchical rule was seen as a valid state organisational system – dynastic government was common to many states prior to the outbreak of war, but did not often survive the challenges that the conflict raised; the new ideologies of democracy and socialism had largely triumphed over such political monarchism by 1918, although it lingered on in some right-wing schools of thought which advocated varieties of authoritarianism, some of which made space for direct monarchical government. For example, the right-wing, radical conservative Carl Schmitt, in his 1922 work *Political Theology: Four Chapters on the Concept of Sovereignty* and his 1928 book *Constitutional Theory*, considered the meaning and purpose of authoritarian monarchical models.[47] However, the few European monarchies in belligerent states that survived the war did so largely as symbolic constitutionally limited entities, stripped of direct political interference with or control over government, with a few arguable exceptions such as the Yugoslav case. In contrast, the end of the war saw the British orchestrate the foundation of a string of politically interventionist monarchies across the Middle East, for example, in Iraq, suggesting that post-war, for key British bureaucrats, the idea of a politically powerful monarchism still had a hold on their thinking, even as in Europe it was disappearing. There has also been a wave of cultural histories of how national leadership mythologies were configured around key European historical figures.[48] The methodology of these studies serves as a useful model, as kingship in First World War Britain lends itself to similar kinds of analysis.

Yet, perhaps the most significant factor has been social change: the decline by the 1990s in those very cultures of class deference, which had so marked the First World War era, meant that historians often simply did not consider the British monarchy – or monarchism – a significant wartime cultural factor worth exploring. It is all too easy to miss the cultural trappings that held greater weight in past societies or operated in different ways. The monarchy was one of these. In the First World War, an age of deference, class culture and religious practice – even if all of these were increasingly contested by the start of the twentieth century – the meaning of monarchy was obviously constructed and perceived differently to today.[49] As William Kuhn has argued, monarchy, and royal ceremonial in particular, represent what cultural anthropologists describe as communities of people speaking 'about themselves to themselves' through central rituals that are 'unusually communicative about the implicit beliefs that underlie their common social life. On these ritual occasions some members of society symbolize what they believe to be essential ideas in their cultural life both for their own benefit and the benefit of others.'[50] The British monarchy in the Great War exemplifies this. Moreover, borrowing from the historian Robert Darnton, the most 'strange' historic occurrences can help us 'to unravel an alien system of meaning'.[51] In other words, where monarchist rituals or beliefs become visible during the Great War in ways that appear odd, inexplicable or jarring with the purported modernity of the conflict, they can be especially revealing. As Roger Chartier writes, one can gain entry into cultures of the past through 'a seemingly incomprehensible, "opaque" rite, text, or act'.[52] David Blackbourn's work on the nineteenth-century Marpingen apparitions offers an exemplary lesson: we should never assume that people in the past did not believe what they claimed to believe so as to dismiss those of their beliefs that perhaps do not match modern sensibilities.[53]

This study draws upon the Annales School's 'history of mentalities' approach, as well as on the new cultural historiography of the First World War.[54] Peter Burke has pointed out how diverse the practice of 'cultural history' now is and how difficult it is to define it: 'one solution to the problem of defining cultural history might be to switch attention from the objects to the methods of study. [...] The common ground of cultural historians might be described as a concern with the symbolic and its interpretation.'[55] The Annales history of mentalities has been described by Lynn Hunt as the study of ideological systems or collective cultural repre-sentations in societies which act themselves as constituents – and even determinants – of social reality.[56] In this approach, 'economic and social relations are not prior to or determining of cultural ones; they are them-selves fields of cultural practice and cultural production'.[57] In other words, the representations of the British monarchy in wartime reflected not only the actions of the royal family and the court but also a collective belief system of meanings that were commonly held about monarchy, including by royals themselves. Behaviour was a product of cultural beliefs and also constituent of them. The study of monarchism here is further inspired by Reinhart Koselleck's pioneering idea of *Begriffsgeschichte*, which encourages historians to explore the history of concepts and their past understanding.[58] It also draws upon the history of emotions – how emotional attachments to the monarchy contributed to individual behaviours: as Daniela Saxer puts it: 'History contributes studies about emotional regimes and ideals that trace long-term historical changes in emotions as well as historically distinct configurations of emotional expression and emotional agency in specific social contexts.'[59] The monarchy is a good example of a form of social 'emotional expression' during the Great War.

Obviously, in an era before public opinion surveys, investigating the cultural meanings of the monarchy raises methodological problems. The source base for this period is skewed towards elites, who were more literate and more powerful in the public sphere; it is difficult to assess how representative they were of broader public attitudes. Moreover, as Andrzej Olechnowicz has pointed out, the existing historiography on the British monarchy overwhelmingly adopts a 'top-down' approach; 'ordinary people's perspectives' have been overlooked.[60] Press reports in the Great War also largely followed a deferential code: their value lies principally in analysing them to see what discourses they were presenting to the public about the monarchy and monarchism. They often operated out of the very cultural constraints of those monarchist beliefs that they also present. Some pro-monarchy stories were also 'planted' by elite figures: for example, Walter Lawrence, the commissioner for wounded and sick Indian soldiers in France and England, 1914–18, wrote an anonymous article praising the queen in *The Indiaman* in July 1915 and was thanked by the king's Private Secretary.[61]

Yet newspapers should not be dismissed as simply official mouthpieces either. Lothar Reinermann in his study found that 'interventions by British government or court officials into newspaper politics were very rare indeed. [...] Freedom of the press was regarded as too fundamental a part of the British way of life.'[62] For the new tabloid press, which 'revolutionized the British journalistic scene in the late nineteenth century', notably the right-wing *Daily Mail*, founded in 1896, the purpose was 'emotionalizing its readership', and presenting particular emotional languages around monarchy was pivotal to this.[63] The press was thus a key force in determining understandings of monarchy. Human interest, sentimental tales of the royals in the Great War sold, something that provides us with insights into what the public liked to read, as much as about how the monarchy wanted to be portrayed. As Catriona Pennell points out, newspapers not only sought to influence public opinion, but also to record and mirror it in order to increase their readership and financially survive.[64] Press sources often reveal popular hegemonic discourses: what was considered acceptable and normative in wartime culture.

Yet the monarchy was also one of what James Joll termed the 'unspoken assumptions' of the 1914–18 British world, which, like most of Europe, was influenced by older honour cultures, not always overtly clarified or explained in written sources.[65] As historian Maarten Van Ginderachter explains: 'when searching for sources that go "beyond" the official rhetoric', historians are 'likely to be confronted with heuristic problems. Documents in which ordinary citizens themselves talk directly to or about "their" royal family are not that widespread.'[66] Even when written sources by ordinary people refer to monarchy, there is 'always an influence of the hegemonic public transcript', what James C. Scott describes as 'the way in which the subordinate publicly address the dominant'.[67] This is particularly the case in any letters from ordinary people which have survived in the Royal Archives, which often make appeals 'that remain within the official discourse of deference'.[68] To what extent such sources reflect the authors' actual individual attitudes beyond standard dominant cultural norms is thus difficult to assess. And as Andrzej Olechnowicz points out, there are questions about how representative such letters are of broader society.[69] Moreover, are they merely 'public transcripts', what Scott terms open interactions 'between subordinates and those who dominate' that reflect back the '*self*-portrait of dominant elites as they would have themselves seen'?[70] Can such letters contain 'hidden transcripts' – 'low-profile forms of resistance' couched in deferential cultural norms?[71] Any reading of such sources requires being alert to these issues. Nevertheless, this study considers that written sources on the monarchy by ordinary people, when analysed carefully, can help us understand personal attitudes and beliefs as well as collective norms.

Moreover, the fact that ordinary people wrote to the monarch is, in itself, revealing. As George V's official biographer Harold Nicolson states, the king received large numbers of letters from ordinary people during the war, which he usually instructed his secretaries to pass on to the government department concerned:

> the King was deluged by a flood of private correspondence. His loyal subjects appear to have regarded him both as the arbiter of justice and the vehicle of bright ideas. He would receive letters, from responsible as well as irresponsible quarters, discoursing upon such varied themes as the administration of the National Relief Fund, the bad relations existing between the Red Cross and the Royal Army Medical Corps, the alleged pro-German utterances of the Head Master of Eton, [...] the visits of society ladies and other tourists to Head Quarters in France [...].[72]

Queen Mary also received letters from the public.[73] It remains unclear how much of this material has survived. Where it has been possible to consult, it provides real insight into the monarchist values of the period.

Assessing how royal figures themselves understood the wartime role of monarchy offers a particularly valuable insight into monarchist culture and its functions but is dependent on ego-documents such as royal diaries. Such sources raise problems of subjectivity, as they, as Mary Fulbrook and Ulinka Rublack have argued, tell us about 'relational personhood' – the idea that ego-documents like diaries are produced for specific purposes with particular audiences in mind and constrained and shaped by social conventions as to what can be expressed or addressed: 'the very notion of a consistent ego or self' in a diary must thus 'be problematized'.[74] Yet here too the source record is not complete. A central figure in shaping the wartime monarchy, Arthur John Bigge, Lord Stamfordham, Private Secretary to King George V, often developed ideas and gathered information through private conversations with his impressive range of contacts; we have written accounts of only some of these encounters.

The centrality of the monarchy to the war effort also should not be assumed. The neglect in the historiography of the monarchy and monarchism during the Great War years may simply stem from the fact that overall it was not that important. The rationale for this book is that the monarchy's significance in the Great War cannot be presumed or discounted but must be carefully assessed across the different war years. This allows us to pick up on fluctuations and change in the monarchy's status and meaning across the war, although pinpointing the origins of historical changes in cultural attitudes is notoriously difficult.[75] It requires using a wide range of sources and drawing upon evidence from the war years but also their aftermath, with all the obvious methodological risk entailed in cross-referencing wartime material with post-war accounts.

To navigate some of these methodological issues, this study draws on the work of Michel Foucault, who argued that all cultural discourses are revealing of power structures.[76] As Jeroen Deploige and Gita Deneckere put it:

> concrete historical work benefits from Foucauldian theories that emphasize the ways in which discourse is tied to institutions and social practices. [...] The linguistic turn is in a sense giving way to a 'historical turn' that remains informed by discourse theory but draws the attention away from questions of representation and back to sites of social practice, conceptualized as the effect of discursive formations that themselves undergo constant processes of change.[77]

In other words, discourses or representations of monarchy during the war related closely to its actual powers and practices – political, social, economic, cultural – and we need to look at this interaction. Jan Rüger's seminal work *The Great Naval Game: Britain and Germany in the Age of Empire*,[78] which explores how navies projected power through cultural display – inspections, visual light spectacles, ship launches and the press – offers a model here. Eva

Giloi's book which explores material cultures of monarchy in Germany – how objects presented and promoted monarchism – is another.[79] As Andrzej Olechnowicz points out, 'the "royalness" of material culture and its impact is another area that requires much further research' for the British case.[80]

This research has much wider implications. The monarchy offers a wide-ranging, unparalleled case study that helps us to examine broader, major questions in First World War and British historiography. One key debate in the existing historiography of monarchy is, how did long-term modernisation occur? David Cannadine has argued that the monarchy adapted to major historical changes by presenting modern innovations as 'traditions'.[81] In contrast, William Kuhn has argued that the monarchy more often renovated existing traditions rather than inventing them as Cannadine suggests, through the renewal of existing or latent royal practices and beliefs.[82] Cannadine's 'invention of tradition' thesis, published in 1983, was closely linked to broader modernisation debates in the late twentieth century about the long- or short-term origins of modern nationalism, by Ernest Gellner, Benedict Anderson, Antony D. Smith and others.[83] By looking in detail at the First World War years, this book shows that both processes existed – invention of tradition and renovation of tradition – and *interacted*. The war saw the renewal and revival of existing, older remnants of monarchical traditions and beliefs, as well as the invention of completely new ones which were given the patina of archaism through the use of the monarchy, such as the burial of the Unknown Soldier in 1920. What matters is less whether a royal cultural practice was of old or new origin but rather the wartime fluctuations in the sacralisation function of the monarchy itself – how it provided a cultural symbolic, of language, artefacts and ceremony, for the British state at war and how this process of sacralisation largely successfully interacted with wartime totalisation.[84] In other words, this book innovates by taking the scholarly debate about how the monarchy rendered rituals or acts 'sacred' or timeless and what this tells us about the modern origins of Britishness or nationalism and applying it to examine the ways in which the monarchy was used to render the war effort itself as sacred as well as the value of this 'monarchy effect' in an extreme wartime period of crisis. In turn, it uses this to assess the extent to which a core bedrock of shared beliefs about monarchy underpinned British culture.

Sacralisation is defined here following the work of William Kuhn and Edward Shils and Michael Young: Shils and Young, writing about the coronation of Queen Elizabeth II, stated that 'a society is held together by its internal agreement about the sacredness of certain fundamental moral standards'.[85] For Kuhn, 'seldom explicitly discussed or even consciously perceived, these fundamental values are "sacred" not in the conventional religious sense, but in the sense that they both attract and generate a large degree of unspoken reverence from different groups within a given society'.[86] The sociologist Max Weber defined the idea of authority in terms of three types: the legal-rational, with a 'belief in the legality of enacted rules', traditional, 'resting on an established belief in the sanctity of immemorial traditions', or charismatic, relying on 'devotion to the exceptional sanctity, heroism or exemplary character of an individual person' and the 'order revealed or ordained by him'.[87] Weber used these definitions to distinguish different types of legitimate authority that characterise different types of society, particularly as they evolved from simple to more complex through history. However, they are also useful as a way of thinking about the multiple ways that monarchy constructed its legitimacy.[88] The British monarchy in the Great War exhibits elements of all three types – with royal authority drawn from traditional beliefs and practices, from legal-rational state structures and from charisma. Biographers and witnesses concur that George V was not a personally charismatic figure.[89] However, to focus solely on the individual in this way neglects the question of the charisma of the Crown itself in wartime. Its symbolic pull, and the monarchist culture with which it was associated, had their own charismatic and traditional powers of authority, which this book examines. This helps us to better grasp the monarchy's actual power at the time: as Frank Mort has pointed out, the Crown's exercise of political authority is inseparable in this period from its use of ritual: 'the constitutional story of the modern monarchy is inseparable from its decorative and ceremonial functions'.[90]

As the philosopher Ernst Cassirer argued, 'societies generally invent and reinvent political myths in times of great political unrest and disorientation'.[91] This was true of the sacralising narratives built around the British monarchy in the First World War, which also had a particularly overtly sacral dimension due to the monarch's relationship with the established Church of England. Robert Gerwarth's definition of myth below reflects well the function of the wartime monarchy:

> myths are popular semiotic narratives, usually based on true historical events or persons, which serve the purpose of fostering the self-awareness and integration of a community. Through mythical narratives political abstractions and complex historical realities can be simplified and [. . .] personalized.[92]

Monarchy depended on cultural mythologies: when Harold Nicolson embarked upon his biography of George V, he was told in all seriousness by George VI's Private Secretary, Sir Alan Lascelles, that the book was 'not meant to be an ordinary biography. [. . .] You will be writing a book on the subject of a myth and will have to be mythological.'[93] The wartime monarchy also generated mythologies: one key finding which appears in this study is how, as the war context changed following revolution in Russia in 1917, a new myth of British exceptionalism developed, that somehow the British monarchy was completely different to Continental variants, because it promoted democracy and egalitarianism and its members worked hard as servants of the people.

This mythologised narrative of British exceptionalism, remarkable given the British royals' Continental familial ties and origins and the fact that both the Italian and Belgian monarchies behaved similarly in wartime, along with other mythic narratives examined here, such as those that stemmed from the monarchy's role in honouring the war dead or comforting the bereaved, would serve to re-sacralise kingship in Britain in potent ways.

The ways the monarchy sacralised the British war effort – whether through invented or renovated traditions, symbols and practices – seems at odds with war historians' assumptions about the modernising dynamic of the 'total' First World War. It suggests arguments that 'Europe broke out of its ancien régime and crossed the threshold of modernity well before 1914' have been exaggerated.[94] As historian Arno Mayer has argued, before 1914, modernisation coexisted with deep-seated older cultural attitudes about hierarchy and dynastic power:

> scholars of all ideological persuasions have downgraded the importance of preindustrial economic interests, prebourgeois elites, predemocratic authority systems, premodernist artistic idioms and 'archaic' mentalities [...] by treating them as expiring remnants, not to say relics, in rapidly modernizing civil and political societies.

For Mayer, '"premodern" elements were not the decaying and fragile remnants of an all but vanished past but the very essence of Europe's incumbent civil and political societies' at the outbreak of war.[95] Symbolic of such older cultural patterns surviving into the twentieth century was the right of British soldiers sentenced to death by court martial to appeal to the king for clemency.[96] This is visible elsewhere too. Even when Roger Casement was facing execution for treason, figures such as Philip Morel and Randall Davidson, the Archbishop of Canterbury, went to Buckingham Palace to personally ask the king to intervene and prevent the execution, highlighting the belief in royal power.[97]

Asserting that archaic monarchist beliefs coexisted with wartime modernisation in the British state – and indeed, often facilitated it, providing the main cultural framework for the packaging of modernisation processes to the British public through sacralised monarchist narratives – is also at odds with the standard comparative arguments about the First World War British and German states at war. These usually portray the United Kingdom as egalitarian and modernising and its German opponent as backward, dominated by powerful elites obsessed with feudal cultural norms and hierarchies – drawing on the famed *Sonderweg* argument of Hans-Ulrich Wehler, which argued the German political system had failed to modernise.[98] With regard to the nineteenth century, David Blackbourn and Geoff Eley have challenged this, arguing that Britain too exhibited dominance by aristocratic elites, oligarchic practices and feudal anachronisms and that its modernising tendencies had been exaggerated; moreover, there was no standard Western path into modernity from which Germany deviated.[99] However, their work did not address the First World War or the monarchy's role in it; it ends with 1914.

Looking at how the British monarchy was at the heart of the British war effort – both culturally and politically – and what this tells us about the ways in which modernising war processes could coexist with, adapt and co-opt older state structures such as monarchy thus tells us about the nature of early twentieth-century British modernity. Did British 'over-traditionalism' lead to 'incurable backwardness', as Tom Nairn has argued, a point echoed by Corelli Barnett and Martin Wiener, who attribute British long-term decline between the 1870s and the present to Britain's political, economic and social elites subscribing to 'beliefs setting supposedly "traditional" and "aristocratic" values over "innovative" and "middle-class" notions'?[100] As Bernhard Rieger and Martin Daunton have pointed out, 'the study of British modernity is in its infancy when compared with the prominence of this field in other national historiographies'.[101] Any examination of wartime kingship calls into question the nature of modernisation in the British context and how it was understood by contemporaries.[102] By looking at the idea of monarchy, it also becomes possible to identify the extent to which Britain reinvented contemporary ideas about, and remnants of, feudal cultures to cope with modern, indeed totalising, warfare – a visible, if curious, wartime paradox. Although, of course, the United Kingdom in 1914 was not 'feudal' by any direct medieval definition, the term is still helpful in understanding the ways that the monarchy and loyalties to the monarch were romanticised by contemporaries.

A further contribution this book makes regards chronological questions. The current historiographical trend in First World War studies is to think in terms of a 'long' First World War. Robert Gerwarth and John Horne have strongly argued that the conflict needs to be seen in terms of an earlier start date and a later end date, from 1911 with the Ottoman invasion of Libya followed by the 1912–13 Balkan wars, to 1923, with the Treaty of Lausanne and the Ruhr Crisis.[103] There is a strong argument that the case of the British monarchy fits this 'long' First World War model because of the crisis in Ireland which began in 1911–12 for the monarchy with the third Home Rule Bill and ended in 1923 with the end of the Irish Civil War, which was partly fought over allegiance to the king, and because of the way that the Great War continued unresolved in some parts of the British Empire, such as Egypt, where a negative war experience helped fuel 1919 revolution and post-war independence. This book ends in 1936, to capture this 'long' war aftermath, and also the fact that the death of George V marked a significant change in the sacralised status of the monarchy due to the impact of the abdication crisis. Examining the British monarchy thus facilitates exploring broader chronological global connections across the 'greater war era', as Gerwarth has termed it.[104]

A note on terminology: that the monarchy was fundamental to *British* wartime identity is one of this book's key arguments. However, British identities in this period stretched well beyond the geographical space of Great Britain on which most of this study focuses. Therefore, the term 'British' here is used in its broadest sense, with an awareness that its meaning was contested at the time, often used in racially exclusive ways and rejected by some populations, both within the then United Kingdom, particularly in the Celtic nations and especially in Ireland, and within the empire. This book seeks to explore the reach of British monarchy discourses in this light, and the term 'British' here does not simply denote the island of Britain but also a broader cultural identity and affiliation. For reasons of scope, however, the whole empire can only be discussed briefly in this book through case studies; the specificities of Wales and Scotland also merit fuller coverage than can be presented here.

If the war ultimately served to sacralise the monarchy this was not an inevitable outcome. This book shows that monarchism in the United Kingdom evolved through a series of phases during the conflict. At the outset, it was a fundamental aspect of Edwardian honour culture, central to dominant political, national and some religious identities. As the war continued, monarchism came under increasing pressure with the growth of war-weariness in 1917 and the rise (albeit rather limited) of republicanism in Britain and demands for the extension of the franchise. The strains of war – in particular the introduction of conscription – resulted in new British definitions of citizenship: instead of being tied to property rights or to residency requirements, the parliamentary vote was increasingly seen as something that service to the nation, and, specifically, war service, merited. These shifts in how citizenship was conceived impacted upon monarchy too – sovereignty was increasingly vested in the mass citizenry, something which had obvious implications for the actual 'Sovereign'. The wartime monarchy responded to these changes in several ways – it promoted an idea of its own wartime 'service'; it accepted a dramatically more egalitarian understanding of the relationship between monarch and individual subject and argued for the extension of the franchise and democracy in an effort to avoid any potential risks of revolution; and it promoted its personal sacralised links to the empire and to the war fallen which created a unique role for the monarchy as a communicative symbolic channel between the British population and a wider imagined population of British 'subjects', both living and war dead. Walter Bagehot's argument in 1867 was that the monarchy 'sanctified government with the force of religion, provided a focus for pageantry and set the standard for national morality'.[105] This remained true of its role during and after the war. The combined effect of the war, and the invention and adaption of royal traditions that it triggered, was to create an aura of reverence around the British monarchy as stoic, uncomplaining and devoutly religious so that by 1919 it was unrecognisable from the bucolic monarchy of King Edward VII, whose reign never truly shook off his press reputation as a 'hedonistic playboy'.[106] The war defined the monarchy in terms of service, hard work, piety, emotional self-control and anti-decadence, helping to explain why the abdication crisis provoked such utter consternation. If the war had re-sacralised the monarchy in new ways after the reign of Edward VII, the 1936 abdication of his namesake threatened to seriously disrupt this.

The outbreak of the war saw a surge in British monarchism and a widespread romanticisation of it. The year 1916 proved a caesura after which ideas of revolution – both in Ireland and Continental Europe, as well as war-weariness, increasingly led to a questioning of the pre-war status of monarchy, pressuring the British court and royals to adapt practices and invent new ones, in response to their perception of a more hostile cultural climate. Anti-monarchist feeling in Great Britain during the war was only ever a minority phenomenon, however; the perception of this threat was more significant than the actual reality, but the perception led to major changes in royal practice and image. For a variety of reasons, not least a successful rationing system that distributed food relatively efficiently across the working classes, military victory in 1918, and a king and queen who astutely responded to the changed circumstances of wartime, eschewing luxury and increasing their visibility, war-weariness did not trigger a revolutionary upheaval against the British state and its royals. If anything, the monarchy's relationship with Labour leaders improved due to their working together to support the war effort.

This book opens with a prelude that sets out the political power of the wartime monarchy, which was the key context for its social and cultural significance. The rest of the book is structured in three parts, to carefully illustrate the fluctuations in the sacralised status of the monarchy across the conflict. Part I examines mobilisation; Part II, changing cultures of deference; and Part III focuses on war commemoration. Chapter 1 looks at monarchist mentalities in the first years of the conflict, 1914–16, and considers how ideas about honouring the king played into concepts of masculine duty and war recruitment before the advent of conscription. Chapter 2 examines whether monarchist beliefs had any impact on wartime behaviour and practices, particularly for combatants. Chapter 3 focuses on the image of the royal body. It looks at how discourses about the royal body evoked older notions of royal 'perfection' and the 'royal touch'. Chapter 4 examines the period 1916–18, arguing that this phase of the war saw a series of discourses that 'de-sacralised' monarchy emerge, looking at revolution in Ireland and the impact of the Russian Revolution in Britain, as well as the counter-discourses that were used to defend the monarchy in response and preserve its sacralised status. Chapter 5 examines the monarchy's engagement with war victory and grief, while Chapter 6 looks at the monarchy's role in the sacralisation of the war dead in post-war commemoration.

Ultimately, it seems bizarre that given the scale of George V's endurance in the First World War that this book reveals – the horrific sights of wounded men he encountered and his personal courage during his visits to the Western

Front – that he has gone down in popular history as a stamp collector and a mediocre king. Famously. Series 3 of Netflix's global blockbuster *The Crown*, released in 2019, sees Prince Philip's character state that George V was 'deadly dull [...] the height of the Great War [...] where was he? He was sticking stamps in his album'.[107] In fact, he was a very astute monarch in a period of unprecedented crisis. The wartime diaries of King George and Queen Mary reveal them as a devoted middle-aged couple who relied on each other in the face of seeing the most awful sights of war-damaged bodies, an extreme workload and meeting war bereaved.

It is also important to ultimately recognise the significance of the precedent that George V set in sticking so rigorously to the limits of his constitutional role, no easy feat in a period of total war when other European monarchs took on military commands and some advisors were suggesting he should claim increased political powers.[108] By remaining so meticulously faithful to the rules of the British constitutional monarchy tradition, George V set an important example of political moderation during war crisis and in this respect protected the balance of power between government, parliament and sovereign at the heart of the British state. Moreover, by privileging the idea of 'democracy' and integrating it into the discourse projected around the monarchy from 1917, and personally reaching out to Labour figures at the same time, George V, Queen Mary and the king's Private Secretary Lord Stamfordham successfully bolstered the reformist strand of socialism, helping ensure that the Labour movement in the UK could work within the state system long term, rather than seek to overthrow it. This royal integration of Labour was seen as invaluable: according to Edward Owens, in the interwar period, 'the media and political elite revered the monarchy as the institution that had anchored Britain's evolution from feudalism to modern democracy, something which chimed with the ideas vigorously promoted by courtiers and allies of the throne that the Crown stood above party politics and that the constitutional sovereign was the unifying symbol of the British people's political freedoms'.[109] With the rise of communism and fascism this idea of the Crown as a bulwark against political radicalism and as an institution that accepted the reformist Labour movement was important.

Through helping steward the monarchy's sacralised image through the war and into the post-war years, King George and Queen Mary ensured its ongoing popularity. All of this was no minor achievement. It helped consolidate the existing British political system in a turbulent historical period and was a factor in interwar Britain successfully avoiding the perils of authoritarianism, fascism and communism, the extreme direct legacies of the war that ensnared so much of Europe. It also created the groundwork for the later, Second World War, image of the British monarchy as a bastion of liberal democracy.[110] George V and Queen Mary's roles in the Great War not only ensured the survival of the monarchy; in the bigger picture, they were a factor in how Great Britain survived the intense strains of 'total war', mass war bereavement and Irish revolution, to emerge as a stable, functioning polity, none of which was inevitable. Indeed Edward VIII, who was quickly tempted to tamper with the system and who was attracted to fascism, illustrates how easily the global political climate could influence a king and how rapidly a different set of royal policies could prove destabilising.

To conclude, the scale of the impact of George V and Queen Mary and the importance of monarchism in British First World War culture has been overlooked, both by historians of monarchy and historians of war alike. We have been left with echoes or residues, shed of their original meanings: the First World War is still often referred to in Britain using the slogan 'For King and Country' without any academic examination or wider public understanding as to why this should be the case – why this particular war was associated with that term. As with Great War monarchism more generally, we lack any understanding of the meaning and weight this phrase once carried, of the war's monarchist context, without which the term cannot make sense. If this study shows the value of reintegrating this history, by launching new debates and questions, it will have served its purpose.

PRELUDE

The Monarchy and Wartime Political Power

Any study of the British monarchy during the First World War must address the forms of political power that it had during the conflict. This was the key context for its cultural significance. Indeed, the monarchy's political role cannot be separated from its cultural one. In the decade before the war, the monarchy's status carried significant political leverage: the British monarch was not merely a constitutional, honorific figurehead, but also closely involved in directly influencing political decision-making. As historian Frank Mort has pointed out, 'historians of the twentieth-century British monarchy have tended to separate the Crown's "efficient" role from its "dignified" functions, to quote from Walter Bagehot in ways that preclude an examination of the ongoing connections between royal politics and ritual symbolism', but the two were actually inseparable in this period; the monarchy, in Mort's words, 'still remained in part a political function of the state'.[1] Before examining in detail the social and cultural significance of the monarchy, we must therefore investigate its political power. The document trail on the monarchy's role in decision-making is far from complete. However, what emerges from the available evidence suggests a more robust and important monarchy in the wartime political sphere than that depicted in the historiography, and that its role was influential in decision-making, diplomacy, patronage and domestic power-brokering. This royal political power is assessed here.

This prelude also explores whether any modern version of the 'kingship mechanism', a term invented by Norbert Elias to define 'the informal power wielded by monarchs in court societies', often through ceremonial culture and ritual, allowed the British monarch to intervene in the political sphere during the war.[2] Elias suggested that the main task of the French kings in the era of absolutism was acting as arbiter between various competing groups and cliques tied to the system and dependent on it, in order to prevent any faction from gaining too much power. Historians Jan Rüger, John Röhl and Nicolaus Sombart have all argued that, in the case of Germany, Kaiser Wilhelm II provided a modern example of Elias's 'kingship mechanism', using his many 'registers of favour and patronage', as well as public rituals, to secure loyalty and increase the power of his 'personal rule' beyond his constitutionally enshrined prerogative.[3] Sombart argues that Wilhelm II sought to establish

'on top of the "primary" power structure – multiform, polycentric, heteroge-
neous, highly unstable and to a large extent autonomous and institutionalised –
a "secondary" system of rules, rituals, ceremonies and all other sorts of activities' which were exclusively directed to and dependent on the kaiser, whose
patronage through this secondary system could advance, and make, careers.[4]
While acknowledging that the constitutional powers of the British king were
more limited than those of the kaiser, this study investigates, as far as the
available sources permit, whether any version of the 'kingship mechanism'
existed in Britain.

The outbreak of the First World War occurred at a key juncture in the
evolution of the British monarchy, which, from the period of Queen Victoria,
had been slowly, in the words of Gladstone, substituting 'influence for power':
this process was ongoing in 1914.[5] The year 1914 thus offers a benchmark –
showing the power–influence equation as war broke out and allowing us to
plot its changing nature in the war years. To be king was, of course,
a constitutionally limited role: the United Kingdom was not an absolute
monarchy.[6] Yet, if the parameters of the constitutional framework of monarchy were broadly clear-cut by 1914, the extent of its cultural and political
influence fluctuated much more. As the German ambassador in 1914, Prince
Lichnowsky noted: 'Although the British Constitution leaves only very limited
powers to the Crown, yet the monarch, in virtue of his position, can exercise
a considerable influence on opinion, both in society and in the Government.'[7]

Belief in honouring the king was part of the political system, as well as part of
ceremonial culture. Royal influence was a significant part of British political
life. It also mattered greatly in foreign policy. As historian Johannes Paulmann
has shown, in Europe in the 'long' nineteenth century up to 1914, royal
influence on foreign policy remained notable, even in parliamentary monarchies, and was key to the cultural framework and structure of international
relations.[8] Edward VII's overseas state visits played a significant role in
British diplomacy, for example, not least in the Entente Cordiale. In his
short reign he visited one or more of the Great Powers at least three times
a year and made sixty-one international trips.[9]

George V too was far from an impotent figurehead in domestic and foreign
policy. Within the limits of his constitutional powers, he was a very active
influence, taking the sovereign's role to be consulted, to advise and to warn
very seriously.[10] Before the outbreak of the First World War, George
V intervened in the political sphere in significant ways. Upon coming to the
throne, he refused to open parliament unless the anti-Catholic clauses of
the Declaration of Accession were removed, which duly occurred. During
the constitutional crisis of 1910–11, he proved very reluctant to accept
Herbert Asquith's advice as Prime Minister to make Asquith a pre-election
pledge to create additional Liberal Peers to give the Liberals a House of Lords
majority; George V delayed and sought additional advice before eventually

agreeing to intervene.[11] In the Irish Home Rule Crisis of 1912–14, the king again became significantly involved in domestic politics, calling, and personally opening, the Buckingham Palace Conference in July 1914, negotiations between political party leaders, intended to resolve the Irish Home Rule impasse, a plan he developed in tandem with Asquith.[12] Asquith believed that 'it is not only within the competence, but at such a time part of the duty, of a Constitutional Sovereign to exert his authority in the best interests both of the United Kingdom and of the Empire'.[13] However, the conference was seen by many Liberals as 'a dangerous constitutional innovation' which 'allowed too much' of a political role to George V.[14] Vernon Bogdanor has described the period 1910–14, the first years of George V's reign, as 'a period of chronic constitutional crisis' during which the sovereign exercised 'real power'.[15]

Domestic constitutional crisis over Ireland famously overlapped in July 1914 with a foreign policy crisis, and here again there was a very significant level of royal involvement by George V. British monarchist culture was a factor in decision-making in the weeks leading up to British entry into the First World War and was particularly visible in foreign policy practices. Two points stand out: first, the German kaiser tried to work through the king to influence the United Kingdom's position vis-à-vis any war between Germany, and Britain's allies – Russia and France. Second, more generally, in a Europe made up predominantly of ruling monarchies, Buckingham Palace was a key channel for communication between Britain and European monarchical states throughout the July Crisis that led to the war; it rivalled the Foreign Office as an entry point to the UK for information and communication with other European states in a way that would not be the case in the post-war era.

With regard to the first issue, it is well known in histories of the outbreak of the war that Prince Henry (Heinrich) of Prussia, Kaiser Wilhelm's brother, visited King George V on Sunday 26 July 1914. Henry believed that, at this meeting, George V had promised him that Britain would remain neutral in the approaching Continental conflict. This information then shaped German decision-making, encouraging it in its move towards war. A number of points bear noting with regard to this incident. First, Prince Henry of Prussia was unlikely to have come to England without the kaiser's permission. Immediately after meeting George V, Henry went to the German Embassy to inform the ambassador, Prince Lichnowsky, and naval attaché, Captain Erich von Müller, of what had transpired, who wired versions of it to Berlin.[16] From the outset, in other words, the Germans hoped to use their royal connections with George V to their benefit and circumvent the Foreign Office and British government.[17] Second, Henry of Prussia had long been a conduit between the two monarchies – George V had informed him of Britain's position with regard to German bellicosity in 1913.[18] So there was ongoing foreign policy exchange of information through royal channels that on occasion circumvented the government and Foreign Office. George V's conversation in July 1914 was not an aberration but a norm. It is clear that there was risk in such a meeting – the king met Prince Henry without asking the Foreign Office first, and the short meeting was private.[19]

Third, the information that George V gave Prince Henry was quite accurate and well informed: at this point the British cabinet was divided on the prospect of war and unclear on whether Britain was obliged to stand by France, and many politicians hoped that Britain could avoid entering a Continental conflict.[20] George V wrote that, in reply to Prince Henry's question about what Britain would do if there was a European war, 'I said I don't know what we shall do, we have no quarrel with anyone & I hope we shall remain neutral.'[21] George V's comments to Prince Henry showed the king's opinion reflected the cabinet situation. In his letter to the kaiser, recounting the conversation from memory, Prince Henry wrote that the king had said 'we shall try all we can to keep out of this and shall remain neutral'.[22] The king's 'hope' was morphed into an expression of intent. This also happened in the German naval attaché von Müller's telegram from London to Berlin on 26 July, which read: 'King of Great Britain stated to Prince Heinrich of Prussia that England would be neutral if war should break out between Continental powers.'[23] The misunderstanding highlighted the risks of royal diplomacy. Prince Henry's slip-up may well have been Freudian wishful thinking, as it is likely, according to historian John Röhl, as well as court advisors at the time, that the prince had been sent to try and get an assurance of British neutrality from George V; he recounted a version of words that fitted what he had hoped to hear.[24] These errors of wording – which appear to be genuine – had enormous consequences. As Röhl points out, the impact of this conversation between Prince Henry and the king on the kaiser's decisions 'in this critical phase of the July Crisis was catastrophic'.[25] It led the kaiser to believe that Germany and Austria-Hungary could act belligerently towards France and Russia without it causing war with Britain.

The kaiser saw the entire July Crisis through the prism of monarchism. He believed in the need for 'solidarity of monarchs' against Serbia, which he considered a regicidal regime, blaming it for the murder of Archduke Franz Ferdinand.[26] He felt, Röhl argues, 'let down in his expectation' that the tsar would oppose the Belgrade 'regicides' and 'as a ruler by the Grace of God, declare his solidarity with him' and Europe's other monarchs.[27] This monarchism was the context for how the kaiser read Prince Henry's reported conversation with King George V and, along with the errors of reporting discussed above, explains his immediate conclusion that Britain had pledged to remain neutral. Moreover, Kaiser Wilhelm and the German regime never understood the limitations upon George V's foreign policy powers in the British constitutional monarchy system. When Admiral Tirpitz suggested a scenario where Britain might declare her support for France, the kaiser retorted that 'I have the word of a king, and that is enough for me.'[28] The term 'word of a king' is hugely significant; it carried weight beyond that of ordinary men for Wilhelm and again invokes ideas of monarchical 'honour'. As Roderick McLean points out, the kaiser fully believed that Britain 'would not go to war against Germany because George V would not allow the British government to intervene'.[29] Wilhelm II believed war ensued because George V had played him false and that, if Queen Victoria, his grandmother, 'had been alive, she would never have allowed it'.[30]

The disastrous meeting between Prince Henry and George V sheds light on the pre-war forms of informal diplomacy that operated between the Continental European and the British monarchies through familial links. It also reveals the substantial confusion in other states about what exactly the role and influence of George V was on foreign policy decisions, a confusion which, as the case of Germany shows, could have major consequences. There is still too little research on this: McLean has highlighted the need for 'systematic investigation of foreign governments' understanding of the British monarchy's political influence'.[31] Throughout the July Crisis, Kaiser Wilhelm communicated directly with George V about the situation, trying to circumvent Foreign Office channels. For example, when on 1 August 1914 the German ambassador in London, Prince Lichnowsky, misunderstood a conversation with Sir Edward Grey to mean that Britain was offering British neutrality and a guarantee of French neutrality if war broke out between Germany and Russia, the kaiser responded to this information in a telegram directly to George V accepting the 'offer'.[32] Likewise when the kaiser's telegram arrived, Grey was summoned to Buckingham Palace to help draft King George V's reply clarifying that Britain had made no such promise.[33]

What appears clear is that the British government and Foreign Office had to work with this situation where royal personal diplomacy was a European norm. George V was also invariably cooperative, quick to share the information he received with them. While the monarch did have private informal, international personal contacts, such as the meeting with Prince Henry, he also took direction from his executive, and these two aspects of his diplomatic involvement frequently overlapped. Thus, the government and Foreign Office worked through the monarchy when they thought it might be advantageous to Britain during the July Crisis. It was *the* key diplomatic channel – among several – which was used to communicate with Germany and Russia, for example. This risked creating ambiguity and confusion both at home and abroad, as the Palace and the Foreign Office were often both simultaneously communicating with foreign states on the same issue, but it also gave British foreign policy additional clout with European monarchies as the word of an anointed fellow monarch, George V, carried far more weight with them than civilian politicians. Despite the constitutional nature of the British monarchy, in 1914 it was operating in a European context where the majority of states were monarchies, often with royal rulers who governed directly, and it was an important mediator between these states and the Foreign Office. What is also apparent is the acceptance – even need – on the part of the British government to develop its response to the crisis through and with the king. This was, in part, in the hope that his close personal and familial relationship with the kaiser and the tsar would have an emotional influence upon them. Also, the veneer of a monarchical foreign policy in a national crisis would protect the politicians from any blame by associating their actions with the revered monarchy in the eyes of the public. Moreover, anxious, overwrought politicians themselves instinctively turned to the king as a reassuring figure, representing tradition, in a moment of acute strain and break with the known. Given this situation, foreign states can hardly be blamed for not being able to work out the degree of power of George V in diplomatic policy. The extent of the king's influence on foreign policy is not clear, although evidently he had some – for example, although he was often given drafts of the telegrams to send to his relatives in Europe, he approved the final versions sent.[34]

Indeed, throughout the final days of the crisis, politicians went to the Palace to communicate with other states, which is indicative of how the royal diplomatic channel trumped the Foreign Office one. The President of France, Raymond Poincaré, also wrote to George V directly.[35] It was also to George V that the Belgian King, Albert I, appealed for British aid upon the German invasion of Belgium.[36] George V's most significant – and well-known – role in the July Crisis was to try to rein in his cousin, the Russian Tsar Nicholas II, and mediate between him and his cousin Kaiser Wilhelm II at the British government's behest, even sending a telegram, presented as 'a direct personal appeal from the King to the Tsar', in the early hours of 1 August in an effort to stop the slide towards war, which had in fact been drafted by Asquith, Maurice Bonham Carter and William Tyrell, Sir Edward Grey's Private Secretary.[37] King George V also sent a 'personal appeal' to the kaiser 'to secure the peace of the world'.[38] Yet, by 1918, when the Armistice was agreed, there was no such process of actual diplomatic negotiation through the monarchy: European foreign relations were now much more publicly the preserve of the Foreign Office.

In contrast, many commentators referred in 1914 to the slide to war in terms of a clash between monarchies: Winston Churchill was critical of the lack of direct action by the king, writing to his wife: 'I wondered whether those stupid Kings & Emperors cd [sic] not assemble together & revivify kingship by saving the nations from hell but we all drift on in a kind of dull cataleptic trance. As if it was somebody else's operation!'[39] Popular culture also reflected this view that international crisis was a monarchic affair: at Madame Tussaud's the management had 'rearranged the wax-models of royal and political personalities into a single display and sent men with sandwich boards round the streets to advertise it', reading 'The European Crisis. Lifelike portrait models of Their Majesties King George and Queen Mary[,] H.I.M. The Emperor of Austria[,]

H.M. King Peter of Serbia and other reigning sovereigns of Europe. Naval and Military Tableaux.'[40] Postcards and war maps showed the king's portrait alongside those of the leaders of Britain's allies; souvenir cloths also carried depictions of the king and allied leaders.[41] To a degree this royalist image of Britain also remained the case for many ordinary Europeans during the war: for example, when, in 1917, the French infantry soldier Charles Burloux carved a walking cane in the trenches with all the European leaders of the belligerent powers carefully worked into the wood, he inserted George V's head to represent the UK, not the Prime Minister, David Lloyd George.[42] Another piece of French trench art from Craonne in 1917, an inkwell fashioned from bullets and shell pieces, had a British penny with King George V's head as its centrepiece decoration.[43] The collection of the Historial de la Grande Guerre at Péronne also has a medallion issued with the heads of Queen Mary and Queen Elisabeth of Belgium in profile.[44] French and Italian postcards often used the figure of King George V to personify Britain, sometimes grouped with the heads of state of other war allies.[45]

What was King George V's own view on the decision to go to war? Here the sources remain incomplete. When it was Serbia alone at stake, it seems the monarchy was less concerned. The king's Private Secretary, Lord Stamfordham, wrote to Walter Lawrence on 2 August 1914:

> At present nothing is definitely settled as to what England is going to do: but Grey is to make a statement in the H[ouse] of C[ommons] tomorrow. What a European Conflagration! And all about a semi barbarous state which has been allowed to grow into a kingdom like Servia [sic].[46]

Stamfordham's views did not always concur entirely with those of George V, but there was frequently very close political overlap.

Germany's ultimatum to Belgium was issued the same day as the communication to Lawrence and changed everything. In 2014, a letter written by Cecil Graves, the nephew of British Foreign Minister Sir Edward Grey, emerged in which Graves claimed that King George V told him in 1933 that he had pressurised Grey to enter the war and to find a reason to justify doing so.[47] Graves wrote that when King Albert I of Belgium sent George V a telegram to notify him of the invasion of Belgium, King George sent it to Grey, advising that the invasion provided adequate reason.[48] A wartime source corroborates this. The Bishop of Chelmsford, John Watts-Ditchfield, recorded in his diary that the king told him on 29 April 1916 that

> Grey was troubled because he had been Foreign Minister before War [sic] and felt he had helped to bring it about whereas[,] said the King[,] I had to urge him on. He came to me[,] said the King[,] and said the people would never stand war and I told him we must go to war and make the people realise we could do no other. The King said our going in when we did saved the situation.[49]

Overall, the evidence suggests that the king's decision to accept entry into the war came quite late in the run-up to Grey's House of Commons speech calling for war on 3 August and was integrally linked to Germany's actions towards Belgium. George V recorded in his diary on 4 August 1914 that 'I held a Council at 10.45 to declare war with Germany, it is a terrible catastrophe but it is not our fault. [...] Please God it may be soon over and that he will protect dear Bertie's life.'[50] It was the writing of an anxious father not a bellicose leader, and it illustrated that the monarch believed Britain innocent of causing the conflict. By 5 August, however, Prime Minister Herbert Asquith was reporting to Venetia Stanley that the king was 'really a good deal relieved that war has come: he could not stand the tension of last week. As you might expect he is becoming very anti-German.'[51] George V certainly believed once Britain entered the war that it had had no other option: as he remarked to the American ambassador, 'My God, Mr Page, what else could we do?'[52] Sir Douglas Haig noted, in notes typed up at a later date, that on 11 August 1914 he had lunched with the king and queen and noticed that

> The King seemed anxious, but he did not give me the impression that he fully realised the grave issues both for our Country as well as for his own house, which were about to be put to the test; nor did he really comprehend the uncertainty of the result of all wars between great nations, no matter how well prepared one may think one is.[53]

The monarchical framing of the war's outbreak here is also notable – the danger to the royal 'house' featuring as a stake of the conflict in Haig's eyes.

The role of the king during the days leading up to British entry into the war remained a highly sensitive subject. When the former American ambassador to Germany, James Gerard, published his memoirs in 1917, he included a telegram from Kaiser Wilhelm II to Woodrow Wilson, setting out the kaiser's belief that George V had pledged to Prince Henry of Prussia that Britain would remain neutral. The censor passed the publication.[54] This was the first time the UK public learned of the incident. Buckingham Palace was alerted by the editor of the conservative *Daily Telegraph*, which was serialising Gerard's book, who showed Downing Street the section on Prince Henry's 1914 visit.[55] Downing Street then 'brought the matter to the King's attention', and Stamfordham took the unusual wartime step of issuing a denial to the press before Gerard's account appeared:

> With reference to a telegram sent by the German Emperor to President Wilson, the 10th August, 1914, which we understand appears in the *Daily Telegraph* to-morrow (Monday), we have the highest authority to declare that the statements alleged by the Emperor to have been made to Prince Henry of Prussia by his Majesty the King are absolutely without any foundation.[56]

It was also 'arranged that the denial should be cabled to all foreign capitals'.

So seriously was this issue taken that, in June 1938, Clive Wigram, the king's wartime Private Secretary and now Keeper of the Royal Archives, wrote to *The Times* to again rebut the claim when Captain Erich von Müller, former German naval attaché in London in 1914, revived it. Wigram stated that 'I was Assistant Private Secretary to the King in 1914 and His Majesty often talked to me about this conversation with Prince Henry of Prussia.'[57] It was obviously key, given the war was presented to the British public as an act of German aggression, to ensure that there was no suggestion that George V might have had any role in misleading Germany into deciding to attack France on the grounds that Britain would remain neutral; the tenet of sole German responsibility for the war was central to British – and Allied – wartime understanding, and had underpinned the Treaty of Versailles reparations clauses. By 1938, it was also a changed world where the idea of a British monarch being so dragged into foreign policy as George V was during the July Crisis was inconceivable. However, Wigram's recollection that George V 'often talked' about that key conversation with Prince Henry suggests that the king himself may have regretted Henry's misinterpretation of their meeting and his words – otherwise why continue to discuss it? Clearly, it remained a moment of some importance to him.[58] Wigram's letter to *The Times* also omitted any actual detail of the 1914 conversation itself – he avoided any citation of what the monarch actually reported to him that he had said in 1914. He merely hinted that the king had always been consistent that England would come to France and Russia's assistance 'under certain circumstances'.[59]

All of this highlights the monarch's ongoing 'soft' political power in 1914, which operated through networks of contacts, patronage and influence as well as through the more visible structures of the constitutional monarchy and its important role in the political sphere. In private, throughout the war, George V was vocal in advising politicians and others and remained extremely well informed through a dense network of elite contacts and his two private secretaries, Arthur John Bigge, who by the First World War was already Lord Stamfordham, and Clive Wigram (later 1st Lord Wigram of Clewer), who were both former officers and nominally remained on the active list after joining the royal household.[60] Moreover, Lord Stamfordham, through his seat in the House of Lords, kept a close watch on all political intrigues, networks and events and acted as the eyes and ears of the king at parliament. Stamfordham also corresponded and met with a wide range of key political and military figures throughout the war and was also a close friend of the Archbishop of Canterbury, Dr Randall Davidson. Stamfordham, the son of a Northumberland vicar and a veteran of the Anglo-Zulu War, had already been Private Secretary to Queen Victoria.[61] He was effectively the key royal advisor and civil servant on whom King George V depended and the principal influence on royal decisions. While other figures in court and church circles provided the king with information and advice, such as the Bishop of Chelmsford, the Canon of Southwark, and the Archbishop of Canterbury, who was a close friend of the king's, Frederick Ponsonby Baron Synonsby, Clive Wigram, Reginald Brett Lord Esher and indeed Queen Mary, most decisions were taken in agreement between the monarch and Stamfordham.

The monarchy was also directly updated on the war and consulted by the military. A system of 'King's Messengers' ensured that correspondence passed unimpeded between the monarch and his commanders at the front without any external person reading the material. In one instance Sir Ian Hamilton feared that the King's Messengers might themselves impart negative observations of the Gallipoli campaign to the monarch, and his staff prevented them from going up to the front.[62] Sir Douglas Haig also sent the king his private diaries in batches during the war to read, as did General Sir Horace Smith-Dorrien, evidence of the reach of monarchy if ever it was needed; the king was actually allowed by his subjects to read their journals, while a whole range of generals and colonels, including Lieutenant General Sir Henry Rawlinson, General Sir Hubert Gough, Colonel (later Major General) William Lambton, General Sir Ian Hamilton, Lieutenant General Sir William Birdwood, General Sir Edmund Allenby and Field Marshal Sir John French corresponded with the king or his private secretaries.[63] Royals also held key military roles: the Duke of Teck, the king's brother-in-law, was for a period Haig's military secretary. His cousin, Prince Arthur of Connaught, served as aide-de-camp to both Sir John French and Sir Douglas Haig. Important state and imperial positions also had close royal links. The king's uncle, Prince Arthur, Duke of Connaught, was Governor General of Canada until 1916 and played an important role in wartime mobilisation there.[64] King George V was also very close friends with 'Eddy', the Earl of Derby, who set up the Derby Scheme for increasing war recruitment in 1915 and was later Secretary of State for War from 1916–18.[65] Privy Counsellors were also a source of information: at Gallipoli, the Earl of Granard told Sir Ian Hamilton that "'I feel it my duty as privy Councillor to write the truth of all that has occurred out here to the King. Perhaps under these circumstances you would prefer that I should not serve under your command." Hamilton replied that in wartime Privy Counsellors did not count and that all became soldiers.'[66] He nonetheless immediately ordered for Granard's letters to be censored. It appears Privy Counsellors did indeed still count. Journalist Ellis Ashmead Bartlett even claimed that Hamilton 'hates Granard like poison because he knows that nothing can stop his corresponding directly with the King and in telling him the truth.'[67]

In terms of patronage, the king was consulted on all important military appointments throughout the war. The British monarch's views were always taken into consideration by political and military decision-makers, and, even if they were not automatically followed, on a frequent number of occasions his private suggestions were adopted. Even the cynical Asquith noted he needed to gain royal support: 'By an odd convention all our Sovereigns (I have now had to deal with *three*) believe that in Army and Navy appointments they have a special responsibility and a sort of "divine right of Kings" prerogative. Anyhow they have to be humoured and brought in.'[68] Asquith's acerbic tone should not surprise: in 1916, the Bishop of Chelmsford warned Lord Stamfordham that he 'could not say [that the] King was popular. He was respected' and that 'his hold was probably weakest in the upper classes'.[69] Yet aristocrats could be openly cynical, and indeed critical, about the personalities of individual royals, as Frank Mort and Kenneth Rose have shown, while nevertheless fully supporting the Crown culturally and politically as an institution, like Asquith.[70] Moreover, they often differentiated between revering the structures of monarchy and being flippant about individual royal family members with whom they socialised.

The king's patronage role was central throughout the war. This was largely outside the public eye. He was absolutely instrumental in the removal of Sir John French as Commander of the British Armies on the Western Front in December 1915 and in the appointment of Sir Douglas Haig as his replacement, who was well connected at court through his wife.[71] Likewise, George V was a key figure in ensuring that William Robertson was appointed as Chief of the Imperial General Staff (CIGS).[72] The king was also a key support to Lord Kitchener as Minister for War during press attacks on him by the Northcliffe papers during the shells crisis of 1915. When John Fisher was removed as First Lord of the Admiralty in 1915, the king suggested – and got – Arthur Balfour as his replacement.[73] When Lloyd George became Prime Minister, he 'deferred' to the king's suggestion of Sir Edward Carson for the First Lord of the Admiralty role.[74] The monarch was used to exercising his influence on political decisions, even below prime ministerial level. Lloyd George's secretary and mistress, Frances Stevenson, wrote in her diary on 30 November 1916 that the king had sent a message opposing Lloyd George's decision as then Secretary of State for War to dismiss Sir John Cowans as Quartermaster General, which had 'made D. very angry, as he said the King had no right to try and use his influence in that way'.[75] Yet, for all Lloyd George's protestations, he subsequently kept Cowans in post. As questions grew regarding the competence of Sir Douglas Haig in 1917 and 1918, the king resolutely supported him, a significant factor in Haig being able to continue in command against Prime Minister Lloyd George's opposition. Moreover, although the king could not force the retention of Sir William Robertson as CIGS in 1918 against Lloyd George's moves to remove him, he did try to prevent it, and it took Lloyd George some time to successfully outmanoeuvre him.[76] The monarch even directly requested in 1917 that Lord Hardinge should still be made ambassador to France, despite having been discredited in the Mesopotamia Commission Report.[77] Hardinge was ultimately appointed to the role in 1920. When the wife of a British diplomat angered the king by jeering the kaiser upon his arrival into exile in the Netherlands at the end of the war, her husband was prematurely retired within months.[78]

It also appears clear from a brief overview of the monarch's role that, throughout the conflict, King George V had significant direct political influence on central issues. On occasion he directly influenced the cabinet: in October 1915, Lord Crewe reported to him that, with regard to the size of the War Council, he felt 'sure that after what Your Majesty stated at his audience on Wednesday that this action by Your Majesty's Ministries will be approved'.[79] The king also wrote a letter on 23 August 1914 urging all parties in the Irish question to recognise 'the need on the part of almost everybody for some sacrifice of cherished conviction' to get a resolution on the Home Rule impasse following the outbreak of the world war.[80] Asquith showed the letter privately to the nationalist and unionist leaders in order to influence them.[81] On 19 July 1915, the cabinet meeting began with Asquith reading his colleagues a letter from the king which suggested that Lloyd George should be sent to Wales to help end a miners' strike by addressing the miners 'in their own language'.[82] The cabinet at once decided to send Lloyd George. Monarchism was clearly an influence: the cabinet further noted that if the strikers continued to refuse to accept the terms they had been offered, serious consideration would be given to 'strengthening the law by making such offenses treasonable as acts "aiding and abetting the enemies of the King"'.[83] A further clear indication of the role of the king as the most powerful wartime government advisor appeared in 1916 when Stamfordham chastised Asquith that in the 'hurry of war' old 'forms and customs' must still continue and 'such communications as replies to the German government in the Baralong case ought to be submitted for the King's approval before they are despatched by the Foreign Office'.[84] This indicated the scale of royal oversight over foreign communications. The Baralong case was an incident where the Royal Navy was alleged to have shot German sailors after their submarine sank rather than taking them prisoner, as reported by American witnesses; it mattered to the international propaganda war. Stamfordham's message suggests that it was normative for the king to read and approve communications with foreign governments – a colossal degree of royal supervision.

The monarch played a key role in ensuring the formation of a coalition government in December 1915 and crucially supported Kitchener being retained as Minister for War in the new coalition government against efforts by politicians to remove him.[85] Crucially, in December 1916, when Asquith resigned as Prime Minister, the king, who hoped to keep him on, asked him to stay his resignation until Asquith could see his Liberal cabinet colleagues the next day.[86] The king also played the key role in ensuring that there was no general election when Asquith stepped down – he opposed the idea of holding an election in wartime. George V told the Bishop of Chelmsford as early as April 1916 that his view was that 'there must not be [a] General Election. Said it would be criminal folly – a million men could not vote – it wd [sic] divide nation. If Conservatives came in they would not tolerate L. G. and a peace party would be formed.'[87] Thus, when the crisis came in December the same year, George V already knew what outcome he would accept and pursued it. On 5 December 1916, when George V invited the Tory Andrew Bonar Law to form a government after Asquith's resignation, he refused Bonar Law's request to dissolve parliament and hold an election.[88] The king then hosted a small conference, of Asquith, Bonar Law, Lloyd George, Balfour and Arthur Henderson, representing the Labour Party, in the hope that they could hammer out a new National Government; ultimately, the conference failed and the king then sent for Lloyd George to form a government.[89] The king also intervened on multiple domestic issues, including against reprisals against German prisoners of war and by suggesting that women manufacture shells to fill manpower gaps.[90] He wrote to the Home Secretary to improve the treatment of enemy aliens and conscientious objectors, even securing the release of two interned members of a German musical band.[91]

In February 1917, in an effort to circumvent Haig, Lloyd George tried to place the British army under the command of the French General Robert Nivelle at the Calais Conference in France without telling the king beforehand, in a direct challenge to 'the King's own prerogative in subordinating his army to a foreign power without his consent'.[92] The monarch strenuously and successfully objected. When, in 1917, the king decided that the United Kingdom should rescind its offer of asylum to the Russian royal family – his own relatives – the government followed through and withdrew their offer; the fact that this had been the king's decision was kept secret until Kenneth Rose's biography in the early 1980s.[93] The king urged the quick deployment of a British military force at Archangel and Murmansk in 1918; this happened.[94] When Lloyd George wished to take on the role of Minister for War as well as Prime Minister in April 1918, the king was instrumental in preventing this, in what John Grigg described as 'royal influence over a modern prime minister on an issue of the first importance'.[95] Lloyd George admitted in a letter to the king that he thought 'there is great force in His Majesty's objections' and followed the king's advice.[96] The king, Lloyd George, Stamfordham, Sir Henry Wilson and the Archbishop of Canterbury also all met on 20 October 1918 to discuss, in detail, the British reaction to American President Woodrow Wilson's peace note exchange with Germany.[97]

In terms of foreign affairs, the royals also played an important wartime role, long forgotten. Raymond Poincaré, the French president, frequently conveyed important information to the British government and military through conversations with George V during his visits to France; on occasion, he consulted directly with the king about war decisions.[98] The French asked King George V for more troops to aid Serbia and discussed French plans for a big push in 1916 with him.[99] The Queen of the Netherlands and the Kings of Denmark and

Sweden wrote to George V, with their protests against the British naval blockade's constraints on their trade.[100] In the case of Britain's wartime allies that were monarchies, such as tsarist Russia, Italy, Greece and Belgium, older intra-royal diplomatic practices and contacts proved particularly useful. On 7 December 1915, objecting to the decisions of the Calais Conference and Lord Kitchener's strategy, Tsar Nicholas sent a telegram to King George V putting 'all my hope in your influence' to intervene.[101] When the King of Spain wanted permission to inspect British hospital ships, he wrote to King George V directly.[102]

King George V played a particularly key role in liaising with the Italian monarchy.[103] At a key impasse in negotiations to bring Italy into the war on the side of the Allies, with Russia holding out on the deal that Britain was offering Italy, Asquith wrote 'we may be driven to playing our last diplomatic card – a personal message from the King to the Czar'.[104] The king duly sent a telegram to the tsar and, following this, the Russian Foreign Minister withdrew his objections; the agreement was then signed within a week.[105] The King of Italy, Victor Emmanuel III, also asked George V directly for British military assistance for Italy in 1917.[106] The Prince of Wales played a significant role too. He visited Italy on the way back from his April 1916 tour in Egypt and then served with the British army on the Italian front from the winter of 1917 into spring 1918; during these periods in Italy, he spent a good deal of time with Victor Emmanuel III and toured the front with him.[107]

The March 1917 Prince Sixte de Bourbon-Parma peace initiative further highlights the importance of King George V. When the prince approached the French with a mooted peace offer from the Emperor Karl I of Austria-Hungary, French President Poincaré advised him to 'expound Karl's proposals to the King and Lloyd George' – the inclusion of King George V here is key, suggesting his importance in war decision-making.[108] On receiving a copy of the Emperor Karl's proposed peace offer from the French, Lloyd George drove to Windsor the next day to discuss it with the king.[109] Suspicious of the Austro-Hungarian proposal and wanting to know the Italian position on it, Lloyd George even proposed that, 'under the cover of a state visit' to the Western Front, King George V and President Poincaré of France should meet Victor Emmanuel III 'and quiz him on whether a peace approach had been made' to the Italians.[110] This all shows George V at the heart of the war's secret diplomacy. In the end, the Italian Foreign Minister, Sidney Sonnino, delayed the proposed Western Front meeting, which ultimately never took place. But the role planned for George V is highly revealing and suggests his significance in weighing up such initiatives. He was also kept directly informed by his own channels of information on the Italian army and king: during the conflict, Brigadier General Sir Charles Delmé-Radcliffe, Chief of the British Military Mission attached to the Italian Army in the Field, regularly wrote confidentially to Stamfordham. For example, on 7 June 1918, Delmé-Radcliffe wrote to

Stamfordham of the Italian monarch's views on the Prince Sixte of Bourbon peace feelers, to warn him that the episode had sowed suspicion that Italy would be 'sold' by its allies.[111]

This was far from the only incident where peace feelers were channelled through the British monarch. For example, George V recorded in his diary for 15 April 1915 a 'long interesting talk' with a Danish go-between named Hans Niels Andersen, acting for King Christian X of Denmark, who had 'just seen William also Nicky and comes from Christian who proposes that when the right time comes, Copenhagen should be chosen to discuss and sign peace and Christian would be ready at any time to bring this about'.[112] In 1916, the king's Private Secretary, Lord Stamfordham, met a German theologian, Dr Battin, twice, in February and December, through the auspices of the Archbishop of Canterbury, Randall Davidson; on both occasions Battin had come from meetings with key Continental political figures, including Aristide Briand, Prince Max of Baden, Gottlieb von Jagow, Arthur Zimmermann and the German chancellor, and set out what the various parties hoped for by way of any peace deal.[113] In December 1917, the king liaised with Lloyd George regarding a trip made by Jan Smuts to Switzerland to sound out Count Mensdorff, the king's relative and former Austro-Hungarian ambassador to the United Kingdom, on the possibility of a separate peace with Austria-Hungary or the Ottoman Empire.[114] Stamfordham noted in August 1918 that there were rumours that the king could lead in negotiating a peace. However, he did 'not think the king could move and so far he is more inclined to the "knock out blow" party'.[115] In sum, elements of the pre-war European system of international royal diplomacy continued to operate during the war, albeit often discreetly. George V was part of this.

The British monarchy was also key in Britain's delicate wartime relations with Greece, which remained neutral until 1917. George V's biographer Harold Nicolson goes so far as to state that it was the king's main foreign affairs preoccupation.[116] In 1915, George V strongly supported his Foreign Minister Sir Edward Grey's proposal to offer Cyprus to Greece in exchange for Greek entry into the war, describing the island as 'something of our own' and 'a powerful asset to bargain with'.[117] The increasing unpopularity in Britain of George V's cousin, King Constantine of Greece, for his pro-Central Power stance caused alarm at court and was another of the British monarchy's pre-war connections that the war disrupted.[118] However, royal diplomatic contact continued: the Greek king's brothers, Prince George and Prince Andrew, came to London to ask George V to use his power to intervene with King Constantine in 1916, as the latter's pro-German views had caused a rift with the pro-Allied Greek politician Eleftherios Venizelos, who had established a provisional government in Salonika in defiance, threatening Greek neutrality.[119] George V followed up by intervening with his own government in a letter on 4 September 1916, suggesting that the Prime Minister rein in

Britain's French allies in their attempts to exploit this clash to bring Greece into the war, as it was undermining its king; the damage to monarchism that such a French policy entailed concerned George V more than Constantine's pro-German attitudes, which is indicative of a sense of international pan-royal loyalties continuing even in wartime.[120] The king feared that France 'as a Republic [...] may be somewhat intolerant of, if not anxious to abolish the monarchy in Greece. But this I am sure is not the policy of my Government, nor is it that of the Emperor of Russia', who had also written to George V to protest the matter.[121] The British monarch believed a gentler approach to Constantine might yet bring Greece into the war on the Allies' side.[122] The methods of royal influence used here are illuminating: George V ended his letter stating 'I do not wish to interfere in the action of my Government, but I regard it as my duty to place on record my views upon this question at the present moment.'[123] Within a day the British ambassador in France had warned the French government to amend its approach in Greece.[124] Political heft was often wielded through letting ministers know the king's will, and relying on their monarchist inclinations to follow it, rather than direct orders. For the rest of 1916, the crisis between Greece and the Allies continued, for Britain, to be largely played out in private communications between George V and his royal cousin.[125]

In particular, in the wartime relations between the United Kingdom and Belgium, royal diplomacy flourished. George V's brother-in-law, Prince Alexander of Teck, served with the British military mission to the Belgian army, resulting in a particularly close relationship with the Belgian monarchy as the Belgian King, Albert I, directly commanded the Belgian armies in the field from 1914 and, in 1918, also acted as Allied northern group commander in Flanders. Thus, the close personal relationship between him and George V, who met many times during the conflict, was an important diplomatic and military connection. It also, however, placed pressure on King George V to live up to the wartime image of heroic royal masculinity so successfully adopted by his Belgian counterpart.[126] King Albert did not hesitate to write to George V to ask him to stop British aviators from bombing Belgian towns, a clear indication of the power the British king was believed to hold; this was particularly significant as Albert was no ill-informed figure but knew the British political situation well.[127] The link was profoundly personal: for much of the war, for safety, the Belgian royal children stayed in the UK with Lord Curzon and his family. Prince Leopold was sent to Eton, where King George's son, Prince Henry, was also at school.[128] In July 1918, King George V even invited the Belgian king and queen to the UK for the official celebrations of his twenty-fifth wedding anniversary.[129] When the Belgian royals were able to re-enter Brussels after the war ended, the British royals cemented this Allied victory in a reciprocal visit. British royal diplomacy in the wake of the Armistice was also clear with regard to France: King George V, the Prince of Wales and Prince

Albert visited Paris in late November 1918 as part of victory celebrations.[130] In other words, although the collapse of monarchies across Europe at the end of the war weakened the value of the British monarchy in Continental European diplomacy, it did not completely destroy it, and the victory moment even briefly bolstered it.

Yet George V also experienced setbacks and came up against the limits of his own power to effect political change during the war. He was unable to influence the outpouring of anti-German xenophobia towards those of foreign descent or with German connections: in 1914, for example, he found himself powerless to prevent his relative Prince Louis of Battenberg being hounded out of his position at the Admiralty against George V's wishes or the appointment of Lord Fisher as First Sea Lord to replace him in October 1914.[131] In 1915, George V wished for the whole of the war effort – War Office and army command – to be placed in Lord Kitchener's hands, 'to invest the Secretary of State for War with executive powers as commander in chief of the Imperial Forces'; the government rejected the idea.[132] The king also strongly opposed the idea of the Salonika campaign; it ultimately went ahead nevertheless.[133] He was unable to prevent Lloyd George being made Minister for War upon Kitchener's death in 1916 or to stop Beaverbrook gaining a baronetcy or a cabinet appointment as Chancellor of the Duchy of Lancaster.[134] George V's opposition to holding a general election after the war ended in 1918 was also overruled.[135] The monarch also wanted Asquith to be part of the British delegation to the Paris Peace Conference in 1919, but Lloyd George rejected the idea.[136]

In fact, during his premiership, Lloyd George sought to increase the power of the Prime Minister vis-à-vis the monarch in ways that are indicative of the degree of political status that the king had enjoyed before the Welshman came to power. Lloyd George's cavalier attitude to communicating with the monarchy drew protests from the king; his introduction of typed cabinet minutes which were generally circulated replaced the personal handwritten letter reporting on cabinet meetings which had traditionally been sent by the Prime Minister to the monarch. He also sought to keep the king in the dark with regard to military strategy, regarding which Asquith had always consulted the monarch. Lloyd George on occasion delayed sending cabinet minutes to George V, leaving him uninformed about political decisions. The king was annoyed in spring 1917 to discover the cabinet had decided to send the Foreign Minister, Sir Arthur Balfour, on a mission to Washington without consulting him; he considered it ill advised for the Foreign Minister to travel so far away in time of war.[137] On 4 March 1917, Stamfordham wrote to Lloyd George complaining that the king had only received very rudimentary minutes of the 2 March War Cabinet meeting, which omitted any details of what was discussed regarding the Irish question.[138] In this case, Lloyd George appears to have been distracted by his uncle's funeral.[139]

On 6 April 1917, Stamfordham wrote to Balfour to ask for advice, as the king had been upset to learn from the minutes of the Imperial War Cabinet that it had authorised the Prime Minister to send a telegram to President Wilson on behalf of the empire 'assembled in the Imperial War Cabinet' welcoming American entry into the war:

> His Majesty is deeply pained at what he regards as not only a want of respect, but as ignoring his very existence. The Country may wish to have a Republic but so long as they elect for a Monarchy there are certain traditional observances and duties which the Government cannot disregard with reference to the Sovereign. Surely one of those is the recognition that all Messages of the nature of the above to the Chief of a State should emanate from the Sovereign.[140]

Stamfordham appealed to Balfour 'as an old friend' to help 'save the King from such treatment.'[141] Balfour's response made clear the oversight was an accident: 'I do not remember the resolution of the Imperial War Cabinet to which you called my attention but I am confident that the last thing that was ever intended was to ignore or belittle the position of the Sovereign', who, he wrote, gives 'unity and stability to the Empire [. . .].'[142] He pointed out that the wording of the resolution was 'unfortunate' and that in the actual telegram which he had 'the honour of drafting for His Majesty his position as spokesman of the Empire is most clearly and definitely expressed'.[143] Here it appears that the tension between the king and Lloyd George against the backdrop of the February Revolution in Russia was causing George V to see republican intent where there was none. Civil servant Thomas Jones believed the king's anger over the communication to Wilson was directly due to his upset at the message of congratulations that Lloyd George had independently rushed off to the new provisional Russian government after the February 1917 revolution, a tactless move in royal eyes given the deposed tsar was a relative.[144]

Yet if Lloyd George was no republican, he was a reformer who wanted more power for the Prime Minister within the monarchic system. Despite Stamfordham's pleas, the lack of information continued – in March 1918, for example, the king only learned from a Foreign Office telegram that Philip Kerr had been sent on a mission to Switzerland. 'I am sure the Prime Minister will agree', wrote Lord Stamfordham, 'that the King should be informed on such matters'.[145] In April 1918, Lloyd George made cabinet changes without consulting with the king first, leading Stamfordham to write to him that 'I cannot disguise the fact that His Majesty is not only surprised, but hurt, that the ordinary procedure of consulting with the Sovereign with regard to such important changes in his Government has not been followed'.[146] The king learned of the dismissal of General Sir Hugh Trenchard from the post of Chief of Air Staff from the newspapers and the replacement of Lord Bertie, British ambassador to France, by telephone 'shortly before the news was made public', issues on which previous governments would have consulted him; they were also changes with which he strongly disagreed.[147] These reactions to Lloyd George's decisions indicate the power the monarchy actually could exercise – and traditionally had done. It was precisely because he did not want the king to intervene – or stop – some of his plans, that Lloyd George did not inform him of them. Frances Stevenson noted that it was even the king's habit to send Lloyd George little notes of admonishment when the latter as prime minister made a speech that he did not like.[148]

Lloyd George claimed his workload was responsible for some of these issues which strained the relationship between him and the monarchy.[149] However, personal views mattered too. No outright anti-monarchist or republican, Lloyd George was sceptical of many royal traditions and, as a liberal radical from a Welsh Nonconformist tradition, particularly disliked the elite privileges of the aristocracy. Some indications of this were subtle: the Prime Minister's secretaries did not rise to their feet when the king's Private Secretary, Lord Stamfordham, entered the room; on one occasion, Stamfordham was left waiting in the hall of No. 10 Downing Street on a wooden chair 'as if in a railway waiting-room', again indicative of how previous governments had granted the monarchy considerable access and prime ministerial deference.[150] Others were less so. It is clear that Lloyd George sought to undermine royal input into the honours system by trying to allocate honours without consulting the monarchy first.[151] Although by 'ancient custom' the monarch could award an honour to a subject without ministerial advice, the vast majority of wartime honours went to names put forward by the Prime Minister, which the king then either approved or rejected.[152] It was this latter mechanism that Lloyd George tried to circumvent. When Max Aitken was offered a peerage without the king being consulted, Lord Stamfordham wrote to Lloyd George that 'His Majesty was surprised and hurt that this honour should have been offered without first obtaining his consent. [. . .] the King recognises it is impossible for him now to withhold his approval. But [. . .] His Majesty commands me to say that he feels that the Sovereign's Prerogative in this respect should not be disregarded.'[153] When a similar incident had occurred under Asquith's premiership, the latter had apologised swiftly; in contrast, Lloyd George continued his behaviour.[154] Historian Ian Beckett has pointed to 'the increasing limitations of the royal prerogative in the face of the machinations of a Prime Minister such as Lloyd George who knew that he was virtually irreplaceable'.[155]

Yet, overall, Lloyd George's reform of the prime minister–monarchy relationship was relatively limited to breaches of protocol regarding when and how information about decisions was communicated to the monarch. Moreover, the king had also complained to Asquith at times during his premiership about not feeling informed.[156] Throughout the war, the monarchy retained its influence over military appointments and successfully reasserted its direct control over who received honours when Lloyd George sought to usurp it. There is no evidence Lloyd George wanted to abolish the monarchy and, as Chapter 4 will show, he saw its value in helping to win over war-weary striking munitions workers in 1917. After the war's end, he and the king exchanged increasingly warm personal messages.[157] By May 1919, the monarchy relied on him as a defender of the status quo against Bolshevism, Stamfordham writing that the king hoped that Lloyd George would soon return to the UK, as 'things both foreign and domestic cause anxiety'.[158] In sum, the extent of 'decline' in royal power under the Lloyd George administration suggested in the historiography should not be exaggerated.[159] Monarchist beliefs and pro-monarchy discourses continued to have considerable political influence even during the Lloyd George premiership.

Overall, examining the role of the king in wartime British politics can only provide limited insights in terms of assessing the full extent of how the conflict impacted upon the monarchy's powers. The results must remain inconclusive without further sources becoming available. What is clear is that George V continued to exercise patronage and was involved in political decision-making, often in ways that have left little paper trail. Indeed, some of the king's influence simply resulted from political figures trying to second-guess what might or might not please the Palace or from an indication from Stamfordham that the king or queen might prefer a particular outcome, rather than from a direct statement by the monarch himself. The king's interventions could be and were sometimes overruled by political decision-makers; nevertheless, they mattered, they were carefully weighed up by politicians and others, and were part of the wartime political decision-making apparatus of the state, and they were often successful.

This, however, was not the case of a true full 'kingship mechanism' to match Norbert Elias's original definition for the early modern period – King George V did not play individuals off against each other to balance rival power factions. However, it does distil something of Nicolaus Sombart's interpretation of how Elias's 'kingship mechanism' operated at the kaiser's court. There was a 'secondary system', of royal influence, patronage, honours, ritual and ceremony that existed within British politics, alongside a 'primary system' of parliament and the executive.[160] Although this British 'secondary system' was constitutionally politically much more limited than that which operated through Kaiser Wilhelm II's court for Germany, and King George V respected those constitutional limitations, it nevertheless was still present. However, unlike in the German case, there is no evidence of the king seeking to accrue personal power – or develop any personal rule – through this secondary system during the war; rather he sought determinedly through this 'secondary system' only to maintain the *existing* powers of the Crown. The British 'kingship mechanism' by the First World War was a very weak one, in comparison to the German. The kaiser, whose political and military power had been all but entirely ceded to his generals, Paul von Hindenburg and Erich Ludendorff after 1916, still retained a more powerful direct patronage role in appointing commanders.[161] Yet, in the kaiser's declining overall powers, if in little else, the two monarchies were becoming more similar as the war went on, as Wilhelm II became less directly politically and militarily in control.

Moving beyond political decision-makers, assessing the royals' cultural role can help shed more light on the question of the monarchy's power and how it changed across the war period. Here the use of the monarchy in mobilising Britain and its empire for war in 1914 emerges as particularly revealing.

PART I

The Role of the British Monarchy in Cultural
Mobilisation for War

1

Monarchist Mentalities and British Mobilisation, 1914–1916[*]

1.1 Introduction

The United Kingdom offers a fascinating case study on the importance of monarchy as a factor in motivating societies to go to war, as its unique circumstances render its role particularly visible.[1] Unlike many other European monarchies that entered the conflict, the United Kingdom did not have conscription; it was also a constitutional democracy and a multi-national state with a global overseas empire. Its small regular army was inadequate for a major international conflict, and it had to create a popular, and unified, consensus for war that was powerful enough to create an army of citizen volunteers in a largely free society. Thus, the British monarchy offers a test case for the value of monarchy as a cultural force that helped motivate society to mobilise and men to fight at the beginning of the First World War.

The monarchy's political and military roles mattered, but its role in mobilisation also went far beyond this. Its part in successful cultural mobilisation – defined in John Horne's words as 'the engagement of the different belligerent nations in their war efforts both imaginatively, through collective representations and the belief and value systems giving rise to these, and organizationally, through the state and civil society' – was crucial.[2] Monarchy served as a sacralising factor that featured among early war motivations, although it was never the only reason as to why people supported or tacitly accepted the conflict in the first years of the war, and assessing its weight for ordinary people remains very difficult.

This chapter explores the role that monarchism played in cultural mobilisation for war in 1914–16 and how the royal family itself engaged with this process. It focuses on the period before Britain introduced conscription, when the issue of voluntary recruitment was at its height. It examines the relationship between ideas of honour and kingship in Edwardian Britain at the outbreak of the conflict, before looking at how monarchism, based upon

[*] Earlier elements of this chapter appeared in the following edited volumes: Merkhens and Müller, eds., *Sons and Heirs*; Glencross, Rowbotham and Kandiah, eds., *The Windsor Dynasty*; I am grateful to these editors for their suggestions.

these ideas, was used to engage people with the war effort, particularly in recruitment campaigns and to motivate men to volunteer. It explores the meaning of the omnipresent phrase 'King and Country', as well as the role of the Prince of Wales. The focus here is on the island of Britain; the empire is discussed in Chapter 2 and Ireland, which in many ways represents a special case, is covered separately in Chapter 4.

The first two years of the war saw a wave of enthusiastic 'sacralisation' of the British monarchy, some of which openly embraced romanticised, pseudo-feudal ideas, which then began to decline from 1916 on. As the sociologist Maurice Halbwachs argued, 'social milieux consciously elaborate a past which corresponds to changing ideological parameters or new political contexts'.[3] This was the case in Britain as it responded to the outbreak of war by emphasising romantic myths of monarchy. The monarchy projected what might be termed a 'dynastic present-ism' – the idea that it connected all British subjects, past and present, both in the UK and overseas, by embodying the essence of Britain's previous and current histories. On the sudden outbreak of a global war, this projection of stability and timelessness mattered: as David Cannadine has pointed out, 'in a period of change' monarchy can be deliberately presented to give 'an impression of con-tinuity, community and comfort, despite overwhelming contextual evidence to the contrary'.[4] As Jay Winter argues, 'the upheaval of war formed national stereotypes [. . .]. "Englishness" was redefined after 1914 in terms of the wartime and post-war assertion of a vaguely defined but palpable set of English "traditions" and their appropriation by British conservative politicians, writers and artists.'[5] The monarchy was part of this, depicted as embodying a 'natural' and perennial English hierarchical and historic societal order – with the sovereign at its pinna-cle – which predated the modernising socio-economic and political developments of the nineteenth and early twentieth centuries. In 1914, it was not perceived as solely a product and reflection of a capitalist class system, even within leftist circles; it had a broader romantic and historic, talismanic image.

Class mattered, of course. 'The Crown is the apex of the social pyramid; it sets the fashion and gives the tone', wrote German ambassador Prince Lichnowsky.[6] Yet focusing on class alone does not capture the full concept of dynastic loyalty and monarchist culture that existed in 1914. The reality that the monarchy was at the top of the class system always coexisted with its self-projection as being outside class dynamics: dynastic loyalty to the king was frequently presented as something that transcended class – was indeed class-less – with all subjects supposedly equal in the eyes of the Crown. Moreover, at a time when the state was rapidly developing modern, often faceless, bureau-cracy as never before, the discourse of monarchical loyalty provided a cosy, nostalgic juxtaposition of an imagined unchanging, affective, direct vertical fealty between subject and king. Such monarchical beliefs mattered: 'dis-courses were not innocent descriptions of reality, but weapons in contests for some form of power'.[7]

1.2 'Honouring the King': Monarchical Honour Culture in 1914

In Britain, older nineteenth-century concepts of honour, grounded in a monarchical understanding of society and honouring the king, played a significant role in the monarchy's influence on cultural mobilisation in the first two years of the war.[8] This process both renewed older ideas about monarchy in British society and went hand in hand with reinvention, with the new sometimes presented as ancient tradition.[9] Examining how ideas of 'honouring' the king featured in mobilisation allows us to explore this. It reveals that early war Britain was a democratic hybrid of modernisation and older monarchist belief systems and traditions.

To understand what the concept of 'honouring the king' meant in mobilisation in 1914–16, we must first examine how contemporaries conceptualised 'honour'. As Mark Girouard has argued, from the late eighteenth century onwards, reworkings of concepts from medieval chivalry – including honour – became popular in England.[10] For Girouard, this revival of chivalry created 'ideals of behaviour, by which all gentlemen were influenced, even if they did not consciously realise it', and the First World War both 'brought Victorian chivalry to its climax and helped to destroy it'.[11] More recently, the work of Stefan Goebel has reinforced the finding that chivalric tropes were key to Great War culture and also shown the extent to which ideals of chivalric honour actually survived the war, frequently appearing on war memorials after the conflict.[12]

Girouard and Goebel show us the extent to which chivalric ideas of honour were widespread, but investigate these as a cultural style. In reality, honour was also a collective sociocultural belief system. Britain in 1914 was an honour-based culture. Contemporary sociology theories about how honour-based societies operate are useful here in helping us conceptualise the function of honour in British society in 1914.[13] Mark Cooney, for example, sets out the close connection between masculine status and fighting in honour-based cultures: to maintain his honour a man need not defeat his opponent, but he must display a *willingness* to fight him; First World War British culture reflects this process, where so many men were prepared to volunteer willingly for a battlefield upon which death from shellfire was far more likely than any actual combat where they personally defeated an opponent.[14] Honour-based cultural codes had proved remarkably flexible in adapting to Edwardian modernisation. As the historian Ute Frevert has argued, the European states that entered the war in 1914 were honour-culture societies, with codes and behaviours predicated upon ideas of status, respectability and reputation that were based upon highly gendered notions of individual and societal 'honour'.[15] From this widespread belief in honour sprang a whole range of other immensely powerful sociocultural imperatives – duty, loyalty, obedience – all necessary to retain one's honourable status. 'Honour' carried real weight. In 1914, it was both a domestic and an international relations entity of *pragmatic* value that influenced decision-making; it was not simply something that was purely symbolic or an empty rhetorical flourish. It had tangible, real functionality as a principle of social organisation. To give one's 'word of honour' was a powerful individual cultural obligation – a contractual expression – that carried an impera-tive obligation of fulfilment, be it in the business, political or familial world, different from other expressions of everyday speech. It was a form of sacralised speech act that was infused with moral meaning in Britain, drawing upon older Protestant ideas of the divine within the sacred biblical 'word'.

In sum, British society at the start of the war shared a collective belief in 'honour' and operated through shared cultural honour codes of behaviour. A romanticised idea of monarchy was integral to this.[16] The role of the royal family, their input into mobilisation, combat, morale and awarding medals, was of crucial importance as the monarchy served as a leitmotif for the cultural beliefs, built around ideals of honour, for which many Britons believed they were fighting.

One clear way in which honour presents in this period is in terms of royal honours – a system of recognition of achievement by the king that was underpinned by a belief that the monarch could bestow 'honour'. The whole British 'honour' system was predicated upon the belief that 'the Crown is the fountain of Honour', as Lord Stamfordham, King George V's Private Secretary, explained to Lloyd George in a 1917 wartime memorandum, referring to the concept behind the award of royal honours. The language and thinking are revealing.[17]

What underpinned this system of monarchical honours, however, and gave it meaning was a widespread collective belief in the existence of royal, personal, familial and national 'honour'. Britain's entry into the First World War was publicly justified in a language deeply loaded with honour references – to protect the honour of Belgium, of international law and treaties and of Britain's good name in keeping its word, of its reputational integrity.[18] Sir Edward Grey, in his speech to the House of Commons on 3 August 1914, referred to how he 'would like the House to approach this crisis in which we are now, from the point of view of British interests, British honour, and British obligations' and how 'if, in a crisis like this, we run away from those obligations of honour and interest as regards the Belgian Treaty, I doubt whether, whatever material force we might have at the end, it would be of very much value in face of the respect that we should have lost'.[19] In a sermon given at St Canice's Cathedral Kilkenny on 6 September 1914, the Archbishop of Dublin, John Henry Bernard, stated that 'we are fighting for honour. A nation's honour needs to be tenderly guarded, just as the honour of a man or the honour of a woman needs to be guarded.'[20] A postcard marking the outbreak of war showed George V's portrait, with the caption 'through war unsought to "peace with honour"!'[21]

A belief in honour, which particularly infused British public school life, helps explain how a former Etonian serving in the First World War, Lionel Sotheby, could write in all seriousness, 'To die for one's school is an honour.'[22] Indeed,

Girouard argues 'all those who had been at public schools, [...] all Boy Scouts, past and present, all Cadets, all members of boys' clubs and boys' brigades, all readers of the right adventure stories in the right magazines', knew 'exactly what was expected of them. [...] Giant forces of loyalty to king and country were ready to be triggered off, submerging all doubts in the process.'[23] A schoolboy at Rugby, Patrick Gray, wrote of his relief that England had declared war, as 'there was an awful feeling that we might dishonour ourselves'.[24] Both the 1908 and 1911 versions of the British Baden-Powell scouting movement's laws had 'a scout's honour is to be trusted' as the first law. The pre-war National Service League and the Moral Education League sought to promote character training which instilled 'personal qualities of service and honour'.[25] In pre-war circles, influenced by ideas of muscular Christianity and militarism, the 'ideal was articulated of a re-invigorated Christian Commonwealth enthused by a new army of Christian knights, for whom spiritual honour, as exemplified by the modern versions of the Arthurian legend and the codes of medieval chivalry, was to be the highest aim'.[26] Monarchism was obviously central to this Arthurian ideal.

'Honouring' the king thus must be seen within this context of what honour meant. Although it has to be emphasised that it is extremely difficult to show causation, because such beliefs are often inherent or general assumptions rather than openly articulated in sources, a belief in 'honouring the king' did exist in 1914–16. In particular, a British idea of masculine honour, which was associated closely with serving and honouring the king, performing one's manly 'duty' to him, and a specific understanding of kingship as a relationship between monarch and people, was a motivating factor in military mobilisation.

Such concepts were taught young: Baden-Powell's 1908 *Scouting for Boys: A Handbook for Instruction in Good Citizenship* set out how each scout must take 'the scout's oath, that is you promise, *on your honour* [italics in original], three things'; notably, the first of the three was 'To be loyal to God and the King'.[27] In a long letter to the Eton College *Chronicle* in 1904, Baden-Powell set out his conception of what 'honour' meant within a boys' movement, as an idea fundamentally linked to loyalty to the monarch:

Form of Engagement
The duties of the knights of old and their retainers were these:

1) To fear God
2) Honour the King

  [...] I promise on my honour, to be loyal to the King and to back up my commander in carrying out our duty in each of the above particulars. (Each member will sign his name in the space below this.) *Note* – if a fellow breaks his word of honour by not carrying out the above engagement after signing it, he incurs one punishment only, and that is *Dismissal*, because he is no longer fit to be a comrade of the others.[28]

Honour here was interwoven with monarchical reverence, and the price of losing one's personal honour was total social ostracism. Thus, individual 'honour' was presented as a precious personal possession – a spiritual characteristic – to be zealously guarded. By 1914, the Boy Scout movement had a little under 150,000 members and was the largest youth movement in the UK.[29] This link between scouting, monarchy and honour was not purely rhetorical: it surfaces in wartime perceptions. *Tring Parish Magazine,* in an obituary for Private Archibald Halsey, killed on 21 September 1916, aged 19, and a former Boy Scout patrol leader, noted: 'The first promise of the Scout is: "To do his duty to God and King". Archie was trying to keep that promise when the shell burst in the dugout on September 20th, somewhere in France.'[30] Archibald Halsey had been part of a scout troop reviewed by the king in 1911.[31] As the aristocrat John Manners left for the Western Front, after volunteering in the first month of the conflict, he gave his mother a note he had written that stated:

> Mon ame a Dieu
> Mon [*sic*] vie au Roi
> Mon coeur aux Dames
> Et honneur pour moi.[32]

> [My soul to God
> My life to the King
> My heart to the ladies
> And honour for me]

When war broke out the monarchy was understood to embody British honour in a particular form of leadership role. In his 6 September 1914 sermon, the Archbishop of Dublin, John Henry Bernard, elucidated the importance of kingship:

> For us the words 'God save the King' mean much more. They express, first of all, a sentiment of personal devotion to the sovereign [. . .]. And they are charged with emotion, as we remember that the King is the symbol and bond of national unity. The Empire is far-flung. It is not one in race, or in speech, or in religion. Dark races and white races; Mohammedans, Hindus, Christians; Protestants and Roman Catholics; they all stand in the same relation to the King. He is the visible bond, uniting these diverse forces and aspirations. He is the symbol of the continuity of the Empire which he rules. And so the prayer, 'God save the King', is a solemn prayer for the maintenance of our free national life.[33]

Of course, Bernard was speaking in an Irish unionist cultural context, but his definition of what monarchy meant as a mobilising force in 1914 reflected the meaning of British monarchism more generally. It was necessary to honour the king by defending him – Bernard went on to describe the duty of young men to their 'King and country' in time of war, including volunteering to fight.[34]

The concept of honouring the king was particularly clearly articulated later in the war in a comment by the radical English nationalist Horatio Bottomley, the editor of the right-wing newspaper *John Bull*, who wrote in the *Sunday Pictorial* in April 1917:

> I am neither fawning courtier nor servile sycophant – but I honour the King. To say that I do so because of his personal virtues would be an impertinence. To place him on a pinnacle of individual superiority over and above his fellow men would be time-serving hypocrisy. I loved King Edward because he was just one of our selves and I doubt not that King George makes no claim to be, except by heredity, anything more. But I honour my King *because he is my King.* Just that.[35]

For Viscount Esher, a highly conservative courtier, writing in 1918, honouring the king included a belief in his infallibility:

> By inherited tradition, by upbringing, by surroundings, his [a king's] judgment is assumed to be superior and his decisions are undisputed. When he speaks *ex-cathedra* upon matters of social order, his word is final. He can afford to impose restraints, and frame rules of conduct, that men and women are ready to obey, because they believe the sovereign to be above social pressure and to be free from partisan prejudice. The King belongs to no party and to no class. [. . .] That the King can do no wrong is not only a convenient constitutional maxim; it is the honest opinion of the mass of the people.[36]

That Bottomley and Esher felt it necessary to spell out this monarchical belief system in 1917 and 1918 is telling. By the latter years of the war, and particularly following the Russian Revolution, established collective cultural understandings of monarchy in the UK were under scrutiny; Esher and Bottomley sought vigorously to defend the 1914 monarchical status quo and to spell out why honouring the king mattered. For this reason, their explanations help to elucidate what the concept of honouring the king meant.

Such ideas about 'honouring the king' were, in fact, something of a resurrected phenomenon: as David Cannadine has shown, between the late 1870s and 1914 there was a fundamental change in the popularity of the British monarchy, which for much of the nineteenth century had been the subject of newspaper hostility, mockery and public scepticism; by contrast, by the time of Victoria's death it had become venerated, a trend concomitant with the revival of chivalry that Girouard has identified and the late nineteenth-century rise in British discourses emphasising the importance of 'honour.'[37] By the reign of Edward VII, Cannadine argues, the monarchy had become 'virtually sacrosanct' in English newspapers.[38]

Although they were most vocally presented by the upper and middle classes, beliefs in honour went largely unchallenged in 1914. Aside from a few radicals like George Bernard Shaw, before the war, even among the Labour and suffragette movements there was no universal rejection of the idea of honour; while some members argued that the idea of sexual honour constrained women, for example, others utilised standard languages of masculine and feminine honour culture as part of their campaigns.[39] A debate in the Canadian parliament, however, suggests that new ideas were beginning to appear there with regard to one aspect of honour-based society – royal honours. Robert Borden, the wartime Canadian Prime Minister, recalled in his memoirs how in January 1914 the Canadian parliament debated a bill to 'abolish titles of honour in Canada'.[40] The bill's proposer declared that 'democracy in itself does not contemplate class honours and therefore it is a violation of the principle of democracy and of the will of the people that they should be established'.[41] Defenders of retaining honours, by contrast, argued that 'the principle, itself, [...] is not wrong in our Empire. It has in the past resulted in great good, and will [...] in the future [...].'[42] Sir Wilfrid Laurier argued against the bill too and pointed out that the honour system could not be abolished through a parliamentary bill in any case, but only through the king, 'who alone bestows such honours', a revealing comment.[43]

Ultimately, references to 'honour' in statements by or about the monarchy must be read as collective cultural texts. As Philip Williamson has pointed out:

> to expect literal meaning from royal language is to misunderstand its purpose, which was not descriptive but exemplary – to express and endorse public values. The more the monarchy had become elevated above sectional controversies, the more convincing and useful it became in symbolizing and universalizing values which most public and voluntary bodies considered essential for the general interest. [...] The values projected upon and expressed by the monarchy were 'ideological' responses by various groups to particular early twentieth-century conditions.[44]

Royal discourse, including phrases like 'honour the king', were a reflection of wider historical cultural values. The king's speeches and statements, in particular, were a collaboration which merged the monarch's input with a public discourse of Establishment beliefs about kingship rhetoric. This insight also clearly helps us to understand the function of monarchism in British society more generally during this period – constructed to convey cultural values as much as literal truths but also influenced by elite political interests. Nevertheless, honouring the king – and believing in the meaning of personal honour as part of this process – were part of the public values that these discourses promoted. These beliefs, in turn, played a role in war mobilisation.

1.3   Monarchism and the Legal Framework for War

The monarchy's role in mobilisation also had profound legal dimensions. A royal message to both Houses of Parliament was required when mobilisation was ordered while parliament was sitting.[45] Margot Asquith, the Prime Minister's wife, described watching her husband dramatically declare the arrival of 'a message from His Majesty, signed by his own hand', mobilising the army reserve, to cheers in the House of Commons on 4 August 1914.[46] The Speaker then read the message aloud to the House. Significantly, the population of the United Kingdom in 1914 were legally defined as *subjects* of the monarch, rather than as citizens; this was also the case for all those living in the dominions and colonies of the British Empire, the very term 'dominion' in itself revealing a profoundly monarchist mentality in the conceptualisation of imperialism.[47] The only exception was the populations of British protectorates, which were considered as territories under the protection of the British Crown, whose indigenous populations were classed as British-protected persons.[48] It was not until the 1948 British Nationality Act that the legal status of 'citizen' was introduced in the United Kingdom, although the term does appear in First World War sources often interchangeably with the more frequently used 'subject'.[49] As Randall Hansen points out, allegiance to the king was a cornerstone of English common law and implies

> two conditions: first, the bond is a direct, unmediated relationship between King and subject, and, second, any privileges attached to one's status as subject are granted by the sovereign and are exercised at his pleasure; they are not claimed by the subject against his sovereign. These features distinguish a 'subject' from a 'citizen'. The latter enjoys his status through membership in a community enjoying the same status and makes claims against the state based on this membership. The essentially feudal concept – everything within the realm of the Lord belongs to the Lord – remained unaltered as Britain entered the imperial age.[50]

Property and personal freedoms in the UK in 1914 were held under the protection of the King's Peace, the legal concept that the monarch protected public order and his representatives upheld it. Likewise, immigrants to the UK before 1914 resided there legally under 'the King's Peace' – the idea that as long as they obeyed the laws of the land they were under the monarch's protection.[51] All cabinet ministers were the king's ministers; their appointments had to be approved by the monarch. Even if the king was constitutionally bound to accept his Prime Minister's decision on the selection of ministers, he could advise on it. Likewise, all civil servants operated through the status of 'servants of the Crown' who were 'by law employed "at the pleasure of His Majesty"' and whose status and pensions were thus 'by gift rather than by right'.[52]

Language also tellingly reveals the monarchical structures that underpinned the legal dimensions of the war effort. The 1914 emergency powers brought in to respond to the outbreak of war were termed 'the Defence of the Realm Act' (DORA), defining the state as a kingdom. DORA 'conferred on His Majesty in Council power to make Regulations during the present

War for the Defence of the Realm'.[53] This included not only regulations affecting the armed forces, but also 'the rights of private citizens'.[54] Powers transferred to the Crown under DORA included the right to intern individuals without trial and purveyance rights for the Crown to 'requisition premises without compensation'.[55]

The use of the monarchic framework of the state as a means of managing wartime governance rapidly expanded. The war would see parliament's influence temporarily reduced as the residual powers of the Crown were used by an over-stretched government to meet the demands of the conflict. There was considerable use made by the government of Royal Proclamations, and of Orders in Council whereby primary legislation was made in the name of the king by the Privy Council using the royal prerogative. Technically this bypassed parliament, allowing the executive and Crown to legislate without it.[56] The Clerk of the Privy Council, Sir Almeric Fitzroy, noted at the start of 1915 that in 1914 the Council had already met thirty-seven times, 'or three times in excess of the mean'.[57] Fitzroy was often responsible for getting a Privy Council quorum, which was a minimum of just three Privy Counsellors, together quickly when meetings were called at the last minute to pass urgent government legislation.[58] The system was considered so invaluable that, unusually, when the king suffered an accident in 1915, the queen was then empowered to hold Councils on the king's behalf for the rest of the war in the case that he was indisposed or away, so that it was not disrupted or delayed.[59] This wartime use of the royal prerogative to legislate through Orders in Council was unusual both in scale and reach. It should also not be confused with the statutory form of Orders in Council, which also operated, which saw Orders in Council made in accordance with an Act of Parliament.

In practice, the king's approval of any Orders in Council was a formality; he simply assented to orders drafted by his government. However, concerns were raised by Labour activists about the wartime use of the Privy Council in this way by the government and what this meant for civil liberties and parliamentary scrutiny.[60] Indeed, the Privy Council was used at times to deal with labour unrest: on 4 September 1918, a council was hurriedly called because of a threatened strike of employees of industrial cooperative societies in northern England, in order to issue a draft proclamation applying the part of the Munitions Act that made arbitration compulsory against them; while Lloyd George attended, this move was his action in concert with the monarch and two other counsellors, not a cabinet decision.[61]

The Privy Council was also often the occasion for the king to receive additional information about political problems by speaking privately with an attendee afterwards or beforehand.[62] The structures and mechanisms of monarchy were clearly at the heart of how the wartime state actually legislatively functioned. These developments set the groundwork for the

1920 Emergency Powers Act, which transferred some of the powers of DORA into the interwar period and gave the king the power to dissolve parliament, declare a state of emergency and appoint a new Prime Minister.[63] None of this suggests a wartime weakening of the monarchy's political roles.

The extent to which the individual subject was legally defined through monarchy was exemplified when, in 1920, the Chancellor of the Exchequer, Austen Chamberlain, announced that the government would hold German reparations for the benefit of the Crown, as such reparations were paid as compensation directly to George V as recompense for damages done to his subjects.[64] By this legalistic monarchic formulation, all reparations received from Germany were the property of the Crown – as representative of the state – and the government could retain them and distribute them as it wished – rather than direct compensation which had to be paid to individual subjects who had put in claims for specific wartime damages. The underlying message was that the individual subjects' financial losses could be corrected by a payment *to their monarch*; this legal formulation clearly echoed older honour ideas whereby a harm done to a subject was a harm done to the king. The subject in this formulation was a damaged possession of their monarch, and the compensation thus went to the Crown – on behalf of the state – and not the individual subject, who was to receive none of it.

This decision to use the Crown's prerogative in this way did not go unchallenged. In 1925, the Civilian War Claimants Association was founded to challenge the Treasury, which it argued was sheltering under the name and prerogative of the sovereign to withhold paying out money paid by Germany to compensate civilians who had suffered war damages. The Association was at pains, however, to state that it blamed the Treasury for this situation and that 'Our Sovereign [. . .] has nothing to do with the matter' and 'cannot from his position express any resentment that his name should have been used in this way'.[65] The king, it noted, 'has ever been ready to give unsparing personal service in answer to the call of the poor and needy', and the association of his name with the Treasury's decision was 'odious'.[66] The king remained sacrosanct, even for those objecting to aspects of the monarchical system. Some civilians even took a case for compensation for individual war damages by bringing a 'Petition of Right' against the Crown, an ancient method of bringing an invasion of the subject's rights to the notice of the sovereign, ironically using archaic legal trappings of monarchy to protest at how the monarchic structure of the state had been used against individual reparations.[67] The case went to the King's Bench, which, in its final decision, in 1931, found against them. As this legal example illustrates, even after it ended, the war could still be conceptualised in financial terms as a conflict between sovereigns, and monarchism underpinned the entire legal existence of the British subject at war.

1.4   Religious Belief and Wartime Monarchism

The idea of honouring the king was also closely associated with the divine and the monarchy's religious power – as Defender of the Faith and Supreme Governor of the established Church of England, the monarch had a specifically sacralised status and was also spiritually linked to his subjects through the Church of England's liturgical prayers for the king. In Scotland, the monarch also had close ties with the established Church of Scotland. Indeed, all Church of England clergy undertook an oath of allegiance to him during their institution, as did all parliamentarians throughout the empire and in Westminster; mayors too took an oath to the king, as did cabinet ministers, who pledged 'not to disclose confidential matters'.[68] Crucially, the king's honour – to which his subjects did homage – was perceived as granted to the monarch from God. The king was a divinely anointed figure, the moment of coronation one that transfigured the man through holy oil to become king, in an act that set him apart from ordinary people, with strong parallels to the distinguishing of the priest through ordination.[69] The Archbishop of Canterbury wrote to George V on 22 June 1911 that he had consecrated the king on behalf of the empire and as 'the spokesman of a Christian people which desires to invoke the blessing of the Lord God Himself upon its Sovereign' and who are praying that God will grant them 'at their head a "consecrated" man [...] a man who deliberately means, by the help of God, to lead a life of "service", [...] of manly purity and justice and truth'.[70] The *Illustrated London News* used religious imagery in its presentation of the new Queen Mary, with her photograph surmounted by miniature images of Christ and alongside an image of Mary, Jesus's mother.[71] Andrzej Olechnowicz has described coronation as representing 'a quasi-ordination and consecration'.[72] Philip Williamson has noted that twentieth-century British kings 'customarily spoke in quasi-priestly terms, bestowing God's blessings, invoking God's help, offering thanks to God'.[73] This was frequently the case for King George V's public declarations in the Great War.

The idea of the king as protector of his people in 1914 thus not only invoked a battlefield role as head of his armies, or a political paternalist obligation to care for subjects' welfare, but also a powerful spiritual dynamic; kingship was a quasi-sacerdotal role. Here the king's position as custodian of the country's honour was one that had intangible religious dimensions: the monarch was protector of religious honour, and his subjects, in honouring him through their service and praying for his well-being, thereby honoured God as well as the state. To be honoured by the king, whether through medals or other recognition, was to receive a portion of honour from one upon whom it had been bestowed by God.

In sum, the monarch was still a sacralised figure at the start of the Great War, as Supreme Governor of the Church of England but also as a focus for more informal kinds of spiritual folk loyalties and belief systems. This is clear from the king's role in several highly popular wartime prayer events. These reflected a much older tradition, long in abeyance, whereby the monarch directly called subjects to special church services to supplicate God for deliverance in time of national peril and ordered fast and thanksgiving days.[74] Between 1915 and 1918 these traditions were 'reinvented' in several ways, largely at the behest of the churches.

Initially, wartime National Days of Prayer for the fate of the war effort were planned by the churches, in consultation with the monarchy, and then 'publicly approved' by the sovereign and announced 'by the King's wish'.[75] Voluntary religious cooperation with the monarchy drove this. Distinct from nineteenth-century Special Days of Worship, often held to mark royal personal events, such as a wedding or the birth of an heir, wartime National Days of Prayer were organised directly by the leaders of the various churches, led by the Archbishop of Canterbury on behalf of a range of denominations, rather than the monarch, as George V refused to resurrect the original early modern format. There was no state or government order to worship as there had been in earlier centuries or exercise of the royal supremacy, nor was the king acting in his capacity as Supreme Governor of the Church of England, although it is unlikely that the average churchgoer was aware of these distinctions in the king's role. In the first years of the war, the king simply endorsed the arrangements made by the religious leaders, and, at their behest, issued the appeal to worship, asking 'the churches and congregations to pray for the nation and its people. [...] the sovereign published a personal request'.[76] Prime Ministers only became involved from 1917–18.[77]

However, in January 1918, a National Day of Prayer was specifically presented as a personal initiative of the king acting as symbolic head of the British nation, although still not in any official ecclesiastical or constitutional capacity.[78] This associated the monarchy particularly closely with wartime religiosity. As historian Philip Williamson argues: 'For the King to give his approval, as from late 1914, for National Days of Prayer publicly arranged by church leaders was straightforward, without risk of controversy or of harm to the monarchy's reputation. But for the king himself to take the initiative and issue the call to prayer', which happened in January 1918, seemed 'to have risks', with George V and Stamfordham both concerned that it might damage the monarchy in the eyes of the non-religious or worse, be poorly attended.[79] Lord Stamfordham pointed out to the Bishop of Chelmsford in April 1917 that 'people would not give over drinking because [the] King told them and they would not pray if he told them to'.[80]

Yet, in fact, there was a marked difference in response: the wartime National Days of Prayer were widely observed and supported by the public in the 1914–18 conflict, and the new tradition only died out after the Second World War.[81] Prayer, it seems, was more of an accepted royal domain than abstemiousness. National Days of Prayer clearly blurred the lines between monarchical tradition and wartime modernisation: the mass public response appears a traditional reflex reaction to the combined status of God and monarchical appeal, while the way they were organised and the fact that they were observed not only in the Church of England but by other Christian denominations made them an innovation. For the first 'national day of prayer in January 1915, the public sales of the Church of England's service alone reached almost three million copies'; in August 1916, 20,000 people gathered at one prayer meeting in Princes Street Gardens in Edinburgh, while in August 1918 'a similar number' gathered in Hyde Park on a National Day of Prayer.[82] For the National Day of Prayer in January 1918, public houses, cinemas and places of entertainment 'voluntarily closed as a mark of respect'.[83]

In July 1919, the king also revived an older practice, directly issuing a Royal Proclamation to 'appoint special worship' for a Sunday of thanksgiving in July 1919 to mark the Versailles Peace Treaty in the UK and across the empire, a very popular gesture. As a Proclamation this was a more traditional direct use of royal power than the National Days of Prayer, even if it was coupled with an innovative ecumenical request for denominations other than the Church of England, and indeed other faiths across the empire, to participate.[84]

All this was illustrative of the broader sacralised status of monarchy in 1914–1918. For example, the tradition of the sovereign personally distributing alms to the poor at a religious service on Maundy Thursday had fallen into abeyance by 1914; the Lord High Almoner usually distributed the alms on the king's behalf. However, during the war, Queen Alexandra, King George V's mother, began attending the Maundy Thursday service in person. By 1932, George V would personally distribute alms at the service, the first time a sovereign had done so since 1698.[85] As Philip Williamson notes, the war marked an increase in royals attending public worship: 'Except for specifically royal events, it had been rare for previous sovereigns to attend public worship, and very rare indeed for them to be present at great church services, even for national occasions.'[86] The war resulted in this occurring frequently, including the king attending the 'national' post-Armistice thanksgiving services, not only in the Church of England, but also the Church of Scotland and the English Free Churches, and sending a representative to the Roman Catholic service.[87] This emphasised the king's own piety but also re-presented the older sacralised role of the monarchy in new ways.

The monarchy was constantly associated with wartime spiritual leadership. Army chaplains' cap badges were designed with a Maltese cross surmounted by a royal crown; Jewish chaplains wore a similar badge with the Star of David surmounted by a crown. The monarchy and religion were combined in this symbolism. During the conflict, the king received numerous private requests that he should support a 'state-proclaimed [...] "Day of Humiliation"' whereby the people would atone for their sins to win God's favour in the war.[88] The Archbishop of Canterbury opposed this, preferring National Days of Prayer instead. When George V made his first public appearance after a serious wartime fall from his horse, at an event in memory of the war dead at the Royal Albert Hall on 5 February 1916, Stamfordham wrote to the Archbishop of Canterbury to ask whether he might encourage clergy to attend, to give both the event and the king's recovery a clear religious dimension. The Archbishop insisted it remain an entirely secular occasion without clergy, to avoid offending those within the Church of England who objected to praying for the dead.[89]

Religious belief was closely integrated within the monarchist world view: a 1914 War Office pamphlet publication for troops was entitled *With the Colours for God, King and Country: Psalms and Hymns for Soldiers in the Field* (Edinburgh, 1914). In British Great War culture, the words 'God save the King' in the national anthem were thus not merely lyrics but, for the devout, prayer – echoing the prayers for the king in Church of England religious services. As the Archbishop of Dublin, John Henry Bernard, stated in a sermon on 6 September 1914: 'Let us pray, above all, for faith, that God, Who can save, Who can give deliverance to kings, will give us His strength. [...] And as we thus pray, our prayers take up the words of the old prayer of our fathers, God Save the King.'[90]

The two dimensions of monarchism – national and spiritual – clearly openly overlapped when the national anthem was itself sung in a religious context. In 1915, at the end of the service held to mark the anniversary of the outbreak of the war, which the king and queen attended at St Paul's Cathedral and which was intended to 'inaugurate the second year of the war by invoking God's help', the service ended with the congregation singing 'God Save the King', and the crowd outside the cathedral also joined in.[91] For Sir Almeric Fitzroy, Clerk of the Privy Council, attending, 'the roll of drums and crash of sound, with which the National Anthem opened, seemed the vibrant echo of an unflinching purpose: no whisper of doubt or misgiving clouded the splendour of the dedication which King and people made of themselves before the altar of God and the consecrated ashes of the dead'.[92] Again, in January 1917, when Irish-Canadian troops were welcomed to a Church of Ireland service in Armagh, the sermon concluded with the singing of 'God Save the King'.[93]

It is noteworthy here that the anthem-singing was *part* of the religious service and followed the singing of religious hymns, which were described as hymns of 'petition'.[94] Church hymns and monarchist national anthem were clearly interchangeable as forms of supplicating God in this particular religious context. The phenomenon surfaced more broadly: when, in 1916, the Devon and Cornwall Baptist Association, Exeter District, held their spring meeting, a 'loyal toast to the King was heartily given' at the close of the luncheon, 'with the singing of one verse of the National Anthem'.[95] Such words and gestures were not merely empty rhetoric: as historian John Wolffe suggests, often the 'use of religious forms and language in public life' was still 'founded on the conviction that direct contact is being made with God, or at least with something transcendent'.[96] Even those opposed to the war effort revealed this widespread norm: Philip Snowdon's wife Ethel declared in a speech to the Independent Labour Party at Woolwich on 30 July 1917 that she was against the national anthem, as she 'wanted to know the reason why she should pray for the King', she stated, 'just because he was the son of his father'.[97] Indicating the changed climate of 1917 following the Russian revolution, police noted that her declaration 'evoked considerable enthusiasm'.[98] For the Archbishop of Canterbury, Randall Davidson, writing to the king in June 1917, the connection between monarchy and public prayer went without saying:

> Of this Your Majesty may be assured. Thoughtful men and women, all the Kingdom through, are quietly, even though silently, appreciating Your Majesty's inevitable anxiety and the daily stress and are giving the support of their [...] confidence, their loyal personal attention and, in very many cases, their earnest prayers.[99]

Again, on 21 August 1918, in a letter praising George V for the example he was setting in attending church services, the Archbishop reiterated the spiritual dimension to the king's wartime leadership:

> Will Your Majesty let me say – from absolute and direct knowledge – how much reality is being given to the prayers for the Sovereign (apt otherwise to be merely formal) by the knowledge throughout the Empire of what Your Majesty has done and is doing in connexion with the war and those directly or indirectly engaged in it. I have heard it again and again said 'Our prayers for the King and Queen have a new ring about them now, for everybody knows how they are [...] stimulating and heartening people by daily word and act.'[100]

He went on to refer to 'a new sacredness to the loyalty of those who think and care and pray'.[101]

Clearly, even the Archbishop of Canterbury here acknowledged that prayers for the king could function in various ways, as a routine part of church life – merely 'formal' – or as profound moments supplicating God's aid for the monarch, illustrating the difficulty of analysing the spiritual history of the king's role. A 1918 Salvation Army wartime publication entitled 'Serving the King's Men', however, suggested that there was an understanding of the power of the duality of religious and earthly languages of kingship and loyalty. It related how serving their earthly king overlapped with troops finding the service of Christ, the heavenly king, describing soldiers on the Western Front attending a service at which Mary Booth spoke, where 'at the conclusion of that Service fifty soldiers, one after another, raised their hands as tokens that they henceforth would serve their God as well as serve their King'.[102] On 18 June 1917, the Daily Record and Mail noted in a report on the king and queen attending church in Newcastle that 'it was appropriate that the King, at the close of a week in which he has received abundant evidences of the homage of loyal subjects, should himself go to pay in turn his homage to the King of kings'.[103] A *Daily Mail* postcard showed the king during one of his front visits, at prayer, head bowed at the front of a throng of troops, heads similarly bowed, attending church in a makeshift chapel.[104]

The impact of religious belief mattered, shaping how kingship was seen during the war and its aftermath, which, it should be noted, saw a rise in both Anglican and Nonconformist church memberships.[105] Indeed, as late as the 1950s, surveys showed that around 30 per cent of the British population believed that the monarch was specially chosen by God.[106] The overt sacralisation of monarchy through religion was a highly visible part of the war effort. The king's message to all ranks in the Royal Navy and Army in December 1917 was a typical example: 'The nation stands faithful to its pledges, resolute to fulfil them. May God bless your efforts and give us victory.'[107] The king's word was depicted as channelling national faith and divine intercession. The response in the conservative *Daily Telegraph* conveyed a similar sacralised understanding of kingship: 'If in all things we act in the spirit of the King's assurance, we shall have nothing with which to reproach ourselves in the coming year.'[108] Monarch and people were depicted in this exchange as in a spiritual bond; living up to the king's exhortation was both honourable and protective – the phrase the 'spirit of the King's assurance' suggested that a people who obeyed would ensure that the king's assurance – his blessing – would be granted by God. Religious cultures were integral to the idea of honouring the king.

1.5   Monarchism in Military Culture

British military cultures too suggest that monarchism was relevant to mobilisation in the first years of the war. Military discourse was particularly infused with the idea of loyalty to the monarchy. From ships named after members of the royal family to honorary regimental positions for royals or the prefix 'royal' being granted to army departments as an honour, such as the Army Chaplains' Department, which became the *Royal* Army Chaplains' Department in 1919, monarchism was part of military group identities. Military service was also presented as a personal, sacralised, individual bond between monarch and subject, not soldier and state. Commissioned officers in the pre-war British army received a certificate that emphasised this: for example, the certificate sent to Stanley Steadman read 'To Our Trusty and well beloved Stanley Joseph Steadman Greeting: We reposing especial Trust and Confidence in your Loyalty, Courage and good Conduct do by these Presents Constitute and Appoint you to be an Officer in Our Land Forces from the Sixteenth day of July 1913.'[109] The certificate carried a facsimile of the royal signature and was sealed with the royal seal.

At the outbreak of the war, the king issued a message to his troops, described in some press quarters as a royal 'blessing', reinforcing this bond: 'You are leaving home to fight for the safety and honour of my Empire', it stated, 'I have implicit confidence in you, my soldiers. Duty is your watchword and I know your duty will be nobly done. I shall follow your every movement with deepest interest [. . .] indeed your welfare will never be absent from my thoughts. I pray to God to bless you and guard you and bring you back victorious.'[110] The message was widely reproduced in the press and in a variety of postcard designs, often with the king's portrait.[111] This culture also applied to the navy, to which the king sent a similar message.[112] Sir David Beatty, upon his appointment to the command of the Grand Fleet, viewed his war role within a subject–monarch framework, writing to the king: 'I pray God grant me a right judgement in all things, to enable me at all times to prove worthy of the Trust that Your Majesty has honoured me with.'[113] Most famously, Kitchener's note of guidance to British troops in 1914, which was to be kept in each soldier's active service pay book, stated: 'You are ordered abroad as a soldier of the King to help our French comrades against the invasion of a common enemy. [. . .] Do your duty bravely. Fear God. Honour the King.'[114]

During the war, the king's body was also used to visually endorse the war effort and the military, by embracing a more militarised image. There is a detailed historiography on the early modern and nineteenth-century royal body and its display, but it excludes the First World War period.[115] In fact, as Andrzej Olechnowicz has pointed out, 'modern royal masculinity remains almost wholly unstudied, either in terms of how kings and princes imagined themselves or how their male personae appealed to their male and female subjects'.[116] This is surprising: after all, the king's was the most symbolically important public male body in wartime Britain. If we draw upon John Tosh's idea of plural nineteenth-century cultural masculinities, whereby dominant masculinities were constructed in opposition to others more subordinate, such as the working-class male, then clearly royal 'manliness' and masculinity mattered.[117] David Cannadine has argued that key to the survival of the British monarchy was the fact that it was 'shorn of its traditional priestly, governing and warrior roles; reinvented during Victoria's time as an imperial, ceremonial, welfare and family monarchy'.[118] Yet, in his embrace of a more martial wartime image, George V reversed this trend for the duration of the conflict.

From the outset of the war, the king's image took a distinctly military turn.[119] He was frequently depicted wearing military and naval uniform, having decided to wear it in public on a constant basis. The king even gave 'away most of his civilian wardrobe'; the only new clothes he ordered during the war were uniforms.[120] Through wearing different military outfits, the royal body could perform a wide range of armed leadership roles that spanned the different army and navy services. 'He very soon adopted military or naval

Fig. 1 The meeting of King George V and President Poincaré of France at the British Headquarters at Merville, France on 1 December 1914, by Herbert Arnould Olivier (© Estate of Herbert Arnould Olivier and Crown Copyright UK Government Art Collection, UK Department for Digital, Culture, Media and Sport, art collection number 3808)

service uniform as his normal dress', wrote George V's biographer John Gore in 1941, 'a sound decision which had a good effect on the country and increased his popularity'.[121] As a newspaper reported on the king's visit to munitions factories in Coventry in 1915: 'He was accompanied by his khaki-clad staff officers, and was himself attired in khaki.'[122] The report was subtitled 'Workmen's Cheers for Khaki-Clad Monarch'.[123] The press approved of this militarisation of the male royal image, noting that the king and queen exchanged portraits at Christmas 1914 of the Prince of Wales and Prince Albert in their wartime uniforms.[124]

A painting by Herbert Arnould Olivier, shown in Fig. 1, emphasises this military image of monarchy: both George V and the Prince of Wales are in military uniform, unlike the French President, who is in civilian clothing. One factor here was that the monarchy felt it had to set a leading example for British masculinity in wartime and encourage voluntary enlistments. However, the king and his sons' image also reflected idealised masculine wartime roles, including that of traditional royal military leader or warrior, as well as the monarchy's long association with the military. The king and his two eldest sons were constantly depicted in the press as 'at war'. The press emphasised that the future Edward VIII (David) was taking risks at the Western and Italian fronts and that the future George VI (Albert) was in danger in the navy, including serving in battle at Jutland; he also visited the Western Front and served with the new RAF, a risky activity given the frequent mechanical problems with planes in this era. Even the schoolboy Prince Henry was photographed in his

Fig. 2   King George V working in his tent in Buckingham Palace Gardens with his Private Secretary Arthur John Bigge, Lord Stamfordham, in June 1918, The Royal Collection Trust, RCIN 2108037 (© Her Majesty Queen Elizabeth II, 2020)

Officers' Training Corps uniform at Eton, training to fight.[125] His younger brother Prince George was less visible; nevertheless, his father wrote to him, aged 12, in August 1914 to enquire if his teacher, Mr Hansell, was instructing him about the war: 'He should read the accounts in the papers to you every day, as you ought to know what is going on.'[126] Here were echoes of the traditional princely education in warfare. By 1916, aged 14, Prince George was enrolled in the Royal Naval Cadets.[127]

The king also increasingly carried out his work from a tent, set up at Buckingham Palace, which resembled that of a general on campaign. Images of him working in it, in 1918, depicted him identically to a military leader and were reproduced as postcards, as shown in Fig. 2.

This was the monarch presented as wartime decision-maker. The image was not a propaganda ruse – George V frequently referred in his diary to working long hours in the tent. Although he had used a tent before the war, it now became a deliberately emphasised part of his visual image, which it had not been before the conflict.[128] Even the king's home front duties were redefined: as John Gore wrote, the king created a new order of his days which indeed differed little from the routine of a Commander at the seat of war. For him, the business of State and ceremonial functions took the place of the Commander's tactical plannings and strategical conferences, but most of his innumerable duties of inspection were very much on the lines – though many times multiplied – of those of a Commander-in-Chief in the field.[129]

This adoption of a martial image matched the trend among contemporary monarchs of belligerent states across Europe, which was one of projecting male action, competition, power and command.[130] Kaiser Wilhelm II of Germany spent much of the war at General Headquarters, where he attended daily situation briefings; King Albert I of Belgium had direct personal command of his army from 1914; Tsar Nicholas II of Russia took charge of his from 1915. Crown Prince Rupprecht of Bavaria was a notably successful army commander, while the tsar's brother, Grand Duke Mikhail, who had lived in Britain before the war and was close to the British royals, served as a skilful frontline commander on the Eastern Front.[131] Victor Emmanuel III of Italy, even though he did not directly command, became known as 'the soldier king' because he was constantly touring the front.[132] The kaiser's two sons, Prince Heinrich as Commander of the naval forces in the Baltic and Crown Prince Wilhelm as Commander of the 5th Army, were granted important personal command positions due to their royal status, but not their competence; although their undeserved promotion, as well as that of the kaiser's other sons, to 'high rank and [...] cosy sinecures' would ultimately damage the German monarchy, at the outbreak of war this was not clear.[133]

Given this European context, it is not hard to see why George V militarised his image. It was a way to sustain the monarchy's influence with the military and also to ensure that no general overshadowed its status. It also served to compensate for the fact that, although George V was Commander-in-Chief of the British armed forces, long-standing constitutional convention was that this royal prerogative was delegated to the government. Yet, in September 1915, Alexandra Churchill claims, a proposal was made that George V 'should take command of the army himself'; in response, Esher pointed out that the king was 'just as qualified as the Tsar who has done this in Russia'.[134] Churchill does not specify who made the suggestion, but it was not taken up. However, the fact that it was ever made is remarkable.[135] It illustrates the tension that existed around the monarch's authority as Commander-in-Chief and the government's actual powers – delegated from the monarch only by convention – to decide military policy and instruct the commanders in the war's various theatres, which surfaced periodically during the war. The mentality was already visible during the Curragh Mutiny in Ireland in March 1914, when Sir Arthur Paget, the General Officer Commanding the troops in Ireland, tried to sway putative mutineers by stating that his instructions were 'the direct orders of the Sovereign' and not 'those dirty swine, the politicians'.[136] The king strongly objected that his name had been used in an attempt to undermine government authority, but Paget stood firm, stating that 'all orders to the army' were always 'the King's'.[137] Royal authority definitely held greater cultural cachet with the army than Downing Street did. As historian Ian Beckett points out, during the war,

> one significant remaining part of the royal prerogative was the monarch's role as titular Commander-in-Chief of the armed forces. [...] For most soldiers, the Crown represented a higher form of authority than that of government. By posing, first and foremost, as servants of the Crown, soldiers could distance themselves from what was perceived as the squalid nature of politics.[138]

Moreover, while George V was scrupulous about following the constitutional norms, within these limits he did frequently directly encourage and warn with regard to specific strategic and operational decisions; he also exercised considerable influence on appointments and dismissals in the armed forces, although in keeping with constitutional convention he accepted those that ultimately went against him.[139] It is no surprise that Sir Douglas Haig reported to and consulted with the king as much as with the government which actually instructed him. The power dynamics were thus somewhat triangulated between Downing Street, the Palace and Haig and remain murky. George V, while careful never to undermine the government, was fully informed on military decisions and let his opinions on them be known behind the scenes; while not actively commanding, he should not be seen as merely a powerless figurehead either.

The monarch's military status was also built upon older notions of faithful allegiance which bound him or her in what was seen as a sacred relationship to each individual subject of kingdom and empire, with the reciprocal obligation upon monarch and subject to 'serve' and 'protect' each other, duties which took on a particular resonance in wartime. This formed the core of the oath of attestation taken by recruits to the British army during the war, who swore 'by Almighty God that I will be faithful and bear true Allegiance to His Majesty King George the Fifth, His Heirs and Successors, and that I will, as in duty bound, honestly and faithfully defend His Majesty, His Heirs, and Successors, in Person, Crown, and Dignity against all enemies, according to the conditions of my service'.[140]

It is difficult to assess if such oaths to the monarch were taken seriously or were merely perfunctory. Although in a civilian context, Harry Cartmell, the Mayor of Preston stated in a speech on 9 November 1915:

> You will have noticed, gentlemen, that whilst most of the usual ceremonies on the installation of a new Mayor are dispensed with on this occasion, it is still considered necessary to impose the oath upon a Mayor continuing in office. Fidelity to the reigning king is now-a-days so much

a matter of course that one might almost be excused for regarding the oath
as being a survival, along with other picturesque ceremonies that accompany the induction of a new Mayor.[141]

Cartmell revealed the widespread normative culture of monarchism – fidelity
was 'a matter of course' – but also the banal perception of its trappings.
However, his wording choice – 'might *almost* be excused' – suggests that the
oath still carried weight as did the fact that it continued to be necessary when
the other induction rituals had been dispensed with due to wartime exigencies.

In military circles, there is some evidence that the oath that recruits took to
the king did matter. When the Germans attempted to convert Irish prisoners
of war in Germany to join a new Irish Brigade to fight against the British in
Ireland, some of the prisoners referred to their oath of allegiance to the
monarch. One former prisoner, Private James Wilson, stated that he was
told by a German priest that 'your oath of allegiance is only a passing
fancy'.[142] Wilson retorted that 'I was taught in school that an oath was binding
in the sight of God and I refuse to break it.'[143] A royal biographer commented
after the war in 1929 that

> while the civilian is loyal to the principle of the monarchy, the soldier is
> loyal to the person of the monarch. The National Anthem played by
> a military band on parade is fraught with real significance: the stiffening
> of the military salute is something much more real than the casual hat-
> raising of the civilian male. [...] The recruit's oath of attestation has for
> him far more meaning than might be popularly imagined.[144]

The comments are revealing of the physical homage paid through the anthem
to the monarchy, which went beyond its monarchist wording 'God save the
King' – the raising of hats, the stiffening of subjects' bodies. They also allude to
a public perception by 1929 that the military oath was not that important. The
author, however, contradicts this, based on his Great War experience, referring
to how, upon victory, soldiers 'struck the note of unswerving loyalty, not to the
principle of the Constitution but to the person of the King. At that juncture the
soldier knew only two lodgments for his loyalty: the officer – typified by the man
who had led him to victory in the field, and the exalted, if remote, individual to
whom he had taken his oath.'[145] Military identity was grounded in monarchical
subjecthood.

As a war volunteer in military training, the writer C. E. Montague wrote on
29 December 1914 of a major who, when reading 'the Army Act to
B Company', suggested that a 'civilian's hat may be removed by other means
than by kicking if he does not take it off at "God save the King"'.[146] King
George V himself marked the reciprocal bond of honour between king and
servicemen through physical acts denoting respect: one of his favourite music
recordings was of the 1907 song 'The Wreck of a Troopship', in which troops
going down with their ship meet death with three cheers for 'his gracious

Majesty the King'. It was played regularly after dinner at Buckingham Palace, 'everyone present standing to attention at the end'.[147]

Further insight into the military sacralisation of monarchy was revealed in a discussion between Lord Kitchener as Minister for War and Lord Stamfordham, the king's Private Secretary, in November 1914. Kitchener felt that, with regard to providing the newly recruited wartime battalions of the army with colours, 'No one [...] can give Colours but the Sovereign, by whom they are, in theory, supplied, though of course in practice by the State.'[148] Kitchener feared that if colours were given in any other way 'there would be an end to all the tradition, veneration, and sanctity with which Colours are now surrounded'.[149] The monarch rendered the colours sacred.

Kitchener's own personal monarchism mattered: in popular parlance, the New Armies he raised of volunteers were often referred to as 'Kitchener's armies', which posed a potential challenge to the established military language of monarchism and threatened to supplant older terms such as the 'Crown Forces' or 'King's Men'. His devout monarchism, however, ensured that, ultimately, the terms complemented – rather than rivalled – each other. According to one biographer, for Kitchener, the king was 'his liege lord to whom not only loyalty and honour were due but devotion and reverence'.[150] His own untimely death in 1916 also ensured that Kitchener did not overshadow the king's popularity, unlike German General Paul von Hindenburg, whose celebrated hero cult rapidly eclipsed his royal master, Kaiser Wilhelm II. Kitchener, along with most other British generals, was in thrall to an ideal of monarchism; he constantly kept the king informed and took his role of obedience to the monarch very seriously. His audiences with the king were regular and reported in the press.[151] Even the famous Alfred Leete poster, which first appeared on the front cover of the magazine *London Opinion* on 5 September 1914 and which used Kitchener's image and pointing finger to recruit with the slogan 'Your Country Needs You', had the words 'God save the King' emblazoned, at Kitchener's insistence, across the bottom when it was rapidly reused as propaganda by the Parliamentary Recruiting Committee.[152] Field Marshal Sir William Robertson revealed the monarchical mindset that underpinned this culture when he praised Kitchener at the end of 1915 as one who 'stands higher in public opinion than any other public servant of the King. [...] He is a loyal and honest servant of His Majesty which is more than we can say to the same extent of others.'[153] Loyalty to the monarch here is presented as a measure of an individual's political honour. Upon his death, drowned when his ship hit a German mine while en route to Russia in 1916, Kitchener's role was described in outrightly monarchist language by Lord Esher: 'I am sorry for the King', he wrote, 'who has lost a great subject.'[154] This discourse permeated widely: Sir George Arthur wrote to the monarch of how Kitchener had frequently mentioned that 'the King's unstinted and unswerving support enabled him (and perhaps alone enabled him) to carry into being the vast military scheme of which the fulfilment was accomplished the very day on which the wise and faithful servant of the King was called home'.[155] The bond depicted was exclusively one between monarch and subject, not the state.

Any breaches of this norm were considered shocking: in 1916, Lord Stamfordham and the Archbishop of Canterbury were appalled to hear that the Tory MP, Frederick E. Smith, who was Earl of Birkenhead and attorney general, 'joked unseemably [sic] about the king, ridiculing him' at a dinner hosted by the military general, Sir Ian Hamilton.[156] The Archbishop acerbically remarked that 'it is hoped that he was – as is apparently often the case – in an "after dinner" condition'.[157] Nevertheless, he considered it 'disloyal' to the monarch and was shocked Sir Ian Hamilton could 'tolerate it'.[158]

As this example shows, we must be careful not to assume that 'honouring the king' was always universally adhered to, even if it dominated official military discourse. Alan 'Tommy' Lascelles, later a royal private secretary, blamed British cultural understatement and reserve for a lack of monarchist zeal among troops he fought with on the Western Front, remarking on 27 August 1915 that

> I honestly believe that if in the thick of Hooge or Festubert an English officer had so far forgotten himself as to shout 'Cry God for England, Harry and St George', or something similar, all his brother-officers within earshot would have come up in shocked remonstrance and said, 'I say, old chap – really! You must keep your head, you know. It's no time for play-acting.' But if he'd shouted 'Let's all go down the Strand, And have a banana', or 'Buck-up, Aston Villa' (which is a football club), everybody would have been charmed.[159]

He revealingly alluded to Britain's monarchist culture as part of fighting 'naturally':

> Why on earth should the English today, after twelve months' fighting, be ashamed of fighting naturally? I'm sure the French don't carry on in that ridiculous way, and of course the Germans and Russians don't. Every now and then, at a church parade, or on the march, the men sing 'God save the King', or the 'Marseillaise', as if they meant it, but they are invariably thoroughly ashamed of it a moment later.[160]

A very different view from an anonymous artilleryman was provided in a letter to the radical left-wing newspaper *Justice* on 3 May 1917 which suggested a more fluid and irreverent linguistic attitude to monarchy in the barracks, following the February Russian Revolution:

> And is Tommy Atkins loyal? Well, in barrack rooms it is always — the King, — — the King, and I dare not write the key letters to the foregoing dashes, but let the Editor of the 'Daily Mail' ask any Tommy to fill in the

blanks for him and he will find it very vulgar vernacular. He can learn also that the majority of the voluntarily enlisted in the New Army, whilst labelled by the professional politician, pressman and parson with a desire to fight for 'God, King and Country', are only concerned with the defence of the latter, and are beginning to get a glimmering of the truth that after the war – a further fight may be necessary to ensure that 'our country' shall be ours in reality.[161]

Ernest Thurtle, the later Labour MP, who had himself previously opposed the monarchy, recalled in his 1945 memoirs regarding his Great War service that his Commanding Officer would always propose a toast to the king at the weekly Grand Mess, 'in his most impressive voice: "Gentlemen, I give you the toast of the Honorary Colonel-in-Chief, His Majesty the King"', itself very revealing of how monarchist everyday cultures worked at war.[162] However, during the Battle of Cambrai in winter 1917, some junior subalterns began to mock the toast:

> Thus it came about that for several Grand Nights in succession, after the C.O. had proposed the toast of the evening, and we all rose and said 'The King' as we drained our glasses, voices would come from the ante-room saying 'The Stationmaster at Camberley' or 'The Bank Manager at Frimley', or some such phrase.[163]

Thurtle attributed this to 'a sense of humour, strong drink, and a "to-morrow we die" feeling'; the offenders were not punished but dealt with by some 'straight talking'.[164] However, he also noted a rise of anti-monarchism among troops, triggered by the Russian Revolution and manifested in 'the unwillingness of the troops to sing "God save the King" in church when on parade. This became so obvious that the C.O. took notice of it and addressed both officers and men on the subject.'[165] Thurtle believed this was caused by 'war weariness [...] plus the fact that the Kaiser was generally held to be responsible for the war. This had been linked up, mainly by American propaganda, with the "king business" as a whole, and something of this had percolated down to the troops.'[166] He asserted that this period of anti-monarchist discontent was short-lived, however, due to the improvement of the military outlook and the image of the king and queen as 'conscientious'.[167] Another private recalled how, towards the end of the war, 'we were so fed up we wouldn't even sing "God Save the King" on church parade. Never mind the bloody King, we used to say, he was safe enough: it should have been God save us. But we worshipped the Prince of Wales.'[168] An important context here was that military law – which applied to all members of the army – listed in the Army Act, under miscellaneous military offences, section 35, using 'traitorous or disloyal words regarding the Sovereign' as an offence liable to court martial, with the potential punishment of being cashiered for an officer; a soldier could suffer imprisonment for this offence.[169] It remains unclear, unfortunately, how many, if any, ever did.[170]

In sum, this section has sought to show the primacy of the monarch–subject relationship in how official military culture presented the conflict. The relationship between monarch and subject – usually presented as a romantic one of loyalty and mutual trust – was invoked throughout the war to smooth military challenges that varied from recruiting volunteers to mitigating the horrors of anonymous battlefield death. This built on the pre-war idea of an 'emotional economy in which the monarch was pledged to the mass of the people through affective ties of mutual dependence'.[171] Dynastic loyalty to the king was used to create a sense of coherence and unity in the military and meant to transcend the home nations' local nationalisms.

1.6   The Language of Monarchy in Mobilisation

An analysis of monarchist language further shows how these discourses of monarchy were used to motivate the British population to support the war.[172] Common terms like 'Crown Forces', 'Soldiers of the King', 'the King's uniform', 'the King's Armies' or 'the King's men' functioned as vectors for monarchism.[173] The more cynical 'taking the King's shilling' also served to describe someone entering British military service. Language conveyed a whole range of contemporary meanings and assumptions about the importance of the monarchy. For example, Arthur Osborn of the 1st Birmingham Battalion Royal Warwickshire Regiment referred in a 1914 letter to the future 'success of the "Birmingham Boys" as soldiers of the King', implying success was interpreted in relation to their identity as troops of the monarch.[174] A. K. Foxwell wrote of her munitions work as 'the business of entering His Majesty's Service in the Arsenal' in July 1916 and how, upon receiving her number and rule book, 'we are now definitely His Majesty's servants in Woolwich Arsenal'.[175] In 1916, the attorney general Frederick E. Smith could open his prosecution of Sir Roger Casement for treason against the king by stating that it was 'the most heinous crime', while the judge 'later directed the jury: "it was the gravest known to the law", and (in wartime) "almost too grave for expression"'.[176] The judge's view was not meant as hyperbole and indicates attitudes to wartime treason, while Frederick E. Smith, who had made personal jokes about King George V in private, staunchly upheld the monarchy in public, again illustrating how elites differentiated between royal personalities and the monarchy as an institution.

Understandings of kingship – and the duty to honour the king – were very evident in the way the language of monarchy was employed. It should be remembered that, in some instances in everyday speech during the First World War, speakers, when referring to the king, would add the words 'God Bless Him' after speaking his name as a form of worshipful language or hallowing: for example, in 1918, Patricia Wilson wrote this traditional verbal act as follows when describing the royal family on the Buckingham Palace balcony: 'Well the

King (God Bless Him) came out with the Queen and Duke of Connaught and Princess Mary in VAD uniform.'[177] When referring to the British monarchy, the nouns king and queen were also *always* capitalised by contemporaries, signifying their cultural weight; frequently pronouns referring to them were too. The term 'King and Country' likewise was usually capitalised. J. G. A. Pocock's ideas on the history of political thought are useful here. Pocock explores what he defines as 'sub-languages': 'idioms, rhetorics, specialised vocabularies and grammars, modes of discourse or ways of talking about politics ... distinguishable language games of which each may have its own vocabulary, rules, preconditions and implications, tone and style'.[178] British monarchism in the First World War likewise had its own 'sub-language' that permeated society both within the UK and its empire in a range of ways.

From an early age, monarchism was part of language. As one schoolgirl, Enid Prichard of Kensington, wrote to Buckingham Palace, 'Dear King, Please will you not put quite such hard words in your speeches because at my school we have them for dictation. Your speeces [sic] a [sic] very interesting but there are hard words in them.'[179] Thomas Baker Brown, a lower-middle-class boy from Newcastle, who fought in the First World War, wrote in his unpublished memoirs of how 'in our "war" games at school, the British, or the English, always won, or, if they lost, fighting against fearful odds, they would be expected to fight to the last man, and would die with "God save the King" on their lips. This was Patriotism [...].'[180] Brown recalled how boys collected cigarette cards issued by the main tobacco firms with series on kings and queens and how one boys' weekly magazine contained a story 'Kaiser or King' which depicted Germany attacking London.[181] The culture of childhood was infused with monarchy: when King George V and Queen Mary visited Liverpool before the war, 60,000 children greeted them in a football stadium, while at Manchester another 75,500 pupils were similarly marshalled to see them, while teachers gave special lessons on the monarchy in British history.[182] During the war, books for children referenced the monarch: *The Child's ABC of the War* listed 'G's for King George, the fifth of that name, the Crown and the guardian of England's fair fame.'[183] The *Belgian Relief Fund's Children's Painting Book* contained a cartoon of a boy who had eaten all the Fry's chocolates but was excused because he had 'eaten the health of the King with them'.[184]

Above all, the most popular manifestation of wartime monarchical culture in language was the frequently used phrase 'For King and Country'. Despite its ubiquity in 1914–18, it has not been subject to any detailed historical analysis. The term itself dates back to at least the 1680s, although it lies outside the scope of this study to definitively track how the term, or its equivalent, 'For Queen and Country', were used in British wars before 1914. It surfaced infrequently in publication titles in the two decades before the Great War: it was the title of a popular 1896 novel about the American War of Independence and of a book by Agnes Weston in 1911.[185] There is also some evidence for the occasional use of the wording 'For Queen and Country' or 'For King and Country' in relation to the Second South African (Boer) War.[186] One of the most popular songs of that conflict was Leslie Stuart's 'Soldiers of the Queen' of 1881.[187] But the omnipresence of the term 'For King and Country' in 1914–18 appears to have been new. No equivalent scale of use has been found for nineteenth-century wars or for the Second South African (Boer) War, suggesting that its sudden mass popularity in the First World War was indeed specifically linked with the importance of monarchism in that conflict.

The phrase 'For King and Country' served as an easy shorthand slogan for British patriotism, and it is difficult to measure how much its wartime use by individuals invoked a conscious monarchist loyalty. But its frequent appearance and the fact that it was chosen for memorial inscriptions suggests the monarchist component was regarded as significant in wartime culture. The popularity of the phrase clearly captured something important for the population about what they were fighting for. More broadly, the term 'For King and Country' reflected the fact that kingship was romanticised as part of a broader romanticisation of war that both Samuel Hynes and Paul Fussell have successfully argued infused British popular understanding of the First World War at its outset.[188] Monarchy was largely narrated in a romantic style by the mainstream press and in memoirs and political and military language. This was particularly evident in 1914–16, but even beyond 1917, when monarchy became politically a much more contested concept and its image changed, some romantic narratives were still mobilised to defend it from any republican or communist detractors.

It can be difficult to assess trends in language in the past with any degree of accuracy. However, Jay Winter's work has pioneered the adoption of a statistical approach using Google N-Grams.[189] Google N-Grams provide us with graphs which plot the number of occurrences of a given word or term over time based on a database search of over 6 million scanned books produced between 1800 and 2000: N means the number of times a given word or term appears in print in a particular year. As Winter points out, the N-Gram approach has its limits. It does not plot how a given word or term was used in a text, its meaning or the connotations it had in the publication, whether positive or negative. It also does not indicate how many, if any, of these publications were actually read or how widely or by whom. Moreover, the assessment is by language – English – not by country of publication, so it is not possible to differentiate UK publications from those published in English elsewhere. This said, the N-Gram does allow a broad insight into changes in the frequency with which the term 'King and Country' appeared in print over time. As Winter argues, N-Grams, 'while limited, are still significant in pointing towards differences over time and space in the printed vocabulary of societies at war'.[190]

Table 1 *Google N-Gram of the term 'King and Country', 1900–39.*

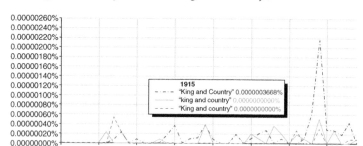

The N-Gram of the term 'King and Country' in Google Books for the period 1900–39 shown in Table 1 reveals a jump in publications mentioning the expression in the period 1914–15, coinciding with the high point in the United Kingdom of the war mobilisation of volunteers for the army, suggesting it mattered in the mobilisation process, as well as a second spike in the use of the term around the period of peak memorial construction and unveiling in 1918–20, when the phrase appeared on innumerable war memorials.[191] It also highlights a very significant jump in the use of the term for the early 1930s. This coincides with a period when there was a boom in war memoirs and literature, suggesting that the expression remained closely associated with the memory of the British Great War experience. A number of songs from the interwar period also used it.[192] The Silver Jubilee and illness of George V in 1935 may, of course, have been a factor in this later surge; another may have been the famous, and controversial, Oxford Union debate in 1933, 'That this house will in no circumstances fight for its King and Country'.[193]

The phrase 'For King and Country' carried real weight at the outbreak of the war – there was a sense of obligation to serve monarch and country within the honour cultures of Edwardian society that the term reveals. It was a key imperative expression, used to trigger a cultural duty reflex across the United Kingdom, and not bland, empty rhetoric. For example, when the pro-women's suffrage Women's Social and Political Union, in a radical patriotic turn, changed its journal's name to *Britannia* in 1915, it added the dedication 'For King, Country and Freedom'.[194] As the Reverend Espine Monck-Mason wrote in a letter to Holy Trinity Parish Magazine, Colchester, Essex on 29 August 1914, 'I am anxious to have an accurate list of all those who have gone from this Parish to serve their King and Country, either abroad or at home.'[195] The Sunday School Union published a pamphlet, *In Touch with God: For Soldiers and Sailors on Active Service for Their King and Country* (London, 1915). The expression 'For King and

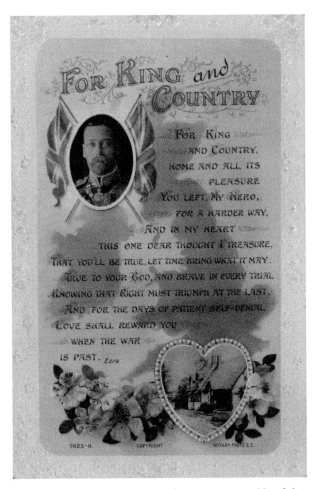

Fig. 3   A King and Country postcard, c. 1916: 'A message to a soldier fighting in World War I, sent by a loved one at home', with inset of King George V, accompanied by a rousing verse, encouraging him to do his best 'For King and Country' (Photo by Hulton Archive/Getty Images, 3428103)

Country' appeared on innumerable postcards, such as the example in Fig. 3, illustrating that it was an accepted feature of war motivation for non-elites, and a slogan which ordinary purchasers often chose to send. In a market saturated with a wide range of war-themed postcards, such choices were significant. 'For King and Country' was a term that clearly sold.[196] For example, Alf Swettenham's mother sent a postcard to her son serving on the Western Front with an image of flowers and the caption 'To my SON serving King and Country'.[197]

'For King and Country' was clearly embedded in home front life. The radical anti-war Glaswegian socialist, William Gallacher, even noted its use in Glasgow in 1914 by those who opposed the war:

> The famous Kitchener poster affirmed that 'Your King and Country need you', but wherever you read this you could also read:
>
> > 'Your King and Country Need You,
> > Ye hardy sons of toil.
> > But will your King and Country need you
> > When they're sharing out the spoil?'[198]

The term 'King and Country' shows how monarchy was central to *British* cultural ideas about identity during the war and the way it amalgamated *English* identity into broader concepts of what constituted Britishness. Historian Simon Potter has questioned whether it is 'too simplistic to emphasise a single "national" British culture or identity' for this period.[199] He is surely correct; nevertheless, if there was one shared thread, it was the monarchy. There was always a tension at the heart of the monarchy between Englishness and Britishness; this was true before and during the war. As Jeffery Richards points out, 'so often in the heyday of Empire *English* [. . .] meant *British*'.[200] Jay Winter has also pointed to the way Britishness and Englishness were often used interchangeably by First World War contemporaries.[201] Ideas that stemmed originally from English monarchism had a hegemonic reach, through being absorbed into the British identity of the monarchy, which stretched far beyond the geographical boundaries of England proper.

Those parts of Britain that were not English were thus subsumed into this culture of monarchy. The same British monarchical discourses, with Englishness at their core, could be projected onto Ireland and the empire more widely, forming unifying cultural codes across nationally disparate territories around the idea of dynastic loyalty to a king who was both 'British' king-emperor and 'English' king. Gestures were made to other national identities within the United Kingdom, such as the royal family's use of Scottish titles when in Scotland or the investiture of the Prince of Wales, held at Caernarfon Castle in Wales for the first time in 1911, but the overarching British identity of the monarchy, developed from the Act of Union onwards, always sat awkwardly with the dominance of England in its historic identity.[202] The German origins of the nineteenth-century royal family actually helped before the war to dilute this imbalance towards England. The monarchy's ever-increasing emphasis on its British identity before 1914 had the same aim.

Using the term 'King and Country' offered a way out of this bind. In 'King and Country', 'country' is deliberately ambiguous – King George V reigned over four home nations, England, Ireland, Scotland and Wales, and 'country' was suitably open to allow the term to invoke dynastic loyalty across all of these territories and the wider empire too, a complex metaphor for Britishness outside a UK setting, projecting the relationship between king and country upon imperial lands.[203] For example, Canadian soldier and British emigrant to Canada Private John Cowles, on 29 March 1916, wrote of 'club members who are serving our King and Country'.[204] The king and his heir embodied the concept of the hereditary, historic bloodline that projected a sense of seamless continuity between England's past and its British present; they personified and familiarised history in a unique way; they also enacted a similar function for the empire which they 'embodied' in dynastic terms. The term 'King and Country' intermeshed dynastic loyalty with that of *Patrie*, as central to British personal identity: duty is owed *both* to monarch and to country. The two elements – king and country – coexist symbiotically in the expression: you could not have one without the other in the symbolic universe of British statehood and empire in 1914. They were, if not one and the same, a perpetual intertwined and coalescing double act, which behoved citizen-subjects everywhere to defend them. Unsurprisingly given this context, the highly versatile term 'For King and Country' appears far more frequently than any reference to the 'state' in popular British mobilisation.

All this helps to explain why the monarchy found the idea of nation and nationalism difficult. First World War British monarchism always prioritised dynastic loyalty over nationalism or a UK 'state' identity. As James Loughlin points out, with regard to Ireland, although relevant more widely, at the start of the reign of George V, the king 'was central to Unionist plans, not just because of the latent constitutional powers a crisis might permit him to exercise, but because he was the embodiment of the nation in a context where the United Kingdom as a state had failed to engender emotional attachment', what Loughlin describes as its 'lack of state national consciousness'.[205] Tom Nairn's description of British 'monarchical nationalism' even argued that 'a pure genetic myth – Protestant, aristocratic consanguinity – has been made to stand in for the usual collective ideology of popular nationhood', thereby facilitating the incorporation of different British internal national identities under the umbrella of dynastic allegiance, as well as those of the wider empire.[206]

Indeed, in many respects, Britishness, in 1914, was a form of dynastic loyalism which was profoundly *anti-nationalist*. In fact, David Edgerton points out that the United Kingdom was an anti-nationalist state construct until the 1940s.[207] Nationalism posed a real threat to a German-heritage dynasty reigning over a multi-national United Kingdom of four nations and multiple empire territories. Jonathan Gumz has shown how Austria-Hungary's state model, which was similarly based upon dynastic loyalty to its emperor from members of very different nationalities within the country, fell apart in 1914–18 under the pressures of totalising war and rising nationalism.[208] Aware of this danger, the British monarchy needed to rise above internal nationalisms, ensuring dynastic loyalty took precedence, and override their becoming too powerful; in the case of Ireland, it notably failed. Nationalism was thus a danger to it; the concept of the United Kingdom was built on a dynastic, not a nation-state, principle. Britishness was thus intrinsically monarchist in conceptualisation as well as function; the idea of a UK state 'nationalism' – what Tom Nairn satirised as 'Ukania' – does not work for the 1914–18 conflict.[209] Indeed, David Edgerton suggests that the term 'British nationalism' was an impossibility in this period: 'nationalism was in British understanding an ideology which threatened the empire, and indeed the nation, not something a British nation could itself have'.[210] If, during the First World War, there was occasional reference to a 'British nation', it was a vague, pan-British ideal that referred to a 'nation' spread across the empire and which also had white racial connotations. As Kathleen Paul has argued, despite the existence of 'imperial nationality', there were 'practical divisions within a theoretically universal subjecthood' which created 'an inclusive formal nationality policy and an exclusive informal national identity'; the latter privileged white British heritage, meaning 'British subjects of colour were repeatedly prevented' from exercising their 'customary rights of subjecthood', as 'within a political community that included all members of the empire/commonwealth, there existed an exclusive familial community defined by blood and culture', an imagined global community of white British origins.[211]

The First World War monarchy generally was very cautious about any use of 'British nation' terminology, preferring dynastic wording such as 'my people' or 'my Empire'. George V was carefully measured in his wartime public statements, with an emphasis on dynastic loyalty as the core of pan-Britishness and empire as motivating war identities for his subjects and an avoidance of English jingoism or nationalism. British identity in 1914 was thus built around loyalty to 'King and Country' or, in its global variant, to 'King and Empire'. Hence why individuals were referred to as subjects of the king before they were described as state citizens in any modern European, post-1789 sense.

1.7   Monarchism and Reactions to News of War

This centrality of monarchy to British identity helps explain why large crowds spontaneously flocked to Buckingham Palace from the evening of 2 August 1914 onwards, as George V reported in his diary. On 2 August a crowd of '6000' gathered and, when the royal couple appeared on the balcony, gave them a 'great ovation'.[212] On 3 August the crowds were 'very large', and the king wrote that 'we were forced too [sic] go and show ourselves on the balcony three different times at 8.15, 9.0 and 9.45. Tremendous cheering.'[213] This process, of spontaneous crowds gathering in the evening and the royal family being called for and having to go out onto the balcony, continued each night from 3 August until Sunday 9 August, when a crowd of '50,000' gathered.[214] Catriona Pennell, in her analysis of mobilisation in 1914, points out that photographic evidence shows that the crowd on the evening of 3 August 1914 was 'mostly middle-class young men in straw hats' – in other words a particular demographic.[215] Pennell points out that, while 100,000 Londoners flocked to central London upon news of the Armistice in 1918, on 4 August 1914, the 'estimated number of people gathered outside Buckingham Palace [. . .] varies between 1,000 and 10,000'; even the top figure would represent only 0.2 per cent of the total 7-million-strong population of the city.[216] The crowd of 50,000 on 9 August was obviously considerable, but it too represented a performance of monarchism by particular demographics. Thus, it appears that it was the cohort most likely to immediately consider volunteering in the war – middle-class young men – who sought to see the king, by going to the Palace in the evening, during this period of early August. Indeed, it suggests that they needed to see him, as part of coming to terms with the realisation that the country was going to war. This was partly about reassurance – the king was a point of stability in an uncertain week – but also about checking that the monarch endorsed the war, and that the duty reflex of serving king and country was thereby correctly to be invoked. This process also occurred in other countries – the kaiser was thrilled by the middle-class crowds who flocked to the Berlin Schloss; monarchist Russian crowds formed too, with about a quarter of a million people gathering in St Petersburg hoping to see the tsar.[217]

The rush to Buckingham Palace was perhaps also subconsciously about invoking an older historic tradition whereby British monarchs 'sent' their people into battle. This is alluded to by a later account by George V's biographer, the popular historian and English nationalist romantic Arthur Bryant, who describes the crowd at 11 p.m. on 3 August as the ultimatum to Germany expired (midnight German time) in terms of monarchism and 'honour':

> As that tremendous hour struck the people looked instinctively to the man who embodied the permanent tradition and honour of these islands. It was no hysteria that moved those dark, shouting crowds that stood before the Palace [. . .] but something far deeper. In that inspired moment – insane though it may seem to many of the present generation – the nation had no doubts. There were, indeed, none that any honourable man could reasonably have.[218]

The sheer scale of the crowds and the way they took the royals by surprise and demanded them – rather than the other way around – again indicates the significance of monarchism when it came to going to war. Mark Hayman has noted how initially a minority on the radical left sought to mock this, only to realise that the war's outbreak had led to an increase in pro-monarchy patriotism:

> In August 1914, when crowds gathered in front of Buckingham Palace to demonstrate their patriotic enthusiasm [. . .] George Lansbury's anti-war

> *Daily Herald* mocked them as 'maffickers', and identified them as mainly
> lower middle-class clerks and shop assistants. The King was similarly
> mocked, and characterized as a leader of the war-mongers. As the war
> progressed, such verbal attacks became a rarity. Patriotic sentiment and
> the King's role as symbol of a nation at war made them dangerous or
> politically unwise.[219]

Indeed, the socialist *Daily Herald*'s sales slumped with the outbreak of war and
shift of mood.[220] A similar reaction occurred in Loanhead, near Edinburgh,
when a meeting of the pacifist Independent Labour Party on 4 August had to be
abruptly ended due to the 'number of interruptions received by people who
supported the King and Sir Edward Grey'.[221] Crowds would also later sur-
round the billboard placed at the base of the empty plinth on Trafalgar Square,
where an extract from George V's comments was posted: 'we are fighting for
a worthy purpose and we shall not lay down our arms until that purpose has
been achieved. *The King.*'[222]

The power of monarchism as a means of endorsing the war effort was
also visible in the impressive rush of donations to the Prince of Wales's
National Relief Fund, a charitable fund launched in response to the
outbreak of the conflict. Wedgwood Benn recounted to Lord Riddell
how the king and queen attended the first appeal meeting at York House:

> On the table was a huge pile of cheques – the result of the first day's appeal.
> Benn said to the King, 'In future there will be no need for a tax-gatherer.
> Your Majesty will be able to dispense with the Chancellor of the
> Exchequer. To provide public funds it will only be necessary to make an
> appeal such as the Prince made yesterday. In two days we have got
> £400,000, which is more than a good many taxes produce in a year.' The
> King laughed [. . .].[223]

This was, of course, meant as a joke, but it also hit on the royal family's very real
support of voluntarism in civic life and suspicion of increasing state bureaucracy or big government, as well as its ability to convince people to donate
money.[224] By September 1914 the fund had raised the vast sum of £2,063,000,
mostly from small individual donations.[225] Businesses encouraged their customers to support the fund in their advertising to highlight their patriotism.[226]

By the end of the war, a myth developed that the monarchy had not been
visible enough in 1914. In 1917, the *Globe* newspaper claimed that Asquith's
government had shown 'a marked tendency to belittle the influence of the
crown' and that 'the incalculable advantages which the possession of our
ancient monarchy provides' had been 'most foolishly thrown away'.[227]
A 1918 press commentary noted of the king that they ought to have 'planned
more display for him. This was an hour when the very pomp of Kingship could
be wisely employed.'[228] These later views are more revealing of fears for the
monarchy in light of the outbreak of European revolution than of the reality of

the first phase of the war and the king's actual role in cultural mobilisation, which had, in fact, been significant and highly visible: on the second anniversary of the outbreak of war in 1916, crowds again flocked to Buckingham Palace, indicating how monarchism continued to underpin wartime identities in the United Kingdom.[229]

Ultimately, monarchy helped shape the pattern of British voluntary mobilisation in 1914–16. Would mobilisation for war have happened without a monarchy? In all likelihood, yes, but it would have taken very different forms. If one makes the comparison with Republican France, for example, a conscription state, it is hard to find a leadership figure to whom perennial individual loyalty was directed in 1914 in a comparable way to the British monarch or equivalents for the cultural associations of 'honouring the king'; likewise, there is no direct equivalent of the term 'for King and Country' or of crowds gathering at Buckingham Palace to seek out the royal family in the week during which war broke out. One has to turn to the other major European monarchies – Germany and Russia – to find parallels, with the kaiser's speech from the Berlin Schloss in August 1914 the closest analogy. Although his words, 'Now I know no parties or confessions; today we are all German brothers', were deeply political, abandoning his traditionally partisan stance against specific political parties such as the Social Democrats and the Catholic Centre Party in Germany, and illustrate the much greater direct political power of the king-emperor in the German system, they also emulated for the first time George V's choice to make the British monarchy impartial in its treatment of political parties.[230] The romanticised sacralisation of monarchy at the outbreak of the conflict was common to many European countries, even if the British case differed due to its lack of conscription and its monarch's limited constitutional powers.

1.8   Monarchist Discourses and Recruitment

Monarchist discourses were particularly evident in war recruitment. They help us understand how men were culturally invoked into volunteering for war, particularly in the first two years of the conflict, in a country without conscription. This should come as no surprise: after all, a large proportion of working-class men did not have the vote during the First World War, so the basis of their personal relationship to the state for which they fought was that of *subjecthood* – as subjects of the monarch. The importance of the monarchy's interactions with troops, such as wartime troop reviews, visits to the wounded and medal award ceremonies, thus takes on a new significance, as it constituted the most personal tangible experience of the British state that many disenfranchised soldiers had had to this point. The government urging them to volunteer was one in which those without the vote had no say; the king and royal family, in contrast, represented a personal tie of loyalty that built on a long cultural history and belief.

The term 'King and Country' was frequently used in recruiting publicity, as ideas of military duty were profoundly associated with gendered notions of male obligation to honour the king by defending him. It evoked a cultural imperative to serve the monarch. On 7 August 1914, the day after parliamentary approval was granted for the size of the army to be increased by 500,000 men, Kitchener's preliminary 'call to arms' was published in the newspapers under the heading 'Your King and Country Need You', which referred to the urgent need for men to join 'His Majesty's Regular Army [. . .] in the present grave National Emergency'.[231] Recruitment posters frequently invoked the monarchy – many using the term 'King and Country' – particularly those produced by the Parliamentary Recruiting Committee in the first two years of the war, as shown in Fig. 4.[232]

The aim was to trigger cultural honour code reflexes: the duty of the male subject to voluntarily fight for the monarch out of loyalty. As a recruitment poster for the Royal Fusiliers (London Regiment Battalions) stated:

> You don't want to see that day [of compulsion] come – nor do we. But there is only one way to prevent it and that is for you, and all of us who are young and healthy, to cheerfully don the King's uniform, and play a manly part by doing a man's work in defence of all an Englishman holds dear – his King, Home and Country.[233]

This quotation highlights the embodiment of language in material culture: the term, the king's uniform, was indeed literal. Monarchist symbols such as crowns were often part of regimental crests, emblazoned on uniform buttons, monarchy literally woven into the fabric of clothing and, in the case of buttons, holding the uniform (and metaphorically the soldier's body) together.[234] The Territorial Force Association of London announced on a recruitment poster produced in April 1915: 'Men of London, In August last, on behalf of the Association of the County, I appealed to you to give thirty thousand Territorials, in a few days, to the King.'[235] Newspaper adverts for recruitment ended with the words 'For King and Country' or 'God Save the King'.[236] The *Western Morning News* carried a letter calling on footballers to enlist which was also being sent to each player in the Cornwall County Football Association, which concluded 'Your King and country need you!'[237] A flyer for a 'great free meeting' at the Chiswick Empire for 'recruiting for the war' on 5 November 1914 had a portrait of George V at its centre.[238] Some posters were even more explicit, as Fig. 5 illustrates. The South Midland Division formed a cyclist company in December 1915; this poster, with its overt monarchism, was intended to draw in recruits for this new unit. The following visual depiction in Fig. 6 of the concept of king and country also appeared on recruiting posters, highlighting the ubiquitous understanding of the phrase, which did not require verbal explanation.

Fig. 4 Parliamentary Recruiting Committee, Poster no. 74, 1915, 'Come into the Ranks', NAM 1977-06-81-39 (© The National Army Museum, London. Image reproduced courtesy of the Council of the National Army Museum, London)

In a similar play upon popular awareness of the king's image, a 1915 war loan poster depicted the monarch's profile on a coin, punning that 'The British Sovereign will win', in a call for the public to invest in war loans, the word 'sovereign' serving as a clever double entendre (Fig. 7). Such overlap between the visual and material cultures of monarchy also influenced soldiers, one officer describing the king as 'looking like a big, rather worn penny' during a royal visit to the front.[239]

The honour imperative upon men of military age to serve the king by volunteering was also reflected in ordinary people's attitudes. The Rev.

Fig. 5   Recruitment poster for the South Midland Division, Art. IWM PST 4893 (©
Imperial War Museum)

Canon Brunwin-Hales wrote in St-Mary-at-the-Walls Parish Magazine in
September 1915 that

> Window cards, showing the number of members of a household who have
> responded to the call for King and Country, can be obtained, free of
> charge, from any of the Clergy or District Visitors, who will gladly supply
> them. They are of a handsome design, with a picture of the King and of the
> British Isles, and we should like to see them displayed in every house that
> has sent a man or men to the Colours.[240]

Such cards occurred in other forms too, as Fig. 8 shows.

The idea that the war was being waged, in part, for the monarchy was
widely conveyed. On visiting a factory in 1915, the king was told by a foreman
that the workers 'are working like heroes. There is not one of them in this
department who would not work till he dropped for the sake of his King and
County.'[241] The *Dundee Evening Telegraph* in August 1915, reporting the

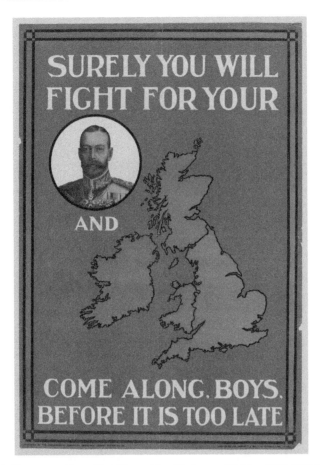

Fig. 6   Parliamentary Recruiting Committee, Poster no. 83, May 1915, NAM 1981-09-26-1 (© The National Army Museum, London. Image reproduced courtesy of the Council of the National Army Museum, London)

death of a former Dundee Corporation official at the Dardanelles, headlined the story 'For King and Country'.[242] The *Daily Sketch* on 1 October 1915 ran a headline on its front page, above a photograph of the monarch addressing a group of seated, wounded, recuperating troops, stating 'Your King and Country Thank You.'[243] The Mayor of Preston in a speech on 31 December 1914 referred to how 'The response to the call of King and Country has been magnificent.'[244] When University College Cork student Vincent McNamara was killed at Gallipoli, his professor wrote part of an obituary for him, stating that 'when the call came for men for King and Country, Vincent McNamara felt it his duty to offer himself'.[245] As historian

Fig. 7   Parliamentary War Savings Committee poster, July 1915, Art. IWM PST 10135
(© Imperial War Museum)

Niamh Gallagher points out, these comments would not have been written if
they did not reflect views in the university at the time.[246] The examples are
endless: the term 'For King and Country' was omnipresent in the first two
years of the war.

The use of monarchism in recruitment was highly gendered. Masculine
honour was closely linked to honouring the king; failing in this lessened
a man's value. In Coulson Kernahan's 1915 memoir, *The Experiences of
a Recruiting Officer*, a girl encouraged a boy to enlist with the words 'Show
you're a man, Harry. We shall all be proud of you if you do, for we don't

OF THIS HOUSE
IS SERVING HIS KING
AND COUNTRY IN

Fig. 8   War card, Mary Evans Picture Library, 10728467

want, any of us – do we, girls? – to have a man who isn't a man, and won't do his duty to his King and country to-day.'[247] In another example, this time from Parliamentary Recruiting Committee propaganda, a poster directed at London women declared: 'If your young man neglects his duty to his King and Country, the time may come when he will *neglect you*.'[248] Yet recruitment propaganda aimed at women also sometimes tempered its monarchism: in its 1915 pamphlet, 'Women and the War', which targeted a female audience, the Parliamentary Recruiting Committee emphasised: 'When we say to our men, "Your Country Needs You", we do not mean that Parliament, or the Government, or Lord Kitchener, or the King, or Mr. Asquith needs them. It is Britain – British cottage homes, British women and children, peaceful fields and villages – that need them.'[249]

The importance of monarchism to recruitment was also illustrated by the surge in new music using the term 'King and Country' in the first two years of the conflict; in the second half of the war this phenomenon all but disappeared, suggesting the introduction of conscription made it less relevant, as well as possibly shifting attitudes to the early war romanticisation of the monarchy.[250] Indeed, the overall prominence of the First World War use of the term 'For King and Country' may well have initially stemmed from its popular use in music, in particular, the way that it was mobilised in music hall recruiting songs, echoing monarchist themes that were already popular in music before the war.[251] A few examples illustrate the general trend: Paul Rubens wrote the famous 1914 song 'Your King and Country Want You', which was published by Chappell Music at the outbreak of the war as a 'Women's Recruiting Song' intended to be used to encourage men to volunteer, with the famous lines 'Oh! We don't want to lose you but we think you ought to go; For your King and Country both need you so.'[252] The song raised £500,000 for the Queen Mary Work for Women Fund and was recorded by some six different artists in 1914 alone, including, most famously, Helen Clark.[253] The same year, Lawrence Wright Music published 'Your King and Country Need You', with words by Paul Pelham and music by W. H. Wallis and Fred Elton: 'Have you seen the Royal Proclamation? Caused by War's alarms, Words addressed to all the population, Calling us to arms! [...] a great and glorious thing, To know the answer to the call, Is each one ready, great or small, So Britain's Sons will one and all, Now sing "God Save The King"!'[254] Yet another popular 1914 song by Huntley Trevor and Henry Pether was also entitled 'Your King and Country Need You'. Such songs were widely sung: in January 1915, a war fundraising concert organised by the 'Children's League of Pity' in Co. Cork in Ireland listened as a teenage solicitor's daughter, Violet Foley, sang 'Your King and Country Want You'.[255]

That these were all 1914 recruiting songs highlights the importance of monarchism as something that could persuade men to volunteer to fight. Yet, as late as 1916, the song 'By Order of the King', written by Albert MacNutt and M. F. Kelly and sung by the group Imperial Quartet, roused its listeners with the chorus:

> By order of the King
> (God bless Him)
> We'll fight and win or die
> 'The Empire and the King'
> (God bless Him)
> Is the nations [sic] cry
> Our countrys [sic] pride are fighting
> 'God bless them and victory bring'
> For they are gladly dying
> Just to keep the old flag flying
> By order of the King.[256]

Note again the insertion of the blessing after the uttering of the word king here.

It is, of course, difficult to assess what effect such music had. However, some soldiers were influenced by such monarchist rhetoric. Private Henry Bridge noted a marching song written to the tune of 'Men of Harlech' – rather ironically a song that originally celebrated the Welsh withstanding an English siege in the fifteenth century – which emphasised in Bridge's version that it was 'for the Empire we are fighting / Wrongs 'gainst others we are righting', all of which was for 'King and Home uniting'.[257] This use of monarchist language helps to place in context the later irreverent war song 'We are Fred Karno's Army' – Fred Karno being a music hall act and, by the time of the war, a popular euphemism for chaos and disorganisation. Sung to the tune of the hymn, 'The Church's One Foundation is Jesus Christ her Lord', the replacement of 'King's army' is 'Fred Karno', which is subversive, even if sung as a form of humour.[258]

Those promoting recruitment clearly *believed* in 1914 and 1915 that portraying military service as a duty to the monarch carried weight with men. The culmination of this came in late 1915, when, with recruiting numbers on the wane, the king issued a personal appeal for men to volunteer, in the form of a Royal Proclamation. The text appeared in newspapers on 23 October, intended to coincide with the promulgation of the 'Derby Scheme', which called upon men to attest their willingness to serve.[259] The appeal was the result of months of engagement between Buckingham Palace and the government on the recruitment question. In June 1915, the king wrote to Asquith of his desire to see registration carried out to assess the number of eligible male combatants in the UK; at this point the monarch still hoped that 'we shall not be obliged to come to compulsion'.[260] The National Registration Act followed on 15 July 1915, according to which all men and women between the ages of 15 and 65 years of age in Britain had to register; the certificate issued to each individual that had successfully registered had 'God Save the King' written in block capitals on it.[261] On 24 August 1915, the king met with Kitchener, Asquith, Grey and Balfour to discuss the possibility of introducing conscription: Asquith noted that 'we four sat in conclave with the Sovereign on the subject of compulsion for nearly two hours: a very unusual proceeding'.[262] The degree of consultation with the monarch is revealing of his influence. The king realised from this meeting that conscription would have to come before the following year.[263] By October, he was urging Asquith to make public the number of recruits that Kitchener estimated that the army needed.[264] In sum, George V took a direct role in attempting to solve the 1915 recruitment crisis and monarchism was a key cultural element in how elites conceptualised dealing with it. The Derby Scheme was communicated to the public in ways that co-opted older monarchist cultural codes to bolster its impact.

The Derby Scheme was named after its instigator, Lord Derby, the king's close friend and newly appointed Director General of Recruiting, who made sure of the king's support for it and met with the monarch immediately before announcing it.[265] Buckingham Palace closely coordinated the Royal Proclamation with him. On 11 October 1915, in the run-up to announcing his Scheme in the press on 16 October 1915, Lord Derby noted to a meeting of the main coordinating body for promoting recruitment – the Joint Recruiting Committee (which had just been formed out of a merger between the older Parliamentary Recruiting Committee and the Labour Recruiting Committee) – that, with recruiting proving increasingly difficult, 'the ordinary propaganda is really now of very little use' and that 'it was his intention to discontinue the general poster campaign, and to exhibit only localised map posters with a message from the King, if that could be arranged'.[266] Monarchism was clearly considered the last impetus still working to convince men to volunteer.

The material culture of the Derby Scheme emphasised monarchy as a core British value: men who attested for service under the scheme but chose to defer it were given a grey armband with a large red crown upon it, the royal symbol signifying willing loyalty to serve the king by taking up arms but also conveying royal protection from accusations of cowardice, as the armband showed everyone the wearer was not a shirker.[267] By 18 October, Lord Derby could inform the Joint Recruiting Committee that 'a message from the King would be forthcoming on Saturday morning and it was agreed that it should be issued as a simple and dignified poster in two sizes and that facilities should be given for the reproduction of the message in the Press'.[268] On 20 October 1915, an emergency night-time Privy Council meeting was called by the king due to a 'suddenly arising matter connected with the war and necessitating an order in Council'; this was in response to a cabinet crisis over divided opinions on any future compulsory service bill.[269] Although the Royal Proclamation was already planned, the cabinet crisis served to make it even more important: if it helped the Derby Scheme to success, then perhaps a compulsory service bill – and the cabinet clashes over it – could be avoided.

The 'King's Appeal', issued just days later, on 23 October 1915, is highly revealing. It shows the depth of hope placed in a personal, direct call from the monarch to bolster recruiting, as well as contemporary monarchist beliefs that war service and patriotic duty to the sovereign were intermeshed:

> To my people: At this grave moment in the struggle between my people and a highly organised enemy, who has transgressed the laws of nations and changed the ordinance that binds civilised Europe together, I appeal to you. I rejoice in my Empire's effort, and I feel pride in the voluntary response from my subjects all over the world, who have sacrificed home, fortune, and life itself in order that another may not inherit the free Empire which their ancestors and mine have built. [...] I ask you men of all classes to come forward voluntarily and take your share in the fight.[270]

The king wrote to Queen Mary that 'I hope my appeal in the papers will have the desired effect of getting the recruits we want.'[271] His intervention was indeed well received. One enthusiastic observer noted to the writer Edward Legge: 'People in high fettle. King's noble appeal has "fetched" everybody. Magnificent response, but only just beginning. [...] Couldn't have believed that those few simple, but well chosen, words would have been so startlingly effective in less than two days.'[272] The *Daily Telegraph* described it as 'a ringing summons to duty which cannot and will not be ignored by the King's loyal subjects'.[273] For *The Standard*, the royal imperative carried greater weight than that of politicians: 'Once again the King has said just the right thing at the right time ... We confess we much prefer the King to his Ministers, not only on the obvious ground of loyal duty, but because he sees facts and states them plainly.'[274] Note the reference here to the 'obvious' ground of loyal duty – highlighting again the collectively understood nature of unspoken monarchist norms and assumptions of the period. The recruiters' faith in the honour-culture imperative to serve the monarch yielded results. There was an increase in recruitment figures for October and November 1915. In each of these months twice as many men volunteered as had done in September of that year. However, volunteering rates plummeted again in December.[275] The King's Appeal produced a surge, but it was only temporary and not large enough to stave off the introduction of conscription in January 1916.

The monarchy also supported recruitment in other ways. Those involved in promoting recruitment received royal thanks: Baroness Orczy, author of *The Scarlet Pimpernel*, received a letter of commendation from the king for her efforts in enrolling 20,000 women to be 'female recruiters' in her Active Service League in 1914.[276] During 1914 and 1915, ordinary families who had contributed many male members to the armed forces received individual letters from the Keeper of the Privy Purse, Frederick Ponsonby, sent on behalf of the monarch, expressing the king's praise for their patriotism. One such letter, to Mrs Baulsom in April 1915, expressed

> His Majesty's appreciation of the patriotic spirit which has prompted your eight sons and two sons in law [*sic*] to give their services at the present time to the Army and Navy. The King was much gratified to hear of the manner in which they have so readily responded to the call of their Sovereign and their country and [...] to the great cause for which all the people of the British Empire are so bravely fighting.[277]

In June 1915, Mrs Rhind in Elgin, who had six sons serving, received an identically worded letter.[278] As in the case of Mrs Rhind, such letters of praise from the monarch were often reported on extensively in the press, which depicted them as a major accolade.[279] The *Dundee Evening Telegraph* reported that Dr Gowan of South Shields received a letter from the king congratulating him on having six sons in the army.[280] In November 1915, the liberal paper *The Scotsman* reported that Mrs Chapman of Twickenham received a 'letter from the King' congratulating her for having six sons serve.[281]

The *Western Chronicle*'s account of one such royal letter highlights how the recipient treated it as a venerable object: Mrs Amos Hull, who received a letter of praise from the monarch for having five sons serving in the army, was visited by a journalist reporting on the arrival of the letter, who described how 'It was taken down from the wall where it was been [*sic*] hanging in a neat frame.'[282] In Hull's case, the *Western Chronicle* reported that 'while Mrs Hull was an in-patient of Salisbury Hospital a gentleman visiting the institution heard of the remarkable record of her family and he took steps to bring the facts to the notice of His Majesty, with the result that in due course Mrs Hull was agreeably surprised to receive the letter'.[283] In December 1915, a similar letter from the Keeper of the Privy Purse was received by Mr John Crack, who worked on the estate of the Hervey family at Ickworth House, conveying 'the honour to inform you' that the 'King has heard with much interest that you have at the present moment five sons serving in the Army' and expressing the king's 'congratulations' and 'appreciation' of this 'example in one family of loyalty and devotion to their Sovereign and Empire'.[284] It was an example that proved costly. Three of the Crack sons would die during the war: two killed in action; one of a heart attack while on military service in India.[285]

Such letters continued to be sent throughout the war, a significant bureau-cratic effort by the monarchy: in August 1917, in the context of the debate about introducing conscription to Ireland, the one part of the UK where it had not been introduced, the *Londonderry Sentinel* reported that the king had written to Mrs Bailey of Ashtead, who had nine sons and two sons-in-law 'serving with His Majesty's Forces'.[286] The wording of these letters was fre-quently identical, suggesting that the missives were mass-produced from a template.[287] Yet they show the ongoing powerful projection of an imagined direct relationship between monarch and subject, even if the reality was that these letters also illustrated advancing anonymous bureaucratic state modern-ity: formulaic reproduced texts sent out by the Keeper of the Privy Purse on the king's behalf to families the monarch did not usually know, they were cultur-ally received and understood by recipients and the broader public as sent *personally* by the monarch in an act of individual royal recognition. Moreover, the fact that the monarchy committed resources to send out such letters suggests that providing direct royal praise to individual subjects was of importance to it as well. A humorous newspaper article even reported that a man, arrested for drunkenness, pleaded for mitigation on the grounds that he had been celebrating receiving a letter of congratulation from the king because he had four sons in the army; the charges were dropped when he showed the letter.[288] The fact that such wartime letters were also preserved by families after the war substantiates the argument that monarchical culture played a role in wartime patriotism.

This background helps to explain why, in August 1918, a vicar's wife, Mrs Bircham, from Barnard Castle wrote to Queen Mary for help, requesting that the sole surviving son of a local family, the Smiths, who had already lost five sons in the war, be removed from danger; the queen's Private Secretary replied, conveying the queen's sympathy and stating that Queen Mary had passed on the request to the war authorities. Wilfred Smith, the last surviving son, was duly moved away from the front and posted as close to home as possible.[289] Bircham's appeal was a clear instance of the monarchy being seen as the intimate protector against wartime injustices by government or army.

Dissenting comments, too, illustrate the degree to which a kingship imperative was being weighed in men's decision to go to war and was not always enough. The Rector of Stoney Massey reported how a young 1916 conscript in Essex explained that he had declined to volunteer earlier in the war because 'He felt he owed a greater duty to his mother at home than to King George, for his mother had done much for him, whereas the King, so far as he knew, had not rendered him any service!'[290] On another occasion in July 1916 a socialist conscientious objector, Robert Gunn, a cooper in Perthshire, stated before the tribunal investigating his request for exemption from conscription that 'he was a Republican and would swear allegiance to no King'.[291] In a telling exchange, the Lord Provost asked him 'Do you know that allegiance is heaven's first law?', to which Gunn replied 'I don't believe in heaven.'[292]

The other end of the spectrum was represented by Frank Beck, land agent on the King's Sandringham estate and a Captain in the 1/5th Battalion of the Norfolk Regiment, a Territorial Force Battalion, who wrote to Sir Frederick Ponsonby, Keeper of the Privy Purse, in spring 1915, to request 'the King's consent' for him to return to his regiment before they were sent abroad to fight.[293] The 1/5th Battalion of the Norfolk Regiment included E Company, often known as the Sandringham Company, which drew a large number of its men, including Beck, from the royal Sandringham estate and household.[294] As the monarch was his employer, Beck's request in itself is not proof of monarchism influencing his decision, but its phrasing is; Beck wrote: 'if the company has the opportunity of serving their King in the field the after effect will have a very good influence on the estate for many years'.[295] George V sent a special telegram message of 'best wishes' to 'the Sandringham Company' on the eve of its departure for the front; they replied: 'most loyal and heartfelt thanks for your Majesty's most kind message. Their one desire is to prove themselves worthy of their King.'[296] The company would be virtually annihilated at Gallipoli, along with its battalion. Frank Beck was among those reported missing, never found.[297]

Recruitment both reflected, and exacerbated, a deep association between fighting in the war and loyalty to the monarchy in popular cultural attitudes. This continued to matter for some throughout the war. As signaller George Soper wrote from the front on 2 May 1917, 'we shall not see home till the whole show is over, worse luck. Well, it is all for our King and country so we will have to stick with it.'[298] But such views were questioned by others as casualties mounted. Vera Brittain recounted in her 1933 post-war memoir *Testament of Youth* how, by 1916, her impression was that 'even the spirit of the *Punch* cartoons, once so blithely full of exhortations to stand up "For King and Country", had changed to a grim and dogged "Carry On!"'[299] By 1918, when invited to tea by a cleric, she recalled responding with rage that 'At that stage of the War, I decided indignantly, I did not propose to submit to pious dissertations on my duty to God, King and Country. That voracious trio had already deprived me of all that I valued most in life'.[300] Although recounted in a post-war source, Brittain's 1918 rebellion is indicative of the social norms of others against which she was protesting and suggests that at middle-class tea parties the concept of kingship was still an unquestioned factor in wartime motivation.

Of course, Brittain's memoir was published the same year as the famous Oxford Union debate, 'That this house will in no circumstances fight for its King and Country', which, in many ways, marked the most significant critique of the term, so the 1918 rage she described in her autobiography may also have been influenced by this 1933 climate of rebellion. Oxford Union passed the motion 275 votes to 153 on 9 February 1933, but the degree of shock that this result met with again indicates that, even as late as 1933, 'For King and Country' retained a charismatic – even sacralised – appeal in many quarters.[301] The debate, however, set a powerful new precedent, challenging the idea of 'King and Country' as symbiotic, interwoven values worth dying for. 'For King and Country' was no longer an unexamined, commonly held social assumption as it had been for much of British society in the Great War.

Post-war disillusionment with the language of 'King and Country' was also illustrated by former munitions worker Peggy Hamilton, who ended her 1978 memoir with a pacifist verse which highlights the extent to which the First World War remained associated with the slogan 'God save the King', as well as the degree to which later decades had seen increasing scepticism regarding its wartime use:

> *Gott strafe* England
> God save the King
> God this and God that
> And God the other thing
> The Nations in a frenzy shout
> Good God, says God, I've got my work cut out.[302]

To conclude, in the First World War personal masculine honour was deeply intertwined with 'honouring' the king by doing one's duty to him, including military service in wartime. Monarchist discourse particularly infused British society in the first two years of the war, in postcards, posters and ordinary language. However, it also had its limits and, in a relatively liberal society, was never universally binding for everyone: in 1915, the language of kingship had powerful enough implications for the Prime Minister to admonish Admiral

Fisher upon his resignation with a note that began 'In the King's name I order you to remain at your post.'[303] Fisher, albeit a maverick character, nevertheless still resigned. The cultural power of the wartime British monarchy was based on popular perceptions of honour, not absolutist coercion, and its potency was never all-consuming.

1.9   Mobilising Kingship and Honour Obligations: The Prince of Wales in 1914

Royals too were affected by the monarchist discourses which were part of British wartime belief systems. A case study of the role of Edward, the Prince of Wales, in the first months of the war, illustrates the powerful potency of the cultural duty to honour the king by serving him in military action. As heir, Edward was meant to act as an exemplary model to young British men but was also set apart by his role as monarchical successor. He found himself in a deeply contradictory position in 1914 when Kitchener issued his call for military volunteers; he was expected to lead Britain's young men by example, but, due to his unique royal status, also refused permission to take on a combat role at the front. The pressure he felt to perform his duty as a man to the monarch and serve in battle, what he understood as meeting the demands of contemporary honour codes, was not feigned but a deeply held world view. He was not just a son of the king but also a subject, interpellated by the cultural construction of a masculine duty to fight for 'King and Country' in 1914 as much as any other young man. Indeed, as future head of the honour system, he was particularly bound to uphold such codes.

However, in contrast to earlier periods of history, by the outbreak of the First World War in 1914, the shedding of the heir to the throne's blood in battle had become taboo, in part because by 1914 contemporary kingship in Britain had come to be seen as no longer predicated upon personal success in military conquest but upon civic relationships with the political sphere.[304] Thus, at the start of the conflict, Edward was barred from going to France with his regiment, the Grenadier Guards, by Lord Kitchener, the Minister for War. Edward's personal desire to fight, expressed in his diary as early as 3 August 1914 was, he suspected, unlikely to be acceptable. He wrote of how he was 'terribly depressed as of course the only topic was the war & I haven't the remotest chance of getting out with the expeditionary force. The knowledge that I must remain in London (for some time anyhow) totally devoid of a job of any description is becoming almost intolerable.'[305] Despite the fact that he had been spending the summer in military training with the Life Guards, Edward's position as heir to the throne meant he would be prohibited from fighting. In seeking to keep Edward on the home front, Britain was protecting its heir to an unusual extent compared to other Western European monarchies: the Belgian King, Albert I, who served as commander-in-chief of his armies during the war, had his heir, the future Leopold III, a very young teenager, serve as a private soldier for several months; the Bavarian and Prussian heirs directly commanded in the field, although not at physical risk.[306] While among elite British circles there was a desire to protect the heir from war death or disability, for Kitchener the real danger was not that Edward would be killed in battle but that if he was allowed to serve in combat he might be captured by the Germans, which, given the honour status of the monarchy, would have been a significant blow.[307]

The role of heir to the British throne in 1914 was thus a paradox: the princely body was paradoxically more transcendent, privileged, precious and sacralised, but also more constrained, than that of the ordinary subject. It was an intensely corporeal role, both in terms of conceptualisation and restrictions. The basic concept of the king's heir drew upon projected cultural ideas about biological hierarchies of descent, birth order and bloodlines; yet these beliefs ironically also meant that the 'sacred' princely heir's body was in practice also physically inhibited in war from honouring the king as others did. As firstborn male offspring of his father's marriage, Edward was protected to a degree that did not apply to his younger brother Albert, the only other of the king's sons who was of military age during the conflict and who served in the navy, including in the Battle of Jutland. Albert, like any sailor in the battle, ran the risk of drowning should his ship be sunk; his war service was a source of immense anxiety to his parents.[308] The king's three Battenberg nephews, Prince Maurice of Battenberg and his brothers Leopold and Alexander, likewise were allowed fight. Alexander and Maurice fought in dangerous locations on the Western Front with no special protection: Alexander wrote to his mother on 15 September 1914 of battle that 'Lots of us were shot down getting back, and I was so exhausted that I finally fell. I knew I could run no further, so crawled for over 300 yards on my stomach, whilst the ground round me was simply riddled with bullets. I confess I thought it was the end.'[309] Alexander's brother Maurice was killed, aged 23, the following month. Significantly, the letter from Sir Douglas Haig, forwarded to the War Office, conveying news of Prince Maurice's death, referred to how 'in peace and war he has done his duty to King and Country', a note added by GHQ, again illustrating the monarchist ideal behind war sacrifice, including that of princes.[310] Even Prince Leopold, who had always suffered from poor health – very likely due to haemophilia – went to the front in 1914, although later in the war he appears to have been promoted out of harm's way.[311] By contrast, the Prince of Wales's exposure to any risk was viewed very differently. As the *Ladies' Field* reported on 3 October 1914, 'it is the proud privilege of our Brigade of Guards to be found wherever the fighting is thickest; this is something they regard as their right. The danger to which they are exposed is, therefore, very great and it is almost out of the question that the Heir-Apparent should be allowed to risk his life in the general mêlée.'[312]

Edward, who had been commissioned as an officer in the Grenadier Guards in August, felt humiliated: 'Papa told me he wouldn't allow me to go out with the 1st Batt. I am to be transferred to the 3rd Batt.', Edward wrote in his diary on 8 September. 'This is a bitter disappointment.'[313] The 3rd Battalion were due to remain all winter at home at this point. Edward described the decision as having 'broken my heart'.[314] It was unsurprising, however; Lord Stamfordham, the king's Private Secretary, had vivid memories of accompanying the former French Empress Eugénie to Southern Africa to see the spot where his friend, her son, Prince Louis Napoléon, another royal prince who had insisted on going to war, was killed by a Zulu attack in 1879.[315] On 14 September 1914, Edward went to the War Office to see Kitchener to protest: 'He is now a g[rea]t fat bloated man and he talked to me about not going out with the 1st batt. putting forward various "excellent" reasons for this. As a consolation he offers me a job on French's staff in 3 months time!! A pretty rotten contrast to my g[rea]t wish.'[316] The next day, Edward went to barracks to watch the men of the 1st Battalion, with whom he had trained, leave for the front: 'it was one of the most terrible moments of my life when they marched out of barracks leaving me behind'.[317]

From the very outset of the war, the press picked up on rumours circulating in London about the prince's hopes of fighting. *The Times* erroneously published a report on 7 August 1914 that he was to go 'upon active service', and the popular *Daily Sketch* later also implied Edward was 'for the Front'.[318] The War Office even had to take the unusual step of issuing a statement of explanation to the press in September 1914 as to why Edward was remaining at home, claiming it was because he was continuing his training and making clear that the prince was being kept from the front by Lord Kitchener rather than of his own volition:

> Last night the War Office issued the following statement through the Press Bureau. The Secretary of State for War was approached by His Royal Highness the Prince of Wales who urgently desired to accompany the 1st Battalion of the Grenadier Guards now under orders for the front. As his Royal Highness had not completed his military training Lord Kitchener submitted to his Majesty that for the present it is undesirable that his Royal Highness should proceed on active service.[319]

Edward was thus forced to remain in London, excluded from combat, yet at the same time expected to serve as the leading example of perfect wartime young martial British masculinity in accordance with his dynastic status as future head of the honour system – an inherently contradictory position. For instance, the upper-class magazine *Tatler* described him as 'A Royal Example to the Young Unmarried Men of the Empire', above an image of him marching in khaki with the Grenadier Guards in London.[320] His role with the Guards was used to endorse recruitment to the armies. Crowds turned out to watch his every route march in London with his unit, something he found deeply embarrassing.

Edward found this very public experience of being kept back in London deeply humiliating. He shared in the war fever of the aristocratic young men he socialised with: in August, for example, he went keenly to the theatre with friends 'hoping to see war films'.[321] Edward's status had not isolated him from broader societal trends regarding the male duty to honour the king by fighting. He wrote revealingly to Lord Esher in November 1914: 'I long to be serving with my rgt. and going thro' the campaign in the proper way. I hate leading this comfortable and luxurious life when all my friends are getting hell in the trenches.'[322] Efforts were made to provide him with compensatory roles. He was given the honour of carrying the company colours during route marches and he went frequently to the Admiralty to be briefed on the progress of the war at sea. He was made head of a new, highly successful, Prince of Wales's National Relief Fund, to alleviate domestic distress in the UK resulting from the war, which was launched with an appeal to the public in his name in August 1914. However, none of this could overcome the contradiction of his position, being described in the press as 'Our Soldier Prince' yet barred from leaving for the front with his colleagues with whom he had trained.[323]

After ongoing and sustained lobbying, Edward won a significant concession: he was ultimately allowed to leave England to serve on Sir John French's staff in November 1914 in what was intended as a safely protected environment. However, once in France, although Edward was never allowed a combat role, he became adept at pushing the boundaries of where he was allowed to go – in the difficult, provisional conditions of the Western Front it was simply far less practicable, or possible, to monitor the prince in the way that was the norm in London; moreover, with the advent of conscription by 1916, it became increasingly awkward to publicly protect the prince more than other men. Edward benefited from considerable freedom of movement, unprecedented for a modern Prince of Wales, and indeed anonymity, once he went among the troops, resembling, in his uniform, just another junior officer – something he relished. Although initially his first position on Sir John French's staff saw Edward safely ensconced at the General Headquarters of the British Expeditionary Force at St Omer, he was later attached to the less restrictive locations of 2nd Divisional Headquarters and 1st Army Corps, both at Béthune, and in September 1915 he was appointed to the staff of the Guards Division, working for Major General Lord Cavan, in which role he was able frequently to visit the front lines to inspect trenches or boost troop morale and to wander the rearward areas relatively freely as part of his staff work, which often involved mapping tasks and independently planning, organising and supervising supplies on the ground. Edward also visited Egypt in 1916 and accompanied Lord Cavan's corps to the Italian front during the conflict. The end of the war saw him attached to the Canadian Corps.

The press response to Edward's posting to France in late 1914 was largely positive: 'the Prince's enlistment proved a valuable aid to recruiting and doubtless the announcement that he will now join the Expeditionary Force will have a similar effect', *The Standard* reported on 17 November, upon news of his departure 'for France'.[324] In contrast to court circle views, there was a degree of consensus in the press that the heir could be at the battlefield and might be placed at risk. In 1914, reporting generally and erroneously implied that the prince was to face real danger through his initial posting – the *Daily Telegraph* referred to the prince 'now at the front' and due 'to receive his baptism of fire at what is probably the critical moment of this vast struggle' and how 'the respect and good wishes of the entire country accompany him on his great errand'.[325] Another report mentioned a further incentive for Edward's departure: the *Daily Chronicle* claimed, albeit mis-leadingly, that 'all the Kaiser's sons are at the front or wounded and in hospital'.[326] Only the *Pall Mall Gazette*, the voice of elite society, empha-sised that Edward must be better protected than ordinary soldiers due to the importance of his role as heir, because 'the life of the Heir to the throne is not his own. It is Britain's; it is the Empire's', effectively an assertion of complete public ownership of Edward, as the illustration in Fig. 9 also suggests.[327]

Above all, however, 1914 newspapers adopted the rhetoric of honour culture in their descriptions, affirming how the prince acted as a proxy for the monarchy as a whole, a spiritual vector for the personal, intimate relationship between king and people: 'the nation deeply appreciates the implied sacrifice of the King in thus consenting to the eager desire of his eldest son to bear his part in the war. No stronger link between Sovereign and subjects could be forged than this of comradeship on the battlefield', the *Evening Standard* commented.[328] The *Pall Mall Gazette* wrote of how English 'lads' fighting alongside the prince 'in days yet far distant, if GOD may send victory and a safe return, [...] may be able to say, "My KING and I fought together for freedom and for right."'[329] The choice of capitalisation conflated the divine and the monarch, the romanticisation of kingship overtly evident in ways that would disappear from the press later in the war. There was also a clear message that Edward's service embodied solidarity across the class system: 'The know-ledge that palace and cottage are sharing the risks of this momentous campaign will inspire further confidence and will touch the people's imagination as few other things can do', the popular working-class *Daily Sketch* reported.[330] Court circles were pleased with the positive narrative: Lord Esher noted in 1914 that 'The Prince of Wales is doing splendidly, and is popular with everybody, owing to his hardihood and simplicity' and, in 1915, 'tried to make' Queen Mary who, he noted, was proud of her son's war contribution, 'see that after the war thrones might be at a discount, and that the Prince of Wales' popularity might be a great asset'.[331]

H.R.H. THE PRINCE OF WALES
With the Grenadier Guards.

H.R.H. PRINCE ALBERT
On H.M.S. "Collingwood."

FOR THE EMPIRE!
The King gives his two Sons to the War.

Fig. 9   'For the Empire! The King Gives His Two Sons to the War', postcard c. 1916, Mary Evans Picture Library, 10997342

The press depiction of the 'soldier prince' encapsulated the romanticised views of monarchy and honour that still existed in 1914. Press accounts related that Edward had gone to battle 'in defence of the national honour and the liberties of Europe'.[332] There were many references to the last time a Prince of Wales fought in France (the fact that he had fought *against* the French was glossed over in most references): 'the last Prince of Wales to leave this country on a warlike expedition to French soil was the Black Prince who won the great victory of Poitiers in his second foray into France in 1356'.[333] 'Stirring days of the Black Prince recalled. The romance and chivalry of far off days are recalled by the news that the Prince of Wales has gone to the front', reported *Lloyd's Weekly News*; the *Daily Telegraph* referred to Edward winning his 'spurs'.[334] The *Pall Mall Gazette* typified this tone:

> It is five hundred years and more since a Prince of Wales was with a British Army on the battlefield. Edward, the Black Prince in full vigour of his manhood brought back great victories for the arms of Britain, a Royal prisoner and the proud yet humble motto, 'I serve.' Once more a Prince of Wales is in the field, an English lad scarce grown out of boyhood, eager to do his duty and to have his share in the victory which shall crown the righteous war. Edward the White Prince goes forth, not to lead armies into impossible situations, nor to issue vainglorious proclamations to his men, but, true to his motto, to serve. With him go the thoughts and prayers of each one of his Royal Father's subjects. Many and many another English lad in the spring-time of life has gone or is about to go and many a one will not return. All the flower of British youth which is facing death with high courage and incurious eyes is for us personified in the gallant young Prince.[335]

This kind of press language illustrated the surge in romantic monarchism which marked the outbreak of the war, indicative of how masculine honour, duty and the romance of war were bound up with languages of monarchy in the first two years of the conflict.

Despite the positive press reaction, however, Edward's main war purpose was still seen to be physical survival to inherit his predestined sacred kingship, as well as his biological destiny, to reproduce and carry on the dynastic bloodline; this overruled all other social and political demands, including the obligation to fight for his monarch. Lord Stamfordham wrote to the Prince of Wales in October 1915, after hearing that his driver had been killed by shellfire while Edward was inspecting trench lines: 'BUT, Sir, you who are so thoughtful of others, will not, *I feel certain*, forget Lord Cavan & the heavy weight of responsibility resting upon him in his Command & remember that your safety, your Life, so precious to your Country, is *another* care which circumstances [*sic*] has devolved upon him.'[336] The *Daily Sketch* in January 1916 reported an incorrect rumour that the prince was to be recalled from France to London:

> It has been agreed [...] that the Prince of Wales shall not return to the front. A great deal of work for which he is needed awaits him at home and he will now be plunged into all that business of chairmanship of commit-tees and so on in which his grandfather got his training as a Sovereign. He is, no doubt, very disappointed, but he has himself to thank for he systematically got himself into dangerous positions – quite an improper proceeding for the heir to the throne.[337]

Edward's wartime mobilisation was always caught between the conflicting honour codes that interpellated the heir, as subject, duty bound to fight for his monarch, and as future king, obligated to physically survive to later metaphysically embody the state.

1.10 Conclusion

Overall, the ways in which Edward's war 'duty' was contested and evolved reflected the complex changing relationship between kingship and honour discourses in Britain in the First World War that this chapter has examined. It provides further evidence of the surge in the romanticisation of the monarchy at the outbreak of the conflict and highlights the tensions between the monarchy's promotion of war service, the role of monarchist beliefs in voluntary recruitment and the gap between the monarchy's claims that all subjects were equal before the king and court circles' desires to protect and privilege the heir. This micro-history supports the broader claim made in this chapter as a whole: that monarchist cultural beliefs were prominent in public discourses and were an important framework for how Britain mobilised for war. Kingship more broadly and the prevailing 'culture of monarchy' were also key to British self-mobilisation. Yet what was the relationship between these cultural discourses of monarchy and the actual behaviour of ordinary individuals? The next chapter turns to this question.

Monarchist Culture and Combatant Practices

2.1   Introduction. Kingship: A Combatant Belief?

Monarchist discourses were clearly widespread as part of British mobilisation for the First World War. Yet, to what extent did they have any tangible effect on social *practices* and behaviours during the conflict? While an idea of 'honouring the king' was evident in discourses around recruitment and societal mobilisation in the first two years of the war, did it have any lasting impact on keeping men fighting *after* they enlisted, once they encountered the horrific realities of the Western Front? Chapter 2 assesses these questions. It examines the extent to which monarchism featured in combatant war experiences and morale. This allows for an insight into the extent to which monarchist cultural discourses had any real impact on troops.[1]

Connecting monarchical discourse and soldiers' actual motivations for fighting remains extremely difficult. Ideas about honour and monarchy were only ever one factor among many influencing societal behaviours. There is a large, sophisticated historiography on soldiers' varied fighting motivations in the Great War; monarchism does not appear in it.[2] The monarchy is also not frequently referred to in British soldiers' letters. Thus, one has to be wary of overemphasising monarchy, and this chapter does not claim that it was one of the leading factors in troop endurance in trench warfare; the sources are far more vocal on food, sleep and the importance of support from immediate family at home to morale. These caveats stated, this chapter shows that monarchism did matter to many combatants, indicating that it was a broadly held cultural belief of some significance, and a constitutive part of individual and collective combatant wartime identities and morale.

This chapter opens by analysing the impact of the king awarding honours to combatants and inspecting troops. It then explores responses to the monarch's visits to the troops on the Western Front. This is followed by an assessment of the role of royal philanthropy to the troops by examining the Princess Mary Gift Box, an initiative of King George V's teenage daughter. The chapter then examines the particular meaning of the monarchy for imperial troops. The last section of this chapter analyses the impact of the Prince of Wales on the

Western Front, a case study which shows how practical royal involvement in the military effort could popularise the monarchy, as well as providing insights into how honour culture evolved. It ends by looking at evidence from letters written during the abdication crisis of 1936, which reveal the extent to which the war generation continued to see their wartime military actions in terms of service to their monarch.

2.2   Kingship at War and Honour Exchanges

To turn first to the impact of the monarchy's role in awarding honours for gallantry: the British honour system was perhaps the most concrete embodiment of Great War honour culture. Its tangible honour practices, such as royal investiture ceremonies presenting orders, awards and medals, had an influence upon servicemen's wartime morale, and that of their communities more broadly. This becomes all the more evident when one considers the sheer scale of the honour system during the conflict: the king personally conferred with his own hands 50,000 awards for gallantry; the scale of this royal activity was far larger, however, as other male royals, including the Prince of Wales and Prince Arthur of Connaught, also awarded medals to troops.[3] Royal investiture ceremonies were widely reported in the national and local press and took place in the United Kingdom and also during the king's visits to the front. They were often major events: for example, on 15 January 1916, the king decorated 300 officers in the ballroom at Buckingham Palace, including seven recipients of the Victoria Cross.[4] Military figures also presented medals, but royal presentations received by far the greater press attention.

Medals were the most visible form of material royal honour culture during the conflict. They were metonyms for actions in the field that involved lauded characteristics such as bravery, courage or self-sacrifice. Through awarding the medal, the monarch not only honoured the individual on behalf of his people but also symbolically sacralised the talisman he handed over, which represented the brave deed. The person would now 'wear' some of the king's divinely ordained 'honour', which, through awarding medals, was incorporated onto the clothing of his subject. Pinning on medals was thus a powerfully intimate act of bestowal of the monarch's honour to be incorporated into the subject. It also represented a profound encounter with the 'royal touch', which was still a sacralised and ritual interaction during the war.[5] A poem in the *Yorkshire Evening Post* in 1917, entitled 'V.C.', written by Ethel Kideon, expresses this view of medal ceremonies as a transfer of monarchical honour: 'There's a proud and happy Mother, Living somewhere in the land; For her son has been to see the King, Who took him by the hand, Speaking kingly words of greeting, As to an honoured guest, And he came back to his Mother, With a Cross upon his breast.'[6] The capitalisation of the word 'Cross' hints at a religious reference to Christ, a theme further evident in the poem's later verses, blurring royal medal-giving with divine sacralisation. The poem describes VC winners as 'Kings of men who walk amongst us, Britain's bravest, and her best', again highlighting the king's bestowal of an element of royal honour upon them through their award.[7]

Medals thus represented both the old and the new in the First World War: on the one hand, medals for acts of extreme gallantry harked back to an older era when the monarch – not the state – rewarded the individual in time of war, and to a romanticised ideal of individual combat feats, which ill matched the realities of anonymous industrialised trench warfare; on the other hand, service medals became mass-produced and ubiquitous as the conflict developed, until, ultimately, in 1919 the decision was taken that every man who had served in the conflict would receive a medal, the British War Medal 1914–18, to commemorate the fact. This was a modern democratic development which still drew upon the older idea of medals as an honorific monarch–subject exchange: the front of the medal depicted the head of King George V.[8] Approximately 6.4 million of these silver medals were issued. Significantly, members of what were known as 'Native' Labour Corps, for example, the Chinese, Maltese and Indian Labour Corps, only received bronze versions, of which far fewer were issued, this mark of lower esteem a sign of both racial discrimination and the lower status of labourers compared to combatants, even though many of the former also came under shellfire at the front and lost their lives.[9] As the war went on, many medals were also issued by post without any royal investiture ceremony.[10]

Defining new categories of who should receive medals was one of the most powerful prerogatives of the monarchy at war. Initially it used it sparingly, with the king even suggesting in 1914 that the award of naval medals should be deferred until the end of the conflict, a policy that Winston Churchill successfully challenged, pointing out a man might die between 'his act of Gallantry and the end of the War'.[11] In 1914, a new medal, the Military Cross, was created for gallantry by officers only; in 1916, at the king's insistence, a new medal, the Military Medal, was introduced for bravery by other ranks, highlighting the increasing awareness at Buckingham Palace of the need to widen the social range of those the monarchy was honouring.[12] The same year the decision was made by the Army Council that the next of kin of fallen medal winners could receive the award on their behalf at any of the king's investiture ceremonies, which were held twice weekly in an effort to deal with the scale of medal presentations required as a result of the war.[13] George V found such ceremonies personally difficult. In his diary in 1916, the king described giving a widow her dead husband's medal as 'very painful'.[14] In some cases, widows brought very young children up to receive their dead father's medal.[15] The young son of Captain Harold Ackroyd was handed his dead father's Military Cross by the king at an investiture in 1917, standing beside his grief-stricken mother, who 'was keenly affected but bravely restrained her emotion [...] the youngster looked wide-eyed at His Majesty and appeared not to understand, whereupon the King opened the case, showed him the decoration within, told him it was well won by his brave father, and patted his head in a fatherly and sympathetic way'.[16] Some investitures were filmed: Mr and Mrs Ball, the parents of Albert Ball, a leading British ace pilot, collected their son's medal, and the film footage shows very clearly their sense of deference and pride – Mrs Ball curtsies twice and they very warmly shake the king's hand.[17] Albert Ball was a war celebrity due to the cult of ace pilots; the monarchy here used a traditional format to honour a new kind of aerial war hero, made famous through press celebrity, through the equally modern medium of film.

In 1917, at the suggestion of Lord Esher, the wartime monarchy created a new order for civilians – the OBE, Order of the British Empire. It allowed ordinary people from a wide range of backgrounds, both men and women, to have their war work honoured.[18] The inclusion of women was a radical novelty, as 'before 1917 the honours system scarcely recognized female existence, much less female distinction'.[19] The inception of the OBE was a direct response to revolution in Russia and the ongoing discussions on the extension of the suffrage. Labour MPs and 'trade unionists, including some with syndicalist sympathies, were prominent among the first recipients' and the first OBE ceremony saw insignia presented alphabetically.[20] The tactic was obvious: radical Glaswegian socialist William Gallacher wrote in his memoir of how in 1917

> at that time a whole host of Labour Party and trade union leaders were holding out their hands for tawdry decorations, such as C.B.E., O.B.E. and the rest of them. [...] Not only was the Government handing out shoddy 'honours' to all and sundry among the Labour Party and trade union leaders, but some bright spark conceived the wonderful idea of passing out medals to the factories. 'The men in the factories are "doing their bit" as well as the men in the trenches. Let us honour them. And surely, if we "honour" them, they'll turn their backs on the wicked path they've been following and devote themselves to "their King and Country."'[21]

In response, he recounted, the workers of one torpedo factory outside Greenock voted for their medal to go to the lavatory attendant.[22] On 1 September 1917, the socialist *Herald* newspaper declared that thirty-two 'Labour men' had been placed 'in a new order of chivalry, *from which it is the highest honour for a Labour man to be excluded*'.[23] However, many Labour leaders responded positively to receiving wartime honours and the increased outreach from the king and queen towards them that the war had brought. As Ramsay MacDonald sharply rebuked Gallacher at the Liverpool Labour Party Conference in 1925: 'I may go to Buckingham Palace or Balmoral Castle now and again but you can't call that the camp of the enemy.'[24] By the end of 1919, 22,000 OBEs had been awarded.

Also in 1917, the monarchy announced a new decoration to be given to all those who had served in the old British Expeditionary Force of 1914, the idea of the king's uncle, Prince Arthur, the Duke of Connaught.[25] These changes were a hybrid of modernisation and tradition – the idea of royal 'honours' for exceptional subject acts was an old one, premised on concepts of honour, fealty to the sovereign and royal sacralisation, but it was now more egalitarian in the sense that it was possible for a much wider range of people to receive awards.

Individual reactions to receiving honours from royals varied. For some bereaved families medal ceremonies with the king were a moment of pride, even giving meaning to their loss. The family of Lieutenant Colonel John Collings-Wells, killed in March 1918, dressed up and travelled to London to collect their son's VC: 'Father in London clothes and high hat and I, in my best frock and hat', his mother wrote in a letter, noting carefully how the king congratulated them on having such a gallant son and expressed his sympathy.[26] She wrote that the king described Collings-Wells's action as 'one of the bravest and most wonderful during the war'.[27] After the ceremony, the parents were mobbed by crowds of people in Green Park 'who wanted a glimpse of their son's Victoria Cross'.[28] The *Globe* newspaper reported in February 1918 that Mrs Healey from Co. Waterford 'received from His Majesty's hands the Albert Medal' awarded to her dead son Michael who was killed saving others during a bombing drill accident in France, the wording emphasising the importance of the monarch's personal royal touch.[29] Interactions with royals at investitures were the subject of much public and press curiosity: 'It is quite easy to talk to the King' said Mrs Healey in an interview with a journalist afterwards. 'He conversed in homely fashion with me. He expressed deep sympathy with me in my loss and congratulated me upon having had such a son. He also talked about the food situation and hoped that I did not have to wait in queues.'[30] Here we see the type of 'human interest' newspaper reporting style on the monarchy that Frank Mort has identified originating in the pre-war period, which was a staple press genre during the war.[31] The direct speech of those who had met with the monarch was very frequently reproduced in press accounts, and such reports also often included what the royals had said to them as if a direct quotation of royal speech.

There was a constant emphasis on how the king's ordinary humanity surprised people who were nervous of meeting revered royalty and anticipated grandeur. The working-class mother of Jack Cornwall, who had been posthumously awarded the VC for his bravery during the Battle of Jutland, reported how 'I was very shy when I went into the Palace' but the king 'shook hands with me very warmly, and talked to me, and then all my nervousness flew away [. . .]. He was so kind that I almost forgot I was talking to a real King.'[32] Brigadier General Foster Hall, by contrast, described the process in 1916 as highly streamlined: 'go in one by one to the King in next room. Bow. He hangs the medal on a hook on your tunic, shakes your hand, and says a word or two. [. . .] another bow and go out.'[33] The scale of public interest in royal investitures was such that supporters of the monarchy realised it could be utilised to enhance its popularity. The Archbishop of Canterbury, Randall Davidson, suggested in 1918 that 'It would make a huge difference if more of the things which *are* done – giving decorations etc. – were done in public. Even those who can't go to such would read about what had happened, and their "cousins and aunts" would go.'[34] He told the king in May 1918, 'why not before a few thousand people, instead of before twenty in the Throne Room?'[35] By the end of the war, investitures had been made open to the public. This, the Archbishop noted, 'has been very popular'.[36]

For some Indian soldiers too, honour was perceived as received through the royal touch during investitures: Subedar Major Sundar Singh Bahadur wrote in October 1915 that 'On the 14th, the Emperor gave me two medals. He decorated me with his own hands in his palace in London. [...] The occasion did me very great honour. [...] And I was only a poor Jat!'[37] Subedar Dhan Singh Lama was struck by the fact that, after his investiture, 'When I came out of the Palace, many distinguished Sahibs and Memsahibs shook hands with me.'[38] The royal touch could confer a status that overcame racial difference in an imperialist world, the white crowd outside the Palace eagerly shaking an Indian soldier's hand. On 11 January 1915, the *Daily Sketch* front cover story was that Queen Mary had given a flower to a wounded Indian boy in hospital who had 'lost his leg' but 'won his Queen's admiration'.[39] Here the startling implication of equating losing a limb to the 'reward' of royal esteem highlights the value assumptions of contemporary monarchist press discourses. Investitures also appear in numerous wartime visual sources, photographs and artists' images, such as in Fig. 10.

Monarchist beliefs also infused the broader public praise of medal winners. When in June 1918 a ceremony was held in Kirton to honour a local VC winner, Harold Jackson, the chairman of the Parish Council, Alderman W. Dennis, JP, making a presentation of gifts to Jackson, declared: 'Your King and your country are proud of you and your friends and the citizens of Kirton are especially proud and we are delighted to do you honour in this, the only way that lies in our power.'[40] The concept of honour exchange is clear here: the public honouring the man honoured by the king. It is also evident in letters of congratulation sent to VC winner Lieutenant C. G. Bonner: 'it is exceedingly difficult to express in words what we all feel at this juncture', a letter from Bonner's former work colleagues stated, 'but we are proud that during all our business careers we have been associated with one [...] whose efforts have been such as to have justly merited so great an honour at the hands of our esteemed and respected King'.[41]

For some awardees, the prospect of meeting the revered monarch was terrifying: the artist Ellis Silas recalled encountering a 'considerably agitated' young officer in a room at Buckingham Palace, awaiting with an 'embarrassment that this was almost panic' the 'ordeal' of receiving a decoration for valour and who remarked 'that he would rather be in front-line trenches'.[42]

1916: THE KING PRESENTING THE VICTORIA CROSS TO MRS. WARNER, THE MOTHER OF A FALLEN HERO.

On November 16, 1916, the King presented Victoria Crosses to parents and next-of-kin of heroes who had won the decoration but had not lived to wear it. Among the recipients was Mrs. Warner, of St. Albans, to whose son, Private Edward Warner, Bedfordshire Regiment, the V.C. was awarded for most conspicuous bravery.

Fig. 10   *Illustrated London News*, 25 November 1916, front page depiction: 'Her Son's V.C.: The King Presenting the Victoria Cross to the Mother of a Fallen Hero', Mary Evans Picture Library, 10725550

Another officer, Captain Arthur Lord, 'was nervous and forgot the second bow', when receiving his Military Cross from the king at Buckingham Palace; his letter to his father began 'the investiture is over and I am still alive'.[43] Another war veteran and VC winner, officer Reginald Haine, recounted in a 1973 oral history interview that

> King George the Fifth was a remarkable man. [...] He had a wonderful memory [...] There were quite a lot of us at this investiture [...] about a dozen V.C.s altogether that he invested but when he spoke to us, he spoke about the battalion chiefly and it was astounding his knowledge of the battalion and the officers in it [...] he enquired after individual people. And I found that I met him on several other occasions later on and he never forgot a thing; he never missed a trick that man.[44]

Haine admitted in his 1973 interview that 'as a matter of fact I in my desk I have got the original investiture thing'.[45] Investitures had a long-lasting impact.

2.3   Royal Troop Inspections in Britain

Another way in which we see monarchist beliefs evident in wartime cultural practices is through the numerous royal troop inspections that the king carried out, which were intended to reinforce the symbolic honour-based relationship between the sovereign and each military subject. George V made 450 visits to troops during the course of the war, according to his biographer Kenneth Rose.[46] In fact, throughout the conflict, no division left Britain to go to the front 'without first being inspected by His Majesty'.[47] Indeed, due to the king's frequent visits to Aldershot to inspect troops about to leave England, his presence became a sign to soldiers that they were imminently due to leave for the war. As one wartime publication by Alexander Hammerton and Herbert Wilson stated, 'It became a tradition with the British Army that "First you're trained; then you're polished up; then the King comes; and then you're off!"'[48]

Elites believed royal inspections mattered. Margot Asquith described the king's review at Blandford of a naval division earmarked for Gallipoli in romantic terms: 'The whole 9,000 men were drawn up on the glorious downs [. . .]. *They marched past perfectly*. I saw the silver band [. . .] coming up the hill and the bayonets flashing – I saw the uneven ground and the straight backs. [. . .] The King was pleased and told me they all marched wonderfully.'[49] A journalist reporting on the king's inspection of the new Welsh Guards regiment described a thunderstorm that broke out just before the men's royal march past as a divine intervention, conflating royal inauguration and spiritual baptism.[50] On 25 September 1914, George V also recorded a positive informal reception from soldiers at Aldershot in his diary: 'Went for ride and saw a great many of the troops drilling, there are over 60,000 here now. Rode by the long valley and on coming home all the Highland Brigade who are camped outside here gave me a great ovation.'[51]

Troops' actual attitudes towards such home front inspections varied, however: many soldiers' diaries referred to them in passing without emotion; some displayed indifference. Trooper Frank Stone's diary prosaically recounted in October 1914: 'Inspection of South-East Mounted Brigade by King George. His Majesty gave us a good report. My horse was crippled so had to use Sgt Websters [*sic*]. Had an awful ride and during practice of inspection was nearly squashed to bits when advancing in regimental line.'[52] Private Dan Joiner was disappointed not to see Lord Kitchener, but only the king, when the latter inspected his unit near Rugby in 1915:

> we were casually informed 'The King is coming to day [*sic*].' We never had such a shock in all our lives. [. . .] Instructions were given out what had to be done when the King was sighted. The word ran along the line. 'The King has arrived.' This was a signal to cheer. The King came riding down

the line at the Salute, not a smile to be seen on his face. I personally looked more closely at his Staff in the hope of seeing Lord Kitchener. I must say I was more interested in seeing 'that' man than anyone else. However he was not there, so I concentrated my vision on the other personality. [...] The King had a word to say to all men with medals. There were a good many, we were thereby enabled to have a good look at him. He certainly resembled his photograph a little. The sad look on his face was, however, the outstanding feature. [...] He undoubtedly looked martial as he sat his horse and took the 'Salute'.[53]

'It was quite good fun in a way but I am very glad it is all over and we can get back to business again. Ceremonial drill is of little use to machine gunners', noted Captain N. J. Ainsworth of his experience of being inspected by the king at Devonport in 1915.[54] Private Thomas McIndoe, inspected in May 1915, recalled how 'everything had to shine, even the tips on your boots' and how the monarch took the salute 'on a dais' at Stonehenge, a powerful symbolic backdrop.[55] For Rifleman J. Anderson Johnson, however, his division's inspection in 1915 on the Salisbury Plain evoked medieval tropes of pageantry:

> [...] being on a slight rise we could see the whole Division, their bayonets flashing in the sun, while behind us, rank after rank, stood the waggons of the Divisional Transport and Artillery. As the King rode forward to the saluting base, a tall flag staff with the Royal Standard, the order 'Royal Salute, Present Arms' was given by the General Officer Commanding the Division (Major-General Lord Gleichen) and the massed bands played 'The King'. His Majesty then rode slowly down the full length of the parade and, returning to the saluting base, took the salute as we marched past [...]. Wheeling into position, three cheers were raised for the King and, as they crashed out, our caps were raised in the points of bayonets and rifles above the clouds of golden dust rising from the trampling of 20,000 men, horses, and guns. His Majesty bid us 'Farewell and God-speed' and as we returned to quarters he left by car for Ludgershall, escorted overhead by ten aeroplanes in battle formation.[56]

The sheer scale of the inspection Johnston witnessed indicates the effort put into inculcating a bond between monarch and soldier at the point of departure from Britain for the war.

The impact of such inspections was mixed; they appear to have impressed troop participants less than those which the king carried out behind the lines on the Western Front, discussed later. However, they reveal the extent to which monarchical ritual and display underpinned the British military mobilisation of men for war and the juxtaposition of older pageantry and symbolism with modern weaponry – royal standards and aeroplanes integrated into a mass monarchical spectacle.[57] For the mobilisation of the navy, which had to occur rapidly on 29–30 July 1914 when the whole navy passed secretly with darkened lights through the Straits of Dover, a grand visual display was impractical, but a monarchist culture was likewise in evidence. The king sent a message of support to Sir John Jellicoe, commander of the Grand Fleet:

> At this grave moment in our national history I send to you, and through you to the officers and men of the fleets of which you have assumed command, the assurance of my confidence that under your direction they will revive and renew the old glories of the Royal Navy and prove once again the sure shield of Britain and of her Empire in the hour of trial.[58]

Again the imagery blended archaic kingship and modern technology, as the postcard in Fig. 11 illustrates.

Fig. 11   Postcard of king and Royal Navy, Mary Evans Picture Library, 10950001

Following the Battle of Jutland in 1916, the navy too saw the ritual performance of wartime kingship, when the monarch travelled to Scotland to inspect the fleet, carrying out a review at sea of the whole fleet assembled, visiting each ship and making a speech and also inspecting thousands of Jutland veterans at Rosyth dockyard, where the men marched past him. 'I am rather proud of the feat which I have performed', King George V wrote to Queen Mary afterwards, 'I have visited, inspected, and have been seen by the whole of the officers and men of the Grand Fleet in three days.'[59] The wartime function of such royal troop reviews, as rituals of power and display, developed out of nineteenth-century roots. It fits with Scott Hughes Myerly's work on military spectacle in the late nineteenth century and Jan Rüger's work on such events in the pre-war British and German navies.[60] Rüger has found that fleet reviews operated as a way of opening up new cultures of patriotic mass politics before 1914. Similar processes were clearly at work in wartime royal inspections of the army, fleet and shipyards.[61]

2.4   Responses to the King's Visits to the Western Front

George V made six visits to the Western Front during the conflict – one per year in 1914, 1915, 1916 and 1917, and twice in 1918. He also visited it immediately after the Armistice in 1918. Responses to these visits provide further insight into whether monarchist cultural discourses had any practical significance in sustaining the war effort. As Frank Mort has argued, reactions from the troops to the wartime 'discourse of royal patriotism were unpredictable. Some pledged themselves to the king and his family as the embodiment of an imperial ideal, while others adopted satire or mockery to criticize royalty's imperfections; yet as serving soldiers almost all were forced to negotiate the wartime impact of the king and his sons in uniform.'[62]

The king visiting his armies at the front was an innovation that depended on archaic, sacralised ideas about the personal bond between the loyal soldier and his monarch. This explains why George V felt so strongly that he had to see as many of the troops as possible during his trips. On his first visit, from 29 November–5 December 1914, George V believed that he had managed to see 'all the troops out here in the last three days except those actually in the trenches'.[63] The Daily Mail reported the same point: 'During the King's visit to his army in the field his Majesty was able to see practically all the troops except those actually in the trenches.'[64] The reference to the army as 'his army in the field' again highlights how the language of kingship infused the understanding of the war effort. In 1914, the British Expeditionary Force was still relatively small, and the king's visit involved large numbers of troops lining the roadside as he passed in his car, so the claim was not implausible.

The trips to the front thus stemmed from George V's strong sense of personal responsibility for his troops, believing that his duty was to be present with them as much as possible in wartime and to watch over their welfare. He wrote to Queen Mary during the 1914 visit that '[they] seem to approve of my having come out here. I don't really care if they don't as I am doing what I consider is my duty.'[65] Queen Mary shared such attitudes, writing to him that he must 'have felt so proud of being their King! I know I should be.'[66] Haig thought this royal faith in the troops could be naïve, noting during his 1914 trip: 'The King seemed very cheery but inclined to think that all our troops are by nature brave', underestimating the work that commanders had to do to sustain morale.[67] By visiting troops on the Western Front, the king reinforced the personal bond of loyalty between the individual and his monarch, which was at the core of military service, thereby, he believed, strengthening his army. Within the lexicon of Great War honour culture, the king's visits represented an exchange – by his presence in France, he honoured those risking their lives in his name; they, in turn, honoured him by their sacrifices. As one soldier, H. G. Gilliland, described it: 'A holder of the King's Commission must carry out the spirit in which that commission is given – the path of duty, even unto death, in whatever circumstances that path may lie [. . .].'[68]

The bond worked both ways: troops not only served the king; he also took stewardship of them. The king's visits to the front allowed him to monitor how his men were being treated. He 'took personal pains to investigate cases of alleged unfairness' towards his servicemen, wrote Harold Nicolson in his authorised biography.[69] Lord Stamfordham, the king's Private Secretary, wrote of how 'One feels now, more than ever, that if an injustice is done, or likely to be done, to an Officer in the Army, His Majesty is the proper person to look into the subject.'[70] Stamfordham's reference to officers is telling: most individual royal interventions appear to have related to them, as under military law officers were entitled to a right to complain to the monarch, although the king did also demand improvements where any poor treatment of other ranks came to his attention.[71] Theoretically, a convicted soldier or officer could also petition the monarch to have a court-martial finding set aside under the royal prerogative of mercy but, in practice, in the case of court-martial death sentences in the First World War, the monarch fully delegated the role of final arbiter confirming sentences to the Commander-in-Chief in the Field.[72] However, in one case it appears that the king did intervene on behalf of two Guards officers who had been accused of fraternising with the enemy on Christmas Day 1915; as a result their sentences were suspended and they were returned to duty, overruling Haig's wish to punish them.[73] When Germany selected a group of captured upper-class British prisoner of war officers for reprisal treatment in 1915 in retaliation for the British government's segregation policy towards German submarine prisoners, at least two of the men appealed for help to the king: Captain Ronald Stewart-Menzies wrote to Stamfordham, while Lieutenant Lord Garlies wrote to Lady Fitzwilliam, whose husband saw the monarch frequently, to pass on the request.[74] Lord

Stamfordham noted to the Prime Minister's secretary that 'The King feels very strongly the fact that these Officers are appealing to him personally.'[75] In sum, George V understood kingship in wartime as a sacralised, symbiotic personal relationship between the monarch and his servicemen, whereby each honoured the other.

Thus, George V's front visits were designed to highlight his concern for troop welfare, and the press emphasised this, as well as their simple nature. The simplicity was a direct attempt to distance the king from the ostentatious kaiser, widely vilified in the United Kingdom and blamed for causing the war, which risked tarnishing all monarchical regimes. The denigration of the kaiser evoked an older discourse of the tyrannical king, with its echoes of the English Civil War depiction of Charles I. This was a dangerous media climate for the British royals, particularly given their German connections.[76] In planning the 1914 visit, Clive Wigram wrote of how 'The King would probably only come over with two or three of his Household and not in any way ape the German Emperor with a full Military Staff and large Escort.'[77] George V travelled with a very small entourage: a staff of eight went on his first 1914 visit, which included Sir Frederick Ponsonby, the Keeper of the Privy Purse; Captain Sir Charles Cust, the king's equerry; and the Hon. Sir Derek Keppel, the Master of the Royal Household; two footmen; two chefs and a valet – a dramatically pared-down contingent compared to pre-war royal travel; in addition he had a small security detail provided by the police.[78] He travelled exhausting distances: his seven-day August 1916 trip covered 800 miles.[79] The king ate food en route during his trips from a travelling hunting box brought over from Sandringham.[80] Symbolically, on Christmas Day 1918, the front page of the popular *Daily Sketch* newspaper showed a photograph from the king's Western Front visits depicting him eating a sandwich, standing against a flat-based railway wagon truck on which his lunchbox lay open.[81] The projected image of novel royal simplicity during front visits had an impact. A Salvation Army worker from Essex wrote to Lord Stamfordham to say that the king's 3–14 July 1917 visit to the front had helped to 'remove' the taint of 'German influence and power from the Court'.[82]

In fact, throughout the war, the king sought to get as close to the fighting as possible. During his winter 1914 front visit, he briefly experienced the battlefield 'live', akin to a nineteenth-century commander, writing in his diary of how:

> We were only about three miles from the enemy's trenches. Ypres, Ghelevelt [sic], Wytschaete, Messines and Mont Kemmel being easily seen with glasses. Mont Kemmel was being shelled as the Germans think it is an observation station which it is not, they have left our hill severely alone although people are killed in the village just below us. Saw

> our guns bombarding the German trenches and in return the Germans
> sent back one or two 'Black Marias' into poor Ypres and onto Mont
> Kemmel. Ypres is quite destroyed and I could see the Cathedral and
> celebrated Halle in ruins. While on the hill I received message by tele-
> phone from Major Baird and Officers of the Gordon Highlanders in the
> trenches.[83]

The telephone call was clearly designed to enable the monarch to feel as if he
was with his troops in their actual battle. Since the actions of George II at the
Battle of Dettingen in 1743, a protocol directly forbade a British monarch and
his heirs in direct line from taking an active role in war.[84] King George
V compensated through his front trips, writing a public message to his troops
after this winter 1914 visit that, although he could not 'share in your trials,
dangers, and successes', he was constantly thinking of them.[85] On
8 August 1918, the king also witnessed the start of the battle of Amiens with
General Horne.[86]

    Yet, the First World War was a conflict where it was not necessary to fight to
be in danger. Front trips involved a degree of risk. The sea crossing ran the
gauntlet of German submarines; more prosaically it also made the king
violently seasick on many occasions. In 1915, when the king and French
President Poincaré were walking through a French communication trench,
Frederick Ponsonby, who was with them, reported:

> three shells burst over our heads, the nearest one about four hundred
> yards off. I, at first, thought it was a bit of stage management, but on
> talking to my neighbour, one of the Generals, I ascertained that the
> Germans were actually shelling the place. [. . .] If, by a fluke, a shell had
> burst in the trench, what a bag the Germans would have had![87]

The papers of the king's equerry, Sir Charles Cust, described how on
26 October 1915, while the royal party 'were in the communication trenches,
the German Batteries fired three shells over their heads'.[88] Sustaining the
norms of royal deference during front visits proved increasingly difficult –
on 27 October 1915, Cust noted rather insensitively that 'His Majesty was
received with a Royal Salute, after which the Troops filed past in fours. There
was one Band, but the cornet-player had been killed the week before and 4
others wounded in the trenches, so the music was not of the 1st order.'[89]

    For his visit from 8–15 August 1916, the first to take place during a major
battle – the Somme – the king expressly wished to stay as close to the firing line
as possible, but this was vetoed by Sir Douglas Haig, who arranged for the
monarch to stay 40 kilometres behind the lines, to avoid the royal convoy
congesting the roads.[90] During this visit, the king again witnessed the fighting
'live' through field glasses. Stamfordham noted that 'it was most interesting to
look down upon the scenes of the desperate fighting at places like the plateau of
N.D. de Lorette, Mametz, Fricourt and watch the pounding of the enemy

trenches about Wytschaet [sic].'[91] In 1916, the king also began to go to recently shelled locations where the risk was very real; this pattern continued in his later visits. Philip Gibbs, then special correspondent in the field for the *Daily Chronicle*, was present during the king's visit to a dangerous shell hole in recently hit Béthune, writing: 'Some of us standing there were nervous because the King lingered so long. At any second another shell might have come and another shell crater as big as this might have opened the earth at his feet.'[92] He related: 'There was no reason why at any moment there should not have been a black puff of German shrapnel over the King's head. There is no life insurance in these places, and the King took the risk like other men, and thought no more about it.'[93] Sir Basil Thomson, the head of the Criminal Investigation Department at Scotland Yard, wrote in his diary on 26 November 1916 that 'Vivian [my son] said that the King had greatly increased his prestige at the front by his coolness under fire. Most soldiers and civilians under shellfire for the first time showed nervousness. The King showed not a trace of it. My Superintendent Quinn, who had been with the King all the time, confirmed this.'[94] In July 1917, King George V noted in his diary that 'Shortly after we left Vierstraat the German artillery shelled the place as well as Wytschaete.'[95] At Bailleul, he 'saw just across the street a house which was destroyed by a German bomb two nights ago, all the windows on the street were smashed'.[96] After the king left Messines, the town suffered a bad air raid, attributed by contemporaries to the Germans trying to kill him.[97] In 1936, Silver Jubilee coverage in the *Illustrated London News* reproduced a photograph of the king walking in a trench with the caption: 'when King George was more than once under shellfire: His Majesty inspecting trenches during his visit to the Western Front in France in 1918'.[98]

George V never showed any concern about the physical risks involved in his front visits, perhaps a result of his naval training in his youth, in contrast to others on his tours, such as the Prince of Wales, who commented at length on the fear that he felt at experiencing shelling. The king never mentioned in his diary what it felt like to be close to shellfire.[99] Of course, bravery in the Great War was all relative, and the king's courage in his front visits was nowhere near the scale required of his men who faced going over the top. But it was recognisable bravery to his contemporaries nevertheless. There were real concerns for the king's safety. His itinerary was kept secret, his trips only revealed in the British press after his return.[100] When George V suffered a serious equestrian accident during his October 1915 front visit, members of his retinue back at his base immediately presumed he had been shot: an equerry 'rode up out of breath and almost incoherent with anxiety' and 'all of us [...] thought at first the King had been shot at by the Germans and might even now be dying'.[101] After this injury, Queen Mary requested daily reports on his welfare during his front visits.[102] By 1916, extensive security arrangements were being made to allow for a rapid evacuation of the king during his front visit if required.[103] George V clearly put himself in locations that were risky enough for his entourage to be worried. It was ultimately somewhat ironic that the king avoided the dangers of shellfire only to be thrown from his horse while at the front in 1915; the biggest risk to the monarch's body in modern war proved to be the one most connected with acting out an older, kingly 'warrior' role of reviewing his troops on horseback, a role he was frequently depicted in in 1915 war propaganda. The cover of the *War Illustrated* even depicted a drawing of George V astride a prancing black charger with the caption 'our king goes to the front'.[104]

The most important of George V's front visits took place from 28–30 March 1918, at a moment of major crisis for the British forces, dramatically pushed back following the start of the Ludendorff Offensives on 21 March. The king's spontaneous decision to visit the front at this point was a dramatic, risky and exhausting gesture of solidarity, born of anxiety. His diary on 22, 23 and 24 March repeatedly mentions being 'anxious'.[105] The army had too little notice of the visit and no capacity, in its ongoing retreat, to prepare for his sudden three-day dash to France, and he saw the war in the raw, including newly wounded men awaiting treatment. The king covered huge distances by car around a mobile, collapsing front, attempting to boost morale and support his troops. Haig later wrote to the king of how 'heart and soul the Army is behind you, Sir. In March things looked black indeed [...]. Your Majesty's presence and kindly words brought home to one and all how very much our King is Head of the Army.'[106] Haig's sycophantism towards the monarchy should not cloud the fact that this trip was a radical act. Had Britain been completely defeated at this point, the monarch would have been associated with the military rout.

Reactions to the innovation of a modern British king visiting a war zone varied. Elites were invariably enthusiastic. At General Headquarters (GHQ) in 1914 when the first visit was being planned the view was that

> a sight of the King and a few words from him will do a world of good and will delight the troops (Sir John has visited a good many lately and from all accounts his visits are much appreciated) much more will [be] those of the king.[107]

Clive Wigram, the king's secretary, writing of the monarch's 1914 visit, stated: 'The visit I think was a great success and everybody seemed delighted to see His Majesty.'[108] Likewise, the king received a letter of praise from the Bishop of Ripon.[109] The editor of the conservative magazine *The Spectator* wrote to the king of his trip that 'I did not realise how great the effect would be. You must feel very happy about it all.'[110] A fictionalised propaganda novel – published to encourage recruitment – described the 1914 trip as 'the great surprise for the British troops in the field. The King himself came over from London, and visited headquarters, the hospitals and his gallant troops in the trenches. The enthusiasm was unbounded and a sergeant unbosomed himself [. . .] by saying he "reckoned His Majesty was a real sport.'"[111]

The king's later visits also won elite praise. Commander-in-Chief Sir Douglas Haig wrote of the king's 8–15 August 1916 visit that

> I cannot adequately explain what a real pleasure it has been to every one of us to see Your Majesty moving about amongst the troops. The universal wish is that 'the King should come and see us oftener!'[112]

Haig also reported very positively on the monarch's spring 1918 trip at the height of the Ludendorff Offensives:

> The coming of Your Majesty amongst his troops at this critical time has been immensely appreciated by us all and it has shown to all ranks the very keen interest which the King personally takes in the work of his soldiers in the field. After what Your Majesty saw of the Army in France last week, I feel sure that no assurance of mine is needed to prove that the troops, in spite of fierce fighting for so many days, still preserve their courage unabated, their determination unshaken and their confidence in final victory undiminished.[113]

The Archbishop of Canterbury, Randall Davidson, wrote to the king on 21 August 1918 that

> The visits to the front have been – if it is not presumptuous of me to say so – exactly right, coming at the proper moments in our history and avoiding both the fussiness of perpetual intervention and the coldness of a mere outside spectator. It is a role of extraordinary difficulty and I shd like Your Majesty to know how deeply we do appreciate the manner in which the task is discharged.[114]

Sir Almeric Fitzroy, the Clerk of the Privy Council, concurred, even believing that the troops 'achievements' in August 1918 were directly inspired by the king's fifth front visit, which took place that month.[115]

Realpolitik was clearly a factor in some of these positive attitudes. The pull of monarchy was such during the king's visit to the front in 1914 that Frederick Ponsonby noted: 'all the Generals had left their commands to come and pay their respects to him'.[116] This, Ponsonby felt, made it imperative that the king should never visit the front during a major offensive lest, if it were unsuccessful, critics blame him for interfering or distracting. During his 1915 visit, Sir John French still came all the way to Boulogne to welcome him, something the king criticised.[117] Alongside monarchist beliefs, the king's key patronage power in the army obviously played a role here. Royal visits were a chance to make a good personal impression to advance a military career. For example, Haig's profound monarchist beliefs and career needs often overlapped. He was devoted to the monarchy, fully believing that his 'sole object is to serve my King and Country', but

George V's support was also key in helping Haig face down political decisions he disliked, so visits were useful occasions to foster their relationship.[118] Visits also promoted the war effort. The king's 1917 visit to the front saw him meet with Australian troops, an encounter which their commander, then Lieutenant General, William Birdwood wanted publicised in Australia, as 'They value such things very much out there and I feel confident that it will help recruiting which is what the commonwealth government is always asking us to do.'[119]

For those officers in the midst of the fighting, a royal visit could come as a boost. Regimental Officer (later Major General) V. G. Tofts wrote:

> I remember one day in France when we had come out of the front line after a rather bad spell with very many casualties and we were reviewed by King George V with General Haig and several other Generals. We were thrilled to see the King but as regards all the Generals and the staff all we could think about was how clean and smart they looked.[120]

Oliver Lyttleton, serving in the Grenadier Guards, experienced a royal inspection immediately before an attack: 'we expected and feared a battle speech, but the King talked to us in the most down-to-earth way: an example of timely tact'.[121] Colonel Stewart Cleeve was very impressed by the king's interest, 'vast knowledge' and questions to him in 1918 about technical gun settings; Cleeve met the king on 8 August 1918, and the monarch, having just come from seeing the start of the Battle of Amiens, ordered Cleeve to fire his heavy artillery gun on Douai station, a 'King's shot' that directly hit a German troop train.[122] Writer C. E. Montague, serving at the front, wrote of how he was presented to the monarch at Cassel, describing George V positively as 'full of good humour and goodwill'; Montague noted wryly, however, that he dined in a hotel room 'reserved for our meals and those of the King's detectives'.[123] By contrast, striking a dissenting note in response to a royal visit, officer Raymond Asquith, the Prime Minister's son, wrote from France, where he was serving with the Grenadier Guards: 'The King came to see us this morning, looking as glum and dyspeptic as ever', a somewhat harsh criticism given touring the Western Front was hardly calculated to inspire joy.[124]

Other rank reactions shed more light on how monarchism functioned at the front, revealing that while many viewed the king's visits positively, soldiers had little agency to dissent. Some troops genuinely were boosted to see the monarch, although this was often because he reminded them of home. Private Herbert Empson, serving with the London Field Ambulance RAMC, connected the sight of the king on 9 August 1916 with thoughts of home, recording in his diary:

> An event of unusual interest took place today, when the King with Sir Douglas Haig and staff passed through the village on their way to Mt S. – I was on duty at the time so I could not go down to the main road to see

him pass, but I saw the cars and clouds of dust. Many of the boys and patients were down on the road and we heard hearty cheering when His Majesty and party went by. [. . .] Later the royal party returned and again I saw the motors and clouds of dust! It was a very fine day and my thoughts went back a month or two to an equally brilliant day when His Majesty inspected our Division in Blighty just behind Scratchbury Hill, near Warminster. We were then eager for France but now I think most of us are even more eager for home. Nevertheless it is nice to know that after two short months, the King again saw our Division; this time at work in earnest and that he had the pleasant duty of presenting awards for gallantry.[125]

H. T. Madders noted in 1918 that 'Our Div. has been complimented by the King and are having a few days rest; thoughts of the Home Fires [. . .]', suggesting the psychological connection between the idea of home and the familiar image of the king which hung in homes and public buildings in this period.[126] After the king had visited a YMCA improvised canteen in a Western Front dugout in July 1917, the men put up a sign that stated 'Patronised by H.M. the King'.[127]

George V often recorded in his diary that ordinary soldiers responded favourably when he appeared. For example, on his first trip in December 1914, driving to Estaires, he saw 'roads lined by troops who were all in reserve, they cheered as we passed. Saw some men dressed in clothing to prevent frost bite consisting of fur skins for the body and sacks filled with straw for the legs.'[128] The weather could indeed make such visits difficult for troops. Captain A. St. John Blunt noted in his diary that when it rained just before the king arrived for an inspection, he and his men even had to clean the roads ahead of the royal visit.[129] Canadian soldier Wilbert Gilroy, writing on 2 November 1915, described a visit in prosaic terms, asserting the king received his troops, rather than the other way around:

> The king received us the other day, accompanied by Prince of Wales, and a drove of generals and other dig's [sic]. He is quite the same old George, and appeared pleased with us in general. The prince is a poor little chap who looks as though he ought to be at home. But he is game to the core, they say.[130]

Private A. Wells's diary sheds further light on what such visits were like for combatants:

> we have received orders to parade on the main western Beauval road. The King was going to pass through the lines. We paraded each side of the Road. The King wished to see us and thank us. He, the King, with the Prince of Wales and Sir John [French] walked down the centre of the Road and he would stop at the end of each Squadron and give us a little speech[.] Of course we got orders to take off our caps and give him cheers for him and England.[131]

Likewise, the papers of the king's equerry, Sir Charles Cust, note that, during the monarch's October 1915 trip to France, 'the King visited the Indian Convalescent Depot under Major Jeudwine, where all the patients were drawn up and gave three cheers for His Majesty'.[132]

Given this context, in which soldiers performed cheers for the monarch in a ritualised way and were often photographed doing so for war propaganda (Fig. 12), it is difficult to interpret whether cheering indicated monarchist attitudes: on the one hand cheering was generally ordered, but this does not indicate whether soldiers found the order congenial or not. For Second Lieutenant John Gamble, cheering indicated enthusiasm: 'Did I tell you we had the King here last week? He had a big review, and the troops didn't half cheer. Guess it would penetrate to the firing line, and "old Bosche" would be getting the wind up, and expecting an attack.'[133] In another case, Private Joseph Elley reported on a winter 1915 inspection that

> Well we had a visit from the King & we had the honour of being <u>one</u> of the Regts he inspected, [sic] He came to a place about 5 miles from the <u>Firing Line</u>. He did not say anything to the troops, but we were pleased to see that the

Fig. 12 'Troops Cheering the King', from the Field Marshal Earl Haig Collection, National Library of Scotland, (106) X.33013 (Reproduced courtesy of the National Library of Scotland)

King [was] taking so much interest in the men so we cheered with all our might.[134]

Police Superintendent Quinn, who accompanied the king as his security detail, described his July 1917 visit to the front to his superior Basil Thomson on 15 July 1917: 'the King visited various army areas, and in each the men lined both sides of the road for miles, cheering with the greatest enthusiasm'.[135]

However, there is also evidence that orders to cheer the royal visitor were sometimes refused by 1917: veteran Raynor Taylor recounted in an oral history interview in the 1990s that when a Welsh unit, exhausted from fighting, came out of the line during the Ludendorff Offensives and were ordered by their officers to stand and cheer for the king's car, the men did not cheer. The incident likely took place on 30 March 1918. Significantly, there were rumours of low morale in the British army in this period as well as a more challenging climate for the monarchy following the Bolshevik October Revolution.

> And eh the battalion was halted along a roadside for the usual ten minutes and eh we were called upon to stand up because the king was coming along this road and eh we were expected to cheer the king when he came along. Eh we stood up – it was an order – we all eh we stood up – no such thing as standing to attention – we stood up just from where we were and this eh cavalcade came along the king in this car and the attendants in other cars behind and the officers of course they did cheer their hurrah but I've no recollection of any of the men because after a period in the, up in the front line you weren't in any mood to cheer anybody [. . .].[136]

It was all a marked contrast to the monarchism of 1914.

The interviewer pressed Taylor further, resulting in a series of revealing comments on the disjunction between the acute monarchism of the cheering officers compared to the men, who muttered rude remarks, illustrating a connection between war exhaustion and anti-monarchism. Taylor indicates there was still a reluctance to openly break monarchist taboos about respecting the monarch and protest loudly. He also highlights that the king, who passed by rapidly in his car, would have been unaware of the men's failure to cheer; clearly some of the king's positive impressions of his front visits were projections of how he believed his troops to be responding rather than how they actually always reacted:

INTERVIEWER: Did they actually tell you to cheer?
TAYLOR: Oh yes, yes. Eh.
INTERVIEWER: Did the men shout anything or [. . .] what happened?
TAYLOR: No, I never heard, I never heard in the particular part where I, I never heard any of the men cheer but the officers of course did, they [sic].

INTERVIEWER:	Did they shout?
TAYLOR:	Oh yes, hurray hurray, oh they lifted their steel hats up you know.
INTERVIEWER:	The officers did?
TAYLOR:	Oh yes.
INTERVIEWER:	What did the men do? Did they say anything or?
TAYLOR:	Nothing at all only, listen, a lot of very crude and rude remarks.
INTERVIEWER:	They actually made remarks?
TAYLOR:	Oh yes amongst themselves, of course, not didn't [sic] shout them out or anything like that you know. Oh no there was no display of animosity in that respect.
INTERVIEWER:	So it was more muttering?
TAYLOR:	Oh yes, oh yes. Mind ye a motorcavalcade it doesn't take, it's only, it's only a flash past, it's gone you see.
INTERVIEWER:	So would the king have been aware that you weren't cheering?
TAYLOR:	I don't think so. I very much question whether he thought that.[137]

Despite the speed of the king's car, Taylor recalled getting a good view of him, as it was an open-topped car to allow troops to see the monarch. Although one must bear in mind the fact that Taylor was speaking in the 1990s, so influenced by later changed attitudes to monarchy, his prosaic summary of the king, 'Well he were a little fella with beard you know', highlighted that the monarch's visits did not always inculcate awe.[138] Royal sources also suggest there were sensitivities around 1918 visits: Major General Arthur Daly, in a letter on arrangements for the king's December 1918 visit to the front after the war had ended, emphasised that where the king met groups of men on his trip, the officers would stand 'furthest away', so that 'His Majesty would see the N.C.O.s and men first', an indication of nervousness that ordinary soldiers resented being presented last, seeing it as indicative of their lesser status to that of officers.[139]

Taylor's interview also highlights how the press manipulated the king's visits into monarchist propaganda: the Paris edition of the *Daily Mail* came up the line and Taylor recognised men from his unit in a photograph that was intended to show the monarch receiving a positive welcome from his troops. For Taylor, 'it was a propaganda photograph to show to the people at home how, eh, the king was right up in the firing line and how the troops welcomed him and that was the background to the story which was being written at the time'.[140] The photograph showed the officers cheering. The fact that the other ranks had not actually cheered was covered up.

In fact, press propaganda reports during the conflict constantly emphasised the troops' cheering during each of the king's visits to the front in the war years, suggesting that this practice mattered intensely to affirming home front and Establishment confidence; for example, in April 1918 troops' cheers were apparently described as so loud by *The Times* that 'the cattle peaceably grazing half a mile off stopped munching and raised their heads to see whence the noise came'.[141] It is interesting that, despite being at the front at war, this sacralising ritual of cheering – and ordering cheering – continued, and continued to be emphasised, even when offensives were taking place. Cheering the king was, in fact, a rather atavistic courtly practice, oddly transposed onto a modern battlefield. The image of the men, still being ready to acclaim their king was something that mattered in propaganda terms for journalists and their readers, viewed as comforting and reassuring, both as an indication that the men's morale and patriotism remained strong but also in its bringing royal practices – with all their long associations with stability, historic traditions including war victories of the past, and peacetime home rituals – to the front.

There are other examples of how the personal experience of royal visits and their propaganda value often merged. When Bombardier C. R. Collins wrote to his sister Grace regarding the king's July 1917 front visit in very appreciative terms, his words found their way into a newspaper:

> We had a pleasant surprise today. We had a visit from the King and Prince of Wales today – it was kept secret till the last minute of course. I must not tell you where but I can tell you he ran a greater risk than I would ever have dreamed of to come right up to the firing line. He came right by where we buried three of our chaps only last night and if you ever hear anyone say the King only goes to the base you can give them the lie direct. He has aged considerably since I last saw him but the Prince looked fine and well. I can tell you it cheered us up a great deal. God bless him. I am a patriot and he has had some worry; you can see it in his face. I only hope that his appearance to us is a sign of better times in store. If only Fritz had known. I don't think it right for him and the Prince to take such risks but I can assure you he had a hearty welcome.[142]

The letter extract was later published in the *Morning Post* in July 1917; the fact that a copy exists in the Royal Archives suggests that royal permission was sought before it was published.[143]

Press reactions to the king's front visits were overwhelmingly positive. Extensive reports appeared on all of the king's trips, accompanied by official photographs, communicating the idea that the king was present with his soldiers at war. Yet it was not until George V's 1916 visit to the front that journalists were allowed to accompany him.[144] This greater direct press access coincided with the vacuum left by the death of Kitchener, which the cult of the monarch now had to fill. His 1916 Somme visit was also filmed for the official production 'The King Visits His Armies in the Great Advance'.[145] Its cinema popularity ensured a sequel: 'The Royal Visit to the Battlefields of France', a film of the king and queen's 1917 trip.[146] By 1917, the king found time to receive 'the British and Allied correspondents' who were working with the British Army; a similar reception was planned for his August 1918 front tour.[147]

Overall, the press reports on the king's tours presented him as providing royal leadership and stewardship of his armies, protective, solicitous, stoic and encouraging. In the first years of the conflict, the cultural archetypes for the role of a British monarch at war that the press presented in its reporting of the tours were those of English history – Shakespeare, Agincourt, Dettingen – of inspiring speeches and of leadership in battle. George V's innovative front visits were likened in the wartime press to 'leading' his men on the battlefield – even if he could not do so in battle itself. While there is no evidence of any expectation that as a modern constitutional monarch he would go into battle with his men, there were frequent press reports and official photographs that associated George V with a battlefield presence, showing him watching the fighting from afar through binoculars, walking newly captured territory and meeting the wounded in base hospitals.[148] The press revelled in images showing the monarch acting the same as any ordinary officer in a front location, uniformed, walking in or clambering over trenches, covered in mud, wearing a Brodie helmet (Fig. 13).[149]

Fig. 13   King George V on Wytschaete Ridge, Flanders in Belgium on 4 July 1917, during a tour of the Western Front, IWM Q 5586/154448839 (Photo by Lt. J. W. Brooke/Imperial War Museums via Getty Images)

Reports made much of his voluntary choice to abnegate himself in this way and of his visits to areas that had recently been shelled, and simple accommodation and food, as a sign of his honouring his men who were fighting for him. These visual and written narratives had power precisely because such royal risk-taking and solidarity with troops was not expected of sacralised royal bodies, due to their different, protected status.

The king was also regularly photographed with his generals during his visits, suggesting his connection with the war planning and strategy, and his over-sight and surveillance of troop welfare, an image of military leadership at the martial limit of what was possible for his constitutional role. He was also constantly photographed awarding honours, pinning medals onto troops in impromptu front area ceremonies or knighting generals in campaign tents and chateau headquarters.[150] All of this was suggestive of a military king and brought the monarchy to the soldiers in a direct way. It also showed the commitment of the monarch to his men, strengthening the sacred image of a direct monarch–soldier relationship.

The same message was conveyed in illustrations: a sketch by the war artist Fortunino Matania which was widely circulated in the press showed the king on his 1914 trip to the front, bareheaded before a war grave, his body language communicating honour-coded meanings: 'the sovereign leaning forward rather than standing erect, in a religious act of homage'.[151] Here honour-culture codes were clearly visible in the artist's impression, which also reflected the fact that George V did behave in this way when he encountered British war graves on his front visits.[152]

The press always emphasised that the visits were popular with the troops. Cheering soldiers marching past or lined up to acclaim the king were a common theme in photographs and reports. Press reports and photographs thus not only created a belief in the king's popularity, but also enhanced it in reality by showing soldiers a monarch who prioritised visiting them, reducing any danger that a more popular general or politician might undermine his role. Yet, although press reports on the front visits were invariably sycophantic in tone, they could also show subtle changes. A *Times* editorial on the August 1916 visit, entitled 'The King and His Soldiers', stated:

> The news that the KING has again visited his Armies in France and the General Order which he has graciously issued to them will be read with deep gratification by all his loyal subjects. HIS MAJESTY has seen every-thing with his own eyes – trenches, captured dug-outs, batteries, and prisoners. Above all he has seen, and been seen by, hundreds of thousands of his men. [. . .] HIS MAJESTY showed the fearlessness of his House in insisting upon investigating 'unhealthy spots', well within range of the German guns, and their tenderness in the homage he paid to the dead. His soldiers, we are told, agree that he is 'a real sport'. The term is not courtly,

but none, we are confident, could sound more gratefully in the ears of an English King.[153]

The editorial is highly revealing. The underlying sense of dynastic and national tradition – his *House*, an *English* king, *homage* – is sacralised language from an older era. The king's bravery is emphasised. Yet, alongside this depiction of the royal body as a dynastic, historic entity is the sense of the royal body at risk – from shells at the front – a metaphor for the risk that the war more broadly entailed for British royalty in the upheavals it was bringing. This is brought home by the mention of royal gratitude in the final sentence – suggesting the king needs to be *grateful* to still be praised by his soldiers given what they are enduring on his behalf and the apologetics for the fact that the men now speak of him using uncourtly – informal – language. By 1916, the war was changing expectations of royalty – something *The Times*, the voice of the Establishment, seemed to be awkwardly navigating.

The king's front trips were believed to have been a propaganda success and also to have had a positive impact on the image of the monarchy. Indeed, wartime press motifs were so powerful, they resurfaced in interwar writings. 'He was the first British Sovereign to appear in the field since George II fought at Dettingen, and was everywhere received with enthusiasm', gushed one popular history of George V's reign.[154] A 1930s biographer noted that, during George V's March 1918 visit, 'he stayed at a château close to the field of Agincourt'.[155] The innovative front tours were thus presented as part of a historic, sacralised tradition of English kings offering leadership to their combatants in war – even if, in George V's case, his solidarity was more one of stewardship of his armies than actual military decision-making. As the journalist Philip Gibbs wrote in 1936: 'The King being a soldier at heart as well as by virtue of his supreme office was not satisfied to remain at home whilst his troops were engaged in a terrific struggle against the most formidable foe that British warriors have ever had to face.'[156]

It is useful here to briefly draw the comparison with Kaiser Wilhelm II, whose visits to the front 'were always carefully staged'; he made no spontaneous trips akin to George V's in 1918.[157] In fact, he rarely visited the front at all. Supposedly Supreme War Lord, in charge of his armies, he spent most of the conflict 'a hundred or so kilometres from the front' at his 'Great Headquarters' at Koblenz, then Luxembourg, Charleville, Pless and Bad Kreuznach, where he went for leisurely pleasure drives every afternoon, as well as walks in the woods, and was visited regularly by the kaiserin.[158] He took his weekends 'off' in Bad Homburg, a Hohenzollern castle in Germany; by spring 1917, he spent most of his time there.[159] When he did leave Headquarters he still went nowhere near the fighting. Kaiser Wilhelm II's visits were 'confined to the relatively safe area well behind the front line', as he 'had to be kept out of harm's way', and he was widely considered to have 'only the vaguest notion of conditions at the front'.[160] An Austro-Hungarian delegate said the kaiser's rare visits to his front troops reminded him of 'Potemkin villages' and gave 'the Supreme War Lord little sense of the conditions in the trenches'.[161] They took place very far behind the front line in safe areas and involved 'inspections and parades' often 'with music' just as on the pre-war parade ground.[162] One observer who accompanied the kaiser to the eastern front in 1915 noted that the totally 'unwarlike character of the arrangements' was 'embarrassing' and that these 'so-called front visits, which go nowhere near to the front, only serve to cause resentment among the troops, who have to endure long marches and parade drill when the Kaiser puts in an appearance'.[163] It was a marked contrast with George V's sympathetic concern for troop morale during his front trips. By 1917, the kaiser's failure to show adequate support for his men had hugely undermined his power.[164] Crown Prince Rupprecht of Bavaria, who commanded a German Army Group, was shocked when, during a troop inspection on the Western Front in December 1917, the kaiser 'brought greetings and a message of support' from Field Marshal Hindenburg to the men. Rupprecht was appalled that a reigning monarch 'should appear before his soldiers as a mere spokesman for one of his senior officers'.[165] But by this point Hindenburg was the de facto leader of Germany's war effort, not Wilhelm II, and had usurped the troops' faith and loyalty too. Getting front visits wrong, in other words, could cost a monarchy all respect among its soldiers and much of its power with its military. George V's visits were, overall, far more successful in bolstering his popularity.

One final way of assessing the king's visits to the front is a series of essays written by working-class and middle-class schoolboys about the monarch for Mass Observation after his death. In late 1937, it collected 512 school essays on the theme 'The Finest Person Who Ever Lived' from boys aged 8 to 18 'at schools in Westhoughton, near Bolton, Lancashire and Middlesborough in north-east England'; 46 of them were on King George V, who was the most popular choice after Jesus, on whom 80 essays were written, although it is not clear from the archive if the boys had a free choice in who they wrote about.[166] All too young to remember the war, they indicate views they must have picked up from society around them, offering a good barometer as to how the king's wartime role was remembered after his death by parents and teachers. Over half of the 46 essays on George V mentioned the late king's visits to the Western Front and charitable aid to ex-servicemen.[167] As one 12-year-old schoolchild wrote: 'I think the finest person in the world is King George V. He is the finest person in the world because he did so much for the world in the world war. When the Great War was on the King went fighting with the English men.'[168] For 10-year-old A. Bushell, King George V was the finest person who ever lived because 'in time war [sic] he went to see the troops in France'.[169] D. N. Guest, also 10, wrote 'I think King George the fifth was the best man that ever lived because he was the best king and ruler, [sic] And what he did in the war.'[170] In December 1937, J. B. Kershaw wrote 'During the Great War, the late King George V visited his troops in the trenches, and it was

the small things like this that made him so popular.'[171] Ten-year-old
G. R. Harrison wrote that 'the finest person that I have ever heard of is King
George the V. [sic] Because he fought for England in the great war. [...] He was
a strong well built man, and always let his sons do as other men in the war did.'[172]
For 15-year-old P. R. Newton, King George V 'was a king who in the war was
many times in the trenches under fire speaking to the soldiers and cheering them
up. [...] All through those years of terror he was continually on the western front
with the soldiers.'[173]

Numerous essays made the connection between the king's wartime hard
work, his visits to the front and his popularity: R. Hulme, aged 14, wrote that

> During the four troublesome years of 1914–1918 the king visited all ranks
> of the British army, who were participating in Great War [sic]. He went to
> the firing line and spoke to many soldiers, he visited hospitals and joined
> in with the nation in their trouble. These actions also go to give him a good
> character and make him well liked.[174]

What is clear here is that there was evidently a popular idea that George V had
been at the front in danger and that this had boosted his long-term popularity
and reputation. In this regard, the children's impressions, while vague, and in
some cases distorted, were not totally inaccurate: the king had been put at risk
during some of his trips to the front during the war, and he had met large
numbers of his troops. What is also clearly evident is the idea of the king as
a national model and exemplar of moral wartime behaviour; in these essays
George V's front trips made him a heroic leadership figure.

2.5 Royal Philanthropy to Combatants: The Princess
Mary Gift Box

Royal charitable mobilisation to support the troops offers another important
example of tangible cultural practices where we can see the monarchy–subject
relationship operating during the war. The monarchy mobilised – and was
mobilised – in myriad ways for wartime philanthropic endeavours. These
included *Princess Mary's Gift Book*, in support of the Queen's Work for
Women Fund, and *The Queen's Gift Book* by John Galsworthy, sold in aid of
Queen Mary's Auxiliary Hospitals.[175] This work was popular, judging by the scale
of the public response it generated.[176] At the outbreak of the conflict, Queen Mary
wanted to avoid the chaos that had marred aid provision during the Second South
African (Boer) War. She took the initiative, organising both the new wartime
Prince of Wales's 'National Relief Fund' and enlarging her existing needlework
charity into a much larger, national organisation, now renamed as Queen Mary's
Needlework Guild, which took on the role of coordinating the production and
delivery of knitted comforts, made by volunteers, to the troops.[177] By June 1915,
the latter had over 60,000 members in London alone and had sent more than

200,000 items of clothing to troops via its collection point at Buckingham Palace.[178] Queen Mary also became President of the Army Nursing Board.[179] When a Women's Army Auxiliary Corps was established during the war, it was renamed after a year as Queen Mary's Army Auxiliary Corps, partly to enhance its status.

The queen's most innovative charitable role, however, was setting up the Queen's Work for Women Fund, a subsidiary of the National Relief Fund, which provided relief work for unemployed working-class women who had lost their jobs due to the war. It resulted from a 1914 meeting between the queen and feminist socialist Mary Macarthur to discuss the problem of unfair competition between Queen Mary's Needlework Guild of volunteers, knitting war comforts for the troops, and working-class women doing the same work as paid labour. Macarthur noted that she had 'positively lectured the Queen on the inequality of the classes, the injustice of it'.[180] The Queen's Work for Women Fund saw the two women work together, developing a friendly relationship. It was run by a central committee, chaired by the Marchioness of Crewe, on which Macarthur and fellow feminist socialist activist Margaret Bondfield also sat, although the Fund's rates of pay were low, leading Sylvia Pankhurst to accuse Macarthur of betraying women workers.[181]

The Queen's Work for Women Fund illustrates how, time and again during the war, the king and queen utilised their wide network of contacts to arrange meetings with individual Labour and Trade Union figures, to listen closely to their expertise on social justice issues, and to use this to realign royal actions and image accordingly. This began well before the revolutionary year 1917: in October 1914, the king recommended to Asquith that he raise pensions for war widows as 'His Majesty doubts the country agreeing to a pension of 5/- for a woman who has lost her husband fighting for his country.'[182] Royal patrician democracy was closely tapped into industrial grassroots information through these channels of intimate meetings and the personal rapport they established; this was a major strength of the monarchy in this conflict. The process of charitable patronage permitted royal women, in particular, an important public presence – both symbolic and practical – as well as significant interactions with their subjects.

The most famous royal wartime philanthropic action, however, was the Princess Mary Gift Box, which aimed to send a gift to each individual soldier and sailor for Christmas 1914. It was funded by the public in response to an appeal by the king's teenage daughter, Princess Mary, launched through a public letter in the press on 16 October 1914, in which she asked readers:

> I want you all now to help me to send a Christmas present from the whole nation to every sailor afloat and every soldier at the front. On Christmas Eve, when, like the shepherds of old, they keep their watch, doubtless their

thoughts will turn to home and to loved ones left behind and perhaps too, they will recall days when as children themselves they were wont to hang out their stockings.[183]

In this, her first ever official appeal, the princess's language was imperative. However, the appeal was also infused with religious references, likening the troops at the front to the watching shepherds of the nativity, connecting monarchy and God.[184] Again, the cultural power of royal interpellation was invoked to mobilise charitable war aid and the image of the princess was used on the Princess Mary Gift Box to fuse the will of the people to provide their servicemen with a Christmas gift with the traditional role of the royal family as embodying the nation. A gift from the princess and a gift from the people was portrayed as one and the same thing. It was also an act of communication; as Helen Hackett has written: 'Monarchs become cult-objects by being turned into artefacts: portraits, statues, a profile on a medal [. . .].'[185] Historian Eva Giloi points out in her work on the Hohenzollern dynasty:

> what other sources can historians draw upon to assess the views of private individuals, few of whom wrote overtly about their experience of the monarchy? The material culture of monarchy offers one such alternative source, especially if understood according to Arjun Appadurai's conception of 'the social life of things'. [. . .] objects in motion [. . .] can 'illuminate their human and social context' in the way they moved between individuals.[186]

The war saw a huge outpouring of royal imagery on commercial products – tin lids were a popular place to depict King George V as central to the war effort (Fig. 14).[187] The image of the princess on the Princess Mary Gift Box thus actually drew on a broader trend.

The Princess's Appeal raised £162,591 in total, well exceeding its target of £100,000. Most of the money came from 'thousands of small gifts sent by ordinary people from all parts of the United Kingdom', although there were some substantial donations from wealthy individuals.[188] Manufacturing the boxes and their contents was organised by a volunteer committee and provided home front employment at a point when parts of the economy had suffered a downturn due to the outbreak of war; the army had the responsibility of delivering them.[189] The brass gift box bore the image of the Princess Royal on the lid, a gendered, symbolic 'care-giving' ritual, clearly personalised to appear as if directly from the teenage girl. It contained a Christmas card as well as a full-length photograph of the princess in a feminine white dress, together with tobacco or cigarettes, a pipe or a tinder lighter or, in boxes for Indian troops, sweets. In many cases, it arrived together with a 1914 Christmas card to soldiers from the king and queen (reproduced in Fig. 22 later in this book), creating the impression of a family care package to troops.[190] It echoed tin boxes of chocolates sent by Queen Victoria to troops serving in the Second

Fig. 14   Example of a tin decorated with wartime monarchist imagery, Mary Evans Picture Library, 11034465

South African (Boer) War and the 125,000 boxes of chocolates distributed to schoolchildren on the occasion of King George V and Queen Mary's pre-war visit to Manchester.[191] The Princess Mary Gift Boxes also tapped into the long-established tradition of collecting royal souvenir memorabilia, and it is likely that recipients had already encountered commercial royal images on mugs, plates or tins, a material culture that continued apace during the war.[192] Yet the boxes also associated the princess with a violent, deadly environment and became part of the material culture of the trenches.[193] This was even explicitly alluded to in their contents (Fig. 15). Nicholas Saunders points out that 'bullet-pencils' were included in the Princess Mary Gift Box sent to non-smokers; the pencil was designed to resemble a bullet and fitted into a metal bullet-casing lid.[194] Only the cult of monarchy and honour can explain how it was appropriate for British society to send a photograph of a teenage girl, together with a mock bullet, to an all-male, violent trench world. The princess was meant to epitomise the honour of the women of Britain the men were fighting for. The gift boxes not only reflected monarchist power, but also broader societal naïveté and innocence.

    It is difficult to comprehensively assess how the Princess Mary Gift Boxes were viewed by troops, but they appear to have been respectfully received.

Fig. 15   A Princess Mary Gift Box from the collections of the Historial de la Grande Guerre, Péronne, catalogued as Boîte offerte aux officiers en 1914 par la princesse Mary 12 AFU 8.3 (Reproduced by kind permission of the Historial de la Grande Guerre, Péronne (Somme) and © Aurélien Roger)

Over 2.6 million servicemen and women received one. Lance Corporal K. M. Gaunt noted on 25 December 1914: 'We have received a very nice card from the king and also a card, cigarettes and tobacco in a beautiful box from Princess Mary, which I must try and keep.'[195] Like medals, the Princess Mary Gift Boxes were metonymic honour exchanges between royals and subjects. One 1914 novel tellingly reveals the ways in which the gift box was perceived:

> with their rations the night before had been brought up pleasant surprises from home in the shape of a card for every officer and man from the King and Queen, inscribed, 'May God protect you and bring you safe home! – Mary R., George R.I.'; while from Princess Mary came a pipe, tobacco and cigarettes and a small gilt casket with a portrait of the Princess. 'Well, this is jolly thoughtful', said Oliver as he opened his packet. 'It's an honour, my boy', replied Vivian; 'and when we shake off this mortal coil, these relics will be handed down or up, as the case may be, together with our medals, to our relatives.'[196]

The religious language here, which quoted the actual wording of the royal Christmas card, enhanced the idea of the monarchy's spiritual role; the ambiguity of God bringing men 'safe home' was clearly deliberate, as it could mean either home alive or to the heavenly home. The fact that the Princess Mary Gift Boxes were rapidly associated with miraculous acts of saving soldiers' lives further highlights this, with the royal link associated with powers of divine intervention. 'Princess Mary's gift boxes have been the means of saving a number of lives amongst the men at the front', reported the *Manchester Courier and Lancashire General Advertiser* in 1915.[197] It reported that 'the most recent one is that of Private A. Johnson of the 1st Royal Warwickshires', who was shot in the leg and chest, where his Princess Mary Gift Box deflected the bullet. Johnson admitted he had expressly kept the gift box in his chest pocket as protection, wanting something solid to cover his heart: '"My wife" he said "wrote asking me why I did not send the gift box home as others were doing but I answered her letter by telling her I would sooner carry it through with me."'[198] His bullet-marked gift box was displayed by his hospital bedside.[199] E. Robinson of the Royal Naval Division, wounded in the leg at the Dardanelles, wrote to his mother from hospital of how a bullet had hit his Princess Mary Gift Box, carried in his breast pocket, and this had saved him.[200] A hospital matron sent Princess Mary a gift box that had similarly saved the life of a private in the 1st Battalion of the Irish Guards, Private Brabston, together with the bullet that had struck it.[201] Such stories serve to reinforce the idea that the monarchy retained an association with the sacred.

It is not difficult to see the ways in which the Princess Royal, who was constantly presented in the wartime press as a model of virginal girlhood and who bore the name Mary, would see her royal Christmas gift associated with protective powers in war. These factors combined hint at a subliminal cultural association between the princess and Mary the mother of Christ. Yet, even without these deeper interpretations, the gift box was a welcome reminder of the bond between monarchy and army. General Rawlinson was one of those who wrote to the king's Private Secretary, Clive Wigram, at Buckingham Palace to convey his thanks:

> I received last night a charming little packet containing pipe, tobacco and cigarettes which I am told is sent me by Princess Mary. It is just what I want, for my pipe is rapidly coming to an end, and tobacco is not too plentiful. The least I can do to show my gratitude is to return to H.R. H. one of my Xmas cards. Will you give it to her for me and say how much we all value her kind gift of tobacco and cigarettes.[202]

Another anonymous officer at 2nd Corps Railhead less tactfully sent Princess Mary a gift box that he had found at the bottom of a trench when the liquid mud was pumped out in 1915.[203]

However, not all were appreciative. In the collections of the Historial de la Grande Guerre at Péronne there is a satirical trench-art version of the Princess Mary Gift Box in which a wooden coffin has been created to mimic it, shown in Fig. 16. The message is stark: the personal bond between royalty and individual soldier is a deadly one that leads to death in war. This trench art, a subversive message of rebellion against monarchist rhetoric, suggests that there were soldiers who rejected the hegemonic culture of monarchism.

The idea of the royal personal gift to the troops as a gesture of support continued throughout 1915. In September 1915, Queen Mary ordered 'Sir Courtauld Thomson to take to the Dardanelles some wallets or packets and also some small writing blocks for the wounded which he told me w[ou]ld be greatly valued as a *personal* gift from me.'[204] Significantly, the royal gift box present was not repeated for Christmas 1916, however; the king and queen were dissuaded from attempting it, at the request of the military authorities. They were informed that even sending cards was impossible, as there was no spare shipping and storage capacity and that 'it would be impossible to undertake the transport and distribution of the cards'.[205] The experiment of using mass gift-giving as a way to retain the direct link between monarchy and soldier would not be repeated.

Fig. 16   Trench-art version of a Princess Mary Gift Box reworked as a wooden coffin, from the collections of the Historial de la Grande Guerre, Péronne, catalogued as Coffret artisanal en forme de cerceuil, 21 ART 4.3 (Reproduced by kind permission of the Historial de la Grande Guerre, Péronne (Somme) and © Aurélien Roger)

However, on the home front, rituals of gift exchange between royalty and subjects did continue. In July 1918, the king and queen's silver wedding anniversary became a focal point for war-effort fundraising. The royal couple received a donation of £53,000 from the City of London which they accepted for charities of their choice.[206] They also issued what became known as the Silver Wedding Appeal, asking ordinary people not to send gifts to Buckingham Palace, an indication that this had been a previous norm on such occasions, but instead to donate any gold or silver they had to the British Red Cross Society for the care of war wounded.[207] Mayors of cities across the country were tasked with accepting the silver donations.[208] Royal rituals around gifting for anniversaries, however, still required recognition and some direct connection with monarchy: in Mansfield the local mayor recorded each donation and sent a list to the Palace of those who had made one.[209] In many towns, the donations of silverware made by ordinary people were personally received by the mayor in the town hall and displayed there.[210] In Barnstaple the church bells were also rung.[211] The *Westminster Gazette* reported that 'Silver of all kinds poured into the collecting office of the British Red Cross Society. [...] The gifts were made in commemoration of the royal silver wedding, and ranged from the complete set of family plate of the Earls of Ashburton to the twenty shillings in 1918 coins presented by "an old maid". [...] Two ladies gave silver which they had received on their own silver wedding days.'[212] Again the meaning of this shared sacrifice of silver in honour of the monarchy must be contextualised: silver was a mark of respectability, gifted to brides when setting up home. It had pride of place as part of a domestic establishment for those who could afford it and was passed down in families. To donate it was therefore a mark of significant esteem and a clear sacralising gesture of honouring the monarchy, particularly noteworthy coming just months after Russia's Bolshevik revolution. The wedding anniversary itself was marked with church services, bunting and a 'royal progress' through central London, with postillions dressed in 'royal blue', as well as an 'address of loyalty and homage' from 2,500 women war workers, who marched from Hyde Park to Buckingham Palace.[213] Thus the traditional and the innovative coalesced.

In fact, traditional gift-giving remained a prominent feature of royal wartime encounters more generally throughout the war. Following the king's first visit to France in 1914, for example, a typical range of gifts were distributed to those who had played a role: brooches were given to the two French maids and the housekeeper of the king's accommodation; the chef was given gold monogram links; Captain J. Ellis of the SS *Brighton*, which transported the king, received a tie pin with a gold crown, diamonds and pearls; the mess steward was given a cigarette case; the chauffeurs silver watches and Superintendent Patrick Quinn of the security detail received a pencil case.[214] Captain Ellis was too awestruck and 'nervous at writing you direct' to send his thank-you letter directly to the monarchy and instead sent it via the General Manager of the London, Brighton and South Coast Railway, which managed his ship, to the king's Private Secretary, Clive Wigram. Ellis requested: 'will you kindly convey to His Majesty the King my most grateful thanks for the valued souvenir of the great honour accorded me'.[215] Any gift from the monarchy could provide a real psychological boost: the king sent General Horace Smith-Dorrien a gift, as a sign of his support, when the latter had been sent home by Sir John French. Smith-Dorrien responded: 'Will you say, that under existing circumstances I appreciate the King's thought more than words can express. [. . .] it is not very easy to keep cheerful just now, and that being remembered in this way by the King and Queen has acted as a powerful tonic.'[216] Some ordinary soldiers also appear to have treasured items associated with royalty: one private wrote in 1915 of how he would keep his Jewish soldiers' and sailors' prayer book which contained a message from the king 'among Their Gracious Majesty's [sic] gifts'.[217] In some cases, of course, royal gifts were viewed in more mercenary fashion: Sub-Lieutenant Hussey of the Royal Navy wrote in 1918 of his disappointment that, upon meeting royalty during the king, queen and Prince of Wales's visit after the Armistice in 1918: 'In the forenoon I had to do Flag Lieutenant's job with the Queen and Lady Beatty at Queensferry and in the afternoon flunkey work in the Royal Barge. I was simply furious as I didn't get a cigarette case out of it as Kemble did last year.'[218]

Overall, the war saw traditional forms of royal philanthropy, based on volunteerism and public monarchist loyalties, increasingly working symbiotically with the state, reflecting trends towards the more systematic, modern organisation of aid that the war instigated.[219] In 1916, the king made a huge donation of £100,000 to the British Treasury, to be used as the government saw best – a tacit recognition that the monarchy now needed the state to channel its assistance to its suffering war subjects.[220] It was also intended to ward off any public criticism that the monarchy had profited because its Civil List income remained the same during the conflict while its spending was greatly reduced due to its wartime economising. Fritz Ponsonby, the Keeper of the Privy Purse, informed Asquith, with regard to the donation, that 'If his Majesty carries out what economies he can and hands over all the savings [. . .] no one later can accuse him of having made money out of the war.'[221] Ponsonby, even in 1916, anticipated 'a bad time' for monarchy when the war ended, with 'strikes and possibly anarchy' and saw this donation as a protective measure.[222] The Chancellor, Reginald McKenna, and the Prime Minister were concerned that, while the king's donation might provoke 'eulogies of the Press', it would also result in pressure on 'members of Parliament and others to follow his example' and provoke them, in reaction, into raising the issue of the monarch not paying income tax.[223] Ponsonby, in a letter to McKenna, pointed out that the king 'did not agree' with this conclusion and felt that, given that the court had made savings on entertainment expenses due to the war, 'the public may rightly ask what is being done with the Balance' and that 'the only answer that is likely to satisfy them is that His Majesty has handed it all to the Exchequer'.[224] The king felt that there was 'no analogy' between the position of the 'Sovereign and Members of Parliament or people living in an unofficial capacity', and therefore the king's gesture could not be seen as an example others would feel obliged to follow, a revealing choice of language suggesting that the king saw his life as living in an 'official capacity'.[225] Ponsonby stated to McKenna that 'It is most important that the King should take some definite steps to show his willingness to participate in the national economy to meet the expenses of the war.'[226] He added that the king wanted McKenna to see the Prime Minister again and tell him that the king insisted on handing over the money to the Exchequer and making a public announcement that he was doing this, despite the Prime Minister and Chancellor's initial opposition to the plan; they had suggested a subscription to a charity instead.[227] In other words, the politicians were overruled, an example of the way the monarchy's power worked behind the scenes. This incident is further revealing of royal influence's limits too, however. Ponsonby informed McKenna that 'His Majesty feels sure that the Prime Minister would be able to prevent any discussion in the House of Commons, either upon the amount handed over, or upon the question of the income tax.'[228] McKenna wrote back that 'it is perhaps right to point out that the Prime Minister has no power to prevent allusions to the subject in the House'.[229] The suggestion that the Prime Minister might censor parliament's ability to criticise the monarch is revealing of the extent of royal expectations regarding politicians' duty to protect the monarchy's reputation. McKenna's response is indicative too, however, of where the limits of this lay.

The king's predictions proved right. His move was widely praised in the press. The *Daily Mirror* devoted a poster to the news, with the headline 'The King's 100,000 gift', above a photograph of King George V.[230] Such gestures were immensely popular, publicly perceived as royal generosity, but they also indicated how, by 1916, royal charity was increasingly an obligation, undertaken in order to preserve the royals' popularity, not merely a 'gift'. As the state, due to the war, recognised it had legal obligations to support the war wounded with pensions and to provide separation allowances for their families, so the monarchy – as part of the state – also channelled funds into state aid rather than distributing it themselves.

Yet, wartime royal philanthropy also shows that monarchism was more than an abstract discourse: it was evident in practical actions, donations and gifts, that represented symbolic exchanges of honour between individual subjects and the monarchy. Some of this helped sustain troops' sense of self-worth – and hence, to some degree, although it should not be overstated, their morale, and it also served to consolidate home front patriotic mobilisation.

2.6   Monarchism and the Mobilisation of Colonial and Dominion Troops

The monarchy's wartime role was not, of course, restricted to the United Kingdom. The monarchical concept of subjecthood underpinned the whole framework of the British Empire's war effort. It provided a constructed, pan-imperial connection between all subjects of the Crown, whose loyalty was always supposedly cherished equally in the eyes of the king-emperor, however unequal they may have been before local laws, which invariably privileged the empire's white populations.

In theory, British subjects throughout the empire were all equal through their allegiance to the king: as Randall Hansen states, a 'fundamental feature' of royal allegiance was its 'indivisibility; all subjects enjoy precisely the same relationship with the monarch and no distinction can be made between them'.[231] This purported 'uniformity of British subjecthood' was an ideal very dear to King George V and Queen Mary, however much of an illusion it was, given that, in reality, the British practice of empire was riven with racial discrimination and that the 1914 British Nationality and Status of Aliens Act had given 'statutory recognition to the practice of distinguishing between British subjects'.[232]

The honours system certainly did not treat subjects uniformly: black subjects fighting on the war's African fronts were far less likely to be nominated for an award than their white comrades, for example, but some of these problems were structurally outside the control of King George V. Endemic racism affected who was put forward for awards for gallantry by commanding officers and also which fronts were prioritised as most important by the army in sending in nominations, marginalising those with predominantly black and Indian troops in Africa and the Middle East. The vast majority of gallantry awards went to Western Front *combatants*, but it was War Office policy not to use black colonial troops as combatants in Europe on racial grounds, thus lessening their opportunity to receive a medal. It was also the War Office and army which established many of the wartime racial hierarchies, such as that combatants had a higher status than 'native labourers' on the Western Front, and this was a key factor in the latter receiving a bronze British War Medal rather than the silver that combatants obtained. During the war, George V countered some of this discrimination, awarding the first VCs to Indian soldiers; he also intervened in 1915 on the side of the Colonial Office in its efforts to establish a West Indian Regiment, the British West Indies Regiment, as a new infantry formation in the British army, against War Office objections to Caribbean men serving as combatants. The War Office grudgingly gave way, and the regiment was formed by Royal Proclamation, but the men were still excluded from fighting and given labour-unit tasks on the Western Front; although they were ultimately allowed to take part in combat, this was restricted to outside Europe.[233]

The monarchist system, with its idealised, romanticised assertion of indivisibility and equality of British subjecthood, in fact, in many ways, served as a complicit fig leaf that obfuscated the empire's racial discrimination and racialised hierarchies, which operated at every level – in the army, in colonial and dominion legal systems, in prison systems, in education and in pay, to name but a few flagrant areas. It was an important conceptual facilitator of empire on the home front too: John Mackenzie has even argued, within Britain there existed a widespread 'imperial nationalism, compounded of monarchism, militarism, and Social Darwinism, through which the British defined their own unique superiority vis-à-vis the rest of the world'.[234] The monarchical framework was ultimately a key factor in enabling the British imperial project to sustain its own self-image as a liberating force in the face of these wider discriminatory contexts; if, under the aegis of empire, all already had equal status as royal subjects, then complaints of discrimination could be dismissed as groundless. Nevertheless, it was the conceptual framework of indivisible and equitable allegiance that framed the monarchy's rhetoric to empire during the war and also the responses at grassroots level of many of its subjects, of all racial backgrounds, too, a significant number of whom appear to have believed in it.

It is, of course, impossible to cover the whole empire's relationship with the monarchy during the war here.[235] The focus of what follows is to trace how the monarchy was emphasised in the mobilisation of the British Empire in the first two years of the war and, where sources permit, how this played out in the attitudes and actions of troops – white, black and Asian – from Britain's overseas possessions.[236] As in Britain, the question of volunteerism was key at the outset of the conflict: in a phase of the war without conscription, the appeal to men across the empire was framed in terms of a dynastic loyalty to the king-emperor. When the United Kingdom went to war on 4 August 1914, the entire British Empire automatically also entered the conflict.[237] This was the last occasion where this was the case, as the dominions later successfully lobbied that their consent would be required for entry into any future war on the side of Britain.

Monarchist belief does appear to have played a role in mobilising certain empire populations to enlist. However, we must be careful to avoid any generalised assumptions. There were key differentiations between groups. In the case of the white populations in the dominions, attitudes could vary greatly. For example, francophone and anglophone Canadians differed in their support for Britain and the monarchy; so did the Afrikaaner and English-speaking populations in South Africa, due to the legacy of the Second South African (Boer) War; parts of the Afrikaaner population rejected the British war effort. In Australia, while there was enthusiasm for Britain's cause among much of the white population, those of Irish Catholic heritage often rejected the monarchy. The outbreak of war saw a surge of patriotism among

Australians of white British descent: singer and composer Peter Dawson recalled how he was giving a concert when news of the conflict arrived: 'Everyone started to cheer, and someone started to sing "God save the King", which the accompanist soon led with the piano. More cheering, and then "Rule Britannia" was sung. More excitement and cheering, and again we all sang "God Save the King."'[238]

For indigenous populations across the empire sources are few and fragmented. Those which do exist often privilege the voices of white witnesses over those of colonised black and Asian peoples. A focus on sources that relate monarchism as a war motivation also risks marginalising the more coercive aspects of imperial war mobilisation, such as forced recruitment, which were used against some indigenous populations. What follows examines available material on Indian, Caribbean and African subjects, but it is key to point out here that much of this material has been filtered through colonial officialdom – for example, censored letters from Indian troops are the main sources used for Indian views of monarchy, while the memoir of Stimela Jason Jingoes from Lesotho who served in the South African Native Labour Contingent was co-written with white authors, and the material from black African voices in the Royal Archives used here was written to praise a royal visit and forwarded by colonial officers. For these reasons, it is important to adopt the historian Michelle Moyd's approach, reading 'the available sources in two directions – against the grain and along the grain. Reading against the grain reveals evidence that the authors may not have intended to produce but which nevertheless helps us see otherwise invisible aspects' of colonised peoples' histories, while 'reading materials along the grain' exposes the views and decision-making of white witnesses.[239]

For all of the above reasons, any conclusions here about the role of monarchism in imperial war mobilisation remain very tentative. However, two key points are clear. First, the monarchy was at the centre of how the war – and supporting the war effort – were represented to populations across the empire in the first two years of the conflict. In Canada, the emphasis on monarchism from Britain in the war mobilisation even triggered a political backlash. Robert Borden, Canadian Prime Minister during the war, in his memoirs recalled the anger in Canada at the Governor General, Prince Arthur, Duke of Connaught's wartime attempts to directly represent the king and play an active role in the decision-making around military mobilisation.[240] Historian Ian Beckett also refers to the annoyance of Canadian politicians at Prince Arthur reviewing Canadian troops before they left for Europe, in direct representation of the king, who took this role without controversy in the United Kingdom.[241] Second, if we turn to assess how these representations influenced war motivations as the conflict went on, there is a distinction visible between white dominion troops, who largely took the monarchy for granted, and black and Asian colonial units in Europe, where the relationship with the monarch was seen as a potential emancipatory tool in gaining greater freedoms out of the war.

To turn first to how the monarchy was used in imperial mobilisation: here the evidence concurs that the idea of loyalty to the king-emperor played a prominent role in war mobilisation discourses across the empire, used to create a personal, direct link with the United Kingdom for both white and indigenous populations. Young men of the Bahamas were urged in a 1915 recruitment poster to 'put yourself right with your King' by enlisting; in 1918, the king's portrait still featured in the centre of a Bahamas recruitment poster.[242] In October 1915, in conjunction with his King's Appeal for recruits in the United Kingdom, discussed in Chapter 1, George V issued a parallel appeal to the empire that, according to historian Richard Smith, 'appeared to contradict the racial considerations of colonial governments and the War Office', as it 'virtually coincided with the announcement, in the *London Gazette*, of the formation, by Royal Proclamation, of the British West Indies Regiment, and suggested that his majesty's subjects would be admitted into the military fraternity on equal terms'.[243] The King's Appeal stated:

> At this moment in the struggle between my people and a highly organised enemy who has transgressed the Law of Nations and changed the ordinance that binds civilized Europe together, I appeal to you. I rejoice in my Empire's efforts, and feel pride in the voluntary response from my Subjects all over the world who have sacrificed home, fortune and life itself, in order that another may not inherit the free Empire which their ancestors and mine have built. I ask you to make good these Sacrifices. [...] In freely responding to my appeal, you will be giving your support to our brothers, who, for long months, have nobly upheld Britain's past traditions, and the glory of her Arms.[244]

The wording is remarkable. It combines an acknowledgement that German aggression has changed 'the ordinance that binds civilised Europe together' with an appeal for non-Europeans to come and put this right. It is made explicit here that 'civilised' Europe is no longer able to sustain its civilisation without non-European help, a significant upending of pre-war imperial hierarchies even if still framed in an older world view of dynastic duty owed to the British monarch by his subjects. Older sacralising monarchist discourses thus interact with more modern egalitarian ideas here.

The choice of language, 'our brothers', is particularly egalitarian, used to imply that both the king and his subjects are in a familial relationship, even equal brotherhood, not only with each other but also with those already serving in the war. Given this appeal was aimed at populations of many different racial backgrounds, this assertion of brotherhood marks a dramatic shift in the language of monarchy to the imperial subject – particularly the non-white imperial subject. All this marked a radical break, depicting royal need for help. As Dieter Langewiesche has pointed out, 'as an imperial institution, in terms of power politics, the monarchy did not present itself minimalistically in any way until well into the twentieth century'.[245] Pomp was designed to communicate 'the monarchy's power structure' in the empire and 'the remote absent British monarch was present in the pomp of the empire as a powerful ruler', particularly in the colonies, where the constitutional limitations on his role were often not made clear to local populations.[246] This was the context for these significant, sudden shifts in rhetoric in 1915.

Contemporaries recognised this as a radical moment. In Jamaica, the King's Appeal was read out in the island's churches, triggering a wave of patriotic enthusiasm and monarchism. A poem in the Jamaican press by Tom Redcam, entitled 'Gentlemen, the King', effectively summed up this mood: 'List to the words of the King! List to the summons they bring! Patriots, stand up for the right, Buckle your armour for fight!'.[247] Richard Smith points out the importance of monarchism in mobilising Jamaican war volunteers.[248] W. G. Hinchcliffe urged men to volunteer in response to the King's Appeal, as its language of equality, he believed, heralded a remaking of the empire upon more egalitarian lines:

> the time is now on us when brothers will be compelled to know each other as brother without thinking of race, nationality, colour, class, or complexion. Therefore those who are not yet standing on the road platform of humanity, and are shirking the duty which the Empire demands of them, they need not be argued with, for the mandate will soon come down from the Throne.[249]

Even the radical Marcus Garvey's Universal Negro Improvement Association, founded in Jamaica in August 1914, passed an oath of loyalty at the outbreak of the First World War.[250]

Historian Timothy Winegard's recent study also found that, where indigenous populations of the dominions – Newfoundland, Canada, Australia, New Zealand and South Africa – supported the war, the idea of loyalty to the king was a significant factor.[251] Stimela Jason Jingoes, who originally came from Lesotho and was living in South Africa when war broke out, also recalled that monarchism influenced him. He was particularly affected by a song published in the newspaper *Leselinyana*:

> Europe is our work
> Of our head the King.
> Who are going? – Boys!
> Who are going? – Girls!
> Europe is our work.[252]

Jingoes related how 'When I read words like these, my blood rushed in my veins and I felt, *Why should I hesitate? I must go and die for my country and my King!*'[253] Jingoes did indeed volunteer for the South African Native Labour Contingent when recruiting began in September 1916, giving up a well-paid secure job.[254] Monarchy appears to have been an emotional pull factor in his decision, and he was not the only example. W. B. Yiba declared he enlisted because 'I answered the call of my King.'[255] In fact, members of the educated African elite supported recruitment for the South African Native Labour Contingent, believing showing loyalty 'to King and Country' would bring them political leverage after hostilities ended.[256] Albert Grundlingh points out that, while many of those recruited for the South African Native Labour Contingent were dragooned or joined for pecuniary reasons, monarchism was also a genuine motivation, particularly for educated Africans.[257] However, the overall numbers of volunteers did not meet British expectations, suggesting that those motivated by monarchism were not representative of wider black attitudes. Throughout the conflict, declarations of monarchist loyalty often came from elites within colonised populations: on 1 August 1916, a group of five Somali leaders, including Sheikh Ismail Isahak and Sheikh Madar Ahmed, wrote to King George V that 'we are ready and anxious, at Your Majesty's behest, to perform whatever is in our power. [...] We are loyal, having no thoughts of other Governments; and there need be no doubt regarding this, while Your Majesty is exercised with the troubles of the present war.'[258] Upon Kitchener's death in 1916, the Chief of the Basuto sent a message of condolence to the monarch: 'We cry with the King, we cry with you [...] and all His Majesty's servants.'[259]

Monarchy was also central in representing the war to the Indian population, as Santanu Das's work reveals.[260] In August 1914, 'King-Emperor George V sent a message to the "Princes and People of My Indian Empire"' which appealed for aid.[261] The native princes in particular responded with gusto, 'competing with each other with offers of men, money and material'.[262] The Nizam of Hyderabad wrote that his father had supported Queen Victoria in 1887 when 'danger merely threatened the borders of the Indian empire. I should be untrue alike to the promptings of my own heart and to the traditions of my house if I offered less to His Imperial Majesty King George V, in this just and momentous war.'[263] Each Indian recruit swore an oath to the king-emperor on joining his regiment.[264] The goddess Kali, it was claimed in one Bengali newspaper, *Bengalee*, 'had declared her support for George V', while Pandit Ram Prashad Sharma, one of India's leading astrologers, predicted that 'the alignment of the five planets via the sun – would ensure "His Imperial Majesty's decisive victory"'.[265]

This monarchist representation of Britain's cause in the war appears to correlate with loyalty to George V serving as an important motivation for Indian troops in Europe. Sources on Indian troops' attitudes towards the monarchy are rare. The most substantial information comes from their censored letters, which David Omissi has edited.[266] These letters, often dictated by the sender to a literate friend or officer and selected for posterity by the censor, raise issues regarding how representative they are and to what extent they actually reflect their sender's real attitudes. However, these letters frequently refer to the king-emperor, suggesting the British monarchy was an important prism through which the war was understood by Indian troops. Omissi describes the 'person of the King-Emperor, who is mentioned in the letters far more than any other individual' as hugely significant in 'the sepoys' mental universe'.[267] He concludes that Indian soldiers had a 'very clear sense of personal duty to the King' and some believed that by 'performing this duty, they could almost become his near relatives'.[268] As he notes, 'it is surely significant that soldiers chose one "royal" formula rather than other, equally acceptable, "Indian" or "nationalist" ones. The mention of the King is simply too frequent and too heartfelt to be reducible to calculated self-interest or scribal formulae.'[269]

The British played upon these loyalties: every Indian soldier received a picture of King George V as a New Year's Day present in January 1917.[270] A Sikh soldier sent his home, writing:

> I have sent you thrice before pictures of His Majesty. As you framed those and put them up on the wall opposite the door, so do the same with this portrait after framing it. Worship it every morning when you get up. This is an act of religious merit, and the portrait will be a memorial. Every morning, pray to the Guru that He will give victory to the King.[271]

Indian troops on the Loire were encouraged by an Order of the Day that declared 'You will fight for your King-Emperor and your faith.'[272] A royal farewell parade was held when the Lahore and Meerut Divisions were withdrawn from the Western Front in November 1915, with the Prince of Wales reading a personal message from the king.[273] On the king's birthday in 1917, the Indian 'mutineers' of the 15th Lancers (who had refused to fight near Islamic holy shrines in Iraq), other than ringleaders, were released to work in the remount depot of the regiment, associating the monarch with direct powers of clemency.[274] The term 'for King and Country' also appeared in Indian letters: Jan Mahomed Khan wrote in July 1917 from France of how 'the loyal soldiers of India are fighting for their King and country in France [. . .] the whole nation is preparing to sacrifice itself for King and country'.[275] Jemadar Ganda Singh wrote of how he fought for the royal standard.[276] A wounded Sikh wrote of how 'our father the King-Emperor of India needs us'.[277] Many wrote of how to die on the field of battle in the service of the king meant automatic entry into heaven, and the whole war was also understood as a clash of various kings.[278]

Yet, this profoundly personal interpretation of the king-emperor's relationship to his Indian subjects also meant that he was looked to to fix war grievances. One wounded Indian, Mir Dast, who was decorated with the VC by the king during his visit to Brighton, submitted a petition to the monarch to ask that Indians who had been wounded not be returned to the front once well but sent back to India.[279] Written on the envelope were the words 'Let no one except the King open this.'[280] Returning the wounded to war was a source of major resentment for Indian troops; eventually the policy was changed, although it is not clear if there was any royal intervention.[281]

Indian family members' letters to their relatives serving on the Western Front also often referenced the king. In 1916, Kaisar-i-Jahan wrote to her brother that 'we are all praying that God may give victory to our King'.[282] Lehna Ram wrote to Heta Ram, working in a Supply and Transport Corps at Marseilles, that 'God will give victory to our King.'[283] For his part, 6-year-old Abdul Ghafur wrote 'what would I not give to be a soldier of the King! [...] Our King is now the chief King in the world, and it is our duty to help him. I am always thinking how I can kill the King's enemies or give my life for him.'[284] Sirfaraz Khan wrote of how 'it is very difficult to get such a King [as we have got]', while Gurmukh Singh informed his relative in France that 'certainly Europe is not our native land; but it is the native land of our King, George the V; and you should therefore esteem it better than your native land and fight with your whole heart'.[285] Sarup Singh related in late May 1917 that 'the Rajput's offspring who does not desire to engage in this war and to help his King and country, is no true son of a Rajput'.[286] Another letter writer stated that 'our King [...] is the protection of our race'.[287]

As in the Caribbean, in the case of India, the war was seen almost immediately as a moment of opportunity when the terms of empire – and imperial monarchism – would be reformed. One Lahore newspaper, the English-language *Panjabee*, discussed on 15 August 1914 how the issue was one of 'enabling the Indian community to feel that they too can have their rightful share in the defence of the Empire .... The distinction that has hitherto been made in this respect between Indians and other classes of the King's subjects is galling to the self-respect of the Indian [...]. The distinction must be removed if Indian loyalty is to be placed on an active and satisfactory footing.'[288] The distinction referred to was the 'policy within the British army of withholding the King's Commission from the Indian officers'.[289] The entire framework of this grievance and its contestation was presented here as a monarchist one – the king's subjects were not all entitled to hold his Commission. The exclusion of Indians from the prestigious status of officers who held the King's Commission was symbolic of their second-rate position in relationship to whites and undermined their purported equal treatment by the monarchy. Here we see the clash between imperial discourses about the monarchy's concern for all subjects, regardless of race, and the realities of the empire's racial discrimination. The demands of the war rapidly forced attention to these contradictions, particularly given the monarchy's emphasis upon racial equality in its appeals to the empire for support for the British war effort. Some actual reforms had to be made to sustain this rhetoric or imperial recruitment would be put at risk: by 1917, nine Indians became the first to be granted the regular King's Commission.[290]

As the war continued, such tensions around race became particularly acute: the monarchist enthusiasm which the king's 1915 Appeal to Empire had generated collided with the realities of the empire's racial hierarchies. It had interpellated whites and indigenous populations equally as royal subjects called to aid their monarch in his hour of need. Yet, in practice, wartime military treatment remained based upon racial discrimination.

The monarchy tried to navigate this contradiction through carefully controlled interactions with black and Asian service personnel. These were, in turn, presented to the public in ways that enhanced the monarchy's sacred aura. This was not new and reflected the way in which the 1911 Delhi Durbar had been used to convey the power of the monarchy over the Indian population. The king, in particular, was presented in the wartime British press as the supreme mediator with the 'exotic racial other' on behalf of his white subjects. Notably, this discourse served to increase the status of the monarchy among the empire's and Britain's white populations, presenting the king as a special interlocutor who could navigate the cultural distance between them and those colonised peoples depicted as most alien, 'uncivilised' and even frightening, and keep them loyal to the imperial system. This discourse suggested that, because of his sacred, anointed, spiritual role with its mystic and ancient elements, the king-emperor was uniquely placed to relate the empire to the supposedly superstitious, mystic, primitive and spiritual Indians and Africans in a way that was not possible for mere ordinary politicians.

On the other hand, some press elements also posited this more cynically: the less 'civilised' peoples of the empire were presented as believing in monarchy in simplistic and overly childlike and literal ways, presented as entertaining or endearing because they were considered so unsophisticated. Whether one was depicted as loyal in the 'correct', reserved British way or in a more childlike manner was defined by one's status in the empire's racial hierarchy and also, to some extent, one's class status too; even working-class white Britons were at times depicted as holding overly sentimentalised or superstitious monarchist beliefs by middle-class journalists. However, in the case of working-class white beliefs, these were often depicted as naïve but touching, whereas monarchist superstition attributed to non-white subjects was portrayed as entertaining and as evidence of white racial superiority. In sum, official wartime interactions between the monarchy and black and Asian subjects conveyed the 'otherness' of monarchy and its sacred power, using the foil of the racial 'other'.

One such interaction was the visits of royals to wounded Indian troops convalescing in hospitals in Britain. As Andrew Tait Jarboe has argued, hospitals for Indian troops during the war 'functioned as "imperial sites" – they had the added burden of reintroducing and reinforcing for British and

South Asian audiences alike the ideologies of imperial rule'.[291] The choice of the Brighton Pavilion, the most famous of the UK hospitals for Indian war wounded, exemplified this. Built as a royal palace, it reflected both British orientalism in its architectural style, which could provide a suitable imperial backdrop for home front propaganda images of recovering Indian wounded, and a close association with royalty, intended to impress Indian patients. As David Olusoga points out, every propaganda image of the Indian wounded there 'reinforced the message that the king and queen cared so deeply for their Indian subjects that they had dedicated one of their palaces to their care'.[292] On 25 August 1915, the king, queen and Princess Mary visited the Royal Pavilion Hospital at Brighton, and, in an elaborate investiture ceremony on its lawn, 1,000 wounded Indians gathered to watch eleven of their comrades receive decorations for gallantry.[293] The Viceroy of India believed that the work done in the Indian hospitals had increased British prestige in India and 'also the attachment the lower classes have to [King George V]'.[294] There is some evidence this may have been true: one Indian soldier wrote home praising the medical care in the Royal Pavilion Hospital and noting that 'Our hospital is in the place where the King used to have his throne. [...] The King has given a strict order that no trouble be given to any black man in hospital. Men in hospital are tended like flowers, and the King and Queen sometimes come to visit them.'[295] A sub-assistant Indian surgeon, Abdulla, wrote of the royal visit to the hospital in August 1915 that 'there was great excitement'. The king 'stayed nearly an hour in the hospital and spoke very kindly to the patients, asking about their condition. The sight of the Emperor delighted the hearts of all.'[296] Despite these expressions of loyalty, however, Indians had their freedom to leave the hospital to visit the town withdrawn during the war because of concerns regarding them mixing with the local white population.[297]

Another key example of carefully staged royal interactions was the inspection of colonial troops. While the sources are fragmentary on this process, we do have one case that is well documented that can be examined in detail. In July 1917, GHQ in France decided that black South African recruitment would improve if the king inspected a selected group of men from different companies of the South African Native Labour Contingent during his front visit. GHQ wrote revealingly to the king's Private Secretary Clive Wigram that only 14,000 of the 50,000 labourers requested of the South African government had arrived at the front and that the army badly needed more: 'recruiting in South Africa wants a stimulant'.[298] The army also needed to convince the 14,000 labourers it already had to stay on for a longer period of war service. The men's white South African officers were key intermediaries in setting up the royal inspection, assuring GHQ that 'they anticipate the best effect from the proposed parade before the King'.[299] The white commanding officer of the South African Native Labour Contingent, Colonel S. M. Pritchard, also drafted the speech the monarch made to the black labourers, containing what Pritchard believed 'represents the sort of thing which will appeal to the natives', and it was repeated afterwards by interpreters in the men's own languages.[300] It emphasised themes of loyalty and recruitment. It is not clear whether the king had any input into the wording.

The planning for the royal inspection thus reveals that it was GHQ and white South Africans who believed that monarchism would appeal to black African labourers, projecting their own cultural assumptions about its importance upon them: 'Those attending will be some 40 selected representatives of all the principal native tribes of South Africa and the impression made on them by the ceremony will at once permeate through the units in France and through that channel to the recruiting fields in south Africa.'[301] The Palace received a list of the white officers who would be attending; an attached internal GHQ note stated that 'In addition to the White Officers mentioned on attached list there will be about 40 Native Chiefs; I hope to have a list of their names ready tomorrow but I do not suppose you will require them as they are all unpronounceable.'[302] The military disregard for the naming of the colonial black subject is a striking indication of their lesser status and of the pervasive racism towards them.

The inspection took place at Abbeville on 10 July 1917. In his speech, the king stated that he had 'great pleasure in seeing you who have travelled a long distance over the sea to help in this great war' and thanked the men for their work in this 'world-wide war' which was 'second only in importance to that performed by my sailors and soldiers who are bearing the brunt of the battle'.[303] The reference to coming in 'second' place was telling. The king also noted that their efforts proved 'the loyalty of my native subjects in South Africa' and also praised the services of 'natives of South Africa [...] to my Armies in German South West Africa and in German East Africa'.[304] He asked the men to convey his wishes for more reinforcements for the Native South African Contingent to 'your Chiefs in South Africa'.[305]

However, the king's speech also contained quite radical ideas too, which suggested equality of freedoms for subjects of different races: 'But you also form part of my great Armies which are fighting for the liberty and freedom of my subjects of all races and creeds throughout my Empire', it stated.[306] 'Without munitions of war', the speech continued, 'my Armies cannot fight; without food they cannot live. You are helping to send these things to them each day and in doing so you are hurling your spears at the enemy and hastening the destruction that awaits him.'[307] The orientalist reference to 'spears' was integrated with very modern languages of liberty and freedom and emancipatory promises, in keeping with the recruitment propaganda to the empire. The speech was a microcosm of the tensions created by using monarchist loyalties to mobilise the empire through discourses of equality between royal imperial subjects and the reality that the monarchy was being used by the military to recruit black Africans who were treated worse than whites. Given the South African Native Labour Contingent was officered by white South Africans, including its commander, who held rigid beliefs in racial segregation, the encounter with the king occurred against a background context of South African racism which undermined the monarchy's agenda to promote the idea of a personal monarch–subject relationship between the king and black British subjects throughout the empire.

The racialised assumptions are further visible in the internal correspondence about the inspection: Evan Gibb at GHQ wrote to Clive Wigram afterwards that

> After the ceremony at Abbeville on the 10th the natives were despatched to the nearest group of Native Companies where they were presented with a bullock to celebrate the King's inspection of them. [. . .] Several other natives made most appreciative utterances and all were agreed that the King had acted as becomes a Great Chief in presenting a bullock to them for slaughter![308]

Gibb referred to the effect of the 'ceremony on the native mind' and reported that twenty-five of the men were now being sent back to South Africa to stimulate black labour recruitment.[309] According to Stamfordham, the king 'was much amused at your description of the delight caused by the presentation of the bullock and that His Majesty's action in the eyes of the natives have [sic] been kingly'.[310] The monarch's reaction to Gibb suggests that even he found elements of his own imperial depiction somewhat ridiculous – the pretence here that George V was an African chief. There is also clearly evidence of condescension in the attitude shown to black South African culture.

Yet, significantly, King George V's own diary entry for his 10 July 1917 inspection of the South African Native Labour Contingent men is entirely matter-of-fact without racial remark or racist slur, as indeed is his diary writing in general: 'I inspected Native Labour Contingents from South Africa and the officers in charge of them. Made them a speech which was interpreted in three different languages.'[311] The king did not engage in openly racist commentary in his private writings, unlike many of his contemporaries, including his own son Edward, Prince of Wales.[312] The derogatory terms which appear in his wartime diary were for the *Germans* – referred to as Hun or Boche – not for colonised peoples.[313] Overall, it seems the king himself believed in the monarchist ideal of a king-emperor who treated his subjects equally, regardless of any perceived differences of race or creed, and prioritised the monarch–subject relationship above all else, although this conclusion must remain provisional pending further archival investigation.[314] He was paternalist, but could be surprisingly progressive on self-rule, and his instincts were towards the humane end of the spectrum, in a period when, for British imperialism, coercion and racial discrimination were normative tools of empire.

Fig. 17   King George V inspects South African Native Labour Company, 10 July 1917, from the Field Marshal Earl Haig Collection, National Library of Scotland, C2088 (Reproduced courtesy of the National Library of Scotland)

Indeed, monarchism and imperial racialisation related in complex ways. Fig. 17, an official photograph of the inspection, as well as other photographs of the event, shows that the black labourers were pointed out to the king by a white officer using his cane, while Queen Mary hovered in the background. In this case, the structure of the inspection parade – troops presented in rows for display before the dominant 'royal gaze' – was the same as that for white soldiers, who were also physically arrayed for royal inspections during the war in ways that made clear hierarchical class and military power structures. Yet, the king's body also mattered in terms of presenting the hierarchies between white dominant and black and Asian subordinate imperial masculinities. Indeed, during the war the king's body, visually contrasted with its subjects in such photographs of the monarch encountering black and Asian colonial subjects, was used to convey the monarch as the ultimate representative of hegemonic white maleness and British imperial power.

Yet, as with the 'King's Appeal to Empire', the royal body could also be subversive of racial hierarchies. Royal hegemony could be represented in ways that saw the kingly body aligned with the non-Western cultures of his subjects, which arguably also disrupted imperial assumptions about 'oriental' masculinity as 'other' and distant. For example, to bolster recruitment in India, a portrait was made in 1914 of the King as Colonel-in-Chief of King George's Own Lancers of the Indian Army, in full uniform, wearing an Indian turban; the image was widely reproduced in the United Kingdom, including in *The Sphere* and in the *War Illustrated*, and artists also adapted colourful versions of it for Indian propaganda (Fig. 18). The monarch in this image embodied power and military force through a visualisation of Indian imperial leadership that borrowed from indigenous cultures. In this regard, the monarchy could act as a vector for blurring and hybridity. The monarchy was thus a complex component of empire, and its direct interactions with its black and Asian subjects – awarding medals or visiting them in hospitals, for example – could promote their status in ways that arguably subverted contemporary imperialist racialised assumptions about their purported 'primitiveness'.

It is difficult to assess what black South African labourers actually made of the experience of royal inspections. We have two accounts to draw on here. The first, sent by Gibb to Wigram, relays the appreciation and loyalty of Walter Dwane, a headman from Lady Frere District in the Cape Province, who made

Fig. 18   'The King Emperor as Colonel-in-Chief, Lancers, Indian Army', 1914. King George V (1865–1936) in military uniform during the First World War' (Illustration from H. W. Wilson, *The Great War: The Standard History of the All-Europe Conflict*, Vol. 1 (London, 1914); photo by The Print Collector/Print Collector/Getty Images, 463958025)

the following speech upon returning to his company after King George V's 10 July 1917 inspection:

> I wish to express to you my thanks for this great day on which we have seen our King. It is a day which will never be forgotten in my lifetime. This day is a blessing to me. I always desired to see the King but when he appeared it seemed as if it were a dream. I thought of the war and his great responsibilities. My heart was grieved but I comforted myself with the knowledge that I have come here to help and with the prayer that the Lord may give him victory. I feel confident that with God's help our great King will be victorious. There is no fear with me now. [...] I am filled with valour in consequence of having seen my King. I have no hesitation in saying that the Xosa [sic] Tribe is loyal and that we all hope that the King's Armies may be victorious. I also thank the Officers who have charge of us for giving us this opportunity of seeing our King.[315]

Dwane's speech actually makes a series of quite radical assertions, couched in the language of monarchical loyalty. First, the fact of giving a speech in reply to the one that the king had given the labourers was in itself an assertive act – that of claiming the right to respond to the monarch, albeit after the event was over. Second, the assertion of religious faith – that the black subject will pray to ask God to intercede to help the white king – is also a powerful assertion of equality. Finally, the reference to the Xhosa tribe is key – Dwane, as a senior figure of power in his own community, like the other selected men, was asserting that his own people had *chosen* loyalty – and by identifying them in this way foregrounded their independent agency and, tacitly, their existence as a people with their own culture. The second source reveals how some black labourers interpreted the king's speech in terms of the equality that monarchism promised the wartime royal subject. On 12 July 1917, M. L. Posholi wrote of being inspected that 'we saw him, George V, our King with our own eyes. [...] we are indeed in the midst of great wonders [...] because we personally heard that we blacks too are British subjects, children of the father of the great Nation, trusted ones and helpers, and that we are cared for and loved'.[316] Indeed, for many of the educated Africans present, the king was the supreme symbol of imperial power and British justice, a counterbalance to military racism.[317]

Such beliefs help to explain why black South Africans in a labour unit on the Western Front wrote a letter to King George V complaining of their living conditions, rather than to army commanders or to politicians. All black labour contingent members were confined to secure camps when not working, effectively treated as prisoners, to prevent their fraternising with white troops, labourers or civilians, at the insistence of the South African government. According to South African Native Labour Contingent member Koos Matli, stationed in Camp Griffiths, the black labourers were upset because their camp had endured aerial bombardment from German planes and they were effect-ively left defenceless, incarcerated, in the face of such attacks:

> nearly every evening we were attacked by the enemy planes and we had nothing to defend ourselves with. This camp was twice in flames during enemy attacks. We formed a committee and after some discussions agreed to send a letter to England. We wrote the letter and explained our condition. We addressed the letter to His Majesty King George V. We gave the letter to one of the soldiers to post for us, since we were not allowed to go out of Camp.[318]

As this case illustrates, for all that monarchist rhetoric was used to mobilise indigenous populations of the empire, it proved hollow against the racist hierarchies of imperial governments. After the war, the South African Government refused to award its Native Labour Contingent a war medal or even allow them to receive the medal awarded by King George V to 'native' labourers of the British Empire; they thus received no medals for their service.[319]

Hopes for greater equality grounded in wartime monarchism also emerged in the case of Jamaican volunteers. Some NCOs in the British West Indian Regiment serving in Palestine produced a petition at their unfair treatment on the grounds that 'the majority of the men of the British West Indies Regiment are taxpayers ... and loyal subjects of His Majesty, and we feel that this discrimination is [...] an insult'.[320] In 1930s Jamaica, the Moyne Commission, investigating poor living conditions, received statements from ex-servicemen who referred directly to their 'supreme sacrifice for King and country' and their right to more equitable treatment.[321] According to Richard Smith, after the war a Colonial Office official remarked that most Jamaicans had no attachment to Britain or empire beyond 'a strong loyalty to the person and crown of the sovereign'.[322] In fact, it was, Smith claims, this 'attachment to the monarch' that sustained the Jamaican war effort, in part because the monarchy was associated with reining in the plantocracy and colonial official-dom, and with emancipation.[323] In sum, in wartime, black colonised popula-tions projected very high hopes onto the monarchy as a potentially liberating force which it failed to fulfil.

Because the monarchy promised equality of all subjects in direct relation-ship to the king, it offered a higher plane of appeal, which could be called upon by black and Asian troops in an effort to challenge the military and colonial discriminations based on race that they faced. Monarchy thus offered alternative discursive uses and motivations for these groups in the First World War that it did not to white subjects. This whole process also fundamentally illustrates the wartime interaction between modernisation processes – in this case, the drive for greater racial equality – and sacralising discourses of monarchy and kingship beliefs. Indeed, such beliefs about royal power and duty to subjects were integral to debate about empire reform. The redefinition of the monarchy's image during the war as a bulwark of British democratic freedoms, discussed further in Chapter 4, also helped inadvertently to undermine imperial racial hierarchies by raising the question as to why some imperial subjects could access democracy and civil rights to a much greater degree than others, based on race. In July 1919, the Society of Peoples of African Origin wrote directly to the British Minister for War, utilising the language of monarchism in its demand for black Africans to be included in the planned 'peace march' in London, 'voicing the heartfelt wishes of all Africans at present in England, to express the hope that Africa will be represented in the "Peace March" by at least a detachment of her Sons who have served their King and Country in the Great War'.[324] The same year, the South African National Congress deputation sent to England incorporated King George V's July 1917 speech at Abbeville to the South African Native Labour Contingent into its petition to the monarch, reminding him that he had told them that his armies were fighting for 'liberty and freedom of my subjects of all races and creeds throughout my Empire'; why then had these been denied to them following the war?[325] Their petition, however, was not transmitted to King George V, and the deputation's request to meet the king was refused by the Colonial Office.[326] A speaker at the Transvaal Native National Congress in South Africa in April 1919 pointed out that they had been 'assisting the Kingdom' in these great wars and that 'King George himself had said that natives should have their freedom.'[327] Here the rhetoric and image of the monarchy clashed with the reality of its actual constitutional powers: in the case of South Africa, the king could not even ensure that his black South African subjects received his war medals. The irony was that, as the immediate post-war period saw the empire become *more* important to the status of the monarchy in Britain, given the loss of much of its European foreign relations influence, bringing it more power at home, the cleavage between its rhetoric of equality of subjects and the reality had never been more visible to its disempowered, black and Asian colonised populations.

It is important to note the agency of the king in this image of the monarchy as a paternalist protector of empire troops and labourers. The evidence suggests that King George V took his royal relationship with colonial subjects very seriously. With regard to South Asian populations, who were situated higher than those of black ethnicity in the British Empire racial hierarchies of the time, King George had good, even close, relationships with elite Indians such as Sir Pertab Singh, the Regent of Jodphur, who dined with him at Buckingham Palace; the Prince of Wales also visited his rented home in France.[328] In fact, the 700 plus Indian native princes who ruled about one third of India under the British were crucial to imperial control, and the British monarchy played a key diplomatic role in liaising with them.[329] After the war, George V employed Indian veterans as orderlies.[330]

Indeed, the monarchy was constantly publicly presented as having a special relationship with Indian troops by dint of the king's title of Emperor of India, which was, after all, the purported 'Jewel in the Crown' of the empire.[331] In the case of King George and Queen Mary, a real relationship with India had been well developed through their pre-war visits there, and both felt a profound sense of personal duty to Indian troops serving in Europe.[332] For example, in November 1914, the king intervened with the newly appointed Commissioner for Sick and Wounded Indian Soldiers in France and England, Walter Lawrence, making clear that his role was to drastically improve their treatment:

> The King was delighted to hear from your letter to Lord Stamfordham that you have been appointed a Commissioner to look after the Indian wounded. His Majesty knows that they are safe in your keeping and that the deplorable conditions at present existing will soon be remedied and regularized under your supervision. Lord Curzon would do no good by writing to the papers and it would be much better to put things straight without the Press knowing anything about it.[333]

This missive is very typical of how the wartime monarchy operated, making its wishes clear, without actually ordering anything and out of sight of public knowledge. In fact, the king was behind Lawrence's appointment. George V informed the Viceroy of India that he had thought the accommodation for Indian troops on the Western Front very unsuitable and had asked Kitchener to improve things; the latter responded by appointing Lawrence.[334]

The wartime image of a monarchy that treated all races equally was one that George V also promoted after the war ended. In 1920, he insisted that Indian princes should be represented at the unveiling of the Cenotaph ceremony.[335] The Prince of Wales was chosen to unveil the post-war memorial to the Indian war dead erected on the English South Downs in 1927, while the same year, in New Zealand, the Duke of York unveiled the Te Arawa Memorial at Rotorua, one of only a few war memorials erected by the Maori to their war dead, which had a statue of King George V at the top and images from Arawa beliefs and history carved into the body of the memorial, an explicit visualisation of a direct – if hierarchical – relationship between monarch and non-white subject.[336] The memorial text read: 'erected by the Arawa tribes in perpetual remembrance of their sons who in the Great War loyally upheld the cause of their God, their country and their King, 1914–1919'.[337] It was the monarchy's recognition of black, Asian and indigenous Australasian troops' and labourers' sacrifices that helped to sustain hopes that it would promote post-war changes for the better for their status in the empire.

The role that the monarchy played in motivating white troops from the dominions was notably different. This took place in a context where white imperial populations were already developing a sense of independence from Britain before the war and had their own agency to effect change through their own prime ministers and wartime structures such as, from 1917, the Imperial War Cabinet. Among white dominion troops a range of quite different reactions emerge towards monarchy, and its utilisation as an emancipatory discourse is missing. For some, monarchism was clearly a profound part of their identity, as Australian Signal Engineer, Sapper D. G. McHugo's 1917 Christmas card design, which reproduces the slogan of British conservative party imperialists from Empire Day 1916, illustrates in Fig. 19.[338]

Fig. 19 Christmas card, 1917, from Australian Signal Engineer, Sapper D. G. McHugo, Imperial War Museum, Documents 8877, Box Misc. 82 item 1249 © Imperial War Museum

Arthur Burrowes from Sydney wrote to his daughter of how he 'saw the King, Queen, Prince of Wales, Princess Mary, they were driving along in a beautiful carriage, with four beautiful horses pulling it, and two men (called Postillions) on two of the horses, and the two men had beautiful clothes on too, so everything was beautiful', a description redolent of royalty as fairy tale.[339] For Canadian Amos Mayse, royalty was associated with deep patriotic kinship and one united British identity. Writing about a service at St Paul's Cathedral in London, he described how

> [...] I sat or knelt right opposite the royal pew in which there were the Duke & Duchess of Connaught with Princess Patricia – Princess Victoria & her Mother Queen Alexander [sic] & Princess Mary daughter of King George, there were others whose faces were familiar but whom I could not name, & when the people passed up for communion to the alter [sic] rail I was amongst the first lot – after the Royal Party had taken their places, the vacant places were filled up by any soldiers present, & I found myself kneeling by the side of the Princess Patricia – it was a service I shall long remember, they used the old cups etc – I suppose some of our Emerson Baptists friends would think that I had wandered from grace if they heard this, but I do know I seemed to get very near the heart of things & very close to God, as I knelt & sat thro the services, after the service I wandered around a little to see the tombs & monuments, our great soldiers & sailors lie buried here, chief of whom are Wellington – Nelson – Napier & General Gordon with a memorial tablet to Kitchener.[340]

Canadian John Cowles wrote of how, on receiving a copy of a magazine from home, 'I was very interested in the list of club members who are serving our King and Country. I knew there were a lot serving but I had no idea there were so many.'[341]

By contrast, for other Canadian troops, the monarchy was experienced through royal troop inspections, which they reported on in mundane terms. Canadian Bertram Cox wrote in 1917 of how 'We were inspected by the King (George V) and Queen Mary about 2 weeks ago; he was dressed in officer's uniform and is exactly like the pictures one sees of him.'[342] Canadian Samuel Ball wrote prosaically: 'We was [sic] inspected by the king last Saturday. We had sports last Sunday all day. Our Coy. won the first prize in a Machine Gun competition.'[343] But, in other cases, there was notable indifference or even anti-monarchist sentiment from dominion troops. White South African Ellis Newton's unit was inspected by Queen Mary before leaving Britain for the Western Front, because King George V was indisposed due to his 1915 accident. Newton's account was irreverent:

> To-day we were inspected by Her Majesty the Queen and Her Royal Highness Princess Mary and it was not half an Indaba'. Although not such a big affair as most of us expected. At any rate it is generally the performance that has to be gone through before regiments go off to the front. The King also sent a message of 'Kiss me Good-Bye' which General Lukin read out to us.[344]

When Newton was killed not long afterwards, his mother received a sympathy letter from one of his comrades, who wrote of how 'I was wounded shortly after Ellis gave himself to his King & Country', placing a monarchist spin on his death that diverged from Newton's own much more cynical attitude.[345] Frank Mort has also found that

> Australian and Canadian soldiers demanded monarchy as spectacle and entertainment, especially from those who claimed tourist-style leisure while on leave in London. Their writings reflected the popular appropriation of monarchy through real or imagined proximity to the king and the Prince of Wales. This demand for familiarity was particularly marked among the Australian forces, whose egalitarian nationalism often centred on exposing royalty's human imperfections and those of the English social elites.[346]

In the case of Australian combatants, Kathryn Cook has found a range of responses. There is not only considerable evidence of excitement and adulation when they encountered the Prince of Wales during his visit to Egypt, but also irreverence at his slender physique and short height, his timidity and his youth, as well as a rejection of ideas of royal privilege.[347] Some Australian troops also reacted negatively to Western Front inspections by the king or the princes Edward and Albert.[348] However, she traces a significant rise in enthusiasm for the Prince of Wales among Australian Western Front combatants in 1918, after he had served with Australian units there. Both Cook and Mort found Australian combatants were relatively open in criticising monarchism. Mort cites one Australian, Private John McRae, who was deeply moved at seeing 'our King' with his 'sad, sweet smile' and 'deep voice', but who acknowledged that 'Royalty' was 'by no means universally popular amongst the boys', as tradition 'is not acknowledged generally by Australia's sons'.[349] Another Australian private commented of a royal inspection in early 1919 that 'we are polishing irons and bits for a visit from the King or Prince of Wales. What do we want him for, he's not been fighting & is only a man', heroising his fellow combatants in contrast to royalty.[350] Major Frank Weir, an Australian officer, stated in a letter home on 26 December 1918 that 'There is talk of the PRINCE coming out to review us – educating a man for a job I doubt he will ever get – & our men are restless [...].'[351] This phenomenon of cynicism towards the monarchy, if not actual outright rejection of it, was more clearly articulated by dominion soldiers than in British sources. It also affected Australia's official war historian, the journalist Charles E. W. Bean, famed for his reports from Gallipoli, who objected to the British monarchy as the centre of feudalism and snobbery and promoted what he saw as Australia's classless society and egalitarianism in his wartime writing.[352] It seems that, for white dominion troops, monarchy was more of a contested motivation during the war than for their British counterparts or even for indigenous colonial troops, although here one must be wary of our limited sources on these men's views.

Ultimately, if 1914 saw the monarchy call on all subjects of the empire equally, regardless of race, by the end of the war the actual situation was changing. The monarchy increasingly saw a future where white settler dominion populations were forging a new relationship with it, while its role towards black and Asian populations remained unchanged. This dichotomy was key to the later ways in which the empire was reconfigured towards the end of the war, which will be discussed in Chapter 4. It also shaped the role that monarchy played for combatant troops from the empire.

2.7   Democratising Kingship and Inspiring Combatants? The Role of the Prince of Wales

One final important factor that bolstered the monarchy's popularity among troops was the role of Edward, Prince of Wales, who spent much of the conflict as a staff officer on the Western Front. As representative of the future of the monarchy, the Prince of Wales was an integral part of the moral economy of wartime, serving as a constant illustration of the ways in which the royal family were participating in the national sacrifice that total war entailed. His Western Front experience thus offers a valuable case study for how individual, practical royal behaviour towards troops could affect popular monarchist beliefs and cultural support for the monarchy, as well as how the honour cultures of 1914 evolved.

Edward's 1914 proactive lobbying to be allowed to fight had been seen very positively in the press: 'what young man of spirit in any rank of life would not have "kicked"?', wrote the *Daily Sketch* approvingly in its report referring to Edward's refusal to accept being initially prohibited from going to France.[353] He was further lauded for his desire to be treated as an ordinary junior officer, his basic billets and his rejection of luxury. Frequent press stories recounted how the prince went among the troops virtually unrecognised and moments where he was mistaken for an 'ordinary' British officer at the front were played up, reflecting a longer British literary trope of the king who goes incognito among his people to ascertain their needs in 'prince and the pauper' fashion, but also new war expectations of monarchy sharing in its people's hardships. As the conflict dragged on, long beyond initial expectations, and the extreme nature of battlefield violence became publicly known, representations of Edward, as a prince in France who was roughing it akin to any other man of military age, became increasingly important to the monarchy's overall wartime image. The honour culture of 1914 was supplanted by new press languages of monarchy as promoting equality, which approvingly emphasised Edward's attempts to act as a 'democratic' prince, based on his supposed love of anonymity and rejection of privilege. This dovetailed with the monarchy's growing concern, as the war continued, to be seen to be sharing the burdens of the conflict with the people and as in touch with public suffering and the demands for social change that the war was bringing. This new 'democratic monarchy' image helped to distance the British monarchy from vilified German 'kaiserism', but it rapidly also became a broader strategy for court advisors who wished to avoid the war triggering any anti-monarchy feeling or resentment in Britain on the basis of any association with socio-economic inequalities.

This press discourse was not manufactured, but reflected Edward's actual behaviour. His war diary reveals how he worked all-night shifts on staff work; he sometimes slept in his 'office' on a camp bed.[354] In September 1915, he wrote in his diary of how he spent one evening 'put on sort of police work at the [cross]rds at the W. entrance of the town [...] to regulate the traffic & was there standing in the rain & mud till nearly 9.00!! And it was some job too sorting all the waggons & limbers as they streamed in from the West.'[355] The Prince of Wales standing in mud, anonymously directing traffic in the rain, highlights the kind of physical deprivation Edward deliberately sought out in France, which endeared him to the troops. He also visited the wounded in Casualty Clearing Stations. Indeed, Edward's workload, tasks and living experiences were very similar to those of an ordinary junior staff officer, particularly after he was appointed to the staff of the Guards Division. However, Edward was also still an honour proxy for his father – a vector for information that the king could trust, as well as a surrogate. The prince reviewed troops at the front and on occasion distributed medals, a continuation of older honour cultures associated with the monarchy ideal. He also was a source of information for the king regarding British army generals, their performance and military attitudes to British politics more generally.

At a personal level, however, Edward's 'democratic' behaviour overwhelmingly stemmed from his upset at not being able to fight like other men. He wanted to be useful to the troops and act 'ordinary', strategies that he employed to cope with this and with war stress more generally. His diaries continually lamented his prohibition from combat, which he clearly felt was emasculating and humiliating. In December 1914, he went up the line to visit the 2nd Battalion of the Grenadier Guards at Le Touret, about a mile from the frontline trenches, but was singled out by a superior, who spotted him and 'told me to return to Bethune [sic] as I was too close!! Bloody having to say good bye to them all & it did bring it home to one how wretched it is to be the bloody P. of Wales!! I almost broke down & had an awful walk back to 2nd Div. HQ.'[356] His discomfort at not being able to share in the war's dangers was thus often relatively public to other combatants. Edward felt an outcast, barred from the central purpose of fighting and dying with honour in battle that dominated the lives and caste culture of the officers with whom he socialised. Their deaths only exacerbated this: 'Papa gave me the very sad news that poor Cadogan had been killed; he will be a really great loss to me for he was such a good kind chap.

I shan't have a friend left soon.'[357] Edward clearly felt deeply insecure about his ongoing special protected position as heir: 'I am in the depths of depression realising at last that there is no job I can take on out here & so am really the only man out here who has nothing to do or anything to work for', he wrote in March 1915.[358] A Christmas card he sent in 1915 highlights his obsession with war combat (Fig. 20).

Unable to participate in that supreme test of Edwardian masculinity which the First World War battlefield represented, Edward looked for substitute moments of danger, acts of bravado, which he used both to exhibit his courage to others and to test his own mental and physical strength. This often involved circumventing the unwritten boundaries of how far forward in the trench system he was allowed to go. In July 1915, he spent a night in the trenches, writing to the king that 'my impressions that night were of constant close proximity to death, repugnance from the stink of the unburied corpses . . . and general gloom and apprehension'.[359] On several occasions in 1915, he came under shellfire; his driver was killed while waiting for him to return from a tour of front area trenches. On 31 December 1915, he wrote of how, while he was visiting an observation post, the Germans began 'shelling all round the O.P. hitting the house a few yds in front & the house next door & put some just over but unpleasantly near. So we got down into an excellent dugout below on the ground floor.'[360] Edward tried to overcome the genuine fear he felt

Fig. 20   A Christmas card sent by Edward, Prince of Wales, in 1915, Magdalen College Archives, University of Oxford MC P163/14 (Reproduced by kind permission of the President and Fellows of Magdalen College, Oxford)

when he came under shellfire by deliberately and constantly exposing himself to this experience.

The fact that the Prince of Wales was prepared to take such risks, without official approval, and that, without actually having to place his life in danger, he chose to do so, endeared him enormously to the troops. It was common knowledge that he could have chosen to stay safely in staff officer quarters far behind the lines, given he was employed as a staff officer. Press reports generally endorsed the view that he was putting himself at risk, often reporting soldiers' accounts of his actions: Private A. Butler, the Coldstream Guards, in a letter to his parents, passed to a newspaper, described the Prince of Wales as a brave hero: 'only last night he passed me when the German shells were coming over. [...] I hope, please God, he will come home safe and sound, and without a scratch.'[361] Another report, headlined 'In His Element: The Prince of Wales at the Front', described how Edward had 'been near, and often in, the fighting line for months although little has been published in this country'.[362] Trooper Percy Hodges of the 10th Hussars stated in the *Newcastle Journal* that 'The Prince is often in the danger zone, and the men are very proud of him.'[363]

Other unpublished sources corroborate that the Prince's risk-taking endeared him to combatants. A British officer, Alan Maciver, serving at a particularly dangerous front position at Passchendaele, recounted in a later oral history interview how 'at that time we literally hardly ever saw any officer from any higher formation'.[364] Maciver noted on one occasion they had not

> seen anyone from divisional headquarters for six weeks [...] The only really senior commander, senior officer, I ever saw, top officer, during this period was the Prince of Wales who had insisted on being taken up to the front line and he came up with the Corps chief staff officer and I had quite a long interesting conversation with him.[365]

Maciver's interjection of the words 'top officer' to describe the prince – who visited him in a position that other commanders feared too much to venture to – is very revealing. Another officer, Captain Alexander Scotland, recalled Edward arriving on site immediately after the German aerial bombing of a Casualty Clearing Station to question him about what had happened.[366] It is clear from such sources, as well as from his own diary, that on many occasions Edward did run real risks.[367] This mitigated against any potential accusations which could have arisen that as a staff officer he had shirked the hardships and dangers of the frontline – an accusation that, by contrast, dogged the kaiser's eldest son Crown Prince Wilhelm.

Edward's personal experience also provides an insight into the trajectory of the war experience in general and into the construction of elite masculinities. His feelings expressed in his diary moved from optimism, a powerful sense of duty and belief in the British cause in 1914–15, into pessimism and terrible war-weariness by 1916. Like many ordinary officers on the Western Front, he struggled to cope with the difficult living conditions, long working hours, war bereavements and homesickness and sought to let off steam in excessive partying when on leave. Edward's diary and letters depict a growing disillusionment with the war and with his own role – 'Here beginneth the 5th volume of my diary & may it see the end of this bloody war!!' he wrote on 20 July 1916.[368] Edward also increasingly resented the military approach to attrition, writing in his diary in July 1916 of a conference he attended in 1st Guards Brigade Headquarters with Lord Cavan (whose nickname was Fatty) that

> The conference was re the taking of Hill 29 High Command Redoubt which Geoffrey had told Fatty (in writing) was a terrible gamble!! So Fatty had assembled these g[rea]t soldiers to tell them that Guards DIV had got to take on this Hill 29, as it was an order from the C. in C. no matter the difficulties. He explained how future operations depended on the capturing of this high position tho. he must have hated doing this and I could see he was worried. Several people have told me that the whole plan of attack seems to them impossible and mad. Of course Haig doesn't think of the poor buggers who will have to do the 'P and P' for this and orders Fatty to ignore the difficulties. What can he do but order the attack despite contrary advice?[369]

If the war was making Edward more questioning about the conflict's cost, it was also changing public expectations of his role. As the war went on and men were conscripted, the assumption developed among the British public and the press – if not among all court and Establishment circles – that the heir to the throne *should* share in the conflict's dangers in the same way as every other male subject of military age. The popular perception was that Edward was incurring real risks in France. By 1918, these views were so strong that when Edward happened to be in London on leave when the Ludendorff Offensives were launched, George V's immediate reaction was one of horror:

> One evening at Buckingham Palace my father suddenly looked up from his war maps and said: 'Good God! Are you still here?' [...] he told me I must be off by morning, adding that he could not have me seen around London with the British line broken and the Army with its back to the wall. I left immediately.[370]

The 1914 relationship between honour and kingship had evolved – even elites now recognised that it was important to show no special treatment towards the heir to the throne; what was 'honourable' now was that the heir should be at risk, democratically sharing the danger of war. What, in 1914, had been portrayed in the press as a generous, benevolent, voluntary gesture by the king of sharing the nation's war effort, in granting his heir's wish to serve in France, was now a non-negotiable popular demand – the king's sons could no longer be seen as entitled to any preferential protections. Edward's role thus provides valuable insights into how monarchy honour culture changed in the Great War. Service to the monarch, which the honour mentality of 1914–16 had demanded, had led to wartime mass death. This threatened to make monarchy a target for war-weariness and to raise accusations that it had been a factor which had created the war carnage. Edward's efforts to experience war danger earned him a reputation for heroism and a 'democratic' image in the British media, which bolstered the popularity of the monarchy among combatants.

The evidence for this appears in letters sent to Edward during the abdication crisis in 1936 by ordinary war veterans, many of whom mentioned how important his wartime service had been to them. The fact they retained these attitudes so long after the conflict had ended provides an invaluable, unique insight into the extent to which his behaviour had indeed mattered to combatants in wartime. One letter on 2 December 1936 from a group of ex-servicemen, calling on Edward to retain the crown, declared: 'We remember your coming into our trenches on the Somme under heavy shell fire and we are your servants now as we were then.'[371] R. C. Smart, a former Captain in the Royal Engineers, wrote, after Edward's radio broadcast announcing his abdication, that 'As I in company with countless thousands listened to your words this evening my thoughts went back to war years when you visited my old Tunnelling Company in front of Bethune [sic] north of the Hohenzollern. Now as then Sir you are to all ranks a man of courage, high honour and purpose [. . .].'[372] Two days later, Norman Hudson, who described himself as ex-Private 2184, 23rd Royal Fusiliers, wrote to Edward:

> But for my own comfort and however useless if may be I write to record the gratitude and respectful affection of one of those countless thousands of men of your own age who had the honour of serving with you and seeing and feeling those things which you also saw and felt during the days of the War. It is the earnest wish of all those men that Your Highness may now find that rest and happiness which you have earned so well.[373]

Ben Richards wrote simply to '"Our" Royal Highness' that 'You will pardon me writing to you as an x-private [sic] soldier; you are in my opinion a man, you went through it like the rest of us, you have removed your crown but we would have loved to see you on the throne.'[374] Arthur Cross wrote 'as an ex-serviceman who served in His Majesty's Army in France, Belgium and Italy from 1914–1919' that 'we as ex-servicemen cherish the many happy memories of your personal presence with us on the Battlefields of Europe and I for one do love, Honour and obey you'.[375] Significantly, many of the approximately one hundred letters still retained in the Royal Archives that were sent to Edward from the public at the time of the abdication set out the writer's wartime service credentials by way of mitigation or justification for the writer's boldness in attempting to write to such a senior royal figure directly, an indication of the ongoing awe in which royal status was still held.

A number of letters also reveal a sense of strong distress for some veterans at the idea of Edward abdicating: Field Marshal Sir William Birdwood wrote to Edward of his 'sleepless nights' over the king's troubles and his anguish at not being able to be of help to him: 'you must know how absolutely and entirely devoted I have been to you ever since we served together in Egypt 21 years ago – later on in France [. . .].'[376] MP Major A. N. Braithwaite wrote of how 'Those of us who have served with you in the war and since in public life feel that nothing can be quite the same again.'[377]

While the vast majority of letters were supportive, wishing the king well in his marriage decision, one rare critical letter was sent by J. O. Roach, who felt that Edward should put country above his personal love interest. His words again indicate the importance of monarchy in the world view of First World War combatants, as well as how the abdication was changing this. Roach was so disenchanted by it that he indicated he was questioning his personal loyalty to the monarch for the first time.

> I am rather younger than his Majesty, I held his father's commission during and after the war, and I took the oath of allegiance 'to his Majesty King George V, his heirs and successors'. If the worst came to the worst, I should rather hope to be released and to take a fresh oath of allegiance to 'England, a constitutional and democratic country'. For the first time in my life I should feel the personal allegiance to be unsatisfactory, as no longer identifying itself with the highest interests of the county. [. . .] May not any one of his subjects be required to sacrifice their very lives in his name? [. . .] Are we to believe that all this talk of service, of loyalty to our country and our fellow men is nothing but an unhappy bluff? What an example.[378]

Roach's was not the only letter to reveal the ongoing importance of the oath of allegiance to the monarch in British culture. The MP, Henry Scrymgeour-Weddenburn, wrote to Edward to ask how he could take an oath of loyalty to a new king without having 'Your Majesty's express command to do so', as he could not feel that the abdication had 'released him, in the light of God, from the allegiance which he owes to Your Majesty'.[379] This suggests that in wartime too the oath had been important.[380]

It is important to contrast the letters sent to Edward from the general public during the abdication crisis with those sent to the Prime Minister, Stanley Baldwin, whose archives contain about eight times as many such letters in comparison, virtually all supportive of Baldwin's role in handling the abdication and opposing King Edward VIII's proposed marriage, even while often also lamenting the latter's loss as king.[381] They contain far fewer mentions of the First World War or of an individual's veteran past or Edward's own war service. In other words, Edward's war service was a factor that influenced those who viewed him more favourably in 1936 and also appears to have disposed ex-servicemen to view him positively.

For those of Baldwin's correspondents who did mention the war, it was as a claim that war service gave them upon the behaviour of the monarchy and state. One writer asked that Edward and Wallis Simpson be exiled, noting that 'As the wife of a true Briton who fought 3 ½ years in the last war, I feel we have a right to this. My husband lost everything by joining up when England was calling and now we are both getting old and no prospect of being able to save.'[382] Another writer, Mrs Findlay, noted that 'If one pauses to think for a moment of the men of Great Britain and the Empire who are called upon to lay down their lives for their King and Country surely the King too must make sacrifices?'[383] What also appeared was the idea that the throne mattered more than the veteran – or indeed the war. One letter writer declared that 'Ten days ago, like many other men, I was frightened for the Throne. Now, much as I am sorry that our friend and comrade of the Army in France has gone, we all feel better and we know how much we owe to you Sir.'[384] Baldwin during the abdication was 'faced with an issue heavier even than the problems which confronted your predecessors during the war', stated another correspondent, in all seriousness.[385] A few ex-servicemen's associations also wrote to Baldwin praising his conduct: Runcorn Branch of the British Legion, for example, conveyed 'our appreciation of the result of your diplomatic handling of the recent Constitutional crisis' and pledged allegiance to the new King.[386] Evesham and District Service Men's Club likewise wrote to Baldwin to inform him that their 300 members, 'ex-servicemen of varying political opinions', were grateful for how he had resolved the 'recent anxieties'.[387]

In sum, the abdication rendered visible the cultural belief systems built around monarchy during and after the First World War, which were usually unspoken collective assumptions. Here perhaps is the clearest indication of the long-term legacy of the association of duty to the monarch with Great War military service that was such a fundamental part of wartime mobilisation in Britain and evidence that ideas of loyalty and duty to the king, as expressed in the oath of attestation, had a deeper meaning than mere platitudes. As historians have shown, war motivation for combatants was, of course, highly complex, based upon a wide range of factors, impossible to disaggregate.[388] But monarchism, long ignored, was surely one of them. What was also evident in the wake of the First World War is the sense that the subject had a claim upon the monarch's behaviour and a right to assert it in letters. This went beyond the older ideas of petitioning a king; this was the grassroots version of the new image of the British monarchy that emerged from the Great War, of monarchy as democratic and existing only by public consent.

2.8   Conclusion

Combatants were affected by the monarchist beliefs and practices which helped mobilise British society and parts of the empire for war in the early years of the conflict. However, while they all faced interacting with military monarchist culture, this process differed in its degree of impact between individuals and between troops from Britain and the different empire populations. Moreover, combatant attitudes to monarchism among troops from Britain appear to have become more contested in the last two years of the war, with more incidents of indifference or covert rejection appearing. This coincided with the impact of conscription. The press and elites overwhelmingly emphasised the popularity of the monarchy among combatants throughout the war. Yet, the reality was that combatant monarchism was always being negotiated. Royal behaviour was key: the king's front visits and the Prince of Wales's war service mattered in ensuring that occasional incidents of dissent never damaged the overall general popularity of the monarch among servicemen during the war.

After 1916, the concept of honour was clearly no longer as powerful a discourse in mobilising recruitment, although it still had cultural force. The unquestioning idea of a duty imperative to go to war for 'King and Country' to preserve one's masculine honour had weakened; the fact that conscription was required highlighted this shift. With it came a change in the role of the king in relation to his army: this was no longer an army of volunteers or professional regulars who had effectively 'chosen' to serve him; now the *state* was very clearly imposing military service. It was interposing itself into what had been seen as a direct honour relationship between military and monarch; even if many soldiers had always pre-1914 enlisted for financial reasons, this image of an honourable relationship had still mattered, particularly for officers. Moreover, it had been greatly energised and evoked as a trope after the sudden outbreak of war in 1914, when Britain faced raising a new, mass volunteer army. Conscription, by dint of its sheer scale, necessitated a vast increase in state bureaucratic support for, and intervention with, the army, which, along with its expansion in size, lessened the direct royal link with servicemen.

George V responded by trying to sustain the sense of a unique bond between the monarch and the ordinary combatant as a direct affective connection as much as possible, one which bypassed the complex faceless state bureaucracy and institutional structures. His tireless inspection of troops before they left the United Kingdom, awarding of medals in investitures and visits to the Western Front, where he sought to be seen and indeed meet as much of the army as possible face to face, highlight this. Likewise, the fact that the king issued a letter to each returning British prisoner of war upon their repatriation after the conflict ended, describing them as 'our gallant officers and men', similarly testifies to his desire to preserve kingship in military culture as a personal bond even after the Armistice; although the letter was mass-produced, it included a sophisticated facsimile reproduction of the monarch's personal signature, which created a personalised effect.[389] The king's efforts to preserve tradition, by emphasising the personal, the individual and symbolic honour interaction between monarch and subject, had the corollary of making the monarchy appear approachable and human, at a moment in history when industrial warfare had made battle faceless, mechanical and anonymous. The monarchy offered an antidote to the modern terrors of Great War anonymity precisely because the king resisted modernising the monarch–subject relationship with his troops. To refer back to Blackbourn and Eley and the feudalism debate, set out in this book's introduction, the role of the British monarchy in mobilisation discourses and engagement with combatants reveals that British wartime modernity successfully retained, reimagined, projected and built upon older feudal languages and structures in the face of total war modernisation processes, and that this was, in many ways, a strength.

The monarchy was a direct agent in sustaining those sacralising aspects of honour culture which supported its popularity. The king's visits to his troops 'in the field' to praise and urge them on, with their echoes of Henry V, his awarding of medals for 'gallantry', do appear to have boosted morale, as indeed did the war service of other members of the royal family. The discourse of equality in the treatment of imperial subjects suggested modernising reform of empire could be obtained through sacralised dynastic loyalty. The monarchy was presented as historic, constant, reliable and virtuous in its British wartime manifestation. Ultimately, there was a very close symbiotic relationship between the modernisation processes that the war necessitated, such as creating a mass army, and sacralised monarchist belief systems.

Ironically, as the relationship between the British monarch and the living soldiery weakened in 1916, with the decline in the idea of an honour obligation of duty to go to war for one's king and the rise of the conscript state, the relationship between the king and the *dead* soldier dramatically strengthened. Importantly, it was in the sphere of commemoration that the most powerful discourse of kingship remained in Britain after the war: the ongoing popularity of the term 'For King and Country' on war memorials in its immediate aftermath testifies to this. It would not be until the literature of disenchantment period after 1929 that the high rhetoric of patriotism regarding the war dead would be radically challenged, and with it, some of the language of monarchism, including this phrase. But from 1916 on, kingship was no longer a cultural code that could be taken for granted in British society in the way that it once had been and was reinventing itself in significant respects. Loyalty now had to be earned by the monarchy, not assumed.

PART II

The Emperor's New Clothes

Changing Cultures of Deference

3

The Royal Body in Wartime

3.1 Introduction

Chapter 3 looks at how the royal body was portrayed in cultural discourses and how this related to actual behaviours during wartime encounters between royalty and their subjects. It argues that studying the royal body in this way – how it was portrayed, culturally gendered and deferred to – offers us valuable insights into the monarchy's status and how royalty sustained a sacralised leadership function in wartime society. It focuses upon two key themes – how discourses of royal 'perfection' and of the 'royal touch', that echoed much older notions of royalty, were adapted and sustained during the Great War – arguing that their cultural representation was reflected in social practices.

Wartime interactions between royal bodies and those of their subjects show that while the war made the royal body more visible and more accessible than ever before, it still retained a sacred aura, allowing an idea of physical contact with royalty as something associated with awe to survive in new ways into the early twentieth century. The king remained linguistically entitled to use the plural royal 'we' – a combination of the physical royal body and the body politic of the state it represented. The royal body was used to promote ideals of perfection, both in its physical wartime behaviour – endurance, frugality, self-denial, indefatigable energy – and its moral stances, and interaction with it was depicted as improving a subject's well-being.

Again, here we see a close interrelationship between the modernisation processes that the war brought – for example, the rapid construction of mass medical facilities for hundreds of thousands of war wounded, advances in medical techniques and transport – and pre-war cultures of monarchism and ideas about 'perfect' royal leadership. Royal hospital visits – an older tradition with sacralised overtones about the 'royal touch' – helped to convey a sense of continuity and dignity to the new, highly modern, medical universe that the war created on the Western Front and in the United Kingdom. Here cultures of monarchist deference were depicted as providing a temporary morale boost to the wounded, who were disorientated by war injury and by being in hospital, as well as a break from routine for the medical staff who cared for them and a reminder of peacetime life. As the symbols of national and imperial honour, royals, in turn, conveyed 'honour' upon the recipients of their visit, giving meaning to their wartime roles. British monarchist cultures adapted relatively successfully to the medical strains of modern total war.

In fact, the preservation of elements of awe around the royal body was embedded within modernisation processes: greater wartime accessibility was about projecting sacralisation, not diminishing it. The war saw increased press access to the royal family, which fuelled wartime mainstream news-paper narratives describing the royal body in particular ways that evoked its special status. The conflict also saw the royal body become accessible virtu-ally, in film and photographic form, in new ways, which gave its cultural power greater reach; while this trend had begun before 1914, the war vastly accelerated it.[1] The 1916 War Office documentary film of the king's visit to the Western Front during the Battle of the Somme, 'The King Visits His Armies in the Great Advance', proved hugely successful, highlighting this wartime trend in increasing royal cinematographic visibility; it was followed by the films 'The King's Visit to the Fleet' and 'The Royal Visit to the Battlefields of France'. Luke McKernan has pointed out how the war was also the key factor in increasing the presence of the royals in newsreel films, in particular from 1917, at the point when the British propaganda effort switched from focusing upon neutral powers to domestic home front morale.[2] Philip Williamson has also noted the increased reach and frequency of royal speeches in the early twentieth century: 'the monarchy became more vocal. As the royal family's activities and visits increased, so its members made more speeches and issued more messages, heard or received more public addresses, and attracted greater media commentary.'[3]

These changes in the media presence of the monarchy happened at the same time that actual encounters between ordinary people and royalty became more frequent. The war accelerated experiments in greater accessibility to the royal body which had been pioneered in the 1912 and 1913 royal tours to industrial areas which saw the king and queen visit a worker's cottage and descend into a mine.[4] Through wartime royal visits to factories, shipyards and hospitals, through royal troop inspections, through the large 'tea parties' hosted by the royal family for wounded soldiers at Buckingham Palace, through tours of the front and through medal investiture ceremonies, the royal presence and the royal touch became democratised; royalty was now not only visible in the distance, in carriage processions for ceremonial occasions, for example, but also was a close encounter, sometimes involving a handshake or the pinning on of a medal, as well as personal conversation, for whole classes of society which had not previously been granted such close access.[5] All of these different encounters presented wartime subjects with close impressions of the royal body and helped to construct the contemporary understanding of monarchy.

Yet, paradoxically, as the royal presence became less distant, the press – and many witnesses of close interactions with royalty – emphasised the distinct sacralised status of the king and queen.

Although the power of such ideas had waned by the early twentieth century, they were still present in British society during the First World War; modernisation and sacralisation overlapped. The king's body had a particular status, expected to help mediate the war experience to the population. This often surfaces where sources relate the gap between the kingly body's actual crowned status and George V's wartime behaviour or appearance – the royal choice to show solidarity with wartime ordinary subjects when visiting them or eschewing luxury was emphasised as a powerful action of royal generosity precisely because the cultural status of the kingly body was perceived as different to that of its subjects. Press reports and contemporaries frequently expressed a sense of being honoured by encounters with the royals in ways that suggested the sacralised difference of the royal body; even critical accounts were often framed in terms of surprise that the king was so like an ordinary man, comments very revealing of cultural expectations that a king should be or would be more different or exceptional in person and physical presence. In particular, when, due to the exigencies of wartime and the royals' own outreach initiatives, working-class subjects found themselves eating or drinking in the royal presence, their accounts expressed a sense of this as a breach of norms, exciting, often welcome, but unexpected and unusual, a breaking of taboos.

Sight of the royal body was always anticipated as a formal experience; when Prime Minister Herbert Asquith rushed to Buckingham Palace at 1.30 a.m. on 1 August 1914, he recorded that 'one of my strangest experiences' was sitting with the king, who was 'clad in a dressing gown', having been woken to approve the draft of an urgent telegram the government wished to send to the tsar to prevent war.[6] The monarch in sleeping attire was a breach of taboo – so unsettling as to rank as one of Asquith's 'strangest' life experiences even though it was, in fact, only a man in pyjamas, hardly in ordinary life, something to merit this level of disquiet. The royal body was anthropologically differentiated by its cultural meanings, and its proximity in night attire was a disruption of hierarchies and boundaries that was profoundly stressful for Asquith. In an indication of this normative culture of extreme public deference, Philip Gibbs, the journalist, wrote of the shock in 1914 before the war when, during a theatre performance, some women suffrage protestors 'rose in a body and actually *shouted* at the King'.[7] Gibbs italicised the word 'shouted' to emphasise the breach of convention.

How the royals dressed, moved and touched people and ate with them were all important cultural messages about wartime changing social conventions – and about what sacralised dimensions of royalty also could not be changed or compromised upon even in a time of national crisis. Wartime royal deportment and clothing were carefully observed. As Frank Mort has argued, there was constant 'close scrutiny of the body, physiognomy and character of leading royals, especially when they were presented in contemporary still and moving images'.[8] The *Daily Telegraph* commented extensively on the royal family joining informally in Christmas festivities in 1916 at a London hospital, including on the comportment and informality of the royal children.[9] This contrasted with the start of King George V's reign, when coverage of the royal body had focused on 'formal, officially sanctioned profiles intended for specific state occasions' and included coronation souvenir booklets, photographs of the Delhi Durbar and 'iconic images of the king on the new coinage and on the first postage stamps of the reign. In these textual sequences, the royal body was variously depicted as majestic or gracious, or as the human embodiment of imperial power; it was rarely informal.'[10] The war saw the ceremonial sacralised image of the royal body interact closely with more direct, intimate subject–royal encounters, but the power of the latter was closely related to the former.

The more visible and more accessible wartime royal body was, of course, profoundly gendered in ways which could display, enhance or even subvert monarchical power. As historians such as Joan Wallach Scott and John Tosh have long argued, gender is a primary way to signify the relations of power in society and its construction changes over time.[11] Royalty represented a major locus of social, cultural, economic and political power, but these dimensions constantly interacted with gendered power dynamics.[12] This must be examined in terms of how gender was 'embodied', drawing upon not only gender historiography but also the historiography of the body, for example, the ideas of historian Lyndal Roper, that culturally gendered behaviours are enacted upon a biologically sexed male or female body.[13] Roper has argued that the historical body is not only biological but also embodies cultural scripts; 'even the experience of embodiment itself might be constructed through culture'.[14]

The meaning of 'king' or 'queen', in other words, was not just a set of gendered representations projected arbitrarily onto individuals but also interacted with their sexed physical bodily realities. Queen Mary's fecundity as a mother of six, for example, was a biological, physical, female role that was often mentioned as connecting her specially with other mothers of all backgrounds.[15] Cultural wartime messages about her role as a queen and woman were based upon perceptions of her biological history of childbearing, perceived as a universal experience uniting mothers in a unique way, particularly mothers of soldiers. The wartime gendered male image of the king was likewise profoundly embedded in the understanding of his biological health and its masculine physical performance of monarchy. The king's frailty after his fall from his horse in 1915 had to be downplayed: given the symbolic intertwining of the monarch's 'two bodies', *pace* Kantorowicz, weakness in the man might suggest weakness in the state at war.[16]

Monarchy also helped to model gender norms for the public, helping shape understandings of self-identity and provoking different responses among male and female audiences. Frank Mort has found that 'men and women differed significantly in their wartime attitudes to the crown', finding that for some middle-class women the monarchy represented 'mystique and magic' and 'patriotic royalism was understood in culturally conservative terms', as they empathised with female royals and 'identified with a hierarchical vision of British and imperial society that the monarchy symbolized'.[17] By contrast, Mort finds that upper-class aristocratic women were less deferential and more sceptical.[18]

There is a detailed, and growing, historiography on the ways in which the First World War's violence was rendered visible upon, and rewrote cultural scripts about, the masculine body but which has also thus far neglected the British monarchy.[19] The war's impact upon the socialisation of, and the cultural meanings constructed around, the female body has also been analysed in-depth.[20] Yet, what was the relationship between these new wartime processes of 'dismembering the male' or redefining female roles and older cultures of the body – particularly the sacred royal body?[21] In particular, how did the new wartime visibility of the damaged, vulnerable male body, and the cultural fragmentation of masculine strength that this presented, interact with a key European tradition of the perfect 'royal' body which symbolised the strength and power of the *Patria*? As Ana Carden-Coyne noted of the Great War, 'shellshock as a result of modern war was situated within both class and gender frameworks, as a "crisis" of masculinity'.[22] The wartime image of the royal body operated constantly within this context of masculine 'crisis'. The male body in military uniform, symbolically held together with royal symbols on badges and buttons, which was blown apart on the battlefield, was literally fragmenting together with the royal insignia it was wearing; the hospitalised troops the king and queen visited presented physical and mental wounding which challenged assumptions about male strength.[23] The royal body's image was a counterbalance, offering stability, status, coherence and awe. Presenting it as perfect – exemplary, intact, secure, healthy, caring and self-controlled – thus mattered as a means of conveying that the state too embodied these characteristics. The war therefore saw ongoing discourses that emphasised the perfection of the royal body – which shared continuities with pre-war peacetime sacralisation discourses – but which also were meant to reassure that the disorientating and challenging wartime 'crisis of masculinity', and more broadly of gender norms, had not reached the physical embodiment of the state. The perfect royal body even appeared on 1914 war souvenir badges to be worn by the subject in support of the war effort, blending royal body, war and the subject's own corporeality.[24] This chapter will now explore the depiction of royal 'perfection' in more detail, before examining in what ways sacralised discourses of the 'royal touch' adapted to wartime and were present in royal practices such as visiting the war wounded. It concludes with an analysis of how monarchist cultures interacted with war disability.

3.2   Discourses of Royal 'Perfection'

One of the main functions of the royal body in wartime was the ongoing display of its 'perfection'. It was constantly depicted in hagiographic wartime and post-war accounts as untiring, energetic, unflagging, self-disciplined, full of stamina and self-controlled. The wartime royals were 'for ever smiling and bowing and waving, never showing the exhaustion or the dull despair which filled their souls', according to one historian.[25] The press constantly portrayed the king's body as exceptional. The *Daily Telegraph* in 1914 depicted the king's purported remarkable powers of memory: how, on meeting random wounded men, he was able to identify their unit and ask for news of their officers, citing one wounded man saying 'He seemed to carry the blinking army list in his 'ead!'[26] This echoed older narratives of the royal body as exemplary and indomitable. George V's physical stamina was depicted as somehow transcending the normal constraints of middle age. The kingly body, and also that of the queen, endured, suffered, never gave up, indefatigably symbolic of the national body politic and its endurance and continuity in wartime, presented as undergoing gruelling physical demands in solidarity with their subjects. For example, the *Dundee Evening Telegraph* reported that 'King George works overtime', stating that:

> The public hardly realises the amount of work the King does. It may be said His Majesty is never idle. He never has been, but now in this war of wars King George is working overtime like the munition workers and like the vast majority of his subjects. Some day, when the time comes for history to be written, an account of His Majesty's engagements and all his doings would surprise everybody. It would show a devotion to duty and to his people that must have been and is now a considerable tax on his physical powers.[27]

As one post-war biographer noted: 'All unobtrusively, this quiet middle-aged gentleman, growing grey in the service of his people, doing his job steadfastly and faithfully as any soldier in the line, had crept into the heart of the nation.'[28] This paralleled the wartime mythologies of the tireless monarch devoted to his people in the leadership cults built around King Albert I of the Belgians and the Italian monarch Victor Emmanuel III. Such depictions were part of the sacralised 'othering' of the royal bodies from those of their subjects. As one 10-year-old schoolgirl wrote in an essay in 1937, 'their blood is not like ours'.[29] Even royals themselves believed in royalty as a blood caste: Queen Mary fretted that she was not of 'full' royal blood due to her morganatic ancestry, while the former Edward VIII, in later life, stated that he was one of 'only three completely royal persons left alive'.[30]

A key dimension of the wartime sacralisation of kingship was also how the royal body was portrayed as exemplifying moral perfection – stoic, self-controlled, performing and promoting idealised wartime values of British society, a public tableau upon which expectations of wartime moral virtue were projected and acted out. It was also used to express sacrifice and spiritual penance on behalf of the country and empire. This drew upon older religious tropes of the king, as God's anointed, appealing on his people's behalf for divine intercession in wartime.

This context helps to explain the *multiple* 'King's Pledges' that the king publicly announced, which saw the king and queen renounce a range of physical pleasures in order to set an example. A wide range of foods were barred from royal palace menus, with the royal couple eating frugally for the duration of the war, alcohol was banned from court and they also renounced the theatre. Typical was the King's Pledge limiting the use of flour and eschewing pastry.[31] Significantly, the royal couple cut back on palace food before official rationing was introduced in late 1917, at which point they were issued with ration cards along with their subjects; their symbolic example preceded government obligation.[32]

George V applied this austerity ruthlessly to all encounters, telling his chef not to worry about the choice of food when high-ranking military generals were dining with him, 'for this was wartime and they should be grateful for anything'.[33] Many of the main events of the royal season, including horse racing, were cancelled during the conflict, so the royals forewent most of their pre-war entertainments; the one exception was shooting at Sandringham, which continued; the king, however, gave away most of the shot birds to worthy causes, including war hospitals in France.[34] Large amounts of produce from the royal estates were given to wartime good causes, the royals symbolic-ally feeding the people while depriving the royal body of luxurious foods. Evidence of public reception of such gestures is rare: one woman, Violet Clutton, noted privately that she was inspired by the king, who had 'done away with all grand dinners at the Palace and will only have what is absolutely necessary'.[35] The monarch was generally seen as offering moral leadership: on 8 September 1914, for example, as public anger peaked at the Football Association for continuing to hold matches despite the outbreak of war, F. N. Charrington, an East End Temperance worker, 'sent a telegram to the King, asking for the playing of football to be banned during the war'.[36] The appeal was to George V, not the government.

Most famously, in 1915, the king took a 'King's Pledge' to abstain from alcohol for the duration of the conflict.[37] Lloyd George believed that war productivity was being affected by working days lost due to alcohol use and thought that the power of the monarchy could be used as a means to reduce alcoholic consumption. He wrote to Stamfordham that the cabinet felt 'that, if the King took the lead in [this], the nation would follow him', suggestive of a belief in powerful royal public influence.[38] For the monarchy, the issue was both avoiding being seen as privileged and leading by example. The king's Private Secretary, Lord Stamfordham, wrote to Lloyd George that, 'If it be deemed advisable, the King will be prepared to set an example by giving up all alcoholic liquor himself and issuing orders against its consumption in the Royal Household, so that no difference shall be made, so far as His Majesty is concerned, between the treatment of rich and poor in this question.'[39] The King's Pledge to renounce alcohol for the duration of the war was announced in the press on 1 April 1915.[40] For George V, it was not an easy gesture: 'This morning [. . .] we have all become teetotallers until the end of the war. I have done it as an example, as there is a lot of drinking going on in the country. I hate doing it, but hope it will do good.'[41] Yet, neither the House of Commons nor the general public responded in kind, although the writer C. E. Montague believed the king's action had improved his standing with the working class, finding that 'The one good word that the average private had for bestowal among his unseen "betters" during the latter years of the war was for the King. "*He* did give up his beer" was said a thousand times by men whom that symbolic act of willing comradeship with the dry throat on the march and the war-pinched household at home had touched and astonished.'[42] Even in the cabinet only Kitchener gave up alcohol in response.[43] It appears there were limits to the extent to which the monarchy could now influence subjects' behaviours. Moreover, the whole issue highlighted the differing degrees of sacralised and modernised views of monarchy that coexisted and jockeyed for dominance during this period: Margot Asquith reported that when Queen Alexandra's old Court Chamberlain enquired of Lord Lincolnshire as to whether 'the PM and his household' were 'following the King's lead', Lincolnshire replied that 'it is not the PM's place to follow the King's lead, but for the King to take a lead from the PM'.[44]

Yet, to focus on the king giving up alcohol and luxurious foods for the war solely as an effort to change subjects' behaviours misses some of its meaning. It was also to ensure the monarchy did not appear privileged, to convey its sharing in war sacrifice, and this dimension of the King's Pledges was successful. They were about reframing the image of the royal body to communicate a *moral* sharing of national sacrifice. This had strong religious dimensions. It was surely no coincidence that among the most positive responses to the king's abstinence pledge occurred at the United Methodist Church conference in 1915, which sent a pledge of loyalty to the monarch, giving 'devout thanks to Almighty God for the high ideals of the royal House'; Methodists could sign a personal King's Pledge abstinence card, which encouraged them to follow the monarch's example.[45] The royal body was being used in a symbolic wartime intercession for the nation and empire, reflecting the king and queen's religious belief system that the outcome of the war was in divine hands and victory had to be merited by ensuring God's favour through moral behaviour. For example, on 7 November 1917, the king declared that 'victory will be gained only if we steadfastly remember the responsibility which rests upon us, and in a spirit of reverent obedience ask the blessing of Almighty God upon our endeavours'.[46] George V's pledges were profoundly linked to cultures of sacralisation around monarchy, invoking older English religious languages about physical mortification of the flesh leading to spiritual renewal and divine favour, combined with the symbolism of the king's 'dual' body as both a physical and a national entity. The king's physical body, sacrificing, doing penance, as a way of keeping faith with the symbolic national body, that of king and people, which was in war crisis, signified an almost puritan, spiritual gesture by the monarch that suggested a supplication of God for victory in return. This had powerful overtones to a public largely still literate in the King James Bible. The Royal Pledges' intention to also 'mortify' British subjects in a social sense, by shaming them into following the king's example and also abstaining, and sacrificing luxuries, cannot be understood without recognising their deeper religious context.[47]

Such meanings surface in a 1916 letter from Lord Halifax, in Randall Davidson, the Archbishop of Canterbury's papers, calling for even greater royal public penance. 'We have all, individually and collectively, a great deal for which to repent', Halifax noted, suggesting that the 'King and Queen walk in procession to St Paul's Cathedral, accompanied by all their people; [...] let the clergy and their parishioners fall into the procession as it passes'.[48] At St Paul's 'the Miserere and the Litany would be solemnly sung'.[49] The whole event would be 'a National act which would impress the whole world and secure the blessing of God'.[50] Stamfordham and the Archbishop of Canterbury rejected the idea as 'Medievalism'; Stamfordham even feared the king would react cynically.[51] But both knew well that this was the religious context within which royal self-sacrifice or Royal Pledges operated. Stamfordham supported the king issuing a personal appeal for a wartime National Day of Prayer in 1917 for these reasons, as it 'culminates H.M. the King's appeal to his people for a supreme effort, for greater self denial, for more strenuous physical labour by invoking their prayers in order to brace themselves to this [...] unified rally of all their resources'.[52] He was aware of an element of risk with regard to less religious parts of the population: 'will the fact of the King saying "let us pray" arouse a spirit of prayer in hearts where it lies dormant or does not exist at all? It is fair to assume that a certain number of people are praying now. But will that number increase at the bidding of the King as head of the nation?'[53] In the event, there was an enormous response; the king calling his people to prayer remained powerful.[54]

How royal rationing was conveyed also echoed historic acts of royal fasting to win God's favour on behalf of the people, of royalty 'embodying' the nation in renouncing luxurious foods for its well-being. The direct spiritual connection being invoked by the King's Pledges was that of the *Patria* as a united 'body politic', with king and people one shared body in combining in these actions of sacrifice. George V was clearly conscious of this at the point when he renounced alcohol for the duration of the war. He told the Prime Minister's wife Margot Asquith in April 1915 that he felt that he had been 'sold', as he had intended his action of giving up alcohol would be backed up by 'drastic' government legislation which would have ensured that he and his subjects abandoned alcohol *together*.[55] He was very aware of the meaning he wanted the Pledge to convey, informing her that 'he wanted to say he was ready to share the sacrifices of the poorest of his subjects'.[56] Royal Pledges were always about the royal body expressing the collective sacrifice of the body politic.

This also helps explain why the wartime King's Pledges went hand in hand with gestures of royalty 'feeding' the people symbolically and literally. Queen Mary, for her part, was frequently depicted in the press in roles that involved handing out food or tea to the public, as was Queen Alexandra, both portrayed as mothering the people by feeding them. In press accounts of these events, which often involved feeding ordinary soldiers at recreation huts or train stations, we find a focus not only upon the royal body as physically nurturing its people, which clearly has a metaphorical dimension to it, symbolising the state, but also upon the novelty – which the press emphasised – of the inversion of class norms, with detailed descriptions of royal women serving in menial waitress roles, a phenomenon which started in 1915 and well predated fears of revolution.[57] Thus, although after 1917 these events were often about giving the monarchy a more accessible and democratic image, they also drew on older ideas of it as part of a just, paternalist, national and imperial order, that took care of its subjects, and traditional well-established notions of royal largesse to the needy, as well as on sentimental, highly gendered narratives of royal femininity as Christian and charitable which dated back well into the Victorian period and earlier. The very real, radical element of these wartime gestures of royal women mingling with working-class populations and serving them food was thus packaged in quite sacralised older concepts of royal grace. The fact of consuming food that had been touched by royalty was a powerfully intimate act, uniting the royal body and that of the subject in quite a dramatic tangible way; this helps to explain the degree of press coverage it received. It became a well-established war phenomenon from 1915 and so raises questions about how the war was reshaping the connection between the royal body and that of the subject from very early on, drawing on older, sacralising ideals about monarchy.

The press emphasised how these events saw royal women joining in with ordinary soldiers and workers: Queen Mary was described as serving dinner at Windsor public kitchen in 1917 to 'working men and women', and as 'waitress' behind the counter at a Stepney communal kitchen in 1917.[58] In

December 1918, Queen Alexandra and Princess Victoria distributed presents and food to repatriated prisoners of war at London Bridge Station.[59] If one takes into account the communal meaning of sharing food as well as the Protestant religious meaning of Holy Communion – as communing together – the power of these gestures becomes clearer, as very close forms of engagement with ordinary people.[60] These occasions were also designed to show the female royals as empathetic and caring: while serving food at Stepney, Queen Mary was given a bouquet by 11-year-old Mary Mitchell, who had witnessed her mother and small niece being killed in an air raid just a fortnight earlier.[61] Queen Mary visiting Stepney so soon after the raid was clearly intended to show the royals as caring for East End Londoners in response to the attack, an act of public sympathy.

The king and queen thus deprived their own bodies while symbolically feeding those of their subjects. Sacrifice was thereby projected as a spectrum that connected all quarters of society; it made the king metaphorically one with his people. Such sacrificing *together* was a form of spiritually communing, a fact not lost on a still largely theologically literate Anglican population and their king, who took his religious role as Defender of the Faith seriously. It also physically conveyed that the monarch wished to share his people's suffering. For George V, his gestures of minor bodily sacrifice in this way honoured the soldiers' far greater sacrifice in battle and showed solidarity with home front shortages. In its ongoing wartime asceticism, service and work ethic, the king's body was portrayed in terms of imitating the 'servant' king, invoking religious and priestly meanings. This reflected the zeitgeist: serving soldiers were bombarded with propaganda that likened war death to a fulfilment of Christian duty and a sacrifice that imitated that of Christ.[62] Such ideas would outlive the war: as Philip Murphy points out, Cosmo Lang, who became Archbishop of Canterbury in 1928, emphasised that the monarchy must put 'duty before personal happiness: the central motif was therefore one of self-sacrifice following in the steps of Christ himself'.[63]

This helps explain the extent to which the Royal Pledges were enforced: royal palaces took war frugality to the extreme, well beyond the norm in aristocratic British homes.[64] Royal chef Gabriel Tschumi wrote of 'austerity, food shortages, restrictions on the use of sugar, butter, eggs and wine and the absence of variety in royal meals' and meat allowed to be served only three times a week to the royal family and household on Queen Mary's orders; this, at a court, where pre-war guests had enjoyed meals of thirteen courses.[65] Marmalade was restricted to a few mornings a week; the menus were dominated by vegetable pies.[66] Frederick Ponsonby's account is instructive: he stated that the food was measured to the extent that 'there was just enough and no more for everyone' so that if anyone helped themselves a little too generously there would be none remaining for any latecomer.[67] When Captain (later Sir) Bryan Godfrey-Faussett, equerry to the king, arrived late to breakfast and found no food left and 'rang the bell and asked for a boiled egg', the monarch 'accused him of being a slave to his inside, of unpatriotic behaviour, and even went so far as to hint that we should lose the war on account of his gluttony'.[68] The idea of being a slave to the body and the use of the term gluttony, associated with sin, highlights the king and queen's attitudes that being abstemious and repressing physical need in wartime was morally and spiritually virtuous; their meagre menu was a shock to many of their wartime guests and long preceded the government introduction of a Public Meals Order restricting extravagance in entertaining large groups, which only came in the last year of the war.[69]

By 1917, the king was also insistent that 'everybody' in Windsor work the land for two hours each afternoon as part of the drive to produce foodstuffs: 'he and the Queen and all in the Castle' took part.[70] This was a specifically wartime understanding of the relationship between the royal body and the *Patria*, particularly the body of the soldier, serving and dying for it: peacetime poverty, which saw subjects die from starvation or, in parts of the empire, famine, did not trigger this kind of royal discomfort about wealth and luxury. Even if the king and queen had been very concerned from the outset of their reign with the living standards of the poor, they did not cut back on food and drink in the royal palaces in response.[71] War was different. Food was rationed at the palaces to the extent that when Princess Mary visiting France after the Armistice was given a cream pudding to eat, her official biographer related that she 'could not restrain her glee' as she had not had such a treat for so long.[72]

However limited George V's wartime sacrifices may appear today, in the context of European monarchy lifestyles at the time they were dramatic: in Britain, and Europe more generally, enormous hereditary privilege and luxury among elites was still the norm before the outbreak of war. Even during the conflict, George V's actions, for example, were in marked contrast to those of the kaiser's sons, who retained luxurious lifestyles; caviar continued to be served at the Prussian court.[73] Compared with the Hohenzollerns, the British royals at war were a model of economy, Crown Prince Wilhelm and his wife Cecilie thinking it appropriate to build their own new palace with over 170 rooms, the Cecilienhof, at Potsdam, during the last two years of the conflict, at a time when German civilians were starving. The pre-war British monarchy had not been without its extravagances: one wartime economy was that Queen Alexandra, King George's mother, who lived in Sandringham Palace, had her budget for flower arrangements in every room reduced.[74] However, its wartime austerity was dramatic. By contrast, in 1917 the kaiser was spending most of his time at Bad Homburg, a Hohenzollern castle in Germany, where he lived in a luxurious manner which was 'hardly distinguishable from peacetime Court life'.[75] The head of the Civil Cabinet criticised the 'peacetime and holiday atmosphere' at court.[76]

The narratives of royal bodily sacrifice, solidarity and sacralisation which the king and queen so successfully performed were much more difficult for their heir, the future Edward VIII. He also tried to practice bodily mortification in symbolic ways during his period serving as a staff officer in France, but proved unable to sustain this. Indeed, the wartime social and cultural expectations that existed to uphold the image of the 'perfect' royal body appear to have badly affected him; he was trapped between these symbolic scripts of the royal body and the realities of life as a Western Front officer where smoking, drinking hard and, in some cases, visiting prostitutes were used as coping mechanisms to deal with the stress of war service. As a young man on the Western Front, Edward faced particular challenges with regard to how to integrate sexual desire into the cultural expectations of the royal wartime body as self-denying, virtuous, moral and disciplined. His insecurities were aggravated due to his short stature and his youthful appearance, as well as the fact that on leaving for France at the age of 20, he had virtually no experience with women and was extremely shy around girls of his own age – his 1914 diary barely mentions girls, except from a far-off distance. Eyewitnesses he encountered in France often described him as a boy: Leo Amery described how, on a visit by the king and the Prince of Wales in 1914 to a staff lunch, 'the P. of W. looked more of a child than ever' (as illustrated in Fig. 21).[77]

He was often viewed as a boy among men by both his colleagues and the troops. C. E. Montague described the Prince of Wales at Cassel as 'blond, infantine, rather lassitudinous, with enigmatic light-coloured eyes'.[78] In November 1914, still adjusting to life in France, the prince wrote in his diary: 'I feel a bit lonely. Papa may come out on Monday!!'[79] The young prince was relieved to see his father during the king's first visit to his troops in the field: 'it is grand his coming out', he wrote in eager anticipation, and he spent hours helping the king in his room with work during the visit.[80] This shows a degree of affection between the father and son, which, as the conflict continued, coarsening Edward's character, would disintegrate. The king's departure left him rather down: 'sad it's Papa's last evening', he wrote on 4 December 1914, and the next day he commented on how he was 'very sorry to take leave of Papa'.[81] The British press described the lonely figure of the Prince of Wales, saluting his father's ship before it sailed for Britain; the Daily Express reported: 'a very boyish little figure standing alone in the rain on the quayside'.[82]

Some of Edward's behaviour almost appears as if he sought to punish his body, for its royal status and divinely ordained, predestined future kingship. Not allowed to fulfil his desire to fight at the front because, as the royal heir, his sacralised body was seen as too valuable to risk, Edward pushed himself physically to the utmost limit – his obsession for punitive daily runs, which saw him run alone in military areas behind the lines for at least half an hour most mornings around 6 or 7 a.m., led to concerns about his well-being.[83] He also limited his food intake to a degree that alarmed observers.[84] All of these

H. R. H. the Prince of Wales in the garden of the Chateau which was his Headquarters in France.

Fig. 21   HRH the Prince of Wales in the garden of the chateau which was his Headquarters in France, NAM 2001-02-256-11 (© The National Army Museum, London. Image reproduced courtesy of the Council of the National Army Museum, London)

efforts reveal a young man seeking to test the limits of his wartime body and to disentangle it from its sacralised protected royal bodily status. Edward resented his body being national symbolic property: for instance, he clashed strongly with his father when he refused to wear the ribbons of the French and Russian Orders that he had been awarded because he felt he had not earned any decorations in battle and so his uniform should be unembellished like that of any other officer who had not earned a decoration; his father ordered him to 'get both ribbons sewn on your khaki at once'.[85] When, in March 1916, the Prince of Wales was told that he was to be sent to Egypt and away from the Guards Division on the Western Front, he was so angry that he *replied rather tartly to the King, and refused to speak to him for several days*.[86] He pursued anonymity at the front to extreme degrees: on one occasion in 1915, during one of his solitary runs near the headquarters of the Guards Division, he was 'held up as a spy by 6 fucking Frenchmen until rescued by a couple of Irish

Guardsmen; I only hope this never gets out!!'[87] On another occasion, in
July 1916, Edward accidentally ran over a French cyclist near the front; he
got the man medical aid and brought him to a French military hospital and was
greatly relieved that his anonymity meant that no one recognised him.[88]
Edward's experience of serving on the Western Front greatly disillusioned
him with regard to ideals of duty and sacrifice, and indeed, kingship itself: after
one narrow escape from shelling on 3 June 1917, Edward returned to his base,
only to be told off by his commanding officer for 'not reading the papers &
taking no interest in World politics!! Of course he is right really & I dont [sic]
attempt to be P of W or prepare for being so, but how I hate all that sort of
thing & how unsuited I am for the job!!'[89] By July of the same year, he stopped
bothering to keep a diary.

For Edward, his royal body was already fragmenting under the pressure of
the war as he experienced huge and upsetting contradictions between his
valuable sacred royal heir identity and his desire to be a young First World
War combatant like his peers and act out the same demanding social scripts of
wartime maleness as they did. Shelling, with its risks of physical disintegration,
ironically also provided him with a fantasy of bodily integrity, as during such
moments he became a combatant like everyone else, albeit briefly, before he
had to return to his staff officer place of safety. Prohibited from a direct combat
role, regularly seeking out shelling was the only means open to Edward to
prove his physical masculine bravery and his strength of nerve, both to his
peers and to himself. For example, on 31 December 1915 he wrote of how,
while watching an artillery strafe from an observation post, he had to take
refuge in a dugout:

> Very good shooting too but then the Boche gave us a few in return [. . .].
> The shelling at the O.P. was fucking while it lasted and I was terrified; but
> it did me worlds of good and it is the best tonic I know!! Would that I got it
> more often for one is apt to get uppish otherwise; it fairly puts one in one's
> proper place!![90]

The sexual language was no accident. The punishment of the royal flesh
described here – 'The shelling [. . .] was fucking' – deliberately elides sex,
punishment and violence. It was a marked contrast to his parents, who
repressed all expression of their sexuality, even in their private diaries.

Edward's wartime role enhanced his popularity but had a formative, coarsening effect on his personality. The young idealist of 1914, who was patriotic,
innocent of women and shy, and who, before leaving for war, had often spent
evenings reading with his father, during his war service became a man who
based his masculinity on machismo, a degree of misogyny and an obsession
with bravado, increasingly alienated from his family. The prince's partying
when on leave during the war became part of this desire to escape his royal
status.[91] Like many troops in France, he frequently witnessed unburied corpses

near the front and became accustomed to the sight.[92] Although he drank less often than his peers, he joined in the communal drinking sessions in the officers' mess, frequently alcohol-fuelled occasions to let off steam for officers shortly due to go up the line to the front. Edward also encountered a new, rakish friendship circle, including Piers Legh and the Duke of Westminster. As the war went on, Edward's closest bond shifted away from his family to his officer comrades: indeed, on 20 December 1916, Edward postponed his leave so as to avoid being in London at the same time as the rest of his family over Christmas: 'I simply couldn't arrive in London to find the family there!!'[93]

In particular, the war introduced Edward to the sexual objectification of women. He wrote on 12 December 1915 of how 'Alby Cator showed us the famous panel of a cupboard which he & others have artistically decorated with obscene pictures of women etc. cut out & pieced together.'[94] By December 1916, his diary evidence shows that he had, partly through the help of his new officer friends, become involved with a French prostitute named Paulette, the mistress of an RFC officer.[95] In April 1917, he began an affair with the courtesan Marguerite Alibert in Paris.[96] Indeed, there is evidence to suggest that, as the war went on, Edward saw the sexual objectification of lower-class women as a way to further compensate for his inability to prove his masculinity to his friends through combat. Writing of his leave in London to his friend Captain Cecil Boyd-Rochfort in May 1917, he recalled: 'A little of the English tart goes a very long way and they aren't a patch on the French ones are they?'[97] During his visit to the Italian front, he wrote of how 'these Italian women are the ugliest collection of bitches I've ever seen and I've hardly seen a fuckable one yet tho I've spent a few hrs in several large towns tho. no time to have a really good look around! So I haven't quite given up hope yet [...].'[98]

The war's impact on Edward's view of women is also clear in a 'filthy French story' he repeated in a September 1918 letter to Mrs Freda Dudley Ward, with whom he had started a romantic affair the same year. The 'story' is, in fact, a joke about rape and venereal disease: 'Un Boche viola une jeune Française dans le pays envahi; après il la dit: "Je vous ai torpillé." Elle répond: "Oui, mais c'est vous qui va couler."!!!' [A Boche raped a young French girl in the occupied territory; afterwards, he said to her: 'I have torpedoed you.' She replies: 'Yes, but it's you who is going to sink.'][99] Edward in this letter reveals a state of mind that is overwhelmed by the war violence around him; the joke is hardly suitable material for a love letter.[100] The retelling of the joke suggests that, removed from London on the Western Front, Edward was losing a sense of normal moral and gendered conventions. While risqué jokes about sex were not unheard of between upper-class men – and indeed married women – in British aristocratic circles at the time, and while ribaldry about the sexual proclivities of French women were part of First World War British army culture, venereal disease was another matter. Likewise, the outrage expressed in 1914 at the 'rape' of 'poor little Belgium', in Britain, and in much of international public opinion, rendered telling a joke about the *rape* of a woman by a German soldier of occupation, to a British lady, notably transgressive behaviour.

Edward's sexual obligations as heir and his newly developing sexual life as an insecure staff officer were, at this point, in complete contradiction: the latter, however, offered a way to compensate for his sense of emasculation at not being allowed to fight.[101] There was an obvious clash being set up here for Edward between the anointed monarchical role his father was presenting of sacrifice, piety, fidelity and physical asceticism and his heir's burgeoning, and increasingly feckless, sexuality. The idea of the priestly function of the royal body – embodying the national war sacrifice, calling National Days of Prayer to supplicate God to save the nation – increasingly constrained how royal war-time sexuality could be depicted, and clashed directly with the developing character of the heir. Excluded from combat, Edward was condemned to never be able to prove his honour as a subject of his monarch. With so many men dead as a result of the conflict by 1917, this was one factor that provoked a sense of terrible masculine inadequacy, self-hatred, guilt and incompleteness in one who had been raised steeped in the old Edwardian honour-culture world. When Edward suffered a nervous breakdown in 1920 during his post-war trip to Australia, it was hushed up and universally attributed to the strains of the tour; yet it may well also have been delayed PTSD from the war experience.[102]

Edward's changed wartime character had to be kept hidden from the public. The image of a morally pure royal family was carefully protected during the war: in 1915, Lord Stamfordham contrived to prevent the sale of love letters from the late Edward VII to one of his mistresses, fearing the letters would reveal 'corruption around the court . . . precipitating a constitutional crisis'.[103] The woman concerned was placed under surveillance, and a helpful inter-mediary who paid off her debts was knighted the following year.[104] Ironically, Edward was developing harsher, callous wartime sexualised attitudes at the same time that the press and his family in Britain began to look for him to marry an Englishwoman. In April 1916, Lord Stamfordham quizzed the Bishop of Chelmsford about his views on whether 'the P[rince] of W[ales] ought to marry a foreign Princess or the daughter of an English nobleman'.[105] The Bishop replied that 'if a wise choice was made the country would rather he married an English girl. [. . .] Germany was out of [the] question and religion came in to Russia and again that it must be remembered that the next thirty years would be trying for the Crown [. . .].'[106] An arranged marriage with a European royal for the Prince of Wales – a norm before 1914 – was rendered impossible by the war. With the German royal dynastic marriage market now inaccessible, and popular attitudes to royalty changing, in 1917 George V declared that British royals were no longer obliged to marry members of other royal families; this opened up the opportunity for his children to marry

British aristocrats instead, a popular move which, some press asserted, would dissociate the monarchy from its German ethnic heritage and further increase its Englishness.[107] Princess Mary would be the first to do so in 1922. The war also eased the welcome for her future husband, Lord Lascelles, with the king informing the Privy Council of his 'greatest satisfaction' that Lascelles was an Englishman and had such a distinguished war record.[108]

The royal couple's second son, Prince Albert, also appears to have found the burden of expectations around royal moral perfection hard to bear in wartime. He took the virtues of stoicism, bravery, self-sacrifice and not complaining extremely seriously, and this created enormous pressure. He endured appalling stomach aches while serving in the Royal Navy during the war. The historian Michael Roper has highlighted the extent to which references to stomach problems often appeared in First World War soldiers' letters as a means of conveying anxiety – stomach ache was often both physical and psychological.[109] Prince Albert was indeed suffering from a physical ailment, a duodenal ulcer – and was operated on successfully – but the immense mental strain he was under to perform his royal role in war impeccably, despite the fear and danger of battle, clearly also aggravated his health issues – stomach ulcers are closely linked to stress. Both of the royal couple's two older sons found it more difficult to cope with the wartime cultural scripts of the moral, superlatively sacrificing royal body than their parents did.

3.3   The 'Perfect' Wartime Female Royal Body

Ideas about the purity of the physical body reflecting that of the body politic have a long history and have been the focus of anthropological study.[110] In the Great War, it is evident that such discourses of royal physical and moral perfection were also highly gendered. This had, of course, long been a big part of the popular appeal of monarchy to different sections of the population. As Imke Polland has pointed out, how Queen Alexandra dressed was a factor in how the monarchy sustained public, and particularly female, popular interest.[111] The idea of the 'perfect', pristine, decorative and immaculate, bejewelled queenly body upon which honour and purity and the wealth of the empire were displayed and projected was evident well before the Great War. The war did not change this. In contrast to King George V, whose khaki-uniformed body was used to promote a military wartime identity that clearly *differed* to peacetime press depictions of him which showed him in dress uniform, full royal regalia or country wear, Queen Mary's visual style did not change in wartime: photographs continue to show her in full Edwardian dress and accessories with no obvious concessions to wartime simplicity or ease of movement.

Queen Mary's careful continuity of dress with pre-war queenly standards of long skirts, high necklines, parasols and wide-brimmed decorative hats illustrated the need to preserve female modesty and conservative physical covering of the female royal body. Her feminine dress was emphasised in images alongside the king's militarised clothing. In fact, Queen Mary's press image was even softened, depicted as more feminine and maternal, from the outbreak of the conflict. Before the war, the gender demarcations in depictions of the royal couple had been more blurred. Countess Airlie, her lady-in-waiting, lamented that, in her view inaccurately, the pre-war press had portrayed Queen Mary as dominating her husband: 'There was never a more false conception of Queen Mary than as a *maîtresse femme*, dominating her husband – a myth which for some reason or other was created about the time of the Coronation [...]'.[112] Yet wartime press reports downplayed this sterner, more assertive image of the queen, emphasising her sensitivity and caring nature. If King George V adopted a more martial wartime image, Queen Mary continued the pre-war feminine norm of *display* of queenly splendour, the regal decorative dimension of the female royal body, which was somewhat anachronistic in a 1914–18 Britain – and royal family – that emphasised wartime frugality. Fig. 22, taken from a royal wartime Christmas card, shows Queen Mary in full courtly dress alongside an image of George V in military uniform.

Such images of the king and queen were common in the First World War, formally displayed on the walls of private homes and offices as well as in public buildings, including schools, libraries and town halls, creating a formal visual royal presence in intimate, as well as public, spaces. The royals encouraged this visual practice – in January 1915, Queen Mary gifted an autographed 'picture of herself and the King' to hang in a YMCA hut for troops at Boulogne.[113] The image of the king in war uniform was thus a feature of the domesticisation of the war on the home front, drawing on George Mosse's point that material objects could help integrate war cultures into daily life; the queen's feminine outfits only served to emphasise the king's wartime martial clothing.[114]

Queen Mary's continuation of pre-war royal norms is revealing. The First World War is usually acknowledged as a point of transition. Gender historiography has often interpreted it as a conflict which changed gender norms, with ideas such as the 'steel man' emerging in Germany in tandem with the industrialisation of the battlefield, for example, or the advent of the concept of the 'new woman'.[115] The depiction of the 'new woman', which overlapped with the later interwar image of the flapper, was an idea that articulated the sense of disruption caused by the visibly new, public roles of the female body, working in manual labour in wartime industry, driving and wearing shortened skirts, factory overalls or having short hair.

In historiography on the body, the war is also seen as a point of change from highly formal cultures of the body to more informal ones. Before the conflict, cultural norms regarding the display of the body in Britain were highly formal – public physical interactions were carefully ritualised affairs, a physical

Fig. 22   The king and queen's Christmas card to the troops, 1914, NAM 1999-11-149
(© The National Army Museum, London. Image reproduced courtesy of the Council of
the National Army Museum, London)

conservatism that spanned class differentials. From doffing caps, raising
bowler hats, saluting, handshakes, polite kisses or bows, acceptable volume
and style of speech, a wide range of intricate formal practices and unwritten
rules framed social interactions.[116] Formal cultural body norms were particularly visible in dress: for both men and women the head was usually hidden by
a hat in public and female hair had to be pinned up and contained once past

childhood. There were particular conservative mores around being seen undressed.[117] Drinking tea or eating in public was similarly formal, bounded by a complex range of rules that varied by class and gender. Unmarried middle- and upper-class young girls were constantly chaperoned outside the home.[118]

The monarchy epitomised such pre-1914 formal cultures of the body in public. In the late Victorian and Edwardian period, monarchy had increasingly been associated with luxury, beauty and elegance and with the royal body being clean, neat and in this way constantly highly differentiated from the dirt, disease and squalor of the poverty of so many of its subjects. Royalty not only embodied hierarchy; they also controlled the bodies of their subjects through deferential rules of behaviour: King George V asked John Watts-Ditchfield to shave off his moustache upon being made a bishop. Watts-Ditchfield complied, describing it as a 'wrench' but noting 'after the King's wish what could I do'.[119] As late as 1917, the Bishop of Chelmsford reported how, at Windsor, 'we all took off our hats' when the royal family appeared.[120] At the reception he attended no one could sit, because the king chose to remain standing; General William Robertson was so exhausted by this that he said that he would 'pay to lean against a chair'.[121]

Thus, the wartime role of royal women offers valuable insights into how these formal pre-1914 cultures of the body altered or adapted in response to the war. In some respects, it challenges the historiography that the war brought change. Royal femininity is one area where we see continuity with pre-war sacralisation of the British monarchy. Queen Mary's image upheld pre-war ideals of the female royal body as immaculate, inviolate, constantly perfectly groomed. Royal women's wartime physical description continued to be used to promote a range of virtues and associate these with the idea of Britishness that the royals embodied.[122] Unmarried royal women were depicted in an idealised fashion that frequently suggested virginal purity and sensitivity. The married royal woman was stylish, tidy and neat and often publicly portrayed as a paragon of virtues bordering on the saintly; for example, the term 'beloved' was used in the title of one biography of the dowager Queen Alexandra, echoing an older religious language of sainthood.[123] Married royal women were, however, at least permitted some idiosyncrasies of character in their press depictions; by contrast, unmarried female royals were narrated in often identical ways as chaste, sweet and sheltered. But both the married and unmarried female body was bounded by constraining cultural frameworks – moving gracefully, tidy hair and clothes, constrained in ways that ensured it was almost homogeneous in the interchangeable descriptions afforded to queens and princesses in the British press.

In both pre-war and wartime depictions, the real physicality of the female body – its illnesses, sexual desires, hunger, pregnancies or even tiredness – was deliberately completely subsumed under a slew of standardised acceptable descriptions and, in particular, accounts of royal women's clothing.[124] The idea of cleanliness – the clean female royal body – was a central symbolic trope to all such reportage and photography. 'Clean' meant unsullied either physically or metaphysically, without moral stain. In the pre-war period, conformity to the sexual mores of royal life, such as submitting to the dynastic, arranged, marriage, was part of how female royals were portrayed – even if the dynastic marriage was invariably sentimentalised as a love match in the press.[125] The royal body epitomised class success, breeding and wealth. It was presented as a lofty, unattainable model of perfection, and this image of the body was an integral part of royal power.

Yet, if these sacralising continuities remained between the pre-war and wartime depiction of the female royal body and its femininity, the locations *where* these royal women were depicted, and the scenes they were associated with, shifted dramatically. During the war, royal women visited, saw and indeed touched bleeding, dying, coughing and incontinent men during hospital visits, as well as shell-shocked war victims. In some ways, this juxtaposition – between royal body and modern war context – only served to enhance the image of female royal cleanliness and pristineness. Yet, in other respects it blended the sacralised royal feminine image with the modernity of total war and modernising change in the status of women.

The First World War placed new demands upon female royals due to the changing expectations of British women at war more generally. Royal women also adopted more informal conduct, serving food to servicemen, for example. The war also led to more blurring of gender boundaries in the kinds of actual work that royals did. With women of all classes taking up war work in support of the war effort, expectations of royal women's work too changed. The initial charitable mobilisation of royalty in the first half of the war established a broader trend: royal women were attributed traditional feminine caring characteristics in wartime in press discourses that depicted them as 'mothering' or caring for the nation and empire at war. Yet, in fulfilling these wartime caring roles, royal women would come into new contact with the population – and with the physical body of the subject – that went far beyond any pre-1914 norm and often challenged royal taboos around dirt, mud, illness and danger. Queen Mary's role as the model of perfect queenly femininity was thus sustained throughout the war against a backdrop of major social change, including for royal women. Indeed, some of the emphasis on Queen Mary's traditional image may even have been in reaction to the wider public fears and concerns that gender changes – such as women's wartime munitions work – raised. Continuities of dress and image hid changes in royal female practices – and indeed may thereby have facilitated them.

As the war went on, female royals were allowed to break free of their usual spheres of action to a remarkable extent, particularly when they emphasised the importance that they should reach out to women subjects doing war work.

The war legitimised allowing royal women to go to new locations to minister to their female subjects, in the guise of inspiring the female subjects of state and empire in their work for the war effort – factories, shipyards, asylums for the shell-shocked, even the Western Front, sites which would previously have been off-limits to them.[126] Princess Marie Louise of Schleswig-Holstein, Queen Victoria's granddaughter, set up and personally ran her own hospital in Bermondsey.[127] Princess Mary between 1916 and 1918 did stints serving food and washing up in a munitions factory canteen at Hayes, together with twenty other upper-class ladies from Windsor; the factory girls even presented her with a special shell by way of thanks, illustrating the integration of war violence into everyday rituals of royalty subject interactions even for female royals.[128]

Yet, any change had to be carefully presented as part of traditional conservative understandings of royal femininity. Within days of the war's outbreak, Queen Mary issued an Appeal to the Women of the Empire, announcing her Queen Mary's Needlework Guild would provide comforts for the troops.[129] In 1915, she requested of the Colonial Office (CO) that it report to her on voluntary war work done by women in the colonies.[130] The Colonial Office was reluctant. A series of CO minutes noted that

> The voluntary work done by women of the Empire outside these islands will presumably not be very large in comparison with the voluntary work which women have done here – as the class of leisured women outside these islands is comparatively small.[131]

The writer doubted the value of trying to get this information. Another minute recorded that 'It will give a lot of trouble to collect the information and if published it will probably be used as a weapon in the feminist controversy after the war. I do not suppose HM would wish that.'[132] Traditional royal female patronage of voluntary charitable endeavours was acceptable; anything potentially promoting feminism was not.

The tension between the Victorian-Edwardian image of purity of the female royal body and the dirt and physical horrors of war was most evident in the visits to the Western Front battlefields by Queen Mary and Princess Mary, which created a new level of juxtaposition of royal female bodies, war dirt and grime. In July 1917, Queen Mary was finally allowed her wish to visit the battlefields, permitted to accompany King George V on his tour of the Western Front that year, although for much of the visit the two pursued separate itineraries. Immediately after the Armistice, Princess Mary would tour Ypres and its hinterland.[133] This posed real challenges. How to continue to present an image of immaculate royal female cleanliness during total war, when, in support of the war effort, the royal family were now expected to visit places which would previously have been out of bounds to queens and princesses? Western Front mud was contaminated with bodily remains, faeces, dead horses and rats; walking through it brought royalty into intimate contact with the flesh and blood of the soldiers who were dying for them at the front. Royal visits to front hospitals likewise brought them close to bodily fluids, blood and pus, and, on occasion, lice. Western Front landscapes were also far grittier, dirtier and, indeed, more dangerous than those royal women had ever been let tour in pre-war Edwardian society. They also faced danger from shelling or munitions lying around, although wartime visits to home front shell factories too were not without some risk of explosion.

The royal responses to this challenge of battlefield filth and mud were very strongly gendered. The wartime masculine visual image of the king emphasised his closeness to the mud and horror of the trenches. Both the king and the Prince of Wales witnessed the unburied dead on the battlefield and touched the earthen defence works and polluted, unsanitary soil of the trench landscape, and this was widely commented on in the press. Edward wrote in his diary in 1915 of how

> There were a few bodies ½ way across but nearly all were beyond 'lone tree' and up against the German wire where the MG mowed them down!! [...] Those dead bodies offered a most pathetic and gruesome sight; too cruel to be killed with a few yds of yr objective after a 300 yds sprint of death!! This was my first real sight of war and it moved and impressed me most enormously!![134]

Journalist Philip Gibbs reported how the king tried to go into an enemy dugout, only to be told by one of the generals that "'I should not go right down, Sir [...] We have not had time to clean them out yet, and they are not very wholesome." The king agreed that there was an evil smell about the place, and did not go into the very depths of it.'[135] Encountering the smell of decomposing dead bodies was part of the male royal battlefield experience. Eyewitness reports also made much of the king picking up souvenirs from the battleground and touching the soil of the Western Front; *The Times* reported that the king 'has climbed in and out of trenches which saw desperate fighting in the early days of the battle of the Somme, has gone into German dug-outs and picked up relics of the battle with his own hands'.[136] Indeed, the king himself treated such items as relics, as the mounted display from the royal collections, with each item labelled 'in his own hand', shown in Fig. 23, illustrates; the reference to the monarch having personally written the captions again illustrates the sacralisation of the royal touch. The king planned his own War Museum and for a period after the war displayed his collection of war memorabilia in Brunswick Tower at Windsor Castle in the 'King's own War Museum'.[137] The Royal Librarian, Sir John W. Fortescue, provided access to the museum to interested visitors.[138] It was disbanded in 1936 with the accession of Edward VIII.

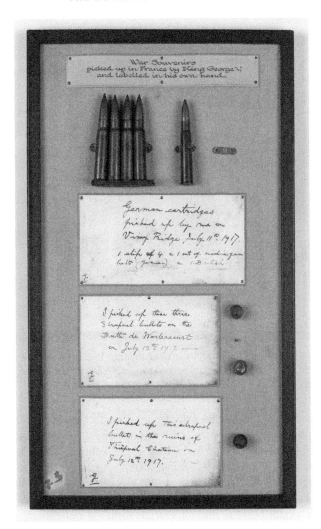

Fig. 23 Souvenirs gathered from the battlefields by George V and labelled by the king, Royal Collection Trust, RCIN 69437 (© Her Majesty Queen Elizabeth II, 2020)

By contrast, press depictions of Queen Mary at the Western Front in July 1917 avoided mentioning mud and emphasised her motherly characteristics and femininity. Indeed, she continued to dress in an extremely feminine, grand fashion, complete with large hat, and often in light-coloured clothing, in marked contrast to the women war nurses and drivers whom she met on her trip, who all wore uniform. The queen's choice of outfits, which made little concession to dressing for her surroundings, complete with elegant parasol as shown in Fig. 24, along with

Fig. 24   Matron-in-chief introduces a matron to Her Majesty, Western Front, 1917, from the Field Marshal Earl Haig Collection, National Library of Scotland, C2023 (Reproduced courtesy of the National Library of Scotland)

her similarly clad lady-in-waiting, served to mask the fact that she was remarkably close to the mud and blood of the war – during her visit she even picked up an entrenching tool that she found in the mud of the Somme – and in her hospital visits she encountered very badly injured men.[139] An entrenching tool was not only for digging trenches but also latrines and on occasion was used as a weapon; items found on the battlefield were also often possessions of the dead. The queen bringing such items home as souvenirs for the royal war museum thus remained a private matter. Her pristine public image – conveyed by her immaculate dress – remained inviolate. The incongruity of the queen's dress appears particularly starkly in Fig. 25, which shows her photographed together with the king and Prince of Wales, both in military uniform, during her Western Front visit.

It is hard not to see such conservatism as in part a public message about the moral probity of the queen; given the attacks on female royals who got their wartime sexual image wrong, like Tsarina Alexandra of Russia, imprisoned since the February Russian Revolution just months before Queen Mary's Western Front visit, such caution makes sense. The queen may well also have shared the views of Princess Marie Louise of Schleswig-Holstein, who wrote in her memoirs of how, despite running a hospital, she never wore a uniform:

Fig. 25   Queen Mary with her husband and eldest son during her visit to the Western Front, from the Field Marshal Earl Haig Collection, National Library of Scotland C2062 (Reproduced courtesy of the National Library of Scotland)

> I suppose I have the strange distinction of being one of the few women who never donned uniform – not even an overall – during either war. Not that I objected to women wearing uniform, but it just did not come my way. I took especial care when visiting my wounded friends to put on my smartest dress and hat, and the men thoroughly appreciated the compliment paid to them.[140]

We also know from the memoirs of the queen's lady-in-waiting, Countess Airlie, that King George V had decided opinions about what his wife should or should not wear, which may also have been a factor in her Western Front sartorial choices.[141] The queen was described by her lady-in-waiting as almost 'early Victorian' in her attitude to her husband: she would not even dare wear a colour he disliked, and 'her style of dressing was dictated by his conservative prejudices'.[142] Queen Mary's style on her tour was matronly even at the time: photographs of her with the younger Belgian Queen Elisabeth, whom she met during her visit, whose wartime style was far more pared down, free-flowing and modern, highlight the elaborate nature of Queen Mary's outfits.[143]

Yet the queen's style was also effective in conveying a sense of normality to some she met on her tour; it was likely even reassuring for some contemporaries that she had made no concession to the war. Frank Mort has found that the wartime 'aestheticization of leading female members of the royal family' was a way of evoking forms of patriotic royalism, particularly in women.[144] In a 1978 oral history interview, Eleanora Pemberton, who was tasked with giving the queen a tour of a Western Front sickbay unit set up for ill VAD (Voluntary Aid Detachment) nurses, recalled how Queen Mary used her umbrella as her signature royal style, as well as a practical tool: 'Eventually I took the queen in to see our quarters and the sick bay and she had, as usual, her umbrella with her and she pointed it "and what are all these little parcels?" I had to explain what all these little parcels were.'[145] Pemberton's interview also indicated the monarchism of her VADs; unwell nurses left their beds in the sickbay at news of the queen's visit: 'I hadn't any patients then because they refused to stay in bed[,] they all wanted to stand by their ambulance.'[146] Pemberton highlighted the visit as a morale boost, associating the queen with the feminine: 'all the staff, the VAD staff were all drawn up outside to be inspected by her, to be visited by her. It was very nice, she was sweet.'[147] This account supports the arguments of Mort, who found that 'nurses' wartime testimonies rarely contained any overt political critique of the monarchy as an institution', with their testimonies highlighting the ritual symbolism that royalty represented for their own 'forms of feminine identity'.[148]

Indeed, beliefs about royal femininity were the central determinants of the queen's 1917 visit. In contrast to both the king and the Prince of Wales, who were allowed to visit dangerous locations, Queen Mary's Western Front itinerary, while tiring, did not allow her to take any risks. Her diary entry on 3 July, her day of departure, describes: 'At 8.30 G. and I left for France, G. to visit the Front, I to visit hospitals.'[149] It was the king who would venture to the battle areas, while the queen, based at different locations, visited the wounded far behind the lines, and her visit was intended as a complement to that of her husband; there was no question of her visiting France without him. Indeed, prior to 1917, even her wish to accompany him had been refused, to her disappointment: she wrote in November 1914 when the king left for his first visit to his armies in the field of how she 'felt very sad' at seeing him go, as 'for all these years I have thank God been able to accompany you on all important journeys during our married life, so I feel it rather having to stay at home'.[150] In July 1917, she was also accompanied by her son, the Prince of Wales, and her brother for much of her trip to France while the king was elsewhere visiting his men; male relatives' presence, in other words, lent propriety to her tour. This highly gendered division of labour and of image was visible in one of the most prominent public commemorations of this royal visit: artist Frank O. Salisbury's mural painting 'Their Majesties, King George V and Queen Mary Visiting the Battle Districts of France, 1917', painted in 1917 and added to the mural sequence on English history at the Royal Exchange in London.[151] The top half of the mural depicts the king in uniform, in a vigorous masculine pose, atop a muddy hill, looking at the battlefield with his generals, with Haig pointing out something to him, the Prince of Wales, in uniform, standing nearby; the bottom half shows a separate scene of Queen Mary, in civilian dress, visiting the wounded in hospital, bowed over a patient.

Queen Mary spent most of her time visiting hospitals at Boulogne, Etaples, Albert, Rouen, Abbeville and Amiens, none of which in July 1917 was at particular risk, although it was emotionally demanding.[152] Her lady-in-waiting, Countess Airlie, recalled: 'We visited many hospitals – British, Australian, French, Belgian – the endless succession of beds had a terrible sameness of young faces and broken bodies. Some of them were cheerful places, clean and well-organized, but others were old and grimy Hôtels Dieu with layers of dust on the floors and the indescribable stench of death and sickness hanging in the air [. . .].'[153] By contrast, the Queen's diary generally records a positive account, emphasising her enthusiasm and excitement: 'After leaving Abbeville we had tea on the roadside and heard the guns in the distance. A most wonderful day.'[154] She was also interested at seeing Chinese labourers and German prisoners of war at work.[155] Her trip included just one visit to actual trenches, and these were old, long disused ones – at Pozières – part of the Somme battlefield of the previous summer and now far from the new German front line following the German retreat of spring 1917 to the Hindenburg defences. Sir Julian Byng gave her this tour and 'explained all about the battle where he commanded the Canadian Division. It was intensely interesting to see it all and the awful devastation. We got out and walked a little just to see the remains of the trenches and dug outs.'[156] Countess Airlie recalled it far less positively, noting that, to the sound of the guns in the distance, 'We climbed over a mound composed of German dead buried by their comrades [. . .]. Over this devil's charnel house nature had thrown a merciful veil of gently creeping plants.'[157] Airlie was disturbed by the battlefield detritus of old rifles, helmets and water bottles, 'pathetic reminders of human life', and described the queen's face as 'ashen and her lips were tightly compressed. I felt that like me she was afraid of breaking down.'[158]

Queen Mary's own account, however, mentions no emotional upset. In fact, she was keen to continue closer to the front that day. When the queen wanted to go further on to Baupaume, Byng told them it was not possible, as 'the King had spoken to him personally over the telephone and had made him promise to let us take no risks', although he did admit to her when they lunched at his headquarters that there was an unexploded shell that had landed under the floor of the room next door.[159] Although she did witness explosions from a distance, as shown in Fig. 26, she was kept well out of harm's way. Indeed, the closest she came to seeing the impact of the war was when by chance she encountered muddy troops newly arrived from the front to Boulogne: 'Had the luck to see 1,500 of our men coming back from the line and going to the rest camp at B.'[160] An internal memo in the Royal Archives confirmed that, on 4 July, 'At Wimereux her Majesty quite unexpectedly met about 1,500 men back from the Lens front on their way to the Rest Camp. They all heartily cheered after the

Fig. 26   Queen and her party witnessing some explosions, 1917, from the Field
Marshal Earl Haig Collection, National Library of Scotland, C2040 (Reproduced
courtesy of the National Library of Scotland)

Queen had talked to some of the officers and men.'[161] This encounter was
photographed, and the juxtaposition of exhausted grimy troops and the
immaculate queen made for a powerful propaganda image and implied the
queen had been closer to the front than she actually had. Her lady-in-waiting,
Countess Airlie, recounted the incident:

> One of the most important visits of the tour was to the Headquarters of
> the W[omens] A[uxiliary] A[rmy] C[orp]s. As our cars drew up there we
> were confronted with the sight of 1,500 men just detrained for a rest from
> the fighting at Sens [sic]. Covered with mud, bleary-eyed and haggard
> from fatigue, they stared blankly at us. The Queen said softly to Colonel
> Fletcher . . . 'I want to speak to those men.' There were tremendous cheers
> as she crossed over to them. [. . .] Seeing cameras being directed towards
> her she whispered to me . . . 'I suppose I shall go down to posterity
> reviewing my troops with two of my women aides-de-camp!'[162]

The quotation highlights the degree to which the queen's tour was intended to
occupy a carefully gendered feminine space, in contrast to the king. The idea of

a female royal reviewing troops was not new; Queen Victoria had carried out this role, for example. Both Queen Mary and Princess Mary were Colonels-in-Chief of regiments. What was subversive, however, was the notion of a female 'aide-de-camp', hence the emphasis in portrayals of this incident upon her femininity. Douglas Haig's response to learning of the event also reinforces this highly gendered view of her role – he said he was pleased about the encounter because it might serve to bolster the popularity of the WAACs to be seen in the queen's company, as they were, he claimed, unpopular with the soldiers.[163]

Fig. 26 also highlights again the question to what extent the royal visits to the war were a form of philanthropically minded war tourism or even war 'slumming', to employ a concept from historian Seth Koven's work. Koven has noted that, in the half century preceding the Great War,

> Britons went slumming to see for themselves how the poor lived. They insisted that firsthand experience among the metropolitan poor was essential for all who claimed to speak authoritatively about social problems. To a remarkable degree, the men and women who governed church and state in late-nineteenth- and twentieth-century Britain [...] felt compelled to visit, live, or work in the London slums at some point in their careers of public service. [...] We will never know precisely how many men and women went slumming, but the fact that slums became tourist sites suggests it was a very widespread phenomenon.[164]

This trend – which had, as Koven shows, become almost a social expectation – may well have influenced the king and queen in their decision to visit industrial areas of the north of England early in King George V's new reign.[165] It also clearly reflected the wartime advice they were given by figures such as John Watts-Ditchfield, Bishop of Chelmsford, who urged them to be more visible and to visit urban working-class areas more in order to quell any rise in anti-monarchism, particularly after 1917.[166] But the idea of slumming – the expectation that society's leaders should visit those enduring hardship so as to acquire expert knowledge and thereby bolster their authority and right to speak on the problems faced by the general population – clearly also underpins the constant visits to the Western Front by politicians, writers and, indeed, royals. Figures as varied as the writer Edith Wharton, Winston Churchill and Lord Northcliffe all took tours.[167] The king's own equerry, Sir Charles Cust, gushed enthusiastically about a sightseeing trip he made to the front in October 1916: 'I met an artillery officer, Major Lyster Taylor, and asked him whether it would be possible to get a little nearer to the front line. [...] We went up Fish Alley to get there, and I could see the front trenches [...].'[168] Cust described it as 'the most interesting trip that I have ever had in my life'.[169] Lord Stamfordham wrote to the Archbishop of Canterbury in August 1916 that he was 'jealous' that the Archbishop 'went much further to the front' than he had been able to go.[170]

This is not to suggest any indifference to the suffering of war on the part of such visitors; the war maimed, dead and wounded were constantly visible. Rather, the idea of war tourism helps us to understand the degree to which contemporaries understood the conflict was an historic event – epoch-making – and wanted to witness it as part of seeing history unfold live, as well as an acknowledgement that, alongside its horrors, the Great War was also *interesting* for observers who could tour quiet or rear-area sites in relative safety, and see new technological developments, problem-solving work to overcome logistical and other challenges, and a scale of enterprise that even soldiers often found fascinating. Visits to the Western Front for VIPs were relatively common, carefully controlled and they were kept away from danger, and this was also the case for the visit of the queen in 1917 and Princess Mary just after the end of the conflict in 1918. At court, there is evidence that mental parallels were being drawn between visits to the Western Front and the king and queen's visits to northern industrial towns. Frederick Ponsonby wrote to Brigadier General Lowther, ahead of the king's trip to the Western Front in 1915, of how

> I am sending under separate cover the Royal Standard and Crown which are usually fixed to the King's motor when he goes on industrial tours. If you think they would be suitable, will you have them fixed to His Majesty's car in such a manner as to make The King's presence in the car unmistakeable?[171]

Yet, unlike other VIPs, the king was able to choose his own route and largely roamed freely by car around the front zone, including stopping at dangerous locations; the Prince of Wales also often chose to visit dangerous areas. By contrast, royal women's tours fit more closely with the pre-war 'slumming' concept and always had to strike a tentative balance with male ideals about what was suitable for royal femininity.

Queen Mary during her visit to the Western Front called at multiple hospitals, including a range of medical facilities for dominion troops and Casualty Clearing Stations and inspected various forms of war work, from hangars to ammunition dumps, railway depots, signal and machine-gun schools, ordnance stores and French women carrying out fabric repairs.[172] Her lady-in-waiting on the tour, Countess Airlie, recorded that 'It was an exhausting tour – we were often so tired at night that we could only collapse on our beds [...].'[173] Yet, Queen Mary recorded in her diary a range of tourist stops as well. On 7 July, she recorded in her diary a visit to the site of the Battle of Agincourt. The following day: 'At 2.30 we motored to where the Battle of Crecy had been fought in 1346 and saw the cross put up to the memory of John King of Bohemia. It was probably the first time that a P[rin]ce of Wales had visited the scene since Edward the Black Prince was there at the time [of] the battle.'[174] On 9 July, she toured Amiens Cathedral, and Abbeville Cathedral the following day. The itinerary for Wednesday 11 July included visiting the 'Australian general hospital, a French hospital and a wonderful Belgian institution for making artificial limbs. Drove back via Jeanne d'Arc's chapel and lunched at our chateau.'[175] Queen Mary was combining a string of intense hospital visits in which she saw wounded men – the sights of war – with the historic sites of northern France. The overlap between royal philanthropy, war tourism and ordinary sightseeing is striking and differed dramatically to the king's timetable, which included no leisure visits to historic sites. King George V even spent his wedding anniversary on this July 1917 visit away from Queen Mary, out of his sense of duty to visit as many of the soldiers at the front as possible.[176]

The gender themes visible in Queen Mary's visit to the front in 1917 were also clear in Princess Mary's only trip to the area, on 20–30 November 1918, after the war ended, as the queen's representative, specifically to see the contribution of women war workers. Her biographer of 1922, Mabel Carey, was at pains to assert that 'she had long pleaded to be allowed to go across the Channel, but had been told, like so many other girls of her own age during the war, that her duty lay at home, where she was of more use in heartening up the "rear-guard" by her presence amongst them'.[177] This exculpatory sentence effectively aims to explain why other British women went to do war work overseas while the king's daughter remained at home. On her visit, Princess Mary wore the uniform of a commandant of the VAD of the British Red Cross Society. Most of her trip was spent visiting VAD and Queen Mary Army Auxiliary Corps (QMAAC) units, hospitals and convalescent and recreation camps, as well as, like her mother, some sightseeing in Rouen of the cathedral and St Maclou and other historic sites, including where Joan of Arc was burned.[178] Again, like her parents, she brought home a collection of 'war souvenirs', some that she had discreetly picked up herself and some which were gifts from the units she visited, including both *objets d'art* and inscribed items made out of shell parts.[179] The gift-giving rituals of her visit again highlight the importance of ritual exchange of items between royals and subjects in wartime monarchist culture.

Gendered perceptions dominated Princess Mary's whole visit and its depiction. On her arrival, the girl who was meant to drive her was supplanted at the last minute by a male officer who 'was afraid to trust his royal charge to the girl driver of the Chief Controller's car, much to her chagrin'; the girl driver was deliberately humiliated in what was a clear kick back against the changes to gender roles that women's war work in France represented.[180] The following day, the princess 'entrusted herself to feminine chauffeurs' for the first time 'and she was much impressed at the absolute capability and excellent driving of the two girls'.[181] George V had had a female chauffeur drive him in Brighton in 1918; however, Princess Mary, the most sheltered of young girls, was a different matter.[182] Her supposed freedoms in France and Belgium are remarkable in highlighting how restricted her life was compared to ordinary middle- and upper-class girls of the same period. The tour saw her stay in a hotel for the first time and also her first meal in a public dining room as well as her first public speech. More daringly, she also took a short ride in a whippet tank.[183] Pains were also taken to avoid her meeting anyone unsuitable: for example, only QMAAC girls with perfect conduct-sheet records were allowed to attend the concert given in Princess Mary's honour in Rouen.[184] During her tour, the closest Princess Mary got to the former front line was when she was shown a shell hole where a Zeppelin had bombed a camp for women war workers at Abbeville in spring 1918 and when she was allowed – in an excursion added in at the last minute to her itinerary – to visit the ruins of Ypres town.[185] Yet both sites had radical, grisly associations for a young princess associated with royal purity. For the trip to Ypres, which was considered to bring the princess to the actual former front area, 'men drivers were substituted in the royal cars' to replace the women drivers yet again, as the journey was 'three to four hours [...] on incredibly bad roads, worn by perpetual heavy traffic'.[186]

In a further echo of 'slumming', the press and other contemporary accounts continually emphasised whenever any member of the royal family ate or slept in less than luxurious conditions during a Western Front visit. Princess Mary was no exception: Mabel Carey noted that the Princess and her lady-in-waiting slept in a wooden army hut one night and, at one of her stops, Princess Mary was given 'an ordinary mess lunch, with the usual rations [...] and ordinary army cutlery drawn from ordnance stores', as the Deputy Controller had 'on purpose' chosen not to get 'special silver and glass for the occasion. She guessed, and rightly, that Her Royal Highness had come out as a girl war worker and not as a Princess, and it was the chance of doing the "real thing", even in details such as these, that really appealed so much to her.'[187] The visit to France and Belgium thus allowed Princess Mary to role play at experiencing the war in the way that some other girls of her own age actually had. The fact that this meal was a performative act of 'normality' within a monarchist framework was highlighted by the fact that the cook insisted on making an extra special luxurious cream pudding, undermining the idea that the princess was just an ordinary girl.[188] Moreover, when the princess spontaneously attempted to thank the cook in person, older scripts of deference immediately reappeared, highlighting the different, segregated nature of the perfect female royal body:

> the Q.M.A.A.C. cook [...] in an agony of embarrassment hurriedly retreated behind the scullery door. But, nothing daunted, the Princess followed after her and shook hands vigorously in the neighbourhood of the sink! The cook, who had enlisted early in the war, was greatly overcome by the Princess's thanks and kind words – 'Me with my dirty apron on, and all ...' she was heard to exclaim in dismay after the royal visitor had departed.[189]

Carey's dramatic exclamation mark after the word 'sink' speaks volumes about the disruptive nature of this kind of bodily interaction between royal and subject and the need for constant wartime contextual framing to justify and render it acceptable. The war allowed these kinds of carnivalesque upturnings of social norms – the princess eating rations with ordinary cutlery, touching the 'dirty' cook and seeing the sink. It is in these purportedly transgressive or innovative details in Carey's narrative that the extremes of monarchist cultures of deference become momentarily visible. Likewise, when the female matrons of the various hospitals and heads of YMCA and Church Army clubs and canteens were presented to Princess Mary, the fact that these were older women who had contributed so much to the war effort allows Carey to state that the princess avoided any 'royal condescension' and 'with a pretty air of welcome, charged with deference [...] as the Queen's representative [...] shook hands with these elder women'.[190] As in innumerable British depictions of the war, Princess Mary, as a royal, was portrayed as superhuman, returning to London 'as fresh as when she started her tour, and [...] would have been perfectly ready to go through the crowded week all over again'.[191] Thus, the modernisation features visible here, of allowing the princess to visit France without her family in the immediate aftermath of the war, of granting greater accessibility to her, and the rhetoric about a 'modern' princess, were all still embedded within an overarching cultural discourse of sacralisation – the indefatigable, perfect, superhuman and untiring royal body and the sheltered, sweet, feminine royal girl.

3.4   The 'Perfect' English Royal Body

One final obvious aspect of the way that the 'perfect' wartime royal body was presented was in the absence of any overt negative reference to the king and queen's German ethnic origins in the first two years of the war. As their role was to perform the key moral virtues of wartime society, any reference to the German heritage of the king and queen was incompatible with their sacralised status. In fact, the case of the monarchy's German heritage is very instructive of its secure status. The previous chapters of this book have highlighted how monarchy – both as an institution and a belief system in Britain – navigated the first years of the Great War relatively successfully, sustaining, and even enhancing, its sacralised status and playing a significant role in cultural mobilisation. Perhaps one of the most important illustrations of this is the remarkable fact that, until 1917, there was practically no discussion of the royal family's German heritage. Before 1917, only a handful of fringe radical socialist papers, such as the Glasgow paper *Forward*, campaigned against the monarchy on the basis of their German connections: it pointed out in 1914 that the Civil List paid Princess Helena of Schleswig-Holstein, daughter of Queen Victoria, £6000 a year, while her son had taken the German side in the war.[192] There was so little discussion of the monarchy's German background that it was not until 1917 that the monarch felt the need to change the German name of his dynasty. This was remarkably late.

This occurred despite virulent, extreme and widespread anti-German feeling sweeping Britain with the outbreak of the war, the history of which is so well known it needs no detailed reiterating here.[193] As Catriona Pennell and Adrian Gregory have shown, it developed extremely rapidly in 1914 and was marked by spy fever, with widespread rumours of German secret agents and a spike in xenophobia against anyone of German origins, to the extent that many German businesses and migrants changed their names.[194] Indeed, the situation became so bad that a factor in the British government's internment of German males of military age in 1914 and 1915 was, in some cases, their own protection from hostile British populations.[195] In February 1915, Stamfordham wrote to the Prime Minister asking for reassurance on the government's policy on aliens and spies, which was raising disquiet 'even among calm and fair minded people'.[196] In May 1915, the United Kingdom saw its first widespread anti-German riots – the so-called Lusitania riots. Yet, the king and queen and their children – with their well-known German origins and German dynastic name Saxe-Coburg-Gotha – were exempt from this public hostility towards all things German until 1917, an indication of the sacralised untouchable status of British kingship. This did not apply to more distant royal relatives: anti-German xenophobia forced Prince Louis of Battenberg to resign from the Admiralty in 1914, for example, and King George V could do nothing to stop this or the appointment of Lord Fisher in his place, despite the king doing 'all I could to prevent it', another illustration of his hidden role in trying to influence key political appointments.[197] June 1916 saw Stamfordham suggesting denationalisation for certain British princes of the blood who were fighting with Germany – the Duke of Cumberland and the Duke of Coburg – but rejecting stripping British honours from Germans, as many British subjects also held German orders.[198] In July 1916, the cabinet advised the king to 'deprive Foreign Princes who are in arms against the Allies of their British titles and orders, and of their contingent rights of succession' in view of 'the widespread and rising feeling on the subject'.[199]

This time lag in criticising the monarchy's German heritage is all the more surprising given that Queen Mary had been born as a princess of a German principality, Teck, although, as she had been raised in Britain, she spoke English without any German accent.[200] Moreover, in the case of Russia, royal status was no protection in wartime from accusations of treachery: the Tsarina Alexandra's German origins were constantly used against her in the press and stoked significant public hostility towards her, as well as anti-monarchism.[201] In Britain, by contrast, in 1914–16 no similar phenomenon emerged towards Queen Mary, even though she was also known as Mary of Teck. Censorship, of course, played a role here, but there was no shift in press control that would explain why open discussion of the monarchy's German origins first appeared in the mainstream press in April 1917 and not in earlier years. This leads us to deduce that in the first years of the war there was no articulation of public discontent with the royal family's German name and origins because of its popularity and sacralised status. Thus, there was no impetus to change the dynastic name until 1917, when the impact of the Russian Revolution challenged existing wartime discourses about monarchy.

In fact, in the first years of the war, the king's status enabled him to frequently resist anti-German xenophobia in the United Kingdom without this triggering any public decline in his popularity or concern about his loyalties among elites. The king rejected viewing those of German heritage as automatic enemies of Britain and opposed the idea of purging royal palaces of German historic associations – hardly surprising given his own family origins, but illustrative of the exemption that kingship bestowed from the wave of popular anti-German feeling among the population. Indeed, Brigadier E. Foster Hall, invited to Windsor to be awarded the Military Cross in September 1916, was astounded to see that a marble bust of the kaiser still remained in place inside the Castle.[202] George V was notably reluctant to remove the standards of German members of the Order of the Garter from St George's Chapel at Windsor, although ultimately he did so; this issue did reveal some pressure on the monarchy. In 1917, Horatio Bottomley, the xenophobic editor of *John Bull*, which had a circulation of 300,000, would claim that in 1915 he had threatened that if the king did not 'order the banners of the Kaiser and the Crown Prince to be torn from the walls of St. George's chapel' that he would go to Windsor Castle with hundreds of thousands 'and do it for him'.[203] While the king detested German militarism, he did not initially conflate the outbreak of war with detesting everything German; his attitudes radicalised relatively slowly compared to British society as a whole. When Winston Churchill referred to the German fleet as 'rats in a hole' in 1914, George V intervened and warned him to avoid such radicalising language, again illustrating royal power, directly chastising one of his politicians and instructing how they should speak in public.[204] George V thus held to the niceties of nineteenth-century cabinet war etiquette for a considerable period after the war had started, long after popular discourses had begun presenting it as a war of peoples, stoking nationalism and presenting the whole German people as the enemy; his diary for 1914 avoids derogatory terms like 'Hun' or 'Boche'; by contrast, they appear relatively frequently in his diary for later war years.[205] In April 1915, the Palace informed the Prime Minister that 'The king yields to no one in abominating the general conduct of the Germans throughout this war', but rejected the idea of reprisals or retaliation, hoping that Britain would conduct its war 'as far as possible with humanity and like gentlemen'.[206] However, as the conflict continued the king increasingly expressed his anger in his diary at German war crimes, such as the sinking of the Lusitania, the innovation of gas warfare, poor treatment of British prisoners of war and the bombardment of British civilians on the home front and, by 1917, the king accepted the idea of reprisals.[207]

The sacralisation of the British monarchy at the outbreak of the war provided it with a protected space in which to largely ignore wartime xenophobia until 1917. The fact that the royals themselves privately clearly expressed their anger at the German way of waging war also helped their patriotic image among elites. Louis Greig, a frequent guest of the royal family, recorded that they 'do hate the huns' and were 'dying to bombard' German cities.[208] Queen Mary even told the Bishop of Chelmsford that she would rather surrender to Turks than to Germans in the wake of the fall of Kut-al-Amara.[209] Among themselves, the royals had a clear sense of British identity: King George V told the Bishop of Chelmsford in 1916 of his annoyance at learning of a collect that 'referred to England as Fatherland' and he 'would not have it – expression was German not English', but he did not object to 'Mother Country'.[210] Likewise, propaganda pitched the king's use of German to prisoners of war he encountered as humane and an example of British fairness and civilised war behaviour; it was packaged as an example of the British values of the monarchy rather than of its German connections, although this may have been war myth-making, as other sources suggest his German was rather basic.[211] George V, however, recorded in his diary on 15 September 1914 that he 'saw 65 German wounded and 7 of their officers who have just arrived, talked with some of them [...]'.[212] This was the norm whenever he encountered prisoners across the war. Stamfordham wrote to Kitchener on 14 November 1914 stating that the king 'would like to think that when this war is over it would be truly said that we had shown the example in generous and magnanimous consideration of our prisoners of war'.[213]

Even the war's impact on the reputation of the king's cousin, the German Prussian king-emperor, and his system of rule, which was depicted as tyrannical in the British press and myriad propaganda books, had little knock-on effect for the popularity of the British monarchy before 1917.[214] As Lothar Reinermann points out, 'After 1914 cartoons descended to the basest and blood-thirstiest character assassination, [...] depicting Wilhelm variously as butcher, grim reaper or the personification of death, depicted in front of burning houses, violated women, maimed children and murdered prisoners of war.'[215] Some of this was official propaganda: Britain's Ministry of Information commissioned cartoon films 'to lampoon the Kaiser', while from June 1917, Lloyd George's new propaganda agency, the National War Aims Committee, promoted the kaiser's demonic image. Kaiser Wilhelm was described in the British press as 'satanic'; propaganda animalised and pathologised him; he was even depicted as the 'Antichrist'.[216] He was also widely ridiculed.[217] It was an obvious risk for the British monarchy to have a wartime press so focused on expressing the evils of a fellow king – even if King George V shared the media's assessment of the kaiser as being at fault for the outbreak of the war, as indicated by comments in his diaries.[218] The constant denigration of 'bad' monarchism in Germany posed a risk that the public might draw parallels with all monarchism as negative, including that in the United Kingdom.[219] Tsardom also remained unpopular; King Constantine of Greece ('Tino'), a cousin of George V, was intensely disliked for his pro-German views. Indeed, the negative reputation of the pro-German Greek monarchy in Britain worried King George V, but again it ultimately did not impact on the British royals' status before 1917, when, in June, the Allies forced King Constantine into exile in Switzerland; initially the Isle of Wight was proposed, which King George V strongly opposed.[220]

Perhaps the best evidence of the degree to which the British royal family's status was protected from anti-German fervour in the first half of the war is that their links with enemy dynasties did not need to be completely severed. After Britain entered the First World War, George V never communicated in person or by letter with Kaiser Wilhelm again, believing him to be to blame for the conflict and for war crimes; Queen Mary also cut contact with the kaiser, although after George V's death in 1936 she renewed occasional correspondence with him. During the war, Queen Mary also continued to send letters to her elderly aunt, Augusta, to whom she was very close, in Mecklenburg-Strelitz in Germany via an intermediary.[221] Queen Alexandra too continued to correspond with German relatives. It was only in 1917 that this gave rise to some alarm: her daughter, Princess Louise, the king's sister, wrote to Foreign Secretary Sir Arthur Balfour that year about her concern that the Queen Mother, Queen Alexandra's letters could give intelligence to the enemy and damage the royals' popularity, if they became known:

> I know that I may write without any fear of your thinking you must answer or that what I write will not remain safe and private in your keeping and that I remain an unknown identity to all others. [...] Another thing wh. also is very private the great danger of Q. A. communications to her various relations – can you not say it is necessary that all such must pass through the Foreign Office. You might let Sir Arthur Davidson know this quietly that you consider it very important. The feeling just now is very bad and it is not possible to take too much care. Had you not better say all letters from any member of the R. family must go through the FO and of course you personally would have a right to have them privately censored or if needs be quietly retained. Pray excuse my writing this but the gravity of the situation prompts me. Pray destroy this [...].[222]

Princess Louise's concerns are indicative of the fact that 1917 marked a major shift. April 1917 saw the first significant wartime discussion of the British monarchy's German background, a shift that will be discussed in more detail in Chapter 4. It was remarkably late in the conflict. War mobilisation in 1914–16 had so successfully associated the dynasty with both British history and the

patriotic war effort and promoted its culturally sacralised status that questioning its German connections, ethnic background or personal loyalties was
simply out of the question in the first half of the war. The royal body was
exempt from questions of loyalty or heritage in 1914–16, successfully presented in the press as the perfect epitome of British values.

3.5 The Aura of the 'Royal Touch'? Royal Encounters with the War Wounded and Disabled

Exploring the interactions between royalty and the war wounded and disabled reveals yet another example of the merging of traditional ideas of
monarchy with wartime innovations – and the symbiotic relationship that
this process involved. On the one hand, the war led to disruptive – and
radically new – interactions between royalty, in particular, female members
of the royal family, and the ordinary war-wounded male soldier; on the
other, the cultural discourses built around these interactions also drew upon
much older, already familiar, monarchist concepts of the healing 'royal
touch' and reinvented them for the 1914–18 conflict. This was another
important way in which the First World War illustrated the reinvention of
traditional ideas in conjunction with forms of modernisation – in this case
of hospital care. How this intertwined process of innovation and tradition
emerged will be explored here by looking at interactions between royal
bodies and war-wounded and disabled bodies. The religious context is
again important: the association of the king's royal body with priestly
spiritual meanings obviously drew upon the tradition of the monarch serving as a link between God and people. The symbolic assertion of the royal
body eschewing luxury as part of the nation's war effort strongly evoked
ideas of religious penance. This sacred royal body – anointed by God and
suffering with and for its people – was the spiritual cultural framework
within which the power of the wartime royal touch operated.

Overall, British monarchist cultures adapted relatively successfully to the
modernising medical systems of the First World War. In many respects, the
war saw the older medieval idea of the 'royal touch' as healing reinvented for
the era of total war.[223] As Santanu Das has written of the cultural history of
wartime touch:

> At once intense and diffuse, working at the threshold between the self and
> the world, touch can be said to open up the body at a more intimate,
> affective level, offering fresh perspectives on certain issues that repeatedly
> surface in war writings and have become central to contemporary cultural
> thinking: ideas of space and boundaries, questions of gender and sexuality
> or the concept of trauma [. . .]. The immediate post-war years were also
> the time when touch was being conceptualised by men such as Havelock

Ellis in *Sexual Selection in Man* (1920) and Sigmund Freud in *The Ego and the Id* (1923).[224]

Royal touch was one of the most symbolic forms of wartime touch, constantly referenced in the press, but has since been overlooked by historians; it was also a fundamental part of the royals' own experience of the conflict and of the construction of the wartime monarchy. For example, the press frequently emphasised the powerful impact such touch had upon ordinary subjects: 75-year-old Alfred Wilson, a foundry worker, told reporters that the king 'shook my hands right heartily [. . .] and my black oily hand left a lovely mark right across his glove, but he did not seem to care'.[225] Journalist Philip Gibbs described wartime medal investitures as follows, emphasising the royal touch: 'There was also, at the King's hands, the decoration of soldiers and sailors with orders of distinction.'[226] When royal biographer Kenneth Rose discusses the debate among Palace officials, including Wigram, in 1917 as to whether women workers at a munitions factory should remove their gloves to shake hands with the queen, what was at stake was the idea of the *corpus mysticum* and the level of appropriate contact between the ordinary subject and the sacred royal body, the elevated 'royal touch' which risked being rendered banal if distributed too easily outside sacralised healing or cere-monial rite contexts: class is obviously a factor, but it is not the only reason for the discussion.[227] Such issues mattered. When the veteran trade unionist and leading Labour activist and MP Will Thorne met the king in 1917 he was anxious about the physical encounter, telling Lord Stamfordham when he arrived at Buckingham Palace 'that I had been led to understand that one had to do a lot of bowing and scraping when in the King's presence'.[228] Thorne was greatly relieved to discover he need only stand up when the king entered the room. The physical simplicity of this imbued the encounter with a positive glow for Thorne: 'I had expected to meet a haughty, stand-offish man with a highly-polished University twang; but I found him a very different person.'[229] One middle-class witness, Peggy Hamilton, who was working as a volunteer munitions worker at Woolwich Arsenal, described a royal visit as a 'break in the tedium of work in the New Fuse Factory'.[230] She recalled being told 'If the King stops in front of your machine [. . .] don't look up, don't stop working. If anything goes wrong or you have a breakdown, just turn levers and things and try to look as if you are working.'[231] The worker's gaze was not permitted to lift to the royal presence. Hamilton described how 'the King spent quite a long time walking slowly up and down the aisles between the machines, stopping here and there, and he seemed very interested. Queen Mary also visited the factory.'[232]

Thus, the 'touch' dimension of the encounter between royalty and ordinary people was only ever partly democratised during the war; its ongoing sacralised aura was what gave it its power and resonance. This is particularly evident in wartime royal encounters with the wounded, where royal touch had a powerful symbolic function. Such encounters provide valuable insights into how the physical bodily trauma of war was integrated into the national body politic and existing cultural frameworks through the medium of monarchy. Hospital visits and medal ceremonies were constant reminders of the body's bloody, visceral, fluid and fragile nature: the naked revelation of war-mutilated faces and limbs; scarring; missing amputated body parts. Yet, accounts of royal hospital visits in the press were often depicted as a sacralised encounter between the caring royal – epitomising the concern and gratitude of the state and empire – and the wounded serviceman. The royal presence thus provided a narrative to discuss the wounded, in ways that sanitised and ennobled physical war suffering. The language of royal formality and sacralisation served as an invaluable trope that could be used to describe war wounding for a culture that generally repressed any verbalisation about the body's physical messiness in a period still marked by Victorian cultures of prudery. The depiction of royal encounters with the war wounded and also with working-class subjects, whose bodies were frequently represented in cultural discourses of the time as sites of dirt and disease, is thus very revealing. Such encounters again show modernisation processes and sacralisation narratives and traditions of monarchy operating symbiotically. Reverence towards the monarchy and the modernisation processes that the war unleashed coexisted and often successfully sustained each other. For example, naming hospitals after royals had a long peacetime history. During the war, it combined sacralisation of the royals – associating a hospital with the ideal of a caring king or queen as a positive augury – with modernisation trends. In 1916, Frognal Estate in Sidcup, Kent was bought by the British Red Cross and Order of St John and turned into a new Queen Mary's Auxiliary Hospital, known as Queen's Hospital, working on facial reconstruction of war wounded.[233] Plastic surgery was one of the war's most radical medical innovations, framed here through royal auspices.

Visiting hospitalised war wounded was not new: Queen Victoria had done it during the Crimean War.[234] Yet, the scale of such royal visiting was unprecedented in the Great War, as was its widespread media representation. The proximity involved was also new: as this chapter relates, King George V even attended at least two operations. Walkabouts during visits to munitions workers were also a modernisation of his reign, drawing on his pre-war visits to northern England. However, the narratives in which these encounters were presented were much older, royal visits bringing comfort and even healing, echoing notions of the sacred 'royal touch'. The image of the 'perfect' royal body, its demeanour, its energy, was also directly juxtaposed with the wounded and damaged body of the hospitalised military subjects that the royals visited throughout the war, enhancing by default the power of the monarchy in such meetings.

The first point to note is the scale of these encounters. The sheer number of royal hospital visits is startling. This was the case from the very first year of the conflict. Some may well have been quite short, even perfunctory, given the royal couple sometimes visited two or three hospitals in a day. In 1914 alone, King George V's diary entries reveal he personally visited several thousand British soldiers and officers in multiple hospital visits across the early months of the war, in Britain and near the front, as well as over a thousand Indian wounded. This was the royals' most immediate early experience of the realities of the war's violence, and the king's diary offers insights into how this process of engaging with the wounded male body evolved over time and the kinds of psychological coping mechanisms the royal visitors developed in response to seeing the wounded.

The initial entries about hospital visits are relatively upbeat: on 1 September 1914 the king and queen visited King Edward VII's Hospital, where they saw 'the 30 officers who came in wounded last night. They all seemed cheerful, nearly all the wounds are from shrapnel shell.'[235] The following day they visited fifteen wounded officers at the military hospital at Millbank 'who have just returned from the front, one or two are badly wounded, all by shrapnel. In afternoon worked with Bacon at my stamps.'[236] The king was able to retain distance, it seems, from what he was witnessing, and to put a positive morale spin on the mood of the wounded: describing a visit to see 300 wounded and sick soldiers at the London hospital on 3 September 'who have just returned from the front', he recorded them as 'all very cheery and want to go out again'.[237] A hospital visit on 15 September recorded visiting 500 sick and wounded British and '65 German wounded and 7 of their officers who have just arrived, talked with some of them, they seemed pleased to be here'.[238] On 21 September, the king first encountered wounded officers who he knew personally, and he responded to the experience by carefully chronicling their bodily injuries: 'May and I went to Aunt Beattie's hospital in Hill St and saw 14 wounded officers amongst them, young Hardinge, Charlie's son in 15th Hussars who is doing well, shot through both arms and young Stuart Allington's son who was shot in the spine and partly paralized [sic].'[239] Similarly, in October, on visiting wounded acquaintances, the king noted what parts of the body had been damaged: 'Lastly we saw Roxburghe in Mrs Beckett's hospital, he was wounded in the groin but not very bad.'[240] The personal impact of the war was expressed by the king through this detailed listing of fragmented bodies and the technical description of the physical damage. The wounded men's conversations – their voices – are usually not referred to; their wounded bodies and the king's assessment of their war morale have supplanted any recording of their speech, an indication of how the shocking visual power of their wounds distracted from listening to their voices, even though the king often conversed with the wounded. The papers of the king's equerry, Sir Charles Cust, also relate how, during a visit to a hospital in France in October 1915, the king 'for some time talked to the wounded men lying there'.[241] The monarch's recollection of these hospital visits was as visual encounters more than auditory ones, the sight of the injuries dominating in his diary record.

In late September 1914, visiting the wounded at Aldershot, the tone of the king's descriptions darkens: 'saw the 130 wounded men who have just arrived, some dangerous cases'.[242] The start of October saw further, more direct, reference to bodies in jeopardy emerging, describing a visit to wounded officers in King Edward VII's Hospital: 'we saw each of the 30 there, some of them are rather bad, but they are most cheery. Walked in the garden with May.'[243] The immediate juxtaposition of walks or his stamp-collecting hobby after hospital visits to the wounded suggests that following such visits the king had a need for calm and for a return to his set daily routine in their aftermath. The range of terms open to the king to express the experience of seeing the severely injured was limited within the culture of masculine reserve and repression of emotion in which he had been raised. The linguistic coding in his accounts merits emphasis: 'bad' or 'dangerous' were euphemisms for severe injury or life-threatening illness. On 30 November 1914, at Dieppe during the king's visit to his troops in France the limits of this repressed language to express the bodily injuries he is witnessing become clearly visible: 'Walked round the wards and saw the 500 wounded there, some very bad cases which can't recover alas, shot through the head, hospital very well run, plenty of doctors and nurses.'[244] Commenting on a further hospital visit on the same trip, the king noted real fear for a patient he knew: 'Visited No. 6 Clearing Hospital (Col. Fard) at Merville, some new bad cases just brought in and a good many men suffering from frost bites of the feet. Poor Reggie Cake (Scots Guards) came in this morning badly hit by a sniper yesterday in back and chest, bullet not out, I fear he is rather bad but was quite cheerful.'[245] In February 1915, the king wrote in his diary:

> May and I went to Queen Alexandra's Military Hospital where we saw 3 wounded officers and 209 wounded men who as prisoners of war have been released in exchange by the German govt. Most of them have lost a leg or an arm, an eye or both eyes or are paralised [sic] being shot through the head or spine. It was a sad visit and they gave very bad accounts of the shameful way they have been treated by the Germans especially in the camp at Münster.[246]

The adjectives, 'sad', 'bad cases' point to emotional stress for the royal visitor, who could not show immediate emotions of shock or horror at the sight of wounds because this would potentially upset or alarm the patient; in many ways the king, as the most famous hospital visitor, epitomised the paradox that all able-bodied visitors faced in dealing with the power of their 'gaze' upon the wounded or disabled body during the war.[247] Queen Mary, for her part, described hospital visits as 'a very tiring affair' and 'incessant' and 'a great trial' in letters to Lord Esher in 1916.[248]

The second remarkable feature of these royal visits to the wounded is the degree of access that the royal visitors had to seeing the horrors of war. Hospital trips involved encounters that often showed the wounded in raw – and disturbing – physical states. Queen Mary noted in her diary on 18 February 1915 of seeing badly wounded British prisoners of war who had been exchanged home that it was 'very pathetic seeing so many men without arms, legs, eyes, etc.'.[249] On 6 July 1917, during a visit to the troops at the front, the king noted in his diary: 'I went to no. 46 Casualty Clearing Station, walked through most of the huts and saw a man shot in both arms being operated on.'[250] The duty of the royal body was to that of the serving national body politic, which the army, and in particular, its wounded, represented, not to the personal ego of the self; individual needs, including the need to express emotions such as shock, grief and horror, were excised. In October 1915, Queen Mary wrote in her diary of seeing 'victims (men and women) of the Zeppelin raid' on London, at Charing Cross Hospital: 'many very sad cases and one boy of 17 dying having had his lung pierced by a bit of a bomb. Most sad.'[251]

Even during well-planned hospital visits, it is difficult to know the extent to which a royal visitor could be steered away from the worst of the war's horror. A 1959, somewhat hagiographic, biography of Queen Mary noted that during the war 'it was soon noticed [. . .] that if the Queen suspected that hospital officials were trying to show her the less bad or more presentable cases amongst the convalescent or the "disabled" she would at once seek out for herself men who were in a worse way'.[252] Such inquisitiveness was characteristic; the queen took great interest in inspecting other aspects of the war effort, such as factories and charitable donations to her needlework guild, and it is highly plausible that she was equally hands-on in inspecting all aspects of the hospitals she visited. In 1918, Queen Mary specifically sought out wounded who had newly arrived in London from the Ludendorff Offensives.[253] In 1915, moreover, the king's diary records that the king and queen also visited officers hospitalised due to shell shock, again conferring respectability upon them.[254] Given the stigma of shell shock during this early phase of the war – while debates still raged about whether it had biological origins or was purely psychological and its suspected relationship to malingering – this was a significant gesture. Likewise, the fact that the king spoke with German wounded during hospital visits was powerful in setting an example of how the enemy should be treated humanely. Frederick Ponsonby recalled that, during a hospital visit on the king's 1915 visit to the front,

> Some of the men there had been gassed and it was painful to watch them, blue in the face and gasping for breath. I found one was a German and

regretted the pity I had wasted on him; but the King rebuked me and said
that after all he was only a poor dying human being, in no way responsible
for the German horrors.[255]

The quote highlights the graphic nature of the sights encountered in
hospital tours as well as the degree of anti-German fervour; it took
character for the king to show moral leadership in dealing with both
issues. Even Queen Mary was less sympathetic, writing to the king during
the same tour, 'So you talked to a wounded German, and another was
dying from our gas, how horrible! but it was their own fault as they started
using the gas.'[256]

The closest the king came to seeing the appalling state of First World War
military wounded in the immediate aftermath of battle was during his short
trip to France during the Ludendorff Offensives. This massive German attack
was launched on 21 March 1918, breaking through the British lines, and the
king immediately arranged to rush to the front, leaving on 28 March. On
29 March, he recorded in his diary:

> I then visited no. 3 Canadian Stationary hospital at Doullens which is now
> amalgamated with 3 casualty clearing stations which had to retire from
> battle zone; so all the wounded men coming straight from the dressing
> stations. There were over 2000 there, saw some very sad and dreadful
> sights, operations of every kind going on. Drs, nurses and staffs working
> splendidly at high pressure.[257]

This royal visit to the front was organised at the very last minute, at the
king's initiative, in response to the shocking impact of the Ludendorff
Offensives, at a point when the British army was in retreat. The chaos of
the situation is indicated by the improvisation in medical arrangements that
the monarch describes – Casualty Clearing Stations, which would normally
have been relatively close to the front and where the wounded were brought
directly from Advanced Dressing Stations, were now operating out of
a Stationary Hospital, a medical facility usually well behind the lines.[258]
Men arriving at a Casualty Clearing Station had received only the most
perfunctory treatment or tidying-up at an Advanced Dressing Station beforehand, and, during a major battle, sometimes not even that. On this occasion,
and given the impromptu nature of the visit, it appears very likely that the king
was witnessing initial treatment of the wounded coming from battle. His words
'some very sad and dreadful sights' illustrate the degree of horror seen.
Although this was not his first visit to a Casualty Clearing Station – he had
visited them in France since 1914 – such visits were usually organised in
advance and carefully controlled; there was time for the staff to get ready.[259]
On 29 March his visit was sudden; he had been due to meet Haig that day, but
the Commander-in-Chief was too busy with the crisis of the German advances
to do more than briefly greet the king.[260] Hospital staff would have had little

Fig. 27 Queen chats with a patient, Western Front 1917, from the Field Marshal Earl Haig Collection, National Library of Scotland, C2021 (Reproduced courtesy of the National Library of Scotland)

time to prepare and, given the chaos of three Casualty Clearing Stations retreating into their unit over the previous week, were unlikely to have been able to manage much staging of the visit in any case. The date the king, a devoutly religious man, noted in his diary, without comment, was Good Friday.

The king's wartime diaries do not mention touch, and it is not clear how much royal visitors actually had physical contact with patients or how much 'touch' or the inference of contact in sources was simply a metaphor for their presence standing at a bedside. Royal visits to the wounded involved a very specific, almost ritualised, kind of personal interaction, as illustrated in Fig. 27.

Neither King George V nor Queen Mary was physically demonstrative in public, and their hospital visits were very formal in the United Kingdom, although less so during the king's trips to the Western Front; when the wounded attended large tea parties with the royals at Buckingham Palace during the war there was also more direct physical contact, with Prince Albert pouring tea for the wounded, for example. Yet, there is evidence of royalty touching the wounded to comfort

Fig. 28 'Queen Alexandra's Christmas Day Visit to the Wounded', front page of the *Daily Mirror*, 27 December 1915, Mary Evans Picture Library, 11115158

them. Shaking hands also occurred during wartime royal hospital visits. Moreover, photographs also suggest close interaction, for example, the image in Fig. 28 of Queen Alexandra giving gifts to repatriated wounded prisoners of war on Christmas Day 1915, which shows her leaning over the patient's body and touching his hand with hers as she gives him a card.

Likewise, Walter Powell, who was an Army Service Corps (ASC) driver for the king and queen during their visits to the wounded at Chester Castle and Eaton Hall, recalled, in 1985, how the royal convoy

> parked in a semicircle where a large number of wounded NCO's and Tommies were lined up in a half-moon row either seated in bath chairs or on crutches etc. The King and Queen plus all the others got out of the cars, and their Majesties commenced shaking hands and chatting right along the row. Some of the men were without a leg, or an arm, and several were decorated with medals. The King and Queen chatted to most of them. Then [...] the convoy moved off to Eaton Hall, the Duke of Westminster's home. The same drill, but all wounded officers here sat in a half-circle some on crutches, and others with a leg or arm missing, or a head wound – decorations and chat. In fact the King and Queen passed all along the lines, shaking hands and chatting. Many were decorated with a medal – those had a little longer chat![261]

This degree of royal physical contact was quite innovative: after all, this was a period when, as historians such as Edward Owens and Frank Mort have pointed out, royal etiquette meant that royals did not 'wave' at crowds, including when they appeared upon the Buckingham Palace balcony, but bowed or nodded to acknowledge cheers, perhaps an indication of the extent to which the royal body was meant to be formally displayed to the people for their acclaim.[262]

How royal visitors behaved during the encounter with the war wounded could have significant psychological repercussions for the patient, and how the subject behaved was also culturally constrained. On one occasion, the Prince of Wales, visiting a unit for facially disfigured war wounded, reportedly chose to kiss the most badly mutilated man, in a gesture of inclusion; the man had been screened off, as his wounds were considered unsuitable for others to see.[263] Yet, the novelty of such royal interactions in such a formal physical culture meant that it could be stressful for those on the receiving end if they felt that they had not performed the right etiquette correctly. A wounded officer, Lieutenant D. C. Burn, wrote the following account of a royal visit to his hospital ward at Londonderry House in summer 1916:

> I was still in bed and had a 'cage' over my leg and wore a red flannel jacket, and must have looked rather like a monkey – anyhow I think I mortally offended the Queen by not calling her 'Your Majesty', or whatever it should be, for after asking me two or three obvious questions she went away in a 'huff' – at least so it seemed to me. On the other hand I had a long talk with the king about various places I had been to in France, and I found his guttural voice and laugh very engaging.[264]

Burn does not mention touch, but his account reveals the sense of concern about not being able to perform the royal encounter correctly, in terms of his outfit and his way of addressing the queen. The references to appearing like a 'monkey' and to his 'cage' highlight a subconscious fear of not only appearing uncouth but also of being servile – a pet – trapped immobile in bed before the royals.

Royal touch was always about asymmetric power: etiquette dictated that only the royal could initiate touch – for example, offering a hand to shake – but not the wounded subject, even if in wartime the wounded serviceman was a glorified cultural figure. Moreover, the subject was obliged to accept. Touching a royal was otherwise taboo. The encounter between wounded and royal in a hospital context was also one in which the wounded were not only physically, but also culturally, hugely constrained: as Joanna Bourke has argued, 'even when wounded', men in the First World War enjoyed no freedom from 'the tyranny of comportment. Suffering demanded carefully calibrated responses. [. . .] The correct response to pain was a learned hermen-eutics' of stoicism, silence, understatement, where complaining was taboo, a lesson 'repeated time and again by propagandists, medical personnel and fellow servicemen'.[265] Displaying a 'manly detachment from bodily pain' was a cultural ideal.[266] It is in this scenario of formidable repression of verbally articulating physical feeling that royal visits took place; this helps to context-ualise why the simplest of interactions by royals – a smile, a pat of the hand – could carry enormous weight, given how disconnected wounded were expected to be from their own emotions and physical bodies. It also helps explain the royal repression of emotion during such visits. If wounded men were not allowed to cry in pain and this was a mark of patriotism, then royals should also not break down emotionally in public.[267]

This was a difficult cultural standard for all parties – patients and royals – to uphold. In January 1915, the king referred to seeing 'hard cases' during a hospital visit.[268] Such language suggests that the king – within the limited emotional range of expression that he permitted himself in his diary – experi-enced distress at the sights of the damaged bodies that he was witnessing. 'Hard cases', in terms of Victorian and Edwardian masculine emotional language, was a commonly understood euphemism for 'upsetting'. The king reportedly confided after the war to a 'lady of the Court': 'You can't conceive what I suffered going round those hospitals in the war.'[269] The queen, too, found visiting the war wounded difficult: '"We have rebegun [sic] visiting hos-pitals!!!" she wrote to one of her sons in November 1916, "Oh! dear, oh! dear."'[270] Her lady-in-waiting and childhood friend, Countess Airlie, noted in her memoirs:

> The Queen too worried over her sons – the Prince of Wales and Prince Albert were often exposed to danger on the battle-fronts – but she never showed her fears for them. She had so long accustomed herself to veil grief, anxiety and all other emotions behind the smile that is always exacted of Royalty. Very few people suspected how great an ordeal her

hospital visits were to her. She had always been so affected at the sight of suffering that even as a child she once fainted when a foot-man at White Lodge cut his finger badly. But in those war years she trained herself to talk calmly to frightfully mutilated and disfigured men. Sometimes when we left the ward I would see tears glistening in her eyes but she never allowed them to fall. Her habit of self-discipline gave her complete physical control.[271]

Princess Marie Louise of Schleswig-Holstein, Queen Victoria's granddaughter, confirmed that Queen Mary had 'an instinctive horror of illness'.[272]

In public, the wartime royal body – like the state that it symbolised – had to appear constantly orderly, dependable, and never out of control. Even when his horse reared and collapsed upon him, causing him severe injuries, the king's initial response was to try to stand up, and to ask for his cap.[273] Being overcome by emotion would represent a loss of self-control, thus setting a bad example to the people and undermining the image of a well-ordered national and imperial war effort that royal visits were meant to laud and reward. This cultural expectation appears to have been partly generational: Queen Alexandra was the one royal who did constantly display emotions without receiving any undue censure for this. For the king and queen and their children, however, a particular performance of emotional control rapidly became part of wartime monarchical culture. The internal human effort such displays of emotional stoicism required – and the separation of performance of duty from physiological responses to grief and trauma – was a profound form of psychological repression and a fundamental constituent of the royal body at war and its image. As King George V wrote to Queen Mary, describing the effect of the war on him: 'very often I feel in despair and if it wasn't for you I should break down'.[274] He wrote to his friend and wartime naval aide-de-camp, Bryan Godfrey-Faussett, in October 1914 that he was 'too anxious and worried' to enjoy a break from work.[275] John Gore described how, for the king, 'every visit to a hospital containing wounded and maimed men wrung his heart and required an effort of mind discipline, yet he forced himself several times to watch operations in the War Hospitals [. . .]'.[276] James Pope-Hennessy described the queen's constant compassionate smile as an effort of 'self-discipline' as the war went on.[277]

While the historiography suggests Queen Mary found it difficult at times to completely mask her emotions on seeing the wounded, there are no wartime accounts of the king actually crying as a result of a hospital visit, either at a hospital or after leaving one; the male royal body was not allowed to show this kind of public emotion, which would have been associated with weakness and with a lack of dignity as well as being a potential cause of distress to the wounded and their families.[278] Stoicism was a patriotic ideal that had to be upheld. Indeed, accounts of the king even crying in private during the war are very rare. The American ambassador, Walter Hines Page, reported that the king 'wept while expressing his surprise and depression' at a tactless sentence in President Wilson's Peace Note of 18 December 1916 which suggested that 'the objects which the belligerents on both sides have in mind are virtually the same', an indication of his frustration at American neutrality.[279] George V's stoicism was in part due to the king's character: he was not an emotional man, although he was capable of crying. He admitted to weeping, writing that he 'quite broke down' in private when saying goodbye to his daughter Princess Mary upon her marriage in 1922.[280] Even if he did not openly break down, however, the king was clearly affected by seeing war carnage: the memoirs of Lieutenant General Sir Tom Bridges recounted how in 1918, during 'a simple war lunch' at Windsor with the king, queen and Princess Mary, the king 'had been to France and gave a graphic account of the suffering and losses of the troops in the "Back to the Wall" battle. Too graphic, indeed, for the kind heart of Princess Mary, who wept and left the room.'[281] In private, royal emotions could be revealed and were clearly deeply felt.

Yet, there was not only stoicism and repressed emotions but also genuine excitement at a royal hospital visit; as one wounded officer wrote in summer 1916:

> one day we heard that the King and Queen were in the house, and were about to come round the wards. The sisters got into an awful flurry, rushing round dusting this, putting straight that, and generally tidying up. Sister Cole, I think it was, couldn't make up her mind what to be doing when they came in and eventually decided to be sewing [...] and all through the ordeal she stitched away in a furious manner, pausing about every ten seconds to bob a sort of curtsey.[282]

The account is revealing of the way that the royal presence impacted upon subjects' physical behaviours and performances of deference. Royal visits were important occasions for hospitals: Whipps Cross War Hospital erected a brass plaque 'to celebrate the Visit of their Majesties King George V and Queen Mary with H.R.H. Princess Mary to this Infirmary and War Hospital on Saturday, November 17th, 1917, when their Majesties visited the wounded soldiers and the Queen presented the medals and certificates of training to the nurses'.[283]

Monarchism was clearly a relatively embedded wartime cultural norm. Moreover, it went beyond the royal touch to include hospital social and material cultures. A matron at the London Hospital in Whitechapel, a working-class area, wrote of how, at Christmas, many of the patients remarked that

> they had never had such a nice Christmas. [...] Our soldiers had many pleasant surprises. Their Majesties the King and Queen had sent Christmas cards with their photographs and autographs to be distributed.

Then, Queen Alexandra had sent to each man back from the 'Front' a box
of cigarettes with her photograph on the lid of the box. These marks of
personal sympathy from our Royal Family gave keen pleasure.[284]

She also noted how a 'Troup' [sic] of little patients from the children's wards
'by special request, was allowed to march through two of the soldiers [sic]
Wards' and described the 'delight' of the military patients at hearing the
children sing 'Its [sic] a long, long way to Tipperary' and 'proposing three
cheers for the King and for the soldiers!'[285] The connection between the
monarchy and wartime nursing also deliberately promoted patriotism. This
was particularly the case for Queen Alexandra's Imperial Military Nursing
Service. In 1917, Queen Alexandra commissioned a portrait of nurse Edith
Cavell, executed by the Germans in Belgium, with the inscription 'Make her
cause – the cause of mercy – your own', which was distributed as
propaganda.[286] Queen Alexandra also issued an illustrated message to all
Queen Alexandra's Imperial Military Nursing Service personnel serving in
France in December 1914, 'as the President of all the nurses in the British
Empire', expressing 'to every individual nurse' her 'heartfelt and grateful
appreciation of their unselfish devotion and patriotism in ministering to, and
relieving the suffering of, our brave and gallant soldiers and sailors who are
fighting for their King and Country'.[287] The image showed a drawing of an
angel watching over a nurse caring for a wounded soldier, and the whole was
surmounted by a photograph of Queen Alexandra. The association of religion,
sacrifice and royal power was clearly evident.

   As the above has shown, royal interactions with the wounded thus offered
a solution to one of the challenges that the war brought: how to integrate the
new experiences, and public outreach and accessibility of royalty, which were
often disruptive of pre-war monarchy norms, into the mythic, sacralised royal
image necessary to the status of monarchy. This ultimately drew upon new
narrations of older concepts of the 'royal touch'. The discourse of the mythic
'royal touch' was used to frame encounters between royals and the wounded,
and mythologised and sacralised these events. Yet, how did the discourse of
'royal touch' operate? As revealing as the *actual* degree of real historical touch
in royal encounters with the wounded is the insight that such practices provide
into how older cultural discourses of royal healing continued to exist during
the First World War. The war saw widespread narratives about the royals
consoling the war wounded, a process of cultural adaptation, presenting the
royal family as providing comfort to the wounded, drawing upon an older
symbolic of the power of the 'royal touch' as well as upon depictions of royal
women as 'mothering' and 'nursing' the nation in wartime. The reverence that
royal encounters generally provoked was thus mobilised as a means of boost-
ing war morale and presenting symbolic 'healing' or 'comforting' narratives
whereby, through the royals, symbolising the nation, collective empathy and

sympathy could be presented to the war wounded and bereaved. As Ana Carden-Coyne argues, the wounded 'demonstrated the complexity of gender constructs and gendered behaviour in response to the military demands placed on male bodies in wartime and the ambiguous and often anxious social significance of the wounded and disabled'.[288]

One British response to this was to mediate the depiction of the war wounded through monarchist imagery and narratives built around royal visits to them. In fact, the royal body was frequently juxtaposed in photographs and press reports with the mutilated soldier's war body which the king and queen encountered in hospitals, at investitures and in meetings with veterans and with the graves of the war dead that they encountered during visits to the front and to war cemeteries. The strength of the royal body's image – its energy, solidity and power – thus served to reassure and offer a narrative alternative and counterweight to the descriptions of injury and death of British soldiery from the United Kingdom and the empire. The royal body was always presented as coherent and whole, while ordinary male bodies of the nation were being dismembered and destroyed during the conflict and while the empire itself was, during and after the war, fragmenting, as power was divested from London to Ireland and the dominions and calls for self-determination, as well as rebellions and secessions, increased. Narratives presenting the royal presence as comforting the wounded also had deeper, older meanings: royalty could comfort because the monarchy was representative of the British nation, the state and empire, of history and of the body politic. The royal body – representing the body politic – offered continuity, reassurance and, through the wartime debates about the possible marriages of the royal children, the potential for regeneration.

The power of the 'royal touch' discourse was particularly evident with regard to hospital visits by royalty, where it was frequently depicted in the press as bringing 'comfort' to the wounded.[289] While Queen Victoria had visited war wounded from the Crimean War on, the First World War, with its public expectations of equality of sacrifice in society, meant that royal visits to war hospitals took place with an unprecedented regularity – virtually daily during some phases of the conflict and certainly weekly.[290] Such visits had to convey real displays of empathy and actual evidence of personal solicitude; the press praised the extent to which the wartime royal family spent time with the wounded and, in particular, emphasised them talking to them, touching them, bringing gifts for them and listening to them. The press created and supported specific tropes around these royal visits which projected the royals as sympathetic counsellors, solicitous, morale-boosting, all of which invoked the traditional idea of royalty as having spiritual powers of healing. Journalist Philip Gibbs described how, in 1915, 'the King and the Queen often cheered the wounded with personal chats that did much to brighten their weeks of painfully slow recovery'.[291] The Daily Mirror in October 1914 referred directly to 'The Royal Touch' in its report on the queen comforting a dangerously wounded soldier who had begged to see her during her hospital visit.[292] When she reached his bedside the man was unable to speak. Touch and the sheer presence of royalty is conveyed here as a central emotional wartime experience of comfort. On another occasion, the queen asked a man to 'unbutton his shirt so that she might see the spot from which a bullet was extracted'.[293] In a September 1914 royal visit to a hospital, the wounded produced 'from underneath their pillows [...] morbid, precious relics' showing the king the 'bullets and shrapnel that have been extracted from their bodies'; the king was 'fascinated' by X-ray images that depicted the bullets before their removal.[294] In 1917, during a hospital visit, a man offered to have his dressing removed to show the king his wound when the monarch showed interest in the injury.[295] There could be no clearer metaphor for the wartime embodiment of royal duty than this physical incorporation of the battlefield into the flesh of the subject – which the royal gaze now legitimised and honoured. The tangible nature of Queen Mary's interventions also powerfully conveys how the war was putting the subject's body on display for inspection and intervention by royalty – and opening it to new forms of 'royal touch' – in new ways. The wounded body was not a private space but a shared, public part of the monarch–subject relationship.

One *Daily Mail* report in January 1915 particularly epitomised this revival of the language of the 'royal touch', referring to how 'The visit was part of that pilgrimage of pity in which the King and Queen have been to so many hospitals and cheered so many of their soldiers.'[296] It described the responses of Indian wounded: 'What the men say in their own words is this: "The smile of the Queen makes us well", or "The King has been. He has smiled on his servants. Behold! We are cured."'[297] *The Times* in 1914 referred to a sepoy with 'eyes filled with tears' of emotion after a 'beside chat' with the king.[298] The rhetoric of 'pilgrimage' and of healing – although attributed to colonial troops, who are also infantilised in the article's depiction – is presented as a sacralised and normal part of the royal wartime role. Yet, such royal visits were often appreciated by Indian wounded: Sardar Bahadur Gugan wrote in a letter home of his time at Brighton Hospital in 1915 that 'The King and Queen talked with us for a long time. I have never been so happy in my life as I am here.'[299] Another wounded patient, Jemadar Mir Dast, described how 'the King with his royal hand has given me the decoration of the Victoria Cross. God has been very gracious [...].'[300]

Perhaps the most dramatic example of the cultural discourse of royalty comforting the wounded occurred in 1917, when the king saw terribly wounded civilian casualties immediately following a devastating air raid on London on 13 June, the first ever raid by a fixed-wing airplane on the city, which killed 162 people, including 18 schoolchildren at a primary school in Poplar, 16 of whom were under 6 years old; the raid also injured 426 people.[301]

Upon receiving news of the raid, the king spontaneously visited the bombed area within hours. The king also visited two of the affected hospitals, the London and St Bartholomew's Hospitals, as they were receiving victims of the bombing: Alexandra Churchill states that on this occasion the king watched 'doctors administer morphine to women with the hair singed from their heads' and witnessed an operation, while Kenneth Rose allocates merely a passing sentence in his whole biography to the king comforting 'air raid victims still drenched in blood', which, although Rose does not specify, probably refers to the same occasion.[302] As the numbers of victims were so great, operations were being carried out behind screens in the wards, as the operating theatres were full; this was how the king witnessed 'a surgeon [...] busy repairing a shattered limb. [...] He did not leave till the man was made comfortable.'[303] On the evening of the raid, Queen Alexandra and Princess Victoria also visited the East End to express their sympathy with the mothers of the children killed in their school.[304] In the days that followed, Queen Mary and Princess Mary also visited the raid victims in hospitals.[305]

Press reports claim that the king was cheered by locals during his visit to the bombed district immediately after the raid: 'His Majesty's promptitude in thus manifesting his sympathy with the sufferers was deeply appreciated and he was warmly cheered as he drove slowly through the streets.'[306] The *Dundee Courier* described it as

> a kindly act of the King to motor through the area covered by this morning's raid. His Majesty had a warm reception but he was not seeking adulation but desirous of giving consolation. Everywhere King George was frantically [sic] cheered and his very presence gave solace. His Majesty was most distressed at the destruction and loss of life that was caused at a poor school in the East End of London, where weeping mothers for long waited patiently for the corpses of their murdered children.[307]

This incident is revealing: monarchist culture was such that the press could confidently assert the idea that the presence of the monarch brought 'solace' just hours after such terrible destruction of homes and lives. In the disorientation of the experience of the first major airplane bombing raid on the country's capital, seeing the king behaving as normal was a powerful reassurance: the monarchy's charismatic symbolism of stability and continuity over time had a powerful, almost sedating, effect. Only this – and perhaps shock – can explain the assertion that the king was *cheered* in streets that were in such mourning; gratitude may also have been a factor, as this was a poor part of London where such rapid recognition from the monarch of its suffering was unprecedented. We must exercise caution here too: these newspaper reports reflect a broader cultural trend, which historian Susan Grayzel has identified, to mythologise the reaction of British civilians to air raids as stoic and calm, when often the reality was far more nervous and anxious.[308] The fact that the press reports of King George V's actions were juxtaposed with reports of the abdication of ex-King Constantine of Greece clearly also provided readers with a comparison between the virtuous British monarch and his pro-German relatives elsewhere in Europe.[309] Reporting on the king's visit to the raid's victims in hospital, the *Yorkshire Evening Post* described how the king 'spoke to those who were able to talk and left smiling faces everywhere'.[310] This appears hyperbolic: the hospital was so overwhelmed by the disaster that extra operations were taking place behind screens in the wards; many dead children had been taken to its mortuary.[311] And yet, the press report insists on the trope of the royal presence as restorative. In response to the 13 June raid, in a letter to Stamfordham, the king wrote that, although he was against reprisals, the British ought to bomb German towns in retaliation if such air raids continued.[312]

The rapid response to 13 June 1917's devastating air raid was possibly modelled on the pre-war mining disaster at Cadeby pit in 1912, which occurred during the king and queen's visit to industrial areas in Yorkshire, where the royal couple visited the scene hours after the accident and were honoured when a large procession of locals subsequently spontaneously processed to where they were staying to thank them.[313] It also reflected the royal response to the Silvertown munitions factory explosion of 19 January 1917. Whitechapel hospital received thirty-two of the injured, and they were visited by the king and queen and Princess Mary in the first week of February. The hospital matron described it as a 'gracious visit' and noted that 'Their Majesties made a point of speaking to each patient in their usual kind and sympathetic way and they were anxious to hear all details of how they had sustained their injuries.'[314] This testimony again highlights the personal interaction and intimacy of royal wartime meetings with the wounded. Throughout the war, the king regularly visited parts of London that had been bombed; however, the speed of his presence on 13 June 1917 was striking.[315] It illustrated a new urgency to being present with war victims but also how the press worked this into older discourses that sacralised monarchy.

The monarchy's interaction with the war wounded was not limited to hospitals. Royal carriages were sent from Buckingham Palace to convey the wounded from railway stations to hospital.[316] Buckingham Palace gardens were 'placed at the disposal of wounded officers'.[317] Above all, in 1916, the king and queen initiated tea parties for the wounded at Buckingham Palace where men of all ranks were waited upon by members of the royal family and the aristocracy, including Princess Mary, Prince Albert and Princess Beatrice.[318] The Countess of Shaftesbury was photographed wearing her apron under her fur coat.[319] These tea parties were widely reported upon in the press, with particular emphasis on the disruptive inversion of class hierarchies that they represented as royals and aristocrats 'waited' on the wounded soldiers. These social events appear to have functioned akin to the historiographical analysis of 'carnival', where normal social roles were briefly abandoned in a temporary inversion of cultural restrictions to release social pressure.[320] The press emphasised the cheery atmosphere and the uplifting entertainments. The *Daily Mirror* announced: 'The King entertains wounded warriors; Prince Albert acts as waiter to his father's guests', together with a photograph of the prince standing, holding a teapot, beside a table of seated soldiers.[321] The first wave of tea parties were held on three consecutive afternoons at the end of March 1916, with afternoon tea for the wounded in the coach houses at Buckingham Palace, followed by a show in the Royal Riding School; approximately 760–800 wounded men from hospitals across London were invited to each one; later such events used a marquee to host the tea.[322] Stars from the West End performed. The men were 'forbidden from rising when the Royal Family enters the rooms', as the king did not want wounded men struggling to their feet on his account.[323] Queen Mary described the first three 'tea parties' as 'so informal, friendly and nice'.[324] Yet working-class men being served by royals and aristocrats, sitting while royals were standing, all marked an upturning of conventional social norms and class hierarchies akin to the disruptive concept of carnival; the wounded masculine body was briefly freed from the usual constraints of class. According to the *Western Daily Press*, the wounded men 'were all allowed to smoke freely, and it was a joy beyond words to watch these rows and rows of khaki and navy blue clad heroes, who delighted to honour their King and defend their country'.[325] Reporting on the men's response to part of the performance – a comedy act – the same paper noted, without irony, how 'it is curious how we all seem to find it excruciatingly funny to see other people fall about and apparently get knocked all over the place!'[326] Men who had themselves been 'knocked all over the place' laughed at the spectacle of a theatrical enactment of bodily mishap after enjoying royal refreshments in the presence of the sacralised monarchic bodies of the king and queen.

Symbolically, the monarchy was physically *feeding* bodies that had been war damaged in its service in an act of honouring that was a reversal of the norms of class hierarchy and subject homage to royalty; the fact that the royal family and their aristocratic helpers were touching food that entered working-class subjects' bodies was a profoundly disruptive act of direct contact. Acting out this kind of performance was a way for the monarchy to symbolically depict the national body as 'whole' – by bringing the monarchical body and the damaged combatant body together. However, the press reporting on the tea parties, with its focus on the magnanimity of the royal gesture and the novelty of duchesses, princes and princesses serving working-class men, occluded the permanency of the extremes of damage experienced by the wounded body and thereby helped present a brief temporary illusion of reconstruction – for a short moment while enjoying themselves at the party, the wounded men were all presented as happy and well. 'They have been wounded in their country's service, but they did not seem in the least to mind it, and were as merry as the proverbial sand-boys', reported the *Western Daily Press*, effectively infantilising – and racialising – the wounded men, with a term usually employed to refer to colonial indigenous peoples.[327] What is clearly in evidence in such depictions of interactions between the royal and the wounded body is 'the shared social pressure that men should reclaim their masculine dignity in overcoming their wounds and disabilities' that pervaded First World War British society.[328] Hence the monarch had a reciprocal duty to very publicly engage with the war wounded and disabled who were taking on disability on his behalf. The British royal couple performed this role and obligation exceptionally well and comprehensively.

The idea of the 'royal touch' in the press was also a combined male and female royal healing role that the king and queen shared; it was associated with both of them and with historic echoes of the spiritual 'otherness' of royalty. Moreover, the ways in which the war had seen the royal couple adopt older cultural scripts of purifying the royal body, through giving up worldly pleasures of luxurious food and alcohol and through calling for divine intercession in National Days of Prayer, gave the wartime 'royal touch' a renewed quality. The spiritual, ascetic royal body stood for the purified nation – this rendered the physical royal touch sacred; it was physical contact with the sacralised majesty. One should not take this too far: some of the delight at royal handshakes or touch was because it overturned class boundaries and expectations that had surrounded monarchy before 1914 or was simply a break in the monotony of hospital. The wartime king and queen directly touching their lowliest of subjects was a radical break with physical class segregation. But older languages of honour and divinely anointed kingship mattered too.

Indeed, these may even have had a superstitious element. According to the journalist and later interwar editor of the *New Statesman*, Kingsley Martin, superstition around the monarchy lasted into the 1930s, including the idea of the 'royal touch':

> In February, 1936, for instance, a Scottish cleric suggested in the course of a sermon in Edinburgh that a crippled boy who had learnt to walk without crutches had been cured by the 'Royal touch', while many people seem to have believed in the providential character of the 'King's weather' in 1935. [...] I could cite many other illustrations of the existence of a magical theory of Monarchy.[329]

Historian Ross McKibbin, in his study of the period 1918–51, suggests that the interwar monarchy developed a quasi-magical character, stating that 'after 1918' the monarchy had 'a cultural centrality to British life possessed by hardly any other British political institution. What is the explanation for this?', a question that he finds difficult to answer.[330] For Martin this revival of older reverences about monarchy was an early twentieth-century phenomenon:

> In the middle of the last century it needed courage to break the religious taboo, to doubt the literal truth of the first chapter of Genesis or question the scientific basis for belief in the virgin birth. The throne, on the other hand, was frankly criticized in the newspapers and on the platform. In the twentieth century the situation is exactly reversed. Any one could question the divinity of Christ; but until the advent of Mrs. Simpson no journalist dared to attribute a fault to the King of England, or, indeed, to refer to the character of any royal person except in the whispered undertones of worshippers in a sacred place. The Monarchy had become sacred; its sacred character protected by a taboo.[331]

The First World War, with its insertion of older sacralised narratives about monarchy into modernisation processes, undoubtedly helped with this re-sacralisation of monarchy.

Yet, although the king and queen were both part of the wartime discourse on the royal touch, it also reveals strongly gendered dimensions too. Hospital visits often emphasised an image of royal women in wartime as 'mothers' and 'nurses' to the wounded national bodies of the soldiers, a role which drew upon and reinvented older notions of the healing power of the 'royal touch' and which challenged royal taboos around masculine disability and interactions with disabled bodies. Royal women's experiences of the physical horrors of war dirt and blood had to be successfully integrated into existing discourses of the pristine female royal body. This was done by emphasising such royal interactions with war dirt and wounding as part of an overall royal 'nursing' role – royalty was depicted as nursing the nation. This was made explicit in press coverage on Princess Mary when she trained as a nurse in the last year of the war. This reflected something of a European trend among the allies: Queen Elisabeth of Belgium nursed during the war; the Russian Tsarina Alexandra and her two eldest daughters undertook nursing training at the start of the conflict and went on to nurse wounded soldiers, including assisting at operations; the Queen of Romania and her three daughters also nursed the wounded.[332] It also echoed older ideas of royal women in medieval periods, who chose convent life and nursing the sick. The royal nursing narrative thus reflected older sacralised myths of saintly queens and princesses. It was also risky, however: in the Russian case, the image of the tsarina and her daughters as nurses was 'favourably viewed to begin with', but the public mood soon turned.[333] It was seen as inappropriate for royal women to be in such proximity to the male bodies of their subjects – even in a caring role – and spurred all kinds of sexual rumours that tarnished the royal image.[334] In the end, their nursing role was better publicised in the Allied press than in the Russian.[335] As a friend of the tsarina, Lili Dehn, wrote in her memoir: 'the average soldier only saw in the Red Cross an emblem of her lost dignity as Empress of Russia. He was shocked and embarrassed when she attended to his wounds and performed almost menial duties. His idea of an Empress was never as a woman, but only as an imposing and resplendent Sovereign.'[336]

This outcome may well help explain why the young Princess Mary was sent to nurse in a children's hospital and not to care for wounded men. The idea of royal nursing, however, is but one example of a broader process of the royal body being used to reintegrate the damaged bodies of the war wounded into the overall body politic. The idea of the healing power of the royal touch was evident in the depiction of Princess Mary, who, as a Voluntary Auxiliary Detachment or VAD nurse, began working at Great Ormond Street Hospital in June 1918. The association of royalty with nursing was not new in 1914–18, but royals taking a hands-on nursing role was: Queen Alexandra's Imperial Military Nursing Service had been established before the First World War, during the reign of Edward VII, with Queen Alexandra as its patron. In July 1918, the *Daily Record* was among the newspapers which reproduced photographs of the princess in nursing uniform.[337] By the last two years of the war, Princess Mary had become an important, and popular, part of the monarchy's war image. Having scarcely appeared in newsreels before, in 1917 and 1918 she appeared more often than the Prince of Wales.[338] The *Illustrated London News* gave particularly prominent attention to the royal family in its January–March 1918 issues.[339] This coincided with the period when the British felt most besieged, due to Germany's renewed unrestricted submarine warfare campaign. The Prince of Wales featured in several stories and cover images, not as a soldier, but as a skilled worker as he toured mines, munitions works and shipyards, taking up a riveter's hammer on Clydeside, for example.[340] Princess Mary was later featured in nursing uniform. The royal offspring were being used to personify the physical contribution of royal bodies to the embattled home front war effort.

As Fig. 29 highlights, the press emphasis was upon Princess Mary as serving akin to any ordinary member of the war effort, and the deliberate juxtaposition of 'King's daughter' and 'hospital nurse' was intended to attract attention and shock by invoking the implied stereotype of the high-status role of princess with that of menial nursing work. Her appearance was that of a war VAD, even though she was nursing children, not soldiers. Other commentators framed her role in terms of war sacrifice, emphasising the risk of air raids to the princess while she worked at the hospital and of disease as 'a children's hospital is not considered nearly such a "safe" one for the staff as an adult hospital, for amongst the patients of such juvenile years there is far greater risk of infection from such diseases as diphtheria, scarlet fever, measles, mumps, and so forth, than there is amongst older people'.[341]

It was radical for a young unmarried British princess to be allowed to work in a public hospital. The new role marked a clear departure for the image of Princess Mary, which had been associated very much with female purity, innocence and shyness. The historiography on First World War nursing has pointed out that the figure of the war nurse, a woman with power over vulnerable, often immobile, men's bodies, had not only positive but also threatening connotations

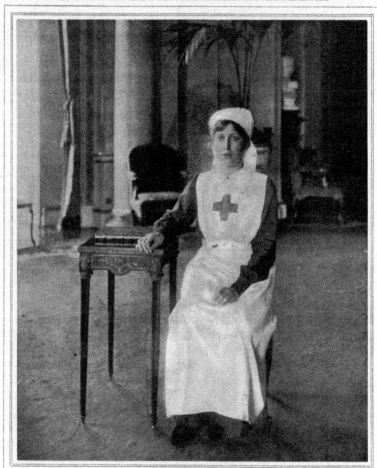

THE ILLUSTRATED LONDON NEWS,

No. 4133.—VOL. CLIII. SATURDAY, JULY 6. 1918. ONE SHILLING.

THE KING'S DAUGHTER AS A HOSPITAL NURSE: PRINCESS MARY IN HER UNIFORM AS A PROBATIONER.

Princess Mary recently began a course of practical nursing at the Hospital for Sick Children in Great Ormond Street, where she arranged to attend on two mornings a week. Her work consists of washing and dressing the babies and helping in the care of older children. In the Alexandra Ward, where she is on duty, her portrait hangs over a cot named after her. She intends to qualify as a fully trained nurse, just as Princess Arthur of Connaught is doing at St. Mary's Hospital. Princess Mary holds the highest certificates of proficiency in home-nursing and first aid. Besides her hospital work, she is Commandant of the Buckingham Palace Voluntary Aid Detachment. In her V.A.D. uniform Princess Mary was present with the King and Queen at the great gathering of Women Workers at Buckingham Palace on June 29, in which her detachment took part.

PHOTOGRAPH BY CENTRAL PRESS.

Fig. 29 'The King's Daughter as a Hospital Nurse: Princess Mary in Her Uniform as a Probationer', *Illustrated London News*, 6 July 1918, Mary Evans Picture Library, 11806729 in First World War societies, with its implicit undermining of gender power hierarchies.[342] Yet the princess's nursing work was, in reality, carefully conscribed and came very late in the war. It was the queen's decision that the princess would work at Great Ormond Street Hospital for sick children.[343] She worked in the hospital two mornings a week from June 1918 and on three other weekday mornings did clerical work at the headquarters of the Voluntary Aid Detachment at Devonshire House, where she had 'her own special little unit, identifiable by special shoulder straps on their uniforms and recruited from amongst the daughters of palace officials'.[344] Yet, however limited her actual weekly nursing time was, the princess did carry out menial nursing tasks, bedmaking, dressing infants' wounds, cleaning and bathing them, as well as assisting at operations and giving injections, although she was spared 'the scrubbing and polishing which usually fall to the lot of a newly joined probationer'.[345] Moreover, she continued her nursing training at the hospital until 1920; it was not limited to the war period, and some of the children she cared for were very seriously ill, some fatally. Mabel Carey's biography, with which Princess Mary appears to have assisted, constantly emphasises the royal touch and its exemplary nature: Princess Mary dressing the wounds of sobbing children with 'that gentleness and deliberation of touch that cause the very least pain possible'; 'sure, deft, fingers'; 'her hands were so gentle and her fingers so sure'.[346] Her own mother Queen Mary noted that the princess had adapted well to nursing in part due to her 'nice light hands'.[347] Expectations of femininity and of royal touch here interacted to help shape how Princess Mary's war role was framed.

Ultimately, the sheer scale of the royal engagement with the wounded and war disabled during and after the war was remarkable and highlights the tension between the idea of the individual bond with the monarch, which was ideologically at the core of how war service was culturally constructed, and the challenges of mass casualties and a modernising wartime healthcare system catering for hundreds of thousands of men. It was a difficult circle to square, preserving the individual royal encounter with the wounded with its historic resonances in the face of such enormous changes. Yet George V certainly tried. The evidence suggests, therefore, that these royal encounters were not merely perfunctory but a real attempt to meet and reach out to the wounded military subject – such connection lay at the core of the British monarchical honour-culture system. After visiting 250 sick and wounded soldiers at the 2nd London Territorial Hospital at Chelsea, the king noted 'it takes a long time to speak to each one'.[348] The military bond in the British and imperial armies was, after all, between the sovereign and his individual subject, not between the citizen-soldier and state; the oath taken was to the sovereign, and the armies were referred to as the king's armies, and soldiers as 'soldiers of the King'. The fragmented military subject's war body – wounded, dying – was thus paying the sacrifice on its flesh for fulfilling its duty to the king. As King George

V observed, on seeing war wounded in hospital uniforms process at the first post-war Derby: 'They've paid the price for us. Without them there would have been no Derby today.'[349] It is important to point out how innovative this very focused royal attention to the wounded body of the military subject by the British royal family actually was. It was a marked contrast with the Hohenzollern monarchy in Germany, for example; as John Röhl points out, 'not once' during the entire war did the kaiser 'ask how many of his own people had been killed or wounded'.[350] While the British royals carried out hospital visits to the war wounded on a vast scale throughout, and after, the conflict, this contrasted with the German Crown Prince, who, although he visited hospitals, admitted that he found it 'difficult' and that 'words of comfort and expressions of confidence in victory' stuck in his throat.[351]

3.6   The Monarchy and the War Disabled

The British monarchy, through wartime hospital visits, thus became closely associated with 'honouring' the war wounded and disabled, the monarchy being associated with the bestowal of national honour upon individuals because of its symbolic role. By shaking hands with the wounded, awarding them medals personally or speaking with them at their hospital bedside, the king and queen conveyed the honourable nature of the war-disabled body and projected both respectability and new status upon it. In turn, the symbolically supreme, healthy and complete 'royal body' was engaged with masculine fragmentation, vulnerability and existential collapse in new ways. Queen Mary, for example, took a particular interest in advances in prosthetic limbs, describing one visit in 1918 in her diary to Roehampton's Queen Mary 'hospital for limbless soldiers [...]. We saw the newest arms & legs & the men showed us what they were able to do. [...] A nice afternoon.'[352] On another occasion, she wrote of going to Brighton to see 'my workshops for limbless soldiers the same as at Roehampton'.[353] In July 1918, she described examining a 'new artificial leg which has just been invented'.[354] Royalty thus helped reduce the stigma around disability and prosthetic limbs but also culturally reincorporated the limbless into the body politic by associating them with the symbolic royal body.

This was a profound shift given how, before the conflict, the idea of any close relationship between disability and royalty had been seen as problematic – and, when it came to royalty itself showing its own instances of disability, such as in the case of George V's youngest son, Prince John, who had learning difficulties, severe epilepsy and possibly autism, taboo. As Prince John's disabilities became more evident as he grew older, he was kept more and more out of the public eye, and his conditions were only made partly known to the public after his early death in 1919 at the age of 13; he spent his last years at a secluded location, Wood Farm, on the Sandringham estate, where his mother visited him assiduously. It was only from the official communiqué announcing his death that his epilepsy was revealed to the public.[355] Such taboos regarding the royal disabled were pan-European. Kaiser Wilhelm II went to enormous lengths throughout his reign to hide the fact that he was disabled, keeping his 'withered' arm out of sight as much as possible. The tsar and tsarina of Russia likewise kept secret their son Alexei's life-threatening haemophilia. In sum, in the pre-1914 world, royal bodies were expected to maintain an illusion of perfect health, completeness and physical perfection, reflecting their symbolic moral virtue and class status and their role as metonyms for the healthy nation, state and empire.[356] The war, however, saw King George V and Queen Mary constantly visit the war wounded and spend time in close proximity with them, which created a different public image of the relationship between royalty and disability; this was no accident. With a disabled son of their own, the royal couple showed great sensitivity towards the issue of disability and pioneered visiting disabled children during their visit to the north of England before the war.[357] While it is not clear if the war shifted attitudes towards a royal themselves having a disability, it certainly saw broad acceptance of the idea of the monarchy honouring the disabled.

As early as January 1915, the king informed Asquith of the need for 'ample provision' by the state for those who were 'permanently disabled' by the war; the motivation at this point, however, was more pragmatic than altruistic, the king believing that recruits were being put off by the risk of being left penniless if disabled in the conflict.[358] As the war went on, the monarchy became more closely involved in the process of specifically honouring the war disabled. In July 1916, the War Office was informed that 'at the express desire of His Majesty the King a special Discharge Certificate is to be given to all soldiers disabled in the present war'.[359] King George V was particularly concerned with preventing the wartime harassment of men who had returned to civilian life as a result of war wounds who were being accused of shirking because they were not in uniform. Thus, in September 1916, the 'King's Silver Badge' (also known as the Silver War Badge), was introduced for those wounded or disabled by the war, which was a lapel pin engraved with the words 'For King and Empire, service rendered'.[360] The idea appears to have followed from a conversation between the king and the Bishop of Chelmsford, who suggested that 'some kind of badge should be given to soldiers invalided home to show they had been to the front'.[361] The king was keen on the suggestion of a badge, as he felt a general campaign medal could not be given until after the war had ended.[362] The King's Special Discharge Certificate and the King's Silver Badge were separate awards – entitlement to the King's Silver Badge did not necessarily entitle a man to the King's Special Discharge Certificate, whereas those awarded a Certificate were entitled to the Badge.[363] The King's Special Discharge Certificate was infused with monarchism: it had a facsimile of King George V's signature under a statement that named the recipient and recorded that an individual had 'served with honour and was disabled in the Great War' and had been 'honourably discharged'.[364] The king thereby, through the facsimile of his personal signature, released the individual disabled serviceman from his service oath to the monarch. Yet, the process of royal approval of the war-disabled body was not a universal one: after the war ended, Lord Milner, Colonial Secretary, opposed issuing the King's Special Discharge Certificates for those disabled in the Great War to 'coloured Contingents', informing the War Office in August 1919 that he was of the 'opinion that the King's Certificates are unsuitable for coloured Contingents generally'.[365] Milner's views reflected his racial prejudices: white disability was privileged over the war disabled from other racialised categories.

When the City of London raised £53,000 as a personal gift for the king and queen to mark their silver wedding anniversary, the royal couple donated it all to the King's Disabled Fund for Sailors and Soldiers and the Air Force, a newly established support organisation to which the king had lent his name.[366] During the war, Queen Mary took an active interest in the rehabilitation of the war disabled through her involvement with a series of wartime Queen Mary's Auxiliary Hospitals.[367] This culture of royal obligation to the war disabled continued into the post-war period. It was clearly no coincidence that, from as early as 1915, the British monarchy was called upon to support the establishment of 'the King's National Roll Scheme' (KNRS) which promoted the employment of disabled ex-servicemen; the Scheme was eventually brought in by the government in 1919.[368] The monarchy would go on to play a significant role in supporting such interwar schemes for the rehabilitation of war disabled. If definitions of what constituted appropriate masculinity in the pre-war world had been predicated upon cultural 'honour codes', then this interwar monarchical action to attribute honour to damaged male bodies and to incorporate them en masse into British honour culture in new, more radical ways marked a profound shift by the royals towards intervention to promote social change regarding the treatment of, and attitudes to, disability – rather than preserving the status quo inherent in pre-war social norms. For a usually highly conservative institution – monarchy and Court – to do this illustrates the extent to which the war challenged the Establishment. Aid was not just symbolic, as the KNRS demonstrates: in the interwar period both the king and queen sought to improve the material living conditions and medical treatment of the war disabled. The king and queen's strong support for the Star and Garter Home for Disabled Ex-Servicemen was another example of this.[369] The king and his sons, Edward and Albert, also appeared in a 'victory film' in aid of St Dunstan's Hostel for blind ex-servicemen.[370] To support the integration of the disabled into the workplace, in particular, was a very radical act, particularly for an institution – the monarchy – that had largely remained aloof in the pre-war period from publicly commenting or intervening on issues of employment treatment or workers' conditions.

The ways in which the KNRS was initially conceived are highly revealing of the power of monarchism in British society in the first half of the war. As Meaghan Kowalsky has argued, the founder of the KNRS, Henry Rothband, cleverly suggested

> an incentive to encourage reluctant employers to participate in the scheme: the appeal to hire disabled men would be sent out by Royal Proclamation. Every business that took up the appeal would be listed on a national Roll of Honour. As further inducement, they would be awarded the King's Seal for use on their correspondence and office stationery. Rothband believed that the prestige of Royal favour would encourage employers to take up and stay with the scheme.[371]

Such ideas remained popular even after the war. When the Scheme was finally established in 1919, the accompanying Royal Proclamation declared: 'it is a dear obligation upon all who, not least through the endeavours of these men under the mercy of Almighty God enjoy the blessing of victorious peace, to make acknowledgements of what they have suffered on our behalf'.[372] Note the ambiguity – 'our' refers both to their disability as obtained while fighting not only on the king's behalf (Our behalf) but also on behalf of the shared British nation and empire, king and people, jointly (our behalf). This Royal Proclamation was by special agreement read 'on four successive Sundays' by ministers of religion in their churches and chapels.[373] The use of a Royal Proclamation, through the Privy Council, sanctified the establishment of the King's National Roll of Employers. The Scheme, which the government supported, could have just been announced by the Ministry of Labour, which backed it. The involvement of royal patronage mattered: as Sir Almeric Fitzroy, the Clerk of the Privy Council, noted in his wartime diary, the Royal Proclamation helped smooth opposition 'on the part of the ordinary ex-soldier to look with jealousy upon the preferment of disabled men to positions which they, who are not in receipt of any pension, think themselves better entitled'.[374]

The role of the monarchy in rehabilitating the male disabled body, during and after the war, by crucially rendering it 'honourable' is thus a very significant wartime development in the relationship between royalty and disability. As a result of the conflict, the symbolically 'perfect' royal body could now engage – and be seen to engage – with the disabled masculine body in new ways, in photographs, in handshakes and touch, in welfare support, in direct affirmation and encouragement. This was clearest on 23 November 1918, when the king, together with the queen and Prince of Wales, reviewed tens of thousands of 'Silver Badge' men in Hyde Park, which the *Daily News* described as follows:

> Saturday's review of Silver Badge men in Hyde Park was marked by unprecedented scenes – scenes which probably could not have happened in any country but this. At least 20,000 men took part in the processions and one

estimate places the number at 30,000. Each man before leaving the parade ground was handed a copy of a message from the King, signed in facsimile in which he wrote: 'Your wounds, the most honourable distinction a man can bear, inspire reverence in your fellow countrymen. The welfare of the disabled in the war is the first claim on the country's gratitude and I trust that the wonderful achievements of medical science, combined with the national and voluntarily supported institutions may assist you to return to civil life as useful and respected citizens. I hope that the splendid spirit of comradeship on the battlefield will be kept alive in peace. As your King I thank you.'[375]

The king's personal letter to the disabled veterans clearly illustrated their honoured status. It also stated: 'We all honour you and admire the ungrudging way in which you have done your duty.'[376] In another speech to the war wounded, the king stated:

> I am glad to have met you today and to have looked into the face of those who for the defence of Home and Empire were ready to give up their all, and have sacrificed limbs, sight, hearing and health. Your wounds, the most honourable distinction a man can bear, inspire deference in your fellow-countrymen. May Almighty God mitigate your sufferings, and give you strength to bear them.[377]

Strong praise and a new understanding of disability as honourable were clearly conveyed here. The idea of the wound as revered by the public gaze, rather than as something reacted to with horror by the onlooker, is a transformative concept. The strange paradox here, of course, is that the royal body was also 'other', segregated, not seen as 'ordinary' and subject to a special gaze by onlookers – that of awe and deference. Thus, two forms of particularly socially differentiated bodies in this period, subject to particular forms of 'gaze', were juxtaposed in this wartime connection between monarch and disabled.

In fact, the Hyde Park event showed how potent this idea of the king bestowing honour on the disabled body was. The parade had been organised at the behest of the War Office, which hoped it might 'calm the growing dissatisfaction of the discharged disabled soldiers'.[378] The royals at the event were thus already nervous when, as the Prince of Wales recalled, there was a sudden commotion and 'as if by a prearranged signal, hitherto concealed banners with slogans were defiantly unfurled. With cries of "Where is this land fit for heroes?" [...] the men broke ranks and made straight for the King, who was quickly surrounded.'[379] The *Daily News* report described how 'the wild enthusiasm of the men culminated in a stampede' towards the royals present.[380] The Prince of Wales feared they wanted to attack the monarch and pull him from his horse, but rapidly realised the disabled ex-servicemen merely wanted to shake the king's hand or simply to touch him: 'I saw with relief that those who were closest were only trying to shake his hand. These men meant no harm: they had merely taken advantage of an opportunity the War Office had all unconsciously given them of laying their grievances before the King in person.'[381] According to the *Daily News*: 'The ranks were broken and hundreds of men shook hands with the King and the Prince of Wales and many crowded around the Queen's carriage and even entered it and shook hands with her. She frequently exclaimed as she shook hands with one of the men "God bless you, boy."'[382] Such was the press of the crowd that the *Daily News* reported: 'At one time it looked as if the King and the Prince of Wales were in danger of being dragged from their horses till a detachment of Life Guards formed a bodyguard for them and piloted them to the outskirts of the crowd. After this the march past took place [. . .].'[383]

It appears that an appeal directly to the king to resolve grievance, almost a feudal concept, was still a potent concept for ordinary British ex-servicemen. And clearly the royal touch remained desirable and talismanic even in the era of the Great War; here was a modern reinvention of the medieval notion of its healing power: King George V's touch as redemptive to the war-disfigured subject's body and sought out by disabled veterans. 'His Majesty shook hands with hundreds of them', according to the *Sunday Post*; other press reports referred to them as 'Silver Badge heroes' greeting King George; the royal handshake, disability and war heroism were all conflated in the reports of this event.[384] Significantly, the sudden and unsanctioned rush to touch the king seemed so disruptive of protocol, which set the king's body as sacrosanct – it was not permitted for a subject to touch it, only the king could bestow 'touch' and it could not be taken at the subject's initiative – that the Prince of Wales thought for a moment a revolution was breaking out. There could be little better illustration of the perceived link between the stability of the British state and the inviolate kingly body: overturning cultural rules that prohibited subjects touching the monarch of their own volition amounted to overturning the state in Edward's mind. Notably, at the event, the Prince of Wales was reassured at the sight that 'Most of the men wore on their lapels the "Silver Badge", signifying their honourable discharge for wounds or other disabilities.'[385] The badge signified that these men were 'honourable', although 'all in plain clothes'; it meant they were former military and their disabilities badges of honour, and, thus, as a crowd, they were less to be feared.[386] Likewise, Queen Mary's portrayal here is revealing of older narratives; rushed by the crowd, she bestowed the royal touch together with a religious blessing. Her photograph album shows how she and the king smiled and engaged the men as they tried to shake the royals' hands, Queen Mary holding a man's hand from her carriage; the king, on his horse, surrounded by exuberant men's faces, reaching hands up to him.[387] The incident fully illustrated how the cultural sacralisation of the monarchy continued to exist, even in the context of socio-economic grievance and post-war political radicalisation, and the tensions which this could generate.

Yet, despite the changes that the war brought to the relationship between the monarchy and the disabled subject, the kingly body *itself* being disabled remained taboo and problematic. Perhaps the most illustrative moment when this became particularly clear was on 28 October 1915, when the king was badly injured – and only narrowly avoided disability – when his horse reared and fell upon him at Hesdigneul during one of his visits to troops at the front. The monarch had to be evacuated by stretcher to a motor ambulance and then to the United Kingdom in a war hospital train – thereby experiencing first-hand the medical services designed for the war wounded and sharing their initial experience of the worry, fear, danger and disorientation of a bad injury; the hospital ship, the *Anglia*, which brought him back to Britain was sunk by a German mine less than three weeks after it had carried the monarch.[388] The king wrote of how, 'During October 29th, 30th and 31st I suffered great pain and hardly slept at all as I was so terribly bruised all over and also suffered very much from shock.'[389] Here the king's own bodily experience was paralleling that of his war-disabled subjects – perhaps also a factor in the scale of his empathy for them during and after the war. Indeed, the king's fall from his horse was narrated in the press as if it was a war injury – his endurance and stoicism, his return on a hospital train intended for the war wounded and his slow and determined recovery all echoed press tropes about war casualties. Even his biographer, John Gore, in his 1941 book, expressly likened the king's conflict experience to a war injury, writing that, for George V, 'as for many a man who went through those years as an adult, the war was an episode, an excrescence, a slice of the years cut from his life, an experience which marked and aged him and brought him permanent physical disability'.[390]

The press also depicted the incident in terms of tropes of royal moral perfection being aligned to physical endurance and stoicism. Despite his severe injuries leaving him unable to sit up, before leaving France the monarch went ahead with decorating Sergeant Brooks of 3rd Bn Coldstream Guards with the VC from his hospital-train bed: 'he knelt down so that I could pin it on his coat', the king noted in his diary.[391] The press emphasised the monarch's fortitude in continuing with the medal investiture ceremony from his hospital-train bed, despite being in pain. Typical was the headline in the *Dundee Evening Telegraph*: 'Pathetic Incident in Hospital Train: His Majesty, Although Lying Helpless, Determined to Honour Gallant Soldiers'.[392] British press languages of the stoic royal body thus drew upon real royal behaviour. Queen Mary suffered neuritis in her right arm and shoulder in 1917; her doctors advised her to rest, but she refused, dedicated to continuing her wartime royal work.[393] The king and queen themselves clearly shared the cultural beliefs in the exemplary function of the physical stoicism and morality of the royal body, thereby consolidating them. Here too we can see how the wartime cultural expectations built around masculine soldierly behaviour – endurance, bodily sacrifice, self-command – were influencing existing pre-war ideals about royal bodies' 'perfection' and exemplary behaviour.

The king's physician Sir Bertrand Dawson wrote that George V's injuries were

> more serious than could then be disclosed. Besides the widespread and severe bruising, the pelvis was fractured in at least two places and the pain was bad, the subsequent shock considerable [. . .] How well I remember that insistant [sic] urging of G.H.Q. that we should get the King to England before the Germans had time to bomb the house, indifferently sheltered in a small wood, and how we insisted we must wait until there had been some recovery from the shock and time enough to know there were no internal injuries.[394]

Dawson's words reveal the concern at making the king's true injuries publicly known, the monarchical body's vulnerability and possible disability being a deeply problematic suggestion for contemporary wartime British culture. A subversive reaction to the king's accident also highlights this: in a 1994 oral history interview, Private John Hall recalled of the king's accident that 'of course everybody said he was drunk'.[395] Royal physical imperfection – falling from a horse – was immediately aligned with *moral* imperfection and associated with rumours at the time regarding whether or not the king actually kept his own wartime pledge to abstain from alcohol. In the moral economy of wartime, any hint that the monarch did not keep up his side of the monarchy–subject equation of sacrificing together had potentially huge dangers for royal popularity.

It was four weeks before the king was able to walk, and his biographer Harold Nicolson reported that 'Those closest to him realised thereafter that he was never quite the same man again.'[396] Winston Churchill recalled how, when, a few months after the king's accident, he 'took leave of him, on resigning from the Cabinet, I was shocked at his shattered condition and evident physical weakness, which had of course been hidden from the world'.[397] Even though a bulletin announcing the king's accident was released by his doctors in France almost immediately after it happened, the full extent of the incident was kept quiet, thereby preserving the image of the intact and invulnerable monarchical body – as a metaphor for the British *Patria* it could not be allowed to be projected as weak or collapsing in wartime.[398] Queen Mary's biographer, James Pope-Hennessy, claimed that, following the accident, 'King George V, who had never been a robust man, was often in actual pain. This pain, bravely concealed, told upon his nerves and thus upon his temper.'[399] The endurance of physical pain, largely hidden from the public, was thus part of the royal war effort.

3.7   Conclusion

The end of the war would see the royal family further embrace new, more informal, cultures of the body. When Princess Mary had her official court debut, which had been delayed due to the war, on 10 June 1920 – the first evening court function to be held since 1914 – full state dress for the ladies was abolished: 'feathers and veils and the regulation court trains were dispensed with by Royal sanction'.[400] Prince Albert – the future George VI – promoted fitness and outdoor recreation during the interwar years. New royal charities were set up around these issues and successfully fundraised to dramatically increase youth access to sporting facilities; of particular note was royal work with the National Playing Fields Association and the Industrial Welfare Society. In the 1930s, as historian Ina Zweiniger-Bargielowska has shown, the royals pioneered a national fitness movement which had the support of the government, Labour leaders and the Trades Union Congress; in 1935, the King's Jubilee Trust Fund was set up to raise money to expand amenities for 'physical recreation' for teenagers.[401] In 1921, Prince Albert, as Duke of York, established the first of his Duke of York camps with the aim of promoting cross-class bonding – bringing teenage public-school and working-class boys together in an effort to create greater social cohesion following the First World War.[402] This was partly a royal response to the war, which had unleashed communism in Russia and triggered royal fears of revolution in the United Kingdom which, it was hoped, greater inter-class solidarity would avoid.

The war had also created a generation of young royals with far greater experience of social interaction with the middle and working classes as a result of their work during the conflict. Not only had two of the elder royal children worked for sustained periods outside of traditional royal educational roles and court circles – Princess Mary as a nurse and the Prince of Wales at the front – they had all carried out innumerable visits to hospitals, factories and shipyards and been part of the new communicative culture of conveying royal intimacy to subjects, handshaking, one-to-one conversation, posing for photographs, sitting with the wounded. While Prince Albert's war service in the navy was a more conventional royal education, he shared these new royal experiences of interaction with the subject, in particular, in his service with the RAF at the end of the conflict, which helped inspire his interest in the physical training of young men.[403] His post-war camps took this process further, mingling the bodies of those from different classes on the sports field and in campsite activities just as they had been mingled together in death on the Western Front. Cross-class bodily contact was fundamental to this idea of sport and games creating social cohesion; it took the wartime royal experience of touching the subject's body during formal war visits to hospitals, medal ceremonies or factories, in solidarity with war suffering and sacrifice, a step further, bringing both royalty and upper-class boys alike into relaxed, informal physical contact with the working-class body. The boys were allocated to groups of 20 (made up of 10 boys from industrial backgrounds and 10 from public school backgrounds) who shared a tent and played sports and games as a team; at least 6,000 boys had attended the camps by the end of the 1930s.[404]

At these camps, Prince Albert too became a participant; the royal body was now symbolic of a new post-war world of generally easier social interactions, which abandoned the stiff formalised rituals of the pre-1914 era. Initially, the prince visited each camp only briefly, but, from 1927, he participated more in the activities and wore shorts and an open-neck shirt rather than the lounge suits and bowler hats of his first visits.[405] One staff member at the Duke of York camps described seeing him 'ducked in the sea by his exuberant guests'.[406] This was not equality – the whole function of the camps was to bring the profoundly socially *unequal* into contact with each other, under the aegis of the royal presence, which made it permissible, in the hope that through physical sporting contact they could accept each other and thereby unify the body politic. In other words, in the immediate aftermath of the war, the royal family realised that using the body to communicate could be a highly effective way of stabilising the monarchy – a lesson to which the experience of the conflict had surely contributed.

The First World War changed the relationship between the monarchy and the body in many different ways, and it is not possible within the scope of this chapter to encompass them all. However, it is clear that the war had a real impact in permanently altering how British royalty was socially permitted to interact with the body of the subject. Royals had to engage with the physical bodies of their subjects as war disabled, wounded and dead in complex ways and had to ensure that their actions did not offend or undermine the status of the monarchy at a time when Britain was engaged upon a modernising total war effort and post-war democratising reforms. The monarchy thus had to steer a careful path between successfully upholding as much of its traditional role as possible while also not seeming an anachronism. Yet, what is also clear is the ways in which older scripts of royal 'perfection' and of the power of the 'royal touch' upon the subject in need of healing were reworked during the war in discourses that sacralised the wartime work of the royals.

Ultimately, the monarchy during the First World War was tangibly 'embodied' in particular ways that reworked cultural concepts of 'honouring the king' and adapted them to the era of total war. These concepts appeared in codes of social practice: when interacting with the physical presence of royal individuals, for example, or touching them, or in royals' physical obligations of behaviour such as the suppression of public emotion and sustaining formal demeanour. The bodies of the war mutilated and dead proved disruptive challenges for existing pre-war codes, some of which were abandoned, as is clear from the way the king and queen opted to interact with the wounded subject's body during their hospital visits, which went far beyond any pre-war norms. Likewise, some of the codes survived, such as the taboo on subjects touching royalty at their own initiative. The monarchy, and ideas about the royal body, thus had hugely significant roles in performing wartime bereavement, compassion, rehabilitation of the disabled and religious ideas of penance, often in directly physical ways, through shifting cultures of the body at war. They also had a powerful resonance in representing the national and imperial body politic. The sophisticated performance of these roles by King George V and Queen Mary was well received by the British public, and this, in turn, was a significant factor in stabilising the position of the British monarchy in an era of enormous social and political change. War cultures of the wartime royal body ultimately served to reinforce older culture codes, about the sacralised, distinct role of monarchy and its innate power.

4

De-Sacralisation Discourses

Challenges to the Monarchy's Status, 1916–1918

4.1 Introduction

What became of kingship in the second half of the war? In what ways did cultural sacralisation of the monarchy continue? How did honour cultures evolve or fall away? Chapter 4 looks at de-sacralisation discourses in wartime society and explores how far cultures of deference regarding monarchy were challenged by wartime change. It shows that de-sacralising the British monarchy was a key part of the campaign for independence in Ireland in 1916–22 and that this had cultural, legal and political ramifications. By contrast, the available evidence suggests that the increase in critical attitudes to the monarchy within Britain remained more limited and that, even where the idea of monarchy was challenged in the abstract, King George V and Queen Mary continued to be personally respected, and, in many quarters, popular, although in an era before public opinion polls popularity is difficult to assess. This chapter analyses the effect of the counter-narratives that the monarchy put forward in the wake of the Russian Revolution and concludes that these were largely effective. It covers the second half of the war, 1916–18, to examine how the monarchy's status and image shifted in this period.

One change is immediately clear: the rise of particularly politicised narratives about monarchy in this phase of the conflict. The current historiography on the British monarchy has long pointed to 1917 – the year of the Russian Revolution – as a catalyst for longer-term modernisation processes rooted in the late nineteenth century, which saw the monarchy successfully adapt to the era of mass politics and increasing democracy.[1] Yet, as the previous chapters have shown, the First World War years were not simply a catalyst for ongoing modernisation, but also revived and reinvented cultural discourses and practices that served to sacralise monarchy, particularly in the war's first two years. This chapter will examine how the second half of the war saw the rise of de-sacralisation discourses – public narratives that contested the monarchy's status or even its existence. It will consider the extent to which these discourses actually represented a threat to the British monarchy's position, as well as the monarchy's own response to them.

This chapter makes a series of key arguments. First, it contends that the impact of the Russian Revolution in 1917, which came as a great shock to the British royals, can only be understood in light of the history of the monarchy across the war as a whole. The Russian Revolution was not a stand-alone moment but interacted with the sacralisation processes and dynamics that the monarchy had sustained and promoted from the war's outbreak as well as with the events of 1918, when a series of royal dynasties collapsed across Continental Europe. Moreover, the period 1916–18 must be read together; 1917 was the middle of the wartime period of challenge for the British monarchy, not its starting point. On 18 November 1916, the Assistant Police Commissioner Basil Thomson noted in his diary that he was 'sent for to go to Buckingham Palace to-day to have a talk with Lord Stamfordham on pacifism and labour matters, about which the King seems to be concerned'.[2] Revolutionary crisis for the British monarchy began domestically in the United Kingdom in April 1916, in an internal attempted revolution in Dublin with the republican-led Easter Rising, and reached its peak with the news of the execution of the Romanovs in summer 1918 and the revolutions across Continental Europe in the final weeks of the war. The 1916 Easter Rising galvanised a rise in republican ideology across the island of Ireland, a close and immediate threat to Britain, with its large Irish Catholic immigrant communities, and one which would play out in the Irish War of Independence that followed immediately after the First World War. Irish republican anti-monarchism was strident and extreme: this chapter suggests the de-sacralisation narratives it presented regarding the British monarchy serve to highlight the relative moderation of those that appeared on the British Left in the wake of the Russian Revolution.

Strikingly, the revolution that actually occurred to disrupt the United Kingdom – that of Ireland – has received far less attention from historians of the British monarchy than the revolution that was feared but never materialised, that of a Bolshevik revolution in Britain. Ireland, after all, was not the core of the monarchy's everyday, lived world, in the way that Britain was. Courtiers were far more exercised about the potential Bolshevik peril to the dynasty in the wake of revolutionary upheaval in Continental Europe, and their focus is reflected in that of the monarchy's historians, who emphasise the year 1917 as the key wartime moment when the status of the British monarchy was challenged as a result of revolutionary ideas stemming from the Continent.[3]

Second, this chapter assesses the impact of the Russian Revolution and the de-sacralisation narratives that it triggered. It finds that the crises of 1916 and 1917 – the introduction of conscription, the Easter Rising, increasing war-weariness and the Russian Revolution – did indeed lead to changes in what could be said publicly about monarchy in wartime. It suggests that the Russian Revolution triggered a breaking of discursive taboos, allowing for the questioning of monarchy in new ways. These, in turn, caused panic at court, leading to changes in how the monarchy presented itself which also had an impact in its press image.

In the second half of the war, the image of the monarchy became less romantic, although it remained highly sentimentalised in the tabloid press; there was a new emphasis on the British monarchy as uniquely democratic and as serving the people's will. This chapter explores the scale of the alarm that events in Russia triggered for the king and his courtiers – in part because of the fact that the deposed tsar was the king's cousin but also because revolution in Russia was followed by other anti-monarchist revolutions elsewhere on the Continent. As historian Richard Bessel has written, the First World War was 'the great catalyst for revolution in the twentieth century [. . .] in a deeper sense, if we understand revolution more broadly as the erosion and dissolution of established hierarchies and the reconstruction of societies as well as polities on the basis of new concepts, allegiances and structures of power and authority'.[4] It is in this light – in terms of triggering revised approaches by the monarchy to sustaining its revered status among the British public, which often included blending old traditions and new innovations – that the Great War was revolutionary for the throne.

Third, this chapter explores how far the alarm at court reflected the reality of any spread of anti-monarchism among the British public. It provides evidence to suggest that the king and queen remained popular and that, although the Russian Revolution changed the discursive climate, it did not trigger a rise in widespread anti-monarchist feeling – or any real republican movement – within the island of Britain. This chapter argues that de-sacralisation of the monarchy in the second half of the war remained relatively limited: it was much more about a reconfiguration of certain discursive taboos – criticism of monarchy was now possible, including openly demanding that the monarchy reform and questioning what its role should be in the future post-war world – than about actual changes in public behavioural responses to the monarch or physical threat. Some caution is necessary here: the source record is incomplete. Lloyd George was advised by Maurice Hankey, the wartime secretary to the cabinet, not to include his planned chapter on the tsar's asylum request in his memoirs, for example. Lloyd George's secretary stated that 'some parts of it made him feel that it would be premature to publish – for instance the reference to the anti-monarchical movement that was developing in England at the time. Hankey thought that the King would object to this [. . .].'[5] Yet, even taking source limitations into account, outright criticism of the king and queen remained very much a minority action in 1917–18, even within the Labour movement. No less a figure than the Prime Minister, Lloyd George, struggled to significantly reduce the king's political influence, as this chapter's examination of how monarchism thwarted his attempt to try the kaiser reveals. Indeed, as the quotation above shows, avoiding offending the king even affected what Lloyd George's memoirs could contain.

Finally, this chapter argues that successful counter-discourses about the value of the British monarchy were used to sustain its power in the second half of the war, in the wake of challenges from Ireland and Continental European revolutions. It looks, in particular, at how the monarchy's loss of its diplomatic role as an interlocutor with Continental European governing royals, with the overthrow of the monarchical order across vast swathes of Europe by 1918, was swiftly replaced by an increasing emphasis upon its sacralised role as the keystone of the empire.

A note here on methodology: for Chapter 3 it was possible to juxtapose cultural discourses about the royal body with actual practices, which can be traced through primary source evidence from encounters between royals and subjects and from material history. However, for Chapter 4, such a juxtaposition has been much more difficult. While in the case of Ireland there is widespread legal evidence of cases of anti-monarchist behaviours, what at the time was termed 'sedition', for Britain, the source base on anti-monarchist practices or behaviour during the war is far thinner. The monarchy certainly believed that it was under threat from a rise in radical socialist attitudes following the Russian Revolutions of February and October 1917. Yet, while cultural discourses shifted in some press quarters and at some political rally speeches, it has proved very difficult to trace any examples of actual anti-monarchist *practices* developing. In contrast to Ireland, royal insignia were not ripped off buildings or royal statues toppled in Britain, and the trappings of monarchy – oaths of allegiance, processions, mass investitures, newsreels of the royals in cinemas – continued to function without protest. Both monarchists and socialist radicals alike claimed that the war had brought major change in attitudes to the monarchy, but these did not play out in significantly changed collective behaviours towards royalty in Britain; quiescent, and often enthusiastic, crowds continued to gather for any royal appearance. For this reason, we must be cautious in accepting any claims about the reach of anti-monarchism in 1917–18 that came from interested groups with a strong stake in the debate, such as courtiers, small-circulation radical left-wing press newspapers and trade-union militants. It is unclear to what extent these reflected widespread popular changes in public attitudes more generally. The historian Frank Prochaska has examined the rise of 'republicanism' in Britain in 1917, but again, his findings relate largely to an increase in anti-monarchist discourses and fears among interested cohorts – militant labour circles and courtiers.[6]

For the Second World War, Mass Observation sources exist to provide us with insight into how ordinary people reacted to cultural discourses about the monarchy; by contrast, for the First World War we have only very limited evidence to answer this question. Yet, the rise in critical discussion of monarchy in Britain in some press quarters in 1917–18 that Chapter 4 shows suggests that it was not war censorship that was 'hiding' a wave of popular mass anti-monarchism – anti-monarchist ideas were clearly permissible in the British wartime public sphere in press debates, pamphlets, books such as H. G. Wells's *In the Fourth Year* (1918) and in radical militant labour circles in this period. Rather, it indicates that there was something of a disjunction between this rise in anti-monarchist cultural discourses in 1917–18 and the actual manifestation of anti-monarchist behaviours and actions among the general public. The former was very visible; the latter barely evident at all, including in police archives, suggesting that the practices of monarchism were not as threatened by the shift in public debate as one might expect. This would help to explain the sheer scale of crowds who thronged to see the king and queen during their processions around London by carriage immediately after the Armistice, with working-class areas such as Lambeth and Kennington showing widespread displays of loyalty. The royals themselves were surprised at their popular reception and at the degree of support they were shown, having believed in the fears of their courtiers that anti-monarchism was rising in the last two years of the war. It seems the fears regarding anti-monarchism in some press debates, such as that in *The Times* in April 1917, did not reflect the majority of the public's attitude to royalty. Indeed, many workers still got their perception of the monarchy from its sentimental and hagiographic depiction in tabloids such as the *Daily Mail*. In sum, as Chapter 4 will show, anti-monarchism in Britain remained limited in its impact, but the belief that it was on the rise following revolutions on the Continent shocked the monarchy into rapidly and radically developing its pre-war and initial wartime outreach to the working class and its association with democracy. Here again the modernisation of the monarchy that the war brought was only one part of the story, which was as much about the integration of widespread traditional working-class loyalism and popular monarchism into the monarchy's image in 1918 as it was about the monarchy's new engagement with the media and with the Labour movement's leaders out of fears of revolution.

Ultimately, revolutionary change in Continental Europe and in Ireland could have triggered a dynamic *de-sacralisation* of monarchy that risked undermining the processes of royal sacralisation that operated in British society shown in the previous chapters. For the kinds of revolutions occurring – the radical rise in Ireland of anti-monarchist secessionism from the United Kingdom catalysed by the 1916 Easter Rising and its aftermath, in increasing accusations regarding the royal family's connections to Germany, and in socialist and communist overthrows of crowned heads of state across Europe – were all about demystifying monarchy, revealing it not as the eternal manifestation of the nation and empire but as a political system that could be replaced with better and more modern and egalitarian alternatives. These did not find mass support in Britain, because the counter-narratives around monarchical sacralisation ultimately proved stronger.

4.2 Ireland: The First Wartime De-Sacralisation Challenge to the British Monarchy

What might a real wartime cultural de-sacralisation challenge to the British monarchy look like? In the case of Ireland, we get some indication. The First World War proved a radical catalyst for monarchist and anti-monarchist political discourses on the island, and both were central to mobilising and radicalising the public in what has become known as the Irish 'decade of revolution 1912–23'. The Irish case merits considerable attention here for multiple reasons. Ireland was the one part of the United Kingdom where anti-monarchist republicanism became a potent political and cultural force during the era of the Great War. However, its triumph was never total: when twenty-six counties of Ireland gained their independence in 1922, it was as a dominion within the British Empire, with the king still head of state. Moreover, Ireland was a case where monarchism had strong supporters at the start of the war among the unionist 20 per cent of the island's population and one where, like elsewhere in the United Kingdom, King George V enjoyed a largely positive personal image, following a successful visit to the country in 1911.[7] It thus illustrates what factors sustained monarchism, as much as what factors could promote and spread anti-monarchism in a politically polarised wartime context. The wartime evolution of Irish monarchism thus offers an analysis of a contest between negative and positive monarchist discourses, key to shaping identities on the island in this period, with the unionist community, north and south, expressing fervent forms of monarchism in many respects, while republicans increasingly defined monarchism as the epitome of British identity and radically rejected it.

Cultural attitudes to, and languages of, monarchism and anti-monarchism in Ireland during this period of war and revolution therefore clearly matter. Yet there is much we do not know. How were these radicalised by the outbreak of the Great War in 1914? How did radicalisation foster political violence, given changing attitudes to monarchy were central to ideas about violence and political legitimacy in Ireland during this period? And how did the mindsets of monarchism and anti-monarchism enable or inhibit solutions to political violence in the final compromises of both partition and Free State? As argued throughout this book, the British monarchy should not be written off as a meaningless symbol: as in Britain, in Ireland monarchy in this period was a powerful cultural belief system and legal framework, supported and rejected on these grounds, which explains why it triggered such strong emotions. Yet the pro- and anti-monarchist cultural dimension to Ireland's independence struggle in this period has not received much historiographical attention, despite the fact that it was so central to the violent culture wars that broke out between unionist and nationalist Ireland, and ultimately between the Free

State compromise and the idealised Republic; the historiography on the British monarchy and Ireland has overwhelmingly focused on earlier periods.[8]

It is also important to note that Ireland, as part of the United Kingdom state during the First World War, was part of a transnational circulation of wartime languages about the British monarchy: Irish republican discourses after the 1916 Easter Rising and into the War of Independence spread to Britain, particularly through Irish emigrant communities, but also beyond these to socialist and later communist British militants and to the wider empire.[9] Republican propaganda in the Irish War of Independence was highly sophisticated and often backed by significant parts of the American and British press, such as the *Manchester Guardian*. In a similar fashion, British imperial and domestic languages of kingship and of monarchism circulated to Ireland, and Irish unionists' monarchist discourses spread beyond the island of Ireland. In sum, the increasing antagonism between monarchism and anti-monarchism during the Irish revolution was a dynamic that was transnationally influential in a way that has not yet been subject to academic scrutiny. The full scale of this cannot be covered here for reasons of scope; however, there is clearly a question as to why the monarchy was not more endangered in Britain by the languages of republicanism coming out of Ireland, particularly in 1917, when there was a rise in internal British domestic questioning of the monarchy following the Russian Revolution. One speculative answer could be that Irish wartime republicanism actually *strengthened* the monarchy in the long term by directly associating anti-monarchism with rebellion against the war effort, with alliance with Germany – the 1916 rebels' gallant allies – and with an Irish Catholic 'other' still largely viewed as racially and culturally inferior in Britain and thereby tarnishing it. Another answer is that Irish unionist propaganda successfully emphasised the value of the monarchy to the population of Britain, presenting it as meaningful, as determinant of ethnic and national identity and in a positive light, under threat from violent republicanism between 1916 and 1921. A key factor too was that Irish republicanism revolved around challenging monarchical 'sovereignty' solely on the basis of Irish nationalism – a basis which was not transferrable to Britain itself. Ultimately too, the independence of the Irish Free State in 1922 ensured that the most fractious part of the British Isles, the part that had most contested the monarchy in the previous decades, had now seceded, allowing the monarchy to consolidate its domestic position in the remaining regions of the United Kingdom. From a Continental European historical perspective an obvious question is: how did the British monarchy survive in Ireland in this broader era of anti-monarchist revolution that emerged across the Continent in the second half of the Great War, which swept away numerous European dynasties? Ireland – with its revolutionary turmoil and violence, which had such a strong anti-monarchist dimension in 1916–23 – seems an anomalous case, to find that the British monarchy would ultimately emerge as head, albeit symbolic and contested, of the new Irish Free State in 1922, given the degree to which the Irish revolutionary pattern fitted with successful anti-monarchist revolts elsewhere. This section explores these issues in detail, examining attitudes to the monarchy among different sectors of the Irish population and why the monarchy ultimately proved central to the compromise of the Anglo-Irish Treaty of 1921.

To turn first to unionism: at the outset of the First World War, ironically, relations between the monarchy and the unionist community were at a low ebb over the Home Rule Crisis. Tensions had been building for some time: in the Ulster Solemn League and Covenant of 1912, which the vast majority of unionist men individually signed, while women made a parallel 'declaration', unionists pledged as 'loyal subjects of His Gracious Majesty King George V' to stand by each other 'in solemn Covenant' to defend their 'cherished position of equal citizenship in the United Kingdom [. . .] using all means which may be found necessary' to defeat Home Rule, devolved government for Ireland.[10] Two forms of identity – of subject but also of citizen – are radically asserted here. The primary bond of the Covenant, moreover, was less to the king than to each other as a religious Protestant community under God. The implication of 'all means necessary' was that unionists would rebel against the king's parliament and army should the third Home Rule Bill succeed, which would de facto also be a rejection of the king and his assent to it. The Covenant thus asserted not unconditional 'loyalty' but *bounded* loyalty, a statement that the king's subjects had indissoluble rights that even the monarch, in granting assent to a parliamentary bill, could not override. The very term 'loyalism', used to refer to unionist cultural and political identity, referenced the British *Crown* not the government, but it was clearly under strain in 1914.[11] Concerns about the degree to which unionist officers in the British army would remain loyal to the Crown in the event they were asked to act against any hypothetical Ulster Unionist rebellion over Home Rule even surfaced during the Curragh Mutiny of March 1914.[12]

The situation worsened due to the king's granting royal assent to the Home Rule Bill in September 1914, although an accompanying Suspensory Act 'effectively delayed its implementation indefinitely during the war'.[13] The government also promised that later amending legislation would exclude Ulster. Nevertheless, unionists, who had petitioned the king to refuse assent and not to sign the bill, were outraged. Their demands, however, would have been a Crown breach of constitutional norms whereby the monarchy would have rejected parliament's will, an indication again of unionist ambivalence when it came to respecting the actual conventions of the modern British constitutional monarchical system. The southern unionist community also felt their interests had been ignored, while northern unionists across Ulster held 'protests against the King. Pictures of George V were booed and members of congregations in some Protestant churches walked out when the national anthem was played', powerful acts of de-sacralisation.[14] By contrast, when the

House of Commons was formally informed of the Royal Assent on 19 September, a Labour MP, Will Crooks, began to sing 'God Save the King', and others joined in, evidence of support for the monarchy, seen as having upheld the rule of parliament on the Home Rule issue.[15]

There was also, however, disappointment with the monarchy on the moderate nationalist, pro-Home Rule side in Ireland due to the failure of the king's personal initiative – the Buckingham Palace Conference – of July 1914, which had aimed to resolve the Home Rule impasse by bringing unionist and nationalist leaders together, but failed to reach a settlement. It was convened at a point where there was real fear that civil war would break out in Ireland over the issue, prompting the king to act. Radical nationalist Kevin O'Shiel recalled how

> That conference can be said to have represented the last straw of hope for a tolerable settlement of the Irish question along strictly limited and constitutional lines. [...] it seemed to Irish Nationalists that, seeing that the King had directly and actively intervened, an All-Ireland Parliament would, with proper safeguards to allay Ulster apprehensions, at last result. [...] Hence it was that Nationalists were frankly surprised and disappointed at the Conference's failure. They were sure that once the King had taken a hand in it, success must follow.[16]

These sentiments rapidly evolved, however. In particular, the First World War saw two key trends: first, the sacralisation of the monarchy as a key motivation in wartime mobilisation and sacrifice by Irish unionists, both north and south, who made it central to their war identity; second, a major increase in the visibility of long-standing, anti-monarchist attitudes amongst the Irish nationalist population, particularly in the wake of the 1916 Easter Rising. These anti-monarchist attitudes aimed deliberately at de-sacralising the monarchy and so were the antithesis of unionist wartime beliefs, setting up a direct clash of war cultures. In fact, a particular dynamic emerged in Ireland between monarchism and anti-monarchism in this period. The binary of monarchism–anti-monarchism is used here deliberately, rather than that of monarchism versus republicanism. For what is clear from looking more closely at the evidence is that republicanism's rise was uneven between 1912 and 1921 among Ireland's nationalists – it took time to come to dominance. The extent of commitment to republicanism in the Ireland of 1916 remains hotly debated, with Fearghal McGarry arguing that many of the Irish Volunteer Force who took part in the Easter Rising were not actually ideological republicans but rather separatists for whom the future structure of an independent Irish state remained vague: 'although the Rising is now synonymous with republicanism, its ideological significance was less apparent at the time: many rebels fought for Irish freedom rather than a republic'.[17] This was in contrast to Irish Republican Brotherhood (IRB) members who led the Rising and were, of course, republican in outlook, but far fewer in number. Although the question remains debated, the nationalist population at large appears to have still been predominantly pro-Home Rule prior to the Rising, although war-weariness was having a significant radicalising effect.[18]

Opposition to the British monarchy in Ireland already had deep roots, which made it a potent rallying force for nationalism in general. There had long been an established anti-monarchy folk culture among parts of the Irish population, particularly the Catholic peasantry.[19] The Irish rebellion of 1798 was inspired by American and French republicanism, and the Great Famine of 1845–9 and the Land War of the late nineteenth century had seen surges of resentment of the British monarchy. Irish connections with America – the world's most successful republic in the mid-nineteenth century – to which a million Irish peasants emigrated during the Great Famine period, were pivotal here; the USA served as a model for what a republic might achieve. It inspired an Irish separatist and republican movement known as Fenianism, active from the 1850s, and led by connected organisations, the secretive Irish Republican Brotherhood in Ireland and Clan na Gael, its American wing, which provided funding and ideological synergies.[20] In 1867, this Fenian republicanism was clearly in evidence in the Irish Republican Brotherhood's declaration on the eve of its failed uprising, which referred to the 'curse of Monarchical Government'.[21] The centenary celebrations of 1798 in 1898 also revived republican ideas.[22]

Irish separatists' opposition to the British monarchy was aggravated by the monarchy's own historic, and dogged, anti-Catholicism. Historian James Murphy has rightly pointed out, however, that we should be wary of projecting the Irish nationalist rejection of the British monarchy in the early twentieth century back upon earlier periods and that nineteenth-century Irish national-ists often differentiated their antagonism towards constitutional union with Britain from their loyalty to the British monarchy; he argues it was only in the era of Parnell that anti-monarchism increasingly became a badge of nationalist conviction.[23] Moreover, opposition to the British monarchy in Ireland was not the sole territory of advanced separatism or republicanism before 1914, but also could be found among mainstream supporters of Home Rule, alongside less anti-monarchist positions in the same movement. The Home Rule cam-paign could accommodate a spectrum of views on the British monarchy, from support and toleration to indifference and hatred. This plurality was closely connected to the blurred late nineteenth-century lines between Fenianism and the Home Rule movement. As historian Matthew Kelly points out, until the Irish Parliamentary Party split in 1890, some Home Rule politicians 'still tried to secure their separatist rivals as collaborators, protecting the ideological interests of advanced nationalism for strategic and ideological reasons', while others of its MPs 'felt the advantage of distancing themselves from the Fenian tradition'.[24] Following the party's reunification in 1900, however, this plurality started to become strained: 'there was growing ideological divergence between separatists and constitutionalists after the home rule party's reunification in 1900'.[25] Nevertheless, within the Home Rule movement before 1914, Irish nationalist anti-monarchism had still managed to coexist with more moderate opinions. Before 1914, in other words, monarchism versus anti-monarchism was not the extreme polarising divide it would become for Irish nationalism by 1919 or the dominant credential for proving a nationalist political identity.

Moreover, by the outbreak of the First World War, Irish republicanism was very much a minority movement in comparison to Home Rule, which had united much of the Irish nationalist population around the relatively moderate political aims of greater devolved government for Ireland within the United Kingdom. Separatist propaganda during the war accused the Home Rule movement of supporting the monarchy, but this assumption requires further nuance: historian James McConnel has shown that radical anti-monarchism also existed within the Home Rule movement to a greater extent in the Edwardian period than is sometimes assumed.[26] For example, the Irish Parliamentary Party, the party that led the Home Rule campaign, opposed parliament voting for the Civil List settlement of 1901 of payments to the royal family, mocking 'the monarchical system as a violation of Irish liberty'.[27] It also boycotted King George V and Queen Mary's visit to Ireland in 1911. However, after the third Home Rule Bill of 1912 passed, the position of the Irish Parliamentary Party with regard to the monarchy was shifting to become more positive. George V's reforms upon his accession in 1910 – in particular his softening of the monarchy's anti-Catholicism – were key here. His successful meeting with the Catholic Archbishop of Dublin upon his arrival at Dublin City Hall during his and Queen Mary's 1911 visit to Ireland had created good feeling among moderate Home Rulers. Likewise, Lord Aberdeen, as Viceroy, had worked hard to improve the monarchy's image among nationalists, taking considerable effort to make the monarchy appear receptive to Roman Catholic grievances by 1912. This was accelerated by what was seen as King George V's genuine attempt to act as neutral arbiter at the July 1914 Buckingham Palace Conference on Home Rule, which was positively regarded by moderate nationalists. In sum, these factors, coupled with the outbreak of war with Germany, led to the Home Rule movement letting go of much of its anti-monarchist positioning. This left the path freer for republican propagandists to claim after 1914 that they were the sole true representatives of the tradition of Irish Catholic peasant hostility to the British monarchy. As historian Matthew Kelly argues, John Redmond failed to hold together a strong coalition of nationalist support during the war, and his 'intensified imperial conception of home rule' saw radical nationalist separatists break with the Home Rule movement: 'Redmond's advocacy of imperial home rule left his ideological flanks exposed.'[28]

The outbreak of the First World War saw the Irish Parliamentary Party move further away from its more anti-monarchist elements and towards compromise. Its leader, John Redmond, believed it needed to rein in its more radical anti-British wing. Long a moderate, he saw Ireland's security and economic interests as best served by devolved government within the United Kingdom and the British Empire. This now appeared particularly acute in view of the scale of German aggression on the Continent and the German invasion scares that swept Britain and Ireland in 1914. In this Redmond was not alone: Catriona Pennell has shown how, in the first months of the conflict, there was a widespread rallying in support of Britain's war effort in Irish towns and cities.[29] For Redmond, supporting the British government's war against the Central Powers would offer proof of nationalist Ireland's loyalty and trustworthiness, thereby tying the British government into implementing Home Rule after the war ended, despite unionist opposition. Although careful to keep his distance from the monarchy, Redmond was not an anti-monarchist; indeed, many historians describe him as a loyalist and an imperialist.[30] He certainly supported the idea of the British Empire and developed a good personal relationship with King George V, whom he met for the first time in 1914 as part of the king's attempt to resolve the Home Rule Crisis.[31] The king confided to the Bishop of Chelmsford on 30 April 1916 that he 'liked Redmond' and 'thought it a good thing if he was Prime Minister of Ireland but Carson and Ulster would never agree'.[32]

Redmond's decision to support the war split the Home Rule movement. The pro-Home Rule nationalist militia – the Irish Volunteer Force – established in 1913 to oppose its unionist counterpart, the anti-Home Rule militia, the Ulster Volunteer Force, split in September 1914 over the war. The vast majority of the Irish Volunteer Force opted to support the British war effort; renamed the National Volunteers, many of these men volunteered for the British army in response to appeals from John Redmond, taking the oath of attestation to the monarch as part of the standard army entry procedure. A much smaller minority, the pre-war more radical separatist and anti-monarchist wing, who rejected the war, remained known by the organisation's original name, as the Irish Volunteers. John Redmond later joined with King George V in taking the salute of Irish regiments about to leave for France, a moment described by journalist Michael MacDonagh: 'with bands of pipers wearing the saffron kilts of the ancient Gaels, playing national airs, and carrying green flags'.[33] Lieutenant Stephen Gwynn, a Home Rule MP, addressed a recruiting meeting in Killarney in June 1915, where a banner read 'Boys come and join to fight for Ireland. God save Ireland and the King.'[34] A rapprochement with monarchism was evident for the Irish Parliamentary Party.

The repositioning of the Irish Parliamentary Party cleared the way for the small republican movement to utilise older Irish folk cultures of opposition to the British monarchy to win broader support. The existing anti-monarchist tradition in Ireland did not disappear in the initial wave of support for the British war effort that spread across the country in 1914: for example, in November that year, the following speech was made at a radical nationalist demonstration against the dismissal of a government employee: 'Mr John Milroy said they were told "Your King and country need you", but they had no King, and they had no country but Ireland. They would have none of it. That Empire which they were asked to serve had done all that inhuman ingenuity could do to crush and destroy their nation.'[35] Anti-monarchism offered a broad and simple established brand for advanced nationalists to utilise to undermine the dominant Home Rule movement; it was also less abstract than republicanism. Republicans became very successful at portraying, and stigmatising, the Irish Parliamentary Party as a monarchist party during the Great War, painting it as one of 'castle' Catholics, a derogatory term implying docile subservience to monarchy. This was particularly effective once the war started to go badly in 1915, with disastrous losses to Irish units at Gallipoli. The surge of wartime monarchism in Britain at the outbreak of war in 1914 may also have been a factor in triggering a concomitant rise in Irish separatist anti-monarchism in response. This fits with historiographical arguments that the Easter Rising was triggered as a last-ditch effort to revive the separatist cause, a reaction to a sense that Irish support for Fenian separatism was on the wane rather than buoyant. Using anti-monarchist discourses and propaganda thus offered an effective way to win broader support for attacks on the British government and state by a minority movement, which republicanism, promoted by the IRB, represented in 1912–16. When Patrick Pearse read the Proclamation of Irish Independence at the start of the Easter Rising in 1916, declaring an Irish Republic, he was very clearly emphasising republicanism as the key differential between his brand of separatism and the devolution model of the Home Rulers. The very words of the Proclamation, 'We declare the right of the people of Ireland to the ownership of Ireland, and to the unfettered control of Irish destinies, to be sovereign and indefeasible', repudiated the British concept of sovereignty as invested in a monarch.[36] The choice of a 'Proclamation' to declare independence also directly asserted a counter-form of republican proclamation to the royal wartime Proclamations of the British king.

Irish unionism sought, by contrast, to show Britain the value of the union, through the scale of Irish unionists' wartime sacrifice, emphasising that unionists were fulfilling their duty to the king, in the hope that this would lead Britain to abandon imposing Home Rule upon them. Loyalty to the Crown was a central tenet of this wartime unionist identity, both north and south. At the Annual Prize Giving event for the Methodist School, Wesley College, in Dublin on 17 December 1915, the Principal Rev. Dr Irwin declared in his speech that 'We are not a little proud of the response our old boys have made to the call of King and Country.'[37] Almost 300 former pupils were serving in the army and navy. Church of Ireland parishes in the south of Ireland, which were predominantly unionist, produced elaborately decorated rolls of honour listing the names of all those serving 'for God, for King and Country' with 'His

Majesty's Forces by sea, land and air' (for another example, see Fig. 30).[38] The Ulster Volunteer Force (UVF), the northern unionist militia set up to oppose the implementation of Home Rule, volunteered en masse for the British army to serve in the war. Monarchism was a core identity in war for these troops.

Fig. 30 Wartime roll of honour from St Barnabas's Church of Ireland Parish, from www.irishwarmemorials.ie (© Michael Pegum)

J. L. Stewart-Moore, who enlisted in September 1914 in the 12th battalion of the Royal Irish Rifles and found himself serving largely alongside UVF men, described how, in his camp of four thousand men, 'I went to sleep every night to the strains of Orange ditties such as: "Come back to Ireland those who are over the sea, Come back to Ireland and fight for liberty. They are flying the flag, the harp without a crown, so come back to Ireland and keep popery down."'[39] The importance of the 'crown' as a symbol here is self-evident. The Easter Rising thus appeared not only as an attack on the British state but a betrayal of the personal virtues of loyalty and duty to the king – and in wartime too – hence the scale of the unionist moral outrage, particularly in Ulster. Their pre-war anger at King George V over Home Rule was long forgotten due to the conflict with the Central Powers. Ultimately, unionists fighting and dying in the war were doing so for the king; rejecting him was to reject the war dead, fallen on his behalf. Hence why for unionism it was such an emotional issue.

This helps explain why loyalty to the British monarch was key to discussions about Irish war service in 1914. Some young nationalists, frustrated at the delay in implementation of Home Rule and conflicted over what to do regarding war recruitment, attempted to compromise by offering to serve the war effort in Ireland. National Volunteers in Cork in January 1915 provided voluntary guards for key bridges, for example. But this effort was disbanded by the British military, Brigadier General Hill stating that he would not 'allow citizens who do not belong to the Crown forces to bear arms in defence of the realm'.[40] The monarchist language was typical, reflecting the centrality of loyalty to the king to unionist wartime cultural values. The Lord Lieutenant for Dublin City and County, the Earl of Meath, wrote to John Redmond on 15 August 1914 stating that 'as H.M. L[ord] Lieut. to County and City of Dublin I am most anxious to support and encourage all efforts to raise forces for the defence of the British islands, as long as I am assured that such forces acknowledge allegiance to King George, and are prepared to pay respect to His Majesty in the usual manner required of British troops'.[41] The Earl of Meath had heard 'rumours' that the leadership of the Volunteers disagreed about this matter.[42] He asked John Redmond for 'a written assurance that by giving official support and encouragement to the Nationalist Volunteers [. . .] I shall in no way fail in any loyal duty to His Majesty, the King'.[43] Monarchism in this context was not only a cultural backdrop: it was also determining political decision-making.

Monarchism was also central to the way that republicans understood Irish support for the war effort – support that dismayed them. Katharine Barry Moloney, the sister of one of Irish republicanism's most celebrated martyrs, Kevin Barry, wrote of how 'Shoals of the young men I knew were volunteering in 1914 for the British army. I was first brought up against reality in the Grafton Picture House when I found it impossible to stand for "God Save the King" during a performance.'[44] The anthem was a particular point of contestation in Ireland. The nationalist writer Ernie O'Malley described how, in the months before the 1916 Easter Rising, 'Three men were sentenced to three months for singing "God save the King" in an unseemly way'.[45] By autumn 1918, a recruiting meeting in Kingstown (Dún Laoghaire) was interrupted when rival factions began singing 'God Save the King' and the republican 'Soldier's Song'.[46] Another such meeting in Galway the same month was disrupted by hecklers shouting 'Up Redmond', 'Up King George', and 'Up de Valera'.[47]

Ordinary Irishmen serving in the British army also included monarchism as one of their key frameworks of interpretation of the war. In March 1916, Private John Cronin of the Munster Fusiliers, who had been held prisoner in Germany, described the treatment of Irish prisoners who had refused to change sides and join the Irish Brigade that the German army was recruiting in conjunction with Roger Casement to support an uprising against British rule in Ireland: 'we got starved in trying to make us join the Hun's Brigade but thanks to the men they stood firm although dying with the hunger for they were a credit to king and country'.[48] Private David Tormey, another former prisoner of the Germans and a regular in the Royal Army Medical Corps from Ballycumber, stated that when asked to join Casement's brigade he had replied that he 'was proud to say he had served faithfully under three sovereigns'.[49] On 23 December 1915, Sergeant John Brooks, serving with the 2nd Royal Dublin Fusiliers at the front, wrote to Monica Roberts in Dublin that 'I know things at home must be very quiet as everyone has someone out fighting for King & Country'.[50] When, shortly after the Easter Rising, German troops put a placard up in front of their trenches that stated 'Irishmen, why will you fight for England when they are shooting your wives and sisters in Dublin?', Munster Fusilier Lieutenant Francis Biggane, a Catholic, retrieved the sign under cover of darkness and 'later presented it to King George at Buckingham Palace'.[51] The obvious meaning of this gesture was to convey Irish loyalty to Britain, but also directly to the person of the monarch.

Although increasingly contested, monarchism appeared on the Irish home front too. In June 1918, Alice Russell, from Co. Limerick, who described herself as 'a soldiers [sic] wife', wrote directly to King George V to pass on 'information about the Sinn Feiners if it is wanted there [sic] conduct is something awful. [...] anything in the world I know I will let you know[,] I love England my husband is a soldier fighting at the front for his King and Country'.[52] In remembering the war, a direct monarchist motivation also appears in some Irish sources: when Emily K. Harris, former matron and commandant of the British Red Cross hospital in Corrig Castle in Kingstown (Dún Laoghaire), found herself faced with eviction in 1926, she wrote to King George V for help because, during the First World War, she had nursed 'to make good the ravages of warfare, by building anew the wornout, maimed tissues and bodies of the sons of Your Majesty's vast Empire, fighting for the glory of their King. For the honour of the Regiment, as a soldier's daughter, I did my duty, without pay, serving my King for Love.'[53] Her letter was, at King George V's command, transferred to the government of the new Irish Free State.[54]

Notably, although opposing attitudes to the monarchy in Ireland did largely overlap with religious affiliation during the First World War, these divisions were more blurred in the pre-1919 period than they would later become: the numbers of Protestant nationalists and Catholic monarchists were significant. Kevin O'Shiel, a later Garda Commissioner, recalled a row between a nationalist Protestant, Edward Millington Stephens, and an unnamed unionist lawyer at a King's Inns dinner just before the 1916 Easter Rising: the unionist was awaiting his commission in the British army and decried what he saw as the low rate of Irish volunteering for the First World War: '[...] the loyal young man lost his temper and told Stephens he should be ashamed of himself for not wearing the King's uniform. Stephen's [sic] replied that the only uniform of the King he ever hoped to wear was the broad arrow of the felon.'[55]

The 1916 Easter Rising again highlighted the degree to which the British monarchy underpinned the entire political and cultural framework of the state during the First World War: the British monarch's role in Ireland was far from that of a figurehead but a central part of the political and legal configuration of wartime power, particularly due to the Defence of the Realm Act. For example, on 26 April 1916 the introduction of martial law required the king's personal approval, as George V recounted in his diary:

> Lord Crewe came down and I held a Council at 5.15 to declare Martial Law in Dublin, where the Sinn Feiners rose two days ago and have barricaded themselves in some of the houses, there are several thousands [sic] concerned. Two Brigades have been sent to Dublin to Liverpool which will make 12,000 troops there besides the police.[56]

John Redmond, speaking in the aftermath of the Rising, referred to the insurrectionists as 'traitors', a remarkably loaded monarchist term.[57] The whole conceptual legal framework on which the Rising leaders were tried by court martial and executed was the crime of treason to the Crown, and the fact that civilians could be court-martialled, rather than tried in the civilian courts, was due to the Defence of the Realm Act of 1914. Kingship – and a monarchist culture – thus underpinned the discourse of the trials and the unionist and British response. The executions of the Rising leaders greatly disillusioned many Home Rule supporters: in September 1916, Tom Kettle, former Irish Parliamentary Party MP, who had been greatly upset at news of the Rising, would pen his famous poem before his death in battle, 'To My Daughter Betty, the Gift of God', in which he conveyed to his infant child that he fought for his faith and no earthly king: 'Know that we fools, now with the foolish dead, Died not for flag, nor King, nor Emperor, – But for a dream, born in a herdsman's shed, and for the secret Scripture of the poor.'[58] The rejection of all forms of temporal monarchism by this erstwhile Home Ruler was clear, as was the suggestion that adherence to Christianity supplanted it.

The outcome of the Rising radicalised the republican use of anti-monarchism as a means of winning public support. The executed IRB Rising leaders were firmly committed republicans and saw their role as upholding an Irish republican tradition dating back to 1798. They had organised the Rising together with James Connolly, the leader of the Irish Citizen Army, a radical socialist workers' militia, which was also closely linked with anti-monarchism. In September 1914, in reaction to the push for Irish nationalists to volunteer for the British army for war service, the Citizen Army had hung a large anti-monarchist banner on its headquarters, Liberty Hall (Fig. 31), with the message: 'We serve neither King nor Kaiser but Ireland', a message that it also promoted as a banner front page heading on its newspaper the *Irish Worker*.[59]

Committed Irish republicans promulgated rabidly anti-monarchist propaganda in the wake of the Easter Rising, together with narratives that conflated monarchism with the evils of the war, as a way of undermining support for the monarchy in Ireland. As Ben Novick has pointed out, advanced nationalist 'propagandists cried out against the futility and waste of King George's war'.[60]

Fig. 31   Armed members of the Irish Citizen Army parade outside Liberty Hall in Dublin under their anti-monarchist banner, Keogh Collection, National Library of Ireland Ke198 (Image reproduced courtesy of the National Library of Ireland)

Seamus O'Sullivan's 1916 ballad on the Battle of Jutland reflects this further, as the names of the ships sunk – called after members of the British monarchy – drew a direct connection between royal agency and death: 'Queen Mary had a thousand men their like we'll never see again, Because they're food for fishes now.'[61] This radicalisation around anti-monarchism rapidly became hardline: in July 1916, in the Palace Cinema in Cork, some of the audience hissed at newsreel images of the king and queen visiting wounded soldiers; even the war wounded were now suitable targets of anti-monarchist opprobrium.[62] At Westminster, Major Newman 'suggested banning cinema showings of images of the king or British troops, to prevent clashes between pro- and anti-war film goers'.[63] Ultimately a military police guard was stationed inside the cinema 'to detect hissing'.[64] War-weariness also facilitated this Irish republican instrumentalisation of anti-monarchism to promote their cause. In 1917, Tadhg Barry wrote a poem in memory of a friend who had fought against the Easter Rising rebels – there were many Irishmen in the British army units sent to put down the Rising – and who was then killed in France, serving with the Royal Dublin Fusiliers, which stated: 'Oh, would when Kings quarrel, Their own blood would be shed, And not like cowards snarl, Whilst slaves must fight instead.'[65] The implication was that the king was cowardly, forcing others to fight in his place. By using the war to attack monarchism, Irish radical nationalists pioneered processes that would later be used elsewhere in revolutions in wartime Europe to bring down royal dynasties. Ireland, in other words, was part of a much broader international zeitgeist across Europe in channelling a radical propaganda of anti-monarchism into a modernist, revolutionary mass movement coming out of the strains of the First World War. The republican separatist movement was also plugging into much older latent anti-monarchist narratives in Irish history as a way of radicalising Irish nationalism. Anti-monarchism was easy to grasp, had readily visible and available symbols to contest and fitted with revolutionary languages emerging elsewhere.

This discourse was aimed at radicalising those more moderate nationalists who had been indifferent or tolerant of the monarchy, particularly among the Home Rulers. Irish nationalism was not uniformly republican in the IRB mould at the time the Rising broke out or even immediately in its aftermath.[66] Republican propaganda had to make it so. For example, while the IRB led the Rising, the foot soldiers of the insurrection were largely those members of the Irish Volunteer Force (IVF), the voluntary militia set up in 1913 to support the implementation of Home Rule, who had rejected supporting Britain in the First World War in September 1914. The degree of their personal republican convictions varied.[67] There was also a range of opinions among the nationalist intelligentsia. The Fenian republican ideal was not the only separatist model before 1914. Some favoured an idea put forward in 1904, by Arthur Griffith, a nationalist journalist and founder of Sinn Féin, for Ireland to form part of a dual monarchy with Britain – similar to Austria-Hungary – as a solution to the problem of Irish self-determination. Griffith's suggestion was always controversial among more extreme Irish radical nationalists, but its existence shows that the British monarchy did feature in some pragmatic advanced nationalist circles as part of a compromise solution for Irish self-rule.[68] Its longevity is also significant. The execution of the predominantly IRB Easter Rising leaders hugely raised the profile of republicanism and badly damaged Home Rule, as did the conscription crisis of 1917–18 and the way that the republican IRB effectively worked to co-opt Sinn Féin in the wake of the Rising, but advanced nationalist leaders were still debating what form of state an independent Ireland might have, with options including a potential dual monarchy for quite some time. According to republicans Desmond FitzGerald and Ernest Blythe, before and during the Easter Rising, even the Irish *Republican* Brotherhood leaders, Joseph Plunkett and Patrick Pearse, considered that, if Germany won the war, they might accept a German prince as king of an independent Ireland for strategic reasons.[69] The kaiser's youngest son, Prince Joachim, was the suggested candidate. Ernest Blythe pointed out that the Irish population were not theoretical purists on republicanism in 1916, confusing it with simply meaning separatism and independence, with which a constitutional monarchy was not incompatible.[70] Garrett FitzGerald, Desmond's son, also emphasised that the image of Europe's leading republic, France, as an anti-Catholic regime made republicanism suspicious to Ireland's devout Roman Catholic population.[71] Historian James Loughlin argues that a dual monarchy solution found 'substantial support' within the radical nationalist and separatist Sinn Féin movement as late as 1917. Edward MacLysaght, an unofficial observer for Sinn Féin at the Irish Convention of 1917, even proposed a dual monarchy as a solution to the forum as a 'view endorsed by "the great bulk" of the movement'.[72] Even Lloyd George wrote during the Anglo-Irish Treaty negotiations in 1921, in which Griffith took part, that 'Irish leaders are struggling to establish principle [*sic*] which we cannot accept – namely alliance with Empire as a sovereign and independent state on the old Austria-Hungary model', which he described as 'foreign to the British constitutional system' and futile given the 1918 fate of Austria-Hungary.[73] There were also vague suggestions and rumours that George V's daughter Princess Mary could become queen of Ireland and establish an Irish monarchy, which did not receive any support.[74] While the Sinn Féin convention of October 1917 declared a preference for a republic, it was accompanied by a statement proposing a referendum to settle Ireland's constitutional form. The global context mattered here. Before the end of the Great War, a republic appeared a difficult dream. Only two Western modern states – the USA and France – offered models. By 1918, the final year of the Great War saw a string of nationalist revolutions establish republics across Central and Eastern Europe. The IRB's republican ideal became significantly more plausible in this context. It was no coincidence therefore that it was the December 1918 general election campaign where Sinn Féin, steered by IRB figures, finally fully committed to an Irish republic and nothing else as its future separatist state model, leading to the newly established clandestine Irish parliament, Dáil Éireann, declaring an independent Irish republic in January 1919. By 1919, the Irish Volunteer Force would change its name – significantly – to the Irish *Republican* Army, a clear political message of anti-monarchism. Yet, even then, as Aidan Beatty has shown, much of the propaganda of Irish republicanism utilised older notions of ancient Irish monarchy – High Kings of Tara or Brian Boru, for example.[75] Monarchism continued to remain acceptable if it was ancient and Gaelic.

The sheer scale and extreme nature of anti-monarchist language and culture that Irish republicanism promoted in its propaganda thus make sense in this light. It was about ensuring that republicanism replaced any alternative rival models of separatist statehood for Ireland, as well as the old Home Rule movement, in an uncertain period. It was also about challenging unionist values and any lingering Catholic pro-monarchy sentiment in the country. These factors mattered if the IRB and its heir, the galvanised Sinn Féin movement that came out of the Easter Rising, were to resurrect the older Enlightenment Irish republican tradition of 1798 as hoped. Anti-monarchism, a traditional rallying cry for Irish peasant grievance, thus became a profound, and extremely held, totem of the Irish revolutionary republican campaign to a degree that it never had been for the Irish Parliamentary Party, nor indeed would be for many later independence movements elsewhere in the British Empire.

The material cultures of monarchism thus rapidly became a fraught issue in Ireland's culture wars of this period and in polarisation dynamics. Terms like the 'King's uniform' or 'King's shilling' had powerful implications – such terms were never empty rhetoric but embodiments of newly radicalising political loyalties and mobilisations. This helps to explain the store that Irish Parliamentary Party leader John Redmond set on trying to design and get approval for a new badge for the 16th (Irish) Division, which was made up largely of nationalist war volunteers for the British army; draft sketches of the badge emphasised shamrocks and had no royal symbolism.[76] As the public mood became more radically separatist after the Easter Rising, the visual and physical everyday material culture of monarchism – uniforms, postboxes, stamps, coinage, statues – became sites of profound contestation, and often attack. Historian Eva Giloi has worked on eighteenth- and nineteenth-century material cultures of monarchism to show how processes in these earlier centuries embedded visual and material cultures of monarchy into everyday life; the Irish revolution saw widespread efforts to reverse – and eradicate – these, particularly from 1919.[77] The violence involved and the intensity that material objects associated with the British monarchy could provoke was indicative of the degree of de-sacralisation that was happening: these were powerful symbols of a monarchy revered by unionists. Now they were being destroyed. The statue of William II in the Boyne Valley was destroyed in 1922. Significant place names with royalist associations were also symbolically renamed: Kingstown in Dublin became Dún Laoghaire and Queen's County became County Laois. Following a local administrative council motion, Queenstown in Cork became Cobh in 1920. By the late 1920s, coinage in the Irish Free State had replaced the king's head with a harp and with farm animals on the reverse sides.

Anti-monarchist political discourses were further radicalised as a response to the embedded role of monarchist language on the British side during the Irish War of Independence 1919–21. In June 1921, for example, the language used at military trials of those involved in Irish Republican Army (IRA) activities is revealing: for example, the charge sheet against Patrick Higgins of Ardra was that he 'DID LEVY WAR AGAINST HIS MAJESTY THE KING by attacking a detachment of His Majesty's troops'.[78] Again here, loyalty to the monarch is of central discursive and legal importance; charges like sedition were regularly used in Ireland, and treason charges appear too, used to condemn those executed after the Easter Rising. This British legal framework helps to contextualise the sheer radicalism of the anti-monarchist beliefs and rhetoric at the heart of Irish republicanism that also existed in the same period. Katharine Barry Moloney recalled that when her 18-year-old brother, Kevin Barry, was awaiting execution in 1920 for his role in an attack that killed three British soldiers, her mother refused to appeal to George V for clemency:

> On Sunday, 31 October, the eve of the execution, a mutual friend of ours and of the family of Sir James McMahon, Under-Secretary, came in great haste to Mother to ask her to send a telegram to King George V. protesting against the execution of her son. [. . .] we were informed that the telegram would, by special arrangement, be immediately conveyed to the British King. Mother refused, on the ground that any recognition by her of the British King would compromise her full support of the Republican Army.[79]

This was a remarkable act of anti-monarchism. Barry's execution went ahead. Such extreme sentiments help explain why, for the most radical republican minority, the oath of allegiance and the trappings of monarchy that the 1921 Anglo-Irish settlement involved were enough to trigger civil war.

Yet, precisely when the majority of the wider Irish nationalist public rejected any role for the British monarchy in the future of Ireland in this period remains very unclear. Rejecting Home Rule, it is important to emphasise, was not the same as fully embracing republicanism, nor was wanting self-rule the same as rejecting the monarchy. This perhaps helps to explain why a role for the British monarchy was still considered feasible in the solution to the Irish question throughout the period 1916–22 by some moderate nationalists, particularly as it appeared to offer the potential for solving the problem of incorporating unionists into any future independent Irish state. Moreover, even during the height of the War of Independence, King George V was still seen as a source of potential solutions. When the imprisoned republican Lord Mayor of Cork, Terence MacSwiney, embarked on his, ultimately fatal, hunger strike in 1920, King George V received petitions from Ireland to intervene and save MacSwiney's life, including 'numerous messages [. . .] from various quarters and from people of different creeds and political parties'.[80] There were genuine concerns, Stamfordham wrote, that people did not understand that the king could not intervene openly in MacSwiney's case, as 'even among the educated public there is an idea that the Sovereign should, in extreme cases, assert his authority. [. . .] His Majesty asks Mr Balfour to tell the public that it is useless their asking the King to release the Lord Mayor of Cork from prison because His Majesty cannot do so unless his Ministers so advise.'[81] In fact, behind the scenes, petitions for leniency were having effect, and the monarchy did try to influence events: Stamfordham also penned a letter suggesting that MacSwiney should be 'taken out of prison' and 'moved into a private house where his wife could be with him' while kept under strict surveillance, as the consequences of his death in prison would be 'serious and far-reaching'.[82] Moreover, the fact that a majority of the Irish public voted for the Anglo-Irish Treaty of 1921, which contained significant monarchist dimensions – dominion status for Ireland, the British monarch as head of state with each member of the new independent Irish Free State parliament taking an oath of allegiance to him or her – suggests that the monarchy was not as universally hated at this point as some of the republican narratives wished to suggest, or at least not hated enough for a majority to jeopardise a peace deal over it. This helps to explain why, for moderates in Ireland and Britain, the monarchy was seen as a potential mediator and as offering a compromise solution to the Irish conflict.

Two further pivotal events illustrate this further: first, the king's opening of the new Northern Irish parliament in Belfast in June 1921, following the partition of the island and the creation of devolved government within the United Kingdom for six counties of Northern Ireland, and second, the battle over having an oath of allegiance to the British monarch incorporated into any future settlement on independent statehood for the remaining twenty-six counties. The question of an oath of allegiance dominated the negotiation of a peace treaty between Britain and Irish republicans in December 1921. Both are points where the weight, ongoing cultural power and meaning of the British monarchy into the post-First World War period are clearly evident.

King George V's decision to travel to open the new Northern Irish parliament in Belfast on 22 June 1921 and the wording he chose for his speech marked a radical intervention by a monarch in UK domestic politics and a major contribution to ending the Irish War of Independence. This intervention stemmed from his long-standing interest in Ireland, which dated back to his accession and his experience of the Home Rule Crisis. Although he held traditional conservative views that Ireland was British, these evolved, initially to accepting Home Rule, later to accepting the Free State.[83] Moreover, he believed strongly that all Irish people, as his subjects, were entitled to their full rights. On Catholicism he was far more open-minded than much of the British Establishment, getting the 'Protestant Declaration', which was profoundly anti-Catholic in sentiment, dropped from his first parliamentary speech and the anti-Catholic clause annulled from his coronation oath. His diary steers clear of the racist anti-Irish attitudes common to the Establishment of the time. Even Sinn Féin did not accuse George V of personal anti-Catholicism. This was the king who, during discussions in 1913 on the exclusion of Ulster from Home Rule, had presciently asked 'if Ulster were left out' whether the 'Protestants would give a promise not to molest the Roman Catholic minority?', and he asked for assurances about this again privately, after partition, from prominent Northern Irish unionists in 1921.[84] The king 'frequently intervened' to warn the Cabinet against its reprisals policy in Ireland, while in July 1921, an American newspaper reported that the king was at odds with Lloyd George's use of repression and had even said 'This thing cannot go on. I cannot have my people killed in this manner.'[85] The Palace was furious at the leak and never publicly acknowledged the king had made such a statement – but the quotation, according to historian James Loughlin, 'has the ring of authenticity'. Moreover, Stamfordham privately admitted to Lloyd George that he had met the journalist concerned to promote the royal view on peace in Ireland.[86] Stamfordham also wrote in May 1921 to the Chief Secretary of Ireland, Sir Hamar Greenwood, to question the government's policy of using violent reprisals in Ireland.[87] George V had shown personal concern for Irish Catholics, even for those who detested monarchy as an institution; he also obviously carried weight with unionists. All this meant that the king could, in 1921, try to serve in the role of arbiter once again between unionist and nationalist, as he had in 1914. It was symbolic monarchy and its history that by 1921 was detested, as highlighted by loaded terms used in republican propaganda. There was some more ambiguity regarding George V himself.

This context helps to explain King George V's risky decision to personally open the new Northern Irish devolved parliament. Lloyd George had advised him that it could be advantageous if he opened the new parliament, which would give the occasion monarchist weight. According to lady-in-waiting Countess Airlie, the king was well aware that he would be exposed to personal danger in making the trip; much of the British press was against it.[88] The Clerk of the Privy Council, Sir Almeric Fitzroy, was so concerned he asked the Lord Lieutenant of Ireland what real risk the monarch ran: 'I was glad to have it confirmed, on his authority, that, so far as the King is concerned, the opportunities of attack are no greater than those which present themselves on any day upon which he encounters a crowd.'[89] A lunch guest, Lord Abingdon, also cynically assured him that the republicans would not attack the king, because the unionists would then probably massacre 'a large section of the Catholic population' in revenge.[90] Queen Mary decided to accompany the king at the last minute, in all likelihood because of her fears that he might be attacked.[91] On the return journey – once onboard ship – the queen admitted as much in front of her lady-in-waiting, stating that 'they could have got any of us'.[92] It was no idle comment; a troop train 'carrying soldiers and horses that had taken part in the visit' was blown up on the way back to Dublin, 'killing three soldiers and a railway guard'.[93] Mary Kenny suggests Queen Mary's presence was unionist leader Sir James Craig's idea and that the queen was asked to also attend.[94] The royal party were driven in open horse-drawn carriages 'at walking pace' through the centre of Belfast, as shown in Fig. 32; Sir Hamar Greenwood, Chief Secretary of Ireland,

Fig. 32 King George V and Queen Mary in Belfast, 22 June 1921, photograph by Alex Hogg (Reproduced from the private collection of Brian Walker with kind permission)

considered too toxic a political figure and too likely an IRA assassination target, travelled separately to Belfast City Hall by a different route – again highlighting that the king was not considered to be as negatively viewed by Irish republicans as the Chief Secretary of Ireland, even if the streets were still lined with security forces to protect the royal couple.[95] Unionism was thrilled and reassured that the king had come to Belfast; by contrast, the Roman Catholic hierarchy and nationalists boycotted the opening.[96] The key unionist politician, Sir Edward Carson, also significantly did not attend the opening of a northern parliament symbolising the end of his original hope that all of Ireland might remain within the Union under direct rule from Westminster.[97] Sacralisation motifs were clearly at work in the unionist response to the monarch's visit. The unionist Lord Mayor of Belfast described 'auspicious' divine approval in the fact the sun came out when the king arrived in the city; another unionist described the opening as a 'fairy-like scene'.[98] In reaction to the king's speech to open the new parliament, among his audience, 'some of the women wept'.[99]

In fact, George V's Belfast speech deliberately invoked this sacralisation and symbolism of the British monarchy. It was intended to awake emotions, of loyalty, of duty, to be steered towards work for reconciliation. It was also deeply personal, and it channelled a sense of his own upset at the horrific violence happening in Ireland. The king invoked his own prayers, a powerful message from a devout monarch in Ireland, a very religious country in this period: 'I pray that My coming to Ireland to-day may prove to be the first step towards an end of strife amongst her people, whatever their race or creed. [...] I appeal to all Irishmen to pause, to stretch out the hand of forbearance and conciliation, to forgive and to forget, and to join in making for the land which they love a new era of peace, contentment and good will.'[100] Well beyond his immediate audience – selected for their loyalty – the broader Irish public also responded positively.[101] George V's moderation was immediately contrasted with the aggressive stance of his government.[102]

This speech had a significant impact on the king's image in Ireland, and his role in creating it rapidly came under scrutiny, particularly given how different the speech's tone was to the public government line, which emphasised force to suppress the IRA and its aims. Even staunch republican Ernest Blythe believed that the king had chosen to reject a 'war to the hilt' speech prepared for him by the British cabinet for the opening of the Northern Irish parliament as he 'had other views about the matter', thereby triggering 'an unprecedented constitutional crisis', as 'the King [...] had not only refused to deliver the speech prepared by the Government, but had produced his own draft', which he had constructed with the help of South African statesman and premier Jan Smuts.[103] Blythe's account was hearsay, based on Smuts's account to Irish republican Desmond FitzGerald and apparently corroborated to Blythe by Winston Churchill, but it shows how Irish republicans, even while they abhorred the British monarchy, believed the monarch personally to be a more sympathetic character than the British government.

Moreover, Blythe's account was not far wrong. The king had indeed intervened directly, rejected initial versions of the speech, and inserted the statement referring to his own personal desire for peace, even if the final version, like all royal speeches, was a multi-authored document. Speeches were often drafted for the king by a range of different figures in this period and then put to the monarch for his input, amendment and approval; they were also often approved in advance by the Prime Minister and the cabinet. Among the regular writers of royal speeches were Rudyard Kipling, Fabian Ware, Jan Smuts, Viscount Bryce, the Archbishop of Canterbury, Randall Davidson and Lloyd George's Private Secretary Edward Grigg. Queen Mary's important speeches were similarly drafted; both her 'letter to the troops' and her speech 'to the women' of Britain were written by the Archbishop of Canterbury's wife Edith Davidson and amended by the queen.[104] The monarch did have an input, however, and this could be considerable: as Lord Halifax noted in November 1918 on a speech by the monarch: 'The King himself took great pains about it. I do not mean that the composition was his, but he had considerable say both as to the points made and the words used.'[105]

Historians concur that the Belfast speech was drafted by Sir Edward Grigg, Lloyd George's Private Secretary.[106] However, given how hostile Lloyd George was to adopting a conciliatory approach in Ireland, it does appear that the king had unusual input into the tone and choice of wording of the speech he gave on this occasion.[107] The conciliatory tone of the speech did not originate with Lloyd George. At the cabinet meeting on 12 May 1921, the cabinet was split on whether it wanted to work for a truce in Ireland or use more repression. Lloyd George was among those who opposed a truce, and he also was adamantly against any offer of dominion status to Ireland's nationalist separatists, arguing that the policy of two Home Rule parliaments, north and south, established in the new 1920 Government of Ireland Act, was as far as he was prepared to go. If it failed, the cabinet planned to enforce crown colony status on southern Ireland; moreover, just days before the king's speech, the cabinet's Irish Situation Committee was contemplating a dramatic escalation of violent repression in Ireland.[108] The royal intervention came after a meeting in mid-June 1921 between the king and Smuts, a dominion premier who was very well informed on Ireland, with close Irish nationalist connections and who, as a Boer who had fought against the British in the Second South African (Boer) War, enjoyed a relatively positive image in nationalist Ireland and was known to be in close contact with the Irish separatist leader, Éamon de Valera. The king had turned to Smuts, who was in London for the Imperial Conference, and invited him to lunch at Windsor Castle on 13 June 1921, after the monarch had become aware of an initial potential draft of his speech for opening the new Northern Irish parliament which had been written by the incoming Northern Irish premier, Ulster Unionist Sir James Craig. Craig's draft had 'greatly distressed' the king, who feared he was to be made a 'mouthpiece of Ulster' in the speech 'rather than that of the empire'.[109] According to Smuts, the king and Stamfordham were 'anxiously preoccupied' about the king opening the new Northern Irish parliament.[110] Lloyd George had 'advised' the monarch that it would be advantageous if the king did so, in all likelihood because Lloyd George felt this would help win over those unionists who rejected partition and wanted all of Ireland to remain in the union.[111] Although he courageously accepted Lloyd George's suggestion to travel to Ireland despite the risk of IRA attack, George V feared that his presence in Belfast could antagonise nationalist Ireland and now requested Smuts to help to draft his speech for the parliament's opening.[112] The next day, Smuts came up with a text emphasising peace and reconciliation, as well as hinting at future Irish dominion status, and shared this with the king and Lloyd George. He also sent the latter a letter, again copied to the king, where Smuts set out that the king's Belfast speech should 'foreshadow the grant of dominion status to Ireland'.[113] It is highly unlikely Smuts would have dared make this suggestion in his letter and draft speech had the monarch not approved the idea; George V was thus ready to concede more on Ireland than his government was. Lord Stamfordham also telephoned Lloyd George on the monarch's behalf to ask the Prime Minister about incorporating Smuts's suggestions into the text.[114] Importantly, this royal intervention took place *before* the government had agreed a final draft of the speech, which was thus superseded by the advent of the more reconciliatory Smuts and the Palace collaborative initiative.[115] The Cabinet's Irish Situation Committee rapidly convened on 16 June, notably with Stamfordham attending to push the king's views, to discuss Smuts's draft, which it found unacceptable, and requested Arthur Balfour to draft an alternative version. Balfour's draft was profoundly unionist, claiming in terms likely to inflame nationalists that Ireland had 'long enjoyed' full political and religious freedom.[116] The king rejected Balfour's draft. At this point, Lloyd George accepted defeat and asked his private secretary, Sir Edward Grigg, who had long argued for a reconciliatory speech approach, to take over the drafting, and it was Grigg who produced the final version, which contained slight traces of Smuts's and Balfour's drafts as well as a statement personally written by the king on his own desire for peace.[117] Grigg's draft then went back and forth between the king and the Prime Minister and Grigg, one paragraph dashed off on headed paper from Chequers for insertion, until finally a wording was found that the king warmly welcomed.[118]

Thus, in this case, it appears royal influence changed the tone of what Lloyd George had initially planned for the Belfast trip. The Archbishop of Canterbury, Randall Davidson, wrote to the king that 'of course I know that the Government accepts responsibility – and will now rather eagerly claim credit – for Your Majesty's Belfast speech. But in the circumstances and manner of its delivery, and in much of its shape and language [. . .] the personal note rings clearly out.'[119] Indeed, the king's efforts at conciliation in Belfast garnered such positive reactions that George V would later offer to open the new independent Irish parliament, Dáil Éireann, after the Irish Free State came into existence in 1922 under the Anglo-Irish Treaty – an offer the Dáil flatly rejected, as it would have clearly compromised its republican aspirations.[120]

It was not so much the reaction of nationalist – or even of unionist – Ireland to the king's speech that had greatest impact, however; it was the reaction in Britain. Here was a royal call to restraint in the Irish conflict, to a new era without direct rule, to respect – a call which clashed markedly with a bitter speech calling for all-out force to repress the Irish which the Lord Chancellor made in the House of Lords virtually simultaneously to the monarch's Belfast trip, a fact which greatly annoyed the king when he later learned of it.[121] The king's words had the effect of undermining the hardliners in the British Establishment – those who refused to accept any change to Ireland's status and supported repression. As the Archbishop of Canterbury warned the king, some men 'both inside and outside parliament' were 'aghast', but impotent, at the king's support for an Irish peace settlement which won the favour of the mass of the British population.[122] The monarch's speech thus had the effect of emboldening a British compromise with regard to Irish independence. As he wrote pointedly to Lloyd George on returning from Belfast, the Prime Minister should not 'lose the opportunity' the speech had created.[123] Following this royal demand for prompt action, the British cabinet decided to invite Éamon de Valera, the leader of Ireland's separatist campaign, to London for peace talks: it was a dramatic U-turn for Lloyd George, who only weeks previously, in May, had been demanding the IRA be hunted down using extreme force.[124] Given Ulster Unionism's emphasis on its loyalty to the monarchy during the war, a royal call to reconciliation also obviously carried great weight with unionists, although there was little time to fully exploit this politically, as sectarian violence re-erupted in Belfast in July 1921, highlighting how on the ground polarisation and security fears rapidly trumped the royal initiative for all sides, including loyalists, purportedly staunch crown supporters who carried out the majority of killings in the city. Huge public crowds turned out spontaneously in London to welcome the king and queen on their return from Belfast. It was clear that, in a society where monarchism was still so deeply influential, the king's wishes for peace so publicly articulated would need to be delivered upon; when the peace treaty ultimately was agreed, Lloyd George telegrammed the king to 'humbly congratulate' him on 'the triumph of the famous Belfast speech from the Throne'.[125] The king was also widely perceived as having shown personal bravery in going to Ireland when republicans threatened his personal safety there, which enhanced the popularity of the monarchy and the power of his message.[126] It was no coincidence that a truce came into effect on 11 July 1921 and official Anglo-Irish peace talks rapidly started in London on

14 July, just weeks after the king's speech – and although there were other factors, such as the IRA's military situation, which played a role, the talks are also an indication of the authority the king held. The king also sent Jan Smuts as his personal emissary to Dublin to meet with Éamon de Valera in early July 1921 when the latter was proving reluctant to accept the talks' offer to directly convey the king's desire for peace, to which de Valera pointedly assured Smuts that he accepted the goodwill of the king but could not believe in the sincerity of the king's government.[127] Smuts's role as a go-between connecting the monarchy and the Irish republican leadership was ultimately a factor which helped hasten the start of the face-to-face peace talks in London between Lloyd George and de Valera later that same month.[128]

The monarchy not only helped promote peace talks; it was also fundamental to the British understanding of potential solutions to the Irish War of Independence. Lloyd George confided in his mistress that the July 1921 peace talks were meant to impress upon de Valera the greatness of the empire and the king.[129] For unionists in Ireland and for the population of Britain, the monarchy was a fundamental ideology that their menfolk had mobilised to defend and perform their 'duty' to in the First World War. This wartime role radicalised the importance of the monarchy but also gave it great authority. One of the paradoxes of this period is that, if the British monarchy provided a polarising symbolic impetus within Ireland, being used to mobilise unionist and nationalist populations against each other, it also ultimately provided the framework – dominion status – for the British exit: the Anglo-Irish Treaty of 1921. The British obsession with the monarchy as the foundation of the entire empire meant that if Ireland retained any link to it, this rendered Irish independence much more palatable on the British side. The ultimate Free State dominion status of the twenty-six counties, which was the solution accepted by the British government in 1921, was underpinned by a profoundly monarchist belief system that meant that if the monarchy survived in Ireland then independence did not mark a British defeat. It provided reassurance. For Lloyd George, for example, who rather ironically was often not considered by the royal court as a particularly committed monarchist, allegiance to the king was the principle 'upon which the whole fabric of the Empire and every constitution within it are based'.[130] If, under the Treaty, part of Ireland had gained independence, it remained part of the monarchist sphere, one of the monarchy's dominions, with the king remaining head of state. In a Britain in which monarchism was the dominant culture this mattered far more to British decision-makers than whether or not Ireland remained under direct British governance by Westminster, even for an anti-IRA hardliner like Lloyd George.

Although both sides recognised that the peace treaty they were negotiating was officially between Irish separatists and the British monarch, Irish negotiators at the Treaty talks never fully grasped the emotional complexity of the British attachment to the Crown.[131] Precisely because of the cultural weight of the monarchy, it remained the one aspect of Britishness that Lloyd George and the British delegation to the 1921 Anglo-Irish peace treaty talks could not renege upon: Lloyd George informed Éamon de Valera that 'we cannot consent to any abandonment however informal of the principle of allegiance to the King [. . .]'.[132] He rejected any form of recognition of the Irish delegation that would suggest 'Irelands [sic] severance from the King's domains'.[133] Hence the long, and torturous, talks over the insistence that members of the Dáil in a new dominion-status Irish Free State would have to take an oath of allegiance to the British monarch. The clash at the talks was a profoundly ideological one between monarchists and republicans: the British side even researched the American oath of allegiance to the constitution to try to find a wording that might fit better with their republican-minded interlocutors.[134] This came to nothing, one minute recording wryly that they had realised what was at issue was not the oath's 'words' but the 'substance'.[135]

Arthur Griffith and Michael Collins on the Irish delegation on 1 December 1921 proposed changing the wording of the oath to: 'I . . . do solemnly swear to bear true faith and allegiance to the Constitution of the Irish Free state as by Law established and that I will be faithful to His Majesty King George in acknowledgement of the Association of Ireland in a common citizenship with Great Britain and the group of nations known as the British Commonwealth.'[136] Needless to say, this version, which is rather different to that which the British proposed, was unacceptable to the British side, which viewed the monarchy in almost mystical terms – the Irish version removed reference to loyalty to the king's heirs and set up a model whereby Ireland 'associated' with the Commonwealth in international affairs but in which the monarch would have no internal role in Ireland, which the Irish delegation argued could then be an 'internal' republic. Griffith's exact idea was that 'for external affairs [. . .] Ireland would recognise the British Crown as proposed, while for internal retaining the Republic'.[137] Griffith told the talks that 'Ireland is not a Colony but a parent race and a separate entity, and that the Dominions would support them.'[138]

The British side was obsessed with loyalty to the Crown as the foundation of the status of all dominions in the British Empire, which all had an equal relationship to their unifying monarch. This was the fundamental principle through which the British government and monarchy were conceptualising imperial reforms in the wake of the changes brought by the Great War. As Frederick Smith, Lord Birkenhead, told the Irish delegation, 'the British people attached the greatest importance to the symbol of the Crown'.[139] Griffith for the Irish delegation rejected this way of thinking. Griffith submitted to the talks that, for the other dominions,

> the Crown to them is a symbol of the external unity of equal states, not of the internal repression of subordinate states. Ireland, on the contrary lies beside the shores of Great Britain, which has been accustomed for

generations to interfere, in the name of the Crown, in every detail of Ireland's life. The desire and temptation to continue interference will remain if the Crown remains, as it cannot be the symbolic Crown that the Dominions know, but will continue to possess the real power of repression and veto which Ireland knows. [...] propinquity imposes on us a necessity for safeguarding our independence which does not arise in the case of the Dominions. The Crown [...] will never menace the Dominions with its powers.[140]

Griffith pointed out that his side's wording of the oath would associate Ireland with Great Britain and the dominions under the Crown and that 'it must be recognised that for Ireland freely to accept the Crown in any capacity is a momentous step on her part in view of history'.[141] For Ireland's delegate, George Gavan Duffy, the Crown 'symbolised a unity based on something real, the tie of blood' and this was why it worked for the other dominions – and Ireland recognised this, he claimed, with its concession that it would associate with the Crown for international issues.[142]

Griffith also pointed out that, under the old Home Rule bills, the Crown – and through it the British government – would have retained supremacy, and right of veto, over the Home Rule parliament. This, he correctly asserted, was not compatible with full independence. The British delegation, for its part, emphasised that, as with the other dominions, the king would act with regard to Ireland on the advice of his Irish government ministers only, and not his British government at Westminster. The monarch by 1919 related to each dominion government separately. For Gavan Duffy on the Irish delegation the issue went beyond the dangers of political interference: 'we cannot agree to use the word allegiance. It is out of date. Loyalty is now due not to Governments but to Nations.'[143]

This ultimately became the core of the row that developed over what wording would be acceptable for the oath of allegiance to the sovereign that Irish parliamentarians would take in the new Irish Free State. The British held the view that

> there were the gravest objections to any proposal to limit or subtract from allegiance. Irishmen could not be both aliens and citizens. [...] The British representatives were willing that the position of the Crown should be the same as the position of the Crown in Canada and in Australia. They could not accede to anything else. They regarded that as fundamental, the real test of common citizenship.[144]

In other words, throughout the British Empire, or Commonwealth as it was increasingly referred to at the talks in the light of Irish sensibilities, citizenship and being a subject of the king were inseparable – a subject *was* a citizen; everyone else was legally an alien. In gaining dominion status within the empire, the Irish Free State could not be exempt – its population remained royal subjects in British eyes, and they continued to have all the rights of British subjects should they choose to exercise them. Indeed, on the British side the belief was that linking Ireland into dominion status modelled on Canada would mean that 'the royal prerogatives of appointing ministers, summoning and dissolving parliament etc. would be maintained in the Irish Free State. However, the subsequent Irish Free State Constitution completely ignored the royal prerogatives.'[145]

The Irish delegation struggled to find a way around this centrality of monarchy to dominion status. Griffith told the talks that 'we are to have a reciprocal citizenship combined only for certain purposes for which we recognise the Crown as head'.[146] This was a non-starter for the British side given their obsession with the Crown as the root of citizenship, which they saw as inseparable from subject status: 'the Crown is the symbol of a common citizenship which makes all subjects of the King one in international law. No man can be a subject of two States. He must either be a subject of the King or an alien, and the question no more admits of an equivocal answer than whether he is alive or dead', noted a British memo.[147] 'Allegiance to His Majesty the King' was regarded as 'vital' for the British delegates.[148] It was the fundament of global British identity – precisely why radical Irish nationalists rejected it. A British note stated that 'The Crown is the symbol of all that keeps the nations of the Empire together. It is the keystone of the arch in law as well as in sentiment. All the Governments of the Empire are His Majesty's Governments.'[149]

Ultimately, the British wording of the oath would win out:

> I do solemnly swear true faith and allegiance to the Constitution of the Irish Free State as by law established, and that I will be faithful to His Majesty King George V, his heirs and successors by law, in virtue of the common citizenship of Ireland with Great Britain, and her adherence to and membership of the group of nations forming the British Commonwealth of nations.[150]

The final text revealed that for the British side it was acceptable to water down the term empire to Commonwealth but it was not acceptable to compromise on monarchist loyalty. Yet even this final wording was the source of controversy in the House of Commons, where, during debates on the Treaty on 14 December 1921, diehard Tories demanded an 'unambiguous expression of allegiance to the Crown' and talked of 'the surrender of the rights of the crown in Ireland'.[151] In truth, the Irish oath was weaker than that which parliamentary members in other dominions had to swear, which referred to being 'faithful' and bearing 'true allegiance' to the monarch, sometimes with the words 'so help me God' added.[152] The Irish oath swore 'true faith and allegiance to the Constitution of the Irish Free State' first, and only to be 'faithful' to the monarch and his heirs and successors.[153] Effectively, what has gone down in Irish history as the much maligned 'oath of allegiance' was in reality an 'oath of fidelity', a subtle difference of wording that highlights how Ireland was a test run for experimentations in new ways of operating for the monarchy within the empire. Moreover, Lloyd George, to soften the blow of accepting a monarchist oath, allowed the new Irish government the right to choose who would serve as 'the king's representative in Ireland', what one commentator described as the 'sterilisation of the Crown', ensuring that while the symbolism of monarchy remained in the Free State, its effective practice was much less likely.[154]

The Irish delegation ironically accepted the point that the Irish Free State would make an annual contribution to the king's personal revenue without much fuss. What mattered was the oath. For de Valera, the oath to a British monarch would 'disenfranchise every honest Republican like the Test Acts against Catholics and dissenters in the past', a reference to the Acts which were part of the Penal Laws whereby any man serving in public office had to 'recognise the king as head of his church as well as head of his state'.[155] De Valera put forward his own alternative to the Treaty, 'Document No. 2', which revised the oath wording as follows: 'I do swear to bear true faith and allegiance to the Constitution of Ireland and to the Treaty of Association of Ireland with the British Commonwealth of Nations and to recognise the King of Great Britain as head of the Associated States.'[156] Such a wording was completely unrealistic for the British side, as it effectively removed the monarchy from any role in the Irish Free State, thus negating 'dominion status', as to be a dominion was by definition to belong, in some form, to the monarchist sphere of the Crown.

The polarising result of these discussions was obvious – the oath dominated the treaty debates in the Dáil and ultimately was a key factor in causing and radicalising the Irish Civil War. Republican member of the Dáil TD Séan T. Ó Ceallaigh's comments on the oath during the Dáil Treaty debates in December 1921 were typical: 'I am opposed to this declaration of fidelity to an alien King because it is an outrage on the memory of our martyred comrades ... and an open insult to the heroic relatives they have left behind.'[157] The widow of republican martyr Terence MacSwiney, Mary MacSwiney, declared against the Treaty that 'Ireland must choose extermination before dishonour', in a direct echo of 1914 romantic honour discourses.[158] For TD Ada English, the oath meant 'they were asked to accept the King of England as head of the Irish State and to accept the status of British subjects', which would be 'a complete spiritual surrender'.[159] Other anti-Treaty figures, including Margaret Pearse, likened the oath of fidelity to the British monarch to 'perjury, as it contradicted the oath they had already taken to the Irish Republic'.[160] For Margaret Pearse, 'an oath to me is a most sacred vow made in the presence of Almighty God': swearing royal allegiance was thus to make a divine pledge in favour of Britishness, in other words, and unacceptable.[161] Anti-Treaty republicans believed that taking the oath would mark Ireland's 'voluntarily accepting the sovereignty over them of the British king' for the first time.[162]

Having mobilised and radicalised Irish nationalism through radical anti-monarchist messaging during and after the Easter Rising, pro-Treaty republicans could not now reverse this process. Ultimately the strength of opposition to the oath of allegiance was a major factor in why many TDs, IRA members and a significant minority of the nationalist population refused to accept the Anglo-Irish Treaty and took up arms against the Free State government in the subsequent Irish Civil War. As historians Liam Weeks and Mícheál Ó Fathartaigh have argued, it was the 'concessions made in the Treaty on Sinn Féin's Irish republican agenda [...] specifically, the oath of fidelity to the British monarch and the dominion status of the state' that 'ruptured the Sinn Féin party in a very arbitrary way', directly leading to the Irish Civil War.[163] A civil war 'Address from the Soldiers of the Republic to their former comrades in the Free State Army' in December 1922 referred to how the Treaty 'makes England's King Ireland's King'.[164] Thus, Ireland's monarchism–anti-monarchism dynamic fuelled a bitter successor conflict which, while the radicals opposing the oath lost, ensured through its propaganda vitriol that their arguments on the oath of allegiance won. The treaty's fudge on monarchism – which allowed a space for northern and southern unionism's monarchist culture on the island – was after the civil war completely untenable. It was later rapidly dismantled once Éamon De Valera took power in 1932.

In sum, what we are dealing with here are histories of emotions as much as politics; contemporary sources all convey the sheer emotion surrounding the issue of the British monarchy's role in Ireland by 1921 for all sides. The importance of kingship ultimately hinged upon the oath of allegiance, and this was so polarising that it led to a civil war by 1922–3, whereas in the Home Rule era monarchy was much less divisive in Ireland and Home Rulers could be both pro- and anti-monarchy to varying degrees within the same party. The First World War had also embedded further the cultural power of the British monarchy, sacralising it as a symbol of the war effort, of Britishness and as the guardian of the war dead and promoting it politically as the fulcrum of the reformed empire for the post-war era, which was now the monarchy's principal international relations focus following the collapse of the monarchical system in Continental Europe. War and revolution had utterly radicalised the British monarchy's meaning in Ireland but also in many ways in Great Britain itself. The First World War had obviously had a huge impact – unionist Irishmen and Irishwomen who served in the war had often died for the idea of Britishness that included the monarchy, sacralising it through blood sacrifice. Many ex-service personnel were very attached to it – particularly unionists, but not only them. The Great War meant that for British and Irish monarchists monarchy was something for which people they loved had died. Monarchism had become a profoundly emotional subject on the republican side too, as the Treaty debates and subsequent Civil War highlight. War violence, together with political violence, had thus infused the meaning of monarchy on the island of Ireland, and also in Britain, by 1921, making it the most emotional issue at the Treaty talks, as played out in the discussions over the oath of allegiance, which reveal radically different positions on both sides. The British monarchy simply no longer carried the same meaning as it had in 1914 for Irish nationalists, the island's unionists or politicians in Britain. It had become a totemic, even existential, issue for all parties. Yet it also, paradoxically, facilitated the compromise that allowed for British withdrawal from twenty-six counties of Ireland. The stakes around monarchism were thus at the heart of the entire Irish revolution.

Even though King George V remained as titular head of state of the new Irish Free State, the dramatic rise of fervent republicanism, which rendered southern monarchism taboo, clandestine and sometimes the subject of violent attention by the IRA, created a real sense of emotional disorientation for those in the twenty-six counties who had identified with the British monarchy. When the southern Irish regiments in the British army were disbanded in response to the establishment of the Free State, their colours were returned to the king at Windsor Castle in a ceremony that highlighted this. John Fortescue, the king's librarian, recalled how 'the King characteristically offered to soften the blow, as far as possible, to all the doomed regiments by receiving back from them their colours and keeping them under his custody at Windsor Castle. The ceremony was one of the most touching that I ever beheld.'[165] In front of an assembled crowd of non-commissioned officers from the regiments, 'The officers in succession carried their colours to the King, knelt before him, kissed the colours and delivered them up to him. The King read a message of farewell to each of the regiments and quitted the hall, leaving most of the officers and non-commissioned officers in tears.'[166] In other words, hardened war veterans *wept* at this interaction with the monarch, which clearly symbolised something profound for them. For one Anglo-Irish commentator, his culture's purpose disappeared with independence, when it was 'shorn of its estates and the opportunity to serve locally in Ireland in the services of the Crown'.[167] Yet the Treaty solution for the Irish Free State actually had not dismantled the monarchy there but rather substituted transnational imperial monarchism for membership of the dynastic UK state model. Royalists in Ireland realised this: 'I confess that I don't like to think of myself as a "Colonial"! Yet that is what it has come to', wrote Church of Ireland Archbishop John Bernard after the Anglo-Irish Treaty was agreed in 1921.[168] For Irish monarchists who found themselves now faced with life in the new Free State, the fact that it was a transition to a more fluid kind of connection with the monarchy, rather than a complete break, helped them to tolerate the new order. Historian Ian d'Alton notes that, for southern Irish monarchists, 'An emotional attachment to the crown, representing connectivity with a residual sense of British values' remained important, particularly as, from 1922, political unionism disintegrated in the Free State, leaving only traces of cultural royalism.[169] A Dublin Anglican cleric hopefully told his parishioners in December 1921: 'Over the Irish Free State we are still to have our King.'[170] The former unionist paper, the *Irish Times*, continued its court and personal columns, headed by the royal coat of arms; Trinity College, University of Dublin continued its royal toasts.[171] It was still legally possible to appeal to the Privy Council. Indeed, appealing to the Judiciary Committee of the Privy Council was inserted into Article 66 of the Irish Free State Constitution and was only removed in 1933.[172] But the reality was that those who had openly shown loyalty to the Crown during the War of Independence would often be harassed – or worse – during the Irish Civil War.[173] Indeed, for much of the 1920s, the British Treasury funded an Irish Grants Committee which compensated Irish loyalists for losses incurred due to their allegiance to Britain. Applicants came from both Protestant and Catholic backgrounds, highlighting the fact that before 1914, Irish monarchism was not a solely Protestant affair. They were asked to 'define the word "loyal"' for themselves: while some mentioned unionism or Protestantism and categories often overlapped, many opted to base their claim on the fact that their behaviour as a 'loyal subject' or their 'loyalty to the British crown' had resulted in their business being boycotted by nationalist customers or their livestock stolen, or in threats to their life forcing them to flee or resulting in family members being injured or killed.[174] 'I was always a loyal subject of the Crown and my persecution was due to my action in assisting to provide comforts for His Majesty's troops during the Great War and to my position in the Orange Institution', wrote John Lang.[175] Catholic applicants in particular, who could not blame religious difference for their treatment, emphasised their loyalty to the Crown as a reason they were targeted.

Given these circumstances, it is little surprise that interwar Irish Free State monarchism became a hidden practice, almost entirely restricted to the circles of the Protestant minority, where it rapidly diminished, particularly among younger generations, and firmly outside the mainstream of the new regime's public life. Instead of being a model for how monarchism could keep a dominion connected to Britishness, as Lloyd George had hoped, Free State Ireland offered a template for its radical rejection. King George V himself would later admit ruefully to Ramsay MacDonald in 1930: 'what fools we were not to have accepted Gladstone's Home Rule Bill. [...] The Empire now would not have had the Irish Free State giving us so much trouble and pulling us to pieces.'[176]

However, this was something of an exaggeration. The outcome of the Irish War of Independence, which left the new Irish Free State within the empire but outside the UK, also left the British monarchy domestically in a better, stronger position to promote a narrative of national coherence across the remaining parts of the UK; what remained – Northern Ireland, Scotland, Wales and England – were, in the majority, far more solidly pro-monarchy territories than the territories of the Irish Free State area had ever been; the monarchy's British national role could thus be consolidated. The solution to the Irish problem – the founding of the Free State, an entity with dominion status which was independent from the UK but retained the king as head of state – also showcased the monarchy's own hopes for its future post-First World War role as the key symbolic imperial connection that could hold the empire together as direct political rule from Westminster over imperial territories was increasingly contested. It also distanced the Crown from a troublesome radical republicanism in Ireland. These trends in Ireland matched those occurring in the monarchy's relationship with Europe, where the British monarchy was rapidly becoming less Europe-focused and more 'national' and 'imperial' due to the war. Above all, the Irish case, with its radical republican iconoclasm towards all symbols of the British monarchy, revealed what real processes of de-sacralisation looked like; in comparison, the challenges to the monarchy in Britain from the reforms of the Lloyd George government and from socialism within Britain appeared weak.

In sum, monarchism and anti-monarchism were broad categories which played complex roles in the Irish revolutionary decade. The small republican movement of 1916 managed to utilise older Irish folk cultures of opposition to the British monarchy, as well as Ireland's Fenian tradition, to successfully win broader support away from the bigger Home Rule nationalist movement, while pro-monarchism formed one of the key belief systems that mobilised unionism in Ireland in this period. Monarchism for the British side in the conflict ultimately offered a way out, by providing the option of dominion status, keeping Ireland within the monarchy system. The monarchism–anti-monarchism dynamic, in other words, both polarised and radicalised the Irish revolution and the conflict between unionist and nationalist, but it also served as a centripetal force that could bring about the ultimate compromise of the Anglo-Irish Treaty. Nationalist resentment at the island's partition would further stoke the longevity and extreme nature of Irish anti-monarchism long after the Irish War of Independence had ended, while northern unionism would continue to cleave to its monarchist identity. As a consequence of all of these combined processes, Irish nationalism was left with a much more militant and long-lived specific antipathy to the British monarchy than appeared elsewhere in formerly British territories, with the first visit by a British monarch to independent Ireland only taking place in 2011, eighty-nine years after independence, an event which required intense security and saw a bomb plot thwarted. Monarchism versus anti-monarchism were ultimately permanently embedded in debates about Irish identities following the polarisation of Ireland's decade of war and revolution, 1912–23.

4.3 De-Sacralisation Discourses and the Russian Revolution

What of processes of cultural de-sacralisation of monarchy in Britain after 1916? Rumours certainly abounded of threats of left-wing revolution at the British Court in 1917 and 1918, dramatically triggered by news of the February Revolution in Russia, which in the Western calendar took place on 8–12 March 1917. These were based upon imagined future scenarios that were shaped by older histories of revolution: as Lord Stamfordham noted on 9 April 1917: 'The Revolution in Russia is bound to re-act upon the other Monarchical Countries. This was the case in the Great French Revolution and again in 1848 [...].'[177] Revolutions have long been understood in terms of historical 'scripts' – the British court in 1916–18 was no exception, looking for patterns that fitted to America in 1776, France in 1789, the German lands in 1848 or the 1870 Paris Commune.[178] Within court circles there were fears about the rise of the Labour Party and that the war was promoting revolutionary socialism, which drove efforts to make the monarchy more visible to the industrial working classes and to highlight its sympathy and support for their immense war sacrifices. Historian Frank Prochaska even points to 1917–18 as seeing an upsurge in republicanism in Britain which exceeded that of the 1870s.[179] This chapter will now examine the rise in anti-monarchist discourses that the Russian Revolution triggered, as well as the broader web of fears that these discourses caused among pro-monarchist elites.

The first key sign that the Russian Revolution had definitively broken the wartime taboo on questioning the role of monarchy in Britain came when the writer H. G. Wells published a letter in *The Times* on 21 April 1917 calling for the formation of a Republican Society 'to give some definite expression to the great volume of Republican feeling that has always existed in the British community'.[180] The letter has gone down as a key moment in the history of British republicanism; Wells wrote it in response to discussion in *The Times* about the future of monarchy in Europe which began on 4 April 1917, when a pro-monarchy letter to the editor suggested that royals should marry spouses drawn from their national 'nobility' to cut the influence of Germany on European royal circles.[181] Another writer informed the editor that the British monarch should take on more power to halt the increasing 'autocracy' of the executive, as 'we are living under a *Monarchy* of historic development' and should 'pay due regard to the personal position of the wearer of the British Crown'.[182] Wells's letter has often been taken out of context. The material in *The Times* in April 1917 was overwhelmingly in favour of the British monarchy: even Wells's letter was accompanied by a resolutely pro-monarchy editorial which described the British monarchy as 'the golden link' of the empire and as a 'chosen kingship, founded on the will of the people and ruling by that will'.[183] The editorial stated that Wells's letter had only been published to show the 'absurdity of "republican"

manifestations in this country' and to quash any 'fantastic analogies' that it
believed risked being 'drawn by the half-educated between the prostrate
autocracy of the [sic] Tsardom and the constitutional Monarchy of the
British Empire'.[184] In this regard, The Times appears to have ended up pre-
emptively triggering a discussion on republicanism and escalating it beyond
its actual prevalence. Yet, Wells's letter remained a discursive blow rather
than any real threat: no republican society was founded in response, and
within two days the pro-monarchist outcry it provoked compelled Wells to
publish a retraction: 'it has been assumed that there is some movement afoot
for the setting up of Republican institutions here ... No such profound
changes as these have been advocated ... We do not wish to discuss the
British monarchy at all.'[185] The swift disclaimer was revealing of the social
pressure that could still be brought to bear upon such radical republican
views at this point.

Wells had, in fact, been virulently supportive of the British war effort in
1914; however, by 1916, he had come to rethink his position, arguing that
dying for 'King and Country' was much the same thing as dying for kaiser and
Fatherland.[186] The strain of the conflict had led him to publish religious
theories and convoluted ideas about the future: 'some people thought that he
had gone out of his mind'.[187] So although his 1917 letter about monarchy came
from a well-known and popular writer, it was also from one who was not
viewed as particularly mentally stable. Far more significant for the Palace than
who had written the letter was where it was published – The Times, Northcliffe
press organ and bastion of the Establishment. As Ernest Thurtle, the later
Labour MP, remarked in his 1945 memoirs, 'it was perhaps not surprising that
Mr. Wells, with his known views and his courage in avowing them, should
write such a letter. What was surprising and significant was that The Times
should have seen fit to publish it.'[188] This was a clear example of the continuation of a relatively free press in wartime Britain. What also mattered was that
it coincided with the appearance of a string of articles in radical socialist
newspapers that also debated what the downfall of the tsar meant for the
future of monarchy. Criticising the tsar was clearly a legitimate current affairs
issue for journalists writing about the outbreak of the Russian Revolution and
its causes; it also brought criticism perilously close to the British monarchy,
which, unlike with the case of the king's other cousin, the kaiser, remained
close to 'cousin Nicky' and his wife.

Much of the April–May 1917 press debate was focused not so much on the
future of the British monarchy, but on Continental European monarchies and
the Continent's monarchical system. The majority of the articles were also not
extreme diatribes calling for the overthrow of King George V. Yet looking
closely at the April–May 1917 press debate on monarchy reveals not only
a sudden wave of debate in the press on the value of monarchy as a state
system, but also the first significant wartime accusations regarding the British

monarchy's German origins. The socialist Henry Hyndman in April 1917 wrote of how the royal family was too German and too close to the kaiser's court; in the same article he rejected asylum for the Russian royals, deliberately conflating the two issues.[189] On 28 April 1917, the *Daily Herald* (at this point briefly known as *The Herald*), a radical left-wing newspaper, in an article discussing republicanism, acknowledged that 'criticism of the King as an *individual* is both rare, trivial and irrelevant; few, if any, kings have been so little exposed to it as our present one', but that 'so far as there is any personal animosity in the country against the reigning house, it is entirely the work of the Jingo press with its screams of "once a Hun, always a Hun"' and that, regarding republicanism, 'we do not believe the issue is of any importance comparable with the economic issue between Capital and Labour'.[190] H. G. Wells wrote in May 1917 in the *Penny Pictorial* of how the British monarchy had to sever ties with German royalty and 'the inevitable collapse of the Teutonic dynastic system upon the Continent of Europe. [. . .] We do not want any German ex-monarchs here.'[191] The *Stirling Observer* wrote on 3 August 1918 of how the war was caused by 'these Willy and Nicky schemes plotting, bartering, and playing with the fate of hundreds of millions of people with no more thought as to what the peoples themselves wished or desired than if they were flocks of sheep on the hillside'; it argued that the war 'will have achieved nothing permanent if it does not make an end of Hohenzollerism and all it stands for'.[192] It was in this regard – breaking the wartime taboo about discussing the royals' German heritage – that press debate posed the most danger to the British throne.

Indeed, Wells was one of the key proponents of this idea of a web of 'Teutonic monarchies' who supported each other, which was a powerful wartime conspiracy idea that appeared in the wake of the February Russian Revolution. In April 1917, he suggested in *The Times* that there might exist a 'trade union' of European monarchies, looking out for their own interests against those of their populations.[193] In his later 1918 book, *In the Fourth Year: Anticipations of a World Peace*, Wells set out his understanding of this idea of Teutonic monarchies in his chapter 'The Future of Monarchy'.[194] He described how 'after 1871, a constellation of quasi-divine Teutonic monarchs, of which the German Emperor, the German Queen Victoria, the German Czar, were the greatest stars, formed a caste apart, intermarried only among themselves, dominated the world and was regarded with a mystical awe by the ignorant and foolish in most European countries'.[195] They enjoyed 'almost universal worship'.[196] For Wells, until the war this 'German kingly caste [. . .] this Teutonic dynastic system' had gone unchallenged; now the conflict had brought 'all monarchy to the question'.[197] Wells believed that

> things march irresistibly towards a permanent world peace based on democratic republicanism. The question of the future of monarchy is

not whether it will be able to resist and overcome that trend [...] it is whether it will resist openly, become the centre and symbol of a reactionary resistance, and have to be abolished and swept away altogether everywhere, as the Romanoffs have already been swept away in Russia, or whether it will be able in this country and that to adapt itself to the necessities of the great age that dawns upon mankind, to take a generous and helpful attitude towards its own modification, and so survive [...].[198]

Yet Wells's harsh critique of monarchy also incorporated suggestions for its reform in Britain which would facilitate its survival and which show that, even for radicals like him, the British monarchy had a special status:

if monarchy is to survive in the British Empire it must speedily undergo the profoundest modification. [...] There are many reasons for hoping that it will do so. The *Times* has styled the crown the 'golden link' of the empire. Australians and Canadians, it was argued, had little love for the motherland but the greatest devotion to the sovereign, and still truer was this of Indians, Egyptians, and the like. It might be easy to press this theory of devotion too far, but there can be little doubt that the British Crown does at present stand as a symbol of unity over diversity such as no other crown, unless it be that of Austria-Hungary, can be said to do. The British crown is not like other crowns; it may conceivably take a line of its own and emerge [...] from trials that may destroy every other monarchical system in the world.[199]

Wells's belief in a Teutonic network of kings was evident elsewhere too in 1917. Harry Snell, later a Labour MP, was quoted in *The Worker* in April 1917 that the kaiser would escape punishment after the war as his relatives would protect him, which was another argument in favour of 'an immediate revival of republicanism'; in another article in the same paper that month he asked if the English people had the courage to follow where the Russians had gone.[200] The editor of *The Spectator*, John St Loe Strachey, wrote to Stamfordham on 27 April 1917 of a growth of 'republican feeling' among Derbyshire miners who believed the king was shielding the kaiser, his 'brother monarch'.[201] Strachey wrote again to Stamfordham on 2 May 1917 of how the working classes, 'who have never been taught the realities of the Constitution, have got it into their heads that the King could protect the Hohenzollerns if he liked, and that he certainly would, because of the supposed Trades Union among Kings'.[202]

The reasons for this sudden April 1917 attack on the British royals' German connections were complex. First, for a small group of political activists, with roots in pre-war militancy, such as the socialist Henry Hyndman or the writer H. G. Wells, with the Russian Revolution offering the opportunity to break down the wartime taboo on questioning monarchy, the monarchy's German associations offered promising potential for undermining its popularity.

Second, while many liberals, as well as socialists, welcomed the spring 1917 overthrow of the absolutist tsar in favour of the Russian liberal democracy the February Revolution promised, these events also triggered deep-seated fears. The revolution was disruptive to a key British ally, raising alarms among the broader public as to whether Russia would stay in the war. Who could the public blame for this disruptive turmoil in a key ally? The terrible wartime leadership of the tsar and his wife were an obvious target: the message that poor monarchical leadership could be costly for a war effort.

Moreover, Ernest Thurtle, wounded in the Battle of Cambrai, noted that as war-weariness increased, parts of the British population actually started to blame the entire monarchical system in Europe for the war – leading to reactions against Britain's own monarchy, seen as tainted by association with this failed international system that had caused the conflagration.[203] In the wake of the Russian Revolution, finally, the British press demonisation of kaiserism was now spilling over into attacks on all monarchy, including the British. As Wells argued, 'we know now that kings cause wars'.[204] The *Sheffield Independent* on 5 April reported that 'The atmosphere of to-day is charged with forces not friendly to monarchy as an institution but least of all to monarchy unlimited'; it described how tyrannical and warmongering monarchies on the Continent meant that now 'the attitude of the average man towards the institution of monarchy is represented by a large note of interrogation?'[205] It argued for the democratising of royal marriage in response, to end monarchy being a caste apart, and pointed out that there are 'good monarchs – every Englishman knows one – and there are bad'.[206] The Bishop of Chelmsford, John Watts-Ditchfield, wrote to Stamfordham on 5 April 1917 of a public belief that the tsar was 'backed by this country'.[207] Any British association with this perceived corrupt Continental monarchical system, with its tyrannical overthrown tsardom and aggressive kaiserism, was now suspect.

The British monarchy in March and April 1917 was quick to fear a possible overlap occurring in the UK between anti-German hostility towards their dynasty and revolutionary Bolshevik or socialist fervour, stoked by war-weariness and events in Russia; after all, it was accusations against the tsarina's German origins that had combined with socialist radicalism in Russia to trigger revolution. When the Bishop of Chelmsford visited the royal family on 28 April 1917 he was told by Lord Stamfordham that 'there was undoubted unrest. That they had heard that the miners in Derbyshire had gone Republican. That people seemed to be waking up to the fact that the Royal House was German in origin.'[208] By May 1917, George V became particularly alarmed on 'being told that people believed he must be pro-German since he had a German name'.[209] In this context, where the Russian Revolution was coinciding with a surge of accusations regarding the British monarchy's links with Germany, the name Windsor was selected purely for reasons of public relations, with Lord Stamfordham the key figure in putting it forward.[210] By

1917, George V accepted the inevitability that 'Germanness' had to be purged from within the royal family as well as without on the field of battle. It was clearly an important personal moment for the king, who held a special Privy Council in July 1917 for the change in the name of the royal family, at which, as Stamfordham related to Arthur Balfour, the king was 'so anxious that not only the present Prime Minister, but all those who have occupied that position and are still living, should be around him on what he regarded as an important occasion so far as himself and his family were concerned'.[211] Not only the name of the royal dynasty changed; the king's Teck and Battenberg relatives also received staunchly British replacement titles of Athlone, Cambridge, Mountbatten or Milford Haven. The action was widely applauded in the press, but even positive propaganda such as that shown in Fig. 33 was double-edged: crowns being swept into the dust were hardly a propitious omen for the future of monarchy in general.

Fig. 33   '"A Good Riddance": The King has done a popular act in abolishing the German titles held by members of His Majesty's family', *Punch Magazine*, 27 June 1917 (Reproduced from *The Year 1917 Illustrated* (London, 1918). Photo by: Universal History Archive/Universal Images Group via Getty Images, 188007253)

This rebranding of the royal dynasty as Windsor is frequently mentioned in passing in histories of the monarchy; far less often is the question asked, why did it work? Several factors seem to explain its success. First, it was pre-emptive. The king acted to patriotically discard his German dynastic name *before* there was widespread popular working-class demand for this action. It was not a measure taken by an unpopular royal family as a last-ditch effort to defend their position but rather one by royals who were widely accepted and whose war work was well regarded. Moreover, the processes of sacralisation of the monarchy that the first years of the war had unleashed had helped to strengthen it. Any controversy about a German name was thus thwarted before it had a chance to spread widely. Second, the history of the British monarchy had many other previous pragmatic examples of dynastic continuity and order being sacrificed in the name of realpolitik, for example, the Glorious Revolution or the Hanoverian Succession. Continuity of royal dynastic name had historically mattered much less than royal continuity of the monarchy itself, from which it could – and had been – publicly detached in Britain when required. Third, if we look at figures like the German-born Elisabeth of Bavaria, who was the extremely popular queen of Belgium during the First World War, it is clear that, for all it was being presented as an exceptional monarchy in 1917, the British case was far from unique. The war could accelerate royal assimilation into a national ideal, just as much as in the case of places like Russia it could undermine it. The risks of failure, however, were real, as the fate of the Russian and Greek monarchies shows. Much depended on how centrally a monarchy was positioned as part of the new kinds of ideas about the wartime 'nation' that the conflict was generating and how effectively it retained this centrality. In the British case, the shared public beliefs that developed that the war was about equality of sacrifice, hard work, endurance, service of others and that these were the values that epitomised Britishness were ones that the monarchy could – and did – utilise and, indeed, promote to remain relevant.

For these reasons, the appearance in such a stalwart mouthpiece of the Establishment as *The Times* of a wartime debate about the values and disadvantages of monarchy as a system gave rise to enormous concern among courtiers. Indeed, how fears of revolution were expressed reveals a collective mentality – borrowing from the ideas of Georges Lefebvre, in his 1932 book *The Great Fear of 1789: Rural Panic in Revolutionary France* – a *grande peur* among court elites and monarchists, in particular, key royal informants: Lord Esher; Clifford Woodward, the Canon of Southwark; Lord Rosebery, the former Prime Minister; Cosmo Lang, Archbishop of York; and John Watts-Ditchfield, the Bishop of Chelmsford.[212] This process was not unique to Britain; Robert Gerwarth and John Horne have shown how across Continental Europe the threat of Bolshevik revolution was the stuff of 'myth and fantasy' for elites.[213] Indeed, they show that in other states such myths and fantasies often led to violence.[214] By contrast, in Britain, they led to reworking the image of the monarchy.

This *grande peur* merits study in its own right as a cultural phenomenon with its own language and assumptions about revolution.[215] Indeed, during the Great War, the Brussels sociologist Fernand Van Langenhove pioneered the study of how collective fears could trigger organisational responses; the historian Marc Bloch endorsed Van Langenhove's work, suggesting that 'a false rumour is always born of collective representations which predate its own birth'.[216] Historians John Horne and Alan Kramer have argued that during the First World War collective fears and false rumours indicate how 'a transient phenomenon of mass self-suggestion interacts with a more permanent substratum of attitudes and beliefs which shape the content of the former and provide much of its force'.[217] In other words, preconceived ideas drawing both on historic precedents and on expectations based on what was occurring in Russia in 1917 shaped how courtiers interpreted events in Britain, leading them to read reality through a distorted prism. They were hostage to collective rumours and fears which coloured the meaning they took from even minor incidents of Labour activism.

Indicative of the degree of paranoia, Colonel J. Unsworth, a Salvation Army worker from Essex, wrote to Stamfordham, again in April 1917, that a friend had told him he had seen 'written in a second class Railway carriage "to hell with the King. Down with all royalties."'[218] The shock at such a very minor display of anti-monarchism is actually more indicative of the general reverence in which the king had previously commonly been held. The graffito was taken as tantamount to a sign of imminent revolution. Likewise, some 'abusive letters', which, according to Frank Prochaska, Lord Stamfordham received in spring 1917, caused real alarm.[219] Unsworth described how 'I have noticed since the news came to hand of the Russian revolution, a change has come over a certain section of the people in respect to their attitude towards the King and the Royal family. In the streets, trains and Buses, one hears talk concerning the high personages mentioned which is very painful at times to listen too [*sic*].'[220] The breaking of monarchist taboo was so personal as to be described as 'very painful'.[221] Given the context of the powerful wartime sacralisation of the monarchy in the first years of the war, which had enhanced its status and reverence compared to peacetime, the fact that suddenly it could be criticised came as a huge shock to monarchists and made the change in 1917 appear all the more extreme for them. But read in the context of actual revolution in Ireland and in Continental Europe, the signs of anti-monarchism picked up on by royal informants in Britain actually reveal very minor incidents or cases where supporters of the monarchy perceived anti-monarchism where the evidence actually does not support the inference they have drawn.

Imaginings of revolution were omnipresent in royal informants' correspondence. The Archbishop of Canterbury, Randall Davidson, reassured

Stamfordham in April 1917 that 'H.M. might have to rely' upon religious people if unrest developed, but they 'look and have looked to the king'.[222] The Bishop of Chelmsford wrote to Stamfordham on 5 April 1917 of how, at the end of the war, 'anything might happen'.[223] He also advocated that the king should meet with two labour MPs, Will Thorne and James O'Grady, about a trip they were making to Russia, as such a royal encounter would 'spike their guns': the imagery of guns highlighted the general Establishment fear of violent Bolshevik revolution.[224] The Archbishop of Canterbury wrote to Lord Stamfordham in 1918 urging more publicity for the war work of the royals and 'small dinners' with those on whom the king 'would have to rely if trouble came'.[225] In January 1918, Lord Esher compared the situation of Britain with that of France in 1870, when defeat in war resulted in the Commune.[226] In a notable choice of language, Lord Beaverbrook described Haig as the 'keeper of the Palace gates', during the spring 1918 clash between his supporters and Lloyd George, implying the moment in 1789 when the mob rushed Versailles.[227] In April 1918, Esher again wrote to Stamfordham, warning him that potential 'centres of disaffection' were increasing daily in number.[228] In April 1917, a letter from the Home Office to Stamfordham warned of 'anarchical movements' and of a 'movement [...] being organized in Labour circles'.[229] By spring 1918, these concerns were occurring in the context of looming possible defeat on the Western Front as the Allies battled the Ludendorff Offensives: military defeat was historically seen as a dangerous trigger for revolution; hence the increasing alarm at court. In May 1918, the Archbishop of Canterbury pessimistically felt that the king's appearance in public made little difference to 'disaffected people who, if riots took place, would loot the shops etc.' but that 'other classes' needed to see the king more and this would bolster the monarchy.[230] By October 1918, Esher's letters spoke of how 'unless tact and sympathy are pronounced features of the demobilization of the vast horde of men and women now employed under government, Bolshevism is inevitable'.[231] The term 'horde' highlights Esher's fear of the revolutionary mob – this was dehumanising language for a working class that consisted mostly of dedicated war workers, after all; the quote also reveals his dislike of big government, which had employed these people, and the fact he refers to both genders also reveals the new landscape following events in Russia in 1917, and in Germany in October 1918, the month he was writing, when women played significant roles in revolution.

Stamfordham's own concerns grew. He wrote to the Prime Minister on 23 January 1918 of the king's concern that the emissary of Bolshevik Russia – Maxim Litvinov – had given a speech in Nottingham and asking if 'the Government intend to take steps to prevent this so-called Ambassador from preaching Revolution?'[232] Stamfordham wrote on 21 October 1918 of how he had heard 'it is often said at I.L.P. [Independent Labour Party] Meetings that the Prince of Wales will never reign' and how he was reading a confidential official report on the 'spread in this country of Bolshevism'.[233] He confided in the Archbishop of Canterbury in December 1918 that 'some suspicions are afloat that there are parts of England in which, if riots took place, the police would not act under authority'.[234] The king even received a letter in 1919 directly from a member of the public complaining that 'nothing is giving rise to more dissatisfaction and disgust than the wholesale giving of titles to pompous mediocrities often unworthy and ignoble [. . .]. It is an insult to the rest of the community. The American and the Frenchman can do his duty by his country without seeking a title as a reward. Why not here?'[235] The letter writer claimed the situation would 'play into the hands of the extremists who want to overturn the present order of things'.[236] The letter is remarkable, suggesting that honour should be protected and not indiscriminately distributed in order to protect the monarchy but also containing the point that republican states could motivate citizens without using monarchical honour codes, hinting that the monarchy – and the honour culture it represented – was not indispensable.

Ultimately, the collective fears and rumours of revolution in Britain had policy implications. The fear of revolutionary contagion from Continental Europe in 1917 lay behind George V's decision that ultimately it would be too risky to allow the Russian tsar and his family asylum in the UK and to pressure Lloyd George and the government into rescinding their offer of a British refuge, which, Stamfordham wrote, would 'cause much public comment if not resentment'.[237] This decision occurred in the spring of 1917 and so was based solely upon an assessment of the situation following the February Revolution and how this had impacted upon the British monarchy; King George V could not have anticipated the Bolshevik revolution of October, which put his relatives in far graver danger. After all, the same period saw him reject the plan for asylum for his cousin Greek King Constantine on the Isle of Wight; cousin 'Tino' went to Switzerland instead, without harm.[238] Yet the fact that George V was able to compel his government to rescind such an important asylum offer to an ally clearly shows the extent of political power that the monarchy could wield on occasion during the war.

The king had initially sent a private telegram to his cousin, the tsar, on 19 March 1917 (Western calendar), following the February Revolution, stating that the revolution had 'deeply distressed me. My thoughts are constantly with you and I shall always remain your true and devoted friend as you know I have been in the past.'[239] In response to a request from the Russian Provisional Government, Lloyd George, in consultation with Stamfordham, agreed that Britain would offer the Russian royal family asylum, and an invitation was sent. However, King George V changed his mind, despite a plea from his government that the monarch 'consent to adhere to the original invitation, which was sent on the advice of His Majesty's Ministers'.[240] It was unlikely the tsar would ever have escaped Russia, but the judgement of George V was that he was too associated with negative ideas about monarchy – in particular absolutism – to be allowed asylum, lest the British public make unflattering connections between the flaws of the Russian monarchy and their own.[241] As Stamfordham wrote to the Foreign Office on 6 April 1917,

> Every day, the King is becoming more concerned about the question of the Emperor and Empress coming to this country. His Majesty receives letters from people in all classes of life, known or unknown to him, saying how much the matter is being discussed, not only in clubs, but by working men, and that Labour Members in the House of Commons are expressing adverse opinions to the proposal. [...] the presence of the Imperial Family (especially the Empress) in this country would raise all sorts of difficulties, and I feel sure that you appreciate how awkward it will be for our Royal Family who are closely connected both with the Emperor and the Empress.[242]

An article in the radical left paper *Justice* on 5 April 1917 by the socialist Henry Hyndman argued for a British republic, stating that 'If the King and Queen have invited their discrowned Russian cousins to come here [...] they are misrepresenting entirely the feelings of us common Englishmen.'[243] Stamfordham underlined these words in his copy and also pointed out the article to the Prime Minister during the meeting on 10 April which resulted 'in the government's U-turn on the offer of British asylum'.[244] Here the monarchy's wishes took precedence over the original government foreign policy decision. Queen Mary confided her views to the Bishop of Chelmsford on 29 April 1917: 'she spoke out vigorously re: Russia – almost violently about the Empress – said "that fool of a woman". She ought never to have married the Czar [...] That the Czar was weak [...] hoped they would not come over here. If they did she did not think she could receive them.'[245]

Even after the news of the brutal murder of the tsar and his family in July 1918 became known in the UK, an extreme act which helped discredit Bolshevism, the court feared the public mood. Stamfordham would write the following to Sir Arthur Balfour regarding the 'difficult question' as to whether King George V should attend the private memorial service for his dead cousin which was being organised in London by a Russian Grand Duchess:

> Queen Alexandra raises the question whether she should go to the private service or send a representative and asks what the King will do. Queen Mary has referred to me. The Czar was up to the time of his death a Field Marshal in the British Army, Col. in Chief of the Scots Greys and a Knight of the Garter. He is a 1st cousin of the King's. He was one of the Allied Sovereigns until dethroned by his Subjects. In ordinary circumstances the King would order Court Mourning and certainly be represented if not personally attend any service in the Czar's memory. On the other hand public opinion is in a hyper-sensitive condition and might misconstrue anything done by the King into sympathy with the counter-revolutionists in Russia anti-democratical [*sic*] etc.[246]

Stamfordham suggested that the king might decline to join in the memorial service 'on the grounds that the government have no official news of the Emperor's death'; even though the British royals had already been given news of the killings there was still some uncertainty until 28 July, when a spy confirmed them to the Foreign Office.[247] Stamfordham asked Balfour: 'But please consider what the King ought to do when the news of the <u>murder</u> is confirmed. I am inclined to think the respect due to an <u>Ally Sovereign</u>, a F. Marshal – a 1st cousin of the King's ought to be shown.'[248] Ultimately, the king was in favour of attendance and was present at the service together with the queen.[249] By 1918, Continental Europe had become a site of revolutions so dangerous that even paying respects to related royal dead – a nondescript feature of the pre-war world – was now in question.

The panic at court was not limited to fears of Bolshevism; there were also fears of a prime ministerial coup. The king's Private Secretary Clive Wigram believed that 'it was the long-term intention of David Lloyd George [...] to destroy the monarchy'.[250] He told the Bishop of Chelmsford he did not trust the Prime Minister.[251] The queen too expressed 'real distrust of Lloyd George'.[252] One of the reasons the king supported Haig remaining as Commander-in-Chief of the BEF on the Western Front was because there were fears that, if he resigned, Lloyd George might hold an election and, in Wigram's words, 'possibly come back as a Dictator'.[253] The king himself was concerned that, if any such election occurred, his own position 'would then be very difficult. He would be blamed for causing a General Election which would cost the country a million, and stop munitions work [...].'[254] The King of Spain's attitude to the allied cause was even tested by the rumours that Lloyd George wished to substitute republican for monarchical institutions.[255]

The impact of fears of revolution or prime ministerial coup cannot be underestimated – they shaped the attitudes of the court and the royal family. They also drove very rapid new discursive shifts to depicting the monarchy as both national and democratic. This was not inevitable: several of the king's correspondents and advisors toyed with the idea of the monarchy shifting to take *more* political power – not less – and standing against the rise of democracy. The socialist writer Bruce Glasier had feared this as early as 1915, writing in a pamphlet of his concerns about the powers available to the king should he choose to use them and that, backed by the armed forces, a British monarch might seize control.[256] In December 1916, Stamfordham asked Hankey, cabinet secretary, whether the king should take 'a more active share in the government of the country', something Hankey counselled against lest the ongoing bad wartime economic and political situation rebound on the monarchy.[257] In April 1917, the Bishop of Chelmsford noted in his diary during his visit to Windsor that General William Robertson had told him that 'he knew crowd of politicians – peers and commons – and said if King would come out in open he would carry country. That men had no animus against King but system and they did not distinguish between Continental and ours. Said Empire would not have President. Quoted Australian who said he would not come over to fight for Will Crooks.'[258] Robertson believed Lloyd George was in league with French socialists and might overthrow the king, ideas which were wild fancies but which carried great weight at court.[259] In February 1918, there were 'questionings' at Buckingham Palace as to what should happen if Lloyd George resigned, with discussion about breaking convention and the king 'making the Speaker Prime Minister' or getting Asquith back.[260] In this febrile atmosphere, in late spring 1918, Lloyd George himself told Hankey that the king was encouraging mutiny when the monarch objected to the removal of General Sir Hugh Trenchard from the post of Chief of Air Staff and of William Robertson from Chief of the Imperial General Staff.[261]

The right-wing Imperial Defence Union also called for the king to assume more political power.[262] On 9 July 1917, it held a meeting at the Queen's Hall, Langham Place, London which was attended by an 'exclusively middle class audience. [...] very high feeling obtained' triggered by air raids on London and the Mesopotamia Commission's report.[263] The extreme right-wing editor of *John Bull*, Horatio Bottomley, addressed the audience and declared:

> The time has come when the people of this country should take things into their own hands. There is a remedy which I have suggested again and again and it is the only remedy. That is to call upon the nominal figurehead of the Nation. You have a king, what is the good of a King if he does not rule. The time has come when the king, I do not care whether he be King George the 5th or anybody else [*sic*]. The King is an institution, a symbol, not a person. Let the crowned head say to his ministers, it is obvious that public opinion is against you, get out of the way. I have power to rule Council, I will select for it men who have no suspicion of personal ambition and I will add to it men of undoubted patriotism and Parliament can rest [...].[264]

Bottomley added: 'It may not be very long – I hope it will not be – when we shall find ourselves marching to Buckingham Palace and telling the King that he must rule or we must.'[265] A police officer reporting on the meeting noted this was followed by cries of '"let us go to-night" and "will you lead us there tomorrow"' and wryly noted that 'Bottomley conveniently backed out of this expedition by replying that His Majesty is at present in France'.[266] Basil Thomson, Assistant Commissioner of the Metropolitan Police, noted that 'I understand that some steps have been taken privately to curb Bottomley's propaganda in "John Bull", but the incident of marching to Buckingham Palace was getting very near the line.'[267] There was a surge to the right in British politics in this period which the monarchy had to watch closely. Only a month after this meeting the National Party was founded, a right-wing, anti-

German and xenophobic party which was particularly strongly opposed to the sale of honours and which focused on the eradication of German influence in British life. The year 1917 also saw the British Empire Union and the Anti-German League, which had merged, become particularly active in England.[268] Given these trends, the change of dynastic name was a prescient move.[269]

Thus, the rise of discourses that were critical of the monarchy appeared on the right as well as the left. King George V was strictly wedded to following the constitution, however. When Sir William Robertson, Chief of the Imperial General Staff, hinted that the UK needed a military dictatorship, the king reacted strongly in defence of parliamentary democracy. Likewise, when it was suggested that 'the King should turn out the politicians and install a military government', his Private Secretary Clive Wigram wrote to Lieutenant General Sir Henry Rawlinson on 18 April 1918 that 'The people, the press and Parliament would not for one moment stand such an unconstitutional act, and it is asking for disaster.'[270] The monarch and Lord Stamfordham embarked instead on focusing on presenting a narrative of George V as a supporter of democracy, a king for the new mass democratic age.

4.4   A Real Threat? Examining the Effects of De-Sacralisation Discourses

How might we go about assessing the degree to which such discourses actually affected the monarchy's popularity in 1916–18? One possible approach is to look at legal history. If one considers the use of legal forms of coercion to protect the monarchy, there is scant evidence of the widespread use of the law to repress anti-monarchist behaviour. The limited use of coercion during the war to protect the monarchy from anti-monarchism is illustrated by the treason laws. Throughout the whole war there were only two cases of high treason in England and Wales, one of which was against the Anglo-Irish nationalist Sir Roger Casement, who was tried and executed in 1916 for his role in the Easter Rising, an execution the king fully concurred with; there was one other case in 1914.[271] The laws on treason illustrated wartime monarchism at its most archaic. Assistant Police Commissioner Basil Thomson noted of the Casement trial that 'in the course of the prosecution the Attorney General invoked a statute passed in the reign of one of the early Plantagenet kings – Edward III, I think – and still operative in cases of high treason'.[272] In 1914, there was also one case of treason felony, the only one for the whole war.[273] The offence of treason felony was defined as acting within the UK or abroad to 'compass, imagine, invent, devise, or intend to deprive or depose' the monarch 'from the style, honour, or royal name of the imperial crown' or any of the crown's dominions or countries or 'to levy war' against the sovereign within the UK.[274] The crime of treason felony also included encouraging any foreigner to invade the UK or any other of the monarchy's British dominions or territories.[275] However, it is important to also look at the statistics on wartime courts martial for the crime of 'war treason'. During the war, military law applied to officers and soldiers, and it included the offence of 'war treason'. Moreover, the 1914 Defence of the Realm Act allowed for the army to try civilians suspected of security crimes by court martial – this meant that during the war some civilians were also tried by court martial for war treason.[276] The statistics for courts martial for war treason are higher than those for high treason or treason felony: the War Office statistics show that 8 officers, soldiers and civilians were tried abroad in general, district and field general courts martial for treason between 4 August 1914 and 31 March 1920 and 163 in courts martial at home for the same offence.[277] Yet again these are not remarkably high numbers, particularly when one considers that war treason included a wide range of security offences and that the figure of 163 home front courts martial also includes 151 civilians tried in 1916 following the Easter Rising in Ireland.[278] The concept behind these laws is as revealing as the figures: treason formulated any action to assist the enemy by a British subject as a personal betrayal of their expected loyalty to the monarch.

This legal history is significant as evidence: as historian Mark Cornwall points out, 'Treason is a ubiquitous historical phenomenon, one particularly associated with regime instability or wartime loyalties.'[279] His study of the practice and prosecution of treason in Austria-Hungary during the First World War reveals that treason trials and executions for treason were prolific in Austria-Hungary at war, matching its internal instability.[280] This was, in part, because in Austria-Hungary the charge of *Hochverrat* – or treason – included not only threats to the person of the emperor, but also 'territorial treason', working to detach a part of the emperor's imperial territory.[281] For the wartime UK, this was dealt with not by treason laws but those concerning sedition: as a result, sedition could include nationalist separatist and/or anti-empire acts that could express anti-monarchism or overlap with it. In the British case, while there was major wartime political concern about sedition in both Ireland and India and use of the anti-sedition laws there, there is no evidence that the laws against sedition were needed to punish English, Welsh or Scottish anti-monarchists in Britain itself during the conflict.

All of this would suggest that anti-monarchism was not a major issue in wartime Britain, even in 1917–18. Some caution must be exercised here: historian Brock Millman has pointed out that the archival documentation on the suppression of dissent by the police, Home Office and intelligence services in wartime Britain is incomplete and has in some cases been actively purged.[282] Edward Owens has also found that 'popular opposition, ambivalence or indifference to the monarchy have not left a deep impression on the historical record', but cautioned that this 'absence of other oppositional voices' may be 'explained by the collection and preservation policies of repositories [...] where positive, adulatory letters from the public that commended the behaviour of the royals and the elites that surrounded them' seem to have been kept more often than critical or negative correspondence.[283] But in terms of records of court proceedings, treason and sedition cases in wartime Britain are rare, indicating very low levels of anti-monarchist public incidents and suggesting that it was not necessary to actually use legal coercive structures to protect the monarchy, even if the existence of these laws may have acted as a deterrent to any would-be anti-monarchist activists.

If legal history can tell us much about the limited use of coercive powers to defend against wartime anti-monarchism, other issues also reveal the monarchy's relatively secure status. In May 1917, when, in the wake of the news of revolution in Russia, a bitter strike wave swept parts of Scotland and the North of England, the cabinet decided that the best way to counter this radicalisation was a major tour by the king and queen of munitions factories and other industrial sites in the affected regions. From the very start of the war, the royal couple had visited war factories and shipyards, in a continuation of their pre-1914 policy of visiting the working classes.[284] However, from May 1917, the scale, range and press visibility of such visits was dramatically increased. The War Cabinet minutes of 11 May 1917 noted that, 'Notwithstanding the strikes now in progress, His Majesty the King should be advised to carry out his intended visit to the industrial areas in the north, and that arrangements should be made for His Majesty to see the leading Trade Unionists in each district.'[285] The Labour MP in the cabinet, Arthur Henderson, was tasked with giving 'effect to this decision'.[286] Furthermore, the War Cabinet also decided on mass publicity for these royal visits, as 'the present restrictions on the publication of His Majesty's movements were unreasonable and that much wider publicity should be given'.[287]

This indicated the scale of royal popularity – not ministers but the royals were believed to be secure in going to strike-hit worker areas, and it was thought that publicising the popular king and queen's visits would mitigate worker discontent. It was also believed that the respect for the monarchy would help to stop the May strikes. It is difficult to imagine this scenario in wartime Central or Eastern Europe. What is particularly striking is that, in a world war triggered by the assassination of a European royal, there was no worry regarding any potential attack on King George V and Queen Mary; nor was allowing militants to meet one-to-one with the king considered a risk to his personal safety.[288] The virtually complete absence in wartime primary sources of concerns or plots regarding any potential assassination of King George V by socialist militants again indicates the very limited and moderate nature of any rise in real anti-monarchism in Britain in this period. Moreover, the way that King George V and Queen Mary were confidently displayed to crowds during their 1917 tours of industrial areas contrasted with the fact that George VI and his consort's visits to blitzed areas from September 1940 were restricted, with 'particular care [. . .] taken that the number of people presented [to the royals is] kept as small as possible and that . . . as little attention as possible is drawn to the visit'.[289] As historian Edward Owens points out, this was only partly for security reasons; these 1940 visits were designed for the press to photograph the king and queen meeting with carefully arranged 'select groups of onlookers and pressmen' because King George VI in 1940 was not a particularly popular figure.[290]

By contrast, the 1917 cabinet conclusion that the king's status still held power in militant labour areas proved right. Assistant Police Commissioner Basil Thomson believed on 16 May 1917 that 'the effect of the King's visit North has been excellent'; he had agreed the previous day that 'as the Cabinet had sent the King and Queen to the strike areas it would be wrong to prejudice the success of their visit by arresting the strikers until they have left the north'.[291] His diary referred to waiting until the king 'would have left the dangerous area', an explicit acknowledgement of the radicalism of the locations where he was being sent.[292] The royals' May 1917 tour covered North West England and included areas where the workers were taking part in the mass strike; among the places they visited were Chester, Lancashire, Flint, Birkenhead District and the Liverpool Docks.[293] The *Driffield Times* headline announced 'royal chats with workpeople' in its report on their visit and noted that, 'After inspecting the docks, His Majesty received a number of the men's leaders, including Mr James Sexton, with whom he talked for some considerable time.'[294] Lloyd George noted in his memoirs of the May 1917 tour that the royal visit to 'the areas where the trouble was most acute' was never 'marred by any kind of unpleasantness' and that instead the 'loyalty of the people was heartened to new vigour'.[295] The cabinet effectively had sent the king to meet with militant worker radicals in the hope that respect for the monarchy would calm anger at the government and bosses. And it worked. The king was personally popular with workers. A *Daily Mail* report on 13 September 1917 noted that, in a speech at Glasgow in summer 1917, Lloyd George had declared that 'there is one man who is working as hard as the hardest-worked man in this country, and that is the Sovereign of this realm', a statement that raised the crowd he was addressing spontaneously to their feet to sing the national anthem.[296] One reason for King George V's popularity, the newspaper reported, was that, by this point in the war, he had personally visited over eighty munitions factories, meeting their labour forces.[297] Another was his presentation as being pro-labour: far from his being depicted as an apolitical monarch, the *Daily Mail* openly declared of the king that 'there is no better friend of Labour in this country or of just and progressive employers, and no one who more heartily desires a saner and friendlier industrial order', describing this as the king's priority.[298] The monarchy's wartime engagement with the left went beyond inviting Labour leaders to Buckingham Palace; it saw a significant realignment of the king and queen's image, presenting them as sympathetic both to labour grievances and to social reforms as part of their necessary solution.

In fact, the royal couple were seen as so good at promoting worker morale that again in June and September 1917 the king and queen were sent to tour munitions factories and shipyards in Northern England and Scotland. In September 1917, the royal couple even visited the most radical region in the country – the 'Red' Clyde in Glasgow – for four days.[299] Notably, the press frequently referred to these visits as royal 'tours', echoing an older idea of the royal progress.[300] The *Southern Reporter* noted that 'the area of the Royal tour' in June 1917 'comprised the huge works in the North-Eastern district, which includes a large portion of the counties of Yorkshire, Durham and Northumberland'.[301] It emphasised the royal 'concern for the welfare of the workers themselves' and how 'these Royal progresses' would encourage war work.[302]

The overwhelmingly positive press tone towards the royal couple mattered in the 1917–18 period. As Frank Mort argues, 'individuals from outside the political and cultural elites who met the royal family did so partly via the imaginative and affective maps provided by the media and also by royalty themselves, who were keen to present a more informal public image'.[303] The 1917 visits to strike-hit regions show that the government believed that the royal couple's popularity was such that their visits to hotbeds of discontent would *calm* rather than inflame the situation, a fact revealing of the strength of wartime monarchism in the UK rather than its weakness.[304] The *Daily Record and Mail* noted that the king's visit to the Clyde saw the 'absolute absence of ceremony and courtly trappings. [...] the King came amongst his people as one of themselves [...] the visit was essentially a democratic one, and in every respect it was carried out on lines diametrically contrary to the rules that used to obtain'.[305] The paper noted that it was not possible to imagine Queen Victoria or King Edward VII 'entering so much into the everyday affairs of their subjects' as King George V did.[306] It boasted that 'the King was as safe amongst the grimiest workers as he would have been at Buckingham Palace or at Windsor', and that 'the democracy of the Clyde' showed that its people were not in awe of the king nor he of them.[307] Nevertheless, precautions were taken: during the visit to the Clyde in September 1917, for security reasons, the royal couple slept on the royal train, which was secretly shunted at night into a guarded tunnel underground between Glasgow Botanic Gardens and Kirklee stations.[308] There are also suggestions that workers, while turning out in huge crowds to see the monarch, interacted with him in a more egalitarian way. During one of the royal trips to the Clyde during the war, the king awarded medals at a huge rally in a stadium; film footage shows him on a central dais, personally pinning a medal on to a wounded man, who is carried up on a stretcher, and on to the uniform of a factory girl, in front of thousands.[309] Each recipient shakes hands with the monarch, but while the bourgeois women in the first part of the film curtsey, the female working-class medal recipients do not.

These successful strenuous visits fitted with Palace policy: Lord
Stamfordham asserted in April 1917 that 'Loyalty to the Throne, in my
humble opinion, must be inspired by the Throne itself and not be the result
of organisation or propaganda.'[310] There was a concerted effort here to build
in wartime upon the successful model of King George V and Queen Mary's
visits to northern industrial areas and mining regions before the war.[311]
George V also tried to influence government policy to ensure better treatment of the poor. On 11 December 1917, Stamfordham informed the Prime
Minister of

> how seriously His Majesty regards the system which compels the poorer
> classes to submit to the inconvenience and discomfort of waiting, some-
> times for hours, in long queues in order to purchase the necessaries of life.
> This morning Their Majesties in going to and from Deptford saw
> instances of these queues, and it brings home to the King and Queen
> the hardship experienced by the poor, while the richer portion of the
> community do not suffer in this respect.[312]

Lloyd George, no fan of George V as an individual, although no outright
anti-monarchist either, would write in his war memoirs of how, 'in estimating
the value of the different factors which conduced to the maintenance of our
home front in 1917, a very high place must be given to the affection inspired by
the King, and the unremitting diligence with which he set himself in those dark
days to discharge the functions of his high office'.[313] This appears to be
accurate: the mainstream press was fulsome in its praise of royal visits to
munitions factories and shipyards. However, it is more difficult to access first-
hand accounts from workers themselves. When middle-class munitions
worker Peggy Hamilton moved from Woolwich Arsenal to a factory in
Southampton, she recalled 'such visits were welcomed as a nice diversion
from which we often extracted some amusement during the long,
monotonous day'.[314] In other words, later in the war, royal visits provided
'amusement', a significant change of tone. Walter Powell, who was the royal
couple's ASC driver during their visit to a TNT factory at Queens Ferry in
May 1917, described the experience as 'a lovely day and one to remember'.[315]
However, during the king and queen's visit to Carlisle in May 1917 there was
also one person on the invite list for presentation to the royal couple who
declined, writing: 'the last thing in the world I want to do is to meet their
Majesties so you may scratch my name out of the affair'.[316] This highlights that
such visits were not universally popular and also that invitees due to be
presented did have a degree of agency to refuse, illustrating that there were
limits to the wartime state control of such events and also to the power of
monarchy. Yet the fact that one could decline conversely also suggests that
those invitees who did accept invitations were not coerced but chose to do so;
the large numbers during the years 1917 and 1918 who opted to greet the king

and queen during visits such as that to Carlisle thus suggests that the royals were genuinely popular.

Visits to munitions factories were not only risky due to radical workers – during a visit to the Chilwell Munitions Factory on 15 December 1916 the king was photographed standing amongst the thousands of live shells in the Filled Shell Store.[317] The risk posed by such munitions was real. The factory saw a substantial explosion on 1 July 1918 that killed 134 workers. Following the monarch's visit, politician Neville Chamberlain wrote to Viscount Chetwynd, the factory owner, with a report from Mrs Clive Wigram, the wife of the king's Private Secretary, who stated that when she dined with the king on 29 January 1917 he was 'very excited' about his visit to Chilwell and declared it 'one of the most remarkable sights I have ever seen – a wonderful place [...] and that he had enjoyed his day there so very much. [...] It is nice for your friends to hear that H.M. appreciates what you have done.'[318] Viscount Chetwynd, replying on 19 December 1916 to a letter of thanks from the king, described 'His Majesty's visit here' as 'keenly appreciated by the large number of His loyal subjects, both men and women, who are working with enthusiasm at the congenial task of filling shells for our Armies at the front [...]. A great honour has been paid to Chilwell.'[319] He referred to the workers' 'pleasure' at the royal visit and the king's 'close personal interest' shown in their work as he passed through the factory.[320] The chasm between the monarchist rhetoric and the reality of the extremely difficult, and far from 'congenial', conditions that munitions workers endured is shocking and again highlights the continuation of older monarchist cultures within the totalising and modernising paradigms of the British war effort.

That royal visits to war factories mattered is illustrated by the contrast with Germany, where the kaiser did little of such work, hastening his downfall. Admiral von Müller warned the kaiser's brother Prince Heinrich that

> In this terrible war which called for such heavy sacrifices from the people the Kaiser must live for his duty alone. Our stay in Kreuznach [German GHQ] too was nothing but a leisurely pastime. No one should imagine that the people don't realise these things. The Kaiser should be far more active, e.g. visiting munitions factories etc. The future position of the Kaiser in peacetime will depend on the Kaiser's behaviour during the war.[321]

If we turn to an examination of the British Labour movement, this too also reveals only very limited opposition to the British monarchy in 1917–18. As Mark Hayman has found, the British Labour movement remained in the majority moderate during the war, and those anti-monarchist views which did emerge largely reflected traditional nineteenth-century radicalism rather than Continental Bolshevism.[322] A huge meeting of over ten thousand people at the Royal Albert Hall on 31 March 1917, organised in conjunction with the

Herald newspaper to celebrate the February Revolution in Russia, expressed 'no hostility to the Crown'.[323] In fact, an informant who attended noted in a report read by Stamfordham and the king that the view of George V was positive:

> 4. Was anything said that might be inferred as its being time for a Revolution here?
>
> No. The condition and status of the English people were accepted absolutely: but I gathered that there was a feeling that absolute Monarchy (such as in Germany) might be modified, if not done away with in Germany before the war was ended. To my mind the general impression at the Meeting was that the King had done very well indeed in his position.[324]

Likewise, a fiery speech against the war and the government in Birmingham Bullring on 3 June 1917 by speaker Jim Donaldson declared:

> They ask you to fight for your King and Country. I have no Country to fight for, have you? Well the only bit of Country I have got, is in my flower pot on the window sill. [...] I don't mind fighting for my King and Country, but I want some Country to fight for, and as regards the King and Queen, well I don't want to say anything about them [...].[325]

The royal couple remained beyond reproach. A police minute noted that 'these "wild and whirling" words do not seem to merit serious consideration'.[326] Even radical left agitation was not particularly focused on overthrowing the British king. A memo by Professor E. V. Arnold of Bangor University in summer 1917 on 'Labour in Revolt', compiled for the Palace, referred to the spread of 'Marxist agitators' through South Wales, Clydeside, Manchester and Sheffield, claiming they could cause violence but were currently peaceful and 'had no designs on King George'.[327] In June 1917, when Robert Blatchford published an article in the *Clarion* contrasting the merits of monarchism and republicanism for the UK, he concluded ultimately in the British monarchy's favour, that 'it is a sheer waste of energy to whip up a revolt against a King who is no more a Kaiser than Old King Cole'.[328]

If courtiers' correspondence was filled with fearful imaginings of revolution, actual British anti-monarchist wartime plots never materialised. When the Labour activist Will Thorne returned from his visit to Bolshevik Russia he was summoned to Downing Street by Lloyd George and told that the king wished to see him immediately; he rushed to Buckingham Palace in a taxi so speedily that he worried that he did not have time to change his clothes.[329] Thorne's swift compliance to a wartime royal invitation and sartorial anxiety was perhaps an indication of the hold that monarchy had gained during the war over even radical Labour activists. He had in 1913 refused to share a platform with the king when he came to Stratford, East London, to open a new reservoir, on the grounds that the royal visit would do nothing to mitigate the 'deep-rooted and chronic poverty' of the area.[330] During the war, however, as Mayor of West Ham, Thorne himself suggested that the king and queen 'might care to visit the hospital at Whipps' Cross' and accompanied them on their visit.[331] Thorne used the occasion while Queen Mary 'was busy presenting gifts' to have 'a rather vigorous talk with the King [. . .] to let him know as much as I possibly could about the terrible poverty of the people. He took a great interest in what I had to say, and the questions he asked made me realise that his was not a formal interest, but a real desire to know the conditions of his subjects.'[332] Thorne clearly kept the letter of thanks he received from Stamfordham, reproducing it in his memoirs a decade later. After the war, when Thorne suggested that the local war memorial should take the form of a new out-patients' department at Queen Mary Hospital, the king's son, Prince Henry, was invited to open it.[333] One must be cautious here: some radical left, labour figures engaged with the British monarchy during the war while remaining pro-revolution and saw no contradiction in this. The Secretary of the Women's Trade Union League, Mary Macarthur, who established a genuine friendship with Queen Mary through wartime philanthropy, also wrote in support of the February Revolution to congratulate Russian women on their part in defeating the tsar, and Beatrice Webb described Macarthur as 'playing with Bolshevik ideas' in 1917.[334] On occasion, the views expressed by labour sympathisers also shocked the royals: they invited F. L. Donaldson, 'the labour parson', to preach at Sandringham, only for the king to be 'a little staggered' by finding out that Donaldson's 'heroes' were 'Ramsay MacDonald, Snowden and, above all, Keir Hardie'.[335]

Nevertheless, intensified efforts by the royal couple to engage with the poorest parts of Britain during the war clearly were undermining elements of pre-war radicalism, but the process was also, as in Thorne's case, linked to the way the war had created common ground where monarchism was associated with British liberal values and patriotism against autocratic, anti-socialist kaiserism. In a similar light, John McGovern, an active labour militant in the 'Red' Clyde area, recalled in his 1960 memoir giving a speech at an anti-war demonstration at Anniesland in Glasgow:

> I had been dealing with Kaiser Bill, the Czar and King George, and said, 'they are three cousins, and the Kaiser and Czar are two of the greatest bloody scoundrels ever known in history, but all the king's horses and all the king's men could never tempt me to say anything against "Our Noble King" except that I was very glad to see that only a month ago he had changed his name from that of Wettin to Windsor'.[336]

It was a very grudging statement of a certain degree of tolerance of the British monarchy; certainly it was an acknowledgement of its difference to the Continental European model. Yet it was also a critique of its German origins, enough for a police inspector present, who stepped into the ring and said, 'You have gone far enough, sir, and I demand your name and address as action may have to be taken against you.'[337] Overall, however, the incident is revealing of both the very limited nature of socialist radicals' attacks on George V and the extent to which any speech against the king was policed; even mildly undermining the sacralised status of the British monarchy could trigger immediate intervention. This may help explain the lack of anti-monarchist trials in wartime Britain and of a strong and visible anti-monarchist movement. The police monitored wartime radical speakers and events, and outright anti-monarchism was one thing to which they would not turn a blind eye, whereas the socio-economic demands of socialism were often tolerated. Speakers had to decide whether it was worth articulating anti-monarchism at the expense of potentially having the rest of a speech, and their wider socio-economic arguments, cut off. It is plausible that police intervention thus ensured that anti-monarchism was often silenced before it could get going at demonstrations.

This is not to ignore the occasions which do reveal public anti-monarchist attitudes towards the British monarchy. In June 1917, over 1,100 labour, socialist and pacifist delegates met at Leeds to mark the February Russian Revolution, where they called for the establishment of soldiers' and workers' councils in the UK.[338] A War Cabinet informant attended, and his secret report was shared with the king. In the view of the informant, the conference was intended to lead to a socialist revolution in the United Kingdom.[339] However, the numbers attending were quite small and the government well informed; moreover, the event was surrounded by a large hostile crowd, who were held back by police, and those who attended were booed.[340] Local hotels also refused accommodation to those attending.[341] Nevertheless, the king was so concerned he quizzed Will Thorne about it.[342] Thorne recorded that 'The King seemed greatly disturbed about the famous Leeds Conference'; he asked Thorne if he thought 'any ill' would come from it and from 'the decisions that were made there'.[343] Thorne's reply that 'there will never be a physical violent revolution in this country' seemed to 'relieve his mind and he spoke to me in a most homely and pleasant way'.[344] Lloyd George, who met with Stamfordham to directly discuss the latter's concerns about 'republicanism' in summer 1917, was inclined to dislike 'too much public talk about Republicanism and Revolution', believing it magnified something Lloyd George thought 'an insignificant movement'.[345] Ernest Thurtle recalled in his 1945 memoirs that, while there was a rise in anti-monarchism in 1917, it only lasted a brief time:

> even if in those dark days our limited monarchy, through no fault of its own, declined somewhat in popular favour, that state of affairs was of brief duration. With the arrival of a brighter war outlook the mood changed with a vengeance, and it was not long before King George and Queen

Mary, by their conscientious devotion to their responsibilities, and by their qualities of heart and character, had lifted the throne to a degree of popularity probably unequalled, and certainly not excelled, in the country's long history.[346]

The Trades Union Congress which met in Blackpool in September 1917 heard 'unprecedented criticism of the monarchy during a debate upon counter-revolution in Russia'; one delegate called for all monarchies to be swept away, while another, the Secretary of the Transport Workers' Union, Robert Williams, stated that 'Kings have gone already, and we are told that the Kaiser must go. Then I say, praise God when there will be a notice "To Let" outside Buckingham Palace.'[347] Yet this was the shattering of rhetorical taboos rather than real threat: the majority of the TUC accepted the monarchy throughout the war. Again, the lack of actual calls for direct violence against British royalty is notable, as is the freedom of speech allowed to Williams to make his anti-monarchist statements.

Aside from political activists, the population at large also showed few anti-monarchist tendencies. Clifford Woodward, the Canon of Southwark, wrote on 8 October 1918 that ordinary people were generally indifferent to the monarchy, but that the poor still had a belief in the 'omnipotence of the throne' and that anti-monarchism was confined to a small minority of those involved in 'active political or socialist propaganda' and was 'theoretical rather than practical'.[348] On 30 October, Assistant Police Commissioner and head of CID Basil Thomson visited Lord Stamfordham, who told him that 'the King remembered all that I had said to him, and said that he had had a very interesting talk and was reassured on the Labour situation; that he intended to adopt my suggestions about his tours [. . .].'[349] The same month the Bishop of Chelmsford also wrote to Stamfordham that 'the vast majority of the working classes are loyal and opposed to anarchy and disorder but their nerves are all on edge'.[350] He might have been writing about himself.

In some ways the British monarchy was simply lucky in terms of timing. While the February Revolution provoked enormous shock and generated debate about monarchy as a system, it was the Bolshevik October Revolution that had far more violent intentions towards royal individuals. News of the October Revolution (which occurred in November in the Western calendar) came just a few months before the Western Front crisis of the Ludendorff Offensives, which began on 21 March 1918. They triggered a rallying of the British home front in response and, by July–August 1918, a push for Allied victory. There was thus little time between November 1917 and March 1918 for Bolshevik violent anti-monarchism to get a foothold before the urgency of war events overwhelmed the news from Russia. Field Marshal Sir Douglas Haig certainly believed victory had been key: 'if the war had gone against us, no doubt our King would have had to go', he later reflected.[351]

This, together with censorship, helps to explain why it was only after the war's end that more evidence of any local spreading of anti-monarchism appears. On 14 November 1918, the Labour Party launched its general election campaign at the Royal Albert Hall, where the event included revolutionary speeches, with a comment again by Robert Williams that he wanted to see 'the Red flag flying over Buckingham Palace'.[352] At the 1918 ILP conference 'several local branches called for the abolition of the monarchy'; this recurred in 1919, but such views never represented a majority of branches, nor did they surface widely in the election campaign.[353] In November 1918 Clifford Woodward, the Canon of Southwark, wrote to Buckingham Palace that at a recent meeting in Southwark to introduce the local Labour candidate 'there was no expression of republicanism'.[354] The December 1918 general election would see all those members of the Union of Democratic Control who had opposed the war lose their seats, some prominent leftist wartime radicals among them.

Finally, there is one further, important example of the monarchy's ongoing status and power in this period – Lloyd George's attempt, declared during his election campaign of December 1918, to try the kaiser for his role in causing the war and in its conduct. George V successfully opposed his own Prime Minister's wish to try the German kaiser. Despite the alienation between the Hohenzollerns and King George V that the war created, a sense of the connection between the British and German monarchies – and common interest in not undermining monarchical status too far even in the interests of punishing the kaiser – saw George V put pressure on his government, in particular, through Lord Curzon at the Foreign Office, to halt plans to try the kaiser in the aftermath of the war.[355] The concerns raised in some sections of the public in 1917 that the British royal family would ultimately protect the kaiser were proved correct.

In fact, the reasoning used in discussions regarding the potential trial of the kaiser reveal the ongoing, powerful and sacralised status of the British monarchy. Lord Curzon, the Foreign Minister, who had initially taken the initiative in proposing the kaiser's trial, following pressure from the king opted to undermine the policy by insisting that a trial in England was not possible.[356] The British Minister in the Hague, Sir Ronald Graham, noted that the king had spoken to him 'most emphatically' against any trial; Maurice Hankey noted that the king on learning of the proposal to try the kaiser was moved to a 'violent tirade'.[357] Haig even regretted the new German Republic, believing that leaving the Hohenzollern monarchy intact would avoid destabilising Europe.[358] Ultimately, Curzon and George V successfully opposed Lloyd George's plans to put the kaiser on trial in London with the argument that the kaiser, as a grandson of Queen Victoria, could not be so humiliated. As Lord Curzon wrote to Lloyd George:

does not there seem to be a certain refinement of severity in bringing the Kaiser here, to the country the most famous Sovereign of which was his Grandmother; where his Mother was born; and from which she was married; where he has constantly stayed as a Royal Guest; and where his Cousin is at the present moment on the Throne?[359]

For King George V, Curzon worried that 'it is putting him in a very delicate and invidious position if his near relative, however great his crimes, is to be tried almost within sight of the Palace where the King lives and where the culprit has so often stayed [...]'.[360] Such concerns would hardly have arisen in any other criminal trial context; royals, even disgraced ones, received deferential consideration. For Curzon, a key factor was 'the sensibilities of the British royal family'.[361] This greatly reduced the chances of any trial ever taking place, as no other state was prepared to host it. George V may also have been influenced by the radical sloganeering of Lloyd George during the December 1918 general election campaign to 'Hang the Kaiser'; in a revolutionary era, proclaiming Britain might execute a fellow royal clearly was not something that Buckingham Palace could entertain. Lord Esher thought the whole idea 'idiotic' and warned a trial might reveal embarrassing aspects of British pre-war policy, such as its degree of support for France and Belgium.[362] King George V himself was reportedly 'furious', particularly as Lloyd George had proposed the London trial without telling him first, and bluntly asked his Prime Minister where the kaiser as a prisoner was to be lodged and if he was going to be brought back and forth from the Tower 'in a black Maria'.[363]

Royal connections with Europe continued to matter: George V received a long joint appeal from the ex-kings of Saxony and Wurttemberg and the ex-Duke of Baden 'appealing to His Majesty on behalf of the German Princes to prevent the extradition and trial of the ex-Kaiser, and throwing the responsibility for such action upon the shoulders of the King'.[364] The Palace warned the Prime Minister that the appeal required a reply, as 'in view of the status of the signatories and the substance of the letter, it should not be ignored'.[365] The pan-monarchist language of the German royal appeal was revealing:

> If the monstrous proposal to demand the extradition of His Majesty, the German Emperor, from the neutral country in which he is residing, in order to bring him to trial, is carried out, the world will behold the spectacle of an independent Monarch, overcome in honourable warfare by the superior forces of the Enemy, being arraigned, against all the laws of War and of Nations, and against the traditions of Christian States, in a Court established by Enemy Powers, and possessing no jurisdiction whatsoever. [...] If Your Majesty, by allowing these proceedings, Yourself raise your hand against the Dignity of a great Ruler, who is your kinsman and was once your friend, every Government and every

Throne, including that of Great Britain, will thereby be placed in jeopardy.[366]

The King of Italy also conveyed to the British that he 'did not like the proposal at all' and thought 'it would be a great mistake to make a martyr' of the ex-kaiser.[367] George V's opposition was very significant: by the end of the war, as historian Isabel Hull points out, Britain had largely rejected reprisals in favour of 'expanding the instruments and reach of law through post-war trials, setting precedents for specific sentences for war crimes, and extending culpability to heads of state and chiefs of armies'.[368] By undermining the chances of trying the kaiser, the extension of international law for war crimes to heads of state was set back decades, and the Treaty of Versailles, which stipulated the kaiser's trial in Article 227, was weakened. Lloyd George was irate, writing to Lord Curzon that if the trial of the kaiser did not go ahead the trials of other German war criminals for prisoner of war mistreatment, submarine war crimes and the execution of Captain Fryatt might also have to be abandoned: 'Is it suggested that we should abandon these prosecutions and let these ruffians go, merely because there is a society objection to the trial of the Kaiser?'[369] For Lloyd George there was 'a class motivation. As a middle class politician, he was keen to see a member of a leading European Royal Family made answerable for his crimes.'[370] By contrast, even though George V considered the kaiser 'the greatest criminal known for having plunged the world into this ghastly war', in 1919 he feared the arrival of German revolutionary ideas about the over-throw of kings and the trial of a monarch on British soil more than he sought Wilhelm II in the dock.[371] The potential echoes to the trial of Charles I were also a factor and featured in some of the discussion about where the kaiser could be accommodated during a London trial.[372] It was all a marked contrast to January 1919, when the king's secretary Clive Wigram wrote that the king trusted that 'no mercy or pity' would be shown to the German General Liman von Sanders and that 'everything possible will be done to bring him to justice' for war atrocities.[373] Similar ideas about inter-royal solidarity were also evident when Archduke Joseph, a member of the Habsburg dynasty, appealed to George V to help Hungary in 1919.[374] The idea that king and government might differ on clemency also appeared elsewhere: even German prisoners of war held in a camp at Redmires, Sheffield in August 1919 hedged their bets by writing *two* petitions for their release – one to Prime Minister Lloyd George, the other to King George V, addressing him as 'Sire' and 'soliciting Your Majesty to give a sympathetic hearing to their wishes for an early repatriation'.[375]

In the debates over the kaiser's trial we see clear evidence of the survival – despite the collapse of so many European monarchies – of the sacralised status of royalty and also of a remnant of a 'royal international'. The historian Johannes Paulmann refers to a 'royal international' to describe the tight network of diplomacy that connected royal leaders in Europe during the early to mid-nineteenth century, defining it as 'as much a heuristic device for investigating the role of monarchy in international relations as a reference to historical proceedings, namely, the search by monarchs themselves for co-operation at a transnational level'.[376] This idea is a valuable one. Even after all the upheavals of the Great War, monarchies continued to coordinate in their own interests. A monarch remained above the law of ordinary citizens. When ex-King Manuel of Portugal needed help disassociating himself from a Portuguese uprising in 1919 he contacted his friend Stamfordham to ask King George V to press Manuel's case with Lloyd George.[377] In 1919, the King of Spain shared letters he had received from ex-Emperor Karl of Austria-Hungary with King George V.[378] The ex-King of Greece also wrote to the British monarch to ask him to intercede for him with Lloyd George.[379] Elements of a transnational royal international survived.

In fact, British royal attitudes to deposed European royalty changed rapidly in the immediate aftermath of the war: King George V welcomed several surviving members of the Romanov dynasty to the UK, including Grand Duchess Xenia Alexandrovna, the dead tsar's sister, whom the British royals then supported financially, and the tsar's mother, the Dowager Empress Marie Feodorovna, for whom the British government sent a warship to evacuate her from the Black Sea to London.[380] Likewise Prince Andrew of Greece and his family, including the infant future Duke of Edinburgh, were rescued from Greece in 1922. The shock at what had happened to the tsar clearly had an impact. In 1920, George V sent a moving plea to his Prime Minister, David Lloyd George, on behalf of civilians who had been supporting General Wrangel's forces in the Russian Civil War, who were fighting against the Bolsheviks, asking that the

> government may yet be able to do something to save if possible the women and children from the terrible fate which will inevitably befall them at the hands of the victorious Bolshevik army. His Majesty understands and appreciates the Governments [sic] refusal to render any further assistance to Wrangel. But in the cause of humanity he feels that we should place any available ships at the disposal of these unfortunate refugees.[381]

Lloyd George firmly replied that this was not possible, because 'it is not only a question of the safe removal of these unfortunate people to a safe place but of their maintenance afterwards [...] in view of the clamour throughout the country and in the House of Commons against increased expenditure, it would be very difficult [...] to finance this further undertaking'.[382] The royals learned from the tsar's fate, however. When the Wehrmacht invaded the Netherlands in the Second World War, the British government even offered Kaiser Wilhelm II asylum, 'with the express approval of George VI'.[383]

4.5   Counter-Narratives: How Pro-Monarchists Re-Worked
the Monarchy's Image

Ultimately, the danger of revolution and anti-monarchism spreading to Britain
was exaggerated by courtiers, elites and the royals alike. The result, however, was
a redefinition of the image of British monarchy in 1917 and 1918. It was now
depicted as a 'democratic' monarchy, based upon kingship by consent of the
people. There was a greater emphasis upon making the monarchy visible and
accessible.[384] It was also projected as a bulwark against extremism: a bastion of
constitutional democracy that protected British people's freedoms, obviating
any need for socialist revolution. Here were the roots of a narrative of British
monarchical 'exceptionalism' that portrayed the British monarchy as different
from its troubled Continental peers in 1917–18. This shift was calculated and
drew particularly upon pre-war experiments in the king and queen's outreach to
industrially militant areas in 1912 and 1913 that historian Frank Mort has
identified as promoting 'a vision of patrician democracy that drew heavily on
traditions of organic, one-nation conservatism' and which drew on traditions of
nineteenth-century Toryism, Anglicanism and philanthropy.[385] This was the
version of democracy that the monarchy and its key advisors now invoked; they
saw this as a form of British democracy that could reconcile the working classes
to the throne and avoid revolution. Although, as Frank Mort has argued, we still
know too little about what type of 'democratic traditions and political languages
defined the monarchy under George V', accessibility for the working classes to
the royals was central to this vision of a direct subject–monarch relationship,
which courtiers saw as at the heart of this kind of patrician democratic order.[386]
One Palace informant, the Canon of Southwark, Clifford Woodward, wrote in
October 1918 of how 'old royal ideas would have to give way to democracy' and
the king become 'far more accessible to the working classes than has ever been
the custom'.[387] In a strange choice of language he referred to how, 'unless we can
seize time by the forelock and adapt ourselves to the new social conditions at
home', both the monarchy and Anglican church would become irrelevant.[388]
Likewise, he suggested both the Crown and the Church of England were under
threat together, as entities associated with the spiritual domain of the nation in
an era of atheistic socialist revolutionary thinking. The Bishop of Chelmsford,
for his part, urged the king to 'come out' more to the public.[389] George V pointed
out that the situation was 'without precedent' and that he had already 'paid more
visits and done more in 3 years than K[ing] Edward did in ten or Victoria in
thirty'.[390] Yet his advisors were convinced the king was not publicly visible
enough, and concerned that Lloyd George was overshadowing him.[391]

Lord Stamfordham, for his part, believed that older cultural ways of per-
ceiving the monarchy were disappearing and that the monarchy needed to
prove its usefulness to survive, if necessary proactively abandoning traditions
to do so: 'I am not concerned', he wrote in a letter to the Canon of Southwark,

'at the possible sacrifice of old traditional ideas and customs regarding Royalty. Some of these have already been sacrificed. Sovereigns must keep pace with the times.'[392] Yet when on 25 November 1918 he summed up his views in writing to the Bishop of Chelmsford, he revealed an ongoing sacralised outlook regarding monarchy, referring to the need to induce

> the thinking working classes, Socialist and others to regard the Crown not as a mere figurehead and as an institution which, as they put it, 'don't count' but as a living power for good, with receptive faculties welcoming information affecting the interests and social well-being of all classes and ready not only to sympathise with those questions but anxious to further their solution.[393]

'A living power for good' retained a moral sacralisation of royal purpose. Moreover, when it came to visibility, modernisation and tradition blended: the king and queen took the advice of the Archbishop of Canterbury in May 1918 that the king should drive 'through the streets in a way which made him more conspicuous. [...] no pomp was necessary, but an open carriage with two horses which would take seven or eight minutes more than a motor to go to some place in London' was a way to ensure the monarchy was seen and retained its aura in a modern age.[394] The king protested that he preferred motors, the queen that open carriages 'disturbed one's hair', but they gave way, and their tour of London after the Armistice was notably in an open carriage, as was their visit to Belfast in 1921.[395] Lord Esher bewailed this reformed use of carriages without pomp: 'Even at the opening of parliament this week', he told the Archbishop of Canterbury in 1918, the Prince of Wales 'was sent down in a carriage without escort or anything to mark him, and nobody knew he was there till he entered the House'.[396] Tradition and innovation were blending; security threats from revolutionaries were also clearly thin on the ground.

George V became quick to advise his contacts of his disapproval of any policies that appeared likely to be seen as unfairly burdening poorer parts of wartime society. Indeed, by the second half of the conflict, the king and British Court circles became particularly keen to emphasise that the monarch wanted to see Britain become even more democratic after the war, accepting the expansion of the suffrage to women and working-class male groups hitherto excluded, as well as an increase in the standard of living of the poor, an unusually radical reformist agenda in comparison to pre-1914 royal concerns.[397] The democratisation of the monarchy's image reflected changing views of sovereignty as something that rested with the *people* as politically defined voters and citizens, rather than solely with the monarch as 'Sovereign' and head of an honour-culture hierarchy and a body of subjects. Hence the increasing references in the press to the king as monarch by popular consent.

In November 1918, Lord Esher wrote to Stamfordham congratulating him on the 'democratization' of the monarchy, which, according to Frank

Prochaska, had by now become palace policy.[398] The image of a democratic monarchy proved effective: when the Labour candidate for Southwark for the 1918 general election was introduced, the crowd booed capitalists and the Northcliffe press but accepted the candidate's words that the 'Throne of England' was 'broad based upon the people's will'.[399] Professor Harold Laski, described by Kenneth Rose as the 'very apostle of republicanism', acknowledged after George V's death that 'He was identified with the spirit of hard work and personal sacrifice that had won the war [. . .]. The Monarchy, to put it bluntly, has been sold to the democracy as the symbol of itself; [. . .] the rare voices of dissent have hardly been heard.'[400] Stamfordham was even furnished with monthly returns showing the number of ex-servicemen working in government departments in 1920 – a way for the king to keep informed about ex-servicemen employment, something he followed closely to ensure that unemployment did not drive ex-servicemen into the arms of communism.[401] A letter the same month from Stamfordham to Lloyd George put royal pressure on the government: 'The King feels sure that everything is being done to find employment for the ex-servicemen whose grievance seems to be a real one.'[402]

As Chapter 3 has argued, the popular stereotype of George V in the historiography is that his ordinariness and thriftiness were what protected his dynasty in an era of revolution.[403] This narrative of George V as modest and ordinary was emphasised in the latter years of the conflict as symbolic of his democratic credentials. The press increasingly referred to the king using the paradigm of the war worker: 'Before the war one might have described him as an eight-hours-a-day man. Since the war he has been anything from twelve to fifteen', wrote the *Daily Mail* of the king's 'hard work' and his 'sympathy with Labour'.[404] Amid rising war-weariness and the outbreak of the Russian Revolution, the king was presented as an exemplary 'citizen' who treated all his subjects equally, a narrative which could undercut any potential Bolshevik anti-monarchist accusations of privilege and elitism. The British monarchy adopted such rhetoric very quickly in 1917–18. But it was also partly genuine. For his part, George V himself fully grasped the need to emphasise publicly his support for democracy. When, in 1919, some cabinet members objected to the 'democratic accents' in the draft of the King's Speech, Stamfordham informed them that the king thought this aspect of the speech 'ought to be strengthened'.[405] At the opening of the Imperial War Museum in June 1920, the king described how 'we owe our success under God not to armed forces alone, but to the labours and sacrifices of soldiers and civilians, of men and women alike. It was a democratic victory, the work of a nation in arms organised as never before for a national struggle.'[406] Rumours of revolution thus triggered the royal family's reinvention, situating them within a narrative of democratic kingship from 1917–18 on.

This redefinition of monarchy was thus pre-emptive rather than a response to any actual revolutionary reality in the UK, but it would stand the monarchy in good stead. By the time of the foundation of the British Communist Party in 1920 – which would share its offices with Sinn Féin, which presented a real revolutionary threat to the UK from Irish republicanism during this period – the British monarchy had already successfully reinvented itself, finally adjusting, as a result of the revolutionary scare of 1917, to the new age of mass politics and popular democracy that had been on the rise since the 1890s.[407] This was modernisation presented as British monarchist exceptionalism – British kingship was depicted as democratic, honest and humble and therefore could continue in the modern age, and this rhetoric served in turn to help sustain its revered status as precious and valuable. The dynastic principle remained sacred but was repurposed as compatible with political change. In reality, of course, these image changes by the British monarchy were not unique to Britain. As Dieter Langewiesche argues, the long-term history of European monarchies that survived the First World War shows 'a process of institutional self-assertion through transformation'.[408] But the 'exceptional British' message proved popular and appealing.

This successful new discourse provided the monarchy with a valuable form of cultural 'soft' power which helped compensate its loss of its pre-1914 status as a diplomatic intermediary with Continental European monarchies. Before 1914, liaising with European royal families, many of whom had huge amounts of political power, such as the kaiser, the Austo-Hungarian Emperor or the tsar, had brought the British royals considerable power in the eyes of the state. As David Cannadine has pointed out, 'during the half-century before the First World War [...] the British monarchy became increasingly entangled with European royalty, largely because of the marriages contracted with the ruling families of the continent by Queen Victoria's many children'.[409] Royal diplomacy, in fact, worked in tandem with the secret diplomacy and concert of Europe approaches of the pre-1914 world and often promoted pan-monarchical interests. This kind of royal diplomacy to Continental Europe was largely destroyed at the end of the First World War due to the conflict sweeping away large numbers of royal dynasties and hence its operational networks and intermarriage systems, leading to the post-war focus in the British case on tours of the empire as a new royal international relations role.[410] Indicative of this was the decline in royal visits to the Continent. The lost diplomatic connections for the British monarchy were not just with those dynasties that had been on the Central Powers side and fell victim to revolution, as the monarchy's successful wartime diplomacy with allied monarchs was also curtailed. The post-war period saw the Italian monarch effectively rendered irrelevant by the seizure of power by Mussolini; the very close relationship with the Belgian royal family, the British monarchy's most successful wartime diplomatic relationship, lasted somewhat longer, until King Albert I's pre-mature death in 1934.

Continental Europe became associated with a fear of revolutionary contagion for the British court, resulting in much looser royal ties with it in the interwar period and a focus instead upon the British Empire as the future of the mon-archy's diplomatic work and power – the increasing political relevance of empire and the need for the Crown to symbolise imperial unity in the light of growing demands for imperial reform from colonised peoples meant empire provided the royal family with a role that brought it considerable power, helping to replace the loss of power that the monarchy faced with the collapse of European royal houses. This shift in royal policy was also a response to the rise in power of the dominions during the war, which drove change: for example, the demand from the dominion prime ministers for greater input into war decision-making, which resulted in the establishment of the Imperial War Cabinet in 1917, and for increased independ-ence, which led to Resolution IX of the Imperial War Conference, which called for a full post-war overhaul of the Imperial Constitution. It was no coincidence that in 1917, for the first time, the king was attended by a mounted 'Empire' escort on his way to open parliament.[411] As Lord Esher warned the king's Private Secretary just before the war ended in 1918:

> Monarchy and its cost will have to be justified in the future in the eyes of a war-worn and hungry proletariat, endowed with a huge preponderance of voting power. I see a great future for the King in connection with the consolidation of "Imperial" control of our public affairs; but imagination and boldness will be required necessitating the abandonment of many old theories of Constitutional Kingship.[412]

Lord Stamfordham held similar views, writing in a letter on 21 October 1918:

> [...] the Crown is the one link that unites those nations – daily becoming more and more *free* nations – of the Empire into one federated whole. Were the King to disappear and be replaced by a President, our Dominions would inevitably break away from the Mother Country.[413]

This became a central PR message of the Palace at the end of the war – one which proved extremely successful. Without monarchy, there could be no empire. It went uncontested, even though the case of Republican France presented an example of an empire that functioned without a monarchy. As Frank Mort contends, 'elite rituals associated with the royal family and the court [...] retained an important place in the political culture of British and dominion diplomacy after the collapse of the old European order in 1918'.[414] The Imperial Conference of 1921 would affirm that 'the most essential of the links that bind our widely spread peoples is the Crown [...]'.[415] Historian John Darwin describes these interwar shifts in the structure of the empire as marking a 'third' phase of the British Empire.[416]

The British monarchy was central to the construction of empire throughout the war, and the conflict's immediate aftermath saw this process greatly reinforced. During the war, the monarchy's status was used to advance British imperial aims through royal diplomacy. Edward, Prince of Wales, was sent to Egypt and Sudan; at Khartoum he rode the battlefield of Omdurman, together with some British officers who had fought in the battle, a 'thrilling' experience of imperialist commemoration for the young prince.[417] When Lieutenant General Sir Stanley Maude took Baghdad, this British action was framed entirely in monarchist cultural terms: 'In the name of my King, and in the name of the peoples over whom he rules, I address you as follows. [...] It is the wish not only of my King and his peoples, but it is also the wish of great nations with whom he is in alliance, that you should prosper.'[418] Personal royal diplomacy was also key to Britain's wartime role in the Middle East, as illustrated by the warm letters exchanged between King Hussein [Sharif Husayn ibn Ali] and King George V in 1918 and 1919; the latter fulsomely praised the Arab revolt and 'those struggling for Arab freedom' against the Ottoman Empire in a letter to King Hussein on 30 September 1918.[419] Even though the post-war settlement fell far short of British wartime promises of Arab independence, when Edward, Prince of Wales, was involved in a train crash in 1920, relations were still good enough that King Hussein sent King George V a note expressing his relief the prince was unhurt.[420] The Prince of Wales also visited Egypt in 1922 to mark the end of the British protectorate there: a delicate trip, as Britain had only granted Egypt limited independence and retained significant control.[421]

The vision of monarchy as the fulcrum of empire was key to Stamfordham, who wrote to the Lieutenant Governor of Burma on 23 January 1917 of how

> Please God out of this hateful War the Imperial idea will become more real, and with it a keener and livelier sense of loyalty to the King-Emperor personally. India has behaved right well regarding the War. [...] The Princes have played up well and have stinted neither their men or money.[422]

The dramatic, long tours of the Prince of Wales to Canada, Australia, New Zealand and India between 1919 and 1925 also offer very clear evidence of this new weight being placed upon publicising and consolidating the personal royal connection with the empire, which served to bolster the monarchy's status at home and abroad in an era of European revolution.[423] Commemorating the empire's fallen war dead was a central element of these tours; Edward as a war veteran and royal heir was seen as the ideal figure to act as a conduit between the monarchy, its imperial future and the sacred war dead, chosen to visit the British Empire to thank it for its wartime sacrifices and renew ties to the monarchy after a war which had seen the rise of nationalism throughout British possessions, with the so-called 'white' dominions, in particular, gaining new status. Between 1919 and 1925, as Prince of Wales, Edward was sent across the empire on a series of visits that covered forty-five countries.[424] His war-veteran status was central to these tours. Upon his arrival in Canada in 1919, for example, reviewing the troops who formed the local guard of honour, Edward 'singled out "my brother Canadians" who had served with him on the western front during the First World War and who were distinguished by their bravery and their "free cordiality"'; he used this shared war experience to claim to his audience that they should look upon him too as a Canadian in spirit.[425] The prince inaugurated Warrior's Day in Toronto in August 1919 to honour Canadian war veterans; 27,000 were present, some of whom mobbed him with their enthusiasm.[426] At Saskatchewan, he met wounded veterans.[427] At New Brunswick he presented war medals to mothers of Canadian war fallen.[428] Throughout his Canadian tour, cameramen singled out moments when the prince encountered war veterans or relatives of the war dead.[429] In New Zealand, the prince met with Maori men who had fought in the war.[430] Edward also visited Australia in 1920 to thank it for its wartime sacrifices; meeting with war veterans was a significant part of this trip, although Lord Louis Mountbatten, who accompanied Edward, would, in 1974, deny that the war was a factor in the prince's tour, arguing that heirs to the throne had traditionally visited the empire 'to get to know the different parts of the Empire and Commonwealth and the people'.[431] On 16 August 1920, in a public letter addressed to Australian schoolchildren, Edward wrote: 'You have a splendid example of patriotism before you in the men and women of Australia who fought and worked and won in the Great War. Your sailors and soldiers thought first of Australia and the Empire.'[432] Newspaper readers in Australia were told that Edward was the 'Digger Prince' who had fought in the trenches.[433] Their shared war was the pivotal experience that gave Edward an immediate bond with his audiences throughout the empire; his tours were not dependent solely upon the loyalty due to the heir but could also draw upon the status due to him as a war veteran. Planning for the Australian tour emphasised war veterans as its primary audience and gave careful consider-ation to how to facilitate veterans with shell shock who might struggle with crowds and noise; at the suggestion of the Governor General, onshore naval salutes were discarded with.[434] As Frank Mort has argued, during these tours, 'unequivocally the Prince was defined as part of the "war generation"'.[435]

By consolidating the monarchy's sacralised role at the heart of the imperial war effort and commemoration in this way, Edward's tours sought to reassert the imperial centre against the forces of self-determination and demands for independence that the conflict had unleashed. Wartime developments had seen the dominions, in particular, gain much greater independent power in exchange for their ongoing support for Britain in the conflict. In 1914, Britain's imperial possessions went to war automatically; by 1917, with the establish-ment of the Imperial War Cabinet, the leaders of the dominions worked together to ensure that they had control over how their war resources, in particular troops, were used. By 1918, it was clear that the old model of pre-1914 empire was dead, and the main debate was on what kinds of reforms were needed, a process that ultimately culminated in the Balfour Declaration of 1926 and the Statute of Westminster of 1931, which removed the ability of the British parliament to legislate for the dominions, and fixed the change of language from 'British Empire' to 'Commonwealth'.[436] Yet the 1926 Balfour formula set out that the components of the empire remained united by 'a common allegiance to the Crown'.[437] It, in turn, increasingly recognised the need for different policies towards different parts of the empire: 'Royalty [...] envisaged a crown that was increasingly understood to be divisible – owned by each dominion, rather than being understood as exclusively British'.[438] The so-called 'white' dominions received pride of place in this rethinking: 'politicians championing the strategy of so-called "progressive empire" focused increasingly on the symbolic role of the king as central to contemporary thinking about the racialized British world'.[439] The refocusing on empire during the war had paid off for the monarchy; in the interwar imperial reforms, it retained enormous status and new purpose.

What was also significant was how, in an age of increasingly prominent anti-imperialist movements and anti-imperial languages, interwar reforms redesigned the monarchy's structural connections with its empire very much in terms of *monarchism*, as a series of separate royal relationships with each individual territory, operating in parallel and independent of each other, a model based on collective royal realms connected to the same monarch, rather than on any universalised crown regime across a global imperium. This, in practice, allowed for an increasingly fragmented monarchist structure of individual regional relationships within the empire, some more independent than others. While the crown was publicly promoted in the interwar period as the sole entity that united and connected the British empire and British people across the globe, what was actually happening, beneath the facade of this unitary interwar imperial role, was that royal structures increasingly promoted separate monarchisms over any more centralised imperialism, although monarchism and imperialism, of course, still closely overlapped in this period. Yet they were becoming much more distinct than they had been in the pre-1914 world. This helps explain why, later, when decolonisation occurred after 1945, many of the former empire's constituent parts could retain a link with the monarchy: interwar structural reforms meant that the British monarchy had already privileged separate monarchist relationships with its individual realms over pan-imperial ones, and the former proved possible to sustain when empire ended.

By the post-war period, the empire was increasingly an arena for key royal diplomacy whereby the monarchy networked on behalf of the British state with increasingly independent dominions, similarly to how it had once functioned across Europe, networking to increase British power with other Continental monarchies. This process largely transferred to the imperial sphere after the war: now the populations and governments of the dominions and India, in particular, were to be wooed and collaborated with, using the monarchy as a key tool for this, rather than incorporated simply as a backdrop to illustrate British power to domestic audiences, as had been the norm pre-1914. The contrast might be summarised as the difference between the Delhi Durbar of 1911, when Indian notables paid homage to King George V and Queen Mary in what was pitched as a sacred, traditional act of fealty, and the Prince of Wales's tours of the early 1920s, when the prince, dressed in ordinary clothing, shook hands with so many subjects he suffered muscle strain.[440] In contrast to the Prince of Wales's tours of the empire, including Canada, Australia and India in the immediate post-war phase, the British royal family's official visits to Continental European states dried up. King George V and Queen Mary did make a state visit to Belgium in 1922, but apart from this the king remained in the UK. In 1912, by contrast, the king had wanted a series of state or official visits to European courts; post-war no such idea was ever floated again.[441] The shift towards prioritising the monarchy's new emphasis upon its function of uniting the empire was further highlighted in 1923 when 'the voice of a reigning sovereign was first heard by media audiences when George V and [. . .] Queen Mary, recorded for gramophone an "Empire Day message to the boys and girls of the British empire"', an intimate gesture, bringing the royal voices into their subjects' own homes.[442] Queen Mary's post-war 'Doll's House' project summed up much of the new vision: a miniature version of a royal palace, each tiny object made to showcase British crafts and industry.[443] It was designed by Sir Edwin Lutyens as a gift from the country to the queen which would be exhibited at the British Empire Exhibition at Wembley Park in 1924.[444] The symbolism was significant. The dolls' house interior contained multiple references to the empire and to the war – a Tommy's photograph, busts of Haig and Beatty, and a sketch of the cenotaph; the war as epic history was thus shrunk into miniature to fit within royal domestic, familial history, symbolising national continuity in dynastic homeliness, a deliberate contrast thereby invoked with the purported militarism and politicking of unstable Continental monarchies.[445] The royal family – their personal world symbolised by the domestic nature of the Doll's House – was now to tie the different empire components together with Britain at their heart, in a familial bond, with each part of the empire having a shared home, in the royal household, not in the United Kingdom state, as the empire's component parts became increasingly independent of Westminster.[446]

4.6   Conclusion

Overall, then, one of the war's most important legacies for the British monarchy was its rebranding as a special democratic case. The conflict saw a carefully crafted message by press, court and politicians that the British monarchy, with its long history of constitutionalism, its limited political power, its purported egalitarian attitudes to all its subjects and its role as the fulcrum of an empire that supposedly promoted the education, civilisation and economic development of its colonised peoples, was somehow unique and progressive. This message was not only promoted by the king but by British elites more generally. The real role of royal influence remained known only to elite circles. When the war ended, Field Marshal Sir Douglas Haig wished to 'publish his appreciation of the king's continued confidence in his command'.[447] George V refused Haig his permission, lest it reveal the extent of royal patronage that Haig had actually enjoyed, which the king feared Lloyd George would view as 'unconstitutional'.[448] The extreme wartime austerity measures introduced by George V also created a sense that in its perceived thrift and eschewal of luxury the British monarchy was somehow 'different' from Continental counterparts. This idea of a British monarchical exceptionalism became a key legacy of the conflict and ultimately protected the monarchy from being tarred by association with the disenchantment with Continental monarchical systems.

It was of course a myth. The British monarchy was still a hereditary monarchy, of German descent, and, although reformed by Lloyd George, who tried to reduce the king's political influence, it was still powerful. But the old 'honour'-based cultural awe for the institution of monarchy, described in previous chapters of this book, had been undermined, and the future looked more uncertain to monarchists. Contemporaries noted the change: Lord Cromer, the king's Assistant Private Secretary, considered that the monarchy was less stable in 1918 than in 1914.[449] Yet, in their performance of wartime 'normality' – visiting ordinary workers in their place of work, factories, shipyards and warehouses – the royals validated the effort and suffering of the British, with, in an inversion of the pre-war honour code, royalty now 'honouring' the people. In effect, this ensured the mystical contract between sovereign and people was both inverted and renewed through the war effort. Irish republicanism was the most direct threat to the monarchy, because it was all about sovereignty, but it was self-limited to nationalist Ireland, whereas British labour and socialist radicals were more concerned with class than sovereignty and largely accepted the monarchy's own justificatory claims that it was above class and not an expression of it.

To conclude, whereas, at the outset of the First World War, kingship was part of a broader honour culture that infused contemporary beliefs and mentalities in much of British society, after 1916, as this chapter has shown, the meaning and weight of 'honouring the king' had changed. The discourse of kingship shifted during the conflict, from one based on tropes borrowed from medieval pageantry, unquestioning martial loyalty and lingering stiff Victorian class hierarchies to one that emphasised kingship as service, thrift and humility, and the king as an ordinary man, a humane, if still sacralised, figure, eager to share in his people's suffering, and the Prince of Wales as a democratic 'ordinary' soldier doing his bit. Kingship as discourse and practice successfully reinvented itself during the war as democratic and dutiful in ways that still shape the modern British monarchy. In promoting new First World War kingship narratives, of the kingly body, of service, of mass sacrifice and of 'honouring' the dead, and substituting them for older, more hierarchical, pre-1914 honour discourses, George V and the royal family helped successfully steer the British monarchy through the crisis years of the conflict. Yet, the monarchy would further restore and reinvent important elements of its 'sacralised' cultural image through how it handled the end of the war.

PART III

The Unknown Soldier

The Role of the Monarchy in Post-War Commemoration

5

The Monarchy and the Armistice

Ritualising Victory, Channelling War Grief

5.1 Introduction: Marking Victory

Chapter 5 explores how the monarchy culturally embodied the transition from wartime to peace during the Armistice period and the year that followed, playing a key role in both the rituals of victory and of war grief. The end of the First World War and its immediate aftermath was a period of ongoing stress and adaptation for the British monarchy. Its role in victory ceremonial and in responding to war grief show the ways in which older cultural practices and new innovations – often packaged as tradition – often coexisted and combined to sacralise it.

This investigation also reveals the extent to which honour-based monarchist concepts survived the conflict: victory ceremonials often 'honoured the king', while the monarchy sought to 'honour' the war bereaved. In particular, the way that the monarchy engaged with war grief became a key means by which it re-sacralised its role in society in the wake of the challenges to its cultural status in the second half of the war. In part, this developed out of new practices that royalty had already adopted during the conflict, such as writing to families who had suffered multiple war losses, but the monarchy's overall post-war role in engaging with the war dead and bereaved would also go far beyond this. This response to mass war bereavement proved key to sustaining the popularity of the monarchy, enabling it to overcome the challenging of its cultural status by republicans in 1917–18 and the broader European anti-monarchist context.

This chapter begins by assessing the monarchy's role in 'performing' victory. With the Armistice of 11 November 1918, the monarchy faced the problematic task of navigating an appropriate new relationship between victory and war bereavement. Its pre-1914 ritual role in celebrating national and imperial victory had to be reassessed and carefully juxtaposed with developing a suitably sensitive approach to the huge numbers of war bereaved and disabled, as well as to the changed socio-political realities and expectations that the war's end had brought. Moreover, the context for these processes was not 'peace', as neither the United Kingdom, where violence broke out in

Ireland in January 1919, nor much of Europe, which in its Eastern and South Eastern regions was wracked by ongoing war, had actually established peace-time norms. For all of these reasons, the celebration of 'victory' or 'peace' was far from straightforward.

The historiography has tended to neglect this core victory–grief dynamic which marked the months immediately following on from the Armistice, focusing more on how societies coped with mass grief.[1] Yet the theme of 'victory' was clearly present in an initial wave of victory celebrations to mark the 1918 Armistice and the signing of the Peace Treaties in 1919. The first British mode of commemorating the war in this period was thus one that emphasised success. But this victory dynamic coexisted with processes of mass mourning and war bereavement, which ultimately came to the fore, supplanting the victory dimension of initial post-war commemorations. Traditional victory celebrations ultimately transitioned into a singular focus upon commemorating the war dead.[2] How this occurred will be shown through this chapter's examination of the role of the monarchy in the period between the Armistice of November 1918 and the Peace Day celebrations of July 1919.

Honouring the war dead began early in the conflict; it was not simply a post-war phenomenon. It had its roots in the war years themselves, in the royal family's experiences of the war's human cost, in their hospital visits, in their experiences of the war fronts and also in their own personal wartime griefs; it was not only a consequence of the Armistice period but reflected longer-term evolutions. How the monarchy honoured the war dead came to matter hugely during the conflict. Kingship was used to venerate war death in battle and thereby stop it becoming banal and anonymous – a real risk with the advent of total industrialised war and mass death on an unprecedented scale for the UK and the empire – and as a way of presenting the monarchy as one that grieved the pain of war, thereby undercutting its association with pro-war militarism and the more militarist aspects of pre-war European monarchical culture. How the royals developed ways of showing empathy with the war grief of their individual subjects before 1918, and how they understood the experience of war loss in their own personal lives, established important new norms which shaped post-war developments, as the second part of this chapter will illustrate. We turn now to the royal role in victory ceremonial, before examining this monarchical engagement with war grief.

5.2   Victory Traditions: Royal Ritual and Ending the War

Despite all the changes wrought by the war, the default cultural response to the first news of victory was remarkably traditional, with monarchist cultural practices central to responses. Royal ritual and display were in fact used to symbolically 'end' the war for the United Kingdom following the Armistice.

Royal biographer Arthur Bryant, writing in 1936, described in mystical terms how 'the end of the War, like the beginning, brought the nation to its ancient shrine, the throne'.[3] Crowds spontaneously gathered at Buckingham Palace on 11 November 1918 at 11 a.m. to mark the Armistice, as recounted by Patricia Wilson, wife of Royal Navy Commander H. M. Wilson:

> This morning at 10.22 I was in the room where the tape machine is (we are simply glued to it always) when I saw news come through 'Armistice signed' – so of course we knew there would be great joy and that people would go at once to Buckingham Palace so off we all went [. . .].[4]

Wilson found herself surrounded by crowds who had likewise rushed to the palace. She provides a valuable account of monarchist culture at the Armistice moment, highlighting it as an immediate response by the public:

> the crowd was simply great but most awfully well behaved in front of the Palace, boys climbed all over the monument, the police tried to keep them down but of course no use, they sat on the heads of the figures and everywhere!! Well the King (God Bless Him) came out with the Queen and Duke of Connaught and Princess Mary in VAD uniform and the crowd cheered like mad and we all sang 'God Save the King': then they went in and the crowd got thicker and thicker [. . .]. Well the crowd yelled and yelled 'WE WANT KING GEORGE' about every moment. Too thrilling for words. [. . .] and the massed band of the Guards came and the King came out again and we all sang 'Keep the Home Fires Burning', Tipperary, the Doxology, all the Allies [sic] anthems and a few others. At the end of each we cheered and yelled We want a speech [sic] and at last the King spoke.[5]

Note the Doxology: religion and royalism were intertwined. Sir Almeric Fitzroy, Clerk of the Privy Council, described the 'instinct' of the crowds 'that lost no time in wending their way to Buckingham Palace', which was a 'call' to the 'Sovereign to share and express their emotions, and should satisfy some that revolution in this country is not likely to be directed against the Crown'.[6]

The occasion was marked by royal solemnity: pages draped the centre balcony with its valance of red and gold.[7] In total, on 11 November 1918 the king appeared on the balcony no less than three times in response to the crowds, as he recounted in his diary:

> At 5.0 this morning the armistice was signed by Foch, Wemyss and the German delegates and hostilities ceased at 11.0. [. . .] The news spread quickly and a large crowd assembled outside and May and I with Mary and Uncle Arthur went on the balcony when the Guard marched off. [. . .] At 1.0 we again went on the balcony, there was an enormous crowd who gave us a wonderful reception, the Guards [sic] massed bands played all the National Anthems of the Allies and a few popular airs; it was an extraordinary sight. [. . .] Worked all the evening, hundreds of telegrams

coming from all parts. [. . .] Showed ourselves on the balcony as there was still a large crowd, the Irish Guards band played.[8]

For the king it was 'a wonderful day, the greatest in the history of this Country'.[9] Queen Mary noted in her diary it was 'the greatest day in the world's history', remarking on the 'huge crowds and much enthusiasm' outside the Palace.[10] The crowds outside the Palace continued for days: the queen noted that in response they went out on the balcony on 12 November twice, once in the afternoon and once in the evening, and again in the evening on 13 November, each time to 'large crowds'.[11] Monarchist display coexisted with radical labour militancy elsewhere, however. Assistant Police Commissioner Basil Thomson noted in his diary for 17 November 1918 that 'side by side with the intense demonstrations of loyalty to the King go noisy revolutionary speeches'.[12] Ambiguity was also visible in Ireland, where, at the Armistice, the nationalists and unionists of East Cavan came together in peace rejoicing with 'cheers [. . .] given for President Wilson and King George' as well as for the British navy, the Ulster and Irish Divisions, Lloyd George and Willie Redmond, only for the area to elect a Sinn Féin MP a month later.[13]

Monarchy was thus a key vector for popular celebration in marking the end of the war. In fact, victory was framed – both at the time and after – as infused with the idea of a special unity between monarch and people. Royal authority was utilised, confirmed and reconsecrated as part of the process of framing victory in terms of the common effort. This was deliberately planned: the Archbishop of Canterbury noted on 3 November 1918 how he and Stamfordham decided that if the war ended 'the King must be prepared to take a leading part personally in speaking, travelling about, processing through the streets, in attending services etc.'.[14] The Archbishop envisaged it all in terms of the king marking 'deliverance', a religiously infused concept for describing the conflict's termination.[15] Stamfordham planned for the monarch to go to the regional cities, including Edinburgh, Manchester and Liverpool, to mark the occasion.[16] The monarch also visited the Fleet at Rosyth. Thus, in the week following the Armistice, 'the King became for his people the hierophant of victory', according to Harold Nicolson, who wrote of how 'on five successive days, accompanied by the Queen', the king processed 'in an open carriage through the poorer quarters of London'.[17] The *Daily Mail* described these tours of the working-class parts of London by the king and queen in glowing terms, the language suggesting again the ideal of symbiosis between monarchy and subjects – a kind of re-enactment of the public at the gates of Buckingham Palace in 1914 when war was declared, except this time, in a symbolic demonstration of how the war had changed kingship, the monarch went out to the people, in London's poorer socio-economic areas:

> The climax of the revelry [. . .] was the passing of the King and Queen through the streets. Without escort save for two mounted policemen they

drove through their delirious people – the King and Queen who, when
thrones are falling like autumn leaves, can ride with only the escort of
a people's love.[18]

The king wrote in his diary of 'nine miles [...] through waves of cheering
crowds. The demonstrations of the people are indeed touching.'[19]
Stamfordham told Margot Asquith that 'the poorest of the poor had clung'
to the royal carriage 'and by special request of the King had not been interfered
with by the police'.[20] The traditional sacralising trappings of monarchy – the
carriage procession – were repackaged with a democratic visibility by touring
working-class districts. Press illustrator Fortunino Matania, who specialised in
royal images, drew the scene for *The Sphere*'s front page (Fig. 34), in a format
that was almost a royalist counter-image to revolutionary crowd scenes.

Some aspects of the victory display of monarchism were clearly projections
of how people felt that the monarchy *should* behave in a situation that was
unprecedented – the end of a 'total' war. As such, these expectations can be
highly revealing of how monarchy was imagined. Admiral David Beatty
believed that the king should 'go out' in a flagship to receive the surrendered
German fleet in person, indicating ongoing monarchist beliefs about for whom
the war had been fought and whose victory actually was.[21] George V was
appalled: 'I don't mean to crow over the fallen enemy', he remarked, pointing
out: 'what would be said of the King who being a Naval officer, had never gone
to sea with his Fleet while mines and torpedo boats were about, but when
fighting is over, he sails triumphantly out as a naval warrior'.[22] It was the king's
own personal decision to refuse and to reject a proposal that blended imagined,
clearly sacralising, traditional notions about a monarch's role in victory
together with modernity, the technology of the industrial fleet.[23] Even though
Beatty's idea never went ahead, it was highly indicative of the aspirations that
existed for monarchists around the monarchy's sacralising role in embodying
and displaying what was a very modern victory. And it reflected naval culture:
an internal order in November 1918 to all ships announced that the
Commander-in-Chief would hold 'a service of thanksgiving' for the victory
which 'Almighty God has vouchsafed to His Majesty's Arms' and all ships were
to do likewise.[24]

There was clearly an overtly religious dimension to the way this relationship
between monarchy and victory was understood. The king and queen attended
a Free Church service of thanksgiving in London at the Albert Hall on
16 November 1918 which was attended by 12,000 people, according to
Queen Mary, as well as a service of thanksgiving at the Guards Chapel the
next day; this was followed by one in Edinburgh at St Giles's Cathedral.[25] The
liberal newspaper, *The Scotsman*, reported how 'It was as if one saw Their
Majesties come down the corridor of ages as we watched the stately procession
pass beneath the flags to the Royal pew. [...] For truly the greatest day of all is

Fig. 34 'King and People in the Streets of London, Armistice Day, November 11, 1918', *The Sphere* front page, 16 November 1918, illustration by Fortunino Matania, Mary Evans Picture Library, 10980897

that in which the King is come to St Giles' to thank God for a victory such as no Empire ever knew.'[26] The report on 22 November by Norman Maclean noted that generations to come would remember that 'the King-Emperor came hither to give thanks and pray when victory was won. It is by these things men live, and in them consisteth a nation's spirit. [...] The King kneeling in St Giles' is the nation confessing its dependence on God – the only giver of victory.'[27] Despite the archaic, sacralising language, the occasion was also one of innovation – it was the first time that a Moderator of the United Free Church had officiated before the monarch.[28] Yet the monarchism harked back to an earlier understanding of kingship. For Maclean, the British monarch had been rewarded with victory by God:

> There are moments when even in a solemn service there falls a deeper stillness: and there came such a moment when prayer was offered for the King and Queen. It is amazing the appeal that kinghood makes to the heart, when kinghood is worthy and noble. And as the prayer arose for the solitary man, alone in his altitude, every heart in that vast throng went forth to His Majesty. It is strange and indefinable. It is of the centuries, and it is of eternity, for to the people still the King is the Lord's Anointed. And the hurrahs in the street are to-day nought but a prayer – that God may bless the King! And over yonder in Holland – isolated, condemned, with all the shouting silenced forever – is he who turned the throne of a mighty Empire into a tool of devilry. [. . .] To feel the atmosphere of love, loyalty, and devotion that filled St Giles' to-day and to think of the fallen Emperors and Kings of Europe is to realise that the judgments of God are abroad in the earth.[29]

The eschatological depiction here of the kaiser and the king is not empty rhetoric – in this religious world view the kaiser has served the purposes of the devil, the king those of Christ. The *Scotsman* report thus depicted royalty in spiritual communion with both the divine and the people: 'And as we sang and prayed the figure of the Christ glowed brighter. The uplifted hands seemed to shed a benediction on the King and Queen and on the people stretched out before them. [. . .] it was as if from the ascending Christ the blessing fell on King and Queen and people.'[30] Here is a clear example of what William Kuhn has argued: the most important royal ceremonies in this era 'were always religious acts', ritual and symbolism expressed broader belief systems and cannot be fully understood without this sacralising context.[31] This was also reflected in the way the prefix 'royal' was used in the aftermath of the war to reward and honour war service: in 1919, for example, the Army Chaplains' Department was awarded the title 'Royal Army Chaplains' Department' in recognition of its war role. The language of royal 'honouring' remained a feature of post-war British culture – another indication of how elements of honour culture survived the conflict.

This was also clear in the decision that the king should make 'a great delivery' by speech to the Houses of Parliament to mark victory, creating a 'new precedent'.[32] This speech was given in person to both Houses in the Royal Gallery on 19 November 1918, when the king also received addresses of congratulations presented by both Houses. The day before, in preparation, the House of Lords and the House of Commons paid tribute to the king in ways which are highly revealing of the fusion of both traditional honouring of the monarch and modernisation rhetoric about democratic kingship. The politicians even went so far as to define the war victory in terms of monarchical stability: on 18 November 1918, Chancellor Andrew Bonar Law proposed that the whole House of Commons present 'an humble Address [. . .] to His Majesty to congratulate His Majesty on the conclusion of the Armistice and on the prospect of a victorious peace'.[33] He noted that the price of the war was not just the war dead but also the collapse of governments, society and civilisation, and 'as a consequence Europe is seething with revolution to-day'.[34] By contrast, Britain and the empire could look forward to the future with 'hope, with courage, and with confidence' because of its strong institutions, and of these, Bonar Law claimed, none was 'stronger, or rests on a more secure foundation, than the Throne. The Throne is the link, I believe, which has held the British Empire together, which has enabled it to play a glorious part in this terrible struggle, and which will in the days to come make the union closer and closer.'[35] Yet, amidst this rhetoric of tribute, Bonar Law sought to emphasise the British monarchy as an institution based on popular consent:

> at this time – when kings, like shadowy phantoms, are disappearing from the stage, [. . .] – our Sovereign is passing daily without an escort through the streets of the centre of the Empire, and is everywhere met with tributes of respect, of devotion, and of affection. These phantom kings have fallen because they base their claim on an imaginary Divine Right. Our King rests secure, because the foundation of his Throne is the will of his people.[36]

One can clearly read in Bonar Law's words an underlying fear that the collapse of European monarchism had engendered in the UK, which helps to explain why supporters of the monarchy rushed to defend it and also sought to differentiate the British royal model from those elsewhere as a way of trying to protect it from the wave of anti-monarchical change sweeping the Continent. This threatening European climate may even have roused some of those usually indifferent to the monarchy to support it. There was a broadly sensed feeling that the era of power of Continental European monarchies had ended due to the war – even Field Marshal Sir Henry Wilson, when unveiling the war memorial at Liverpool Street Station in 1922 just hours before his own assassination, closed his unveiling speech with the lines of Kipling's poem 'Recessional': 'The Captains and the Kings Depart.'[37] Asquith, in his endorsement of the 'Address of Congratulation' to the king, echoed Bonar Law's framing of the British monarchy as a timeless embodiment of the people's will, as well as presenting the First World War as a war between different forms of *monarchical* ruler:

> In the crash of thrones – built, some of them, on unrighteousness, propped up in other cases by a brittle framework of convention – the Throne of this country stands unshaken, broad-based on the people's will.

It has been reinforced to a degree which it is impossible to measure by the living example of our Sovereign and his gracious Consort, who have always felt and shown, by their life and by their conduct, that they are there not to be ministered unto, but to minister. [...] monarchies in these days are held, if they continue to be held, not by the shadowy claim of any so-called Divine Right; not, as has been the case with the Hapsburgs and Hohenzollerns, by the power of dividing and dominating popular forces and popular interests; not by pedigree and not by tradition: they are held, and can only be held, by the highest form of public service, by understanding, by sympathy with the common lot, by devotion to the common weal.[38]

In these speeches the laurels of war were presented not to the government or generals but to the king-emperor, in keeping with much older traditional understandings of war as waged on behalf of the monarch, but also illustrative of the fact that the king as British head of state was the key leadership figure of the UK and the empire, albeit with his role now presented as a natural direct, democratised, corollary of the will of the people. Here was a fusion of older cultural ideas about war victory and monarchy and newer imperatives to somehow refashion the British monarchy as exceptional and democratic in a Europe where monarchical power was increasingly discredited due to the war. Asquith was almost word for word presenting George V as a 'servant king', with its religious overtones. The war had led to this reconfiguration of the British monarchy as a spiritual, moral and organic embodiment of the people's needs and suffering rather than a symbol of privilege. This language in the House of Commons endeavoured to reframe the mystique and myth of British monarchical leadership – as a natural, unelected, performance of the people's will – in ways that unconsciously and unintentionally presaged some of the ideas that fascist leaders elsewhere in Europe would later build upon to justify their power. Yet again older cultural ideas remained present too: Queen Mary described the king's reply to the 'addresses of congratulations from both houses of Parliament' – significant language with its older implication of war victory as something for which a monarch is personally congratulated – as 'an excellent reply sending a message to his people'.[39] Here the rhetoric is of traditional hierarchies of monarch and his subjects.

If both Bonar Law and Asquith's speeches showed the concept of kingship was now built around ideals of merit, humility and service – a more modern take on monarchy – the whole ritual of congratulating the king on victory was a traditional one. Moreover, it was one about which Asquith privately retained some scepticism: he wrote to a friend on 12 November 1918 of the Service of Thanksgiving at St Paul's Cathedral attended by the king and queen that 'as one after another of our female royalties was led up the nave', he had turned to Lady Lansdowne, seated next to him, and asked, 'how long do you think this will last?', referring to the monarchy and noting in his letter that 'I see they have got rid of eight kings in Germany in the course of the last two or three days, and there are more to follow.'[40] Part of the prominent display of monarchism at the moment of victory in 1918, in other words, was an outward show of royalist faith precisely because of inward concerns about the monarchy's future in the post-war world. Yet, as he walked down the nave at the same service, the king confided to the Archbishop of Canterbury that 'the enthusiasm of his greeting in the streets was greater than at any time of his life'; huge crowds had gathered outside to cheer him.[41]

What explains this public acclamation of the king? In part, he symbolised the British victory; there was also a traditional role for monarchy in performing war victory that was being reasserted after the Armistice. The king was also genuinely popular for the war leadership, hard work and sacrifice he had shown. Yet one also cannot ignore the value of royal ceremonial display as a form of letting off steam for the public – as celebration and style – that was welcomed as entertainment after the dull and grey war experience. The Archbishop of Canterbury mused on the strangeness of these vast displays of public support for monarchy against the backdrop of elite fears of revolution. When crowds gathered for the wedding of Princess Patricia of Connaught, in February 1919, he wrote:

> the popular demonstrations in the streets seemed to me to betoken the sort of public loyalty and interest in these royal things which contrasts curiously with the Radical demonstrators who have been at work during the same week in Trade Conference. It is not, so far as I can judge, that these industrial folk are hostile to royalty itself, but they seem to regard the old order of things as having passed away, and I felt that the demonstrations in the streets and the interest in the press all showed that there is a deeper and more widely extended interest in these matters than the ordinary Radical newspapers would ever suggest. Whether this is likely to be an enduring sentiment is another question, but it certainly exists just now, and would have to be reckoned with if agitations of a revolutionary kind were attempted.[42]

Public interest in a royal wedding had clearly not yet been swept away by any revolutionary fervour.

The fusion of older, sacralising, cultural ideas of British monarchy with new innovations was also clearly evident in the response to the signing of the Treaty of Versailles with Germany on 28 June 1919. When news that the treaty had been signed at Versailles reached London, the first reactions were largely traditional. There was a 101-gun salute at the personal order of George V.[43] Large crowds also responded to the news of the peace treaty signing by seeking out the royals. The king noted in his diary how, following news of the signing reaching London at 4 p.m. on 28 June, a large number of people collected in front of the Palace and at 6.0 a salute was fired of 101 guns, May and I and the children went out of [*sic*] the centre balcony and there was a great demonstration of loyalty, one of the Guards bands played in forecourt, we stopped on the balcony for 40 minutes. After dinner I received a letter from the Prime Minister telling me peace was signed brought by Mr Davidson in an aeroplane. At 9.15 we again went on the balcony, a larger crowd than ever, probably 100,000. David and I each made a short speech. At 11.0 then turned search lights on and we again went out. Today is a great one in history and please God this dear old Country will now settle down and work in unity.[44]

There are multiple layers of significance here. First, Buckingham Palace remained the totemic site where the public rallied in moments of historic importance. Second, the king interpreted this behaviour in much older cultural codes and, as a devout man, through a religious framework – as a 'demonstration of loyalty', highlighting that this interaction between crowd and monarch was much more than just a throng gathering at a famous central London site. The spontaneous choice of the monarch and his heir to make speeches reinforced this, as a process of ongoing relationship between monarchy and subjects. Yet there was also the juxtaposition of modern practices too: the letter from the Prime Minister, after all, arrived by aeroplane.

  The monarchy's response to peace also highlighted older monarchist cultural codes and practices that remained present: the signature of what was referred to as the 'Peace Treaty' was announced in the king's 'Proclamation of Peace' on 2 July 1919, a proclamation which was ritually performed in an extensive ceremonial. First, the deputy Earl Marshal and the Officers of Arms, wearing their tabards, assembled at St James's Palace accompanied by Sergeants at Arms, carrying their maces, and proceeded to the balcony in Friary Court, where the trumpets were sounded 'three times by six state trumpeters' before the king's Proclamation of Peace was read by 'Garter Principal King of Arms, Sir Henry F. Burke' (Fig. 35).[45] The Proclamation reading concluded with the words 'God save the King', followed by the singing of the national anthem.[46] The ceremony at St James's was then followed by the gathering processing on foot through London, passing through the Mall, the Strand, Fleet Street, Ludgate Hill, St Paul's Churchyard, Cheapside and Poultry. At a number of key sites, including Trafalgar Square, Temple Bar and Cheapside, the procession halted and the Royal Proclamation was again read out; the trumpets were sounded three times before and after each reading.[47] The heralds wore black silk breeches and stockings; the poursuivants mounted in the procession wore white buckskin breeches, knee boots and golden spurs and carried jewelled swords and golden batons.[48] The Treaty of Versailles was thus given a British reception full of pomp and pageantry that reflected much older monarchist cultural codes. The *Sheffield Daily Telegraph* reported that

Fig. 35   The Public Proclamation of Peace at Friary Court, St James's Palace,
2 July 1919, Getty Images, 646304130 (Photo © Hulton-Deutsch Collection/CORBIS/
Corbis via Getty Images)

Really it did not seem the year 1919 when one's gaze was kept fixedly upon
the principal actors of the ceremony. It was only when the black coats of
the men folk, with tall hats to set them off, came that the Middle Ages
atmosphere was ruthlessly destroyed. [...] we might more easily have
imagined ourselves listening to a Proclamation of the Peace that followed
the victories of the Black Prince or the termination of the Wars of the
Roses. Certainly a few knights in armour would have been in keeping with

all the solemn and archaic business. The presence of photographers, too, was an anachronism. The survival of the ancient custom brought great crowds to town. The route between St James' Palace and the Royal Exchange, where the first and final announcements were made, was thronged with people, who gazed in open-mouthed astonishment at all they saw.[49]

Here again was a fusion of sacralising ideas about what constituted proper monarchical ritual in response to a war victory and new practices, such as large numbers of press photographers now photographing court ritual.

The planning for peace celebrations which followed on from the signature of the Treaty of Versailles similarly involved both innovation and ideas about monarchical tradition. At the king's insistence, a national religious ceremony was rapidly planned in response to the peace treaty with Germany, as 'in His Majesty's opinion the question of rendering thanks to the Almighty ought not to be deferred', while the government, courtiers and civil servants wrangled over when and how the major peace celebrations should take place.[50] A National Service of Thanksgiving in response to the signing of the peace was then organised by Lord Stamfordham and church representatives, to take place on 6 July at St Paul's Cathedral. The service was timed to coincide with similar thanksgiving services to be held nationwide and on the old Western Front. The government agreed the plans.

On 2 July 1919, Stamfordham approved the idea that, before entering St Paul's Cathedral and upon leaving it, the king, queen and other royals would take part in brief religious services on the cathedral steps. Stamfordham noted to the king that this innovation drew upon precedent:

> At the conclusion of the Service, when Your Majesties come out of the Cathedral, the National Anthem will be sung by the people, and the Archbishop of Canterbury will bless the people. This last act was performed by the Archbishop of Canterbury when Queen Elizabeth went to St. Paul's for a Thanksgiving Service after the Armada, but on that occasion Her Majesty also addressed the people.[51]

The national anthem was to be sung as follows, with two new verses added to mark this special thanksgiving moment outside St Paul's:

> God save our gracious King
> Long live our noble King
> God save the King!
> Send him victorious,
> Happy and glorious
> Long to reign over us,
> God save the King!
>
> One realm of races four,
> Blest more and ever more,

God save our land!
Home of the brave and free,
Set in the silver sea,
True nurses of chivalry
God save our land!

Kinsfolk in love and birth
From utmost ends of earth,
God save us all!
Bid strife and hatred cease,
Bid hope and joy increase
Spread universal peace
God save us all![52]

Monarchy's imperial function was emphasised here: the concept of the United Kingdom and its empire as one of diverse nations and races held together by the dynastic principle of the Crown. Indeed, royal significance and popularity was such that the Prime Minister intervened in the planning to insist that 'at such a National [sic] occasion the King should not be separated from his Ministers. Arrangements will be made accordingly that they are accommodated on the steps and will follow in the procession up the Cathedral.'[53] Lloyd George wanted to ensure politicians shared in the royal limelight, a further illustration of the monarchy's popularity. The whole event attracted large crowds, and people lined the streets all the way to Buckingham Palace.[54] Sir Almeric Fitzroy, who attended, described it as 'happily conceived and worthily executed'.[55] The royals on the cathedral steps giving thanks to God for peace was later immortalised in a large mural painting by artist Frank Salisbury for the Royal Exchange, London.[56] Salisbury's image was deeply religious, showing at its centre the king, in naval uniform, bareheaded, hat in hand, standing beside the queen, with their adult children to one side of them, surrounded by clergy as they exited the cathedral, following a cleric in ornate robes leading the procession carrying a cross.[57] At the edge of the foreground were royal trumpeters.[58] Royalty and religion combined. The painting set the figures in almost identical positions to those they had actually taken on exiting the cathedral, as shown in photographs of the event; Salisbury had witnessed the scene in person and had been profoundly moved, particularly by its novel interdenominational nature; ecumenical innovation was worked into a new ceremony on the cathedral steps that was presented to the public as if archaic royal tradition.[59] This mural would become one of three relating to the First World War painted for the Royal Exchange, London to add to its existing sequence of Victorian murals on events in English history. Together with Salisbury's 'Their Majesties, King George V and Queen Mary Visiting the Battle Districts of France, 1917', it meant that two of the three explicitly connected the war effort with the monarchy.

The broader planning for how to mark the eventual signing of the peace treaty with Germany had been in progress since early May 1919, with Stamfordham and the Minister for Foreign Affairs, Lord Curzon, playing key roles. The Treaty of Versailles was signed by Germany on 28 June 1919, and 19 July 1919 was chosen as Peace Day, when the population would celebrate. Stamfordham and Curzon's initial ideas for this event offer a clear illustration of the fusion of older cultural assumptions about monarchy with modernisation processes. Curzon's initial plan was for four days of national celebrations, including 'a great River pageant on the Thames, all the City Guild Barges to be present and it is hoped the King will consent to lead the procession in the Royal Barge', a markedly antiquarian image of kingship to project.[60] Yet Curzon also emphasised the modernising trends the war had unleashed, stating that 'The idea is a democratic celebration.'[61] His proposal for children's entertainments in parks across London and nationwide was based on the plan that these would be 'haunts of the democracy'.[62] Ultimately, even though the king disliked the idea of a barge event, believing it would be too tiring, it went ahead, although not as part of the Peace Day celebrations, but on 4 August 1919, as part of a separate 'Sea Services' commemoration of the war services of the Royal Navy and the Mercantile Marine.[63] The king and queen processed down the Thames on a 230-year-old royal barge, the image of traditional kingship: journalist Philip Gibbs described it as 'The King's water pageant or "Triumph" (as it was called in the old days) [...] this Royal Triumph', invoking the older idea of a monarch processing in a triumphal march to mark victory in war.[64] Even the left-wing *Daily Herald* provided full details of how the public could best see the royal barge as it led the flotilla of boats.[65]

In the planning for the July 1919 Peace Day celebrations it is again evident that the king feared the rise of anti-monarchism when, in fact, these events showed the monarchy was popular. He insisted that the military parade be arranged so that it was not too tiring for the troops involved: 'His Majesty fears that although this kind of display may be pleasing to the people, it is likely to be irksome to and not appreciated by the Troops themselves.'[66] The king was also wary of any extravagance antagonising the public mood. He rejected plans to illuminate Buckingham Palace as a waste of money.[67] He insisted that the peace celebrations 'should be arranged as much as possible for the "People". South London should certainly not be overlooked.'[68] Moreover, Stamfordham noted that

> His Majesty's idea regarding the form the celebrations should take is that every locality should have its own celebrations in its own way at the time that is most convenient to it, he considers that at all events in the country there is a good deal of indifference, if not lukewarmness [*sic*] about the whole thing.[69]

In reality, however, the Peace Day events on 19 July 1919 proved hugely popular, attracting enormous crowds to the main military 'victory' parade through central London, which saluted the monarch as it passed Buckingham Palace, to the park events for children and later fireworks, and to the local festive events around the country. Out of concern for costs, the celebrations were condensed into the one day, Saturday, 19 July, which was made into a special bank holiday for the occasion. The fusion of monarchism and victory was clearly in evidence during the London Peace Day victory parade. The victory procession included a march past the king, who took the salute from those passing the royal stand at Buckingham Palace – a location, *The Times* claimed, where 'throughout the war, in every moment of victory, the people of London have flocked instinctively to make the King a sharer in their joy'.[70] It also described war-maimed men singing the national anthem before the king as

> the noblest tribute king ever had from free people. It expressed all that the Royal House of England has meant to the soldiers of England throughout the past years; but much more than that, it was the tribute of men, approved in the fires of war, to a man whom their hearts acclaimed.[71]

Again, here the core relationship of the soldier was to the monarch – yet, in keeping with the increasing post-war lauding of democracy, it was now also described as a relationship of equals: man to man. The whole of the victory parade, which incorporated delegations from Britain's Allies, including those from republican states, carried out a march past and saluted the British monarch, French Generalissimo Ferdinand Foch and American General John Pershing among them. However, Sir Almeric Fitzroy's observations on the parade reflected the way that the victory mood was increasingly underpinned by grief: 'popular enthusiasm, combined to produce a grandiose spectacle, and one, moreover, inseparable from deeper emotions than the mere hour called forth, for, before and around those who defiled under our eyes, there went an immaterial company, the sacred legion of the lost, who purchased our safety with their blood'.[72]

During the day, the royal family responded to the crowd by appearing on the balcony of Buckingham Palace twice; they also visited Hyde Park to see the festivities, to tremendous acclaim by the crowds. *The Times* reported 'thousands of people cheering and dancing around an open carriage in their anxiety to show their loyalty and devotion to the Sovereign'.[73] The evening's fireworks in many ways echoed the traditional firework displays of the English monarchy for special occasions – a tradition that went back to Queen Elizabeth I. Illustrating the centrality of the monarchy to victory, the fireworks display included making portraits of the king and queen on the night sky and at the end spelling out the words 'God save the King'.[74]

At a local level too, monarchy was also very present in the Peace Day celebrations. The *Devon and Exeter Gazette* published a poem entitled 'Peace Day, July 19th 1919', which stated: 'To-day then, our King, our Country, our men we will cheer, for Peace reigns again – a thing we count most dear.'[75] In Tytherington

in South Gloucestershire, the Royal Proclamation was read at the council school –
the reader, Mr Fry, was specially given the archaic title of 'Constable' for the
occasion.[76] Such centrality of the monarch was also visible in other local Peace
Day celebrations such as the 'Peace Souvenir and Programme of Festivities'
produced for Clevedon-on-Sea, Somerset, which had George V in uniform
prominently displayed on the cover, as shown in Fig. 36. It appears this was
a standard template, as an identical souvenir pamphlet cover, with only the name
of the location changed, also appeared for Ebbw Vale and District's Peace Day in

Fig. 36   Clevedon-on-Sea peace souvenir, 1919 pamphlet (© Clevedon Pier and
Heritage Trust Archive)

Wales.[77] A postcard to mark victory issued by C. W. Faulkner and Co. had the king's portrait under the word 'Victory', surrounded by the royal standard and the flag of St George for England and the Union Jack.[78] Underneath was the legend 'either conquer or die' and a verse from Cowper, clearly intended to refer to the monarch: 'He holds no parley with unmanly fears, where duty bids he confidently steers, faces a thousand dangers at her call, and, trusting in his God, surmounts them all.'[79] This was followed by a line from the king: 'we have continued to the end, buoyed up by faith in our just and holy cause'.[80]

It is important to emphasise that the Peace Day celebrations were not uncontested, however, highlighting the political and social tensions now emerging in post-war British society, particularly in those towns, such as Coventry and Luton, where working-class organisations or ex-servicemen felt excluded from the occasion and serious riots occurred over several nights to coincide with the Peace Day events.[81] In Luton, the mayor was taunted on Peace Day by a hostile crowd as he read the King's Proclamation for Peace Day 1919, due to a decision to ban the National Federation of Discharged and Demobilised Sailors and Soldiers from holding a commemoration of the dead as part of the planned events.[82] A riot ensued and the town hall was burned to the ground. Victory celebrations that did not pay adequate tribute to war grief were already contested, a portent of the shift away from marking victory to focusing upon commemorating the war dead which was rapidly to come. The *Catholic Herald* wrote of Peace Day: 'The great peace day has come and gone. Some "maffickers" have "maf-ficked". Much silly twaddle has been talked. Lloyd George and George V "took the salute somewhere in London".'[83] It was this awkward juxtaposition of monarchist ritual and celebration of victory with mass grief, resentment and economic hardship that was the context for the Peace Day celebrations of July 1919. Ultimately, Peace Day would not remain an annual calendar fixture after 1919; the war would be marked instead with Armistice Day, and the focus by 1920 was upon bereavement, not victory, with the burial of the Unknown Soldier that year. Monarchy was visibly central to this transition, the fundamental element of both victory events in 1919 and the commemoration events built around mass bereavement in 1920 and after. Moreover, the overall conclusion regarding the initial wave of events to commemorate 'victory' in 1919 and those that followed to venerate the war dead is that traditional beliefs and cultural practices survived around and through monarchism, echoing Jay Winter's findings regarding the extent to which war grief was often traditionally expressed.[84]

5.3   Public and Private: The Monarchy's Encounters with War Grief

Central to the development of war commemoration was the way that the war created a newly expanded role for the monarchy as vector for the expression of war mourning and as representative of the broader war-bereaved public, with the royal family embodying what Jessica Meyer has described as 'fictive kinship' between the monarch and his grieving subjects.[85] Ultimately, the monarchy became the central performer of national and imperial war grief rituals both during and after the conflict, devotedly supported in achieving this by the Imperial War Graves Commission and the Church of England.[86] This was not an inevitable outcome, but contingent upon a series of successful adaptations that positioned the monarchy effectively as apt conduits of popular war grief – innovations that read the public mood well. There is considerable value in examining this process in more detail. The monarchy's interactions with war grief were wide-ranging and revealing: they provide an important insight into the way that monarchical culture was embedded within British First World War culture, as well as into different micro-cultures of grief in British society during this period. They also allow us to assess the development of change over time: the monarchy's involvement in commemorating the war dead encompassed both the war years and their aftermath, and in many ways it was the wartime innovations in this regard that set the tone for 1919 as public emphasis shifted from celebrating victory to commemorating the dead. Given the scale of monarchical engagement with war mourning, however, it is not possible to cover all of its dimensions here. The focus of the following section is upon one key question only: how was the monarchy able to successfully incorporate individual and local war grief into narratives of national and imperial sacrifice? It argues much of the groundwork for this success was laid *during* the war, in particular, through innovative royal emphasis on egalitarian treatment of the war dead and bereaved.

This section assesses the gestures, practices and rhetoric that were developed to this end and why they proved such a popular success. It analyses the ways that the royal family successfully engaged with war grief during the conflict, setting out their early emphasis on egalitarian treatment of the war dead. This then laid the foundations for the monarchy's very extensive involvement in commemorating the war dead in the interwar period, which is discussed in more detail in Chapter 6. It is easy to forget that any royal engagement with war grief was a high-stakes activity that could easily backfire: the wrong gesture, any perceived disrespect or opportunism, particularly in a European context where monarchism was being challenged, and war grief could rapidly turn into mass resentment towards royalty. Yet the British monarchy's engagement with war grief successfully created a profound – and idealised – image of social, national and imperial unity, despite ongoing contemporary social and political tensions, which served to stabilise the state. This success drew upon the monarchy's pre-war status under George V as sacralised, moral and traditional, of course, but it also innovated and modernised; the dynamic relationship between older ideals of monarchy and new mass war bereavement led to a new emphasis upon social equality in how royal engagement with war grief was presented. It is also important to note the wartime innovation here that the Great War represented for British society, with the establishment of the Imperial War Graves Commission in 1917: past wars had focused their commemorations on the key fallen royals, generals and battles, not on the mass of other-rank dead soldiery and their grief-stricken families. Already by 1917 this had shifted. Together this explains how, during the conflict, war grief came to consolidate, not undermine, the status of the monarchy and why its wartime narrative of social, national and imperial unity in grief proved effective and enduring into the interwar period and beyond. The shift to a more egalitarian narrative about the war dead during the conflict, which set the later tone for 1919 and after, took several forms for the royals, which we will now explore in two case studies. The first was the way that royal war grief was played down. The second was the way that the monarchy made contact with the individual war bereaved, particularly in royal letters of condolence.

Whereas in previous conflicts royal war grief was the subject of heroisation and ceremony, in the First World War its only relevance was as a means of illustrating in the press that the royals too felt war suffering and shared in its sacrifice and were not immune to the war's toll. Even then, the royal family never dared portray its own war losses as on a par with those endured by the people, which took centre stage. The king lost a nephew, many close friends and his cousin and his family were murdered. But the public narrative of egalitarianism in war death masked these very intimate war grief experiences of the royal family, which could not be seen to be paid any special treatment, as well as hiding the way that the war affected a specific micro-culture of royal bereavement practices. The royals had a key social role: they constantly set the norms of what constituted acceptable emotional behaviour, as national and imperial exemplars. In turn, this also meant that instances of their own wartime mourning had to be subsumed into the formal cultural patterns of stoicism, emotional self-discipline and egalitarianism that they had established for collective war grief. When Princess Beatrice's son, Prince Maurice of Battenberg, the king's cousin and Queen Victoria's youngest grandson, was killed on the Western Front in 1914, his mother had to follow the conventions of royal stoicism and silence, writing privately:

> It is one of those losses one can never get over [...] and it is so terribly hard to sit quietly and resignedly realising that one's dear child, who was like a ray of sunshine in the house, will never be amongst us again in this world. In the midst of all I have much to be thankful for, in that he died a noble soldier's death and without, as I am assured, suffering, and I have two dear sons still spared to me, when so many poor mothers have lost their one and only one.[87]

Her other two sons were also serving.[88] The press narrative emphasised Prince Maurice's loss as one that showed the royals' war experience was akin to that of

ordinary people. However, as the war continued, Maurice was rapidly forgotten in the media and by the public. Indeed, although he sympathised with his
aunt in her bereavement, the king strongly encouraged a narrative of equal
treatment of royal and non-royal war grief.[89] When Prince Maurice's brother
Prince Alexander married in 1917, his brother Prince Leopold was refused
special leave to be best man at the wedding.[90] Princess Beatrice, Prince
Maurice's mother, even lost her battle with the Imperial War Graves
Commission for her son's grave to have a unique headstone of her own design;
it had to be marked the same as all other war graves, something the king
insisted upon.[91] Moreover, the princess's request to lay a wreath at the
Cenotaph on the occasion of its unveiling in 1920 was refused, as it was feared
it would show preference to a royal and as the king thought it 'best that ladies
should not take part' in the actual wreath-laying ceremony at the Cenotaph.[92]
With enormous demand for seats for the service of the burial of the Unknown
Warrior in Westminster Abbey, and other relatives of the fallen being turned
away due to lack of space, there were real concerns about avoiding any
accusations of favouritism regarding the Cenotaph unveiling and the
Unknown Warrior burial which was held immediately afterwards.[93]
Although there was acknowledgement at court that Princess Beatrice was 'in
a special position as a bereaved mother', her request to lay a wreath was also
considered logistically inconvenient by the king, 'as there will be no other
ladies grouped around the Cenotaph'.[94] The Cenotaph ceremony was to be
a masculine imperial and military moment, in contrast with the subsequent
burial service at Westminster Abbey, at which grieving mothers predominated.
Thus, the king ensured that Indian princes were represented at the Cenotaph.[95]
Ultimately, however, a solution was found: Princess Beatrice was permitted to
watch the Cenotaph unveiling from the windows of the Home Office, along
with other royal women, including Queen Alexandra, Queen Mary, Princess
Mary, Princess Victoria and the Queen of Norway, and to also attend the
Abbey burial service afterwards.[96] In contrast to the era of Queen Victoria,
herself a particularly famous exemplar of personal monarchical mourning
following the death of her husband Prince Albert, in the First World War,
royal grief was to be rendered discreet. It was all a marked contrast with the
way that previous royal deaths in war had been distinguished by widespread
public recognition, such as that of Prince Louis Napoléon, son of the Empress
Eugénie, in the Zulu War or Prince Henry of Battenberg, Princess Beatrice's
husband, who died of illness onboard ship while on a colonial campaign in
1896 or Prince Christian Victor of Schleswig-Holstein, a grandson of Queen
Victoria, who died of fever during the Second South African (Boer) War, in
which he served as a staff officer.[97]

   Yet, despite the new invisibility of royal bereavement in wartime, private
personal grief – while never emotionally displayed publicly – was a significant
aspect of the royal experience of the First World War. Princess Beatrice was

obviously deeply affected by the loss of Maurice. Younger royals too grieved their war-dead friends. Princess Beatrice can hardly have been reassured when her son Prince Alexander of Battenberg wrote to her from the front that 'I know now that poor des Voeux is dead, also young Cunliffe and four other of our officers, including Sloper, wounded. Surely your prayers have helped me so far.'[98] In another letter he confided: 'Every moment I miss poor Bob Vereker whom I was so fond of. I trust Lady Gort has had the news very gently broken to her, as she adored her brother.'[99] The Prince of Wales wrote in his diary in 1914 of his friends who had died in the war.[100] The king himself noted in his diary that he felt depressed at the death of 'Charlie Nairne', Lord Charles Mercer Nairne Petty-Fitzmaurice, who had been his equerry and friend for years, who died in 1914, just days after Prince Maurice.[101] On 8 November 1914, the king wrote to Prince Albert describing how devastated his friend Harry Legge was at the death of his son at the front, noting five days later, in his diary, how 'all the best Officers and our friends are going in this horrible war'.[102] When Lord Kitchener, Secretary of State for War, drowned, the king described this loss of his 'great personal friend' as a 'heavy blow' in his diary and wrote to his second son, Albert, that 'I had known him for 30 years and he always told me everything. He has left behind a terrible blank.'[103] Albert received another letter from his mother, which stated that 'Papa is awfully upset.'[104] King George V's grief was such that he broke protocol by attending the memorial service for Kitchener at St Paul's Cathedral; traditionally the monarch did not attend memorial services for his subjects.[105] The German satirical magazine *Simplicissimus* mocked the monarch's pain, with a cartoon of the king and Queen Mary being told the news of Kitchener's death just as they were about to eat fish from the North Sea and recoiling in horror.[106] Innovation coexisted with tradition, however: when Queen Mary's elderly aunt Augusta, the Dowager Grand Duchess of Mecklenburg-Strelitz, an Englishwoman who had long ago married into a German dynasty, died in Germany, in December 1916, Queen Mary received 'many kind letters & telegrams' and also wrote many letters 'in connection with dear Aunt's death'.[107] The normal cultural practices of condoling upon a royal death took precedence over the fact that Augusta was living in an enemy state as a member of an enemy royal dynasty.

The king and extended royal family also experienced direct personal loss with the murder of the Russian royal family at Ekaterinburg in summer 1918. The historiography has long focused on the king's role in intervening to get Lloyd George's government to rescind its offer of asylum to the Russian royals, as discussed in Chapter 4; however, there has been little study of the ways in which the royal family grieved the deaths.[108] Princess Marie Louise of Schleswig-Holstein provides an account of their reaction:

> On one Sunday, we were all assembled in the corridor, waiting for the King and Queen. The King came slowly down to where we stood, and he looked so grave and distressed that our thoughts at once flew to the

fighting in France, and my mother exclaimed, 'Oh, George, is the news very bad?' He said, 'Yes: but it is not what you think. Nicky, Alix, and their five children have all been murdered by the Bolsheviks at Ekaterinburg.'[109]

Queen Mary wrote in her diary of how 'Mama & Toria came to tea, terribly upset at the news.'[110] The king insisted that the dead Russian empress's sister, Victoria, Princess Louis of Battenberg, who lived in the UK at East Cowes, should hear the news in a personal letter from him before it reached the press, which Princess Marie delivered. Upon arrival, Marie told Victoria's husband of the news, giving him the letter, and he then privately broke it to his wife. Princess Marie provides us with a detailed account of the way that initial grief was handled:

> We did not talk at great length about it at all: there was so little one could say. The horror of this ghastly tragedy was too overwhelming for mere words, and just the ordinary expressions of condolence seemed utterly out of place. If I remember rightly, we went down to tea and afterwards Victoria said, 'Let us go into the garden as there is any amount of work to be done and one gardener cannot do it all by himself.'[111]

Princess Marie recalled how they gardened together each day of her stay and also knitted comforts for the troops; Victoria read aloud from books after dinner each evening:

> Victoria did not allow her grief to interfere with the ordered daily routine of life. [. . .] Victoria and I, after that first half-hour we had spent together when I had brought the tragic news of that mass murder at Ekaterinburg, never alluded to it again. I felt instantaneously that it was a subject too poignant and sacred to talk about. She knew I was sharing her grief, and that my silence did not mean careless indifference to what she was suffering, but that it was the only way I could convey my sympathy, by not intruding with expressions of condolence however sincere and well meant. So we worked all day in the garden [. . .].[112]

It is a quite startling account of the silences and stoicism with which grief was handled in royal circles during the war.

The suppression of war grief was also a deeply personal issue for the king's Private Secretary, Arthur John Bigge, Lord Stamfordham, whose young son and namesake, John, was killed in action in 1915. 'If it is God's will that he is to be taken we must be brave', Stamfordham wrote to the king as he waited for news, 'and we shall only be like many many others'.[113] Upon learning of his son's death, Stamfordham wrote 'there is nothing to do but <u>work</u>', seeking meaning in his role as Private Secretary to the monarch.[114] He wrote to his close friend, the Archbishop of Canterbury, Randall Davidson, of the loss of 'our life centre', 'a staggering blow', and indicated how painful it had been to visit a wounded comrade of his son's and see his father and mother there with him.[115] In many ways his loss helps explain Stamfordham's intensified efforts to advise the monarch on the war, as managing the conflict well was now an intensely personal issue: 'Neither you nor I, Mrs Asquith', he said to the Prime Minister's wife, 'would mind our only sons dying in a Waterloo, but in this muddled, mismanaged war everyone feels the uselessness of their losses'.[116] These were bitter words for a man at the heart of the monarchy for which the war was ostensibly being waged. Stamfordham struggled terribly with his bereavement, seeking solace from the Bishop of Chelmsford.[117] The bishop wrote that 'Lord S. and I had a most interesting talk at his request on the soul after death. He is still sore about the death of his son. He asked a number of questions and was most grateful for what I said.'[118] In fact, Stamfordham's grief was such that Clive Wigram, another of the king's secretaries, asked the bishop for help: 'He is much concerned about S. Says he has aged so and urged me to do all I could.'[119] The king himself also mentioned to the bishop that he was 'much disturbed at Lord S. sadness [sic]. It was apt to get on his nerves and S [sic] was indispensable.'[120] Robert Borden, the visiting Canadian Prime Minister, noted that when he condoled with Stamfordham on the death of his son, the latter was 'greatly affected when I alluded to his loss', which suggests Stamfordham was visibly emotional.[121] At the very heart of court life, private grief was affecting relationships and decision-making.

If personal royal grief had to remain hidden, this contrasted with the public duty of care to the war-bereaved subject. This was immediately evident from the start of the war with regard to those employed as staff in the different royal households and estates when war bereavement occurred. John Robertson, a forest labourer at Sandringham killed in the retreat from Mons, was the first royal employee to die in the war.[122] By the end of September 1914 more than sixty members of staff at Buckingham Palace had enlisted, three of whom would be killed within weeks of the conflict starting.[123] At Windsor Castle, Royal Librarian John Fortescue recalled how, with the outbreak of war:

> The Castle staff, moreover, was greatly disorganised owing to the rush of its younger members to join the colours. One of my own men, a fine and very promising young fellow, belonged to the Berkshire Yeomanry, and, of course, had to join his regiment at once. [...] he was manifestly keen after any adventure. I never saw him again. He rose to be serjeant, and as a serjeant was killed two or three years later in Palestine. The King allowed me to place a small tablet to his memory in the library.[124]

King George V and Queen Mary also commissioned a war memorial for the private chapel at Windsor Castle to commemorate their staff. The inscription read: 'To the honoured memory of the members of the royal household who fell in the Great War 1914–1919. A tribute from their King and Queen. These be the souls to whom high valour gave glory undying.'[125] The memorial is flanked on either side by lions holding the king and the queen's standards, while St George killing the dragon forms the centrepiece. The names of the dead are listed in two groups: officers, and NCOs and men.[126] The war was thus integrated into the longer fabric of English history that Windsor Castle and the royal dynasty represented.[127] The division of the dead by rank was not unusual on First World War memorials and did not detract from the war's egalitarian novelty of commemorating other ranks by name and listing them on the same memorials as their officers and, moreover, in a royal chapel.

Both the king and his mother, the elderly dowager Queen Alexandra, went to considerable lengths to try to ascertain what had happened to the men from the Sandringham estate and household who had been serving in King's Company, which included the original Sandringham Company, and were reported missing when it was annihilated at Gallipoli on 12 August 1915, along with most of the rest of its battalion, the 1/5th Battalion of the Norfolk Regiment.[128] The royal family were particularly affected by the loss of Frank Beck, reported missing aged 54, who had served as land agent at Sandringham for twenty-five years, starting to work for the royal family during the reign of Edward VII. The king, wishing the Sandringham Company well in a telegram upon their embarkation, had written 'I have known you all for many years [. . .]'.[129] These were familiar faces, part of the royals' personal universe. The contemporary conservative ideal of the Edwardian class system portrayed it as based upon a paternalistic hierarchy; according to this world view the monarch, as their employer, as well as their sovereign, had a particular duty of care to provide for the Sandringham men; indeed, one press report openly referred to how these men 'were in a double sense servants of the King' as both subject and employee.[130] King George V sent a direct message to General Sir Ian Hamilton, who commanded Gallipoli operations, to ask for information about what had happened to his estate workers: 'I am most anxious to be informed as to the fate of the men of the 5th battalion Norfolk regiment as they include the Sandringham Company and my agent Captain Frank Beck.'[131] The king then telegraphed the little information that Hamilton was able to provide him with to Arthur Beck, Frank Beck's brother, who was acting land agent at Sandringham while Frank was away at war, to keep him and the other families on the estate informed:

> Further enquiries are being made on receipt of which I will at once let you know. I heartily sympathise with all the families who are left in suspense but I am proud that the Battalion has fought so splendidly.[132]

Hamilton would continue to provide the king with updates on the largely fruitless search for news of the Sandringhams' fate, and the king, when he encountered any surviving members of the Fifth Norfolks in his hospital visits, would ask them for news, reduced to making enquiries by word of mouth from the wounded, the same as so many of his subjects seeking missing loved ones.

He would do the same in 1916 when visiting the Somme, asking for information about how two of his footmen, Sergeants Kennedy and Church, had died in the battle.[133] The vicar of Dersingham, where some of the Sandringham men worshipped, stated that 'the King [...] has done every possible thing to ascertain if they are alive and prisoners'.[134] In a private letter to the king, he wrote: 'Will you be so kind as to tell His Majesty how deeply grateful the relations and friends of the Dersingham men in that company are to His Majesty for his kindness.'[135] A sympathy letter from the king and queen assured one widow that 'during the long months of uncertainty Their Majesties' thoughts had been constantly with her'.[136] The king and queen provided Frank Beck's widow with a house to live in at Dershingham in 1917; they also visited her regularly, the king noting in his diary in 1918 that she was 'in a very excitable state again'.[137]

Queen Alexandra, for her part, asked her friend and comptroller of her household, General Sir Dighton Probyn, to make enquiries via the American Embassy in London with the American Embassy in Constantinople for information about Frank Beck and his nephew. Probyn's letter to the embassy on 27 October 1915 described it as 'a matter in which Her Majesty is deeply interested. There is a certain Captain F. R. Beck, for whom Her Majesty has a very great regard having known him personally for some 50 years – ever since his childhood.'[138] Among Frank Beck's 'friends and admirers', Probyn wrote, 'Queen Alexandra ranks the highest'.[139] When no news was forthcoming, Probyn concluded that 'we must, I am afraid, feel certain they have been murdered, or at any rate given up their lives somewhere for their King and Country'.[140] As one biographer noted:

> By the summer of 1915 Queen Alexandra was a very tired woman. Not merely was she exhausted by the nervous strain of her own public appearances; she shared to the full in the general feeling of overwhelming anxiety and grief as the enormous casualty lists lengthened. True, she lost none of her immediate relatives but in almost every one of her letters she grieves for someone, perhaps the son of a friend or one of the Sandringham tenants whom she knew so well. She was also full of anxiety for her many relations abroad.[141]

After the war ended, Queen Alexandra is believed to have influenced the War Office to send a clergyman she knew, the Rev. Pierrepoint Edwards, as emissary to the former Gallipoli battlefields to investigate.[142] The result of his enquiry confirmed that the Sandringham men had died; however, the full details – that he had found a mass grave with 122 men shot through the head – were never passed on to Queen Alexandra for fear of upsetting her too much.[143] The destruction of the Sandringham Company was perhaps the most fundamental instance of the royals' personal world and their public engagement with ordinary subjects' war grief colliding. The fact that the

Sandringham Company's fate remained unknown as they were reported missing in action on the Gallipoli battlefield only added to the private distress of those who knew them.

The royal family's reaction to Beck's disappearance, in particular, was clearly one of grief and an indication of how, while obeying the strict structures of Edwardian class hierarchies, close working relationships, even if cautious and formal, were possible and often formed between employer and staff. But there was also constraint in how much the royals could do for the bereaved of Sandringham: this case could not be treated any differently to that of any other war dead or missing, despite the lost men's close relationship with the royal family. Discreet marks of attention continued, however, long after the war. The king and queen paid for a war memorial on the royal Sandringham estate to the fallen officers and men of the Sandringham Company, which the king personally unveiled in October 1920; they also erected a plaque inside Sandringham Church in memory of Frank Beck.[144] Religion was clearly a key way in which the royal couple coped with the loss; the war memorial design they chose was a 'memorial cross', and George V's short speech when he unveiled it dedicated it

> to the glory of God in memory of the brave men of the Sandringham Estate who have fallen in the late war. May their example inspire us to like courage in the great war against evil. May their memory ever burn brightly in those who here and elsewhere remember their deeds and strengthened by their fellowship look forward to reunion with them on the inheritance of the saints in light.[145]

The speech highlighted how, for the king, war memorial dedications were a profoundly religious duty as well as a secular one; indeed, his speech was remarkably similar to that usually given by a Church of England ordained priest at a memorial dedication, and normally the king was meticulous about not infringing upon the priestly role at dedications.[146] The king then laid a wreath and Queen Alexandra flowers on the memorial. When King George V died in 1936 at Sandringham, one of the very few survivors of the Sandringham Company was among the foresters chosen to keep vigil over the king's coffin, and the guard of honour at Wolferton Station, where the coffin was entrained, was provided by the Sandringham Company of the 5th Norfolk Regiment and 'composed of sons of men who formed the original Sandringham Company of woodsmen and workers on the estate enlisted at the beginning of the war'.[147]

It would be the aftermath of the war that would see the most personal experience of grief for the royal family, however. On 18 January 1919, King George and Queen Mary's youngest son, Prince John, died suddenly as a result of an epileptic seizure, aged 13. Thus, while the royal couple had lost none of their five boys in the war, within two months of the conflict ending, they, like many of their subjects, were grieving a son. The press made this parallel: 'Public sympathy is deep for the King and Queen', reported the *Runcorn Guardian*, 'the more so because of their solicitude for parents whose sons have given their lives in the war'.[148] The *Eastern Morning News* wrote of how the 'King who has for more than four years suffered at heart over the bereavements of his people, brought to grief by war, is now himself stricken and sorrowing, and the Queen whose sympathies had gone to so many thousands of mothers is now a heart-broken mother herself'.[149] It described how the royal couple had carried the prince's ill-health as a private burden during the 'years of war-born anxiety'.[150] Clearly connections were being made between the loss of war sons and the royal parents' bereavement in terms of shared pain. But the press more frequently emphasised Prince John's youth and the fact that his epilepsy had not been widely known; as a 13-year-old child his death could not too readily be compared to that of adult soldiers. The loss of Prince John was treated respectfully, as a private matter for the royal couple; the news reports were brief, and the very real distress shown by Queen Mary, who was devoted to the child, and Queen Alexandra at Prince John's funeral remained private.[151] Queen Mary wrote of how 'It was an awfully trying moment when the coffin was lowered and we were terribly upset.'[152] As during the war, personal royal grief was hidden from view, discreet and subordinated to the royal public role.

During the conflict, a credible narrative of the monarchy supporting social equality in the treatment of the war dead was prioritised over privileging any personal war grief among the royals and their circle. Above all, the king and queen rejected the idea of the monarchy allocating its wartime recognition on the grounds of class or wealth. This showed how astutely the monarchy was aware of broader trends: one of the key social changes that the war brought was a new discourse of equality, which underpinned the introduction of new policies such as the innovation of mass conscription, the burial of officers and men together and the introduction of fairer economic resource distribution via rationing.

This brings us to our second case study: how the monarchy made contact with the individual war-bereaved subject during the war. The emphasis upon treating all war dead and bereaved equally was very evident here. It was clear, for example, in the royal involvement in the new Imperial War Graves Commission, founded in 1917, which had the Prince of Wales as its president and which developed an ethos of treating all war graves equally.[153] The monarchy's relationship with grief was also projected in the press as encompassing the entire spectrum of the British class system, from prince to pauper.[154] And, in reality, the monarchy's engagement with war mourning did indeed span class divisions. From the start of the conflict, the royals attended memorial services for young aristocratic men they had known who had fallen, with the Prince of Wales noting these experiences as 'very depressing' in his diary in 1914.[155] However, heading up charitable endeavours such as the Prince of Wales' National Relief Fund, discussed in Chapter 2, involved the monarchy in trying to mitigate the unequal economic cost of war bereavement and engaging with poorer social cohorts. A further example of this kind of engagement was royal visits to local wartime shrines to the war dead that sprang up in working-class areas. On 10 August 1916, Queen Mary visited a number of streets in working-class Hackney where shrines had been erected to the war dead and those from the locality who were serving in the war. It was described as a personal visit by the queen at the invitation of the local vicar, B. S. Batty, who had encouraged the shrines.[156] The queen's gestures, however, were hugely significant in terms of presenting the royal narrative of equality in war sacrifice: she personally laid flowers at the different street shrines (Fig. 37) and herself presented flowers to two war-bereaved mothers, a profound gesture of inversion of norms in the class culture of the time, where during

Fig. 37   Queen Mary lays flowers at a local memorial shrine and roll of honour on Palace Road, Hackney, August 1916, Mary Evans Picture Library, 12014319

royal visits flowers were usually given to the queen rather than the other way around.[157] One presentation appears to have been planned, the other more spontaneous:

> During her visit the Queen stopped in Balcorne Street and spoke a few sympathetic words to a widow who lost her husband in action last May, and handed her a fragrant bunch of deep red roses. The roll of honour in this street bears the name of 183 soldiers and sailors, and Edith Scotchmere handed to her Majesty a large bouquet on behalf of a brother serving in the Rifle Brigade, receiving in return a bunch of choice carnations. The Queen thoughtfully brought bunches of fresh flowers to place in the vases beside each roll of honour.[158]

In this way, royal honour was used to sacralise war-bereaved, working-class motherhood. The visit was also presented as an equal and intimate war experience across class divisions: the *Yorkshire Evening Post* described the queen shaking hands with one woman who, the paper claimed, told her: 'You're a mother yourself, Queen Mary [...] and you've sent boys to the war. So you know how mothers feel. An' I suppose that's why you are here?'[159] To which the queen agreed. Yet the role of the monarchy projected here was profoundly paradoxical – on the one hand it represented the pinnacle of the class system, hence why a visit from a royal mattered and honoured the street shrine servicemen and their communities; on the other, it sought to convey a shared, direct, intimate relationship between the king and queen and those mourning the war dead that transcended all class divisions and circumvented state bureaucracy.

This process of sacralising the war grief of the individual subject highlighted the way that the relationship between the subject and the monarchy was experienced as one where the latter could validate war loss in ways that brought comfort to the war bereaved. Despite the modernity of total war, monarchical recognition still had powerful resonance; indeed, the modernising and the traditional interacted constantly. For example, large numbers of ordinary families who had suffered war losses received individual private letters or telegrams from the king, produced on his behalf, conveying condolences. Sent by the Keeper of the Privy Purse, such letters formally expressed royal sympathy with the bereaved. One typical case was that of J. J. Morris in Nottingham, who received a telegram on 4 October 1917 stating that 'The King and Queen deeply regret the loss you and the army have sustained by the death of your son in the service of his country. Their Majesties truly sympathise with you in your sorrow.'[160] On 7 October 1916, William England in Yorkshire received a similar telegram.[161] On 1 February 1917, Richard Cotter in Sandgate, Kent received a letter from the king expressing his personal condolences on the death of Cotter's son, a Lance Corporal:

It is a matter of sincere regret to me that the death of Lance Corporal
William Richard Cotter deprived me of the pride of personally conferring
upon him the Victoria Cross, the greatest of all rewards for valour and
devotion to duty.[162]

The letter, which survives in the National Army Museum Archives in
a cardboard gilt frame, was clearly preserved and displayed by the bereaved
family. It appears that similar letters were also sent to Indian war-bereaved
families: 'The family of Gulab Shah have received a letter from His Majesty
himself, sent by the Viceroy, expressing the King's regret at the death of Gulab
Shah', noted one retired Indian soldier in a letter in April 1917.[163]

Such royal condolences were also frequently reported in the press: in
May 1915 the *Dundee Courier* reported that 'His Majesty has sent' a telegram
to Mr David Lumsden, Dalreoch, regarding the death of his son at the front;
the wording of the telegram reproduced in the article was the same as that sent
to J. J. Morris.[164] Not only those who died at the front were recognised: the
widow of an RAMC Private who died of pneumonia at Chatham, Mrs Harmer,
received a letter from the Army Record Office: 'The King commands me to
assure you of the true sympathy of His Majesty the King and Queen –
Kitchener.'[165] Clearly even the briefest of monarchical acknowledgements
was reported. In 1915, the *Sheffield Daily Telegraph*, in an article entitled
'The King's Sympathy', described how 'Mr A. H. Marsden of Kenwood
Bank, Sheffield, has received a letter of sympathy from the King in which the
bravery of his son, Corporal Edwin Marsden, is also recognised.'[166] In reality,
the special recognition was from the War Office; however, the standard
monarchist language of the War Office letter was read as a personal condolence from royalty. The article continued:

Corporal Marsden met his death near Mons, and the communication
received yesterday from the War Office states that by command of His
Majesty: 'I have to inform you that the late Lance-Corporal Edwin
Marsden, of the Royal Engineers, was mentioned in a dispatch from Field-
Marshal Sir John French, dated January 14th 1915, for gallant and distinguished service in the field. His Majesty desires to condole with you on the
loss you have sustained, and to express his high appreciation of the
services of the late Lance-Corporal Edwin Marsden.'[167]

Another example, published in the *Daily Mail* in 1915, reproduced a letter
from Lord Stamfordham to a family who had lost three sons: 'By order of the
King, Lord Stamfordham has written to Mr and Mrs W. L. Field, of Newlands,
Streatham Common, S. W., to express his Majesty's sympathy with them on
the loss of three of their sons in the war.'[168] The condolence letter was then
reproduced in full, in which Stamfordham wrote 'the King realises this is the
third beloved son that you have given in your country's cause' and to 'express
His Majesty's deep feeling of sympathy'.[169]

That so many examples of such individual royal condolence communications could merit newspaper reports highlights the power monarchy still held to bestow status upon the individual subject. It also shows how royal recognition was something to be publicised throughout the locality: naming the recipient so precisely was clearly intended to allow those who knew them to learn of the honour accorded their war dead and acknowledge it. Monarchist culture was thus part of the social fabric of wartime human interactions at local level. A further indication of the significance of royal recognition was the reading of royal condolences at memorial services, such as that for Captain D. Henderson, who was the son of MP Arthur Henderson, the first member of the Labour Party to serve in cabinet, where the king and queen's message was read out.[170] This was particularly noteworthy given that before the war, in 1911, there had been debate among royal advisors about whether or not the king should send a message of sympathy to the then Labour leader, Ramsay MacDonald, on the death of his wife; upon learning of her illness the king had sent a telegram – a degree of contact between the monarch and the leader of Labour that was unprecedented and which raised eyebrows at court according to Frederick Ponsonby. As a result, upon the death of Mrs MacDonald no letter was sent.[171] This illustrates the degree to which wartime royal condolences could serve to create new forms of monarchical engagement with parts of society that before the war had been taboo for such personal contact. There was still some hierarchy to royal wartime expressions of sympathy, however. More prominent political families, such as the Hendersons or the family of Irish Party MP Willie Redmond, usually received more personalised messages.[172]

How were royal condolences received? Some families wrote back to thank the king, such as Emilie Harmsworth, who wrote a letter of thanks to the king and queen, via Lord Stamfordham, for their sympathy on the death of her brother Captain Henry Telford Maffett in 1914.[173] The parents of Australian combatant Terence Garling wrote to King George V via the Governor General of Australia, Munro Ferguson, of a 'silver lining to the cloud' of their son's war death, as it was for 'the preservation of the British Empire'.[174] In the case of the Sprunt family from Hertfordshire, who lost three sons in the war, the royal acknowledgement of their grief mattered to the extent that it was incorporated into the memorial plaque that the bereaved parents erected in St Peter's Church in Berkhamsted (Fig. 38), including the message from the assistant military secretary that 'His Majesty trusts that their public acknowledgement may be of some consolation in your bereavement.'[175] The king's direct message to them was also reproduced on the tablet: 'Your three gallant sons —', 'They died that we might live.'[176] The religious overtones here are clear – the plaque's location, in a Christian church, with these words suggestive of sacrificial death to ensure the life of others, echoes the meaningful suffering and sacrifice of Christ. In fact, a local history shows their third son, Gerald Sprunt, died of wounds in

Fig. 38   Sprunt family memorial, St Peter's Church, Berkhamsted (Reproduced by kind permission of the Parish Council)

unusual circumstances, possibly suggestive of suicide, in October 1919: 'Weary of hospitals and home Gerald volunteered for India and died on the troop ship "Norvana", bound for Bombay, in a bath from heart failure, under sad circumstances.'[177] However, his parents clearly saw him as one of the war fallen; the tablet refers to his death 'in consequence' of war wounds, and frames his loss in terms of the monarch's words, which were important enough to the family to be included on the memorial, adding to its length and presumably its cost.[178] They may also have served to stave off any stigma connected to Gerald's death.

Precisely because the monarchy was held in awe and because subjects believed that war service was partly carried out in its name, the act of royal recognition of the individual fallen combatant or their next of kin was perceived as a significant honour and a gesture of direct – if formal – intimacy between the monarchy, representing the nation and empire, and their subject.

The transfer of royal honour that royal condolence letters or telegrams to the war bereaved represented was partly innovative in its scale and use of technology but also drew on older, pre-war honour cultures, combining the modernity of the bureaucratic state, tracking who should receive such messages, with the older tradition of the king recognising faithful war service. However, if there was an echo of medieval royal recognition of valour, the process was in reality highly modern – this was not the king recognising warriors he had personally served with, as in the feudal past, but a constitutional monarchy sending largely standardised messages through the Keeper of the Privy Purse, to lists of names, and projecting royal intimacy with the war bereaved throughout the county and across divisions of class and region. But the power of such very formal royal recognition of individual war grief lay in its perceived intimacy in the context of a highly formal world of Edwardian class-culture hierarchies and the imagined personal relationship between king and subject that it conveyed. Moreover, in a period of highly formal grief rituals at all levels of society, the royal letter or telegram of condolence was in keeping with how sympathy was generally expressed.

Although such royal condolences were formally conveyed, it would be wrong to see them as feigned; formality in language conveyed dignity at the time, and honouring the war dead mattered enormously to King George V. However, by 1917, there is evidence that there were concerns at the War Office that the message sent from the monarch was too brief and needed softening. The Secretary of State for War, Lord Derby, a friend of the king's, wrote to Stamfordham on 4 December 1917 that 'it has been pointed out to me from the Propaganda Department that the King and Queen's message of sympathy, appreciated as it is, is a little too abrupt, and that something more might be added to give it a touch of patriotism.'[179] Derby enclosed two possible amendments, one drafted by the writer Rudyard Kipling, and the other his own suggestion. Kipling's proposal was rejected as too risky, as it was a template which left a space to fill in the relationship between the bereaved person and their lost combatant, which Derby feared would cause great offence if it was done wrongly: 'the fact of having to fill in the relationship would give rise to an enormous amount of clerical labour and might also result in the wrong relationship being put in i.e. husband for father or brother for husband'.[180] What is clear from this exchange between Derby and Stamfordham is the degree to which the War Office and the monarchy were cooperating in using royal condolences to bolster support for the war effort, as well as working together to construct the monarchy's wartime image. Derby asked that the king be consulted to approve the wording and in case George V felt 'any alteration is desirable'.[181] The king approved Derby's text. In a letter to Kipling, Derby also set forth why he felt the existing condolence wording was not sufficient:

at the present time when a letter goes to the next of kin of anybody who has been killed, the wording is very bald; it is as follows: 'The King commands me to assure you of the true sympathy of His Majesty and the Queen in your sorrow.' That letter is signed by me. It is suggested that we ought to put something more in to counteract the Pro-German pacifist poison which is being freely scattered in stricken homes.[182]

Again here we see evidence of how the monarchy was seen by Lord Derby as a powerful counterweight to the anti-war discontent which grieving families were beginning to show. For Derby, the monarchy, if employed correctly, could bolster the war effort in 1917, just as he had tried to utilise it in 1915 to increase voluntary recruitment, as discussed in Chapter 1. Derby wanted to add overt lines about patriotism to connect the king's sympathy directly to the state's war policies:

> one wants to put in something to the effect that the person to whom he is writing should be told that 'he whose loss you mourn died in the noblest of causes and that the Country will be ever grateful to him for the sacrifice he has made'. I don't want it to be too long or too fulsome, but just something that would make the person who receives it feel that, not only the King and the Queen, but the Nation behind them appreciate what the dead man has given for his Country.[183]

Dynastic condolences were no longer enough; royal sympathy had to be integrated into the propaganda of the state war effort. The final text from Derby, which the king approved, read: 'The King commands me to assure you of the true sympathy of His Majesty and the Queen in your sorrow. He whose loss you mourn died in the noblest of causes. The Country will be ever grateful to him for the sacrifice he has made for Freedom and Justice.'[184]

Sending an individual message of condolence from the king and queen to the next of kin of fallen soldiers upon news of their death during the war appears to have been initiated in late August 1914.[185] It was a specific gesture of royal sympathy that was intended as a particular honour for the Great War dead, and it represented an enormous administrative effort in locating names and addresses of relatives. Its purpose, as a particular bond between monarchy and *Great War* dead, was made clear in a letter to the War Office in July 1920 which stated that the Keeper of the Privy Purse had been approached as to whether 'the King's Message of sympathy should be sent to the next-of-kin of Officers and Soldiers who are killed in Ireland'.[186] The question arose because 'it is understood that the message of sympathy applied to casualties in the Field during the past war', and for this reason 'casualties which may occur in Ireland, or in riots in India, Egypt, or elsewhere in His Majesty's dominion' were not to receive such letters.[187] The king approved this decision.[188] This particularly intimate form of royal condolence was thus seen as something specific to the mass mobilisation of the First World War.

Overall, the monarchy was an important cultural structure used to channel personal war griefs, of all levels of society, into a more formal national and imperial ritual process and history, and this sense of drawing individual grief into the national cause and historic tradition does seem to have comforted some bereaved, if not all; unfortunately we lack the evidence to draw wider conclusions on how the war bereaved reacted. This process, of course, fused the personal individual grief of the subject with the realm, with national and imperial needs. Royal recognition – because the monarchy embodied the state – was a way of incorporating the single loss into the national and imperial history, honour and survival, and doing this in an egalitarian way was central to the success of this monarchist First World War policy.

The year 1919 clearly illustrated the importance of this. The monarchy was used to sacralise victory in the ceremonies that followed the signature of the Treaty of Versailles, many of them involving the revival of older paraphernalia and customs. But it was also the means of creating sacralised innovative egalitarian structures for collective mourning and commemoration: on 7 November 1919 all newspapers carried 'a request from the King for an Empire-wide observance of a two-minutes' silence at 11 am on 11 November'.[189] Lord Milner had presented the idea to Stamfordham, and the king was supportive. George V's statement declared 'I believe that my people in every part of the Empire fervently wish to perpetuate the memory of the Great Deliverance and of those who have laid down their lives to achieve it.'[190] The religious language of 'Great Deliverance' was of archaic monarchist origin, recalling early modern royal ceremonies for deliverance from plague or war, while the idea of a two-minute silence was a radically modern innovation, a pause for reflection akin to a secular Angelus, which was particularly striking when busy noisy urban centres stopped their activity. The silence was virtually universally observed, a powerful example of the fusion of archaic and modernising trends that the monarchy channelled around war grief in response to the Great War. The year 1920 would see this process develop further, as the next chapter on war commemoration will show.

The Monarchy's Role in Sacralising Post-War Commemoration

6.1 Introduction

Chapter 6 explores how, through commemoration of the war dead, the British monarchy retained a sacralised role into the interwar period and in fact reinvented and extended it. The British monarchy innovatively and successfully became central to war commemoration, in particular through how it projected continuity and tradition onto new commemorations, such as the burial of the Unknown Soldier. Its commemorative role ultimately became central to its post-war *raison d'être* and a way of adapting to the societal changes that the conflict had brought. War commemoration was a process that sacralised the monarchy through the latter taking on a key lead role in sacralising the war dead. This process integrated and adapted surviving aspects of older honour cultures into completely new cultural commemorative practices designed in response to the sense of dislocation created by the conflict; older beliefs coexisted with modernisation trends. This, in turn, provides insights into the extent of the ongoing cultural significance of monarchism as a belief system in Britain after the conflict.

Chapter 6 also examines the monarchy's role in paying tribute to war veterans. The monarchy felt duty-bound to engage with war veterans and their needs in the aftermath of the conflict, even if, in many respects, this proved a much more difficult process than honouring the war dead, as the resentments of living veterans, many of whom called for social reforms and in some cases advocated political radicalism, were much harder to incorporate into the monarchy's traditionally apolitical role and even threatened it. The Prince of Wales came to be the focus of the monarchy's outreach to veterans in the 1920s, ultimately largely successfully.

First World War commemoration has a rich, exciting and well-established historiography, which, although it has largely neglected the role of the monarchy, serves as the inspiration for this chapter. Adrian Gregory has examined which groups had the greatest influence over the commemorative process, arguing that in Britain the emphasis was upon bereaved parents; Mark Connelly has explored the way commemoration interacted with local identities in East London; and Jay Winter, who pioneered the field, has considered the relationship between commemorative rituals and how societies coped with mass grief in the wake of the war as well as how commemoration relates to collective remembrance.[1] Winter contends that the modes of commemoration adopted in the UK after the war were predominantly traditional – and often religious in themes or reference; the findings here on the monarchy support Winter's argument. The difficult question as to how war commemoration interacts with collective memory – a contested category which some historians, such as Winter, argue does not actually exist, preferring the term collective remembrance – has been the focus of much of the ongoing historiographical debate.[2] In its assessment of the contribution of the monarchy to commemoration, this chapter will provide new insights into some of these questions, in particular, who had key influence in determining the structure that commemoration would take, the extent, and limits, of the power of the war bereaved to influence commemorative practices and the ways in which the monarchy contributed to creating an initial form of 'collective memory' of the war through engaging with mass remembrance rituals.

As Dominic Bryan has argued, 'whilst commemorative practices appear to be about the past, they are actually about the present and the future. Commemorations are a way of capturing the sacrifices of the past for the legitimation of the political present and the imagined political future.'[3] Thus, marking victory, grief and war service through commemoration processes built around monarchist cultural forms was a way of embedding monarchy into the new, and future, post-war political and cultural framework. As Bryan also points out, 'commemorations are conducted by the utilisation of symbols endowed through acts of ritual' that 'appear to defy time by linking participants with the past. Through culturally embedded practice, the rituals form part of a narrative that imbues groups with a past that suggests they are in communion with those that are being remembered.'[4] The idea of the monarch, through ritual acts of commemoration, communing as God's anointed intermediary between the war dead and the living nation, epitomises this idea of a commemorative space where time breaks down in the symbolic merging of past, present and future. Here the monarchy's value in presenting an illusion of unbroken historic continuity, its projection of dynastic presentism, 'The King is dead, Long live the King', matched perfectly with the need to see an unbroken connection between the fallen and the living nation and its future, for which they were perceived as having died.

The monarch established a new paternal role as 'mourner-in-chief' for the war dead, creating a personal emotive tie between the monarch and the war bereaved. Indeed, members of the royal family represented war mourners at commemorative events in a way that both supplanted and sublimated the latter's grief – and potential resentment or anger towards the state – in the national sphere. Importantly, the majority of British society – including the war bereaved – appears to have approved of, or at least tolerated, this process of allowing royalty to represent them, in particular through a king who highlighted their pain and humbled himself before the sacrifice of the war dead. The monarchy thus served to stabilise British post-war society by incorporating war bereavement into powerful processes of Establishment recognition, while also relegating the war-bereaved public to the place of spectator, rather than actor, in national rituals of commemoration at which the royals took the key roles. Historians, such as Jon Lawrence, have long questioned why in the immediate aftermath of the war the island of Britain remained relatively free of internal violent conflict, in contrast to much of Continental Europe and Ireland; here, in the monarchy's successful navigation of the popular need for symbolic and unifying rituals of state mourning, lies one of the possible contributory factors.[5] Local communities of war bereaved projected the monarch into their shared web of grief, thereby sacralising it through the monarch's association with the spiritual, and with those cultural understandings of honour that had survived the war. By the early 1920s, commemoration emphasised the human cost of the war – grief became the dominant commemorative trope and the monarchy central to channelling this message.

Often new forms of commemoration, such as the burial of the Unknown Soldier, promoted traditional sacralising messages about monarchy. The king was profoundly motivated by what he saw as his obligation to honour the war dead, who had effectively died on his behalf, in his armies or navy, 'for King and Country'. Royal involvement in war commemoration was thus both a new phenomenon – no king had ever performed mourning rituals in the wake of total war before or enacted collective war grief by proxy in the innovative way or on the scale that George V did – and drew on older ideas about monarchical honour. This was not solely the monarchy's initiative. It received direction regarding the form that commemorative ceremonial should take, from figures like Fabian Ware, founder and Vice Chairman of the Imperial War Graves Commission, and the writer Rudyard Kipling. It was an ad hoc process. Lord Stamfordham also worked closely with the king to craft his commemorative role.

If, in 1914, the idea of kingship – as a metonym for the state – had led men to go to war, then it followed that the men who had died in this cause should be honoured by the monarch. Moreover, this had to be done in ways that recognised the changed cultural landscape: understandings of 'honour' by 1918 had shifted, and languages of democracy and equality of sacrifice without class hierarchies were now at the core of what was considered appropriate when selecting ways of 'honouring' the dead. Here the monarchy could emphasise the equal personal bond between the sovereign and each subject – within the UK and across the empire – a trope that worked well, matching the post-war emphasis on creating a more egalitarian British democracy. At the same time, the figure of the king, as the religiously anointed monarch, remained associated with the sacred, so his homages to the war dead were a way of, in turn, sacralising them – his involvement in mourning rituals had a religious and spiritual dimension that mattered. Sacralisation, however, worked both ways: George V bestowed royal honour upon the war dead but also associated the monarchy closely with the sacred reverence that society felt towards the fallen.

The historian Frank Mort has pointed out that under the reign of King George V, the monarch and his advisors pioneered an 'expansive version of democracy [. . .] which embraced political, social, and cultural traditions of inclusiveness in their conservative and traditionalist forms'.[6] This was particularly the case with regard to war commemoration, where the monarchy's paternalistic version of democracy was particularly visible. The pre-war years of his reign had seen George V establish a new role for the monarch as conciliator in response to crisis in parliament and in Ireland and the rise of industrial unrest. As the celebration of victory rapidly dissipated into the bleak reality of responding to mass war bereavement and the need to commemorate the dead, this idea of the king as 'conciliator' came again to the fore. The pre-war 'decision of the king and his advisors to promote the crown as conciliatory and extra-political' now held particular value, as did its close association with the Church of England, the Church of Scotland and Christian belief more widely, as these factors meant that it was particularly well placed to symbolise the mourning of the home nations and the empire, as it was seen as a non-divisive element of the state.[7] The king and queen also remained widely popular as individuals.

How the Crown as a function of the state – and individual royals at a personal level – engaged with war commemoration and the war bereaved would thus become integral to how Britain dealt with the war's legacy. Commemoration consolidated a post-war image of an accessible, democratic and caring monarchy. It also helped sacralise the monarchy in new, highly significant ways that helped sustain it in the turbulent 1920s. To show this, this chapter will explore a number of ways in which the monarchy was part of war commemoration, looking at commemorative languages, the burial of the Unknown Soldier in 1920, the king's 1922 'pilgrimage' to the war cemeteries of the Western Front and the Prince of Wales's engagement with war veterans. Together these reveal how commemorative innovations were presented in royal guises, showing the symbiotic relationship between modernisation and traditional expectations of royal leadership. Commemoration rituals were often new but, conveyed using royal tropes, they helped turn a war that had marked a major break and discontinuity in global history into something connected back to a projected archaic British past, thereby softening the sense of radical change and disorientation that the war had brought. War commemoration reveals modernisation processes working interactively with older ideas of the sacred – the sacred war dead and the revered Crown, which, by honouring the fallen, helped to sustain the monarchy's own sacralisation in an era of anti-monarchist revolution elsewhere in Europe.

6.2   Monarchist Languages and War Commemoration

Language continued to illustrate how monarchism was used to transform war grief into a symbol of national and imperial unity. When, in 1918, a government committee decided to issue an individual commemorative scroll and plaque to the next of kin of the war dead, the scroll's wording read: 'He whom this Scroll commemorates was numbered among those who, at the call of King and Country, left all that was dear to them, endured hardness, faced danger and finally passed out of the sight of men, by the path of duty and self-sacrifice, giving up their own lives that others might live in freedom.'[8] The whole inscription was 'surmounted by a device including the Royal Arms in colour with the initials of His Majesty the King', and the scrolls were accompanied by a standard letter from Buckingham Palace which read 'I join with my grateful people in sending you this memorial of a brave life given for others in the Great War' over the king's signature.[9] The additional letter from the king was considered vital, as 'these Memorials bear upon their face no direct indication as to why, or by whom they are sent', therefore 'His Majesty has been graciously pleased to approve' his accompanying letter which would make clear their connection with the monarchy.[10] The scrolls ultimately proved faster to issue than the plaques and were sent out from mid-1919, with the hope that they could later be issued concurrently.[11] In an example in the Mary Evans Picture Library Collection for Sergeant Charles Edward Brown, the scroll was kept with an image of the dead soldier and his mother, set inside a border which had the flags of the allies and which was topped by a portrait of King George V and the legend 'Faithful to the Empire'.[12]

Clearly the phrase 'For King and Country' continued to be important in the immediate post-war years – reflecting its ubiquity in 1914 as part of the call to men to fight and its power as the slogan that had invoked men in British society to volunteer. However, by 1918 the phrase 'For King and Country' also had another function, when it appeared on war memorials: it conveyed honour upon the dead. There are some parallels here with the French search for a wording that would appropriately mark recognition and gratitude for combatant sacrifice. In France, *mort pour la patrie*, an officially bestowed honour, which appeared on the war graves of those who had died for France in combat in the conflict and which came with generous state welfare benefits for the bereaved families of those granted it, conveyed the honour of the state upon the fallen.[13] Britain had no such official system of a formally allocated term in this way. However, the more informally applied phrase 'For King and Country' lauded the self-discipline of the British dead, their answer to the duty imperative when called and their fulfilment of their manly 'honour'. The term does not mention the 'state', but king and country together serve as metonyms for it.

The phrase 'For King and Country' was thus far from an empty platitude on war memorials; it emphasised a shared British identity. It was frequently independently chosen by committees that had been charged with designing memorials, and which, in many local cases, often contained bereaved family members. It was meant as a comforting recognition of the *success* of the dead in meeting the demands of honour placed upon them, including their duty to their king. Even if honour culture was damaged and undermined by the war, in the immediate post-war years it still carried weight. In other words, mentioning the king in this way on memorials sacralised the dead with some of the sacredness of the monarchy. This process also went two ways, given that so many memorials were located inside churches or on church grounds and that the Church of England played such a key role in so many unveiling ceremonies: the monarch was being associated with sacred religious space and rites. UK war memorials thus frequently blended monarchism with a strong religious dimension, a combination that sat comfortably with the king's spiritual role as Supreme Governor of the Church of England and intertwined duty to king and duty to God. The widespread process of erecting war memorials, therefore, to an extent re-established the importance of the king as transcending the ordinary and representing the spiritual in a way that allowed the monarchy to subtly integrate some of the trend towards emphasising the 'ordinariness' of the monarch and his heir that had developed in the last two years of the war into a new form of monarchical mysticism and myth. The wartime image of the humble, democratic, 'servant' King George V with its Christlike symbolic was thereby firmly merged, through memorials, into what were seen as eternal narratives – the religious narratives of church architecture and liturgies – and the historic eternal narrative of the British people. The term 'King and Country' that appeared on 1914–18 war memorials never specified to *which* British or English king it referred, thereby absorbing both George V and the war dead into the eternal national kingly tradition.

Carefully conceived commemoration, in other words, helped stabilise, sanctify and secure the position of the monarchy and define the revised post-war relationship between kingship and honour. Indeed, it was not until the famous 1933 Oxford Union debate 'That this House will in no circumstances fight for its King and Country' that the expression 'For King and Country' began to fall out of favour and be interrogated.[14] The Union debate itself, however, actually made little direct reference to the monarchy, although Keith Steel-Maitland, future President of the Union and the Oxford University Conservative Association, declared that 'he was proud to defend his King'.[15] The fact that the Oxford Union passing this motion unleashed such enormous controversy, however, showed the extent to which the idea of fighting – and dying – 'For

King and Country' remained sacrosanct to many and central to ideas of British identity as late as 1933; students *rejecting* these concepts was considered shocking. The phrase 'for King and Country' again resurfaced during the Silver Jubilee of King George V's reign in 1935 when, amidst the celebrations, there were constant references to the war dead and ex-servicemen who 'gave so much and lost so much for their King and country in the war'.[16] The mood was more critical towards the monarchy by the 1930s; there were debates about the Jubilee's cost in a time of economic hardship, but King George V retained overwhelming public respect and affection, as shown by the success of the Jubilee events. Much of this was due to public respect for both his wartime role and the monarchy's stewardship of war commemoration.

The use of the monarchy to sacralise commemoration in the wake of the war remained common throughout the 1920s and was clearly a local grass-roots choice: monarchist discourse was popular on memorials at all levels of society. It appeared on rolls of honour listing the names of those who had served, such as that produced by the Midland Railway Company in 1921.[17] Innumerable monuments were engraved with the phrase 'For King and Country'. For example, the monument to Scottish women's war service in the Scottish National War Memorial proclaimed: 'whether their fame centuries long should ring, they cared not over much, but cared greatly to serve God and the King'.[18] The Royal Air Force Memorial on the Embankment in London was inscribed to 'those air forces from every part of the British Empire who have given their lives in winning victory for their King and Country'.[19] Monarchist language not only appeared on such official military monuments, however, but also on individual graves. The grave of Lieutenant A. W. Spencer Molineaux of the Royal Flying Corps at Merridale Cemetery, Wolverhampton, who died aged 20 on 28 July 1916, states: 'He died serving his King and Country.'[20] In St Edmundsbury Cathedral in Bury St Edmunds, Suffolk, the memorial to Lieutenant Geoffrey Charles M. Leech, killed at Arras in April 1917, concludes with the words 'Pro Christo – Pro Rego [*sic*] – Pro Patria'.[21] To give but a few examples of a common trend: the locally erected war memorial in St Nicholas's Church, Pevensey, East Sussex refers to the war dead as having died 'for King and Country', as does the war memorial at Dagnall village, Buckinghamshire.[22] Evidence of a monarchist motivation for serving in the war also appeared on war memorials in Irish Protestant churches. One example is the memorial in Tullow Church of Ireland, Carrickmines, Co. Dublin, to 2nd Lieutenant Geoffrey Monck Hamilton, who 'gave his life for his King and Country at the battle of Ginchy'; St Matthew's Newtownmountkennedy, Co. Wicklow, likewise holds a memorial to its parishioners who 'laid down their lives for King and Country during the Great War 1914–1918'; a personal memorial in the same church commemorates 2nd Lieutenant Henry Geoffrey Hamilton Moore, who died in October 1914 having 'at the call of King and Country left all that was dear'.[23] Some memorials incorporated monarchy in more subtle ways: famed architect Sir Edwin Lutyens placed carved stone imperial crowns above the arches of his famous monument to the British and empire dead and missing of the Somme at Thiepval.[24] The royals were even seen as arbiters of the treatment of the war dead: during the debate about whether or not the Imperial War Graves Commission should permit families who wished to choose a cross in lieu of the standard headstone, Lady Florence Cecil, the wife of the Bishop of Exeter, wrote to the Prince of Wales as President of the Commission requesting he support the option of a cross. Ultimately, in a key debate in May 1920, parliament supported the Commission's case that only the standard headstone be allowed. As one historian, Gavin Stamp, wrote: 'Equality in death, like equality in life, had to be enforced by the state, and the British people had to learn that liberty is incompatible with war, and that once a man had enlisted his body – whether alive or dead – belonged to the King.'[25]

Unveiling war memorials became a mainstay of royal duties throughout the early twenties, again illustrating how closely the war bereaved associated the monarchy with sacralising the fallen. Significantly, the king himself did not unveil very many. In 1927, he turned down an invitation to unveil the Menin Gate Memorial because 'as long as he unveiled no Memorials, the promoters of other Memorials were quite content, but once the King deviates from this line of policy it would possibly arouse great discontent'.[26] However, despite this, George V did make exceptions. In October 1920, he accepted to unveil the memorial to the men from the Sandringham estate lost in the war, and a month later he accepted to unveil the Cenotaph, discussed later in this chapter.[27] In 1922, the king accepted to unveil the war memorial to the men of the London and South Western Railway at Waterloo Station, but on the day was ill, so Queen Mary, who had been due to attend with him, carried out the unveiling on behalf of the King.[28] The king's reluctance to accept war memorial unveilings was perhaps pragmatic: they were such constant occurrences in the five years after the war that the workload would have been impossible for one figure to manage; there was also, as ever, the risk of being seen to favour one bereaved group over another in terms of which unveiling invitations were accepted. Other members of the royal family, however, often represented the monarchy at unveiling events. To list but some examples among many: in 1919, Queen Alexandra unveiled the memorial in Poplar in East London to eighteen children of Upper North School who were killed in the air raid of 13 June 1917.[29] The Duke of Connaught, the king's uncle, unveiled the Royal Artillery War Memorial at Hyde Park Corner in 1925 and a memorial tablet on behalf of the Imperial War Graves Commission in Amiens Cathedral in 1923.[30] The Prince of Wales was particularly active, in 1921 unveiling the memorial on the South Downs to Indian soldiers who fell in the war and the memorial to those of the Dover Patrol lost in the conflict, and in 1922 the Parliamentary War Memorial at Westminster County Hall.[31] In April 1923, the Prince of Wales unveiled the Anglo-Belgian War Memorial in the Rue des Quatre Bras in Brussels to commemorate Belgian aid to British prisoners of war. In Edinburgh, in 1923, the Prince of Wales unveiled the memorial to the Royal Scots Fusiliers who fell in the war, while in 1924 he unveiled the memorial to the British and British Empire war dead at Notre-Dame Cathedral in Paris and his brother Prince George unveiled the Royal Navy War Memorial.[32] Prince Henry, Duke of Gloucester, unveiled the Yeomanry War Memorial in Bury St Edmund's in 1928.[33]

Many traditional elements of monarchism, honour culture and sacralisation of kingship were visible at these ceremonies: for example, in December 1928, Queen Mary unveiled the Mercantile Marine War Memorial on Tower Hill in London, which included a presentation of war widows and orphans of those listed on the memorial to the queen. One observer noted their 'pride and delight' at the 'honour'.[34] The first prayer at the ceremony was for the king, who was seriously ill, calling upon God to restore him to health 'and to the service of Thy people committed to his charge'.[35] The second prayer was for the war dead at sea. The fact that the prayer for the king came first highlights the priorities of what was a normative monarchical culture.[36] Modernity and innovation, however, were also interwoven into the ceremony: the whole event was broadcast by the BBC, the first time that the queen's voice had been heard on radio, creating a new intimacy around the royal role in honouring war bereavement. Sir Fabian Ware wrote in a letter that 'Sir Philip Stott whom I saw in Gloucester on Thursday told me that he had "listened in" in Oldham and that the Queen's voice was "just as if it had been in the same room". An old builder, who is working for me at Amberley came to tell me all about it: he had been deeply impressed and used precisely the same words about the Queen's voice.'[37] It was also the first war memorial that Queen Mary had been invited to unveil in her own right without the king, which was also innovative.[38] The fact that she fulfilled the engagement despite the fact that the king was so unwell was acclaimed as a further mark of the royal couple's dedication to duty and the war dead.[39]

Even if the crowns placed on its structure were discreet, the Thiepval Memorial's Anglo-French unveiling ceremony in May 1932 was also obviously infused with monarchism and with the theme that the missing, named on the monument, had fallen for king and country. The Prince of Wales made a speech at the ceremony and unveiled the memorial, while it was dedicated by the Right Rev. H. K. Southwell: 'To the glory of God and in grateful memory of 73,367 soldiers who gave their lives on the Somme battlefields in the service of their King and Country, but who have no known grave [. . .].'[40] In his speech inviting the prince to unveil the memorial, Sir Fabian Ware, Vice Chairman of the Imperial War Graves Commission, referred to the Commission's work 'to commemorate all those who served the King and who fell in the Great War' and stated that he had been asked to associate the relatives of the dead named on the memorial with this request, as well as the ex-servicemen present, 'comrades of your Royal Highness on these battlefields'.[41] The prince in his speech described how 'I can speak with personal knowledge', referring to the work of the War Graves Commission, 'for I was privileged to take part in the inception of that work during the war [...]. And it gives me very great happiness to see here to-day some of those friends with whom I was associated in this task when the dark storms of war were bursting with unexampled fury on these fair fields around us'.[42] The whole ceremony was broadcast by the BBC in Britain and also throughout the empire and, it was hoped, would have a positive impact on the Ottawa conference, an imperial economic conference taking place that summer: the prince in his speech referred to his pride in the British Empire as one of 'free nations under a common Crown' who 'co-operate for a common object'.[43] The Prince of Wales also said part of his speech in French and spoke of France and Britain together creating a new world of peace among the nations.[44] Both the Prince of Wales and the French President when replying to him at the ceremony referred to the words of George V, who during his 1922 visit to the battlefield cemeteries had described them as a 'massed multitude of silent witnesses to the desolation of war', which, the prince stated, 'will eventually serve to draw all peoples together in sanity and self-control, even as it has already set relations between our Empire and our Allies on the deep-rooted bases of a common heroism and a common agony'.[45]

All this royal diplomacy through commemoration impressed observers, and not only in Allied countries: the German liberal Albrecht Mendelssohn Bartholdy wrote of how at Thiepval

> the Prince of Wales declared that the names of the fallen must form no mere Book of the Dead; they must be the opening chapter in a new Book of Life, the foundation and guide to a better civilization from which war, with all the horrors which our generation has added to it, should be banished. [...] Nothing could be more honorable, in the old sense of the term, than these words coming from the future monarch of a great Empire and a soldier who fought in the War.[46]

For Bartholdy, monarchy still represented the 'old' honour culture of the pre-war era. Monarchism was clearly operating in this Thiepval ceremony at several levels – as a tool of diplomacy towards Britain's French ally, as an intermediary presenting a new vision for a global international political order based on peace, and as a symbol of national and imperial unity. Innovation in how the empire was presented – as based on equal nations under a common Crown – and in how the future world order was envisaged was conveyed hand in hand with traditional ideas of duty to the sovereign and of the acknowledgement that the British war dead had died for their king and country. Potently too, the Thiepval Memorial was to the missing – the soldiers whose bodies had not been found – who could be symbolically represented by the living body of the soldier who embodied the national and imperial dynasty, the war veteran Prince of Wales. Indeed, Fabian Ware commented that, upon his arrival, the prince was surrounded by photographers, 'a great crowd of them [...] like flies around something nasty and oversweet'.[47] The description rendered the living veteran prince's body into one of the war dead being commemorated, attracting pests on the battlefield as it putrefied. This suggests that monarchy could ostensibly channel sanitised scripts about commemoration at events like the Thiepval unveiling, but at other levels onlookers were all too aware of what dying 'for King and Country' had actually meant and even subconsciously resented it.

It is in this symbolic context that the active role of the royal family in the outpouring of post-war war commemoration – the monarchy's work in engaging with war grief and formalising it with national and imperial recognition – has to be seen. It was a method of amalgamation through which the individual war dead could, through the monarchy's performance of collective national and imperial war-grief rituals, continue to serve the cause of UK and empire unity. This was particularly illustrated by the Prince of Wales's unveiling of a war memorial to the empire's war dead in Westminster Abbey in 1926, immediately preceding the opening of the Imperial Conference in London, which brought together the leaders of the British Empire's dominions and colonies with the heir to the throne, thereby attempting to set the tone of unity for the political conference that was to follow just hours later.[48] Prime Minister Stanley Baldwin personally wrote to the heads of the dominions and representatives of the colonies due to attend the conference, stating that the unveiling ceremony would be 'a not unfitting prelude to our Conference if the Prime Ministers of His Majesty's Governments now assembled in London supported His Royal Highness on this occasion' to pay tribute to the war dead, while the final prayer at the unveiling ceremony beseeched God to grant 'that the members of our widespread Empire may ever be bound together in mutual love and unity under our Sovereign Lord the King'.[49] The ceremony threw up the issues of innovation that the war had brought for the monarchy. The Prince of Wales accepted to take part despite initial reservations among courtiers that 'they think there may be difficulty as no Royal Personage has yet, they say, made a speech in a sacred edifice'.[50] Fabian Ware, at the Imperial War Graves Commission, replied that 'the Duke of Connaught had done so when I was with him at Amiens Cathedral and that they may quote this precedent'.[51] The war – and the role of honouring the war dead – had made it acceptable for royalty to speak in the sacred religious space that underpinned monarchical sacralisation, something which previously would have been seen as an impertinence before God.

6.3   The Burial of the Unknown Soldier

One of the most significant acts of the British monarchy in the wake of the First World War was thus to sanctify the war dead. How did the monarchy successfully take on – and adapt – this role in the aftermath of mass war death on an unprecedented scale? As Chapter 5 has already shown, this process did not begin in 1918. However, it was the post-war period that saw its most significant developments and which saw the kingly body – the king's own physical presence or references to the king on memorials – being used to bestow national honour upon the dead body of the soldier in ways that eased the integration of the problematic dead soldiers' bodies back into the national symbolic sphere. The bodies of the war dead were, of course, in reality absent – many had no known graves, and those who did had graves overseas where they fell, not in the UK, unless they had died of wounds in a home hospital. However, the kingly body, with its anointed religious, national and imperial symbolism, was a ready proxy onto which this absence could be projected. The absence of actual dead bodies at so many UK commemorative ceremonies, as Jay Winter has argued elsewhere, was deeply problematic for the bereaved; for some it invoked Christian themes of empty tombs and resurrection, but for others it inhibited grieving, particularly because, for many, it interrupted deeply valued continuities in burying men in family grave plots which could be regularly visited.[52] Hence the role of the monarchy in symbolically commemorating the war dead in ways that obscured the widespread, troubling *absence* of the actual soldiery's dead bodies and which projected eternal national and imperial continuities became particularly important. This was the function of royal figures at war memorial unveiling ceremonies, and it helps to explain the cultural messages projected through the king's role at the unveiling of the Cenotaph and the burial of the Unknown Soldier in Westminster Abbey, both on 11 November 1920, and the king's personal pilgrimage to visit Western Front war cemeteries in 1922. This chapter will now examine each of these innovations in detail.

The royals became the connection between war dead and living nation by taking on the role of symbolic 'primary mourners'. In particular, the physical intertwining of the living king with the dead soldier took on a deep performative cultural value. This was explicit in a new innovation in November 1920, the funeral and burial of the Unknown Soldier or 'Unknown Warrior', an anonymous British combatant body, which came to represent all fallen British subjects.[53] The burial of the Unknown Soldier was a novel act – it fits with Eric Hobsbawm's arguments that many 'ancient' traditions are actually of recent invention.[54] Yet it was given much of its 'sacral' dimension by the participation and veneration of the sacred monarch who, as Supreme Governor of the Church of England, had a particularly important spiritual leadership role. And much of its elaborate planning emphasised kingship as a core part of

British identity, an important choice in a post-war Europe where monarchism was under threat from new political ideas.

This is illustrated by the pressure which was put on George V to unveil the Cenotaph in 1920, a ceremony that directly preceded the burial of the Unknown Solider, which showed the degree to which there was a broad belief in monarchism having a sacralising and unifying national function. Initially the king did not wish to be involved, telling Stamfordham he would not unveil the Cenotaph.[55] Mrs Cazalet, one of the organising committee, wrote to Lord Stamfordham that 'the fact is that the other people on this committee seemed inclined to believe that the King did not wish to unveil the Cenotaph'.[56] Stamfordham replied that 'His Majesty did not see his way to undertake to perform the unveiling ceremony.'[57] Cazalet's response indicated the depth of public feeling; she wrote back that 'His Majesty's decision will be a great disappointment to many people who feel as I do, that as our sons gave their lives for their King and Country we should have liked the King to be the centre figure on that memorial day.'[58] The Prime Minister's office wrote to Stamfordham that the Office of Works, who were responsible for the Cenotaph memorial, were keen for the king to perform the unveiling, as 'It appears to be a general desire that the King should do so.'[59] This proved influential with the king: Stamfordham wrote to Downing Street on 26 September 1920 that, 'If the Prime Minister is interpreting the general desire, which you seem to think exists, that the King should unveil the Cenotaph [...] His Majesty would perform the ceremony.'[60] The *Daily Mirror* reported to the Palace that there were widespread rumours that the king was to do the unveiling; the *Daily Mail* contacted Stamfordham to ask for the king's views on the two minutes' silence.[61] Rear Admiral Donald Hopwood wrote a fulsome letter to Stamfordham on the potential for the Cenotaph to unite the classes and particularly to bring together trade unions, employers and employed; he suggested that their representatives and those of the public services should take part in the unveiling and that 'subsequently no doubt HM might visit the various bodies and this of course he would do better than anyone else in the world'.[62] For Hopwood, monarchism was the chance to create a 'moral nationalisation' of the nation,

> the only kind that will ever be any use and of course infinitely stronger than any other sort. [...] Do you remember Kipling's 'The King's Task' – 'after the sack of the city'? [*sic*] how the young men home from the wars exhibited signs of coming changes and how doubts were expressed as to the future unless their King taught them? Ending 'That is thy task oh King.' This all may be rather visionary!? [*sic*] but it seems we are all in need of a little imagination these days.'[63]

The king pithily responded to Stamfordham 'that the Admiral is too much of a "thinker" and his idea somewhat visionary'.[64] Hopwood's ideas were disregarded, but they highlighted the existential and often sacralised hopes that were being built around the post-war image of the king.

In autumn 1920 the Cenotaph unveiling planning ran into further difficulty when the Archbishop of Canterbury, Randall Davidson, raised objections to the king being involved in dedicating what many Church of England observers feared was a 'pagan' monument, due to its lack of Christian reference.[65] His words reveal the discomfort among some Church of England bishops with the idea of the monarch dedicating war memorials, a role perceived as religious, as dedications were meant to invoke God's blessing upon a monument: 'I see in the papers that the King is himself to open or "inaugurate" or whatever be the word the Cenotaph in Whitehall on Armistice Day.'[66] For some, Davidson wrote, 'the monument is pagan', and the belief that it was a purely secular memorial 'would be inexpressibly augmented were the actual ceremonial to take place at the hands of His Majesty himself without there being a Christian note definitely struck'.[67] Davidson thus revealed that the monarch could not transgress the actual role of the priest at a memorial unveiling. The king himself shared these concerns and was anxious that there should be a religious element to the unveiling ceremony; he suggested a prayer be read by the Archbishop of Canterbury but, for ecumenical reasons, the organisers eventually opted for just a hymn that all creeds could join in with.[68] But, partly to assuage the concerns that the Archbishop of Canterbury had raised, a further solution, originally the idea of the Dean of Westminster, was also put forward by Stamfordham to Davidson: a second event, which would have an explicitly Christian theme – the burial of the body of an unknown British war combatant in Westminster Abbey in a religious ceremony.[69]

> The Dean of Westminster suggests bringing home the body of any 'unknown soldier' of whose graves there are thousands and burying it in nave of W.A. with a big funeral. Rather a fine idea. The King not sympathetic 'Too long since the war ended' etc. etc. but the Dean is to talk to the PM. I believe it would appeal enormously to the Masses and remain for ever as a hallowed spot in the national land.[70]

Again, it was Stamfordham who saw the importance of the king giving way and accepting the idea, realising its power to create a symbolic sacralising moment for both the public and the monarchy. Lord Curzon then proposed, despite the short notice, that this event should take place on the same day as the Cenotaph unveiling, due to happen in just a few weeks' time.

Overall, the planning documents reveal that there was a demand for monarchism as part of the 11 November 1920 ceremonies and that it was seen as an integral part of war commemoration. The king's presence was expected, required, even demanded. While his role was distinct from that of ordained priests in the ceremonies, it was also a sacralised one – he conveyed monarchical 'honour' upon the dead. Indeed, for those planning the Cenotaph ceremony his role came before that of the Archbishop of Canterbury, which was added in as a secondary consideration. The result of the king's involvement was that, on 11 November 1920, the Cenotaph – or empty tomb – was juxtaposed with the Westminster Abbey tomb containing an actual unknown body, with the king the central figure of continuity between both ceremonies. Thus the war dead – and in particular those who had no known graves – were symbolically brought home to both the country and the king for which they had died. If there was an irony in the secular monument representing an empty tomb, while the Christian Abbey, with its culture of resurrection, became the site of the loaded grave, it was missed by the public. The day's ceremonies drew huge crowds, many of whom were war bereaved and profoundly moved. Newspaper reports referred to how the two minutes' silence at 11 a.m. at the Cenotaph unveiling were 'minutes of tense emotion, during which many sobbed aloud', while within the Abbey, where the congregation, already seated at 11 a.m. awaiting the arrival of the coffin of the Unknown Warrior, also marked the silence, 'men sob, and the weeping of many women makes itself heard'.[71]

The body of the Unknown Soldier itself was clearly sanctified through a rhetoric infused with monarchism: his tombstone recorded that 'they buried him among the Kings', thereby symbolically incorporating his dead body into royal status:

> thus are commemorated the many
> multitudes who during the great
> war of 1914–1918 gave the most that
> man can give life itself
> for God
> for King and Country
> for loved ones home and empire
> for the sacred cause of justice and
> the freedom of the world.
> They buried him among the Kings because he
> had done good toward God and toward
> his House.[72]

Note the hierarchical order of causes for which the individual had died – first God, then king, with the rest following after. The *Daily Telegraph*, on 12 November 1920, included the headline 'Brother of Kings: Unknown Buried in the Abbey' and referred to how King Henry V, also buried in Westminster Abbey, had pledged that anyone who shed blood with him at Agincourt would be his 'brother'; thus, the Unknown Soldier 'as a brother of Kings he was given a place in our Abbey yesterday'.[73] This new idea of the people as symbolically part of the royal 'family' helps to explain why the tomb in Westminster Abbey was in stark contrast to the humble grave of the one actual member of the British royal family who fell in the war, Prince Maurice of Battenberg, who, as Mark Connelly and Stefan Goebel have pointed out, was 'the prince commemorated like every other soldier, while the Unknown Warrior was everyman treated as a prince'.[74]

The fact that the king took the role of chief mourner during the unveiling and burial ceremonies, and referred to himself as such in his diary, laying a wreath on the Unknown Soldier's coffin and scattering earth on it during its burial, implied that the Unknown Soldier's tomb was being honoured as if it had the same status as a tomb of a member of the royal family.[75] The coffin was even a sixteenth-century chest made of wood from Hampton Court Palace.[76] The Palace press release stated that 'This morning the King unveiled the Cenotaph in Whitehall. Afterwards His Majesty was present as Chief Mourner at the burial of "An Unknown Warrior" in Westminster Abbey and walked there from the Cenotaph in the Funeral Procession.'[77] *The Scotsman* reported: 'Who that saw the grand funeral can ever forget it? A humble warrior honoured by the nation with the King as his chief mourner [. . .].'[78] The artist Fortunino Matania sketched the burial ceremony, while Frank Salisbury painted it, both emphasising the king as central figure, bareheaded and deferential to his dead subject.[79] In this way the monarchy interacted directly in a new symbolic with the war dead: it incorporated them into the royal sphere by granting the Unknown Soldier pseudo-royal familial status and, by proxy, other war dead too, thereby making the royal family guardians of the fallen.

The war dead – their bodies buried overseas – were thus reintegrated into the national and imperial body politic symbolically through the most significant bodily personification of the British nation, state and empire, the monarchy. Significantly, there was only one Unknown Soldier tomb in London to globally represent all British UK and empire war dead, again highlighting the global nature of 'British nation' identity in this period; it was only in more recent times that Australia (1993), Canada (2000) and New Zealand (2003) established their own such tombs. As *The Scotsman* noted, at the Cenotaph 'most eyes' were upon the coffin of the Unknown Warrior, which had been drawn up by the Cenotaph in preparation for the procession to the Abbey which was to follow, 'who was symbolical of the whole phantom host [. . .] Britain's exiled dead, scattered in graves known and unknown in every corner of the world'.[80] Standing near the coffin, the king paid *physical* homage to the war dead as part of the Cenotaph unveiling ceremony: he bared his head and during the two minute silence stood, facing the Cenotaph, with head bowed in homage to the war dead (Fig. 39).[81] He and his sons also each wore a black armband. For the crowd, these were easily recognisable Edwardian honour-culture gestures of deference, but here they were visually embodied by the *king* towards his dead subjects, something which was radically innovative and a powerful inversion of the normative cultural hierarchies of monarchy and class culture.

Fig. 39 King George V (flanked in rear by Prince of Wales and Duke of York) leading procession for the burial of the Unknown Soldier of WWI, Getty Images, 53370747 (Photo by Mansell/the Life Picture Collection via Getty Images)

Such gestures were also visible during the royal weddings of the early 1920s. During the drive home from her wedding at Westminster Abbey in 1922, Princess Mary's carriage stopped at the Cenotaph, where her new husband Viscount Lascelles saluted and a soldier laid flowers on her behalf. Princess Mary's wedding was a ceremony full of 'reminders of the Great War', including VADs and Red Cross nurses in uniform and a choir which wore their war medals pinned to their surplices.[82] There was some press anxiety about the practicalities of how the bridal procession, and dress, would navigate the tomb of the Unknown Warrior, which forced the procession to split in two.[83] The *Sheffield Daily Telegraph* reported that 'the tomb of the Unknown Warrior was carefully protected with rails, and no foot, whether King or Queen or bride stepped on the sacred spot'.[84] Monarchy thus physically made way for their most honoured symbolic subject – the dead First World War Warrior. Elizabeth Bowes-Lyon, at her marriage in 1923 to George V's second son, Prince Albert, spontaneously placed her wedding bouquet on the tomb of the

Unknown Soldier as she entered Westminster Abbey, a gesture that received widespread public approval and sent out a similar message, that the Unknown Warrior was deferred to by royalty and honoured akin to a dead royal family member.[85] Royal brides to this day have a bouquet laid on the tomb. Ultimately, the location of the grave within Westminster Abbey was highly significant – it was 'positioned so that for ever after no one, not even a king or queen approaching the altar at their own coronation, would be able to avoid side-stepping the grave of the man who had given his life for his country'.[86]

The war dead – their bodies buried overseas – were reintegrated into the national and imperial body politic symbolically through the most significant bodily personification of the state, the monarchy. Acting as chief mourner, on behalf of the 'nation and the Empire', as *The Scotsman* put it, projected the king as both father to his people – a familial relationship with the one dead body being used as emblematic of the country and empire's war dead as a whole – and as representing the war-bereaved individual.[87] But it also had other clear overtones – the king as 'servant' to his soldiery, as bestowing some of his own kingly honour, divinely ordained through the moment of coronation, upon his dead combatant subject. The king's honour was always symbolically bestowed but, rather than through awarding a medal, here it was unusually being granted to a dead unknown body and one already within the process of decay. The king himself had initial concerns about how this would work – he fretted that the body might smell in Westminster Abbey.[88] This presented risks for the monarch in the possible association with the horror and decay of the war's violence upon his subjects. But the religious meanings of acting as a 'servant king' – with its Christ-like resonances – helped to smooth away such possible tensions. The Rev. Alex MacKay-Clarke confirmed such views when he wrote to the king on 12 November 1920, the day after the ceremonies, in words that emphasised the relationship between Christ the King as comforter of the bereaved and the temporal kingship of George V:

Sir,

In connection with yesterday what could be more appropriate than the closing lines of Neale's hymn 'Safe home, safe home in port!'

'The exile is at home!
O nights and days of tears
. . .
What matters now griefs [*sic*] darkest day?
The KING has wiped those tears away.'[89]

Comptroller in the Lord Chamberlain's Department Brigadier General Sir Douglas Dawson replied that the king had appreciated the letter and that the 'words of the hymn to which you refer [. . .] seem indeed appropriate to the solemn occasion'.[90] There was a double 'resurrection' here, insofar as this body was resurrected physically from the soil of the front where it had lain and created into a symbol, transfigured through the bestowal of royal, and thus also national and imperial, honour. But the actual site – in the Abbey – was one that was meant also to emphasise the hope of the Christian belief in a spiritual resurrection. This context thus offered religious consolation to the war bereaved and associated the monarchy with the spiritual.

There was also the element of incorporating the war, such a shocking and disorientating historic rupture, into the continuity of British history through the monarch honouring the Unknown Soldier's body: 'The King [. . .] selected one of his own ceremonial swords to accompany the coffin on its journey home.'[91] George V donated an antique sword that he himself had selected from his private collection, which was placed upon the soldier's coffin before it left the Continent for the UK – a gesture that captured the public's imagination: a 'soldier's gift to a soldier' as the *Sheffield Daily Telegraph* described it, rather inaccurately.[92] *The Scotsman* reported it was a 'Crusader's sword, presented by the King, a relic of long ago, together with, in sharp contrast, the webbing belt and trench helmet that we have associated with modern warfare'.[93] The comparison was illustrative of how the monarchy was used in the ceremony to integrate the cataclysmic historical break that new industrial 'total' war represented into a long trajectory of national history and to spiritualise it by analogy with a religious crusade. The burial of the Unknown Soldier thus both fits the Hobsbawm–Ranger–Cannadine model of a moment of the 'invention of tradition' but also expressed older, long-existing religious and monarchist beliefs.[94]

Overall, this performance of royal rites using the body of a dead British combatant stabilised the position of the monarchy. *The Scotsman* reported how, as the king left and drove away from the Abbey, 'Every head was bared'; the monarch was shown ritual deference by the crowd, a gesture again illustrating the ongoing sacralised power of the monarchy in this period which was so key to why the monarch honouring an unknown ordinary combatant body carried so much symbolic impact.[95] This helps to explain the constant role of royalty in interwar commemoration.

Underpinning all this was another pattern. Wartime National Days of Prayer had seen the monarchy reach out in an ecumenical spiritual leadership role beyond the traditional remit of the established churches, thereby enhancing the sacralisation of monarchy among other denominations and religions. This was both modernising ecumenism and a reflection of older religious beliefs about kingly leadership in a call to prayer. It also reflected a realisation that the monarchy had to broaden its sacralised leadership remit beyond its traditional constituencies. The burial of the Unknown Soldier illustrated this too. The monarchy's role in honouring the war dead at this commemorative ritual, while it included religious ceremony, also made clear the division between the spiritual authority of religion and the temporal authority of the crown, a pattern also visible at other commemorative events attended by royals and in the organisation of National Prayer Days. Although his position was quasi-sacerdotal, the king never wished to encroach on the spiritual authority of religion, and the tension between the monarchy's religious role and the Church's was reconciled at war commemoration events by ensuring the presence of ordained priests who carried out prayers and blessings. This set up a space in these ceremonies for royal honouring of the war dead to provide a secular sacralisation process, alongside the Church role. Thus, the war resulted in the monarchy formulating its sacralisation in ways that associated this not only with the established churches but also with other denominations and religions, as well as with a secular sacredness with which the non-religious could identify. Given the rise in British atheist numbers later in the twentieth century, this First World War shift that allowed monarchical sacralisation to operate both with and beyond religion through war commemoration proved prescient and again extended the monarchy's long-term cultural reach.

The public response to the burial of the Unknown Warrior and the unveiling of the Cenotaph was largely very positive; the ceremonies were seen as dignified and filled a deep need on the part of the war bereaved to see their losses publicly acknowledged. An estimated 40,000 people filed past the grave of the Unknown Warrior immediately after the funeral service on 11 November 1920.[96] The role of the monarchy in performing this acknowledgement was central, something apparent even before the ceremonies. There was enormous demand for tickets to the burial service in Westminster Abbey, and the king received letters from bereaved relatives, and others, requesting a place at the event, to which a standard reply had to be issued that the seats available to the public were being allocated by lottery to mothers who had 'lost all or only sons' and that those without tickets should try to line the procession route instead.[97] Such letters are revealing of the way that the monarch was seen as an important intermediary for his bereaved subjects. Joseph Kaye from Peterborough, who lost his son in the war, wrote to 'His Majesty the King, Sir', asking if his wife, a 'sorrowing mother', could be present at the burial in the Abbey.[98] Kaye noted that 'Your Majesty sent a telegram of sympathy on May 10th/17, since that time we have heard nothing as to his body having been found and receiving interment.'[99] Kaye also set out his family's monarchist and military credentials in the letter: 'I had the honour of serving under Her Gracious Majesty Queen Victoria and your illustrious Father King Edward in the Boer War.'[100] Sydney Turner, writing from Portsmouth to ask for seats in the Abbey for himself and his brother, similarly wrote of how 'My brother has served with your Majesty's Forces in France and I have had the honour of serving your Majesty for nearly 4 years with the British Expeditionary Force in Mesopotamia.'[101] Again the request was framed in powerful monarchist language which showed how individuals situated themselves as subjects within a royalist historical trajectory. Turner wrote:

> Trusting that your Majesty may grant this humble request that we may be able to pay our last respects to our Comrades who so gloriously laid down their lives, for God, for King and Country. That God may bless your Majesty with long life, Peace and Happiness during your reign and that brighter days may be in store for old England is the earnest wish of Your [sic] most loyal and obedient servant.[102]

Mrs Newbold of Surbiton, Surrey, who had 'lost her only two children in the War' and who wished to attend the ceremonies, wrote that 'She now appeals to your Gracious Majesty with every confidence that her appeal will be listened to and granted if possible.'[103] Newbold was also anxious to check if the king permitted next of kin to wear the medals of the dead: 'Your Majesty has requested that all who earned decorations should wear them on the 11th inst. Does that included [sic] the next of kin to those dear ones who passed over. Heartfelt loyal greetings from a very grateful subject.'[104] The king was approached with a certain language of awe and deference: 'Humble Subject' H. C. Bayldon, who sent the king two suggestions of inscriptions for the tomb of the Unknown Warrior and the Cenotaph, wrote: 'Trusting you will overlook any transgression of etiquette I may be unconsciously guilty of having committed in my Patriotic fervour in thus presuming to approach you.'[105]

Such letters are revealing of the attitudes of ordinary war-bereaved individuals, even if one must allow for the fact that those supplicating the king for tickets were, of course, particularly likely to emphasise monarchism. The monarch was still seen as one to whom personal appeals could be made, a moral arbiter between state bureaucracy and subject. This was also the case for ex-servicemen whose organisations were divided over the plans for Armistice Day 1920. When concerns arose that the planning committee had prioritised 'military display' over a place for widows and ex-servicemen at the ceremonies, the National Federation of Discharged and Demobilised Sailors and Soldiers wrote to Stamfordham asking that His Majesty intervene: 'A great deal of feeling has been occasioned amongst widows, dependants and ex-service men generally at the manner in which they have been treated in respect to this matter. [...] It is felt that this is certainly not His Majesty's wish and needs only to be brought to his notice to be remedied.'[106] By contrast, the right-wing association Comrades of the Great War wrote to the king to express their disappointment that the ceremonies would not include a march past the monarch by ex-servicemen 'to show their loyalty once again'.[107] The king responded by insisting to Douglas Dawson, who was organising the ceremonies, 'that some arrangement will be made for representatives from the Ex-Service Men's organisations to take part in the Cenotaph and Abbey Services on November 11th. The King says that everything possible should be done to treat them sympathetically.'[108] Thus, the monarchy navigated this issue by ensuring that bereaved mothers and ex-servicemen were strongly represented at Westminster Abbey and informing the Comrades of the Great War that any review of ex-servicemen's organisations would be too tiring for the king, given the extent of his involvement in the planned ceremonies at the Abbey and Cenotaph. This was not entirely true: a note from Clive Wigram to Douglas Dawson stated that the king feared that any march past 'would probably mean a repetition of the Silver Badge Parade when the King and Queen and members of the Royal Family were mobbed. Further the police will have their hands quite full enough on Armistice Day with the Procession past the Cenotaph and into the Abbey without making arrangements for a "March Past".'[109] Ultimately, the National Federation of Discharged and Demobilised Sailors and Soldiers wrote to thank Douglas Dawson after the event for 'the splendid manner in which the whole of the arrangements were conducted and the great tribute which was paid to the memory of their fallen comrades'.[110] The monarchy, as symbolic embodiment of the state and empire, clearly had an authority which could calm resentments among ex-servicemen's organisations.

Indeed, for some of the bereaved, the king's symbolic role as an intermediary with the war dead on behalf of the state and empire was taken quite literally. Several wrote to the king in the belief that he might be able to tell them if the unknown British combatant being buried was their lost family member: one writer, M. Nathan, from Penge in London, asked 'is there any possibility of it been [sic] my son who was killed in France I have heard the end of him would not bee [sic] traced he had Fair complexion and mole on his left shoulder [. . .].'[111] Rose Else, who appears to have been barely literate, wrote, referring to her fallen son aged 19:

To his most madigester [sic] the King

> Sir I am informed there is to be a Funeral of a Brave Life at London on 11 of November. Will it be my dearest Boy god now [sic] hoe [sic] it will bee [sic] as my youngest Boy was kild [sic] on Oct 2 of 1917 and I canot [sic] get no informatshon [sic] were [sic] he was buried or enething [sic] or enething [sic] that belonged to him and he was the only Boy I had at home to help me. May I ask his Magest [sic] the King if its true all mothers are to com [sic] to the Funeral [. . .] I must pray for all forgiveiness [sic] I the great liberty I have taken trusting his most Magester [sic] the King will let me heare [sic] by return if all is true and I am forgiven by writing.[112]

The symbolic involvement of the king and the royal family in marking the end of the war and honouring the dead was genuinely popular and appreciated. In December 1920, just a month after the burial of the Unknown Soldier and Cenotaph unveiling, news that Buckingham Palace was to host a garden party for VC holders to which the next of kin of fallen VCs were also invited led to a series of letters from members of the public who had lost immediate family in the war, requesting an invitation; this included many whose dead relative had not been awarded a VC.[113] One typical example from Mrs F. Spain, a Royal Navy widow, requested permission to bring her son: 'We have not [sic] an invitation of any kind since my poor Husband has been dead so for my little son sake [sic] I should be glad to come and bring him with me.'[114] Mrs E. G. Sandford wrote in response to 'His Majesty the King's gracious invitation' of how she was 'deeply touched by His Majesty's expression in this, of remembrance of those who have gone'.[115] The garden party at Buckingham Palace was a post-war innovation, which, as the *Daily Telegraph* reported, made 'the way less difficult and less costly for those deserving of recognition to be received' by the royals, avoiding the complicated protocol and dress rules of indoor Palace events and allowing the king and queen to entertain much larger numbers of ordinary people; in 1919, 10,000 invitations were issued for the first garden parties.[116] However, the use of the gardens also ensured that the masses were met outside rather than within the inner sanctum of the Palace, preserving its mystique and privacy. There was, nevertheless, considerable awe among those selected to attend a garden party in the king's own personal gardens. One nurse described 'What sights awaited all those who recd the command to attend', illustrating that the king's invitation was still seen as a command of loyalty and that within the closeted grounds of the Palace was a hidden world of royal 'sights', mysterious and exciting.[117] These factors too help explain why bereaved families were keen to obtain an invitation.

Post-war recognition by royalty also mattered in releasing pent-up grief. One veteran, Basil Farrer, remembered 'the Prince of Wales inaugurating a plaque in the cathedral of Notre Dame de Paris to the million dead of Great Britain and the British Empire. And I did have a feeling of sadness that day.'[118] Indeed, the royals could trigger powerful moments of personal mourning: 86-year-old Florence Corkran of Norfolk, who lost a son in the war, wrote during the abdication crisis to Edward VIII of how

> I have always wanted you to know how deeply touched I was when I heard of the little incident only of Your Majesty's thought and most touching act that night of Armistice Day! When you went in the Field of Remembrance and planted a little cross in memory of the Grenadiers (who all love you so well) may I tell you Sir I cried for ages that day and think that most touching act of Your Majesty was for me the feeling that it included the memory of my darling youngest boy! [...] the memory of that little cross is with me all day always and I want to thank you Sir with my whole heart.[119]

It was rarer to find instances where the war bereaved channelled their anger at the royal family. Amy Beechey, who lost five sons and was presented to the king and queen during the war, apparently retorted, when Queen Mary thanked her for her immense sacrifice, that 'It was no sacrifice Ma'am; I did not give them willingly', although there is no contemporary evidence to support this widely cited quotation.[120] In other instances royal sympathy was met with anguish: on unveiling the war memorial at Vimy Ridge in 1936 after becoming king, Edward VIII was presented to Charlotte Wood from Winnipeg, Canada, who had lost five sons and had two wounded in the war. 'I wish your sons were all here', the king reportedly said to her. 'Oh Sir,' she replied, 'I have just been looking at the trenches and I just can't figure out why our boys had to go through that.'[121] Both cases illustrate the high stakes for the monarchy's image in the long-standing wartime and post-war policy of engaging with the war bereaved. In the post-war period, the war-bereaved mother, in particular, was a figure with powerful societal status, as Adrian Gregory has argued.[122] The older idea of presentations as an 'honour' to those presented to royalty was blurring in such cases into one where they marked the monarchy as honouring and paying its respects to the bereaved relatives, risking it becoming subordinate to their growing status.

6.4   The King's 'Pilgrimage'

The royal role of honouring the war dead culminated in the king's 1922 'pilgrimage' to France and Belgium to visit the war cemeteries, which was a three-day tour, beginning on 11 May, following an official state visit to Belgium. The state visit itself also included an important commemoration, when the king and queen laid a wreath on the grave of Edith Cavell, executed by the Germans. Frederick Ponsonby, who accompanied them, described it as 'quite a simple ceremony, but it aroused a great deal of feeling, not only in Belgium, but also in England'.[123] During his subsequent war-graves visit, the king was accompanied by Sir Fabian Ware from the Imperial War Graves Commission (IWGC) and Field Marshal Earl Haig, recently elevated to an earldom, as his tour guides and three of his personal staff. The king insisted that this was a personal visit, something the press also emphasised. Yet the personal was also deliberately symbolic and communicated as such: he accepted that two journalists, from Reuters and from Havas Agency, would accompany him; some limited access was also ultimately given to the picture press to take photographs.[124] The Topical Budget, a British company that made newsreel film, and which in 1917–18 had been controlled by the War Office as a propaganda outlet, was also granted permission to film part of the trip, after an initial refusal.[125] In exchange, it promised: 'we should not dream of inconveniencing anyone much less trespassing on His Majesty.'[126]

The choice by the king to use the term pilgrimage, with all its religious connotations, was deliberate, as the IWGC noted: 'The French and Belgian governments, when this visit was notified to them, were told that it would be in the nature of a solemn pilgrimage, words which literally express His Majesty's own attitude in the matter.'[127] The idea of the 'king's pilgrimage' to the graves of the war dead again highlighted the idea of King George V as a servant king – with its religious homage to Christian ideas of imitating Christ. The trip involved little ceremonial. It was only on the final day that the king took part in a large wreath-laying ceremony and service at Terlincthun Cemetery. Frederick Ponsonby, who accompanied the king, described the tour to Marshal Ferdinand Foch as 'a personal and private visit' by the king 'to the graves of his soldiers'; Ponsonby, in his memoir, however, claimed the idea of making the visit private was also to avoid the king having to meet the French President.[128] 'Pilgrimage' was both a reference to George V's faith and his understanding of war death within a religious framework, but also a reference to the frequent description in the public sphere at the time of visits by the bereaved to the war graves as 'pilgrimages'. It also conveniently obviated the need for much of the protocol associated with an official visit to foreign countries. The king's pilgrimage was also seen as appropriate in the context of a post-war boom in war tourism: the king should humbly make the same long and tiring journey to out-of-the-way cemeteries that so many of his bereaved subjects were doing.[129]

The whole conceptualisation of a royal 'pilgrimage' to the war graves had obvious sacralising connotations: the monarchy both honouring the fallen and taking command of the sacred duty of stewardship towards them, thereby gaining an invaluable new moral purpose. It was further evidence of George V emphasising the British monarchy's post-war character as humble, spiritual and pared down. If in the pre-war period at the start of his reign the pomp and luxury of the Indian Durbar was his major overseas trip, in the post-war era the 1922 pilgrimage provided a completely different vision of monarchy. The king was to 'live on the train and proceed from the train by car to as many cemeteries as possible in the time'.[130] The itinerary was to be kept secret in advance. George V's pilgrimage was to convey honour upon the war dead through their king personally visiting their graves but was also a deeply personal gesture by a man still coming to terms with the enormity of the conflict and its losses. Those accompanying him noted that the memory of the war 'weighed heavy on him'.[131] In this way the king helped to symbolically further integrate the absent dead bodies into the national and imperial body politic. A telegram to Fabian Ware from the Prime Minister of Canada on behalf of the Canadian 'Government and people' expressed gratitude to the IWGC and to the king for 'His Majesty's assurance that these graves will be reverently and lovingly guarded'.[132]

The tour was also intended to serve the king's war-bereaved subjects in the UK and across the empire, by visiting, on their behalf, cemeteries to which many of them were unable to travel. At Meerut Cemetery, the monarch was shown the different forms of headstones used for Muslim, Sikh and Hindu soldiers and labourers buried or commemorated there after cremation.[133] At Etaples Cemetery, the king met with official representatives of the dominions – Canada,

Australia, New Zealand, South Africa and Newfoundland – and symbolically visited the dominion graves with them.[134] The Victoria League further emphasised this link to the dominions, sending the IWGC a list of names of relatives of men buried in France 'who belong to the overseas Dominions' who were at present 'in or near London' and who it felt should be invited to the closing ceremony of the king's tour.[135] Honour culture and class hierarchies infused the letter, with the Victoria League assuring that the people on its list were 'in every way suitable for such a privilege' and 'how very greatly such a privilege would be appreciated'.[136]

The IWGC fretted over the planning details of the trip. It wanted the king to personally inspect and thank the IWGC workers employed in building and landscaping the graveyards. When it became clear that the king would only inspect the gardeners at two sites, it was suggested that its workers could line the royal route and 'the car could pass them slowly so that they could all get a glimpse of H.M. at any rate'.[137] This again highlights the sheer importance of monarchical recognition to individual subjects. Gardeners at Etaples Cemetery were instructed to 'spring to attention with their hats in their hands on the King's arrival'.[138] There was delight at Albert Camp among those IWGC workers lined up on parade when the king made an unscheduled stop to inspect them.[139] Captain Parker, the Head of the Horticultural Department for the IWGC in France, wrote to Fabian Ware after the visit:

> We have come through troublous [sic] times, now and then, during the past three and a half years and have been engaged in the most difficult and trying part of our task, but the past three days have washed out the memories of those times of stress and have rewarded us a thousandfold. The King has seen our work. He has graciously approved of it in a public speech. He has shaken hands with us and said kind words to us.[140]

Fabian Ware added that 'Parker is not the sort of man to say a thing without really meaning it.'[141] The emphasis here on the royal touch, the royal word, is indicative of how elements of older concepts of the royal body bestowing honour survived the war. Knowing the impact of the king's visit upon the morale of IWGC staff, Ware arranged for 2,000 copies of the letter of thanks sent by the king after the trip to be distributed to them.[142] The IWGC also proposed erecting commemorative plaques stating 'this cemetery was visited by His Majesty' at the sites visited.[143] The French even erected a wooden sign at the French military cemetery of Notre Dame de Lorette to commemorate the road route taken by the king.[144]

The IWGC, and, in particular, Sir Fabian Ware, were heavily involved in assisting the king to make his tour. The cemetery locations were difficult to access, often in remote, war-ravaged areas. There was also the delicate issue of dealing with French and Belgian sensitivities; the IWGC was anxious that the king's visit should not offend Britain's former allies, whose cooperation it needed for its work. However, the king had 'a very strong objection to any representative of the French Government, or French Army, accompanying him on his tour round the Graveyards. The King thinks that it would spoil the whole effect if he were to go round with Foch, or any French Minister.'[145] One sees here the shrewd grasp George V had of appearances and of the importance for the monarchy's post-war image that the visit be projected as a private pilgrimage. The IWGC, however, ultimately ensured that homage was paid to the Allies on whose territory the war cemeteries lay by suggesting that the king visit Notre Dame de Lorette, a large French war cemetery, and lay a wreath there in the presence of Ferdinand Foch, which proved a carefully choreographed piece of diplomacy.[146] During his visit to Ypres, the king also presented representatives of the Belgian government and army with flowers in memory of the Belgian war dead.[147] Likewise, the IWGC ensured that on the last day of the king's visit there was what it described as the 'crowning act of homage', an official ceremony to conclude the tour, when the king, now joined by Queen Mary, who arrived by train from Brussels, unveiled the cross of sacrifice at Terlincthun Cemetery, in the presence of Belgian, French and British representatives, including General de Castlenau and Admiral the Earl Beatty.[148] In this way, the king's private unofficial visit was also a very public one. Terlincthun was highly symbolic given its links with Napoleon and the defence of the channel and the fact that it contained graves not only of British war dead from all three services – army, navy and air force – but also of Allied war dead. Here the king read a speech to close his 'solemn pilgrimage', addressed to

> all who have lost those dear to them in the Great War. [. . .] I feel that, so long as we have faith in God's purposes, we cannot but believe that the existence of these visible memorials will, eventually, serve to draw all peoples together in sanity and self-control [. . .]. [. . .] we remember, and must charge our children to remember, that, as our dead were equal in sacrifice, so are they equal in honour, for the greatest and the least of them have proved that sacrifice and honour are no vain things, but truths by which the world lives.[149]

He referred to the war dead as 'our brothers'.[150] The key themes of the tour were clearly evident – equality of the war dead and their place within a religiously framed and royally sacralised British honour culture. Even a journalist, Henry Benson, wrote that 'in my long career as a journalist it has, naturally, fallen to my lot to witness a very large number of public functions but I have never been present at one more beautiful, more touching or more impressive in its dignified simplicity than the King's homage to the dead at Terlincthun'.[151]

The king was very pleased with how the tour had gone: indeed, so much so that his Private Secretary, Clive Wigram, wrote to ask Fabian Ware to arrange for a commemorative, illustrated book of the tour, *The King's Pilgrimage*, to be published by the IWGC.[152] It remains unclear who exactly wrote the body of the book's text: most was written by Australian journalist Frank Fox, very likely with close input from Fabian Ware and IWGC Commissioner Rudyard Kipling.[153] The publication was carefully controlled: 'no photographs to be included with anybody smiling' was one key instruction.[154] Tactfully, all profits from sales of the publication were to go to charities that assisted the war bereaved to visit war graves of their loved ones overseas. On reading the draft manuscript, the king noted that 'There were one or two small points which His Majesty did not consider were absolutely correct, but in an account of this sort, as long as the main facts are true, the smaller details do not matter.'[155] Thus, the book itself was accepted as an act of commemoration rather than of accurate history. Kipling, who had lost his own son in the war, wrote a poem for the book, which exemplifies the way that monarchism was being intermeshed with war commemoration:

The King's Pilgrimage

Our King went forth on pilgrimage
His prayer and vows to pay
To them that saved our Heritage
And cast their own away.
And there was little show of pride
Or prows of belted steel [. . .]
[. . .]
And the last land he found, it was fair
and level ground
Above a carven Stone,
And a stark Sword brooding on the
bosom of the Cross,
Where high and low are one;
And there was grass and the living trees
And the flowers of the Spring,
And there lay gentlemen from out of
all the seas
That ever called him King.
(*'Twixt Nieuport sands and the eastward lands*
where the Four Red Rivers spring
five hundred thousand gentlemen of those that
served the King.)[156]

The poem deliberately reinforced the message of the personal and sacred relationship between the war dead and the monarch, a theme emphasised throughout the book, which referred to the king visiting the tombs 'in Belgium and France of his comrades' and to him wearing 'the uniform which they wore on service'.[157] Here is a suggestion of egalitarianism – 'comrade' – in the relationship between the monarch and those who died for him. In the description of the king as wearing their uniform, the fallen have also metaphorically become one with him in terms of their honoured status. He embodies the nation and empire that is purportedly their legacy. The equality of the war dead – 'high and low are one' – was also presented as both a natural equality of all subjects in their relationship to the monarch and to Christianity. This was reinforced by the images which appear in *The King's Pilgrimage*, such as the one in Fig. 40, which emphasised the personal, simple nature of the monarch's grief for his subjects and their equality in death before him, indeed for him. The caption, advocating peace, positioned the monarch as a peaceful Christian king, a symbolism readily recognisable to 1922 audiences.

The commemorative book constantly highlighted the spiritual nature of the visit: 'Nowhere did official ceremony intrude on an office of private

" In the course of my pilgrimage I have many times asked myself whether there can be more potent advocates of peace upon earth through the years to come than this massed multitude of silent witnesses to the desolation of war"

Fig. 40 Image of the king in a war cemetery from *The King's Pilgrimage* (London, 1922)

devotion', and the king's mission was referred to as one of 'gratitude and reverence', the same as that of the war-bereaved relatives he encountered.[158] Here the relationship between monarch and subject was portrayed as so intimate that the king's grief for his lost soldiers was equated to that of their own close relatives.

This evidently bordered upon hyperbole, but the tone of the commemorative book was not criticised. Indeed, the encounters between the king and his subjects that took place on this tour clearly had a powerful effect. One war-bereaved mother, Mrs S. A. Heald, who lost her son on the first day of the Battle of the Somme and who was introduced to the king during his visit, wrote of her gratitude to Fabian Ware

> for the honour you gave to me by presenting me to the King. [. . .] I was very proud to tell His Majesty of the great help the Imperial War Graves Officers [. . .] (in 1920) had given me, in helping me to locate my son's grave. He replied 'He was very glad to know.' I remarked if they had been looking for the Prince of Wales's grave, they[,] 'War Graves Officers'[,] could not have done more. I could see you were very sympathetic and it comforted me when you shook hands also.[159]

The Freudian slip in the remark about the Prince of Wales is revealing, suggesting that the king's son returned, whereas hers did not. It was a sensitive issue that the king's adult sons had survived their war service. *The King's Pilgrimage* emphasised that, at Ypres, the monarch had visited the graves of 'his own personal friends', including Prince Maurice of Battenberg, Lord Charles Mercer Nairne Petty-Fitzmaurice and Major the Hon. William Cadogan, which, showing egalitarianism in royal mourning, 'lie among those of their men, marked by the same simple memorials'.[160] The book implied that the king agreed that 'general and private rest side by side beneath the same simple stones, equal in the honour of their death for duty's sake'.[161] The king also met with Australian relatives visiting a grave at Crouy Cemetery and who, an IWGC official reported, 'were given very much pleasure when the King went up and spoke to them. These people will no doubt carry back with them to Australia their very great appreciation of the honour conferred on them by personal conversation with the King.'[162] A photograph of the meeting, however (Fig. 41), shows the grief etched on the faces of the Australian couple. The way that the monarchy's image was transforming is evident: the king appears bowed and ordinary, his stance one of service and humility in this informal meeting, juxtaposed against the strong, leaning, slightly angry, dominant pose of the bereaved father and the awkward sadness of his wife. George V's body language in this photograph is of attempted consolation and deference to his own war-bereaved subjects.

Such royal encounters could have profound emotional effects. During the Terlincthun ceremony, Mrs Barker, from the St Barnabas Hostels organisation,

CROUY BRITISH CEMETERY

THE KING TALKING TO TWO BEREAVED AUSTRALIAN
RELATIVES

Fig. 41   Crouy British Cemetery, the king talking to two bereaved Australian relatives, from *The King's Pilgrimage* (London, 1922)

became 'very distressed' when she was told she would not be able, impromptu, to present the king with a book of photographs of 'certain cemeteries', and a colonel intervened and accepted to pass the book on to one of the king's staff.[163] As the king's visit was a private one, the encounters with relatives of the dead were not planned in advance – indeed, several appear to have happened by chance. The one moment of the tour where royal interaction with individual bereavement was somewhat stage-managed was when the king placed some pressed forget-me-nots, sent to Queen Mary by a bereaved mother 'in the West of England [...] as one mother to another', upon the grave of the woman's son, Sergeant A. T. Matthew.[164] The IWGC internal report noted that 'The King explained that the Queen had asked him in her absence to do this for her and the King of England stooped and placed the flowers on the earth', before asking the head gardener to secure them against the wind and ensure they were watered.[165] This moment on the tour was widely reported and was perceived as deeply touching. A photograph of the king placing the flowers on the grave shows Sir James Allen, the High Commissioner for New Zealand, who had lost a son at Gallipoli, looking haggard, standing beside another, unidentified man in a suit, who appears to be crying.[166]

It seems the appreciation of the king's homage to the war dead was often genuine. When the king and queen made a similar private tour to the British war cemeteries in Italy in 1923, bereaved parents, Mr and Mrs Chutter, whom they had encountered, wrote to Fabian Ware: 'we both felt very honoured by the extremely kind and sympathetic manner in which their Majesties spoke to us at our boy's grave, and we shall always remember with gratitude the attention we received [...].'[167] As with the French tour, the press coverage was sympathetic, in part because the *Times* journalist in attendance was a war veteran who knew Asiago and the Piave 'very well, having fought there for a year, and, alas, I fear many of my friends lie on the former'.[168] The royal couple's visits to war graves were thus encounters with the bereaved at multiple levels, and grief influenced the press's own perception of events and how they conveyed them as much as it did that of the general public.

The role of the monarchy as vectors for public war grief helps to explain its ongoing power in a post-war and increasingly democratic era. Adapting monarchism to channel mass bereavement into effective public ritual helped sustain the British monarchy's popularity. It put old concepts of honour culture to new uses, sanctifying the war dead with the homage of the king as eternal symbol of the state and empire. In fact, such was the success of this symbiotic intertwining of King George V with the mourning ceremonies for the war dead that upon his own death elements of the new rituals created for war remembrance that he had carried out were incorporated into his own lying-in-state and funeral. As Ina Zweiniger-Bargielowska has pointed out, a two-minute silence, a ritual developed for Armistice Day commemorations, was incorporated into George V's obsequies.[169] In 1936, 809,182 people filed past his coffin over four days: over twice as many as would turn out to do the same for George VI over three days in 1952 or for Winston Churchill in 1965.[170] As the journalist Philip Gibbs wrote of George V: 'Why did he take hold of his People's heart so strongly? [...] He never lost his nerve or his confidence in pulling through. He did his duty – a hard duty – through those years of tragic sacrifice. The people remembered that.'[171]

6.5   Paying Tribute to War Veterans: Ex-Servicemen and the War-Veteran Prince

The function of honouring the war dead also extended to the Prince of Wales in his role as President of the IWGC, an important symbol of the integration of monarchy and war bereavement. Edward had begun this role during the war, but it was as the Commission's work expanded in the wake of the conflict that it became more prominent. However, if his father, as king, represented the nation in grief and the state and empire for which the war dead had died, Edward's role was to symbolise the generation who fought. Even if he had not gone into combat, the public knowledge of his exploits at the front made the charismatic young prince into an idealised embodiment of the war veteran.[172] This chapter will now explore how the monarchy engaged with ex-servicemen, whose reintegration into society presented European states with considerable difficulties. It argues that, by using the Prince of Wales's status as a veteran, the British monarchy was able to develop close links with the British Legion and that his role helped to defuse potential anti-monarchism amongst former soldiers. Yet, this came at a cost: Edward's close involvement, and identification, with veterans meant that he rapidly espoused their politics, including supporting rapid reconciliation with Germany and appeasement, which the British Legion endorsed in the hope of avoiding another war. Likewise, it meant that when Edward broke with conventional royal behaviour by the early 1930s, he had a large veteran support base that listened to his political outbursts, potentially making him more difficult to rein in. While the monarchy had long had close associations with war veterans from previous conflicts, the advent of mass conscription and the volatile nature of European politics with the rise of communism and fascism, which in other countries had benefited from some veteran groups' support, meant that ex-servicemen in the interwar period were a cohort it particularly needed to keep loyal. The future Edward VIII's role was therefore key to stabilising interwar monarchism in Britain, and, to some extent, played a similar role in the empire.

Edward's war service had earned him a reputation for heroism among British troops and in the media, which bolstered the popularity of the British royal family at a time of revolution and dynastic upheaval elsewhere in Europe. After the war, the widespread public belief was that the prince had been 'at the front', as numerous wartime press photographs of him in France and Italy had been captioned. This made him a frequent choice for the unveiling of war memorials. In 1923, the Prince of Wales was praised in a speech at the dedication of the Metropolitan Police War Memorial as follows:

> A large proportion of these men were Reservists in His Majesty's Guards with which Division, Sir, you served for so many months. You will therefore specially appreciate the valour of those who fell and it is quite possible that you may have been actually present on occasions when those

casualties occurred, for it is within the lively recollection of all who are
here present that you served almost continuously with the Armed Forces
of the Crown during the War.[173]

Again here one finds the public assumption that Edward was in the front
line in danger. He became the most important symbolic veteran in the state
and empire. This was something Edward encouraged: when he reportedly
made a speech from the balcony of Buckingham Palace on 28 June 1919,
after news arrived that the Treaty of Versailles had been signed, he stated to
the crowd: 'I am very proud to have served with so many of you who are
here.'[174] In 1920, he was still using a photograph of himself in war uniform
on his Christmas card.[175] As late as the 1950s, Edward believed that he was
still remembered as a veteran: 'even now, after three decades, I still meet
men who will suddenly turn to me and say, "The last time I saw you, you
were on your bicycle on the road to Poperinghe" – or Montauban, or any
one of a hundred French villages.'[176] When Edward visited a Welsh mine,
going a thousand feet down the shaft, he found chalked on the wall,
'Welcome to our soldier Prince. Long may he live.'[177] Edward responded
by asking for chalk and writing 'Thank you. Edward. Prince.'[178] Clearly,
even though he was a veteran, Edward felt it was appropriate to drop the
'soldier' in his response. He constantly self-identified as a veteran, referring
to the war generation as 'my generation'.[179] In August 1928, he attended
a service held at the Menin Gate – an event which was part of a mass
'pilgrimage' to the battlefields by war bereaved and veterans.[180] Referring to
his war service at the ceremony when he became a Freeman of the City of
London in 1919, he stated that 'in those four years I mixed with men. In
those four years I found my manhood.'[181] Here he was effectively admitting
the extent to which his masculine identity was intractably linked with the
conflict. King George V himself admitted to his heir that 'You have had
a much freer life than I ever knew [...]. The war has made it possible for you
to mix with all manner of people in a way I was never able to do.'[182] This
reality clearly challenged the king, who feared it had undermined the sense
of distance between the prince and his people: he added to Edward: 'But
don't think that this means you can now act like other people. You must
always remember your position and who you are.'[183]

As the royal heir who had served on the Western Front, Edward had a unique
status with war veterans. He was certainly immensely popular with them.
A recording of a speech he made on Armistice Day in 1927 before veterans at
the Festival of Remembrance at the Royal Albert Hall shows he was received
with rapturous applause. He was treated to a spontaneous round of 'For He's
a Jolly Good Fellow' as well as vociferous cheering.[184] Addressing the crowd as
'old comrades and friends', Edward spoke in a way that emphasised his veteran
status:

> The full sum of that remembrance not I nor anyone can express in words. Each one of us man or woman cherishes dear memories which belong to him or her alone. But beyond those precious, those precious personal recollections there arise also the great memories we can share one with another and these memories should dwell in us not only on this day but on each and every day of the year.[185]

He emphasised wartime comradeship in personal terms, as if he too had fought:

> In the actual day of battle every man who fought by our side was our comrade and our friend. For nine difficult years we have endured the inevitable sombre consequences of war and whether he who fought by our side has fared better or worse than ourselves or whatever his luck may be, he is no less our comrade and our friend today.[186]

Edward emphasised that veterans should work for peace: 'to save ourselves and those that come after us from a renewal, renewal, in an even more frightful form of all that we suffered in the Great War we must in our every action, in our everyday conversations, and even in our very thoughts seek peace and ensue [sic] it'.[187] He ended his speech to further wild applause. As this instance illustrates, the public claim upon Edward was no longer one couched in terms of the honour culture of 1914 and sacred bloodlines but upon the classless community of veteran camaraderie and the legacy of shared wartime sacrifice – one which, by serving, and by risk-taking against official policy to access dangerous areas, Edward had helped interweave into the British monarchy as a new right upon which its assertion to reign was grounded, thereby protecting it in the unstable European 1920s. However, this also laid the foundations for a clash between Edward's desire to be a modern 'classless' charismatic leader, emphases which were also traits of the new fascist leadership models emerging in interwar Continental Europe, and the monarchy's existing structures of kingship. As Clive Wigram remarked, as king, Edward VIII was 'another type of King. One of a new generation, a product of the war.'[188]

As Prince of Wales, Edward frequently appeared at events associated with veteran welfare. For example, in 1921 he appeared alongside Field Marshal Earl Haig, Admiral Beatty and Sir Hugh Trenchard at an event at Drury Lane Theatre to inaugurate 'Warrior's Day', which was a fundraiser by those working in the entertainment industry in aid of ex-servicemen. The prince came onstage to 'a magnificent ovation' and made a speech, which was loudly cheered, stating: 'from my experience on active service and during my journey of tens of thousands of miles throughout the Empire since the war, I can assure you that the cause for which we are pleading to-day is second to none in national importance at the present time'.[189] Such gestures mattered: there was real anger among ex-servicemen about the economic hardship that many experienced in the interwar years. As the chairman of Limavady Urban Council declared in April 1935 during the discussions for planning for King George V's Silver Jubilee: 'there was a lot of talk about decorations but never any mention of the ex-Servicemen. Some of these men who helped to keep the king on the throne were to-day in absolute poverty.'[190] Such views were not limited to county Derry but were widespread in Britain too.

It was also Edward's credibility as a veteran that meant that he was chosen to test the interwar public mood around any royal re-engagement with Germany. The monarchy's contact with Germany in the interwar period was slow and extremely limited, even if some private ties re-emerged more quickly: by 1928, Princess Alice and the Duke of Connaught were writing to German relatives via the German Embassy.[191] A few weeks after the Armistice, Prince Albert met with the kaiser's sister Princess Victoria in Germany. She asked after the British royal family and said that she 'hoped that we should be friends again', Albert wrote to his father.[192] Albert told her 'politely that I did not think it was possible for a great many years!!!'[193] The king never again met or wrote to the kaiser, and interaction with any of the German dynasties remained fraught.

Edward's status as a veteran, however, enabled him to make bold public moves towards reconciliation. He was the royal who in the early 1930s was most engaged in Anglo-German rapprochement, fostering initiatives that brought ex-servicemen from the former enemy states together. In 1935, he supported a proposed visit by British Legion war veterans to Germany in the name of peace and reconciliation with the former enemy, a move which delighted the Nazi press.[194] It was Edward who was even tasked with publicly announcing the visit.[195] Speaking to the British Legion, he stated: 'there would be no more suitable body or organisation of men to stretch forth the hand of friendship to the Germans than we ex-Servicemen who fought them in the Great War and have now forgotten all about that'.[196] His speech coincided with a delicate moment in Anglo-German naval negotiations, causing embarrassment to the Foreign Office, and was even discussed in cabinet; in fact, the cabinet requested that the king show the minutes of the meeting to the prince so that he should realise the 'complications that he had caused'.[197] However, Edward's gaffe may also have been a sign of the monarchy's shifting position: behind the scenes, George V himself was also 'lobbying the Foreign Office in favour of agreement with Germany'.[198]

During the period when Leopold von Hoesch was ambassador to Britain in the early 1930s, Edward, the Prince of Wales, even 'enjoyed visiting the German Embassy'.[199] This role of engaging with Germany, linked to his work with veterans to create a lasting European peace, clearly deeply influenced Edward's personal political opinions. He was already virulently anti-communist, profoundly affected by the murder of his Romanov cousins by the Bolsheviks in 1918; when he met the Soviet Union's People's Commissar for Foreign Affairs, Maxim Litvinov, on 29 January 1936, he spent most of the encounter interrogating Litvinov on how his Russian relatives had died.[200] Edward's opposition to communism and support for reconciliation with Germany to avoid the horrors of another war thus help to explain his later relatively easy transition to full-blown appeasement, a path trodden by many of his contemporaries among British upper-class elites in the 1930s. His later secret wartime discussions with Nazi Germany, revealed after the Second World War in the Marburg files, were the final step on a trajectory that had begun long before. He appears to have spent much of the interwar period believing that any future war would spread socialist revolution, as the 1914–18 conflict had, and that social inequality and, in particular, the poor economic and welfare treatment of war veterans was a risk to Britain's political stability and to the monarchy itself. Hence his championing of veterans' welfare needs, which won him such popularity more generally, and his deliberate interwar development of his image as a 'democratic' prince which had first emerged during the war. In these fears, Edward was, to some extent, mirroring the attitudes of royal courtiers who worried about the rise of the left in interwar British politics, believing it would bring an increase in anti-monarchism. Queen Mary fretted to her son that 'I sadly fear Papa does not yet realise how many changes this war will have brought about.'[201] The left-wing paper, the *Daily Herald*, reported that the turnout for the king's opening of the Imperial War Museum in 1920 was much lower than expected, suggesting a new indifference to the royal presence in some working-class areas that suggests that the fears of courtiers were not entirely imagined.[202]

Indeed, Edward's popularity with veterans was one of the fundamental reasons that his abdication was seen as so dangerous; it may also have been a factor in his decision to pursue his marriage plans. Frederick Maurice, president and founder of the British Legion, wrote on 19 November 1936 that the king had been 'much impressed by his reception at the Albert Hall on Nov. 11th and that this had confirmed him in his decision to go forward with the marriage'.[203] There were rumours that he might use his charisma to set up a rival power base using veteran support. This triggered alarm, given that both Mussolini and Hitler had claimed that they had seized power in the name of war veterans in Italy and Germany when they dismantled democracy.[204] Just weeks before the king abdicated, Prime Minister Stanley Baldwin was given a copy of a letter that Frederick Maurice had written on 19 November 1936 to the king's Private Secretary, Major Hardinge. Maurice relayed his views as to what the attitude of war veterans would be to King Edward VIII's proposed marriage:

> H.M.s immense popularity with the Legion was due to 1) his great position 2) his personal charm 3) his readiness to meet the Legion as a comrade 4) his obviously sincere desire to further the welfare of ex-service men in every possible way. [...] the vast majority of the members

of the Legion did not bother their heads about the King's private life but
[...] the marriage of the King would not be considered a private matter
[...] I was sure that not even the King's great popularity with the Legion
would stand the shock of the proposed marriage. [...] I have [...]
consulted in strict confidence leaders of the Legion, who are in touch
with opinion, in the North, South, East, and West [...] I am confident that
the King could not rely upon the support of the Legion if it were to take
place.[205]

Notably, the status of king, 'his great position', was the first reason given for
Edward's popularity. Even in 1936, monarchical loyalty determined popularity
ahead of any personal attributes of the king himself. The letter had clearly been
passed from someone at Buckingham Palace, in all likelihood Hardinge, to the
Prime Minister, illustrating the degree of shared concern in court and government alike about Edward's veteran support base. There were further worries
that as Duke of Windsor, ex-King Edward might try to sit in the House of
Lords, thereby building a political role for himself; George VI barred him from
this.[206] A charismatic former king with a large following among ex-servicemen
and pro-German inclinations clearly caused alarm. Indeed, the public reaction
to the abdication was a source of great worry to the Establishment. The
abdication aroused powerful emotions: in fact, the Mass Observation Survey
was founded in 1937 precisely because it was believed there was a need for
intellectual analysis of the 'emotion' of the abdication. This also helps to
explain the concerns in 1939 when the former Edward VIII, now Duke of
Windsor, demanded an opportunity to participate in the war effort and was
sent to France to work in a liaison role 'as part of a British military mission to
report back on the French army's preparations'.[207] A Mass Observation study
of the popularity of royal figures in newsreels in 1939 suggested he was the
most popular member of the royal family, and the government and royal
household had to work secretly 'to prevent the duke from visiting British
troops stationed in France', partly so that he did not upstage the king.[208]
When Edward ultimately fled the German invasion of 1940 via Spain, however,
his image was deeply and permanently tarnished.[209]

The Great War's legacy was evidently part of the emotional response to the
abdication and to Edward's image. The idea that the British and empire war
dead had sacrificed themselves for the king remained highly significant in
terms of how the monarchy saw itself into the interwar period. There was
a clear sense of burden: the duty to live up to the extent of this sacrifice. This
context helps to explain the fierce reaction amongst his own family to Edward
VIII's decision when he rejected the crown in order to pursue personal
happiness with Wallis Simpson. Queen Mary informed him: 'It seemed inconceivable to those who had made such sacrifices during the war that you, as their
king, refused a lesser sacrifice.'[210] In a private letter to the Prime Minister,
Stanley Baldwin, she referred to her son's 'failure' to carry out his duties and

responsibilities.[211] Edward's abdication was seen as abandoning a sacred duty not only to the living but also to the war dead and bereaved. His uncle, the Earl of Athlone, wrote to Baldwin 'of the tragic failure of my nephew to recognise his duty [. . .] as an old soldier, I am horrified that one who served with courage during the late war should have allowed his courage to fail him in this affair'.[212] The sacralisation of national and imperial mass death in the war had provided a particular role for the Prince of Wales as a veteran. The abdication crisis should thus be understood as a betrayal of the language of sacrifice and duty espoused by the monarchy during the war and consolidated by commemoration in its aftermath. Placing personal fulfilment over duty was more than an individual failure; it threatened the re-development and re-sacralisation of kingship through the war experience.

The abdication also marked the culmination of Edward's increasing blurring of public and private in ways that had undermined the connection between monarchical reverence and war sacrifice during his brief period as king. Newspaper reports on the unveiling of Canada's National War Memorial at Vimy Ridge in July 1936 reported the inappropriate juxtaposition of war commemoration and pleasure, noting that, following the unveiling, King Edward would go 'direct to Cannes', where he would holiday for a month at a villa he had rented.[213] The unveiling ceremony, which was broadcast on radio across Great Britain, was described as moving. However, it saw King Edward VIII suggest in his speech, heard by millions across the airwaves as well as thousands of Canadian and French pilgrims, mainly veterans and bereaved, present, as well as the French President whose country the Germans had occupied, that the war's causes now looked irrelevant: 'All the world over there are battlefields the names of which are written indelibly on the pages of our troubled human story. It is one of the consolations which time brings, that deeds of valour done on those battlefields long survive the quarrels which drove the opposing hosts to conflict. Vimy will be one such name.'[214] It was hardly tactful.

In the first week of September 1936, Edward fitted in a one-day visit to the war cemeteries on the Gallipoli peninsula at the end of a long yachting holiday in the Mediterranean, which he had embarked upon in August with his mistress Wallis Simpson. The names of those he was holidaying with were widely reported. Although the real purpose of Wallis Simpson's presence on the king's luxury yacht, the *Nahlin*, during his stop-off at Gallipoli was not directly mentioned in the British press at the time, the image of the suntanned, holidaying king, in a dapper grey civilian suit (Fig. 42), breaking his leisure time to pop ashore for what was the first visit of a British royal to the Gallipoli war dead was shocking in its contrast with his father's sombre pilgrimage to France and Belgium over a decade before. Some veterans even complained about the monarch's behaviour, one Australian ex-serviceman describing it as 'a bit thick, his taking that woman with him to Gallipoli'.[215] According to

Fig. 42   Image of Edward VIII's visit to Gallipoli from *The Sphere*, 19 September 1936, p. 456 , Mary Picture Library, 13156681

a letter from Alfred Duff Cooper, Minister for War, to the IWGC, the king's war-graves visit was the 'only official ceremony' that he took part in 'during his holiday'.[216] The new king's different approach to war commemoration was clear from the newspaper headlines: although some referred to Edward's Gallipoli visit as 'The King's Pilgrimage' in an echo of his father's visit to France and Belgium, many mentioned the holiday dimension: 'Tour of Turkish Defences of Dardanelles: Day Spent in Sightseeing'; 'The King's Holiday Talks'; 'The King in Gallipoli: Holiday to End in 12 Days'.[217] *The*

Sphere covered the war-graves visit in a round-up entitled 'Royal Holiday: The Diary of King Edward's Historic Journey on Land and Sea', referring positively to cheers for the king in countries that were '"enemy countries" during the great war', and to 'what a holiday! But then, what a monarch!', captioning its photograph 'A Day at Gallipoli'.[218]

The IWGC and Fabian Ware were largely marginalised in the organisation of the visit, and the planning was last minute. Fabian Ware struggled to get information from the Palace regarding the king's itinerary. Ever dutiful to protect the monarchy's image, however, it was Ware who after the visit sent in a draft letter that Edward VIII might like to release to the press, expressing suitably diplomatic tones of praise about the care taken of the graves, special mention of the empire war dead, thanks to the Turkish government and reassurance in general to the war bereaved.[219]

Clearly Edward had a more cavalier style than his parents in his performance of war commemoration. Edward's personal focus by the 1930s, however, was far less on war commemoration and more on practical forms of intervention – help for hard-up ex-servicemen and international reconciliation. Like many war veterans, he perceived his role as a mission to use his veteran status to prevent any future war and to use the monarchy to preserve peace in Europe. Clearly there was some self-interest in this role too. The enormous demands and new risks to the monarchy's future stability that his father had faced as a king during the First World War, a conflict that toppled multiple European dynasties, was a fate Edward wished to avoid. Even after his abdication, his commitment to this work remained profound: in the BBC archives there is a recording of an appeal for European peace which Edward made as Duke of Windsor from the Verdun battlefield on 8 May 1939. Given the sensitive political context, the recording was never broadcast in the United Kingdom, although it did air in the United States. In it, Edward refers directly to what he saw as his role in preventing another European war and his personal experience of the horrors of the First World War:

> [. . .] as I talk to you from this historic place, I am deeply conscious of the presence of the great company of the dead and I am convinced that could they make their voices heard they would be with me in what I am about to say. For two and a half years I have deliberately kept outside of public affairs and I still propose to do so. I speak for no one but myself without the previous knowledge of any government. I speak simply as a soldier of the last war whose most earnest prayer it is that such cruel and destructive madness shall never again overtake mankind.[220]

It is striking how the ex-king still sought to channel the will of the war dead to bolster his own war-veteran status and political narrative. But it is not a language of monarchism, that the war dead had fallen for his father,

George V, and the dynasty he had inherited, and thus he could speak for them; rather it is the language of interwar veterans' associations with their claim to an eternal comradeship, a oneness of mind and soul, between the veterans and their fallen comrades. It also echoes some of the discourse about the mystical 'Front Generation' of European fascism. Edward called upon statesmen to work together to preserve peace in the name of the dead of the Great War and to this end to work as 'citizens of the world' and not in the pure self-interest of their own states. He remained clearly haunted by what he termed the 'last carnage' – the Great War and the revolutionary chaos it had brought:

> I break my self-imposed silence now only because of the manifest danger that we may all be drawing nearer to a repetition of the grim events which happened a quarter of a century ago. [...] You and I know that peace is a matter far too vital to our happiness to be treated as a political question. We also know that in modern warfare victory will lie only with the powers of evil. Anarchy and chaos are the inevitable results with consequent misery for us all. [...] there is no land whose people want war. This I believe to be as true of the German nation as of the British nation to which I belong.[221]

It was an extraordinary intervention by the ex-king – a last-minute appeal for peace with a speech which effectively placed pacifism above national or dynastic loyalty. In this last appeal, Edward again highlighted his veteran mentality, mirroring the views of many of the European pacifist veterans' movements of the interwar period and the degree to which the war had marked him.

6.6   Conclusion

The honour culture of 1914, with its active political and social dimensions to kingship, had dramatically evolved by the early 1920s. In the wake of total war, the monarchy, as with other parts of British society, would relegate ideas of honour to a more restricted symbolic realm. Kingship was now defined around service, a rhetoric of a monarchy based upon democratic consent and equality and sacralised through the king honouring the war dead. Rather than being the pinnacle of honour in a hierarchical honour culture, the monarch now humbly venerated and honoured his fallen troops. Yet the idea of honour had not completely vanished. It was referenced on the graves of the war dead by individual families and on collective war memorials. It also continued to have a moral meaning, illustrated clearly by the opprobrium faced by Lloyd George when he was found to be involved in the sale of honours for vast sums to finance his political party.[222] King George V wrote to the Prime Minister in 1922 of his 'profound concern' and of 'evident signs of growing public dissatisfaction' at too many honours being given and noting the need for greater checks so they were not given to unsuitable people 'in order to protect the Crown and the Government'.[223] There was anger at the honours system – which remained closely intertwined with the monarchy – being marketised in this way, suggesting that the idea of the honour system becoming corrupt was not accepted and that, rather than being redundant in a post-war era of modernisation, it was still regarded as important enough to defend.[224] An Act to prevent the abuse of the honour system was introduced in 1925 in response to the scandal.

Few in 1918, however, would consider 'honour' as important a factor in international relations as it had been in the July Crisis in 1914. In the political sphere honour culture exited the war greatly diminished; in the social and symbolic sphere it emerged redefined. However, through this shift, the monarchy would ultimately flourish. By sacralising the glorified war dead, the monarchy also sacralised its own role and image. The key way in which informal monarchical power thus remained very potent in interwar Britain was through the monarchy's new role in commemorating total war – and its main achievement – helping society deal with mass bereavement and reframe the war not in terms of bombastic victory but of grief, which better fitted the public mood. Kingship was also now about channelling public mourning in democratic ways – honouring the most lowly soldier as much as a fallen general, something the monarchy recognised very early during the war itself. Other aspects of kingly wartime leadership, such as George V's political influence in the selection of generals during the conflict, were quickly forgotten in its aftermath, supplanted by this honouring the war dead and bereaved kingship function.[225] Likewise forgotten was the role of the king in promoting war recruitment prior to the introduction of conscription in 1916. It was as if, by paying the dead their due honour, the king offset some of what he owed them for dying for him. The royals became custodians of remembrance rites and, in standing in for the war bereaved of the nation and empire, they became themselves symbolically associated with the war bereaved, not the war belligerent, something which enhanced the royal image. In subordinating himself to his own war dead, moreover, the king acknowledged the changed landscape of 1918: the British experience mirrored that all across Europe where, in the aftermath of the war, the combatant war dead became the dominant heroes of society, trumping pre-war class distinctions. Glorified above all other groups, the combatant dead were sacralised to the extent that the king himself bowed before them. By honouring them, the monarchy re-balanced the equation, ensuring it retained a sacralised social and cultural function, which in part offset its reduction of political power under the Lloyd George premiership. However, this role in war mourning took its toll on the king. In 1935, with European political tensions rising again, he shocked Lloyd George with a 'most extraordinary outburst', when the monarch 'fired up and broke out vehemently, "And I *will* not have another war. I *will not*. The last war was none of my doing, & if there is another one & we are threatened with being brought in to it, I will go to Trafalgar Square and wave a red flag myself sooner than allow this country to be brought in."' Even if it cost the monarchy, George V could not face reliving his Great War role.[226]

~

Conclusion

This book set out with several aims. It sought to show the extent to which the British monarchy and British monarchism mattered during the First World War. Monarchism was not unimportant or mere rhetoric; the monarch was not a token figurehead. In fact, it was one of the central British belief systems of the age. More broadly, throughout Europe and its empires monarchism, like socialism or communism or liberalism, was a significant ideology in the public sphere. This book has also aimed to contextualise monarchism as a historically contingent phenomenon, manifesting in different ways in specific historical moments. First World War monarchism, it has shown, merits being assessed not only as a political framework but also as a distinct belief system which existed during the war period and its aftermath. Later twentieth-century manifestations of monarchism must similarly be explored on their own terms: monarchism is not a universal, unchanging concept but a phenomenon particular to its historical circumstances.

This book has also aimed to nuance the existing historiographical consensus that the First World War saw the significant modernisation of the British monarchy. Some modernisation certainly occurred, but it went hand in hand with the deep-seated sacralisation of the monarchy, often through inventing or reviving traditional, even archaic, discourses and practices during and after the war. This occurred to a far greater degree than has previously been recognised. The modernisation of the British monarchy during the Great War can only be fully understood when this sacralisation dimension is included in the analysis, and the idea of any straightforward linear modernisation trajectory in the historiography needs to be problematised more. The honour culture of 1914 did not disappear due to the war. Rather, it evolved into honouring the war dead, honouring the war wounded and honouring the war worker, with the king and the monarchy placed at the heart of this process, as the embodiment of British honour, a continuity with the pre-war period, and as the central figures in commemoration. Honour culture *was* significantly changed by the war, but it also fed into wartime and post-war sacralisation processes which sustained the monarchy. It was transformed and incorporated into the values of duty, sacrifice and service that the monarchy now presented itself as embodying by the end of the conflict.

Although they were politically less important after the war, honour belief systems still retained significant cultural relevance in Britain, especially in terms of their symbolic functions; honour was a key idea in how the war dead were idealised. In this regard, the wartime transition of ideas about honour appears to have closely reflected that of the monarchy, with which they were so closely intertwined. The relationship between honour and the ideal of kingship was not defunct post-war, as the pressure upon Edward VIII to abdicate in the 1930s would reveal, even if it had evolved, illustrated by the fact that breaking honour codes to find personal happiness – as Edward VIII would do in 1936 – now met with a new degree of popular sympathy. Many politicians after the war also still believed in 'honouring the King', although not in terms of the romantic, unquestioned, often servile manner of 1914, and more in terms of supporting and valuing the monarchy as a bulwark against Bolshevism. George V would continue to play a key political role in the interwar period, particularly in intervening in government formation. Moreover, the war generated an important new sacralised myth of the British monarchy as an exceptional monarchy, different, distinct and untainted in comparison to its Continental European peers in its promotion of democracy and service of the people.

All this suggests that the view that the First World War seriously undermined the British monarchy is largely inaccurate, although this was a fear of some contemporary courtiers, journalists and politicians at the time and the conflict did see a change in discourse which allowed for more criticism of the monarchy. In fact, timelines may need new consideration: the findings of this study suggest that it was the abdication crisis of 1936, following the death of George V, whose personal status had been so greatly enhanced by the war, that was the profound moment of 'de-sacralisation' of the British monarchy, followed by its reduced role during the Second World War and the crisis of decolonisation, which largely removed its imperial function and purpose. This study also suggests that the degree of revolutionary anti-monarchism on the island of Britain during the First World War was quite limited. The high point of radical labour came after the war ended, culminating in the General Strike of 1926, and even then it was not specifically focused on destroying the British monarchy as a priority. This study has analysed the radicalism of Irish republicanism during the Irish revolution of 1912–23, which offers a clear contrast as to what radical anti-monarchism actually consisted of during these years; the British labour movement was not in its league.

This sheds further light on the nature of the British state itself at war. Modernisation in Britain during the conflict was uneven, slow and contested in many spheres – the shift to focus more on the sciences in universities, the need to widen the franchise, the necessity of much greater state intervention in economic planning and production, to list but three examples. The monarchy was a key site of contestation where the struggle between those who advocated radical departures from the status quo and those who resisted change completely or sought to repackage it in older processes and practices became very visible. Some credit for adaptive change is due here to the instincts of George V and Queen Mary, who showed empathy with war victims and who were prepared to work long hours and relinquish luxury as part of the royal war effort; here we see particularly dramatic contrasts with both the kaiser and the tsar, the two least successful First World War sovereigns. More broadly, the war as a whole greatly consolidated George V and Queen Mary's pre-war experiments in new kinds of ceremonial performance in terms of visits to industrial areas, by introducing a whole range of new initiatives, visits to the troops at the Western Front, visiting and supporting the war wounded and disabled, mass investitures, that together were ultimately used in support of the monarchy's narrative from 1917 that emphasised its democratic credentials. This process went hand in hand with the re-sacralisation of the monarchy and often involved elements of traditional ceremonial or ritual, as seen in troop reviews, investitures, victory and war commemoration events such as the burial of the Unknown Soldier. If Bagehot emphasised the monarchy's 'dignified' part of the British constitution, focusing on its utility in rational terms, this book has shown the power of the 'sacred' element, a key component of all authority but particularly monarchical systems, and how the experience of 'total war', with its mass mobilisation and death, made this more prominent, not less. In Britain and the empire, partly because of victory, partly because of a political system in which visible decision-making power lay elsewhere, the monarchy was able to reinvent the sacred dimension and use it to democratise itself, thereby renewing its relevance and importance for a new age of popular sovereignty. We do not see the same process or outcome in other countries, such as Russia, Italy, Germany or, indeed, the Irish Free State. In these cases, what Max Weber in 1919 called 'charismatic power' was reinvested differently, in new forms of sovereignty – communism, fascism and nationalism.

The monarchy showed a real aptitude for mastering the new kinds of mass media available during the war – the tabloid press, with its emphasis on human interest journalism, news reels, documentary film, such as 'The King Visits His Armies in the Great Advance' – to project this mixture of innovation and sacralisation. In 1918, the position of Palace Press Secretary was created for the first time. In the immediate war aftermath the royal wedding was reinvented as a mass national public spectacle when, in 1919, Princess Patricia of Connaught became the first member of the royal family to wed in Westminster Abbey in over five centuries; her nuptials were closely followed by similar pageantry for those of Princess Mary to Henry Lascelles in 1922 and Prince Albert to Elizabeth Bowes-Lyon in 1923, blending traditional imagery and modern media approaches to monarchical display.[1] Royal advisors like the Archbishop of Canterbury rapidly realised the popularity and potential of more public royal weddings for bolstering and sacralising monarchism.[2] The media used were modern, in other words, but the message was often a much older one about collective cultural beliefs in royal leadership and its aura, and the reshaping and promotion of their continued relevance. Frank Mort has pointed to the war as bringing 'a partial desacralization of sovereignty, whereby royalty was brought closer to the lives of ordinary people'.[3] In fact, new forms of deferential sacralisation often underpinned such personal wartime encounters. Overall, the monarchy during the First World War proved remarkably successful at responding to the crisis of 'total war' by fusing older and more modern cultural narratives and processes, and the evidence suggests it remained very popular despite the strains the conflict placed on society.

The monarchy's own wartime image reinventions – designed and implemented by royals, courtiers and advisors – helped it get through the European revolutionary era of 1916–23, as did the extent of British monarchist cultural belief systems in society. Victory mattered too, of course. Monarchies in defeated powers faced far greater strains and were much more likely to be overthrown. But the Second World War shows us that military defeat alone does not necessarily create anti-monarchism – the Netherlands and Belgium in 1940 prove a case in point. The relative economic stability of Britain during the First World War was certainly a factor in limiting anti-monarchist radicalism. But the huge cost of the conflict in lives, and the food shortages of 1917, were structural stressors for the state. Moreover, the United Kingdom did not emerge from the war a total victor: the violent secession of twenty-six Irish counties meant it was a truncated UK that entered the interwar period. Yet the British monarchy – and popular cultural monarchism – remained robust, and the ways that the monarchy successfully blended modernisation and sacralisation processes was a significant factor in this. In particular, its projection of Britain's monarchy as a democratic and exceptional, indigenous, unique form of monarchism, separate and different to other European monarchies, was highly effective and durable.

This projection of British monarchical exceptionalism also effectively supplanted the memory of the monarchy's role in recruitment for war in 1914–16, which was rapidly forgotten. The monarchy thus largely escaped the British opprobrium of the 1930s disenchantment with the First World War and its erstwhile politicians and propagandists, and the 1960s anger towards its generals and recruiters. In part, this was also because for later generations it was hard to conceptualise the cultural power of monarchism in 1914 – that it had once had the strength to help raise an army. Later depictions also very fairly recognised that once Britain was at war, George V was constitutionally bound to publicly support the war effort; however, this meant that his private political influence and the degree of agency that he did have has been neglected. As later monarchs faced far fewer constitutional crises, the powers he had exercised also became less visible in any case. This historical amnesia was facilitated by the monarchy's own selective projection of its Great War role, which emphasised democratisation and commemoration.

Well might we ask why all this proved to be the case. Why was the British monarchy so successful at consolidating a role as representing 'Britishness' at war, when it was in fact of German dynastic origin? How did the idea of the British monarchy's 'democratic' monarchical exceptionalism prove so potent when, in fact, it was a myth? After all, there were actually many similarities between the 'exceptional' British monarchy and its Continental peers. The Belgian and Italian wartime monarchies followed many of the same strategies as the wartime British one, visiting troops at the front, eschewing luxury, supporting the wounded, mourning the war dead, resulting in similar degrees of popularity.

To answer these two questions provides us with important insights for our understanding of the monarchy. Myths succeed best where they address a social function. War sacralisation processes – the romanticisation of the monarchy's English roots in the first years of the conflict, in particular – helped to assimilate it and obscure its German heritage at a point where the population of the island of Britain was frightened by the outbreak of war and the collapse of long stable Continental locations into warzones. Emphasising cosy narratives of indigenous royal identity was reassuring in a shocking and disorientating historic period of war upheaval: indeed, such narratives often directly mimicked comforting childhood tales of good royals, of wise leaders in control, of national destiny in secure, divinely ordained and timeless royal safekeeping. Moreover, in the decade up to 1914, the German dynastic origins of the royal family had usually been portrayed in terms of assimilation in Britain's favour: Queen Victoria depicted as a British mother who had wed and propagated *her* bloodline into Continental European dynasties. The hierarchy here was of the British monarchy absorbing foreigners into its line, both at home and abroad, rather than the other way around. The very fact that Victoria's German husband remained Prince Consort and never became king only enhanced this idea. It is not hard to see how, during a war with Germany, in an era when there were common beliefs about heredity shaping behaviour, the notion that the royal family's mixed ancestry displayed the strength of British blood over German, with George V emerging as the epitome of Britishness, might be reassuring and credible. If the royals themselves could vanquish their German connections, if their British blood ancestry could assimilate their German, so too would the realm overcome Germany. This context perhaps helps explain the way that the Windsor name change worked so smoothly.

This narrative of Britishness's success as an assimilatory force also reflected a broader imperial need. Britishness in this period might be best defined as 'pan-Britishness' – an identity which was largely defined by being a royal subject, not a classic nationalism, and which connected people from Canada to Scotland, India to Gibraltar. Unlike most Continental European national-isms, which in 1914–18 were focused upon a close connection to the soil of the *Patrie*, Britishness was not territorially defined in this way – it was not neces-sary to have ever lived in Britain to be British; it was thus always more fluid and needed to be depicted and understood as assimilatory, both of newly con-quered peoples and of third- and fourth-generation descendents of white British settlers. Moreover, while being of white British descent mattered and brought specific racial privileges and status throughout the empire, this was underpinned by racialised concerns that intermixing with other populations – be they white immigrant settlers from other parts of Europe or indigenous locals – might weaken this British racial 'stock' component of the empire's population. Again, this suggests that wartime myths that reinforced the strength of British bloodlines of descent, such as the monarchy's assimilation of its Germanness, had a broad societal and imperial function. The monarchy's increasing sacralisation through its greater emphasis on its role as the lynchpin of empire by the end of the war, in other words, corresponded with the empire's increasing need for the monarchy's identity symbolism.

The wartime monarchy's power to model various versions of both cultural and biological assimilatory 'Britishness' was thus metaphorically valuable at multiple levels. The British monarchy's success in representing 'Britishness' was therefore, in part, due to the success of Britishness itself – as a globalised identity, which was to be found across the span of the empire, and which needed the monarchy to serve as the key cultural motif that it could use to define itself. There was nothing that could replace it in this role in 1914–18, and portraying the royals as Germans was only likely to undermine the unity of the war effort and of the empire as a whole, aims which did not find much home front support. Resources mattered too: while Britain did see strikes, war-weariness and food shortages, these were largely limited and short-term phenomena compared to their equivalents elsewhere, in Russia and the Central Powers, for example, and never coalesced around anti-monarchism. Britain's war consensus thus never came under dangerous levels of social and economic strain, and this, in turn, allowed its monarchist consensus and myths, which helped bolster wartime unity, to continue.

The myth built around the British monarchy's democratic exceptionalism also served a valuable social and political function. While the British monarchy was not exceptional, in many ways British society was. By the late nineteenth century, Britain already lacked a strong peasant class, which was integral to sustaining monarchy in some Continental countries, necessitating its mon-archy to find new power bases in urban working classes much earlier than its Continental peers. With Britain's history of early industrialisation, urbanisa-tion, comparatively faster urban secularisation and imperial overseas emigra-tion, its monarchy was left, by 1914, as the most widespread, enduring common element of cultural identity based on older belief systems to still

survive, as other forms of folk belief, practices and traditions rapidly disappeared and religious identities remained denominationally divided. However,
British monarchism still needed to find new ways to sacralise the institution
that fitted with the modern, urban literate world and thereby renew it into the
future, as its behaviour during the First World War shows. The monarchy was
also central to the political functioning of the state – a system that, with its
reformist approach to the labour question, offered a way to avoid the upheavals
of class antagonism appearing elsewhere with the rise of socialism. Politicians
from all classes believed they could benefit from the current British state
structure, and it was in their interest, as a result, not to stir up anti-
monarchist sentiment. The monarchy itself helped this process by so actively
promoting its own image as a monarchy that cared about Labour issues. It is
impossible to underestimate the degree to which the monarchy's engagement
with Labour mattered – in reducing bourgeois fears of Labour leaders in
particular, but also in perpetuating pre-war working-class monarchism. All
this reduced the attractions of red Bolshevik revolution and, by promoting
a narrative of a loyal working class, also of white counter-revolution. Here too
the myth of the British monarchy as exceptional and 'democratic' fulfilled an
important centrist stabilising social and political function and was used to
communicate to British society a belief in its own virtuous tolerance and
stability. It proved successful and enduring. Similarly, the way the war embedded a narrative that the monarchy must serve the people, be hard-working and
make sacrifices to recompense the people for the war sacrifices that they had
made in its name would later help shape the values of the twentieth-century
reigns of George VI and Queen Elizabeth II.

Ultimately, the British monarchy's First World War success becomes particularly visible if we look at how it helped to shape the monarchy's image at
the outbreak of the Second World War. With King George VI only recently
crowned and amidst genuine concerns about his popularity, courtiers and
press alike emphasised the royal role in commemorating the Great War as
a way of emphasising the value of the monarchy.[4] Nothing could make clearer
that 1914–18 was seen as a period when the monarchy had performed well.
When Queen Elizabeth made her first broadcast on 11 November 1939, it took
place on Armistice Day, 'drawing on the powerful emotions associated with
the memory of the First World War' and the popular memory of George V and
Queen Mary's successes in responding to it.[5] The broadcast was also recorded
by a newsreel cameraman, and the subsequent film shown by Pathé Gazette
interspersed film of Queen Elizabeth with footage of 'the monarchs' observance of Armistice Day at the cenotaph' and of 'nurses and the women's
auxiliary forces on parade as part of the Armistice procession'.[6] Yet this was
to be a starkly different war for the monarchy. Its symbolic role, while still
important, was less visible than in 1914–18 and only mythologised largely after
the conflict. The Second World War saw the 'sidelining of the monarchy', its

status and influence reduced.[7] During 1939–45, the royals were far less visible in the wartime press in comparison to 1914–18. As one man noted to Mass Observation: 'before the war, what royalty did was the only news we got – now all the news is war news so we don't hear much about them'.[8] By the end of the war only 8 per cent of Mass Observation diarists were listening to George VI's broadcasts, while nearly all listened to Winston Churchill's.[9] The contrast between the balance of power in the public depiction of the wartime relationship between George V and his prime ministers, Asquith or Lloyd George, and that between George VI and Winston Churchill, is clear. Churchill was the dominant leadership figure of the 1939–45 wartime state, often keeping government secrets from the king.[10] In 1914–18, in comparison, Asquith's popularity was never at risk of overshadowing George V, while both monarch and Palace alike tried to counter Lloyd George's popularity overshadowing the king – as well as the former's attempts to reduce royal political influence – with a considerable degree of success. Kitchener's premature death also removed the risk of him overshadowing the monarch. Ironically, while Second World War historiography and collective memory has paid more attention to the question of the monarchy's role in the war effort, it was never as successful, or dominant, as its role in the previous 1914–18 conflict. Perhaps here we see the longer-term impact of the damage the abdication did to the legacy of wartime monarchist sacralisation processes or the effects of Second World War social change: the abdication crisis in many ways marked the end of the British monarchy's 'long' First World War. But these are questions for others to explore. It is hoped that by analysing the monarchy and the First World War this book has helped to pave their way.

NOTES

Introduction

1. The first non-academic history was published only in 2018: Alexandra Churchill, *In the Eye of the Storm: George V at War* (Warwick, 2018).
2. For examples of the 'long nineteenth century' approach: William M. Kuhn, *Democratic Royalism: The Transformation of the British Monarchy, 1861-1914* (London, 1996); Roderick McLean, *Royalty and Diplomacy in Europe, 1890-1914* (Cambridge, 2000).
3. David Cannadine, 'The Context, Performance and Meaning of Ritual: The British Monarchy and the "Invention of Tradition", c.1820-1977' in Eric Hobsbawm and Terence Ranger, eds., *The Invention of Tradition* (Cambridge, 1983), pp. 101–64.
4. See for example Antony Taylor, *'Down with the Crown': British Anti-Monarchism and Debates about Royalty since 1790* (London, 1999), which has no chapter on the war but rather a chapter on 1911–19; Frank Prochaska, *The Republic of Britain, 1760-2000* (London, 2000); Mark Hayman, 'Labour and the Monarchy: Patriotism and Republicanism during the Great War', *Journal of First World War Studies*, 5, 2 (2014), 163–79; Matthew Glencross, 'George V and the New Royal House' in Matthew Glencross, Judith Rowbotham and Michael Kandiah, eds., *The Windsor Dynasty, 1910 to the Present: 'Long to Reign over Us?'* (London, 2016), pp. 33–56.
5. Frank Prochaska, 'George V and Republicanism 1917-1919', *Twentieth Century British History*, 10, 1 (1999), 27–51; Prochaska, *The Republic of Britain*.
6. Frank Prochaska, 'The Crowned Republic and the Rise of the Welfare Monarchy' in Frank-Lothar Kroll and Dieter J. Weiß, eds., *Inszenierung oder Legitimation? / Monarchy and the Art of Representation: die Monarchie in Europa im 19. und 20. Jahrhundert. Ein deutsch-englischer Vergleich* (Berlin, 2015), pp. 141–50.
7. Frank Prochaska, *Royal Bounty: The Making of a Welfare Monarchy* (New Haven, 1995); Prochaska, 'George V and Republicanism'.
8. Frank Mort, 'Safe for Democracy: Constitutional Politics, Popular Spectacle, and the British Monarchy 1910-1914', *Journal of British Studies*, 58, 1 (2019), 110.
9. Edward Owens, *The Family Firm: Monarchy, Mass Media and the British Public, 1932-53* (London, 2019); Vernon Bogdanor, *The Monarchy and the Constitution* (Oxford, 1995) p. 34; Vernon Bogdanor, *The British Constitution in the Twentieth Century* (Oxford, 2003).
10. The term 'total war' has been the subject of considerable historiographical debate, and definitions vary. This book uses the term to describe the unprecedented mobilisation of British state and society, while acknowledging that 'totalisation

processes' – the ways that the conflict became ever more all-consuming for states, societies and economies – in the First World War were never complete. For an excellent summary of the debates on terms, see Roger Chickering and Stig Förster, eds., *Great War, Total War: Combat and Mobilization on the Western Front, 1914–1918* (Cambridge, 2000).

11. Prochaska, *Royal Bounty*; Prochaska, 'George V and Republicanism'; Frank Mort, 'On Tour with the Prince: Monarchy, Imperial Politics and Publicity in the Prince of Wales's Dominion Tours 1919–20', *Twentieth Century British History*, 29, 1 (2018), 25–57; Philip Williamson, 'The Monarchy and Public Values, 1910–1953' in Andrzej Olechnowicz, ed., *The Monarchy and the British Nation, 1780 to the Present* (Cambridge, 2007), pp. 223–57; Cannadine, 'The Context, Performance and Meaning of Ritual'.

12. Matthew Glencross, 'A Cause of Tension? The Leadership of King George V: Visiting the Western Front' and Judith Rowbotham, '"How to Be Useful in War Time": Queen Mary's Leadership in the War Effort, 1914–1918', both in Matthew Glencross and Judith Rowbotham, eds., *Monarchies and the Great War* (London, 2018), pp. 153–89, 191–223.

13. Churchill, *In the Eye of the Storm*. Churchill's book includes material in the Royal Archives such as letters between members of the royal family that have not been seen by researchers previously.

14. As rare examples of a cultural history approach to studying the monarchy in the Great War, see two chapters by the present author: Heather Jones, 'A Prince in the Trenches? Edward VIII and the First World War' in Heidi Merkhens and Frank Lorenz Müller, eds., *Sons and Heirs: Succession and Political Culture in 19th Century Europe* (London, 2015), pp. 229–46 and Heather Jones, 'The Nature of Kingship in First World War Britain' in Glencross, Rowbotham and Kandiah, eds., *The Windsor Dynasty*, pp. 195–216. See also Hayman, 'Labour and the Monarchy'.

15. Frank Mort, 'Accessible Sovereignty: Popular Attitudes to British Royalty during the Great War', *Social History*, 45, 3 (2020), 330.

16. Ibid., 329, 330.

17. Ibid., 329.

18. Andrzej Olechnowicz, 'Historians and the Modern British Monarchy, 1780 to the Present' in Olechnowicz, ed., *The Monarchy and the British Nation*, p. 27.

19. Benedict Anderson, *Imagined Communities: Reflections on the Origin and Spread of Nationalism* (London, 2006).

20. See Jay Winter's work on how the war led to a resurgence in religious art motifs: Jay Winter, *Sites of Memory, Sites of Mourning: The Great War in European Cultural History* (Cambridge, 1995); on how the war provoked romanticism: Samuel Hynes, *A War Imagined: The First World War and English Culture* (London, 1992).

21. Mort, 'Accessible Sovereignty', 329.

22. Prochaska, *Royal Bounty*; Prochaska, 'George V and Republicanism'.

23. On Ireland and the British monarchy, see James Loughlin, *The British Monarchy and Ireland: 1800 to the Present* (Cambridge, 2007); Mary Kenny, *Crown and Shamrock: Love and Hate between Ireland and the British Monarchy* (Dublin, 2009).

24. Owens, *The Family Firm*, p. 2. The Great War had a similar effect on the Belgian monarchy, re-sacralising the royal image, according to Maarten Van

Ginderachter, 'Public Transcripts of Royalism: Pauper Letters to the Belgian Royal Family (1880–1940)' in Gita Deneckere and Joeren Deploige, eds., *Mystifying the Monarch: Studies on Discourse, Power and History* (Amsterdam, 2006), p. 234.

25. Philip Murphy, *Monarchy and the End of Empire: The House of Windsor, the British Government and the Postwar Commonwealth* (Oxford, 2015), p. 3.

26. Winter, *Sites of Memory, Sites of Mourning*.

27. One exception is Ian Beckett, who has written a valuable chapter on King George V's relationship with First World War generals: Ian Beckett, 'George V and His Generals' in Matthew Hughes and Matthew Seligmann, eds., *Leadership in Conflict: 1914–1918* (London, 2000), pp. 247–64.

28. On social historians' reluctance to study the aristocracy for a long period, see Ludmilla Jordanova, *History in Practice* (London, 2016), p. 148. For a superb analysis of First World War cultural history, see John Horne, 'End of a Paradigm? The Cultural History of the Great War', *Past and Present*, 242 (2019), 155–92.

29. For example, several studies that have inspired this research do not cover the monarchy in any detail: Adrian Gregory's outstanding *The Last Great War: British Society and the First World War* (Cambridge, 2008) barely discusses the monarchy. Jay Winter, ed., *The Cambridge History of the First World War*, 3 vols (Cambridge, 2014), the best recent overall history of the conflict, does not have a single chapter specifically on monarchy, although it is mentioned in its chapter on civil–military relations. Catriona Pennell's excellent study *A Kingdom United? Popular Responses to the Outbreak of the First World War in Britain and Ireland* (Oxford, 2012) assesses the attitude towards war of the crowds who gathered at Buckingham Palace in 1914 but not monarchism. Thomas Otte's *July Crisis: The World's Descent into War, Summer 1914* (New York, Cambridge, 2014) largely neglects the British monarchy's role.

30. David Cannadine, 'From Biography to History: Writing the Modern British Monarchy', *Historical Research*, 77, 197 (2004), 299–300.

31. On the generals, see Gary Sheffield, *Douglas Haig: From the Somme to Victory* (London, 2016); also Gary Sheffield, *The Chief: Douglas Haig and the British Army* (London, 2012); Elizabeth Greenhalgh, *Foch in Command: The Forging of a First World War General* (Cambridge, 2011); on the historiographical debate on generals, see Heather Jones, 'As the Centenary Approaches: The Regeneration of First World War Historiography', *Historical Journal*, 56, 3 (2013), 857–78.

32. It is not possible to list all the works on German royals in the First World War here, as they are too numerous. However, a leading selection includes: Isabel V. Hull, *The Entourage of Kaiser Wilhelm II: 1888–1918* (Cambridge, 1982); John Röhl, *Wilhelm II: Into the Abyss of War and Exile, 1900–1941*, transl. Sheila de Bellaigue and Roy Porter (Cambridge, 2015); Jonathan Boff, *Haig's Enemy: Crown Prince Rupprecht and Germany's War on the Western Front* (Oxford, 2017); Katharine Lerman, 'Wilhelm's War: A Hohenzollern in Conflict, 1914–1918' in Müller and Mehrkens, eds., *Sons and Heirs*, pp. 247–62; Holger Afflerbach, 'Wilhelm II as Supreme Warlord in the First World War', *War in History*, 5, 4 (1998), 427–49; Annika Mombauer and Wilhelm Deist, eds., *The Kaiser: New Research on Wilhelm II's Role in Imperial Germany* (Cambridge, 2004); Arne Hofmann, *'Wir sind das alte Deutschland, Das Deutschland wie es war ... ': Der 'Bund der Aufrechten' und der Monarchismus in der Weimarer Republik* (Berlin, 1998); Stefan März, *Das Haus Wittelsbach im Ersten Weltkrieg: Chance und Zusammenbruch monarchischer Herrschaft* (Regensburg, 2013).

33. For examples of the long tradition of writers rather than academic historians producing biographies of British royals, see Harold Nicolson, *King George the Fifth: His Life and Reign* (London, 1952); James Pope-Hennessy, *Queen Mary, 1867–1953* (London, 1959); Kenneth Rose, *King George V* (London, 1983); Philip Ziegler, *King Edward VIII: The Official Biography* (London, 1990); Anne Edwards, *Matriarch: Queen Mary and the House of Windsor* (London, 1984); Sarah Bradford, *King George VI: The Dutiful King* (London, 1989). On King George V's image, see Nicolson, *King George the Fifth*; Harold Nicolson, *Harold Nicolson: Diaries and Letters 1930–1964*, ed. Stanley Olsen (London, 1980) and Rose, *King George V*, all of which portray King George as a mediocre personality and downplay the importance of his war work.

34. www.royal.uk/archives, accessed 4/12/2019.

35. British Library (hereafter BL), Add MSS 46722 1890–1918, Boyd-Carpenter Papers, Vol. 6 (ff. 74), unpublished letters from and on behalf of members of the English Royal Family, 1890–1918, Stamfordham to Mr Boyd Carpenter, 7/1/1919, f. 42.

36. Note in Baldwin Papers supplementary catalogue, Cambridge University Library (hereafter CUL), 229–33.X; see also https://discovery.nationalarchives.gov.uk/details/r/f9f9480d-ce81-49ca-8750-e22aab706826, accessed 4/12/2019. Owens, *The Family Firm*, p. 203.

37. For example, the Dutch Royal Archives fall under the management of the royal household: www.royal-house.nl/topics/royal-archives, accessed 4/12/2019. By contrast, the Belgian Royal Archives at the Palais Royal in Brussels are a section of the state archives of Belgium: www.arch.be/index.php?l=en&m=about-the-institution&r=presentation&sr=organisation-chart, accessed 4/12/2019.

38. For a more detailed discussion of these issues regarding the Royal Archives, see Owens, *The Family Firm*, p. 24.

39. Owens, *The Family Firm*, p. 202.

40. On the neglect of the twentieth-century monarchy by academic historians, see Olechnowicz, 'Historians and the Modern British Monarchy', p. 6. For examples of pioneering new studies: Owens, *The Family Firm*; Murphy, *Monarchy and the End of Empire*; Frank Mort, 'Love in a Cold Climate: Letters, Public Opinion and Monarchy in the 1936 Abdication Crisis', *Twentieth Century British History*, 25, 1 (2014), 30–62.

41. Beckett, 'George V and His Generals', p. 260.

42. The historiography of European monarchy has recently undergone a revival, although the First World War period remains largely neglected. See Johannes Paulmann, 'Searching for a "Royal International": The Mechanics of Monarchical Relations in Nineteenth-Century Europe' in Martin Geyer and Johannes Paulmann, eds., *The Mechanics of Internationalism: Culture, Society and Politics from the 1840s to the First World War* (Oxford, 2001), pp. 145–76; Johannes Paulmann, '"Dearest Nicky": Monarchical Relations between Prussia, the German Empire and Russia during the Nineteenth Century' in Roger Bartlett and Karen Schönwälder, eds., *The German Lands and Eastern Europe: Essays on the History of Their Social, Cultural and Political Relations* (London, 1999), pp. 157–81; Merkhens and Müller, eds., *Sons and Heirs*; Johannes Paulmann, *Pomp und Politik: Monarchenbegegnungen in Europa zwischen Ancien Régime und Erstem Weltkrieg* (Paderborn, 2000); Dieter Langewiesche, *Die Monarchie im Jahrhundert Europas: Selbstbehauptung durch Wandel im 19. Jahrhundert*

(Heidelberg, 2013); McLean, *Royalty and Diplomacy in Europe*; Alexis Schwarzenbach, *Königliche Träume: Eine Kulturgeschichte der Monarchie, 1789-1997* (Zurich, 2009); Deploige and Deneckere, eds., *Mystifying the Monarch*; Mark Cornwall, 'Treason in an Era of Regime Change: The Case of the Habsburg Monarchy', *Austrian History Yearbook*, 50 (2019), 124–49; Kroll and Weiß, eds., *Inszenierung oder Legitimation?*; Richard S. Wortman, *Scenarios of Power: Myth and Ceremony in Russian Monarchy*, 2 vols (Princeton, 1995-2000).

43. On the kaiser, the most useful texts are John C. G. Röhl, *The Kaiser and His Court: Wilhelm II and the Government of Germany* (Cambridge, 1995); John C. G. Röhl, *Wilhelm II: The Kaiser's Personal Monarchy, 1888-1900* (Cambridge, 2004); John C. G. Röhl, *Wilhelm II: die Jugend des Kaisers, 1859-1888* (Munich, 1993); John C. G. Röhl, *Wilhelm II: der Weg in den Abgrund, 1900-1941* (Munich, 2008), Eng. transl. *Wilhelm II: Into the Abyss*; Lothar Reinermann, *Der Kaiser in England: Wilhelm II. und sein Bild in der britschen Öffentlichkeit* (Paderborn, 2001); Lothar Reinermann, 'Fleet Street and the Kaiser: British Public Opinion and Wilhelm II', *German History*, 26, 4 (2008), 469–85; Jost Rebentisch, *Die vielen Gesichter des Kaisers: Wilhelm II. in der deutschen und britischen Karikatur (1888-1918)* (Berlin, 2000); The German Historical Institute, *Many Faces of the Kaiser: Wilhelm II's Public Image in Britain and Germany* (London, 2002); Christopher Clark, *Kaiser Wilhelm II* (Harlow, 2000); Martin Kohlrausch, 'The Unmanly Emperor: Wilhelm II and the Fragility of the Royal Individual' in Regina Schulte, Pernille Arenfeldt, Martin Kohlrausch and Xenia von Tippelskirch, eds., *The Body of the Queen: Gender and Rule in the Courtly World, 1500-2000* (New York, Oxford, 2006), pp. 254–78; Matthew Stibbe, 'Kaiser Wilhelm II: The Hohenzollerns at War' in Hughes and Seligmann, eds., *Leadership in Conflict: 1914-1918*, pp. 265–83.

44. Ibid.

45. See Viscount Esher, *After the War* (London, 1918); also James Lees-Milne, *The Enigmatic Edwardian: The Life of Reginald, 2nd Viscount Esher* (London, 1986).

46. See Reinermann, 'Fleet Street and the Kaiser', 473.

47. Carl Schmitt, *Political Theology: Four Chapters on the Concept of Sovereignty* (Cambridge, MA, 1985 [1922]); Carl Schmitt, *Constitutional Theory* (Durham, NC, 2008 [1928]).

48. See, for examples, Anna von der Goltz, *Hindenburg: Power, Myth and the Rise of the Nazis* (Oxford, 2009); Robert Gerwarth, *The Bismarck Myth: Weimar Germany and the Legacy of the Iron Chancellor* (Oxford, 2005); Lucy Riall, *Garibaldi: Invention of a Hero* (New Haven, London, 2007); Laurence Van Ypersele, *Le roi Albert: histoire d'un mythe* (Ottignies, 1995); Valentina Villa, 'The Victorious King: The Role of Victor Emmanuel III in the Great War' in Glencross and Rowbotham, eds., *Monarchies in the Great War*, pp. 225–49. On the myth of Victor Emmanuel III as the soldier king, see also Elisa Signori, 'La monarchia italiana e la Grande Guerra: il mito del "re soldato"' in Marina Tesoro, ed., *Monarchia, tradizione, identità nazionale: Germania, Giappone e Italia tra ottocento e novecento* (Milan, 2004), pp. 183–213. Another example of this kind of leadership mythology analysis approach is Birte Förster's work, *Der Königin Luise-Mythos: Mediengeschichte des Idealbilds deutscher 'Weiblichkeit', 1860-1960* (Göttingen, 2011).

49. On religion, see Philip Williamson, 'National Days of Prayer: The Churches, the State and Public Worship in Britain, 1899-1957', *English Historical Review*, 128,

531 (2013), 323–66; Michael Snape, *God and the British Army: Religion and the British Army in the First and Second World Wars* (London, 2005); Alan Wilkinson, *The Church of England and the First World War* (London, 1996). On class, see Ross McKibbin, *Classes and Cultures, England 1918–1951* (Oxford, 2000); Gregory, *The Last Great War*; Bernard Waites, *A Class Society at War, Britain 1914–1918* (Leamington Spa, 1987).

50. Kuhn, *Democratic Royalism*, p. 13.
51. Robert Darnton, *The Great Cat Massacre and Other Episodes in French Cultural History* (London, 1984), p. 5.
52. Roger Chartier, 'Text, Symbols and Frenchness', *The Journal of Modern History*, 57, 4 (1985), 683.
53. David Blackbourn, *Marpingen: Apparitions of the Virgin Mary in Nineteenth Century Germany* (London, 1993).
54. See Lynn Hunt, 'French History in the Last Twenty Years: The Rise and Fall of the Annales Paradigm', *Journal of Contemporary History*, 21, 2 (1986), 209–24.
55. Peter Burke, *What Is Cultural History?* (Cambridge, 2004), p. 3.
56. Hunt, 'French History in the Last Twenty Years', 217. See also the famous *histoire des mentalités* by Emmanuel Le Roy Ladurie, *Montaillou: Cathars and Catholics in a French Village, 1294–1324* (London, 2013 [1978]).
57. Hunt, 'French History in the Last Twenty Years', 217.
58. For an introduction to Koselleck's work, see Reinhart Koselleck, Javiér Fernández Sebastián and Juan Francisco Fuentes, 'Conceptual History, Memory, and Identity: An Interview with Reinhart Koselleck', *Contributions to the History of Concepts*, 2, 1 (March, 2006), 99–127.
59. Daniela Saxer in 'Forum: History of Emotions', *German History*, 28, 1 (2010), 67–80, 69.
60. Andrzej Olechnowicz, 'Introduction' in Olechnowicz, ed., *The Monarchy and the British Nation*, p. 2.
61. BL, MS EUR F143/64, Papers of Sir Walter Lawrence, Letter from Clive Wigram to Walter Lawrence, 3/7/1915, f. 21.
62. Reinermann, 'Fleet Street and the Kaiser', 471.
63. Ibid.
64. Pennell, *A Kingdom United?*, p. 6.
65. On the idea of 1914 European society as built around certain 'honour' codes, see Ute Frevert, 'Honor, Gender and Power: The Politics of Satisfaction in Pre-War Europe' in Holger Afflerbach and David Stevenson, eds., *An Improbable War? The Outbreak of World War I and European Political Culture before 1914* (New York, Oxford, 2007), pp. 233–55. See also James Joll, *1914: The Unspoken Assumptions* (London, 1968); Avner Offer, 'Going to War in 1914: A Matter of Honour?', *Politics and Society*, 23, 2 (1995), pp. 213–41. For another example of 'honour' discourse, see David Lloyd George, *Honour and Dishonour: A Speech* (London, 1914).
66. Van Ginderachter, 'Public Transcripts of Royalism', p. 223.
67. Ibid., p. 224; James C. Scott cited in ibid., p. 226.
68. James C. Scott cited in ibid., p. 226.
69. Andrzej Olechnowicz, '"A Jealous Hatred": Royal Popularity and Social Inequality' in Olechnowicz, ed., *The Monarchy and the British Nation*, p. 284.
70. James C. Scott cited in Van Ginderachter, 'Public Transcripts of Royalism', p. 224. Maarten Van Ginderachter adopts this approach in his reading of letters from the public sent to the Belgian royal family.

71. Ibid.
72. Nicolson, *King George the Fifth*, pp. 254–5.
73. Lambeth Palace Library, (hereafter LPL), Papers of Dr Randall T. Davidson, Archbishop of Canterbury, private papers, Vol. 13, f. 314, Memorandum of trip to Windsor, 12/5/1918.
74. Mary Fulbrook and Ulinka Rublack, 'In Relation: The "Social Self" and Ego-Documents', *German History*, 28, 3 (2010), 263–72.
75. Hunt, 'French History in the Last Twenty Years'.
76. Michel Foucault, *Discipline and Punish: The Birth of the Prison* (London, 2019 [1977]).
77. Jeroen Deploige and Gita Deneckere, 'Introduction. The Monarchy: A Crossroads of Trajectories' in Deploige and Deneckere, eds., *Mystifying the Monarch*, p. 9.
78. Jan Rüger, *The Great Naval Game: Britain and Germany in the Age of Empire* (Cambridge, 2009).
79. Eva Giloi, *Monarchy, Myth, and Material Culture in Germany, 1750-1950* (Cambridge, 2011).
80. Olechnowicz, 'Historians and the Modern British Monarchy', p. 33.
81. Cannadine, 'The Context, Performance and Meaning of Ritual'.
82. Kuhn asserts that royal traditions were 'altered and adjusted [...], they did not invent them' in a process of renovation of the monarchy: Kuhn, *Democratic Royalism*, p. 13.
83. Anthony D. Smith, *Theories of Nationalism* (London, 1971); Anthony D. Smith, *The Ethnic Origins of Nations* (Oxford, 1986); Ernest Gellner, *Nations and Nationalism* (Oxford, 1983); Anderson, *Imagined Communities*.
84. On total war and totalisation, see Chickering and Förster, eds., *Great War, Total War*, pp. 1–16; pp. 35–54.
85. Kuhn, *Democratic Royalism*, pp. 13–14.
86. Ibid., p. 14.
87. Dieter Langewiesche, 'Monarchy-Global: Monarchical Self-Assertion in a Republican World', *Journal of Modern European History*, 15, 2 (2017), 282; see also John Breuilly, 'Max Weber, Charisma and Nationalist Leadership', *Nations and Nationalism*, 17, 3 (2011), pp. 477–99.
88. Langewiesche, 'Monarchy-Global', 283.
89. See Rose, *King George V*; Nicolson, *King George the Fifth*.
90. Mort, 'Safe for Democracy', 110.
91. Ernst Cassirer, *The Myth of the State* (London, 1946), cited in Gerwarth, *The Bismarck Myth*, p. 3.
92. Gerwarth, *The Bismarck Myth*, p. 6. On debates on how to define myth and its sociocultural functions, see Roland Barthes, *Mythologies* (Paris, 1957); Elizabeth M. Baeten, *The Magic Mirror: Myth's Abiding Power* (Albany, NY, 1996); Frank Becker, 'Begriff und Bedeutung des politischen Mythos' in Barbara Stollberg-Rilinger, ed., *Was heißt Kulturgeschichte des Politischen?* (Berlin, 2005), pp. 129–48; Stefan Berger, 'On the Role of Myths and History in the Construction of National Identity in Modern Europe', *European History Quarterly*, 39, 3 (2009), 490–502.
93. Olechnowicz, 'Historians and the Modern British Monarchy', p. 10.
94. Arno Mayer, *The Persistence of the Old Regime: Europe to the Great War* (London, 1981), p. 5.
95. Ibid., pp. 5–6.

96. It is not clear whether any soldier ever did make such an appeal, as the monarchy had delegated its peacetime military prerogative on this to the Commander-in-Chief in the Field. The king did intervene in the case of the court martial sentence of two officers who had received a custodial sentence. See Chapter 1 of this book.

97. LPL, Papers of Dr Randall T. Davidson, Archbishop of Canterbury, official letters, Vol. 195, f. 192, Memorandum by Randall Davidson, n.d.

98. Hans-Ulrich Wehler, *Das deutsche Kaiserreich, 1871–1918* (Göttingen, 1973); Hans-Ulrich Wehler, *Deutsche Gesellschaftsgeschichte*, 5 vols (Munich, 1987–2008).

99. David Blackbourn and Geoff Eley, *The Peculiarities of German History: Bourgeois Society and Politics in Nineteenth-Century Germany* (Oxford, 1984).

100. Tom Nairn, *The Break-Up of Britain: Crisis and Neo-Nationalism* (London, 1977), p. 29; also Tom Nairn, *The Enchanted Glass: Britain and Its Monarchy* (London, 1988); Bernhard Rieger and Martin Daunton, 'Introduction' in Bernhard Rieger and Martin Daunton, eds., *Meanings of Modernity: Britain from the Late Victorian Era to World War II* (Oxford, 2001), pp. 1–2.

101. Rieger and Daunton, 'Introduction', p. 1.

102. As Rieger and Daunton point out, 'there is not one predominant approach to a topic as multifaceted as the study of the semantics of modernity. [. . .] close readings of historical texts must constitute the focus of explorations that illuminate historically specific meanings of modernity. [. . .] at present there is no generally accepted theoretical definition of modernity among scholars.' Rieger and Daunton, 'Introduction', p. 4.

103. Robert Gerwarth, *The Vanquished: Why the First World War Failed to End, 1917–1923* (London, 2016); Robert Gerwarth and Erez Manela, eds., *Empires at War 1911–1923* (Oxford, 2014); Robert Gerwarth and John Horne, eds., *War in Peace: Paramilitary Violence in Europe after the Great War* (Oxford, 2012).

104. See Gerwarth and Manela, eds., *Empires at War*.

105. Murphy, *Monarchy and the End of Empire*, p. 1.

106. Reinermann, 'Fleet Street and the Kaiser', 473.

107. See Nicolson, *King George the Fifth*; Rose, *King George V*; Churchill's recent hagiographic text challenges this view: Churchill, *In the Eye of the Storm*. Netflix, *The Crown*, Series 3, Episode 2, 'Margaretology', 40:24. Twenty-one million households viewed Series 3 in its first four weeks; it was reported in January 2020 that 73 million households had seen an episode of *The Crown* since it launched in 2016. www.bbc.co.uk/news/entertainment-arts-51198033, accessed 18/2/2020.

108. See Chapters 1 and 4.

109. Owens, *The Family Firm*, p. 2; p. 88.

110. Ibid., p. 4.

Prelude: The Monarchy and Wartime Political Power

1. Mort, 'Safe for Democracy', 110–11; 140. Edward Owens also finds George V made 'calculated interventions in party politics which tested the limits of his constitutional powers', Owens, *The Family Firm*, p. 5.

2. Rüger, *The Great Naval Game*, p. 188.

3. Ibid. See also Nicolaus Sombart, 'The Kaiser in His Epoch: Some Reflections on Wilhelmine Society, Sexuality and Culture' in Nicolaus Sombart and John Röhl, eds., *Kaiser Wilhelm II: New Interpretations. The Corfu Papers* (Cambridge, 1982), pp. 287–312, p. 309.
4. Ibid.
5. Bogdanor, *The Monarchy and the Constitution*, p. 34.
6. In the First World War era, it was the norm to capitalise a range of nouns, including King, Queen, Empire, Crown, Army, Navy, Church etc. This was stylistic convention, as much as an indication of social power. Where primary sources are quoted in this study, the capitalisation of the original is retained. Otherwise, current convention is used, i.e. King George V or Queen Mary where referring to proper names but king or queen where using the noun alone.
7. Prince Lichnowsky, *Heading for the Abyss: Reminiscences* (London, 1928), p. 66.
8. See Paulmann, *Pomp und Politik*.
9. Paulmann, *Pomp und Politik*; Matthew Glencross, *The State Visits of Edward VII: Reinventing Royal Diplomacy for the Twentieth Century* (Basingstoke, 2015); McLean, *Royalty and Diplomacy in Europe*.
10. Bogdanor, *The Monarchy and the Constitution*, p. 69.
11. Roy Jenkins, *Asquith* (London, 1986), pp. 214–15; pp. 218–22 and also later 1913 memo, 'The Constitutional Position of the Sovereign', pp. 543–5. Paul Adelman, *The Decline of the Liberal Party, 1910–1931* (London, 1981), pp. 1–2; Chris Cook, *A Short History of the Liberal Party: The Road Back to Power* (Basingstoke, 2010), p. 52; see David Cannadine, 'Churchill and the British Monarchy', *Transactions of the Royal Historical Society*, 11 (2001), 249–72, for Churchill's views that both Edward VII and George V interfered politically.
12. Loughlin, *The British Monarchy and Ireland*, pp. 271–96. The initial idea appears to have come from the Palace side: see Oxford, Bodleian Libraries, MS Asquith, A.1, Vol. 3, f. 235.
13. Oxford, Bodleian Libraries, MS Asquith, A.2, Vol. 7, f. 145, Cabinet Minutes, 17/7/1914.
14. Ian Packer, *Liberal Government and Politics 1905–1915* (Basingstoke, 2006), p. 72.
15. Bogdanor, *The Monarchy and the Constitution*, p. 35.
16. Röhl, *Wilhelm II: Into the Abyss*, p. 1060.
17. Ibid., pp. 1059–60.
18. Ibid., p. 991.
19. Ibid., p. 1059; John Röhl, 'Goodbye to All That (Again)? The Fischer Thesis, the New Revisionism and the Meaning of the First World War', *International Affairs*, 91, 1 (2015), 153–66; 159–60.
20. Röhl, *Wilhelm II: Into the Abyss*, p. 1059.
21. Ibid.
22. Ibid., p. 1061.
23. Ibid., p. 1060.
24. Ibid., p. 1058; p. 1060.
25. Ibid., p. 1060.
26. Ibid., p. 1066.
27. Ibid.
28. Ibid., p. 1064; Röhl, 'Goodbye to All That (Again)?', 159–60.

29. Roderick McLean, 'Kaiser Wilhelm II and the British Royal Family: Anglo-German Dynastic Relations in Political Context, 1890–1914', *History*, 86 (2001), 487, 502.

30. David Cannadine, 'Kaiser Wilhelm and the British Monarchy' in T. C. W. Blanning and David Cannadine, eds., *History and Biography: Essays in Honour of Derek Beales* (Cambridge 1996), p. 194.

31. Olechnowicz, 'Historians and the Modern British Monarchy', p. 16.

32. Röhl, *Wilhelm II: Into the Abyss*, p. 1095.

33. Originally from www.telegraph.co.uk/history/world-war-one/11002644/First-World-War-centenary-how-events-unfolded-on-August-1-1914.html, accessed 6/8/2019.

34. Herbert Asquith, *H. H. Asquith, Letters to Venetia Stanley*, eds. Michael and Eleanor Brock (Oxford, 1985), Letter from Asquith to Stanley, 1/8/1914, p. 140.

35. HMSO, *Letter of July 31, 1914, from the President of the French Republic to the King Respecting the European Crisis: and His Majesty's Reply of August 1, 1914* (London, 1915).

36. Nicolson, *George V*, p. 247.

37. Herbert H. Asquith, *Memories and Reflections, 1852–1927*, Vol. 2 (London, 1928), p. 7.

38. George Arthur, *King George V: A Sketch of a Great Ruler* (London, Toronto, 1929), p. 295.

39. Martin Gilbert, ed., *Winston S. Churchill*, Vol. 3: *The Challenge of War 1914–1916* (London, 1990), p. 10.

40. Lyn MacDonald, *1914: The Days of Hope* (London, 1987), p. 41.

41. For examples, Mary Evans Picture Library, 10656208, 'This Triple Entente'; 10837628, 'United in defence of the right'; 11034504, the Oxo war map. For cloth examples: 10726610, 'Boys in Khaki, Boys in Blue', music with leaders' images on cloth; 11034368 for another example of this; 11034367, 'National leaders 1914'; 10727905, 'Jutland souvenir'. In the collections of the Historial de la Grande Guerre, Péronne, see handkerchief examples with the Allies' heads of state depicted: 4 LIM 24_3 and 4 LIM 31_3, and 15 FI 6051, which has the Allies' heads of state and the caption 'gloire aux Alliés' on it. Even Stewart's blotter carried the king's face on its 1915 naval image montage cover: Mary Evans Picture Library, 11034099.

42. Stéphane Audoin-Rouzeau, 'An Artifact of War Carved in 1917: The Trench Cane of Soldier/Peasant Claude Burloux', *South Central Review*, 34, 3 (2017), 103–14.

43. Collections of the Historial de la Grande Guerre, Péronne, 4 ART 36_1_b.

44. Ibid., 15 MED 352_1#, Medallion showing the heads of Britain's Queen Mary and Queen Elisabeth of Belgium in profile.

45. For examples, see Mary Evans Picture Library, 10284426, postcard, 'Honneur, Patrie, 1914, L'union fait la force'; 10426511, postcard 1914, 'conflit européen'; 10793383, postcard, 'Gloire aux alliés'; 11989690, postcard, 'sport ai bellico,1914'; 12014362, 'National anthems of the Allies'. See also the collections of the Historial de la Grande Guerre, Péronne: 048354, 1914 card with photographs of 'reine Mary' and 'roi Georges V' on it; 048371#, images of war heads of state with the caption 'united in Freedom's cause'; 049000, images of Allied heads of state with caption 'Nos Alliés'; 064727, sheet music in French for the British national anthem 'God Save the King' with a large photograph of King George V on the cover.

46. BL, MS EUR F143/62, Stamfordham to Walter Lawrence, 2/8/1914, f. 1.

47. 'How King George V Demanded Britain Enter the First World War', *Telegraph .co.uk*, 26/7/2014, retrieved from www-proquest-com.libproxy.ucl.ac.uk/news papers/revealed-how-king-george-v-demanded-britain-enter/docview/ 1548442636/se-2?accountid=14511, accessed 15/3/2021.
48. Ibid.
49. Essex Record Office, ACC.AI3528 Diaries of the Right Rev. J. E. Watts-Ditchfield, Bishop of Chelmsford, 29/4/1916, f. 312.
50. The Royal Archives (hereafter RA), RA GV/PRIV/GVD/1914: 4 August.
51. Asquith, *H. H. Asquith, Letters to Venetia Stanley*, p. 157.
52. Arthur Bryant, *George V* (London, 1936), p. 90.
53. *Douglas Haig: War Diaries and Letters, 1914–1918*, ed. Gary Sheffield and John Bourne (London, 2006), p. 56.
54. George Riddell, *Lord Riddell's War Diary, 1914–1918* (London, 1933), pp. 262–3.
55. Ibid.
56. Riddell, *Lord Riddell's War Diary*, p. 263; John Gore, *King George V: A Personal Memoir* (London, 1941), pp. 288–9.
57. Gore, *King George V*, pp. 288–9.
58. Ibid.
59. Ibid.
60. On Wigram and Stamfordham, see Beckett, 'King George and His Generals', p. 251.
61. Stamfordham's grandson Michael Adeane would serve as Private Secretary to Queen Elizabeth II.
62. Jenny Macleod, *Reconsidering Gallipoli* (Manchester, 2004), p. 127.
63. Beckett, 'King George and His Generals', pp. 251–3.
64. Noble Frankland, *Witness of a Century: The Life and Times of Prince Arthur, Duke of Connaught, 1850–1942* (London, 1993).
65. Mort, 'Safe for Democracy', 117.
66. Macleod, *Reconsidering Gallipoli*, p. 131.
67. Ibid.
68. Rose, *King George V*, p. 186.
69. Essex Record Office, ACC.AI3528 Diaries of the Right Rev. J. E. Watts-Ditchfield, Bishop of Chelmsford, 1/5/1916, f. 325.
70. Mort, 'Accessible Sovereignty', 355; Rose, *King George V*, p. 174; p. 221.
71. Röhl, *Wilhelm II: Into the Abyss*, pp. 256–7; Beckett, 'King George V and His Generals', pp. 256–7.
72. Oxford, Bodleian Libraries, MS Asquith, A.1, Vol. 4, ff. 165–6, Letter from Stamfordham to Asquith, 3/12/1915.
73. Rose, *King George V*, p. 189.
74. Ibid., p. 199.
75. Frances Stevenson, *Lloyd George: A Diary by Frances Stevenson*, ed. A. J. P. Taylor (London, 1971), p. 130.
76. The Parliamentary Archives (hereafter PA), PA LG/F/29/2/6/(b), Stamfordham to Lloyd George, 9/2/1918; Nicolson, *King George the Fifth*, pp. 320–2; Churchill, *In the Eye of the Storm*, pp. 262–7; Hew Strachan, *The Politics of the British Army* (Oxford, 1997), pp. 70–1.
77. PA LG/F/29/1/42, Stamfordham to Lloyd George, 30/5/1917.
78. Rose, *King George V*, p. 231.
79. Oxford, Bodleian Libraries, MS Asquith, A.2, Vol. 8, f. 112, Lord Crewe to the king, Report on cabinet meeting, 21/10/1915. Likewise, in 1921, during talks with

Irish republican separatist Éamon de Valera the king's views were communicated to the cabinet: PA LG/F/29/4/66, Lloyd George report to the king, 13/8/1921. The government's reply to de Valera was also communicated to the king for his approval: PA LG/F/29/4/68, Prime Minister's secretary to the king, 26/8/1921.

80. LPL, Papers of Dr Randall T. Davidson, Archbishop of Canterbury, private papers, Vol. 13, f. 142, King George V to Asquith, 23/8/1914.

81. Ibid., ff. 144–5, Asquith's reply to King George V, 25/8/1914, which Stamfordham shared with the Archbishop of Canterbury.

82. Oxford, Bodleian Libraries, MS Asquith, A.1, Vol. 4, f. 139, King George V to Asquith, 18/7/1915 and MS Asquith, A.2, Vol. 8, f. 69, Cabinet report to king, 19/7/1915.

83. Ibid.

84. Ibid., f. 176, Stamfordham to Bonham Carter, 22/2/1916.

85. Gore, *King George V*, p. 295; Churchill, *In the Eye of the Storm*, p. 137.

86. LPL, Papers of Dr Randall T. Davidson, Archbishop of Canterbury, private papers, Vol. 13, f. 65, Note, 4/12/16.

87. Essex Record Office, ACC.AI3528 Diaries of the Right Rev. J. E. Watts-Ditchfield, Bishop of Chelmsford, 29/4/1916, f. 310.

88. Churchill, *In the Eye of the Storm*, p. 185; Rose, *King George V*, p. 198.

89. Churchill, *In the Eye of the Storm*, pp. 185–6.

90. Nicolson, *King George the Fifth*, p. 255; Rose, *King George V*, p. 172.

91. Ibid.

92. Beckett, 'King George V and His Generals', p. 258.

93. Rose, *King George V*, pp. 212–13.

94. PA LG/F/29/2/13, Stamfordham to Lloyd George, 17/3/1918.

95. John Grigg, *Lloyd George: War Leader, 1916–1918* (London, 2003), pp. 479–81; p. 481.

96. J. T. Davies, secretary to Lloyd George to Stamfordham, 17/4/1918, cited in Grigg, *Lloyd George*, p. 480.

97. LPL, Papers of Dr Randall T. Davidson, Archbishop of Canterbury, private papers, Vol. 13, f. 336, Memorandum, 20/10/1918.

98. Oxford, Bodleian Libraries, MS Asquith, A.1, Vol. 4, f. 219, Stamfordham to Asquith, 12/8/1916.

99. Gore, *King George V*, pp. 296–7.

100. Nicolson, *King George the Fifth*, p. 280.

101. Oxford, Bodleian Libraries, MS Asquith, A.1, Vol. 4, f. 169, Copy of a telegram from the tsar to the king, 7/12/1915.

102. PA LG/F/59/6/1, King of Spain to King George V, 19/5/1917.

103. Churchill, *In the Eye of the Storm*, p. 108.

104. Asquith, *H.H. Asquith, Letters to Venetia Stanley*, Letter from Asquith to Stanley, 31/3/1915, p. 524.

105. Churchill, *In the Eye of the Storm*, p. 108.

106. Andrea Ungari, *La guerra del re: monarchia, sistema politico e forze armate nella Grande Guerra* (Milan, 2018), p. 176.

107. There was considerable press coverage of his stints in Italy: for example, 'Prince of Wales in Italy', *Morning Post*, 12/11/1917. RA EDW/PRIV/DIARY/1916: 23 April; RA GV/PRIV/GVD/1918: 27 March. See also Ziegler, *King Edward VIII*; Churchill, *In the Eye of the Storm*, p. 153.

108. Grigg, *Lloyd George*, p. 88.

109. Ibid., p. 90.
110. David Stevenson, *1917: War, Peace and Revolution* (London, 2017), p. 244.
111. The Imperial War Museum (hereafter IWM), IWM Documents 13120, Box 06/1/ 1, Papers of Brigadier General Sir Charles Delmé-Radcliffe, 06/1/1, Delmé-Radcliffe to Stamfordham, 7/6/1918.
112. RA GV/PRIV/GVD/1915: 15 April.
113. LPL, Papers of Dr Randall T. Davidson, Archbishop of Canterbury, private papers, Vol. 13, f. 43, Memorandum, 6/2/1916 and f. 77, Memorandum, 24/12/1916.
114. PA LG/F/29/1/52, Letter from King George V to Lloyd George, 25/12/1917.
115. LPL, Papers of Dr Randall T. Davidson, Archbishop of Canterbury, private papers, Vol. 6, f. 27, Stamfordham to Randall Davidson, 18/8/1918.
116. Nicolson, *King George the Fifth*, p. 280.
117. Oxford, Bodleian Libraries, MS Asquith, A.1, Vol. 4, f. 78, Stamfordham to Asquith, 22/1/1915.
118. Nicolson, *King George the Fifth*, p. 301.
119. Ibid., p. 281.
120. Ibid., p. 282.
121. Oxford, Bodleian Libraries, MS Asquith, A.1, Vol. 4, f. 224, King George V to Asquith, 4/9/16.
122. Nicolson, *King George the Fifth*, p. 282.
123. Ibid.
124. Oxford, Bodleian Libraries, MS Asquith, A.1, Vol. 4, f. 226, Memorandum, 5/9/1916.
125. Nicolson, *King George the Fifth*, p. 283.
126. Van Ypersele, *Le roi Albert*.
127. Nicolson, *George V*, p. 280.
128. BL, MSS EUR F112/580, Letters to Lord Curzon from Elisabeth, Queen of the Belgians, September 1914–June 1922.
129. Ibid., Elisabeth Queen of the Belgians to Lord Curzon, 1/7/1918.
130. RA GV/PRIV/GVD/1918: 27 November and 28 November.
131. RA GV/PRIV/GVD/1914: 29 October.
132. Churchill, *In the Eye of the Storm*, p. 136. Also Oxford, Bodleian Libraries, MS Asquith, A.1, Vol. 4, f. 137, n.d.
133. Ibid., f. 151, Stamfordham to Asquith, 11/10/1915.
134. Rose, *King George V*, p. 195; p. 207.
135. Ibid., p. 231.
136. PA LG/F/29/2/63, King George V to Lloyd George, 19/11/1918.
137. PA LG/F/29/1/36, Stamfordham to Lloyd George, 5/4/1917.
138. RA PS/PSO/GV/C/K/1080/3 Stamfordham to Lloyd George, 4/3/1917; also PA LG/F/29/1/28 copy.
139. PA LG/F/29/1/29, unnamed secretary for Lloyd George to Stamfordham, 5/3/1917.
140. The National Archives (hereafter TNA), TNA, FO 800/199, ff. 3–4, Letter from Stamfordham to Arthur Balfour, 6/4/1917.
141. Ibid.
142. TNA, FO 800/199, f. 5, Arthur Balfour to Stamfordham, 7/4/1917.
143. Ibid.
144. Thomas Jones, *Whitehall Diary*, Vol. 1: *1916–1925* (Oxford, 1969), p. 29.
145. PA LG/F/29/2/10, Stamfordham to J. T. Davies, 13/3/1918.
146. PA LG/F/29/2/14, Stamfordham to J. T. Davies, 16/4/1918.
147. Rose, *King George V*, p. 207.

148. Stevenson, *Lloyd George*, p. 150.
149. PA LG/F/29/2/16, James O'Connor to Stamfordham, 18/4/1918.
150. Rose, *King George V*, p. 236.
151. PA LG/F/29/1/7, Lord Stamfordham to J. T. Davies, Secretary to the Prime Minister, 11/1/1917.
152. Rose, *King George V*, p. 246.
153. PA LG/F/29/1/2, Lord Stamfordham to Lloyd George, 14/12/1916.
154. PA LG/F/29/1/6, Lord Stamfordham to Lloyd George, Memorandum as to the procedure relating to grants of Honours by His Majesty, 1/1/1917.
155. Beckett, 'King George V and His Generals', p. 260.
156. Oxford, Bodleian Libraries, MS Asquith, A.1, Vol. 3, f. 233, King George V to Asquith, 15/7/1914.
157. PA LG/F/29/3/27, Lloyd George to King George V, n.d. [August] 1919.
158. PA LG/F/29/3/19, Stamfordham to Lloyd George, 9/5/1919. PA LG/F/29/3/21.
159. See Rose, *King George V*, on decline.
160. Nicolaus Sombart, 'The Kaiser in His Epoch', p. 309.
161. Röhl, *Wilhelm II: Into the Abyss*, p. 1108.

1 Monarchist Mentalities and British Mobilisation, 1914–1916

1. The role of the British monarchy in popular mobilisation for war at the outbreak of the 1914–18 conflagration has been largely ignored in the historiography. Leading examples of the most insightful recent historiography on the war experience of 1914 in the UK include Gregory, *The Last Great War* and Winter, ed., *The Cambridge History of the First World War*. Catriona Pennell's excellent study *A Kingdom United?* briefly assesses the crowds who gathered at Buckingham Palace in 1914. Yet none of these studies address in detail the role of the monarchy in helping to mobilise the British population for war.
2. John Horne, ed., *State, Society and Mobilization in Europe during the First World War* (Cambridge, 1997), p. 1.
3. Gerwarth, *The Bismarck Myth*, p. 5.
4. Cannadine, 'The Context, Performance and Meaning of Ritual', p. 105.
5. Jay Winter, 'British National Identity and the First World War' in Simon J. D. Green and R. C. Whiting, *The Boundaries of the State in Modern Britain* (Cambridge, 1996), p. 262.
6. Prince Lichnowsky, *Heading for the Abyss*, p. 66.
7. Olechnowicz, 'Historians and the Modern British Monarchy', p. 9.
8. On how these nineteenth-century cultures evolved, see Mayer, *The Persistence of the Old Regime* and Cannadine, 'The Context, Performance and Meaning of Ritual'.
9. Cannadine, 'The Context, Performance and Meaning of Ritual'.
10. Mark Girouard, *The Return to Camelot: Chivalry and the English Gentleman* (New Haven, London, 1981), preface.
11. Ibid.
12. Stefan Goebel, *The Great War and Medieval Memory: War, Remembrance and Medievalism in Britain and Germany, 1914–1940* (Cambridge, 2007).

13. John G. Peristiany, ed., *Honour and Shame: The Values of Mediterranean Society* (Chicago, 1966); Peter Berger, Brigitte Berger and Hansfried Kellner, 'On the Obsolescence of the Concept of Honor' in Peter Berger, Brigitte Berger and Hansfried Kellner, eds., *The Homeless Mind: Modernization and Consciousness* (New York, 1973), pp. 83–96; Frank Stewart, *Honor* (Chicago, 1994); Donald Black, *Moral Time* (New York, Oxford, 2011); Kwame Anthony Appiah, *The Honor Code: How Moral Revolutions Happen* (New York, 2010).

14. Mark Cooney, *Warriors and Peacemakers: How Third Parties Shape Violence* (New York, 1998), pp. 107–32.

15. Frevert, 'Honor, Gender, and Power'. On the cultural honour codes of bourgeois respectability, see James Connolly, 'Mauvaise Conduite: Complicity and Respectability in the Occupied Nord, 1914–1918', *First World War Studies*, 4, 1 (2013), 7–21. See also William Mulligan, *The Origins of the First World War* (Cambridge, 2010), pp. 133–74.

16. Peristiany, ed., *Honour and Shame*. On First World War societies as honour-based cultures, see Frevert, 'Honor, Gender, and Power'.

17. PA LG/F/29/1/6, Memorandum enclosed in letter from Stamfordham to Lloyd George, 1/1/1917.

18. Lloyd George, *Honour and Dishonour*; Nicoletta Gullace, 'Sexual Violence and Family Honor: British Propaganda and International Law during the First World War', *American Historical Review*, 102, 3, (1997), 714–47; Isabel V. Hull, *A Scrap of Paper: Breaking and Making International Law during the Great War* (Ithaca, NY, London, 2014).

19. Hansard, HC Debate, 3/8/1914, Vol. 65, cc. 1809–32, c. 1823, Statement by Sir Edward Grey to the House of Commons.

20. John Henry Bernard, *In War Time* (London, 1917), pp. 4–5.

21. Getty Images, 151211071, First World War postcard, 1914.

22. Peter Parker, *The Old Lie: The Great War and the Public School Ethos* (London, 1987), p. 96. Quotation is from image caption.

23. Girouard, *The Return to Camelot*, p. 281.

24. Ibid., p. 283.

25. Allen Warren, 'Sir Robert Baden-Powell, the Scout Movement and Citizen Training in Great Britain, 1900–1920', *The English Historical Review*, 101, 399 (1986), 381.

26. Ibid., p. 382.

27. Robert Baden-Powell, *Scouting for Boys: The Original 1908 Edition* (New York, 2007 [1908]), p. 20. See also Michael Rosenthal, 'Knights and Retainers: The Earliest Version of Baden-Powell's Boy Scout Scheme', *Journal of Contemporary History*, 15, 4 (1980), 605–6.

28. Rosenthal, 'Knights and Retainers', p. 604; p. 606.

29. Sam Pryke, 'The Popularity of Nationalism in the Early British Boy Scout Movement', *Social History*, 23, 3 (1998), 310.

30. *Tring Parish Magazine*, November 1916, https://tringhistory.tringlocalhistorymu seum.org.uk/Memorial/Biog.%20Notes%202.htm, accessed 16/12/2019.

31. Ibid.

32. Girouard, *The Return to Camelot*, p. 283.

33. Bernard, *In War Time*, pp. 2–3.
34. Ibid.
35. Horatio Bottomley, 'Hands off the Throne!', *Sunday Pictorial*, 29/4/1917, p. 4.
36. Viscount Esher, *After the War*, pp. 11–13.
37. Cannadine, 'The Context, Performance and Meaning of Ritual', pp. 120–1.
38. Ibid., p. 123.
39. See Nicoletta Gullace, *'The Blood of our Sons': Men, Women and the Renegotiation of British Citizenship during the Great War* (Basingstoke, 2002).
40. Robert Laird Borden, *Robert Laird Borden: His Memoirs*, Vol. 1 (Toronto, 1938), p. 432.
41. Ibid.
42. Ibid.
43. Ibid., p. 433.
44. Williamson, 'The Monarchy and Public Values', p. 231; p. 232.
45. Oxford, Bodleian Libraries, MS Asquith, B.26, f. 1, enclosure, Downing St to Prime Minister, Comments by Sir Reginald Brade on the royal message to parliament concerning mobilisation, 4/8/1914.
46. Margot Asquith, *Margot Asquith's Great War Diary: The View from Downing Street*, eds. Michael and Eleanor Brock (Oxford, 2014), p. 13.
47. In this period, the dominions were also sometimes referred to as the 'white dominions', a profoundly misleading term which hid their multi-ethnic indigenous and immigrant populations.
48. Mark Pearsall, 'British Nationality: Subject or Citizen?', talk given at The National Archives, Kew, 14/4/2014, https://media.nationalarchives.gov.uk/index.php/brit ish-nationality-subject-citizen/, accessed 27/5/2020.
49. Randall Hansen, 'The Politics of Citizenship in 1940s Britain: The British Nationality Act', *Twentieth Century British History*, 10, 1 (1999), 67–95. The status of 'subject of the King' was the basis of British nationality until the 1948 Act: Hansen, 'The Politics of Citizenship', 67. LPL, Papers of Dr Randall T. Davidson, Archbishop of Canterbury, private papers, Vol. 6, f. 38, Notes [on the conclusion of peace], n.d.
50. Hansen, 'The Politics of Citizenship', 70.
51. On the history of the concept of the 'King's Peace' and public order, see David Feldman, 'The King's Peace, the Royal Prerogative and Public Order: The Roots and Early Development of Binding Over Powers', *Cambridge Law Journal*, 47, 1 (1988), 104–7.
52. Laura Cahillane and Paul Murray, 'The Treaty: An Historical and Legal Interpretation' in Liam Weeks and Mícheál Ó Fathartaigh, eds., *The Treaty: Debating and Establishing the Irish State* (Newbridge, 2018), p. 255.
53. Text of Defence of the Realm Act, 8/8/1914, www.legislation.gov.uk/ukpga/1914/ 29/pdfs/ukpga_19140029_en.pdf, accessed 10/1/2020.
54. Nicolson, *King George the Fifth*, p. 112.
55. Ibid.
56. Hayman, 'Labour and the Monarchy', 171–2.
57. Sir Almeric Fitzroy, *Memoirs* (London, 1925), Vol. 2, p. 579.
58. Ibid., p. 633.
59. Ibid., pp. 704–5.
60. Hayman, 'Labour and the Monarchy', 171–2.

61. Fitzroy, *Memoirs*, Vol. 2, p. 683.
62. Ibid., p. 659; p. 637.
63. Nicolson, *King George the Fifth*, p. 113.
64. Anon., *The Civilian War Sufferer: Compiled from the Records of the Civilian War Claimants Association* (London, n.d.), p. 23, citing Hansard, 4 May 1920, Q. 55.
65. Anon., *The Civilian War Sufferer*, p. 20.
66. Ibid., pp. 19–20.
67. Ibid., pp. 15–16, p. 19.
68. Oxford, Bodleian Libraries, MS Asquith, A.1, Vol. 4, f. 223, Stamfordham to Bonham Carter, 23/8/1916.
69. On coronation, see Edward Shils and Michael Young, 'The Meaning of the Coronation', *The Sociological Review*, 1, 2 (1955), 63–81.
70. LPL, Papers of Dr Randall T. Davidson, Archbishop of Canterbury, private papers, Vol. 20, f. 158, Randall Davidson to King George V, 22/6/1911.
71. 'Crowned with the Kings, Their Husbands: Consorts of British Sovereigns', *Illustrated London News*, 27/5/1911, p. 67.
72. Olechnowicz, 'Historians and the Modern British Monarchy', p. 38.
73. Williamson, 'The Monarchy and Public Values', p. 248.
74. Williamson, 'National Days of Prayer'.
75. Ibid., 330.
76. Ibid., 343.
77. Ibid., 330.
78. Ibid., 333.
79. Ibid., 343.
80. Essex Record Office, ACC.AI3528 Diaries of the Right Rev. J. E. Watts-Ditchfield, Bishop of Chelmsford, 29/4/1917, f. 518.
81. Williamson, 'National Days of Prayer', 324.
82. Ibid., 326, 327.
83. Ibid., 324.
84. Ibid., 329.
85. Williamson, 'The Monarchy and Public Values', p. 246.
86. Williamson, 'National Days of Prayer', 344.
87. Ibid.
88. Ibid., 332.
89. LPL, Papers of Dr Randall T. Davidson, Archbishop of Canterbury, official letters, Vol. 195, f. 262, Stamfordham to Archbishop of Canterbury, Randall Davidson, 28/1/1916.
90. Bernard, *In War Time*, p. 15.
91. Churchill, *In the Eye of the Storm*, pp. 118–19.
92. Fitzroy, *Memoirs*, Vol. 2, p. 601. Fitzroy's memoirs are largely a verbatim reproduction of his war diaries.
93. Niamh Gallagher, *Ireland and the Great War: A Social and Political History* (London, 2020), p. 119.
94. Churchill, *In the Eye of the Storm*, pp. 118–19.
95. 'Devon and Cornwall Baptist Association, Exeter District', *Western Times*, 31/3/1916, p. 14.
96. Wolffe quoted in Olechnowicz, 'Historians and the Modern British Monarchy', p. 38.

97. Brock Millman, *Managing Domestic Dissent in First World War Britain* (London, 2000), p. 186.
98. Ibid.
99. RA GV/PRIV/AA48/130, Randall Davidson to King George V, 3/6/1917.
100. RA GV/PRIV/AA48/174, Randall Davidson to King George V, 21/8/1918.
101. Ibid.
102. Frederick A. McKenzie, *Serving the King's Men: How the Salvation Army Is Helping the Nation* (London, 1918), pp. 46–7.
103. 'King and Heroes, Touching Scenes at Investiture, the Royal Tour of Shipyard Areas', *Daily Record and Mail,* 18/6/1917, p. 3.
104. Mary Evans Picture Library, 10639237, *Daily Mail* postcard, 'King at the front, attending church, service in the field'.
105. 'Congregationalist membership rose from 288,784 in 1916 to 290,934 in 1927, the highest figure since 1908. The Baptists similarly climbed from 255,469 members in 1919 to 259,527 in 1926, their highest figure since 1911. The Wesleyan Methodists reached their highest membership since 1906 prior to their reunion with the other Methodist churches in 1932. Anglican communion figures similarly rose from 2,097,000 in 1917 to a peak of 2,390,978 in 1927.' Matthew Grimley, 'The Religion of Englishness: Puritanism, Providentialism, and "National Character", 1918–1945', *Journal of British Studies*, 46, 4 (2007), 887.
106. Olechnowicz, 'A Jealous Hatred', p. 291.
107. *Daily Telegraph*, 26/12/1917, cited in Churchill, *In the Eye of the Storm*, p. 258.
108. Ibid.
109. Templer Study Centre, The National Army Museum (hereafter NAM) 2002-02-516-5, 9/7/1913.
110. *The Telegraph*, 18/8/1914, cited in Churchill, *In the Eye of the Storm*, p. 62. See the report 'The King's Blessing and Leader's Counsel to Our Troops', *Shepton Mallet Journal*, 21/8/1914, p. 8.
111. For examples, see Getty Images, 450522859 and 502237918, First World War postcards, 1914.
112. Churchill, *In the Eye of the Storm*, p. 57.
113. Nicolson, *King George the Fifth*, p. 280.
114. www.firstworldwar.com/source/kitchener1914.htm, accessed 7/12/2015.
115. Kohlrausch, 'The Unmanly Emperor'; Simon Schama, 'The Domestication of Majesty: Royal Family Portraiture 1500–1850', *The Journal of Interdisciplinary History*, 17, 1 (1986), 155–83; Alexis Schwarzenbach, 'Royal Photographs: Emotions for the People', *Contemporary European History*, 13 (2004), 255–80.
116. Olechnowicz, 'Historians and the Modern British Monarchy', p. 30.
117. John Tosh, *Manliness and Masculinities in Nineteenth-Century Britain: Essays on Gender, Family and Empire* (London, 2016).
118. Cannadine, 'From Biography to History', 311.
119. On analysing monarchical imagery, see Helen Hackett, 'Dreams or Designs, Cults or Constructions? The Study of Images of Monarchs', *Historical Journal*, 44, 3 (2001), 811–24.
120. Churchill, *In the Eye of the Storm*, p. 146.
121. Gore, *King George V*, p. 293.
122. 'King George in Coventry', *Coventry Evening Telegraph*, 22/7/1915, p. 3.
123. Ibid.
124. 'Our London Letter', *Exeter and Plymouth Gazette*, 12/1/1915, p. 3.

125. Mary Evans Picture Library, 10698045, Prince Henry in training at Eton, 1915.

126. RA GV/PRIV/AA59/293, letter from George V to Prince George, 17/8/1914, cited in Pennell, *A Kingdom United?*, p. 212.

127. Owens, *The Family Firm*, p. 45.

128. For example, Mabell, Countess of Airlie, *Thatched with Gold: The Memoirs of Mabell, Countess of Airlie*, ed. Jennifer Ellis (Bath, 1962), p. 135 refers to the king working in his tent with Sir William Robertson in summer 1917; James Pope-Hennessy refers to the tent existing earlier in the war for use 'in fine weather': Pope-Hennessy, *Queen Mary*, p. 497.

129. Gore, *King George V*, p. 291.

130. This had a much older history: on how the image of the king was used in Prussian propaganda during the Napoleonic wars, see Karen Hagemann, 'The Military and Masculinity: Gendering the History of the Revolutionary and Napoleonic Wars, 1792–1815' in Roger Chickering and Stig Förster, eds., *War in an Age of Revolution, 1775–1815* (Cambridge, 2010), pp. 331–52.

131. Boff, *Haig's Enemy*.

132. See Signori, 'La monarchia italiana e la Grande Guerra'.

133. Röhl, *Wilhelm II: Into the Abyss*, p. 1119. See also Lerman, 'Wilhelm's War'.

134. Churchill, *In the Eye of the Storm*, p. 136.

135. Ibid.

136. Nicolson, *King George the Fifth*, p. 238.

137. Ibid.

138. Beckett, 'George V and His Generals', p. 248.

139. For an excellent overview of this, see Beckett, 'George V and His Generals'.

140. Text of oath from TNA, WO 339/35077, Territorial Force Attestation of Eric Skeffington Poole, 3/10/1914. Digital copy online at www.nationalarchives.gov.uk /pathways/firstworldwar/transcripts/people/poole_attestation.htm, accessed 3/1/ 2018.

141. Harry Cartmell, *For Remembrance: An Account of Some Fateful Years* (Preston, 1919), pp. 233–4.

142. TNA, WO 141/9, Interview with Pte James Wilson. Interview no. 331.

143. Ibid.

144. Arthur, *King George V: A Sketch of a Great Ruler*, p. 221.

145. Ibid., p. 222.

146. Oliver Elton, *C. E. Montague: A Memoir* (London, 1929), p. 109.

147. Jeffery Richards, *Imperialism and Music: Britain 1876–1953* (Manchester, 2001), pp. 514–15.

148. Oxford, Bodleian Libraries, MS Asquith, A.1, Vol. 4, ff. 35–6, Stamfordham to Bonham Carter, 20/11/1914.

149. Ibid.

150. George H. Cassar, *Kitchener: Architect of Victory* (London, 1977), p. 190.

151. 'Lord Kitchener Visits the King', *Manchester Courier and Lancashire General Advertiser*, 30/11/1914, p. 6.

152. Peter Simkins, *Kitchener's Army: The Raising of the New Armies, 1914–1916* (Manchester, 1988), p. 122.

153. Churchill, *In the Eye of the Storm*, p. 159.

154. Ibid., p. 162.

155. Harold Nicolson, *King George the Fifth*, p. 261.

156. LPL, Papers of Dr Randall T. Davidson, Archbishop of Canterbury, private papers, Vol. 13, f. 66, Note 4/12/1916.
157. Ibid.
158. Ibid.
159. Duff Hart-Davies, ed., *End of an Era: Letters and Journals of Sir Alan Lascelles from 1887 to 1920* (London, 1986), pp. 180–1.
160. Hart-Davies, ed., *End of an Era*, p. 181.
161. RA PS/PSO/GV/C/O/1106/28, *Justice*, 3/5/1917.
162. Ernest Thurtle, *Time's Winged Chariot: Memories and Comments* (London, 1945), p. 56
163. Ibid.
164. Ibid.
165. Ibid.
166. Ibid.
167. Ibid., p. 57.
168. Martin Middlebrook, *The First Day on the Somme* (London, 1976), p. 300.
169. War Office, *Manual of Military Law, 1914* (London, 1914), p. 410.
170. The War Office's own statistics show that, during the period 4 August 1914 to 31 March 1920, a total of 21,039 soldiers, officers and civilians were tried by general, district and field general courts martial in the UK for 'miscellaneous military offences' and a further 30,147 in general, district and field general courts martial abroad, but this category – which included a wide range of other military crimes – is not broken down to indicate what proportion of this figure was ever charged with using traitorous or disloyal words against the king: 'Summary of Analyses of Proceedings of General, District and Field General Courts-Martial at Home for the Trials of Officers, Soldiers and Civilians, 4th August 1914 to 31st March 1920', War Office, *Statistics of the Military Effort of the British Empire during the Great War 1914–1920* (London, 1922), p. 658 and ibid., p. 667, 'Summary of Analyses of Proceedings of General, District and Field General Courts-Martial Abroad for the Trials of Officers, Soldiers and Civilians, 4th August 1914 to 31st March 1920'.
171. Mort, 'Safe for Democracy', 137.
172. On how language can reveal collective war mentalities, see Jay Winter, 'Beyond Glory? Cultural Divergences in Remembering the Great War in Ireland, Britain and France' in John Horne and Edward Madigan, eds., *Towards Commemoration: Ireland in War and Revolution 1912–1923* (Dublin, 2013), pp. 134–44. See also Jay Winter, *War beyond Words: Languages of Remembrance from the Great War to the Present* (Cambridge, 2017).
173. For examples of this language, see Edward Legge, *King Edward, The Kaiser and the War* (London, 1917), p. 119; p. 126. Also McKenzie, *Serving the King's Men*.
174. IWM Documents 315, Box 90/17/1, Capt. Arthur Guy Osborn, 1st Birmingham Battalion Royal Warwickshire Regiment, Letter, 10/10/1914. I am grateful to Alex Mayhew for alerting me to this reference.
175. A. K. Foxwell, *Munition Lasses: Six Months as Principal Overlooker in Danger Buildings* (London, 1917), pp. 23–4.
176. Mark Cornwall, 'Traitors and the Meaning of Treason in Austria-Hungary's Great War', *Transactions of the Royal Historical Society*, 6th ser., 25 (2015), 115.
177. IWM Documents 12767, Box 04/1/1, Letter from Patricia Wilson to Commander H. M. Wilson, n.d., pp. 1–3.

178. J. G. A. Pocock, 'The Concept of Language and the *métier d'historien*: Some Considerations on Practice' in Anthony Pagden, *The Language of Political Theory in Early Modern Europe* (Cambridge, 1987), p. 21, cited in Paul Stock, 'Towards a Language of "Europe": History, Rhetoric, Community', *The European Legacy: Towards New Paradigms*, 22, 6 (2017), 649.

179. PA LG/F/29/4/4, Enid Prichard to King George V, n.d.

180. Newcastle University Library Special Collections and Archives, GB 186 TBB, Thomas Baker Brown (1896–1975) papers, TS memoir, pp. 4–5 and pp. 7–8.

181. Ibid.

182. Mort, 'Safe for Democracy', 133.

183. Mary Evans Picture Library, 11034048, *The Child's ABC of the War*.

184. Mary Evans Picture Library, 11033901, *The Belgian Relief Fund Children's Painting Book*.

185. James Barnes, *For King or Country: A Story of the American Revolution* (New York, 1896); Agnes Weston, *For King and Country* (London, 1911).

186. See I. B., 2011, *An Humble Address to the Livery-Men of London Relating to the Election of Sheriffs by a Lover of His King and Country* (1682), Oxford Text Archive, https://ota.bodleian.ox.ac.uk/repository/xmlui/handle/20.500.12024 /A30983, accessed 13/3/2021, and the anonymous text *The Undaunted Seaman Who Resolved to Fight for His King and Country* (London, c. 1690). See also James Gildea, *For King and Country: A Record of Funds and Philanthropic Work in Connection with the South African War 1899–1902* (London, 1902) and the more unusual mention of the fact that the war in South Africa spanned both Queen Victoria and King Edward VII's reigns: Mildred G. Dooner, *The 'Last Post': A Roll of All Officers (Naval, Military or Colonial) Who Gave Their Lives for Their Queen, King and Country in the South African War 1899–1902* (London, 1903).

187. Richards, *Imperialism and Music*, p. 335.

188. Paul Fussell, *The Great War and Modern Memory* (Oxford, 1975); Hynes, *A War Imagined*.

189. Winter, *War beyond Words*, pp. 99–100.

190. Ibid., p. 100.

191. This is based on a case-insensitive, Google Books N-Gram search of the term 'King and Country' for the period 1900–39, with a smoothing factor of zero. The graph tracks the term in capitals; and the term when the nouns appear in mixed case.

192. John Ishmael Thomas, 'Stand Up for King and Country: A Patriotic Song' (London, 1925); Bruce, 'We Stand for King and Country' (London, 1931); Thomas Bidgood, 'For King and Country: March' (London, 1920); John Masefield, 'A Prayer for King and Country: Unison Song with Male Voice Chorus' (London, 1935).

193. See Martin Ceadel, 'The "King and Country" Debate, 1933: Student Politics, Pacifism and the Dictators', *The Historical Journal*, 22, 2 (1979), 397–422.

194. Galit Hadad, 'La Guerre de 1914–1918, matrice du pacifisme féminin au XXe siècle' in Nicolas Beaupré, Heather Jones and Anne Rasmussen, eds., *Dans la Guerre 1914–1918: accepter, endurer, refuser* (Paris, 2015), p. 335. See also Gullace, *The Blood of our Sons*, p. 126.

195. Robert Beaken, *The Church of England and the Home Front 1914–1918: Civilians, Soldiers and Religion in Wartime Colchester* (Woodbridge, 2015), p. 56.

196. Peter Doyle, *British Postcards of the First World War* (London, 2011). For French cultural analyses of the wartime role of the postcard, see Marie-Monique Huss, *Histoires de famille 1914–1918: cartes postales et culture de guerre* (Paris, 2000); Jean-Yves Le Naour, *La Grande Guerre à travers la carte postale ancienne* (Paris, 2013).

197. Postcard to Alf Swettenham from his mother, reproduced in Michael Roper, *The Secret Battle: Emotional Survival in the Great War* (Manchester, 2009), p. 74.

198. William Gallacher, *Revolt on the Clyde: An Autobiography* (London [1936]; 1949), p. 30.

199. Simon Potter, 'Empire, Cultures and Identities in Nineteenth- and Twentieth-Century Britain', *History Compass*, 5, 1 (2007), 53.

200. Richards, *Imperialism and Music*, p. 506.

201. Winter, 'British National Identity and the First World War', p. 263.

202. On the 1911 investiture, see John S. Ellis, 'Reconciling the Celt: British National Identity, Empire and the 1911 Investiture of the Prince of Wales', *Journal of British Studies*, 37, 4 (1998), 391–418.

203. On this ambiguity, see David Edgerton, *The Rise and Fall of the British Nation: A Twentieth-Century History* (London, 2018), p. 23; pp. 28–9. On cultural mobilisation in all four home nations, see Pennell, *A Kingdom United?*

204. Vancouver Island University, Canadian Letters and Images Project, Letter from Pte Jack Cowles to Balliol Boys Club, 29/3/1916, www.canadianletters.ca/content/document-762, accessed 6/8/2019.

205. Loughlin, *The British Monarchy and Ireland*, pp. 286–7.

206. Nairn quoted in Murphy, *Monarchy and the End of Empire*, p. 2.

207. Edgerton, *The Rise and Fall of the British Nation*, pp. 25–9; p. 30.

208. Jonathan Gumz, *The Resurrection and Collapse of Empire in Habsburg Serbia, 1914–1918* (Cambridge, 2009). See also Laurence Cole and Daniel L. Unowsky, eds., *The Limits of Loyalty: Imperial Symbolism, Popular Allegiances, and State Patriotism in the Late Habsburg Monarchy* (Oxford, 2007).

209. Nairn, *The Enchanted Glass*, p. xvii.

210. Edgerton, *The Rise and Fall of the British Nation*, p. 29.

211. Kathleen Paul, *Whitewashing Britain: Race and Citizenship in the Postwar Era* (Ithaca, NY, 1997), p. 13; p. 26.

212. RA GV/PRIV/GVD/1914: 2 August.

213. RA GV/PRIV/GVD/1914: 3 August.

214. RA GV/PRIV/GVD/1914: 9 August.

215. Pennell, *A Kingdom United?*, p. 40.

216. Ibid.; also Adrian Gregory, 'British "War Enthusiasm" in 1914: A Reassessment' in Gail Braybon, ed., *Evidence, History and the Great War: Historians and the Impact of 1914–18* (Oxford, 2003), p. 72.

217. Röhl, *Wilhelm II: Into the Abyss*, pp. 1109–11; Joshua Sanborn points out that these large patriotic crowds in St Petersburg, and other towns, were unrepresentative of the mood elsewhere in the country, however: Joshua Sanborn, 'The Mobilization of 1914 and the Question of the Russian Nation: A Re-Examination', *Slavic Review*, 59, 2 (2000), 273.

218. Bryant, *George V*, p. 89.

219. Hayman, 'Labour and the Monarchy', 167.

220. For the period of the war it was published weekly only and was known as *The Herald* before reverting to a daily in 1919.

221. Pennell, *A Kingdom United?*, p. 45.

222. Italics on original. Getty Images, 515359592, photograph.

223. Riddell, *Lord Riddell's War Diary*, pp. 10–11.

224. On this suspicion, see Prochaska, *Royal Bounty*.

225. Rowbotham, 'How to Be Useful in War Time', p. 211.

226. Mary Evans Picture Library, 10643246, Dunlop Tyres advertisement, September 1914.

227. 'The King', *The Globe*, 12/10/17, p. 4.

228. Churchill, *In the Eye of the Storm*, p. 47.

229. Ibid., p. 214.

230. Röhl, *Wilhelm II: Into the Abyss*, p. 1109.

231. Simkins, *Kitchener's Army*, p. 39.

232. For examples of recruiting posters referring to the king, see IWM, Art. IWM PST 3289; Art. IWM PST 0952; Art. IWM PST 0581; Art. IWM PST 0302. Also, for an Irish example, National Library of Ireland (hereafter, NLI), EPH F78, 1914. See also multiple examples at https://tringhistory.tringlocalhistorymuseum.org.uk/Memorial/Biog.%20Notes%202.htm, accessed 16/12/2019. Roy Douglas refers to Parliamentary Recruiting Committee posters using the phrase 'your King and Country need you': Roy Douglas, 'Voluntary Enlistment in the First World War and the Work of the Parliamentary Recruiting Committee', *The Journal of Modern History*, 42, 4 (1970), 569.

233. The Liddle Collection, Leeds University Library, Alfred Edward Burdfield, Liddle/WW1/GS/0222 (2/3 Bn Royal Fusiliers).

234. Examples include buttons for the Royal Artillery Regiment and the Royal Air Force.

235. IWM, Art. IWM PST 4465, Territorial Association of London Recruiting Poster, April 1915.

236. For example, '7th Service Battalion, The Royal Sussex Regiment', *Chichester Observer*, 9/9/1914, p. 3.

237. 'Recruiting Boom: Call to Football Players of Cornwall', *Western Morning News*, 10/9/1914, p. 6.

238. Mary Evans Picture Library, 12445317, 'Great Free Meeting at the Chiswick Empire'.

239. Rose, *King George V*, p. 180.

240. Beaken, *The Church of England and the Home Front*, p. 58.

241. *Daily Chronicle*, 19/5/1915, cited in Churchill, *In the Eye of the Storm*, pp. 115–16.

242. 'For King and Country', *Dundee Evening Telegraph*, 24/8/1915, p. 4.

243. *Daily Sketch*, 1/10/1915, p. 1.

244. Cartmell, *For Remembrance*, p. 229.

245. Gallagher, *Ireland and the Great War*, p. 140.

246. Ibid.

247. Coulson Kernahan, *Experiences of a Recruiting Officer* (London, 1915), p. 24.

248. Simkins, *Kitchener's Army*, p. 123.

249. 'Women and the War', Parliamentary Recruiting Committee pamphlet 23 (London, 1915), p. 1, cited in Gullace, *'The Blood of Our Sons'*, p. 48.

250. For 1914–16 examples: William Brett, 'For King and Country: March, Pianoforte, Solo' (London, 1914); Robert Harkness, 'For King and Country' (London, 1914); Ralph Abercromby, 'For King and Country: Military March' (London, 1915); Trevor Huntley and Henry Pether, 'England Calls for Men: Your King and Country Need You' (London, 1914); Elmslie Edgar Emerson, 'You Fight for Your Country and King' (London, 1915); T. O. Kavanagh, 'Fight Boys, Fight: For Your Country and Your King' (London, 1915); James Ord Hume, 'For King and Country: A Descriptive Grand

Military Fantasia' (London, 1915); A. W. P. and H. Taylor, 'To Fight for Our King and Country: Soldiers' Marching Song' (London, 1915). There was even a hymn: B. Mallett, 'Special Hymn for Those That Are Serving Their Country and King' (London, 1916).

251. For pre-war music using the term, see Heinrich Maria Hain, 'For King and Country: March for the Piano and Violin' (London, 1887); T. L. Clemens, 'For King and Country: Hymn for Coronation Day' (Bradford, 1901); James Helsby, 'For King and Country' [March] (London, 1902); Mrs White Purcell, 'For King and Country: March Song' (London, 1909). See also Richards, *Imperialism and Music*, p. 516.

252. Victoria and Albert Museum, https://collections.vam.ac.uk/item/O1274573/ your-king-and-country-want-sheet-music-rubens-paul-a/, accessed 17/12/2019.

253. John Mullen, *The Show Must Go On! Popular Song in Britain during the First World War* (London, 2016), p. 54; Richards, *Imperialism and Music*, p. 337.

254. See the Imperial War Museum copy, www.iwm.org.uk/collections/item/object/ 1502022018, accessed 5/11/2020.

255. Gallagher, *Ireland and the Great War*, p. 146.

256. The song was sung by Donald C. Macgregor, Hartwell DeMille, H. Ruthven McDonald and Howard Russell, among others. Digital images of the original score and lyrics are online at www.youtube.com/watch?v=rlM-0CCV5BE, accessed 13/3/2021.

257. I am grateful to Alex Mayhew for this reference: Manchester Regiment Archives, 3/17/139, Papers of Pte Henry Bridge, 'Marching Song'.

258. Kent Bowman, 'Echoes of Shot and Shell: Songs of the Great War', *Studies in Popular Culture*, 10, 1 (1987), 32.

259. The appeal was widely published in the press. For examples, *Liverpool Daily Post*, 23/10/1915; *Daily Telegraph*, 23/10/1915, p. 9; *Rochdale Observer*, 23/10/1915, p. 7. The 'Derby Scheme' was also sometimes referred to as the 'Group Scheme'.

260. Churchill, *In the Eye of the Storm*, p. 127.

261. See, for an example, the Imperial War Museum's collections, www.iwm.org.uk /collections/item/object/30085183, accessed 8/1/2020.

262. Asquith, *Memories and Reflections*, Vol. 2, p. 109.

263. Churchill, *In the Eye of the Storm*, p. 127.

264. Ibid., p. 128.

265. Ibid.

266. BL, Add MS 54192 B, Parliamentary Recruiting Committee Minutes, Vol. 2, 11/ 10/1915, ff. 9–10. On the PRC, see Douglas, 'Voluntary Enlistment in the First World War'. For press announcement of the Derby Scheme, see 'Lord Derby's New Recruiting Scheme', *Hull Daily Mail*, 16/10/1915, p. 3. For examples of PRC posters referring to 'King and Country', see Philip Dutton, 'Moving Images? The Parliamentary Recruiting Committee's Poster Campaign, 1914–1916', *Imperial War Museum Review*, 4 (1989), 43–58.

267. See Imperial War Museum Collections, Derby Scheme Brassard, www.iwm.org.uk /collections/item/object/30078876, accessed 8/1/2020.

268. BL, Add MS 54192 B, Parliamentary Recruiting Committee Minutes, Vol. 2, 18/ 10/1915, f. 15.

269. 'The King Summons a Night Council', *Daily Mirror*, 21/10/1915, p. 3.

270. 'The King's Summons', *Liverpool Daily Post*, 23/10/1915, p. 4.

271. Churchill, *In the Eye of the Storm*, p. 129.

272. Legge, *King Edward, the Kaiser and the War*, pp. 128–9.

273. *Daily Telegraph*, 23/10/1915, p. 9.

274. *The Standard*, 23/10/1915, cited in Churchill, *In the Eye of the Storm*, p. 129.

275. See David Fitzpatrick, 'The Logic of Collective Sacrifice: Ireland and the British Army, 1914–1918', *Historical Journal*, 38, 4 (1995), 1020.

276. Gullace, *'The Blood of Our Sons'*, pp. 87–8.

277. IWM Documents 8749, Box Misc. 120 item 1851, Royal letter of appreciation of one family's contribution to the armed forces, Keeper of the Privy Purse to Mrs Baulsom, 10/4/1915.

278. 'King Congratulates Elgin Mother', *Dundee Evening Telegraph*, 8/6/1915, p. 4.

279. For other examples of royal letters to families with many members serving, most with identical wording, see 'The King's Congratulations to Mother of Four Sons in the Forces', *Folkestone, Hythe, Sandgate and Cheriton Herald*, 12/12/1914, p. 10; 'A Proud Mother', *Liverpool Echo*, 13/2/1915, p. 4; 'King Congratulates a Leeds Mother', *Yorkshire Evening Post*, 4/5/1915, p. 5; 'Proud Budleigh Mother', *Western Times*, 20/11/1914, p. 8; 'A Mother's Pride', *Wiltshire Times and Trowbridge Advertiser*, 25/12/1915, p. 3. See also the two examples cited in Churchill, *In the Eye of the Storm*, p. 176.

280. 'King Congratulates Elgin Mother', *Dundee Evening Telegraph*, 8/6/1915, p. 4.

281. 'King and Mother of Six Soldiers', *The Scotsman*, 27/11/1915, p. 10.

282. 'The King's Congratulations', *Western Chronicle*, 1/10/1915, p. 2.

283. Ibid.

284. National Trust pamphlet, 'Ickworth and the Great War', available online: https://nt .global.ssl.fastly.net/ickworth/documents/ickworth-and-the-great-war–research-pamphlet-.pdf, accessed 2/4/2019.

285. Ibid.

286. 'A Patriotic Family', *The Londonderry Sentinel*, 4/8/1917, p. 3.

287. The letter Mrs Baulsom received was worded identically to that received by Mrs Bailey and very similar to that received by Mrs Rhind.

288. Churchill, *In the Eye of the Storm*, p. 176.

289. www.bbc.co.uk/news/uk-england-25497900, accessed 19/09/2018. See also www .theguardian.com/world/2018/nov/04/barnard-castle-pauses-remember-five-sons-who-never-came-home-first-world-war-rememberance-day, accessed 4/11/2018.

290. Gregory, *The Last Great War*, pp. 94–5.

291. 'Conscientious Objector's Claims: Field Night at the City Tribunal', *Perthshire Advertiser*, 29/7/1916, p. 3.

292. Ibid.

293. Nigel McCrery, *All the King's Men: One of the Greatest Mysteries of the First World War Finally Solved* (London, 1999), p. 47.

294. E Company was amalgamated in spring 1915 with another company to become C Company and renamed 'King's Company', but the royal family and others continued to refer to it as the Sandringham Company.

295. McCrery, *All the King's Men*, p. 47.

296. Ibid., pp. 48–9.

297. The royal reactions to this loss are discussed in more detail in Chapter 5.

298. Dublin City Library and Archive, The Monica Roberts Collection, Vol. 4, Letter from Private George Soper to Monica Roberts, 2/5/1917.

299. Vera Brittain, *Testament of Youth: An Autobiographical Study of the Years 1900–1925* (London, 1978 [1933]), p. 259.

300. Ibid., p. 450.
301. Ceadel, 'The "King and Country" Debate'.
302. Peggy Hamilton, *Three Years or the Duration: The Memoirs of a Munition Worker 1914–1918* (London, 1978), p. 125.
303. Rose, *King George V*, p.188.
304. This was not the case in all of Europe by 1914, and even in some places where it had become the norm, such as in Belgium, the war revived older ideas that kings should lead their men in war.
305. RA EDW/PRIV/DIARY/1914: 3 August.
306. Lerman, 'Wilhelm's War'; Boff, *Haig's Enemy*.
307. Edward, Duke of Windsor, *A King's Story: The Memoirs of HRH the Duke of Windsor* (London, 1951), p. 109. This memoir must be treated with caution, as Edward's wartime diary contradicts it on a number of points.
308. Churchill, *In the Eye of the Storm*, p. 158.
309. The British Monarchy, Flickr account: Album Prince Alexander of Battenberg, Letter from Prince Alexander of Battenberg to Princess Beatrice, 15/9/1914, www.flickr.com/photos/britishmonarchy/albums/72157646469135840, accessed 4/6/18.
310. TNA, WO 339/7854, Sir Douglas Haig to GHQ, forwarded to War Office, 27/10/1914.
311. Press and other accounts claim Leopold served at the front in 1914 as an infantry lieutenant. M. E. Sara, *The Life and Times of HRH Princess Beatrice* (London, 1945), p. 129. Also 'War Notes', *Derby Daily Telegraph*, 29/10/1914, p. 2; 'Royal Victim', *Hamilton Daily Times*, 29/10/1914, p. 5; Churchill, *In the Eye of the Storm*, p. 71 describes him as wounded.
312. RA NEWS/PRESS/EVIIIPW/MAIN: 1914, Vol. XIV, p. 41: *Ladies' Field*, 3/10/1914.
313. RA EDW/PRIV/DIARY/1914: 8 September.
314. RA EDW/PRIV/DIARY/1914: 13 September.
315. Paul Emden, *Behind the Throne* (London, 1934), pp. 195–8.
316. RA EDW/PRIV/DIARY/1914: 14 September.
317. RA EDW/PRIV/DIARY/1914: 15 September.
318. RA NEWS/PRESS/EVIIIPW/MAIN: 1914, Vol. XIV, p. 12; p. 31: 'The Prince as Guardsman to Go on Active Service', *The Times*, 7/8/1914; 'The Prince of Wales for the Front', *Daily Sketch*, 12/9/1914.
319. Ibid., p. 37: 'The Prince of Wales: Official Statement', *Daily Telegraph*, 19/9/1914.
320. 'A Royal Example to the Young Unmarried Men of the Empire', *Tatler*, 12/8/1914, p. 8.
321. RA EDW/PRIV/DIARY/1914: 28 August. On the close connection between the monarchy and the aristocracy, see Mort, 'Accessible Sovereignty', 355.
322. Churchill Archives Centre, Esher Papers, ESHR 6/9, Letter from Edward Prince of Wales to Viscount Esher, 28/11/1914.
323. RA NEWS/PRESS/EVIIIPW/MAIN: 1914, Vol. XIV, p. 32: 'Our Soldier Prince', *The Queen*, 12/9/1914.
324. Ibid., p. 47: 'Prince of Wales to Join Expeditionary Force', *The Standard*, 17/11/1914.
325. Ibid., p. 48: 'Prince of Wales at the Front on Sir John French's Staff', *Daily Telegraph*, 17/11/1914.

326. Ibid., p. 52: 'Last Prince of Wales to Go to War Abroad', *Daily Chronicle*, 17/11/1914.
327. 'I Serve', *The Pall Mall Gazette*, 17/11/1914, p. 5.
328. RA NEWS/PRESS/EVIIIPW/MAIN: 1914, Vol. XIV, p. 56: 'The Prince in the Field', *Evening Standard*, 17/11/1914.
329. 'I Serve', *Pall Mall Gazette*, 17/11/1914, p. 5.
330. RA NEWS/PRESS/EVIIIPW/MAIN: 1914, Vol. XIV, pp. 55–6: 'Prince of Wales and Prince Albert off to the War', *Daily Sketch*, 17/11/1914; see also 'The Prince in the Field', *Evening Standard*, 17/11/1914.
331. Churchill College Archives, Esher Papers, ESHR 2/13, Diary, 18/12/1914 and Esher Papers, ESHR 2/15, Diary, 15/10/1915, both cited in Glencross, 'A Cause of Tension?', p. 181.
332. RA NEWS/PRESS/EVIIIPW/MAIN: 1914, Vol. XIV, p. 62: 'I Serve!', *Daily Graphic*, 18/11/1914.
333. Ibid., p. 52: '1356-1914: Last Prince of Wales to Go to War Abroad', *Daily Chronicle*, 17/11/1914.
334. Ibid., p. 76; p. 48: 'Prince and People at the Front', *Lloyd's Weekly News*, 22/11/1914; 'Prince of Wales at the Front on Sir John French's Staff', *Daily Telegraph*, 17/11/1914.
335. 'I Serve', *Pall Mall Gazette*, 17/11/1914, p. 5.
336. Edward, Duke of Windsor, *A King's Story*, pp. 116–17.
337. 'The Prince of Wales's Risks', *Daily Sketch*, 17/1/1916.

2 Monarchist Culture and Combatant Practices

1. I am grateful to Alex Mayhew for his assistance in bringing some source material used in this chapter to my attention.
2. See, for example, Alexander Watson, *Enduring the Great War: Combat, Morale and Collapse in the German and British Armies, 1914–1918* (Cambridge, 2008); Roper, *The Secret Battle*; Tony Ashworth, *Trench Warfare, 1914–1918: The Live and Let Live System* (London, 1980).
3. Rose, *King George V*, p. 179; Gore, *King George V*, p. 292.
4. 'Investiture by the King', *Newcastle Journal*, 17/1/1916, p. 6. This scale of event was common: on 13 February 1918, the King decorated 296 'ladies and men' and 308 'officers and nurses' on 2 March 1918: RA GV/PRIV/GVD/1918: 13 February and 2 March.
5. See Chapter 3 for more discussion of the 'royal touch'.
6. 'V.C.', *Yorkshire Evening Post*, 12/9/1917, p. 4.
7. Ibid.
8. www.iwm.org.uk/history/first-world-war-service-medals, accessed 28 May 2020.
9. Ibid.
10. Churchill, *In the Eye of the Storm*, p. 179.
11. Gilbert, ed.,*Winston S. Churchill*, Vol. 3: *The Challenge of War 1914–1916*, p. 88.
12. Churchill, *In the Eye of the Storm*, pp. 177–8.
13. Ibid., pp. 178–9.
14. RA GV/PRIV/GVD/1916: 29 November.
15. 'Investiture by the King', *The Scotsman*, 27/9/1917, p. 4.

16. Ibid.
17. British Pathé online archive, www.britishpathe.com/video/buckingham-palace-investiture-mr-and-mrs-ball-pare, accessed 8/7/2020.
18. Churchill, *In the Eye of the Storm*, p. 243.
19. Rose, *King George V*, p. 258.
20. Ibid.; Prochaska, *The Republic of Britain*, p. 165; Owens, *The Family Firm*, p. 172.
21. Gallacher, *Revolt on the Clyde*, pp. 166–7.
22. Ibid., p. 168.
23. Ibid. Italics in original.
24. Ibid., p. 267.
25. Churchill, *In the Eye of the Storm*, p. 243.
26. Terry Oliver, *For King, Country and Caddington 1914–1918* (Caddington, 2014), p. 13.
27. Ibid.
28. Ibid.
29. 'The King and the Food Queues: Solicitude for Irish Hero's Mother', *The Globe*, 9/2/1918, p. 8.
30. Ibid.
31. Mort, 'Safe for Democracy', 130; 132.
32. *Daily Sketch*, 17/11/16, cited in Churchill, *In the Eye of the Storm*, p. 179.
33. IWM Documents 22414, Box P150, Private papers of Brigadier E. Foster Hall, Diary, 15/9/1916, f. 58.
34. Prochaska, *The Republic of Britain*, p. 166.
35. LPL, Papers of Dr Randall T. Davidson, Archbishop of Canterbury, private papers, Vol. 13, f. 313, Memorandum of trip to Windsor, 12/5/1918.
36. Ibid., ff. 322–3, Memorandum on fourth anniversary of the beginning of the war, 4/8/1918.
37. David Omissi, ed., *Indian Voices of the Great War: Soldiers' Letters 1914–1918* (Basingstoke, 1999), p. 111, Extract no. 164, Subedar Major Sundar Singh Bahadur to Havildar Basant Singh, 19/10/1915.
38. Ibid., pp. 148–9, Extract no. 238, Subedar Dhan Singh Lama to Subedar Major Gopi Ram Lama, 6/2/1916.
39. Mary Evans Picture Library, 11114205, *Daily Sketch*, 11/1/1915, cover.
40. Stanley Naylor, 'Remembrance "Lest We Forget": To the Memory of the Gallant Sons of Kirton Who Unstintingly Gave Their Lives for King and Country in Two Great Wars; 1914–1918; 1939–1945' (BL, unpublished history, Boston, 2008), p. 39.
41. IWM Documents 14178, Box 09/57/1, Private papers of Lieut. C. G. Bonner VC, letter to C. G. Bonner from twenty-six former colleagues at Johnson Line Limited, Liverpool, 19/10/1917.
42. IWM Documents 7218, Box 97/37/1, E. Silas, 'A Royal Occasion', 20/5/1916.
43. IWM Documents 17029, Box 09/34/1, Captain A. J. Lord, Letter of 16/3/1918.
44. IWM Sound Archive, Reginald Haine VC (Oral History), 1973, Catalogue no. 33, reel 5.
45. Ibid.
46. Rose, *King George V*, p. 179.
47. RA PS/PSO/GV/C/O/1106/7, Stamfordham to Col. Unsworth, 9/4/1917.

48. John Alexander Hammerton and Herbert Wrigley Wilson, eds., *The Great War: The Standard History of the All-Europe Conflict*, 13 vols (London, 1914–19), Vol. 10 (1918), p. 20, cited in Churchill, *In the Eye of the Storm*, p. 62.

49. Gilbert, ed., *Winston S. Churchill*, Vol. 3: *The Challenge of War 1914–1916*, pp. 305–6. Italics in original.

50. *Daily Telegraph*, 4/8/1915, cited in Churchill, *In the Eye of the Storm*, p. 84.

51. RA GV/PRIV/GVD/1914: 25 September.

52. IWM Documents 12538, Box 02/55/1, Private papers of F. L. Stone, 26/10/1914.

53. IWM Documents 15403, Box 06/120/1, Dan Joiner, book 1, pp. 10–11.

54. IWM Documents 17992, Box 14/18/1, Captain N. J. Ainsworth, Letter to his father, 9/9/1915.

55. IWM Sound Archive, Pte Thomas McIndoe (Oral History), 1975, Catalogue no. 568, reel 3.

56. IWM Documents 12383, Box 02/29/1, J. Anderson Johnston, The Diary of a Rifleman, p. 7.

57. On medievalism in British commemoration, see Goebel, *The Great War and Medieval Memory*.

58. 'King George's Message to the Navy', *Western Gazette*, 7/8/1914, p. 12; RA GV/PRIV/GVD/1914: 5 August.

59. Letter from George V to Queen Mary in 1916, cited in Churchill, *In the Eye of the Storm*, p. 166. Churchill does not give a source reference for this quotation.

60. Scott Hughes Myerly, '"The Eye Must Entrap the Mind": Army Spectacle and Paradigm in Nineteenth-Century Britain', *Journal of Social History*, 26, 1 (1992), 105–31; Rüger, *The Great Naval Game*, pp. 1–2; p. 192.

61. On George V's personal account of these visits, see RA GV/PRIV/GVD/1915: 17 May, visit to Glasgow.

62. Mort, 'Accessible Sovereignty', 332–3.

63. RA GV/PRIV/GVD/1914: 3 December.

64. 'The King's Return', *Daily Mail*, 7/12/1914.

65. Churchill, *In the Eye of the Storm*, p. 77.

66. Churchill, *In the Eye of the Storm*, p. 75. The same letter is cited in Pope-Hennessy, *Queen Mary*, p. 496, where the wording is quoted as 'awfully proud'.

67. *Douglas Haig: War Diaries and Letters*, pp. 82–3.

68. H. G. Gilliland, 'My German Prisons', quoted in A. L. Vischer, *The Barbed Wire Disease: A Psychological Study of the Prisoner of War* (London, 1919), p. 18.

69. Nicolson, *King George the Fifth*, p. 255.

70. Ibid.

71. For example, BL, MSS EUR F143/62, India Office Records, Clive Wigram to Walter Lawrence, 20/11/14, f. 6. See also War Office, *Manual of Military Law*, p. 415.

72. Gerard Oram, '"The Administration of Discipline by the English is Very Rigid": British Military Law and the Death Penalty (1868–1918)', *Crime, Histoire et Sociétés*, 5, 1 (2001), 93–110. See also G. R. Rubin, 'Parliament, Prerogative and Military Law: Who Had Legal Authority over the Army in the Late Nineteenth Century?', *The Journal of Legal History*, 18, 1 (1997), 45–84.

73. Churchill, *In the Eye of the Storm*, p. 144. No footnote for the source of this information is provided in Churchill.

74. Oxford, Bodleian Libraries, MS Asquith, A.1, Vol. 4, f. 109, Captain Ronald Stewart-Menzies to Lord Stamfordham, 17/4/1915 and f. 112, Lieutenant Lord Garlies to Lady Fitzwilliam, 15/4/1915.

75. Ibid., f. 114, Stamfordham to Bonham Carter, 4/5/1915.

76. See Chapter 3 for more on this wartime problem of the British royals' relationship to Germany. On the image of the Kaiser in Britain, see Reinermann, 'Fleet Street and the Kaiser'.

77. RA PS/PSO/GV/PS/WAR/QQ7/4745, Wigram to Lambton, 5/11/1914.

78. Gabriel Tschumi, *Royal Chef: Recollections of a Life in Royal Households from Queen Victoria to Queen Mary* (London, 1954), pp. 138-9.

79. LPL, Papers of Dr Randall T. Davidson, Archbishop of Canterbury, private papers, Vol. 6, f. 11, Stamfordham to Randall Davidson, 17/8/1916.

80. Tschumi, *Royal Chef*, p. 139.

81. Mary Evans Picture Library, 10725818, *Daily Sketch*, 25/12/1918.

82. Prochaska, *The Republic of Britain*, p. 165.

83. RA GV/PRIV/GVD/1914: 3 December.

84. Glencross, 'A Cause of Tension?', p. 157.

85. 'The King in the Field, Message to the Troops', *Westminster Gazette*, 8/12/1914, p. 7.

86. Churchill, *In the Eye of the Storm*, p. 184.

87. Sir Frederick Ponsonby, *Recollections of Three Reigns* (London, 1951), p. 323.

88. Lincolnshire Archives, BNLW 4/4/8/2, Papers of Sir Charles Cust, Diary of the king's visit to the army in the field, 1915, 26 October.

89. Ibid., 27 October.

90. Lyn MacDonald, *Somme* (London, 2013), p. 218.

91. LPL, Papers of Dr Randall T. Davidson, Archbishop of Canterbury, private papers, Vol. 6, f. 11, Stamfordham to Randall Davidson, 17/8/1916.

92. Gibbs, Philip, ed., *George the Faithful: The Life and Times of George 'The People's King' 1865-1936* (London, [1936]), pp. 254-6.

93. Ibid., p. 257.

94. Basil Thomson, *The Scene Changes* (London, 1939), p. 311.

95. RA GV/PRIV/GVD/1917: 4 July.

96. Ibid.

97. Andrew Rose, *The Prince, The Princess and the Perfect Murder* (London, 2013), p. 56.

98. Mary Evans Picture Library, 10724664, Supplement *Illustrated London News*, 1936.

99. RA EDW/PRIV/DIARY/1915: 31 December.

100. Lincolnshire Archives, BNLW 4/4/8/2, Papers of Sir Charles Cust, Diary of the king's visit to the army in the field, 1915, Friday and Saturday 22 and 23 October. Cust, an equerry, relates that the French police took precautions, and extra sentries were posted. Additionally, four extra sentry posts were allocated to the royal train.

101. Tschumi, *Royal Chef*, p. 142.

102. Churchill, *In the Eye of the Storm*, p. 168.

103. Ibid.

104. Mary Evans Picture Library, 11960975, *War Illustrated*, no. 17, 1915.

105. RA GV/PRIV/GVD/1918: 22, 23 and 24 March.

106. Nicolson, *King George the Fifth*, p. 324.

107. RA PS/PSO/GV/PS/WAR/QQ7/4745, Lambton GHQ to Wigram, 26/11/1914.

108. RA PS/PSO/GV/PS/WAR/QQ7/4745, Clive Wigram to Colonel Sir Harry Legge, 9/12/1914.

109. BL, Add MSS 46722 1890–1918, Boyd-Carpenter Papers, George V to Bishop of Ripon, 25/12/1914, f. 40.

110. Papers of John St Loe Strachey, PA S/13/15/15, Strachey to king, 8/12/1914.

111. Escott Lynn, *In Khaki for the King: A Tale of the Great War* (London, Edinburgh, 1915), p. 342.

112. RA PS/PSO/GV/C/Q/832/124, Sir Douglas Haig to King George V, 20/8/1916.

113. RA PS/PSO/GV/C/Q/832/139, Sir Douglas Haig to King George V, 2/4/1918.

114. RA GV/PRIV/AA48/174, Randall Davidson to King George V, 21/8/1918.

115. Fitzroy, *Memoirs*, Vol. 2, p. 680.

116. Ponsonby, *Recollections of Three Reigns*, p. 314.

117. Ibid., p. 316.

118. RA PS/PSO/GV/C/Q/832/130, Sir Douglas Haig to King George V, 28/2/1917.

119. RA PS/PSO/GV/PS/WAR/QQ18/05707, Letter from William Birdwood to Clive Wigram, 13/7/1917.

120. IWM Documents 14169, Box 67/7/1, Major General V. G. Tofts, 2–8 Battalions Manchester Regiment, Memoir, p. 14.

121. Rose, *King George V*, p. 180.

122. IWM Sound Archive, Colonel Stewart Montagu Cleeve (Oral History), 1983, Catalogue no. 7310, reel 8, describing George V's visit in August 1918.

123. Elton, *C. E. Montague*, p. 190.

124. Rose, *King George V*, p. 169.

125. IWM Documents 11943, Box 02/12/1, Papers of H. Empson.

126. IWM Documents 11289, Box 01/21/1, H. T. Madders, 2/1st Battalion Royal Fusiliers, Diary, 3/4/1918.

127. *The Red Triangle*, 20/7/17, cited in Churchill, *In the Eye of the Storm*, p. 236.

128. RA GV/PRIV/GVD/1914: 1 December.

129. IWM Documents 16149, Box 08/42/1, Captain A. St John Blunt, Diary, 3/12/1914.

130. Vancouver Island University, Canadian Letters and Images Project, Wilbert Gilroy to Em, 2/11/1915, www.canadianletters.ca/content/document-1391, accessed 6/8/2019.

131. IWM Documents 18542, Box 66/160/1, Papers of A. Wells, November 1914.

132. Lincolnshire Archives, BNLW 4/4/8/2, Papers of Sir Charles Cust, Diary of the king's visit to the army in the field, 1915, Thursday 21 October.

133. IWM Documents 12003, Box PP/MCR/82, The 1915–16 letters of Lieutenant J. W. Gamble.

134. Dublin City Library and Archive, The Monica Roberts Collection, Vol. 3, Letter from Private Joseph Elley to Monica Roberts, 8/11/1915.

135. Thomson, *The Scene Changes*, p. 349.

136. IWM Sound Archive, Raynor Taylor (Oral History), 1990–2, Catalogue no. 11113, reels 12, 13, citation from reel 13.

137. Ibid.

138. Ibid.

139. RA PS/PSO/GV/PS/WAR/QQ20/7/484, Major General A. C. Daly to Wigram, 7/12/1918 cited in Mort, 'Accessible Sovereignty', 337.

140. IWM Sound Archive, Raynor Taylor (Oral History), 1990–2, Catalogue no. 11113, reels 12, 13, citation from reel 13.

141. 'King at the Front', *The Times*, 1/4/1918, p. 4.
142. RA PS/PSO/GV/PS/WAR/QQ18/05707, Miscellaneous Folder, Extract from a letter to Miss Grace Collins from her brother, Bombardier C. R. Collins, 4/7/1917. Note again here the use of the reverent 'God Bless Him' when the king is mentioned; also *Morning Post*, 17/7/1917.
143. Ibid.
144. On the press and the king's Western Front visits, see Glencross, 'A Cause of Tension?', p. 176.
145. IWM film 192.
146. IWM film 198.
147. RA PS/PSO/GV/WAR/QQ19/07110/4, Earl of Onslow to Major E. G. Thompson, 6/8/1918, cited in Glencross, 'A Cause of Tension?', p. 178. Thompson was designated the king's guide during his Western Front visit in 1918.
148. See the selection of 110 official photographs taken of the king's visits to the front in the Earl Haig Papers, National Library of Scotland, First World War 'Official Photographs', Royal Visits: https://digital.nls.uk/first-world-war-official-photographs/archive/75201717, accessed 28/5/2020. Some of these were issued to the press.
149. Ibid.
150. This is based on a survey of official and press photographs of the king's visits to the Western Front held in the Field Marshal Earl Haig Collection, National Library of Scotland, in Alamy Stock Photographs, the Imperial War Museum, the Mary Evans Picture Library and the Royal Collections.
151. Mort, 'Accessible Sovereignty', 340.
152. Churchill, *In the Eye of the Storm*, p. 171.
153. 'The King and His Soldiers', *The Times*, 16/8/1916, p. 7.
154. H. W. Wilson, 'Introduction', in Associated Newspapers Limited, *His Majesty the King 1910–1935: Twenty Five Years of a Glorious Reign Told in Pictures* (London, n.d.), p. 14.
155. Bryant, *George V*, p. 104.
156. Gibbs, *George the Faithful*, p. 244.
157. Röhl, *Wilhelm II: Into the Abyss*, p. 1131.
158. Ibid., p. 1132.
159. Ibid., p. 1127; p. 1132. Also Stibbe, 'Kaiser Wilhelm II', p. 269; p. 275.
160. Röhl, *Wilhelm II: Into the Abyss*, p. 1118; p. 1131.
161. Ibid., p. 1131.
162. Ibid.
163. Ibid.
164. Ibid., p. 1118.
165. Stibbe, 'Kaiser Wilhelm II', p. 277.
166. Owens, *The Family Firm*, p. 125.
167. Ibid., p. 128.
168. Mass Observation Online, Topic Collections, Children and Education, 1937–52, 59-4-F, Miscellaneous Essays by School Children, 'The Finest Person Who Ever Lived', Image 3270, G. W. F. Rigby. I am grateful to Edward Owens for alerting me to this source.
169. Ibid., 59-4-H, Image 3836, A. Bushell.
170. Ibid., 59-4-H, Image 3837, D. N. Guest.
171. Ibid., 59-4-H, Image 3842–3, J. B. Kershaw.

172. Ibid., 59-4-H, Image 3844, G. R. Harrison.

173. Ibid., 59-4-H, Image 3852, P. R. Newton.

174. Ibid., 59-4-H, Image 3859, R. Hulme.

175. Rachel Duffett, 'The War in Miniature: Queen Mary's Dolls' House and the Legacies of the First World War', *Cultural and Social History*, 16, 4 (2019), 434; Elisabeth Basford, *Princess Mary: The First Modern Princess* (Cheltenham, 2021), p. 52.

176. Rowbotham, 'How to Be Useful in War Time', pp. 191–223.

177. Pope-Hennessy, *Queen Mary*, p. 488. Rowbotham, 'How to Be Useful in War Time', p. 210.

178. Ibid., p. 214.

179. Pope-Hennessy, *Queen Mary*, p. 492.

180. Cathy Hunt, *Righting the Wrong: Mary Macarthur 1880–1921. The Working Woman's Champion* (Alcester, 2019), p. 119.

181. Ibid., p. 119; pp. 121–2.

182. Oxford, Bodleian Libraries, MS Asquith, A.1, Vol. 4, f. 24, Stamfordham to Bonham Carter, 11/10/1914.

183. 'Princess Mary's Appeal', *Daily Gazette for Middlesbrough*, 16/10/1914, p. 2.

184. Mabel C. Carey, *Princess Mary: A Biography* (London, 1922), p. 73.

185. Hackett, 'Dreams or Designs, Cults or Constructions?', p. 812.

186. Giloi, *Monarchy, Myth, and Material Culture*, p. 5.

187. For examples of pictures of George V as the central figure in wartime tin images depicting the war effort, see Mary Evans Picture Library, 11034471, Slade's Army and Navy Caramels; 11033831, Callard and Bowser Butterscotch; 11033681, Tin of patriotic postcards; other examples: 11033682; 11033821; 11033829; 11034460; 11034467; 11034475; 11034477; 11034481. See also the collections of the Historial de la Grande Guerre, Péronne, 004194#, Tin with the image of King George V and the royal standard.

188. Diana Condell, 'A Gift for Christmas: The Story of Princess Mary's Gift Fund, 1914', *Imperial War Museum Review*, 4 (1989), 72.

189. Carey, *Princess Mary*, p. 74.

190. Ibid., pp. 74–5.

191. NAM 1971-01-29-1, Queen Victoria Gift Chocolate Box, 1900; Mort, 'Safe for Democracy', 133.

192. On royal souvenirs, see Mort, 'Safe for Democracy', 138. For examples of the commercial use of the wartime royal image, see the collections of the Historial de la Grande Guerre, Péronne.

193. See Nicholas Saunders, ed., *Matters of Conflict: Material Culture, Memory and the First World War* (New York, London 2004) and Nicholas Saunders, *Trench Art: Materialities and Memories of War* (London, 2003).

194. Nicholas Saunders, *Trench Art: A Brief History and Guide, 1914–1939* (Barnsley, 2001), pp. 73–4.

195. IWM Documents 7490, Box 75/78/1, L/Cpl later 2/Lt K. M. Gaunt, 1/16 Battalion London Regiment and 4 Battalion Royal Warwickshire Regiment, Letter from Gaunt to Auckland, 25/12/1914.

196. Lynn, *In Khaki for the King*, pp. 343–4.

197. 'Saved by Royal Gift Box', *Manchester Courier and Lancashire General Advertiser*, 3/5/1915, p. 6.

198. Ibid.

199. Ibid.

200. 'Protected by Princess Mary's Gift Box', *Dundee Evening Telegraph*, 24/8/1915, p. 4.

201. Carey, *Princess Mary*, p. 75.

202. The British Monarchy, Flickr Account, Album Christmas 1914, Royal Archives, Rawlinson to Wigram, 26/12/1914, www.flickr.com/photos/britishmonarchy/albums/72157649814564456, accessed 4/12/2018.

203. The British Monarchy, Flickr Account, Album Princess Mary's Gift Box, The Royal Collection, www.flickr.com/photos/britishmonarchy/15459086253, accessed 16/6/2020.

204. Pope-Hennessy, *Queen Mary*, pp. 499-500. Italics in original.

205. *The Times*, 7/12/15, cited in Churchill, *In the Eye of the Storm*, p. 145.

206. Churchill, *In the Eye of the Storm*, p. 290.

207. 'The Silver Wedding Appeal', *Western Times*, 25/6/1918, p. 4.

208. 'Silver Wedding Gifts', *Bucks Herald*, 29/6/1918, p. 5.

209. Carol Lovejoy Edwards, *Mansfield in the Great War* (Barnsley, 2015) p. 127; p. 149.

210. 'News of the West: Barnstaple', *Western Times*, 9/7/1918, p. 6; 'Collection of Silver Gifts', *Coventry Evening Telegraph*, 1/7/1918, p. 3; 'Silver Wedding Gifts', *Bucks Herald*, 29/6/1918, p. 5.

211. 'News of the West: Barnstaple', *Western Times*, 9/7/1918, p. 6.

212. 'The Silver Collection', *Westminster Gazette*, 6/7/1918, p. 6.

213. Churchill, *In the Eye of the Storm*, p. 290; 'The Royal Progress', *Westminster Gazette*, 6/7/1918, p. 6.

214. RA PS/PSO/GV/PS/WAR/QQ7/4745, The King's Visit to His Army in the Field, 29 November to 5 December 1914, List in file.

215. Ibid., Captain J. Ellis to Major Clive Wigram, 10/12/1914.

216. Churchill, *In the Eye of the Storm*, p. 138.

217. Letter from Private W. Bandall, published in the *Jewish World*, 21/4/1915, p. 23, cited in Jonathan Lewis, 'Jewish Chaplaincy in the British Armed Forces, from Its Inception in 1892 until the Present Day' (Unpublished PhD thesis, UCL, 2020), p. 147.

218. Broadlands Archive, University of Southampton Library, MB1/A9 First World War: HMS *Lion* and HMS *Queen Elizabeth* 1916-18, Extract from letter from Sub-Lieutenant Hussey, November 1918.

219. On the Princess Mary Gift Box distribution, see Condell, 'A Gift for Christmas'. On increasing state roles in humanitarian war aid, see Bruno Cabanes, *The Great War and the Origins of Humanitarianism, 1918-1924* (Cambridge, 2014) and Heather Jones, 'International or Transnational? Humanitarian Action during the First World War', *European Review of History*, 16, 5 (2009), 697-713.

220. Churchill, *In the Eye of the Storm*, p. 147.

221. Oxford, Bodleian Libraries, MS Asquith, A.1, Vol. 4, ff. 180-1, Ponsonby to Asquith, 10/3/1916.

222. Ibid.

223. TNA, T 172/396, Letter from Ponsonby to Reginald McKenna, 2/3/1916.

224. Ibid.

225. Ibid.

226. Ibid.

227. Ibid.

228. Ibid.

229. TNA, T 172/396, Letter from Reginald McKenna to Frederick Ponsonby, 3/3/1916.

230. Mary Evans Picture Library, 11034516, *Daily Mirror*, n.d.

231. Hansen, 'The Politics of Citizenship', 69; 71.

232. Ibid., 69; 71; see also Paul, *Whitewashing Britain*, p. 13; p. 26. See also the discussion in Chapter 1.

233. David Olusoga, *The World's War* (London, 2014), p. 294; p. 296. Also Richard Smith, *Jamaican Volunteers in the First World War: Race, Masculinity and the Development of National Consciousness* (New York, Manchester, 2004), p. 55.

234. Mackenzie quoted in Potter, 'Empire, Cultures and Identities', 61.

235. On the impossibility of writing any single universal historical narrative of Britain's relationship with its imperial possessions, see Potter, 'Empire, Cultures and Identities', 53.

236. For reasons of scope, it has unfortunately not been possible to track the history of Australasian indigenous troops in any detail in what follows here.

237. Olusoga, *The World's War*, p. 19.

238. Richards, *Imperialism and Music*, p. 502.

239. Michelle Moyd, *Violent Intermediaries: African Soldiers, Conquest and Everyday Colonialism in German East Africa* (Athens, OH, 2014), p. 24.

240. Borden, *Robert Laird Borden: His Memoirs*, Vol.1, p. 461.

241. Ian F. W. Beckett, 'Royalty and the Army in the Twentieth Century' in Glencross, Rowbotham and Kandiah, eds., *The Windsor Dynasty*, p. 112.

242. Library of Congress, 1915 Bahamas recruitment poster, www.loc.gov/resource/cph.3g11198/, accessed 18/12/2019. Mary Evans Picture Library, 11095240, Bahamas Recruitment Poster, 1918.

243. Smith, *Jamaican Volunteers in the First World War*, p. 55.

244. Ibid.

245. Langewiesche, 'Monarchy-Global', 284–5.

246. Ibid.

247. Smith, *Jamaican Volunteers in the First World War*, pp. 55–6.

248. Ibid., p. 55.

249. Ibid., p. 56.

250. Robert A. Hill and Carol Rudisell, eds., *The Marcus Garvey and Universal Negro Improvement Association Papers*, Vol. 1, *1826–August 1919* (Berkeley, 1983), p. 86.

251. Timothy C. Winegard, *Indigenous Peoples of the British Dominions and the First World War* (New York, 2011); see also Timothy C. Winegard, *For King and Kanata: Canadian Indians and the First World War* (Winnipeg, 2012).

252. Stimela Jason Jingoes, *A Chief Is a Chief by the People: The Autobiography of Stimela Jason Jingoes*, recorded and compiled by John and Cassandra Perry (New York, London, Cape Town, 1975), p. 72.

253. Ibid.

254. Ibid., p. 73.

255. Albert Grundlingh, *War and Society: Participation and Remembrance. South African Black and Coloured Troops in the First World War 1914-1918* (Stellenbosch, 2014), p. 63.

256. B.P. Willan, 'The South African Native Labour Contingent, 1916-1918', *Journal of African History*, 19, 1 (1978), 65.

257. See his comments in Albert Grundlingh, 'Mutating Memories and the Making of a Myth: Remembering the SS *Mendi* Disaster, 1917–2007', *South African Historical Journal*, 63, 1 (2011), 28 and Grundlingh, *War and Society*, p. 63.

258. IWM Documents 10201, Box Misc. 58 item 866, Letter from Sheikh Ismail Isahak, Sheikh Madar Ahmed, Haji Para Ismail, Sultan Deria Hassan and Sultan Geria Gerad to His Majesty, the Imperial King of the British through our Commissioner Archer the Honourable Wali of the Somalis and the Somali coast, 1/8/1916.

259. Churchill, *In the Eye of the Storm*, p. 162.

260. The term 'India' of the war period referred to undivided India under British rule, which encompasses the modern-day states of Bangladesh, India, Pakistan and Myanmar (formerly Burma). Wartime propaganda references to 'Indian' troops thus cover men from multiple ethnic and cultural backgrounds from these areas, as well as Gurkha soldiers from the independent kingdom of Nepal and Pashtuns. Wherever the sources permit, these identities will be referred to; however, for the most part royal interactions with troops from the Asian subcontinent simply refer to them as 'Indians'. On these issues of definition, see Santanu Das, *India, Empire, and First World War Culture: Writings, Images, and Songs* (Cambridge, 2018), p. xxiii.

261. Ibid., p. 44. See also Olusoga, *The World's War*, p. 51.

262. Das, *India, Empire, and First World War Culture*, p. 45.

263. Ibid., pp. 47–8.

264. George Morton-Jack, *The Indian Empire at War. From Jihad to Victory: The Untold Story of the Indian Army in the First World War* (London, 2018), p. 41.

265. Das, *India, Empire, and First World War Culture*, p. 50.

266. Omissi, ed., *Indian Voices*.

267. Ibid., p. 20.

268. Ibid.

269. Ibid., p. 21.

270. Ibid.

271. Ibid., p. 275, Extract no. 483, Jemadar Khisan Singh to his wife, 6/2/1917.

272. Morton-Jack, *The Indian Empire at War*, pp. 117–18.

273. Ibid., p. 294.

274. Omissi, ed., *Indian Voices*, p. 305.

275. Ibid., p. 308, Extract no. 556, Jan Mahomed Khan to Abdullah Khan, 25/7/1917.

276. Ibid., p. 175, Extract no. 290, Jemadar Ganda Singh to Gurandate, 12/4/1916.

277. Ibid., p. 28, Extract no. 7, Anonymous wounded Sikh to his brother, 15/1/1915.

278. Omissi, ed., *Indian Voices*.

279. Ibid., p. 93, Extract no. 128, Yusaf Khan to Harif Khan, 25/8/1915.

280. Omissi, ed., *Indian Voices*, p. 61, Extract no. 68, To the King.

281. Das, *India, Empire, and First World War Culture*, p. 163. Omissi, ed., *Indian Voices*, p. 14.

282. Omissi, ed., *Indian Voices*, Extract no. 248, Kaisar-i-Jahan to Khabit Allah, 16/2/1916, pp. 153–4.

283. Ibid., p. 183, Extract no. 308, Lehna Ram to Heta Ram, 9/5/1916.

284. Ibid., p. 265, Extract no. 459, Abdul Ghafur to Abdul Hakim Khan, 2/1/1917.

285. Ibid., p. 175, Extract no. 291, Sirfaraz Khan to Dafadar Alam Khan, 16/4/1916 and p. 273, Extract no. 478, Gurmukh Singh to Bishan Singh, 30/1/1917.

286. Ibid., pp. 294–5, Extract no. 526, Sarup Singh to Hira Singh, n.d. [late May 1917].

287. Ibid., p. 330, Extract no. 605, Kishan Singh to Gajan Singh, 2/11/1917.

288. Das, *India, Empire, and First World War Culture*, p. 53.
289. Ibid., p. 54.
290. Ibid.
291. Andrew Tait Jarboe, 'Healing the Empire: Indian Hospitals in Britain and France during the First World War', *Twentieth Century British History*, 26, 3 (2015), 349.
292. Olusoga, *The World's War*, p. 91.
293. Jarboe, 'Healing the Empire', p. 355.
294. Ibid., p. 360.
295. Omissi, ed., *Indian Voices*, p. 59, Extract no. 63, Isar Singh to a friend, 1/5/1915.
296. Ibid., p. 92, Extract no. 126, Sub-assistant surgeon Abdulla to a friend, 23/8/1915.
297. Suzanne Bardgett, 'A Mutual Fascination: Indians in Brighton', *History Today* (March, 2015), 41–7.
298. RA PS/PSO/GV/PS/WAR/QQ18/05707, WAR, Visit of King and Queen to France, 1917, R. Maxwell, GHQ to C. Wigram, 8/7/1917.
299. Ibid.
300. Ibid.
301. Ibid.
302. RA PS/PSO/GV/PS/WAR/QQ18/05707, WAR, Visit of King and Queen to France, 1917, copy of letter sent from Evan Gibb, GHQ British armies to Col. J. H. Nation, AAG Advanced HQ, n.d.
303. RA PS/PSO/GV/PS/WAR/QQ18/05707, WAR, Visit of King and Queen to France, 1917, King's Speech to Native South African Labour Corps, Abbeville, 10 July 1917, enclosed in R. Maxwell, GHQ to C. Wigram, 8/7/1917.
304. Ibid.
305. Ibid.
306. Ibid.
307. Ibid.
308. RA PS/PSO/GV/PS/WAR/QQ18/05707, WAR, Visit of King and Queen to France, 1917, Evan Gibb to Clive Wigram, 13/7/1917.
309. Ibid.
310. RA PS/PSO/GV/PS/WAR/QQ18/05707, WAR, Visit of King and Queen to France, 1917, Stamfordham to Evan Gibb, 15/7/17.
311. RA GV/PRIV/GVD/1917: 10 July.
312. Frank Mort, 'On Tour with the Prince: Monarchy, Imperial Politics and Publicity in the Prince of Wales's Dominion Tours, 1919–20', *Twentieth Century British History*, 29, 1 (2018), 45.
313. RA GV/PRIV/GVD/1917: 12 July and RA GV/PRIV/GVD/1918: 5 August refer to Huns; RA GV/PRIV/GVD/1918: 7 August, 3 December and 4 December use the term Boche.
314. This conclusion, however, must remain provisional awaiting further research into George V's papers in the Royal Archives.
315. RA PS/PSO/GV/PS/WAR/QQ18/05707, WAR, Visit of King and Queen to France, 1917, Evan Gibb to Clive Wigram, 13/7/1917.
316. Grundlingh, *War and Society*, p. 99. See also p. 107.
317. Ibid.
318. Willan, 'The South African Native Labour Contingent', 80.
319. Ibid., 83.
320. Smith, *Jamaican Volunteers in the First World War*, p. 126.
321. Ibid., p. 92.

322. Ibid., p. 39.

323. Ibid.

324. TNA, CO 323/807, f. 404, The Society of Peoples of African Origin to the Secretary of State for War, 10/7/1919.

325. Willan, 'The South African Native Labour Contingent', 83–4.

326. Grundlingh, *War and Society*, p. 109.

327. Willan, 'The South African Native Labour Contingent', 83–4.

328. Morton-Jack, *The Indian Empire at War*, p. 413.

329. On the 'native princes', see Das, *India, Empire, and First World War Culture*, pp. 44–5.

330. Morton-Jack, *The Indian Empire at War*, p. 503.

331. Churchill, *In the Eye of the Storm*, p. 87.

332. Nicolson, *King George the Fifth*, p. 165. See also RA GV/PRIV/GVD/1914: 17 November.

333. BL, MSS EUR F143/62, India Office Records, Clive Wigram to Walter Lawrence, 20/11/14, f. 6.

334. Rose, *King George V*, p. 180.

335. RA PS/PSO/GV/PS/MAIN/30880, Wigram to Dawson, 24/10/1920.

336. www.rotoruamuseum.co.nz/blog/2019/03/01/te-arawa-soldiers-memorial-unve iling/, accessed 8/6/2020. Monarchism was also a feature in memorials to white New Zealanders; the war memorial in the village of Matakana from 1920 also includes a statue of George V: https://nzhistory.govt.nz/media/photo/matakana-war-memorial, accessed 8/6/2020.

337. https://nzhistory.govt.nz/media/photo/arawa-war-memorial-rotorua, accessed 8/6/2020.

338. Edgerton, *The Rise and Fall of the British Nation*, p. 20.

339. Mort, 'Accessible Sovereignty', 343.

340. Amos Mayse, Letter, 4/2/1917, www.canadianletters.ca/content/document-9748, accessed 18/12/2019.

341. John Cowles, Letter, 29/3/1916, www.canadianletters.ca/content/document-762, accessed 18/12/2019.

342. Bertram Howard Cox, Letter, 15/8/1917, www.canadianletters.ca/content/docu ment-41692, accessed 18/12/2019.

343. Samuel Ball, Letter, 5/7/1916, www.canadianletters.ca/content/document-1030, accessed 18/12/2019.

344. IWM Documents 13253, Box 05/8/1, Papers of Ellis Alban Newton, Ellis Newton to his sister Madge, 2/12/1915.

345. Ibid., Cecil Trenam to Mrs Newton, 11/8/1916.

346. Mort, 'Accessible Sovereignty', 357.

347. Kathryn Cook, 'The Monarchy Is More than the Monarch: Australian Perceptions of the Public Life of Edward, Prince of Wales, 1916–1936' (Unpublished DPhil thesis, Australian National University, 2017), pp. 60–73, https://openresearch-repository.anu.edu.au/bitstream/1885/117268/1/Cook%20Thesis%202017.pdf.

348. Ibid.

349. Mort, 'Accessible Sovereignty', 347.

350. Ibid., 351.

351. Ibid.

352. John Barrett, 'Historical Reconsiderations VII. No Straw Man: C. E. W. Bean and Some Critics', *Australian Historical Studies*, 23, 89 (1988), 113.

353. 'Second Lieutenant HRH', *Daily Sketch*, 18/11/1914.

354. RA EDW/PRIV/DIARY/1916: 4 and 17 December.

355. RA EDW/PRIV/DIARY/1915: 25 September.

356. RA EDW/PRIV/DIARY/1914: 23 December.

357. RA EDW/PRIV/DIARY/1914: 13 November.

358. RA EDW/PRIV/DIARY/1915: 14 March.

359. Letter from Edward Prince of Wales to George V in 1915, cited in Churchill, *In the Eye of the Storm*, p. 150. Churchill does not give a source reference for this quotation.

360. RA EDW/PRIV/DIARY/1915: 31 December.

361. 'Prince of Wales at the Front', *Newcastle Journal*, 22/5/1915, p. 12.

362. 'In His Element: The Prince of Wales at the Front', *The Graphic*, 17/4/1915, p. 3. See also, for another example, 'Local Tommies [*sic*] Letters: Hastinger Sees the Prince of Wales', *Hastings and St Leonards Observer*, 28/11/1914, p. 4.

363. 'War Sidelights', *Newcastle Journal*, 22/1/1915, p. 4.

364. NAM 1989-08-154, Alan Maciver's memories of the First World War, 2nd Lancashire Fusiliers, Western Front 1915–18, oral interview.

365. Ibid.

366. Alexander Scotland, *The London Cage* (London, 1957), p. 36.

367. See for example his account of being shelled at an observation post: RA EDW/PRIV/DIARY/1915: 31 December.

368. RA EDW/PRIV/DIARY/1916: 20 July.

369. RA EDW/PRIV/DIARY/1916: 19 July.

370. Edward, Duke of Windsor, *A King's Story*, p. 123.

371. RA PS/PSO/GVI/C/019/441–3, Letter from E. Beddington Behrens, late Capt. RFA, to Edward VIII, 2/12/1936.

372. Ibid., Letter from R. C. Smart to Edward VIII, 11/12/1936.

373. Ibid., Letter from Norman Hudson to Edward VIII, 14/12/1936.

374. Ibid., Letter from Ben Richards to Edward VIII, 11/12/1936.

375. Ibid., Letter from Arthur Cross to Edward VIII, n.d. [1936]. The capitalisation of 'Honour' by the writer is significant of its importance.

376. Ibid., Letter from Field Marshal Sir William Birdwood to Edward VIII, 11/12/1936.

377. Ibid., Letter from Major A. N. Braithwaite, MP, to Edward VIII, 10/12/1936.

378. Ibid., Letter from J. O. Roach to Edward VIII, 3/12/1936.

379. Ibid., Letter from MP Scrymgeour-Weddenburn, 1936.

380. There is also evidence that Australian ex-servicemen supported Edward due to his war role: see Cook, 'The Monarchy Is More than the Monarch', p. 282.

381. See CUL, MS Baldwin, Vols 143–50.

382. CUL, MS Baldwin, Vol. 145, f. 236, Edith Donnelly to Stanley Baldwin, 15/12/1936.

383. CUL, MS Baldwin, Vol. 145, f. 269, Florence Findlay to Stanley Baldwin, 11/12/1936.

384. CUL, MS Baldwin, Vol. 145, ff. 265–6, Captain G. S. Fillingham to Stanley Baldwin, 13/12/1936.

385. CUL, MS Baldwin, Vol. 143, f. 9, letter from W. K. Anderson to Stanley Baldwin, 11/12/1936.

386. CUL, MS Baldwin, Vol. 150, f. 101, A. Wilkinson, Honorary Secretary, British Legion Runcorn Branch to Stanley Baldwin, 13/1/1937.

387. CUL, MS Baldwin, Vol. 145, f. 255, C. Knight-Coutts to Stanley Baldwin, 14/12/1936.
388. See Alex Watson's work, for example, for a sophisticated analysis of the range of factors that affected British soldiers' morale: Watson, *Enduring the Great War*.
389. Heather Jones, *Violence against Prisoners of War, Britain, France and Germany, 1914–1920* (Cambridge, 2011), p. 291.

3   The Royal Body in Wartime

1. On pre-war trends, see Mort, 'Safe for Democracy'.
2. Luke McKernan, '"The Finest Cinema Performers That We Possess": British Royalty and the Newsreels, 1910–37', *The Court Historian*, 8, 1 (2003), 63–4.
3. Williamson, 'The Monarchy and Public Values', p. 226.
4. Mort, 'Safe for Democracy', 132; 135.
5. Olechnowicz, 'Historians and the Modern British Monarchy', p. 18.
6. Asquith, *Memories and Reflections*, Vol. 2, p. 7.
7. Gibbs, *George the Faithful*, p. 235. Italics in original.
8. Mort, 'Accessible Sovereignty', 340.
9. Churchill, *In the Eye of the Storm*, p. 187.
10. Mort, 'Safe for Democracy', 131.
11. On gender and power, see the work of Joan Wallach Scott: 'Gender: A Useful Category of Historical Analysis', *American Historical Review*, 91, 5 (1986), 1053–75 and AHR Forum, 'Revisiting "Gender: A Useful Category of Historical Analysis"', *American Historical Review*, 113, 5 (2008), 1344–1430; also John Tosh, 'What Should Historians Do with Masculinity? Reflections on Nineteenth-Century Britain', *History Workshop Journal*, 38, 1 (1994), 179–202.
12. For discussion of this, see Schulte et al., eds., *The Body of the Queen*.
13. Lyndal Roper, 'Martin Luther's Body: The "Stout Doctor" and His Biographers', *American Historical Review* 115, 2 (2010), 352.
14. Ibid.
15. John Hodge, *Workman's Cottage to Windsor Castle* (London, 1931), p. 184.
16. Ernst Kantorowicz, *The King's Two Bodies: A Study in Mediaeval Political Theology* (Princeton, 1957).
17. Mort, 'Accessible Sovereignty', 358.
18. Ibid.
19. Ana Carden-Coyne, *The Politics of Wounds: Military Patients and Medical Power in the First World War* (Oxford, 2014); Ana Carden-Coyne, *Reconstructing the Body: Classicism, Modernism, and the First World War* (Oxford, 2009); Jeffrey S. Reznick, *Healing the Nation: Soldiers and the Culture of Caregiving in Britain during the Great War* (Manchester, 2004); Joanna Bourke, *Dismembering the Male: Men's Bodies, Britain and the Great War* (London, 1996); Julie Anderson, *War, Disability and Rehabilitation in Britain: 'Soul of a Nation'* (Manchester, 2011); Heather Perry, *Recycling the Disabled: Army, Medicine, and Modernity in WWI Germany* (Manchester, 2014); see also Nicholas Saunders and Paul Cornish, eds., *Bodies in Conflict: Corporeality, Materiality and Transformation* (London, 2014); Leo van Bergen, *Before My Helpless Sight: Suffering, Dying and Military Medicine on the Western*

Front, 1914–1918 (Farnham, Surrey, 2009); Deborah Cohen, *The War Come Home: Disabled Veterans in Britain and Germany, 1914–1939* (Berkeley, 2001).

20. Of a large literature on this subject, see in particular Stéphane Audoin-Rouzeau, *L'enfant de l'ennemi, 1914–1918: viol, avortement, infanticide pendant la Grande Guerre* (Paris, 1995), Gullace, 'Sexual Violence and Family Honor' and Susan Grayzel and Tammy Proctor, eds., *Gender and the Great War* (Oxford, 2017).

21. Joanna Bourke's phrase from her famous monograph title, mentioned in previous note 19, on the subject.

22. Ana Carden-Coyne, 'Masculinity and the Wounds of the First World War: A Centenary Reflection', *Revue Française de Civilisation Britainnique* [online], 20, 1 (2015), p. 2.

23. For examples, see Reginald H. W. Cox, *Military Badges of the British Empire, 1914–1918: The Great War* (London, 1982).

24. For an example, see Mary Evans Picture Library, 11984855, 1914 button badge.

25. Pope-Hennessy, *Queen Mary*, p. 497.

26. *Daily Telegraph*, 8/9/1914, cited in Churchill, *In the Eye of the Storm*, p. 65.

27. 'King George Works Overtime', *Dundee Evening Telegraph*, 17/8/1916, p. 2.

28. Bryant, *George V*, pp. 106–7.

29. Mass Observation Online, Topic Collections, Children and Education, 1937–52, 59-4-A, Miscellaneous Essays by School Children, 'The Royal Family', Image 2469, Doris Clough.

30. James Pope-Hennessy, *The Quest for Queen Mary*, ed. Hugo Vickers (London, 2018), p. 132, p. 239.

31. 'Guarding the Food Supply; Use of Pastry in Private Houses; the Meaning of the King's Pledge', *Yorkshire Post and Leeds Intelligencer*, 14/6/1917, p. 10.

32. Churchill, *In the Eye of the Storm*, p. 253.

33. Tschumi, *Royal Chef*, p. 142.

34. Churchill, *In the Eye of the Storm*, p. 146; Tschumi, *Royal Chef*, p. 141.

35. Pennell, *A Kingdom United?*, p. 203.

36. Ibid., p. 79.

37. Gregory, *The Last Great War*, p. 97.

38. M. Asquith, *Margot Asquith's Great War Diary*, p. 90.

39. Nicolson, *King George the Fifth*, p. 262.

40. M. Asquith, *Margot Asquith's Great War Diary*, p. 90.

41. Nicolson, *King George the Fifth*, p. 262.

42. Ibid.; also C. E. Montague, *Disenchantment* (London, 1922), p. 244; Keith Grieves, 'C.E. Montague and the Making of "Disenchantment," 1914–1921', *War in History*, 4, 1 (1997), 44.

43. Churchill, *In the Eye of the Storm*, p. 114.

44. M. Asquith, *Margot Asquith's Great War Diary*, p. 91.

45. Jonathan Curtis, 'Methodism and Abstinence: A History of the Methodist Church and Teetotalism' (Unpublished PhD thesis, University of Exeter, 2018), pp. 181–2.

46. *Daily Mirror* pamphlet, 'The Father of His People: "They Loved Him as a Man"' (London, 1936), p. 7.

47. Gregory, *The Last Great War*, p. 97.

48. LPL, Papers of Dr Randall T. Davidson, Archbishop of Canterbury, private papers, Vol. 6, f. 10, Halifax to Archbishop of York, 14/8/1916. Underlining in original.

49. Ibid.

50. Ibid.
51. Ibid., f. 12, Stamfordham to Randall Davidson, 21/8/1916.
52. Ibid., f. 20, Stamfordham to Randall Davidson, 22/4/1917.
53. Ibid., f. 18, Stamfordham to Randall Davidson, 25/3/1917.
54. See Chapter 1. Also Williamson, 'National Days of Prayer', 326–7.
55. M. Asquith, *Margot Asquith's Great War Diary*, p. 93.
56. Ibid.
57. For some examples of a widespread phenomenon, see 'Queen Alexandra as Waitress', *Birmingham Mail*, 17/1/1916, p. 3; 'Queen Alexandra as Waitress', *Aberdeen Press and Journal*, 15/12/1915, p. 4; 'Queen as Waitress', *Birmingham Daily Gazette*, 18/1/1916, p. 4; 'Queen as Waitress', *Sheffield Independent*, 7/12/1918, p. 7; 'The Queen as Waitress', *Aberdeen Press and Journal*, 7/10/1919, p. 4.
58. 'Queen as Waitress', *Daily Record*, 21/9/1917, p. 3; 'Queen as Waitress', *Ormskirk Advertiser*, 5/7/1917, p. 3.
59. 'Returned Prisoners' Welcome', *The Times*, 27/12/1918, p. 4.
60. The cultural history of food is a field so well developed it needs little detailing here. Alain Corbin has pointed to the acculturation of food and how diet, table manners and who food was shared with are all markers of social status: Alain Corbin, *Time, Desire and Horror: Towards a History of the Senses* (Cambridge, 1995), pp. 1–2; see also Fabio Parasecoli and Peter Scholliers, eds., *A Cultural History of Food*, 6 vols (London, 2016).
61. 'Queen as Waitress', *Ormskirk Advertiser*, 5/7/1917, p. 3.
62. See Edward Madigan, *Faith under Fire: Anglican Army Chaplains and the Great War* (Basingstoke, 2011).
63. Murphy, *Monarchy and the End of Empire*, p. 3; also J. G. Lockhart, *Cosmo Gordon Lang* (London, 1949).
64. Tschumi, *Royal Chef*, p. 128; p. 135.
65. Ibid., p. 128; p. 135.
66. Ibid., p. 141; p. 146.
67. Ponsonby, *Recollections of Three Reigns*, p. 329.
68. Ibid.
69. Rose, *King George V*, p. 177.
70. Essex Record Office, ACC.AI3528 Diaries of the Right Rev. J. E. Watts-Ditchfield, Bishop of Chelmsford, 28/4/1917, f. 513.
71. On their pre-war concerns, see Mort, 'Safe for Democracy'.
72. Carey, *Princess Mary*, p. 128.
73. Lerman, 'Wilhelm's War'.
74. Georgina Battiscombe, *Queen Alexandra* (London, 1969), p. 293.
75. Stibbe, 'Kaiser Wilhelm II', p. 275.
76. Röhl, *Wilhelm II: Into the Abyss*, p. 1132.
77. Churchill Archives Centre, AMEL 6/3/32, ff. 69–71, Leo Amery letter to AFA, 1/12/1914.
78. Elton, *C. E. Montague*, p. 190.
79. RA EDW/PRIV/DIARY/1914: 19 November.
80. RA EDW/PRIV/DIARY/1914: 28 November. On working late with his father, see RA EDW/PRIV/DIARY/1914: 2 and 4 December.
81. RA EDW/PRIV/DIARY/1914: 4 and 5 December.
82. 'Royal Farewell', *Daily Express*, 7/12/1914.

83. See RA EDW/PRIV/DIARY/1917: 7 June, when his superior reprimanded him for running.
84. Churchill, *In the Eye of the Storm*, p. 60.
85. Glencross, 'A Cause of Tension?', p. 182.
86. Churchill Archives Centre, Esher Papers, ESHR 2/15, Diary, 5/3/1916. Italics in original. Matthew Glencross points out that this material was left out of the published version of Esher's Diaries. Glencross, 'A Cause of Tension?', p. 181.
87. RA EDW/PRIV/DIARY/1915: 11 December.
88. RA EDW/PRIV/DIARY/1916: 9 July.
89. RA EDW/PRIV/DIARY/1917: 3 June.
90. RA EDW/PRIV/DIARY/1915: 31 December.
91. For example: RA EDW/PRIV/DIARY/1917: 22 January.
92. RA EDW/PRIV/DIARY/1916: 27 December.
93. RA EDW/PRIV/DIARY/1916: 20 December.
94. RA EDW/PRIV/DIARY/1915: 12 December. See also Rose, *The Prince, The Princess and the Perfect Murder*, p. 21; p. 28.
95. RA EDW/PRIV/DIARY/1916: 16, 18 and 21 December; RA EDW/PRIV/DIARY/ 1917: 3 February.
96. Rose, *The Prince, the Princess and the Perfect Murder*, p. 49.
97. NAM, Transcript of 2002-02-924-3, HRH Prince Edward to Cecil Boyd-Rochfort, 28/5/1917.
98. NAM, Transcript of 2002-02-924-5, HRH Prince Edward to Cecil Boyd-Rochfort, 15/11/1917.
99. Rupert Godfrey, ed., *Letters from a Prince: Edward, Prince of Wales to Mrs Freda Dudley Ward, March 1918–January 1921* (London, 1998), p. 97.
100. Ibid.
101. NAM, 2002-02-924, Collection of papers associated with Edward, Prince of Wales, 1915 (c)–1917; letters written to Capt. Cecil Boyd-Rochfort, Grenadier Guards.
102. PA LG/F/29/4/19, Extracts from letters and telegrams regarding Prince of Wales's health, and advisability of postponing visit to India, June 1920.
103. Rose, *The Prince, the Princess and the Perfect Murder*, p. 161.
104. Ibid.
105. Essex Record Office, ACC.AI3528 Diaries of the Right Rev. J. E. Watts-Ditchfield, Bishop of Chelmsford, 30/4/1916, f. 319.
106. Ibid., ff. 319–20.
107. Glencross, 'George V and the New Royal House', p. 49.
108. Fitzroy, *Memoirs*, Vol. 2, p. 767.
109. Roper, *The Secret Battle*, p. 68, pp. 252–3.
110. As the anthropological study by Mary Douglas argues, it is a mistake to treat bodily margins in isolation from all other margins, contending with reference to ancient Israelite culture that 'the threatened boundaries of their body politic' were 'mirrored in their care for the integrity, unity and purity of the physical body'. Mary Douglas, *Purity and Danger: An Analysis of the Concepts of Pollution and Taboo* (London, 2002 [1966]), p. 153.
111. Imke Polland, 'How to Fashion the Popularity of the British Monarchy: Alexandra, Princess of Wales and the Attractions of Attire' in Frank Lorenz Müller and Heidi Mehrkens, eds., *Royal Heirs and the Uses of Soft Power in Nineteenth-Century Europe* (London, 2016), pp. 201–21.

112. Airlie, *Thatched with Gold*, p. 128.
113. 'The Queen's Gift', *Liverpool Daily Post*, 11/1/1915, p. 4.
114. George Mosse, *Fallen Soldiers: Reshaping the Memory of the World Wars* (Oxford, 1991), pp. 126–56.
115. For an introduction to the impact of these changes, see Detlev Peukert, *The Weimar Republic: The Crisis of Classical Modernity* (London, 1991).
116. For example, Alice, Duchess of Gloucester recalled how, as a small child, she and her siblings had to wear hats and many-layered dresses and had to remain dressed formally at all times, even on hot days: Princess Alice, Duchess of Gloucester, *Memories of Ninety Years* (London, 1991), p. 13.
117. Simon Szreter and Kate Fisher, *Sex before the Sexual Revolution: Intimate Life in England, 1918-1963* (Cambridge, 2010), pp. 268–316.
118. Brittain, *Testament of Youth*, p. 53.
119. Essex Record Office, ACC.AI3528 Diaries of the Right Rev. J. E. Watts-Ditchfield, Bishop of Chelmsford, 28/1/1914 and 23/2/1914, n.f.
120. Ibid., 29/4/1917, f. 517.
121. Ibid., 28/4/1917, f. 513.
122. Polland, 'How to Fashion the Popularity of the British Monarchy'; Kate Strasdin, 'Empire Dressing: The Design and Realization of Queen Alexandra's Coronation Gown', *Journal of Design History*, 25 (2012), 155–70.
123. John G. Rowe, *Queen Alexandra the Beloved* (London, 1925).
124. Polland, 'How to Fashion the Popularity of the British Monarchy'.
125. On the history of the depiction of royal marriages, see Edward Owens, 'All the World Loves a Lover: Monarchy, Mass Media and the 1934 Royal Wedding of Prince George and Princess Marina', *English Historical Review*, 133, 562 (June 2018), 597–633.
126. On the queen's role in mobilising women, see Rowbotham, 'How to Be Useful in War Time'.
127. Marie Louise of Schleswig-Holstein, *My Memories of Six Reigns* (London, 1956), p. 182.
128. Carey, *Princess Mary*, p. 94.
129. Sarah Glassford and Amy Shaw, eds., *A Sisterhood of Suffering and Service: Women and Girls of Canada and Newfoundland during the First World War* (Vancouver, 2012), p. 55.
130. TNA, CO 323/693, f. 377, 'Voluntary work done by women'.
131. Ibid., Minute on file, n.d.
132. Ibid., Minute on file, 2/12/1915.
133. Carey, *Princess Mary*, p. 128; p. 134.
134. RA EDW/PRIV/DIARY/1915: 29 September.
135. Gibbs, *George the Faithful*, p. 261.
136. 'The King's Crowded Days', *The Times*, 16/8/1916, p. 7.
137. www.rct.uk/collection/themes/trails/king-george-vs-war-museum, accessed 11 February 2019. See also Churchill, *In the Eye of the Storm*, p. 182.
138. John William Fortescue, *Author and Curator: An Autobiography* (Edinburgh, London, 1933), p. 237. See also the mention in Edward, Duke of Windsor, *A King's Story*, p. 125.
139. Royal Collections, RCIN 69491, Entrenching Tool With Pebble, www.rct.uk/collectio n/themes/trails/king-george-vs-war-museum/entrenching-tool-with-pebble, accessed

13 February 2019. In all likelihood Queen Mary found this item during her visit to Pozières on 9 July 1917.

140. Marie Louise of Schleswig-Holstein, *My Memories of Six Reigns*, p. 182.

141. Airlie, *Thatched with Gold*, p. 128.

142. Ibid.

143. See NLS, Earl Haig Papers, Official Photographs, Royal Visits, C 2060, Photograph of Queen Mary and Queen Elisabeth together with their husbands in July 1917. During the king and queen's pre-war visit to Paris in 1914, even Frederick Ponsonby had noticed that her dress was 'of a fashion of years before'. Ponsonby, *Recollections of Three Reigns*, p. 301.

144. Mort, 'Accessible Sovereignty', 354.

145. IWM Sound Archive, Eleanora B. Pemberton (Oral History) 1978, Catalogue no. 3188, reel 4.

146. Ibid.

147. Ibid.

148. Mort, 'Accessible Sovereignty', 351; 352.

149. RA QM/PRIV/QMD/1917: 3 July.

150. Pope-Hennessy, *Queen Mary*, p. 496.

151. Mary Evans Picture Library, 10951895, Frank O. Salisbury pictured at work on 'Their Majesties, King George V and Queen Mary Visiting the Battle Districts of France, 1917'.

152. RA QM/PRIV/QMD/1917: 3–14 July. See also Pope-Hennessy, *Queen Mary*, pp. 507–8.

153. Airlie, *Thatched with Gold*, pp. 138–9.

154. RA QM/PRIV/QMD/1917: 9 July.

155. RA QM/PRIV/QMD/1917: 5–6 July.

156. RA QM/PRIV/QMD/1917: 9 July.

157. Airlie, *Thatched with Gold*, p. 139.

158. Ibid.

159. Ibid., p. 138.

160. RA QM/PRIV/QMD/1917: 4 July.

161. RA PS/PSO/GV/PS/WAR/QQ18/05707, War, Visit of king and queen to France, 1917, Diary of Queen Mary's visit to the front, July 1917.

162. Airlie, *Thatched with Gold*, pp. 136–7.

163. Ibid., p. 137.

164. Seth Koven, *Slumming: Sexual and Social Politics in Victorian London* (Princeton, 2006), p. 1.

165. On these tours, see Mort, 'Safe for Democracy'.

166. See Chapter 4.

167. Edith Wharton, *Fighting France: From Dunkerque to Belfort* (New York, 1915); Alfred Harmsworth, Viscount Northcliffe, *At the War* (London, 1916), pp. 35–50.

168. Lincolnshire Archives, BNLW 4/4/8/3, Papers of Sir Charles Cust, 'Diary of my trip to France, October 1916', 7/10/1916.

169. Ibid., 8/10/1916.

170. LPL, Papers of Dr Randall T. Davidson, Archbishop of Canterbury, private papers, Vol. 6, f. 11, Stamfordham to Randall Davidson, 17/8/1916.

171. RA PS/PSO/GV/WAR/QQ06/03330, Fritz Ponsonby to Brig. Gen. H. C. Lowther, 18/10/1915, cited in Glencross, 'A Cause of Tension?', p. 174.

172. RA QM/PRIV/QMD/1917: 3–14 July.

173. Airlie, *Thatched with Gold*, p. 136.
174. RA QM/PRIV/QMD/1917: 8 July.
175. RA QM/PRIV/QMD/1917: 11 July.
176. RA GV/PRIV/GVD/1917: 6 July.
177. Carey, *Princess Mary*, p. 119.
178. Ibid., p. 125; p. 133.
179. Ibid., pp. 140–2.
180. Ibid., p. 121.
181. Ibid., p. 122.
182. Churchill, *In the Eye of the Storm*, p. 289.
183. Carey, *Princess Mary*, p. 124; p. 132; p. 135.
184. Ibid., p. 125.
185. Ibid., p. 123; p. 137.
186. Ibid., p. 137.
187. Ibid., pp. 127–8; pp. 134–5.
188. Ibid., p. 128.
189. Ibid., pp. 128–9.
190. Ibid., p. 130.
191. Ibid., pp. 138–9.
192. *Forward* criticised the monarchy's German connections on 5 December 1914 and again in 1915: Hayman, 'Labour and the Monarchy', 168.
193. See Pennell, *A Kingdom United?*, pp. 98–117.
194. Gregory, *The Last Great War*, pp. 235–9.
195. Matthew Stibbe, 'Enemy Aliens and Internment', https://encyclopedia.1914-1918-online.net/article/enemy_aliens_and_internment?version=1.0, accessed 7/12/2019.
196. Oxford, Bodleian Libraries, MS Asquith, A.1, Vol. 4, f. 86, Stamfordham to Bonham Carter, 4/2/1915.
197. RA GV/PRIV/GVD/1914: 29 October.
198. Oxford, Bodleian Libraries, MS Asquith, A.1, Vol. 4, f. 122, Stamfordham to Bonham Carter, 6/6/1915.
199. Oxford, Bodleian Libraries, MS Asquith, A.2, Vol. 8, f. 187, Asquith cabinet report to the King, 27/7/1916.
200. There is a debate among historians about whether Queen Mary sounded at all German, with Kenneth Rose claiming she had a 'slight guttural accent': Rose, *King George V*, p. 174. However, in an early recording of Queen Mary from 1923 there is little sign of any German accent: 'Empire Day Messages to the Boys and Girls of the British Empire from King George V and Queen Mary', March 1923, www.youtube.com/watch?v=3JyC6qw2D_s, accessed 15/7/2020.
201. Lili Dehn, *The Real Tsaritsa* (London, 1922), chapter 6, www.alexanderpalace.org/realtsaritsa/1chap6.html, accessed 7/5/2020. See also Boris Kolonitskii and Orlando Figes, *Interpreting the Russian Revolution: The Language and Symbols of 1917* (New Haven, London, 1999); William Fuller, *The Foe Within: Fantasies of Treason and the End of Imperial Russia* (Ithaca, NY, 2006).
202. IWM Documents 22414, Box P150, Private papers of Brigadier E. Foster Hall, Diary, 15/9/1916, f. 59.
203. TNA, HO 45/10743, Report by a Metropolitan Police Officer on meeting of the Imperial Defence Union at the Queen's Hall on 9 July, 10/7/1917, p. 6. Gregory, *The Last Great War*, p. 62.

204. Pennell, *A Kingdom United?*, p. 96.

205. RA GV/PRIV/GVD/1917: 12 July and RA GV/PRIV/GVD/1918: 6 August refer to Huns; RA GV/PRIV/GVD/1918: 7 August, 3 December and 4 December use the term Boche; Gregory, *The Last Great War*, p. 62.

206. Oxford, Bodleian Libraries, MS Asquith, A.1, Vol. 4, ff. 94–7, Stamfordham to Asquith, 16/4/1915.

207. For some of George V's criticism of German war crimes, see diary entries: RA GV/PRIV/GVD/1915: 18 February; RA GV/PRIV/GVD/1917: 12 July; also GV/PRIV/GVD/1922: 10 May on Edith Cavell. Also Churchill, *In the Eye of the Storm*, p. 102 and p. 107 on George V's reaction to the sinking of the Lusitania.

208. Geordie Greig, *Louis and the Prince: A Story of Politics, Intrigue and Royal Friendship* (London, 1999), p. 120.

209. Essex Record Office, ACC.AI3528 Diaries of the Right Rev. J. E. Watts-Ditchfield, Bishop of Chelmsford, 29/4/1916, f. 309.

210. Ibid, 30/4/1916, f. 322.

211. Anon., *The King's Pilgrimage* (London, 1922), no page numbers. See Glencross, 'George V and the New Royal House', p. 37.

212. RA GV/PRIV/GVD/1914: 15 September.

213. Nicolson, *King George the Fifth*, p. 255.

214. For examples, see Austin Harrison, *The Kaiser's War* (London, 1914); Anon., *The Real Kaiser* (London, 1914); Emil Reich, *Germany's Swelled Head* (London, 1914); A. H. Catling, *The Kaiser under the Searchlight* (London, 1914); Iconoclast (pseud.), *Is the Kaiser 'The Beast' Referred to in the Book of Revelation and by the Prophets Isiah and Ezekiel?* (London, 1914); Ernest Henry Clark Oliphant, *Germany and Good Faith: A Study of the History of the Prussian Royal Family* (Melbourne, 1914); Morton Prince, *The Psychology of the Kaiser: A Study of His Sentiments and His Obsessions* (London, 1915); Joseph MacCabe, *The Kaiser, His Personality and His Career* (London, 1915); Edward Legge, *The Public and Private Life of the Kaiser Wilhelm II* (London, 1915); W. de Veer, *An Emperor in the Dock* (London, 1915); Edith Keen, *Seven Years at the Prussian Court* (London, 1916); John J. Pearson, *The Nemesis of Germany and Austria* (London, 1916); Theodore A. Cook, *The Mask of the Beast* (London, 1917); Henry D. Houghton, *Is the Kaiser 'Luzifer'?* (London, 1917); Robert Munro, *From Darwinism to Kaiserism: The Origin, Effects and Collapse of Germany's Attempt at World Domination* (Glasgow, 1918); Sylvester George Viereck, *The Kaiser on Trial* (New York, 1937). See also Rebentisch, *Die vielen Gesichter des Kaisers*.

215. Reinermann, 'Fleet Street and the Kaiser', 469.

216. Ibid., 469; 480; 481; 483.

217. Ibid., 482. The extremes to which the British press went over the kaiser may well have echoed long-held British fears about a 'universal monarchy' gaining power on the Continent which originated with Louis XIV and had a long afterlife in British foreign policy preoccupations; the portrayal of kaiserism as hegemonic tyrannical monarchism certainly chimed with this: see Stephen Conway, 'Transnational and Cosmopolitan Aspects of Eighteenth-Century European Wars' in Dina Gusejnova, ed., *Cosmopolitanism in Conflict: Imperial Encounters from the Seven Years' War to the Cold War* (London, 2017), pp. 29–54.

218. He described the kaiser as 'the greatest criminal known for having plunged the world into this ghastly war': RA GV/PRIV/GVD/1918, 9 November.

219. Reinermann, 'Fleet Street and the Kaiser'; Reinermann, *Der Kaiser in England*.

220. See Nicolson, *King George the Fifth*, pp. 311–12; also p. 301 on Constantine's unpopularity in Britain.
221. Pope-Hennessy, *Queen Mary*, pp. 503–4.
222. BL, Add MS 49686, Balfour Papers, Princess Louise to Sir Arthur Balfour, 14/6/1917, ff. 172–4.
223. The royal touch in medieval times had been attributed with the power to heal scrofula, also known as the 'King's evil'. Marc Bloch, *The Royal Touch: Sacred Monarchy and Scrofula in England and France* (London, 1973).
224. Santanu Das, *Touch and Intimacy in First World War Literature* (Cambridge, 2005), p. 6.
225. *Daily Telegraph*, 28/9/1915, cited in Churchill, *In the Eye of the Storm*, p. 118.
226. Gibbs, *George the Faithful*, p. 244.
227. Rose, *King George V*, p. 185.
228. Will Thorne, *My Life's Battles* (London, [1925] 1989), pp. 195–6.
229. Ibid.
230. Hamilton, *Three Years or the Duration*, p. 36.
231. Ibid.
232. Ibid.
233. Andrew Bamji, 'Sir Harold Gillies: Surgical Pioneer', *Trauma*, 8 (2006), 144.
234. Mort, 'Accessible Sovereignty', 342.
235. RA GV/PRIV/GVD/1914: 1 September.
236. RA GV/PRIV/GVD/1914: 2 September.
237. RA GV/PRIV/GVD/1914: 3 September.
238. RA GV/PRIV/GVD/1914: 15 September.
239. RA GV/PRIV/GVD/1914: 21 September.
240. RA GV/PRIV/GVD/1914: 23 October.
241. Lincolnshire Archives, BNLW 4/4/8/2, Papers of Sir Charles Cust, Diary of the king's visit to the army in the field, 1915, Friday 22 October.
242. RA GV/PRIV/GVD/1914: 27 September.
243. RA GV/PRIV/GVD/1914: 1 October.
244. RA GV/PRIV/GVD/1914: 30 November.
245. RA GV/PRIV/GVD/1914: 1 December.
246. RA GV/PRIV/GVD/1915: 18 February.
247. Suzannah Biernoff, 'The Rhetoric of Disfigurement in First World War Britain', *Social History of Medicine*, 24, 3 (2011), 666–85. Also Seth Koven, 'Remembering and Dismemberment: Crippled Children, Wounded Soldiers, and the Great War in Great Britain', *American Historical Review*, 99, 4 (1994), 1167–202.
248. Churchill College Archives, Esher Papers, ESHR 6/8, Queen Mary to Viscount Esher, 7/8/1916 and 19/11/1916.
249. Pope-Hennessy, *Queen Mary*, p. 498.
250. RA GV/PRIV/GVD/1917: 6 July.
251. Pope-Hennessy, *Queen Mary*, p. 499.
252. Ibid., p. 498.
253. Ibid., p. 508.
254. RA GV/PRIV/GVD/1915: 16 February. At least one further such visit by the king and queen, to a 'shell shock hospital at Hampstead', took place as evidenced by a photograph of the visit in Churchill, *In the Eye of the Storm*, p. xxxi.
255. Ponsonby, *Recollections of Three Reigns*, p. 317.
256. Pope-Hennessy, *Queen Mary*, p. 500.

257. RA GV/PRIV/GVD/1918: 29 March.
258. Mark Harrison, *The Medical War: British Military Medicine in the First World War* (Oxford, 2010).
259. Pope-Hennessey, *Queen Mary*, p. 496.
260. RA GV/PRIV/GVD/1918: 29 March.
261. Walter Powell, 'Footman for a Day in the Convoy for King George V and Queen Mary', May 1917, The First World War Poetry Digital Archive, Oxford, http://ww1lit.nsms.ox.ac.uk/ww1lit/gwa/item/7603, accessed 16/1/2020.
262. Mort, 'Safe for Democracy', 126; Owens, *The Family Firm*, pp. 56–7.
263. Fitzroy, *Memoirs*, Vol. 2, pp. 802–3.
264. IWM Documents 12139, Box PP/MCR/173, The First World War Memoirs of Lieutenant D. C. Burn, Vol. 2, chapter 1, April–May 1916.
265. Joanna Bourke, 'Gender Roles in Killing Zones' in Winter, ed., *The Cambridge History of the First World War*, p. 169.
266. Ibid., p. 171.
267. On the Victorian and Edwardian construction of cultures of emotional stoicism, see Thomas Dixon, *Weeping Britannia: Portrait of a Nation in Tears* (Oxford, 2015).
268. RA GV/PRIV/GVD/1915: 9 January.
269. Pope-Hennessy, *Queen Mary*, p. 498.
270. Ibid.
271. Airlie, *Thatched with Gold*, pp. 131–2. Pope-Hennessy also refers to Queen Mary's dislike of seeing suffering, illness or the maimed. Pope-Hennessy, *Queen Mary*, p. 497.
272. Marie Louise of Schleswig-Holstein, *My Memories of Six Reigns*, p. 190.
273. Ponsonby, *Recollections of Three Reigns*, p. 324.
274. Pope-Hennessy, *Queen Mary*, p. 505.
275. Churchill Archives Centre, Papers of Captain Sir Bryan Godfrey-Faussett, BGGF 2/5 part 2, King George V to Godfrey-Faussett, 19/10/1914.
276. Gore, *King George V*, p. 292.
277. Pope-Hennessy, *Queen Mary*, p. 498.
278. Alexandra Churchill suggests the queen did show tears in public after some hospital visits. Churchill, *In the Eye of the Storm*, pp. 88–9; p. 245, based on press reports. In 1912, press reports on the Cadeby mining disaster also suggested the queen wept. Mort, 'Safe for Democracy', 136.
279. Nicolson, *King George the Fifth*, p. 297.
280. Ibid., p. 366.
281. Tom Bridges, *Alarms and Excursions: Reminisces of a Soldier* (London, 1938), p. 216.
282. IWM Documents 12139, Box PP/MCR/173, The First World War Memoirs of Lieutenant D. C. Burn, Vol. 2, chapter 1, April–May 1916.
283. St Bartholomew's Hospital Museum and Archives, RLHINV/551, Royal Visit to Whipps Cross War Hospital Brass Plaque.
284. St Bartholomew's Hospital Museum and Archives, RLHLH/N/7/20, Undated war letter fragment by matron at the London Hospital Whitechapel, p. 1.
285. Ibid., p. 2.
286. St Bartholomew's Hospital Museum and Archives, RLHCI/3/16, Framed colour print of Edith Cavell with inscription.

287. St Bartholomew's Hospital Museum and Archives, RLHPP/BAX/6/1, Christmas Message from Queen Alexandra to all QAIMNS serving in France, December 1914.

288. Carden-Coyne, 'Masculinity and the Wounds of the First World War', p. 4.

289. See press reports mentioning royal touch during hospital visits cited in Churchill, *In the Eye of the Storm*, pp. 64–5; pp. 88–9.

290. See the diaries of the king and queen, which record constant hospital visits to the wounded: RA GV/PRIV/GVD/1914–18 and RA QM/PRIV/QMD/1914–18.

291. Gibbs, *George the Faithful*, p. 244.

292. *Daily Mirror*, 10/10/1914, cited in Churchill, *In the Eye of the Storm*, p. 66.

293. Churchill, *In the Eye of the Storm*, p. 65.

294. Ibid., p. 64.

295. Ibid., p. 245.

296. 'The King-Emperor Talks with Wounded Indians', *Daily Mail*, 11/1/1915, p. 3.

297. Ibid.

298. 'The King at the Front', *The Times*, 2/12/1914, p. 8, cited in Mort, 'Accessible Sovereignty', 338.

299. Omissi, ed., *Indian Voices*, p. 27, Extract no. 4, Subedar Major Sardar Bahadur Gugan to a friend in India [1915].

300. Ibid., p. 94, Extract no. 130, Subedar Mir Dast VC to Naik Nur Zada, 27/8/1915.

301. On the raid, see Susan Grayzel, *At Home and under Fire: Air Raids and Culture in Britain from the Great War to the Blitz* (Cambridge, 2012), pp. 67–8. See also https://historicengland.org.uk/research/current/discover-and-understand/mili tary/the-first-world-war/first-world-war-home-front/what-we-already-know /air/first-blitz/, accessed 4/6/2020.

302. Churchill, *In the Eye of the Storm*, p. 230. Rose, *King George V*, p. 180.

303. 'The King's Solicitude', *Yorkshire Evening Post*, 14/6/1917, p. 4.

304. 'The King's Sympathy', *Daily Mirror*, 14/6/1917, p. 10; 'King in the City: Visit to Raid Area', *Hampshire Telegraph*, 15/6/1917, p. 7.

305. Churchill, *In the Eye of the Storm*, p. 231.

306. 'King Visits the Sufferers', *Lincolnshire Echo*, 14/6/1917, p. 2. See also 'King in the City: Visit to Air Raid Area', *Hampshire Telegraph*, 15/6/1917, p. 7.

307. 'Our London Letter: King Visits Scene of Airplane Raid on London', *Dundee Courier*, 14/6/1917, p. 3.

308. Grayzel, *At Home and under Fire*, pp. 64–92.

309. 'Our London Letter: King Visits Scene of Airplane Raid on London', *Dundee Courier*, 14/6/1917, p. 3.

310. 'The King's Solicitude', *Yorkshire Evening Post*, 14/6/1917, p. 4.

311. Ibid.

312. Churchill, *In the Eye of the Storm*, p. 231.

313. Mort, 'Safe for Democracy', 136.

314. St Bartholomew's Hospital Museum and Archives, RLHLH/N/7/15, London Hospital Whitechapel, Matron's letter to Mrs Bright, 8/2/1917, p. 2.

315. Churchill, *In the Eye of the Storm*, pp. 230–1.

316. Pope-Hennessy, *Queen Mary*, p. 495.

317. Ibid., p. 497.

318. Churchill, *In the Eye of the Storm*, p. 148.

319. *Daily Sketch*, cover, 23/3/1916, p. 1.

320. Mikhail Bakhtin, *Rabelais and His World* (Bloomington, 1984) coined this concept of carnivalesque; several historians have applied it to historical

moments, for example, Fabrice Virgili, *La France virile: des femmes tondues à la Libération* (Paris, 2000).

321. *Daily Mirror*, cover, 22/3/1916, p. 1.

322. 'Woman's World', *Western Daily Press*, 25/3/1916, p. 11; Churchill, *In the Eye of the Storm*, p. 147.

323. Churchill, *In the Eye of the Storm*, p. 149.

324. Pope-Hennessy, *Queen Mary*, p. 502.

325. 'Woman's World', *Western Daily Press*, 25/3/1916, p. 11.

326. Ibid.

327. Ibid.

328. Carden-Coyne, 'Masculinity and the Wounds of the First World War', p. 6.

329. Kingsley Martin, *The Magic of Monarchy* (London, 1937), p. 9.

330. McKibbin, *Classes and Cultures*, p. 7; pp. 14–15.

331. Martin, *The Magic of Monarchy*, pp. 9–10.

332. Dehn, *The Real Tsaritsa*, chapter 6, www.alexanderpalace.org/realtsaritsa/1chap6 .html, accessed 7/5/2020; Anna Vyrubova, *Memories of the Russian Court* (London, 1923), chapter 8, http://www.alexanderpalace.org/russiancourt2006/viii .html, accessed 7/5/2020; Princess Alice, Countess of Athlone, *For My Grandchildren: Some Reminiscences of Her Royal Highness Princess Alice, Countess of Athlone* (London, 1966), p. 158.

333. Kolonitskii and Figes, *Interpreting the Russian Revolution*, p. 24.

334. Ibid.

335. Ibid.

336. Dehn, *The Real Tsaritsa*, chapter 6, www.alexanderpalace.org/realtsaritsa/1chap6 .html, accessed 7/5/2020.

337. 'Queen and Our VAD Princess', *Daily Record*, 16/7/1918, p. 8.

338. McKernan, 'The Finest Cinema Performers That We Possess', p. 63.

339. I am grateful to John Horne for drawing my attention to this source.

340. 'Prince of Wales in Mining Garb during His Western Tour', *Illustrated London News*, 2/3/1918, p. 1; p. 2; 'The Prince of Wales as a Riveter', *Illustrated London News*, 9/3/1918, p. 1; 'Prince of Wales on Clydeside Inspecting the Steering Gear', *Illustrated London News*, 16/3/1918, p. 11; 'Building of the Ship: Prince of Wales a Spectator', *Illustrated London News*, 16/3/1918, p. 7.

341. Carey, *Princess Mary*, p. 100.

342. For an early presentation of this argument, see Sandra Gilbert and Susan Gubar, *No Man's Land: The Place of the Woman Writer in the Twentieth Century*, 3 vols (London, New Haven, 1988–9).

343. Carey, *Princess Mary*, p. 98.

344. Churchill, *In the Eye of the Storm*, p. 304; Carey, *Princess Mary*, p. 100.

345. Carey, *Princess Mary*, pp. 102–3; pp. 110–11.

346. Ibid., p. 104; p. 105; p. 112.

347. Letter from Queen Mary to King George V, 10/8/1918, from the Royal Archives Flickr account, www.flickr.com/photos/britishmonarchy/albums/7215764682480 1886, accessed 16/6/2020.

348. RA GV/PRIV/GVD/1914: 10 October.

349. Airlie, *Thatched with Gold*, p. 144.

350. Röhl, *Wilhelm II: Into the Abyss*, p. 1118.

351. Lerman, 'Wilhelm's War', p. 254.

352. Pope-Hennessy, *Queen Mary*, p. 506.

353. Ibid.
354. Ibid.
355. 'Prince John Dead', *Western Gazette*, 24/1/1919, p. 8; 'The Death of Prince John', *The Sphere*, 25/1/1919 p. 2.
356. As discussed in Chapter 1, the word 'nation' is problematic with regard to the monarchy, as the monarchy represented all four home nations of the United Kingdom as well as the empire. However, contemporary sources on the monarchy often refer to *the* nation – singular – to express a default idea of a single 'British' global nation at war.
357. Mort, 'Safe for Democracy', 119.
358. Oxford, Bodleian Libraries, MS Asquith, A.1, Vol. 4, f. 74, Stamfordham to Bonham Carter, 9/1/1915.
359. TNA, CO 323/720, B. B. Cubitt, War Office to Under Secretary of State, Colonial Office, 17/7/1916, f. 12.
360. Churchill, *In the Eye of the Storm*, p. 178.
361. Essex Record Office, ACC.AI3528 Diaries of the Right Rev. J. E. Watts-Ditchfield, Bishop of Chelmsford, 29/4/1916, f. 314.
362. Ibid.
363. www.iwm.org.uk/history/silver-war-badge-and-kings-certificate-of-discharge, accessed 9/3/2020.
364. Ibid.
365. TNA CO 323/807, f. 474, B. B. Cubitt, War Office to the Under-Secretary of State, Colonial Office, 11/8/1919.
366. Churchill, *In the Eye of the Storm*, p. 356.
367. Duffett, 'The War in Miniature', p. 434.
368. Meaghan Kowalsky, '"This Honourable Obligation": The King's National Roll Scheme for Disabled Ex-Servicemen, 1915–1944', *European Review of History/ Revue européenne d'histoire*, 14, 4 (2007), 567–84. It is not yet clear if the monarchy had decided to support the initiative before 1919.
369. www.surreyinthegreatwar.org.uk/story/star-and-garter-home/, accessed 15/11/2017.
370. Churchill, *In the Eye of the Storm*, p. 356.
371. Kowalsky, 'This Honourable Obligation', p. 569.
372. Ibid., p. 571.
373. Fitzroy, *Memoirs*, Vol. 2, p. 708.
374. Ibid.
375. RA NEWS/PRESS/EVIIIPW/MAIN, Vol. 22, 'The Silver Badge Men's March', *Daily News*, 25/11/1918.
376. IWM Documents 10750, Box Misc. 105 item 1670, Royal letter of appreciation for a disabled serviceman, November 1918.
377. Carden-Coyne, *The Politics of Wounds*, p. 1.
378. Edward, Duke of Windsor, *A King's Story*, p. 128.
379. Ibid.
380. 'The Silver Badge Men's March', *Daily News*, 25/11/1918.
381. Edward, Duke of Windsor, *A King's Story*, p. 128.
382. 'The Silver Badge Men's March', *Daily News*, 25/11/1918.
383. Ibid.

384. 'King Reviews Silver Badgers', *Sunday Post*, 24/11/1918, p. 2; 'King George Reviews the Silver Badge Men', *Leeds Mercury*, 25/11/1918, p. 12.
385. Edward, Duke of Windsor, *A King's Story*, p. 128.
386. Ibid.
387. www.rct.uk/collection/2303834/page-from-queen-marys-photograph-album-includ ing-king-george-vs-meeting-president#/referer/232899/subject, accessed 8/7/2020.
388. Lincolnshire Archives, BNLW 4/4/8/2, Papers of Sir Charles Cust, Diary of the king's visit to the army in the field, 1915, 1 November.
389. RA GV/PRIV/GVD/1915: 28 October.
390. Gore, *King George V*, p. 291.
391. RA GV/PRIV/GVD/1915: 1 November.
392. 'Pathetic Incident in Hospital Train', *Dundee Evening Telegraph*, 2/11/1915, p. 3.
393. Airlie, *Thatched with Gold*, p. 135; Pope-Hennessy, *Queen Mary*, p. 506.
394. Nicolson, *King George the Fifth*, p. 268.
395. IWM Sound Archive, Private John Hall, catalogue no. 14599 (1994), Reel 4.
396. Nicolson, *King George the Fifth*, p. 268.
397. Winston Churchill, *Great Contemporaries* (London, 1941), p. 287; Pope-Hennessy also relates how the gravity of the accident was 'much minimised in the public bulletins.' Pope-Hennessy, *Queen Mary*, p. 501.
398. Ponsonby, *Recollections of Three Reigns*, p. 326.
399. Pope-Hennessy, *Queen Mary*, p. 502.
400. Carey, *Princess Mary*, pp. 72–3.
401. Ina Zweiniger-Bargielowska, 'Keep Fit and Play the Game: George VI, Outdoor Recreation and Social Cohesion in Interwar Britain', *Cultural and Social History*, 11, 1 (2014), 111; 120.
402. Ibid., 111.
403. Ibid., 113.
404. Ibid., 114; 115.
405. Ibid., 114.
406. Ibid., 113.

4   De-Sacralisation Discourses: Challenges to the Monarchy's Status, 1916–1918

1. Prochaska, 'George V and Republicanism'; Hayman, 'Labour and the Monarchy'; Taylor, *'Down with the Crown'*.
2. Thomson, *The Scene Changes*, p. 310.
3. See Prochaska, *The Republic of Britain* for the best overview of British republicanism.
4. Richard Bessel, 'Revolution' in Winter, ed., *The Cambridge History of the First World War*, Vol. 2: *The State*, pp. 126–7.
5. Rose, *King George V*, pp. 217–18. Lloyd George's secretary, Frances Stevenson, reported that he submitted draft chapters of his memoirs to the king for approval, but did not always respond well to the king's input on them. Stevenson, *Lloyd George: A Diary*, 24/4/1934, p. 269.
6. Prochaska, 'George V and Republicanism'; Prochaska, *The Republic of Britain*.
7. Loughlin, *The British Monarchy and Ireland*, p. 277.

8. Loughlin, *The British Monarchy and Ireland* does devote a chapter to this period, but mainly presents a purely political history of the monarchy's role during the period 1919–23, with little on cultural discourses of monarchism and anti-monarchism; James McConnel's article 'John Redmond and Irish Catholic Loyalism', *The English Historical Review*, 125, 512 (2010), 83–111, largely focuses on the Irish Parliamentary Party, while James Murphy's study *Abject Loyalty: Nationalism and Monarchy during the Reign of Queen Victoria* (Washington, DC, 2001) is on the nineteenth century. Aidan Beatty's research looks at the ways that, during the Irish revolution 1912–23, nationalist separatists used positive images of ancient Irish monarchies as part of their nationalist propaganda, ancient native Gaelic monarchies promoted incongruously alongside their republicanism: Aidan Beatty, 'Royalism in Republicanism: The Political Vocabulary of Irish National Sovereignty, 1912–1924', Unpublished paper, open access work-in-progress: www.academia.edu /38553631/Royalism_in_Republicanism_The_Political_Vocabulary_of_Irish_So vereignty_1912-1924_Work_in_Progress,_accessed 7/12/2019. Mary Kenny's *Crown and Shamrock* is a popular survey history covering from Queen Victoria to Queen Elizabeth II.

9. Kate O'Malley, *Ireland, India and Empire: Indo-Irish Radical Connections, 1919–1964* (Manchester, 2008).

10. The text of the Ulster Solemn League and Covenant is available at https://apps .proni.gov.uk/ulstercovenant/image.aspx?image=M0034910003, accessed 10/7/ 19.

11. On the history of loyalism, see Allan Blackstock, *Loyalism and the Formation of the British World, 1775–1914* (Woodbridge, 2014).

12. Nicolson, *King George the Fifth*, p. 238.

13. Pennell, *A Kingdom United?*, p. 181.

14. Ibid., p. 182.

15. www.rte.ie/centuryireland/index.php/articles/home-rule-for-ireland-suspended-until-war-ends, accessed 19/6/2019.

16. Bureau of Military History (hereafter BMH), WS 1770, Kevin O'Shiel, section 4, pp. 466–7.

17. Fearghal McGarry, '1916 and Irish Republicanism: Between Myth and History' in Horne and Madigan, eds., *Towards Commemoration*, p. 46. A similar argument is made by John Dorney, 'Republican Representations of the Treaty: "A Usurpation Pure and Simple"' in Weeks and Ó Fathartaigh, eds., *The Treaty*, p. 74.

18. Senia Pašeta, *Before the Revolution: Nationalism, Social Change, and Ireland's Catholic Elite, 1879–1922* (Cork, 1999).

19. On the long-term history of republicanism in rural Ireland, see Kevin Whelan, *The Tree of Liberty: Radicalism, Catholicism and the Construction of Irish Identity, 1760–1830* (Cork, 1996).

20. Alvin Jackson, 'Widening the Fight for Ireland's Freedom: Revolutionary Nationalism in Its Global Contexts', *Victorian Studies*, 54, 1 (2011), 95–112. Fearghal McGarry and James McConnel, eds., *The Black Hand of Republicanism: Fenianism in Modern Ireland* (Dublin, 2009).

21. Dorney, 'Republican Representations of the Treaty', pp. 73–4.

22. For more on 1798 folk memory, see Guy Beiner, *Forgetful Remembrance: Social Forgetting and Vernacular Historiography of a Rebellion in Ulster* (Oxford, 2018).

23. Murphy, *Abject Loyalty*.

24. Matthew Kelly, *The Fenian Ideal and Irish Nationalism, 1882–1916* (Woodbridge, 2006), p. 6.
25. Ibid.
26. McConnel, 'John Redmond'.
27. Prochaska, *The Republic of Britain*, p. 146.
28. Kelly, *The Fenian Ideal and Irish Nationalism*, p. 6.
29. Pennell, *A Kingdom United?*, pp. 163–89.
30. McConnel, 'John Redmond', p. 84.
31. Ibid., p. 104; Kenny, *Crown and Shamrock*, p. 140.
32. Essex Record Office, ACC.AI3528 Diaries of the Right Rev. J. E. Watts-Ditchfield, Bishop of Chelmsford, 30/4/1916, f. 323.
33. Michael MacDonagh, *The Home Rule Movement* (London, 1920), p. 283, cited in Loughlin, *The British Monarchy and Ireland*, p. 299.
34. Kelly, *The Fenian Ideal and Irish Nationalism*, p. 245.
35. 'Dismissal of Government Employee', *Irish Times*, 21/11/1914.
36. www.museum.ie/en-IE/Collections-Research/Collection/Resilience/Artefact/Test-3/fb71e3dc-2e95-4406-bc46-87d8d6b0ae5d, accessed 11/8/2020.
37. 'Annual Distribution of Prizes', *Wesley College Quarterly*, Fourth Special War Number, 26, 6 (April 1916), 18.
38. The quotation is from a typical example, the roll of honour from North Strand Church, United Parish of Drumcondra, North Strand and St Barnabas, in Dublin, www.irishwarmemorials.ie, accessed 7/11/2019.
39. D. G. Boyce, '"That Party Politics Should Divide Our Tents": Nationalism, Unionism and the First World War' in Adrian Gregory and Senia Pašeta, eds., *Ireland and the Great War: 'A War to Unite Us All'?* (Manchester, 2002), p. 194.
40. John Borgonovo, *The Dynamics of War and Revolution: Cork City, 1916–1918* (Cork, 2013), pp. 34–5.
41. NLI, Redmond Papers, MS 22187/5, Letter from the Earl of Meath to John Redmond, 15/8/1914.
42. Ibid.
43. Ibid.
44. BMH, WS 0731, Katharine Barry Moloney, p. 4.
45. Ernie O'Malley, *On Another Man's Wound* (London, 1961), p. 27.
46. Gallagher, *Ireland and the Great War*, p. 152.
47. Ibid.
48. TNA, WO 141/9 24 K, Statement from John Cronin, Royal Munster Fusiliers, 30/3/1916.
49. TNA, WO 141/9, Interview with Private David Tormey, Interview no. 372.
50. Dublin City Library and Archive, The Monica Roberts Collection, Vol. 3, Letter from Sgt John Brooks to Monica Roberts, 23/12/1915.
51. Borgonovo, *The Dynamics of War and Revolution*, p. 188.
52. TNA, CO 904/214/10, file 389, A letter to His Majesty the King from Mrs Alice Russell, 10/6/1918.
53. Emily K. Harris, Kingstown (Dún Laoghaire), former Commandant and Matron of the British Red Cross Hospital at Corrig Castle to King George V, 10/11/1926, reproduced in John Horne, ed., *Our War: Ireland and the Great War* (Dublin, 2008), p. 253.
54. Ibid., p. 252.

55. BMH, WS 1770, Kevin O'Shiel, section 4, p. 512. On Protestant nationalists, see Valerie Jones, *Rebel Prods: The Forgotten Story of Protestant Radical Nationalists and the 1916 Rising* (Dublin, 2016).

56. RA GV/PRIV/GVD/1916: 26 April.

57. Fearghal McGarry, 'Violence and the Easter Rising' in David Fitzpatrick, ed., *Terror in Ireland, 1916–1923* (Dublin, 2012), p. 40.

58. Full text of 'To My Daughter Betty, The Gift of God', online at www.bartleby.com /103/115.html, accessed 4/3/2020.

59. D. R. O'Connor Lysaght, 'The Irish Citizen Army, 1913–1916: White, Larkin and Connolly', *History Ireland*, 2, 14 (Mar/Apr. 2006), www.historyireland.com/20th-century-contemporary-history/the-irish-citizen-army-1913-16-white-larkin-and -connolly/, accessed 2/7/2020.

60. Ben Novick, *Conceiving Revolution: Irish Nationalist Propaganda during the First World War* (Dublin, 2001), p. 201.

61. Ibid.

62. Borgonovo, *The Dynamics of War and Revolution*, p. 53.

63. Ibid.

64. Ibid.

65. Ibid., p. 186 and footnote 1, p. 305. On Irishmen in British army units that put down the Rising, see Neil Richardson, *According to Their Lights: Stories of Irishmen in the British Army, Easter 1916* (Cork, 2015), p. 4.

66. See Borgonovo, *The Dynamics of War and Revolution*, p. 220 on the debate on these issues in Cork before the 1918 general election.

67. See McGarry, '1916 and Irish Republicanism'.

68. Borgonovo, *The Dynamics of War and Revolution*, p. 21.

69. Ronan McGreevy, 'A Prussian Solution to an Irish Problem: An Irishman's Diary on Prince Joachim and the 1916 Rising', *Irish Times*, www.irishtimes.com/opinion/ a-prussian-solution-to-an-irish-problem-an-irishman-s-diary-on-prince-joachim-and-the-1916-rising-1.4308126, accessed 20/7/2020.

70. Ibid.

71. Ibid.

72. Loughlin, *The British Monarchy and Ireland*, p. 306.

73. PA LG/F/29/4/81, Telegram from Lloyd George to King George, n.d. [1921].

74. The idea was floated by M. T. Judge in his newspaper *Irish Nation*; BMH, WS 1770, Kevin O' Shiel, part 4, p. 592.

75. Beatty, 'Royalism in Republicanism'.

76. NLI, Redmond Papers, MS 15519.

77. Giloi, *Monarchy, Myth, and Material Culture*.

78. BMH, WS 1467, Patrick J. Higgins, Appendix A.

79. BMH, WS 0731, Katharine Barry Moloney, Appendix A, Attitude of Kevin Barry and his family towards reprieve, p. 18.

80. PA LG/F/3/5/12, Stamfordham to Balfour, 27/8/1920.

81. Ibid.

82. Rose, *King George V*, p. 238.

83. Ibid., p. 242.

84. Kenny, *Crown and Shamrock*, pp. 138–9; p. 160.

85. Loughlin, *The British Monarchy and Ireland*, p. 312; Rose, *King George V*, pp. 240–1. On King George V having 'frequently intervened with his customary courage and good sense to warn the Cabinet against the activities of the Black

and Tans and the policy of authorized reprisals', see Thomas Jones, *Whitehall Diary*, Vol. 3: *Ireland 1918–1925* (London, 1971), p. 77.

86. Loughlin, *The British Monarchy and Ireland*, p. 312. PA LG/F/29/4/63, Stamfordham to Edward Grigg, 29/7/1921. PA LG/F/29/4/62, Memorandum, 29/7/1921. Lloyd George told his secretary and mistress Frances Stevenson that Stamfordham was 'evidently the culprit'. Stevenson, *Lloyd George: A Diary*, 29/7/1921, pp. 232–3.

87. Kenny, *Crown and Shamrock*, p. 156.

88. Airlie, *Thatched with Gold*, pp. 148–51.

89. Fitzroy, *Memoirs*, Vol. 2, p. 753.

90. Ibid.

91. Airlie, *Thatched with Gold*, p. 149.

92. Ibid.

93. Loughlin, *The British Monarchy and Ireland*, p. 318.

94. Kenny, *Crown and Shamrock*, p. 158.

95. Airlie, *Thatched with Gold*, pp. 148–9.

96. Loughlin, *The British Monarchy and Ireland*, p. 317.

97. Kenny, *Crown and Shamrock*, p. 156.

98. Loughlin, *The British Monarchy and Ireland*, p. 315.

99. Airlie, *Thatched with Gold*, p. 149.

100. Kenny, *Crown and Shamrock*, p. 161.

101. PA LG/F/29/4/55, Letter from Stamfordham to Lloyd George, 24/6/1921. Also Jones, *Whitehall Diary*, Vol. 3, p. 79; see also O. Geyser, 'Irish Independence: Jan Smuts and Eamon de Valera ', *The Round Table*, 348 (1998), 479–80.

102. Kenny, *Crown and Shamrock*, p. 159.

103. BMH, WS 0939, Ernest Blythe, pp. 128–9.

104. LPL, Papers of Dr Randall T. Davidson, Archbishop of Canterbury, private papers, Vol. 20, f. 194, Queen Mary to Edith Davidson, 18/11/1918. Also Vol. 13, f. 314, Randall Davidson Memorandum, 12/5/1918.

105. LPL, Papers of Dr Randall T. Davidson, Archbishop of Canterbury, official letters, Vol. 196, f. 168, Letter from Lord Halifax to Randall Davidson, 22/11/1918. For another example of how the king amended his speeches, see LPL, Papers of Dr Randall T. Davidson, Archbishop of Canterbury, private papers, Vol. 13, ff. 355–61, Memorandum, 17/11/1918.

106. George V's biographer Kenneth Rose argues that there was no clash with the cabinet: Rose, *King George V*, p. 238; see also Loughlin, *The British Monarchy and Ireland*, pp. 312–13.

107. Loughlin, *The British Monarchy and Ireland*, pp. 313–14.

108. Jones, *Whitehall Diary*, Vol. 3, p. 70; pp. 76–7.

109. Cormac Moore, *The Birth of the Border: The Impact of Partition on Ireland* (Dublin, 2019), p. 47; Geyser, 'Irish Independence', 477.

110. Geyser, 'Irish Independence', 477.

111. Ibid.

112. Ibid.

113. Jones, *Whitehall Diary*, Vol. 3, p. 75, p. 247.

114. Geyser, 'Irish Independence' and PA LG/F/29/4/48, Note on telephone message, n.d.

115. Geyser, 'Irish Independence', 477.

116. Jones, *Whitehall Diary*, Vol. 3, p. 247; p. 76; p. 78.

117. Ibid.; also Loughlin, *The British Monarchy and Ireland*, p. 313.

118. PA LG/F/29/4/50, Paragraph from Chequers. Also PA F/29/4/50, Second draft of speech.
119. LPL, Papers of Dr Randall T. Davidson, Archbishop of Canterbury, private papers, Vol. 20, f. 170, Randall Davidson to King George V, 11/12/1921.
120. Kenny, *Crown and Shamrock*, p. 117.
121. Airlie, *Thatched with Gold*, p. 150; Rose, *King George V*, p. 239.
122. LPL, Papers of Dr Randall T. Davidson, Archbishop of Canterbury, private papers, Vol. 20, f. 170, Randall Davidson to King George V, 11/12/1921. Public support was helped by the fact that Wickham Steed, editor of *The Times*, and Lionel Curtis, editor of the *Round Table*, had been among those arguing the king's speech in Belfast was a peace opportunity. Jones, *Whitehall Diary*, Vol. 3, p. 77.
123. PA LG/F/29/4/55, Stamfordham to Lloyd George, 24/6/1921.
124. Geyser, 'Irish Independence', 478.
125. PA LG/F/29/4/90, Lloyd George telegram to King George V, n.d. [1921].
126. Airlie, *Thatched with Gold*, p. 147; p. 151.
127. Geyser, 'Irish Independence', 479–81.
128. Ibid.
129. Stevenson, *Lloyd George: A Diary*, p. 227.
130. PA LG/F/29/4/77, Copy sent to Stamfordham of Lloyd George reply to Éamon de Valera, n.d. [summer 1921]; see also TNA, CAB 24/128, Lloyd George reply to letter from Éamon de Valera, 1921.
131. PA LG/F/29/4/77, Copy sent to Stamfordham of Lloyd George reply to Éamon de Valera, n.d. [summer 1921].
132. Ibid.
133. Ibid.
134. TNA, CAB 21/247, Suggestion by Mr Tom Jones merging the draft oath of allegiance with the oath administered to representatives and delegates to Congress.
135. TNA, CAB 21/247, Undated, unsigned minute.
136. TNA, CAB 21/247, Oath proposed by Mr Griffith and Mr Collins, 1/12/1921.
137. TNA, CAB 21/247, Conference on Ireland, Meeting of Sub-Conference at the House of Lords [Minutes], 24/11/1921, p. 3.
138. TNA, CAB 21/247, Notes of a Meeting of the Conference on Ireland held at the House of Lords, 24/11/1921.
139. TNA, CAB 21/247, Minutes of Conference on Ireland, Meeting of Sub-Conference at the House of Lords [Minutes], 24/11/1921, p. 2.
140. TNA, CAB 21/247, Memorandum by the Irish delegates on their proposal for the association of Ireland with the British Commonwealth, signed Arthur Griffith, 28/11/1921.
141. Ibid.
142. TNA, CAB 21/247, Conference on Ireland, Meeting of Sub-Conference at the House of Lords [Minutes], 24/11/1921, p. 2.
143. TNA, CAB 21/247, Notes of a Meeting of the Conference on Ireland held at the House of Lords, 24/11/1921.
144. TNA, CAB 21/247, Aide memoire by the Attorney-General, Conference on Ireland, 25/11/1921.
145. Cahillane and Murray, 'The Treaty', p. 244.
146. TNA, CAB 21/247, Notes of a meeting of the Conference on Ireland held at the House of Lords, 24/11/1921.

147. TNA, CAB 21/247, Conference on Ireland, Memo by His Majesty's Government, 27/10/1921.
148. TNA, CAB 21/247, Note in file, titled 'incorporated in S.F.C. 17', n.d.
149. TNA, CAB 21/247, Conference on Ireland, Memo by His Majesty's Government, 27/10/1921.
150. Kenny, *Crown and Shamrock*, p. 163.
151. Mel Farrell, '"Stepping Stones to Freedom": Pro-Treaty Rhetoric and Strategy during the Dáil Treaty Debates' in Weeks and Ó Fathartaigh, eds., *The Treaty*, p. 17.
152. Cahillane and Murray, 'The Treaty', pp. 246–7.
153. Ibid.
154. Maurice Walsh, *Bitter Freedom: Ireland in a Revolutionary World, 1918–1923* (London, 2015), p. 319.
155. Dorney, 'Republican Representations of the Treaty', pp. 74–5.
156. Cahillane and Murray, 'The Treaty', p. 247.
157. Kenny, *Crown and Shamrock*, p. 163.
158. Walsh, *Bitter Freedom*, p. 329.
159. Sinéad McCoole, 'Debating Not Negotiating: The Female TDs of the Second Dáil' in Weeks and Ó Fathartaigh, eds., *The Treaty*, p. 150.
160. Dorney, 'Republican Representations of the Treaty', p. 72; p. 74.
161. Ibid., p. 72.
162. Ibid., p. 67.
163. Liam Weeks and Mícheál Ó Fathartaigh, 'Conclusion: Judging the Treaty' in Weeks and Ó Fathartaigh, eds., *The Treaty*, pp. 226–7.
164. Dorney, 'Republican Representations of the Treaty', p. 75.
165. Fortescue, *Author and Curator*, p. 236.
166. Ibid.
167. William Magan, *Umma More: The Story of an Irish Family* (Salisbury, 1983), p. 381, cited in Gemma Clark, *Everyday Violence in the Irish Civil War* (Cambridge, 2014), p. 85.
168. Ian d'Alton, 'No Country? Protestant "Belongings" in Independent Ireland, 1922–49' in Ian d'Alton and Ida Milne, eds., *Protestant and Irish: The Minority's Search for Place in Independent Ireland* (Cork, 2019), pp. 27–8.
169. Ibid.
170. Ibid., p. 28.
171. Ibid., p. 29; p. 31.
172. Cahillane and Murray, 'The Treaty', p. 254, p. 256.
173. Clark, *Everyday Violence in the Irish Civil War*.
174. Brian Hughes, 'Defining Loyalty: Southern Irish Protestants and the Irish Grants Committee, 1926–30' in d'Alton and Milne, eds., *Protestant and Irish*, p. 35; p. 38; p. 42.
175. Ibid., pp. 34–5.
176. Rose, *King George V*, p. 242.
177. RA PS/PSO/GV/C/O/1106/7, Lord Stamfordham to Col. J. Unsworth, 9/4/1917.
178. On 'scripting' revolutions, see Keith Michael Baker and Dan Edelstein, eds., *Scripting Revolution: A Historical Approach to the Comparative Study of Revolutions* (Stanford, 2015).
179. Prochaska, 'George V and Republicanism'.

180. Norman and Jeanne Mackenzie, *H. G. Wells: A Biography* (New York, 1973), p. 314.
181. 'The Crown and the Nation', *The Times*, 4/4/1917, p. 7.
182. Letter from Civis Britannicus, *The Times*, 6/3/1917, p. 5.
183. 'The "Golden Link"', *The Times*, 21/4/1917, p. 7.
184. Ibid.
185. Mackenzie, *H. G. Wells*, p. 314.
186. Ibid., p. 310.
187. Ibid., p. 312.
188. Thurtle, *Time's Winged Chariot*, p. 57.
189. Prochaska, *The Republic of Britain*, p. 158; p. 161.
190. 'Republicanism', *The Herald*, 28/4/1917, p. 2; p. 3.
191. H. G. Wells, 'The Future of the Monarchy', *Penny Pictorial*, 19/5/1917.
192. 'Current Topics: The War-Makers', *Stirling Observer*, 3/8/1918, p. 4.
193. Prochaska, *The Republic of Britain*, p. 161.
194. H. G. Wells, *In the Fourth Year: Anticipations of a World Peace* (London, 1918), p. 86.
195. Ibid.
196. Ibid.
197. Ibid., p. 87.
198. Ibid, p. 91.
199. Ibid., p. 90; p. 92.
200. Hayman, 'Labour and the Monarchy', 168; 173.
201. RA GV/Q 1104/1, Strachey to Stamfordham, 27/4/1917; RA GV/Q 1104/8 Stamfordham to Strachey, 30/4/1917, cited in Prochaska, *The Republic of Britain*, p. 162.
202. RA GV/Q 1104/10, Strachey to Stamfordham, 2/5/1917, cited in Prochaska, *The Republic of Britain*, p. 162.
203. Thurtle, *Time's Winged Chariot*, pp. 56–7.
204. Wells, *In the Fourth Year*, p. 88.
205. 'The Outlook: Monarchy', *Sheffield Independent*, 5/4/1917, p. 4.
206. Ibid.
207. Prochaska, *The Republic of Britain*, p. 159.
208. Essex Record Office, ACC.AI3528 Diaries of the Right Rev. J. E. Watts-Ditchfield, Bishop of Chelmsford, 28/4/1917, f. 511.
209. Prochaska, *The Republic of Britain*, p. 162.
210. See also Glencross, 'George V and the New Royal House'.
211. TNA, FO 800/199, f. 14, Earl of Balfour, Correspondence with the Palace, 1917–18, Stamfordham to Balfour, 19/7/1917.
212. Georges Lefebvre, *The Great Fear of 1789: Rural Panic in Revolutionary France* (London, 1973 [1932]).
213. Robert Gerwarth and John Horne, 'Bolshevism as Fantasy: Fear of Revolution and Counter-Revolutionary Violence, 1917–1923' in Horne and Gerwarth, eds., *War in Peace*, p. 40. See also Mark Jones, *Founding Weimar: Violence and the German Revolution of 1918–1919* (Cambridge, 2016).
214. Gerwarth and Horne, 'Bolshevism as Fantasy'.
215. George Rudé, 'Introduction' in Lefebvre, *The Great Fear*, pp. xiii–xv calls for historians to look at 'rumour, panic and fear', which are a 'significant dimension in the historical process'.

216. John Horne and Alan Kramer, *German Atrocities, 1914: A History of Denial* (New Haven, 2001), p. 89; p. 91.
217. Ibid.
218. RA PS/PSO/GV/C/O/1106/2, J. Unsworth to Lord Stamfordham, 5/4/1917.
219. Unfortunately, Prochaska gives no source for this claim nor any indication of who sent the letters or how many arrived or exactly when. Prochaska, *The Republic of Britain*, p. 158.
220. RA PS/PSO/GV/C/O/1106/2, J. Unsworth to Lord Stamfordham, 5/4/1917.
221. Ibid.
222. LPL, Papers of Dr Randall T. Davidson, Archbishop of Canterbury, private papers, Vol. 6, f. 19, Randall Davidson to Stamfordham, 21/4/1917.
223. RA GV/O 1106/3, Bishop of Chelmsford to Stamfordham, 5/4/1917, cited in Prochaska, *Republic of Britain*, p. 159.
224. Ibid.
225. Prochaska, *The Republic of Britain*, p. 166.
226. Ibid.
227. Beckett, 'King George V and His Generals', p. 250.
228. Prochaska, *The Republic of Britain*, p. 167.
229. Ibid., p. 160.
230. LPL, Papers of Dr Randall T. Davidson, Archbishop of Canterbury, private papers, Vol. 13, f. 311, Randall Davidson account of his trip to Windsor, 12/5/1918.
231. Prochaska, *The Republic of Britain*, p. 167.
232. PA LG/F/29/2/5, Stamfordham to J. T. Davies, 23/1/1918.
233. Prochaska, *The Republic of Britain*, p. 170.
234. LPL, Papers of Dr Randall T. Davidson, Archbishop of Canterbury, private papers, Vol. 13, f. 375, Memorandum, 8/12/1918.
235. PA LG/F/29/3/23, Mr Macculloch, London, to King George V, n.d., c. June 1919.
236. Ibid.
237. PA LG/F/3/2/17, Stamfordham to Drummond, 5/4/1917; also Rose, *King George V*, pp. 212–13. There is little new to be said on the subject of the tsar's asylum, which is one aspect of the wartime monarchy that has been researched in great detail: see Helen Rappaport, *The Race to Save the Romanovs: The Truth behind the Secret Plans to Rescue Russia's Imperial Family* (London, 2018).
238. Nicolson, *King George the Fifth*, p. 312.
239. PA LG/F/29/1/34, Stamfordham to Major General Sir John Hanbury Williams, Message to Emperor from King, 19/3/1917.
240. Rose, *King George V*, p. 211.
241. Ibid, pp. 212–13.
242. Ibid., p. 212.
243. H. M. Hyndman, 'The Need for a British Republic', *Justice*, 5/4/1917, in RA PS/PSO/GV/C/O/1106/1.
244. Prochaska, *The Republic of Britain*, p. 158. The question of the tsar's asylum has been the focus of much public attention: for the latest book, see Rappaport, *The Race to Save the Romanovs*.
245. Essex Record Office, ACC.AI3528 Diaries of the Right Rev. J. E. Watts-Ditchfield, Bishop of Chelmsford, 29/4/1917, ff. 515–16.
246. BL, Add MS 49686, Balfour Papers, Stamfordham to Balfour, 22/7/1918, ff. 128–31.

247. Ibid. On how the royals received this news, see Chapter 5.
248. Ibid.
249. Churchill, *In the Eye of the Storm*, p. 294.
250. Beckett, 'King George V and His Generals', p. 250.
251. Essex Record Office, ACC.AI3528 Diaries of the Right Rev. J. E. Watts-Ditchfield, Bishop of Chelmsford, 29/4/1917, f. 514.
252. Ibid., f. 516.
253. Beckett, 'King George V and His Generals', p. 250.
254. Ibid.
255. PA LG/F/43/1/5, Rufus D. Isaacs to Lloyd George, 21/6/1917.
256. Hayman, 'Labour and the Monarchy', 172.
257. Rose, *King George V*, p. 201.
258. Essex Record Office, ACC.AI3528 Diaries of the Right Rev. J. E. Watts-Ditchfield, Bishop of Chelmsford, 29/4/1917, ff. 514–15.
259. Ibid, f. 519.
260. LPL, Papers of Dr Randall T. Davidson, Archbishop of Canterbury, private papers, Vol. 13, f. 272, Memorandum, February 1918.
261. Rose, *King George V*, p. 207.
262. Hayman, 'Labour and the Monarchy', 172.
263. TNA, HO 45/10743, Report by a Metropolitan Police Officer on meeting of the Imperial Defence Union at the Queen's Hall on 9 July, 10/7/1917, p. 1.
264. Ibid., p. 7.
265. Ibid., pp. 9–10.
266. Ibid., p. 10.
267. TNA, HO 45/10743, Basil Thomson, memo, 11/7/1917.
268. Gregory, *The Last Great War*, p. 234.
269. William D. Rubinstein, 'Henry Page Croft and the National Party, 1917–22', *Journal of Contemporary History*, 9, 1 (1974), 129–48.
270. Beckett, 'King George V and His Generals', p. 250.
271. Home Office, 2015: Summary of recorded crime data from 1898 to 2001/2, England and Wales, https://data.gov.uk/dataset/f79c8194-93b0-41eb-bba5-56a83fd32f10/historical-crime-data, accessed 10/1/2020. RA GV/PRIV/GVD/1916: 24 April.
272. Thomson, *The Scene Changes*, p. 296.
273. Home Office, 2015: Summary of recorded crime data from 1898 to 2001/2, England and Wales, https://data.gov.uk/dataset/f79c8194-93b0-41eb-bba5-56a83fd32f10/historical-crime-data, accessed 10/1/2020.
274. Text of the 1848 Treason Felony Act, amended in 1891 and 1892, www.legislation.gov.uk/ukpga/Vict/11-12/12/section/3/1991-02-01, accessed 10/1/2020.
275. Ibid.
276. Text of Defence of the Realm Act, 8/8/1914, www.legislation.gov.uk/ukpga/1914/29/pdfs/ukpga_19140029_en.pdf, accessed 10/1/2020.
277. War Office, 'Summary of Analyses of Proceedings of General, District and Field General Courts-Martial at Home for the Trials of Officers, Soldiers and Civilians, 4th August 1914 to 31st March 1920', *Statistics of the Military Effort of the British Empire during the Great War 1914–1920* (London, 1922), p. 658 and ibid., p. 667, 'Summary of Analyses of Proceedings of General, District and Field General Courts-Martial Abroad for the Trials of Officers, Soldiers and Civilians, 4th August 1914 to 31st March 1920'.

278. Ibid., 'Analysis of Proceedings of Field General Courts-Martial for the Trials of Civilians at Home, 4th August 1914 to 31st March 1920', p. 657.

279. Cornwall, 'Traitors and the Meaning of Treason', 113.

280. Ibid., 116; 120.

281. Ibid., 117–18.

282. Millman, *Managing Domestic Dissent*, p. 3.

283. Owens, *The Family Firm*, p. 95.

284. On the pre-war visits, see Mort, 'Safe for Democracy'.

285. TNA, CAB 23/2/54, ff. 162–3, Minutes of War Cabinet Meeting, 11/5/1917, pp. 3–4.

286. Ibid.

287. Ibid.

288. The precedent for this was the king's meeting with a radical local Labour and trade unionist MP, Albert Smith, during his pre-war tour of Lancashire: Mort, 'Safe for Democracy', 127.

289. Owens, *The Family Firm*, p. 231.

290. Ibid.

291. Thomson, *The Scene Changes*, p. 338.

292. Ibid.

293. 'The King's Tour, Munitions Works Visited, Royal Chats with Workpeople', *Driffield Times*, 19/5/1917, p. 4. Also 'King and Queen's Tour', *Western Morning News*, 15/5/1917, p. 3.

294. 'The King's Tour, Munitions Works Visited, Royal Chats with Workpeople', *Driffield Times*, 19/5/1917, p. 4.

295. Grigg, *Lloyd George*, p. 115.

296. 'The King and the War', *Daily Mail*, 13/9/1917, pp. 5–6.

297. Ibid.

298. Ibid.

299. 'The King's Visit to Greenock and Port-Glasgow', *Daily Record*, 17/9/1917, p. 1.

300. The royal couple's pre-war 'industrial tours' had likewise drawn on these older ideas of the royal progress: see Mort, 'Safe for Democracy', 129.

301. 'Their Majesties Tour', *Southern Reporter*, 21/6/1917, p. 4

302. Ibid.

303. Mort, 'Accessible Sovereignty', 330–1.

304. TNA, CAB 23/2/54. Also Prochaska, *The Republic of Britain*, p. 156.

305. 'A Homely Royal Visit', *Daily Record and Mail*, 21/9/1917, p. 2.

306. Ibid.

307. Ibid.

308. In fact, railway preparations for royal train travel were exhaustive in 1917. Each tunnel was checked and monitored by teams of men ahead of the train passing, and a pilot engine travelled the line 15 minutes ahead of the royal train: TNA, RAIL 1014/10, Great Western Railway, Royal journeys, notice of a royal train, Windsor and Eton, Bushbury Junction, 16/9/1917.

309. www.britishpathe.com/video/king-meets-people-at-huge-war-rally, accessed 8/7/2020.

310. RA PS/PSO/GV/C/O/1106/13, Stamfordham to Colonel Unsworth, 15/4/1917.

311. Mort, 'Safe for Democracy'.

312. PA LG/F/29/1/50, Stamfordham to J. T. Davies, 11/12/1917.

313. David Lloyd George, *War Memoirs of David Lloyd George*, 2 vols (London, 1938), Vol. 2, pp. 1162–3.

314. Hamilton, *Three Years or the Duration*, p. 36.
315. Walter Powell, 'Footman for a Day in the Convoy for King George V and Queen Mary', May 1917, The First World War Poetry Digital Archive, Oxford, http://ww1lit.nsms.ox.ac.uk/ww1lit/gwa/item/7603, accessed 16/1/2020.
316. TNA, HO 190/854, Visit of HM King George V and Queen Mary to Carlisle, Mr Meiklejohn to Mr Sanders, 12/5/1917.
317. IWM Documents 10311, Box Misc. 1840, 118/2, 'The Chilwell Story, 1915–1982', p. 42.
318. IWM Documents 10311, Box Misc. 1840, 118/2, Letter from Neville Chamberlain to Lord Chetwynd, 31/1/1917.
319. IWM Documents 10311, Box Misc. 1840, 118/2, Letter from Lord Chetwynd to King George V, 19/12/1916.
320. Ibid.
321. Röhl, *Wilhelm II: Into the Abyss*, p. 1132.
322. Hayman, 'Labour and the Monarchy', 164.
323. Prochaska, *The Republic of Britain*, p. 158.
324. RA PS/PSO/GV/C/O/1106/9 and 10, Notes on meeting held at the Albert Hall on Saturday March 31st to celebrate the recent Russian disturbance.
325. TNA, HO/45/10743/263275, Police report, Meeting in Bull Ring, 3/6/1917.
326. Ibid. Minute on report on public meeting in Bullring, remarks in address made by Jim Donaldson, 13/6/1917.
327. Prochaska, *The Republic of Britain*, p. 165.
328. RA GV/O 1106/45, *Clarion*, 29/6/1917.
329. Thorne, *My Life's Battles*, pp. 194–5.
330. Ibid., p. 179.
331. Ibid., pp. 180–1.
332. Ibid., p. 181.
333. Ibid.
334. Hunt, *The Working Woman's Champion*, p. 128.
335. LPL, Papers of Dr Randall T. Davidson, Archbishop of Canterbury, private papers, Vol. 13, f. 213, Memorandum, 3 February [c. 1918].
336. John McGovern, *Neither Fear Nor Favour* (London, 1960), p. 51.
337. Ibid.
338. Hunt, *The Working Woman's Champion*, p. 128.
339. Prochaska, *The Republic of Britain*, p. 163.
340. 'Socialist Convention on the War', *Manchester Guardian*, 4/6/1917, p. 5.
341. Ibid.
342. Thorne, *My Life's Battles*, p. 195.
343. Ibid.
344. Ibid.
345. Prochaska, *The Republic of Britain*, p. 164.
346. Thurtle, *Time's Winged Chariot*, p. 57.
347. Hayman, 'Labour and the Monarchy', 175.
348. Prochaska, *The Republic of Britain*, pp. 167–8.
349. Thomson, *The Scene Changes*, p. 377.
350. Prochaska, *The Republic of Britain*, p. 171.
351. Langewiesche, 'Monarchy-Global', 283.
352. Prochaska, *The Republic of Britain*, p. 172.
353. Hayman, 'Labour and the Monarchy', 175.

354. Ibid., 171.
355. PA LG/F/12/1/23, Curzon to Lloyd George, 9/7/1919; Nigel J. Ashton and Duco Hellema, 'Anglo-Dutch Relations and the Kaiser Question, 1918–1920' in Nigel Ashton and Duco Hellema, eds., *Unspoken Allies: Anglo-Dutch Relations since 1780* (Amsterdam, 2001), p. 87.
356. PA LG/F/12/1/23, Lloyd George to Lord Curzon, 8/7/1919. For Curzon's very unconvincing denial that George V had influenced him. see PA LG/F/12/1/23, Curzon to Lloyd George, 9/7/1919.
357. Ashton and Hellema, 'Anglo-Dutch Relations and the Kaiser Question, 1918–1920', p. 87; Rose, *King George V*, p. 231.
358. Langewiesche, 'Monarchy-Global', 281.
359. PA LG/F/12/1/21, Lord Curzon to Lloyd George, 7/7/1919, pp. 2–3.
360. Ibid.
361. Ashton and Hellema, 'Anglo-Dutch Relations and the Kaiser Question, 1918–1920', p. 91.
362. Röhl, *Wilhelm II: Into the Abyss*, p. 1197.
363. LPL, Papers of Dr Randall T. Davidson, Archbishop of Canterbury, private papers, Vol. 13, ff. 410–11, Memorandum, 6/7/1919.
364. PA LG/F/12/3/2, Unidentified royal secretary to Lloyd George, 17/1/1920.
365. Ibid.
366. PA LG/F/12/3/2(a), Frederick Augustus, King of Saxony, William, Duke of Wurttemberg (formerly King), Frederick Duke of Baden, signed 22, 26 November and 7 December 1919, to King George V.
367. PA LG/F/56/2/35, Rennell Rodd to Lloyd George, 18/8/1919.
368. Hull, *A Scrap of Paper*, p. 315.
369. PA LG/F/12/1/22, Lloyd George to Lord Curzon, 8/7/1919.
370. Ashton and Hellema, 'Anglo-Dutch Relations and the Kaiser Question, 1918–1920', p. 86.
371. Rose, *King George V*, p. 229.
372. PA LG/F/12/1/23, Curzon to Lloyd George, 9/7/1919.
373. PA LG/F/29/3/3, Wigram to Theo Russell, 10/1/1919.
374. PA LG/F/29/3/12, Appeal to George V from Archduke Joseph, Budapest, 2/2/1919. The Archduke was briefly head of state in Hungary in 1919.
375. TNA, FO 383/502, f. 542, German senior officer, signature illegible, to King George V, 5/8/1919.
376. Paulmann, 'Searching for a "Royal International"', p. 145. However, Paulmann argues that the 'royal international' was never as formal as the later 'socialist international' and that it became moribund with the increasing nationalisation of monarchies after the mid-nineteenth century revolutions and morphed into what he terms a looser 'royal cosmopolitanism'.
377. LPL, Papers of Dr Randall T. Davidson, Archbishop of Canterbury, private papers, Vol. 13, f. 390, Memorandum, 2/3/1919, p. 5.
378. PA LG/F/29/3/16, Stamfordham to Lloyd George, 5/4/1919.
379. PA LG/F/29/4/12, Ex-King Constantine of Greece to George V, 18/5/1920.
380. Ponsonby, *Recollections of Three Reigns*, pp. 335–6.
381. PA LG/F/29/4/32, Stamfordham to David Lloyd George, 14/11/1920.
382. PA LG/F/29/4/33, David Lloyd George to Stamfordham, 15/11/1920.
383. Röhl, *Wilhelm II: Into the Abyss*, p. 1260.
384. Mort, 'Accessible Sovereignty', 328–59.

385. Mort, 'Safe for Democracy', 109; 112. Mort points to the expression 'loyal democracy', which was also used during the royal couple's pre-war industrial tours of Wales and the north of England. Ibid., 124.
386. Mort, 'Safe for Democracy', 112.
387. Prochaska, *The Republic of Britain*, p. 168.
388. Ibid.
389. Essex Record Office, ACC.AI3528 Diaries of the Right Rev. J. E. Watts-Ditchfield, Bishop of Chelmsford, 29/4/1917, f. 517.
390. Ibid.
391. Ibid.
392. Prochaska, *Republic of Britain*, p. 169.
393. RA PS/PSO/GV/C/O/1106/65, Stamfordham to the Bishop of Chelmsford, 25/11/1918.
394. LPL, Papers of Dr Randall T. Davidson, Archbishop of Canterbury, private papers, Vol. 13, ff. 312–13, Memorandum of visit to Windsor, 12/5/1918.
395. Ibid.
396. Ibid., f. 273, Memorandum, 17/2/1918.
397. RA PS/PSO/GV/C/O/1106/30, 'Unrest in the Country', policy suggestions to the Palace from the Bishop of Chelmsford, n.d.
398. Prochaska, *The Republic of Britain*, p. 173.
399. Ibid., p. 171.
400. Rose, *King George V*, p. 229.
401. PA LG/F/7/3/20, Lloyd George Papers, Stamfordham to R. P. M. Gower, 18/8/1920.
402. PA LG/F/29/4/20, Stamfordham to Lloyd George, 4/8/1920.
403. See the presentations of George V in the following, for example: Nicolson, *King George the Fifth*; Rose, *King George V*; Catrine Clay, *King, Kaiser, Tsar: Three Royal Cousins Who Led the World to War* (London, 2006).
404. 'The King and the War', *Daily Mail*, 13/9/1917, pp. 5–6.
405. Jones, *Whitehall Diary*, Vol. 1, p. 76.
406. 'Imperial War Museum: King George's Opening Speech', *Gloucestershire Echo*, 9/6/1920, p. 4.
407. On Sinn Féin's offices, see Prochaska, *The Republic of Britain*, p. 176.
408. Langewiesche, 'Monarchy-Global', 282.
409. Cannadine, 'Kaiser Wilhelm and the British Monarchy', p. 189.
410. Glencross, *The State Visits of Edward VII*.
411. www.britishpathe.com/video/george-v-empire-escort-to-parliament, accessed 8/7/2020.
412. Murphy, *Monarchy and the End of Empire*, pp. 16–17.
413. Prochaska, *The Republic of Britain*, p. 169.
414. Mort, 'On Tour with the Prince', 31.
415. PA LG/F/29/4/64, Lloyd George to King George V, 5/8/1921.
416. John Darwin, 'A Third British Empire? The Dominion Idea in Imperial Politics' in Judith Brown and William Roger Louis, eds., *The Oxford History of the British Empire*, Vol. 4: *The Twentieth Century* (Oxford, 1999), p. 67.
417. Edward, Duke of Windsor, *A King's Story*, p. 121.
418. Lieutenant General Sir Stanley Maude, 'The Proclamation of Baghdad', 19/3/1917, wwi.lib.byu.edu/index.php/The_Proclamation_of_Baghdad, accessed 7/5/2020.

419. TNA, FO 141/781/4, Letters between King George V and King Hussein [erroneously catalogued as 'of Egypt'], 1918–20; Letter from King George V to King Hussein, 30/9/1918.

420. TNA, FO 141/781/4, Telegram from King Husein [sic] to King George V, 14/7/1920.

421. 'Prince of Wales in Egypt', The Scotsman, 10/6/1922, p. 9.

422. BL, MSS EUR F116/44, Stamfordham to Sir Harcourt Butler, Lieutenant Governor of Burma, 23/1/1917, f. 5.

423. On these tours, see Mort, 'On Tour with the Prince'; Chandrika Kaul, 'Monarchical Display and the Politics of Empire: Princes of Wales and India, 1870–1920s', Twentieth Century British History, 17, 4 (2006), 464–88; Hilary Sapire, 'Ambiguities of Loyalism: The Prince of Wales in India and Africa, 1921–22 and 25', History Workshop Journal, 73 (2012), 37–65.

424. Frank Mort, 'On Tour with the Prince', 28.

425. Ibid., 26.

426. Ibid., 39; 41–2.

427. Ibid.

428. Ibid.

429. Ibid., 41.

430. Ibid., 45.

431. Broadlands Archive, University of Southampton, MB1/A15, Prince of Wales' tour to Australia and New Zealand 1920 correspondence 1974–9, Mountbatten to Kevin Fewster, 17/6/1974.

432. Broadlands Archive, University of Southampton, MB1/A15, Prince of Wales' tour to Australia and New Zealand 1920 correspondence 1974–9, Letter from the Prince of Wales, Sydney, 16/8/1920.

433. Mort, 'On Tour with the Prince', 50.

434. Cook, 'The Monarchy Is More than the Monarch', p. 94; pp. 116–17; p. 137.

435. Mort, 'On Tour with the Prince', 33.

436. Owens, The Family Firm, p. 117.

437. Nicolson, King George the Fifth, pp. 470–2.

438. Mort, 'Accessible Sovereignty', 332.

439. Ibid.

440. Mort, 'On Tour with the Prince', 52.

441. Mort, 'Safe for Democracy', 123.

442. Owens, The Family Firm, p. 32.

443. Mary Stewart-Wilson, Queen Mary Dolls' House (London, 1988).

444. Ibid., p. 13. See also Jiyi Ryu, 'The Queen's Dolls' House within the British Empire Exhibition: Encapsulating the British Imperial World', Contemporary British History, 33, 4 (2019), 464–82.

445. Duffett, 'The War in Miniature', 441; 437; Ryu, 'The Queen's Dolls' House', 476.

446. Archbishop Cosmo Lang in his address at the 1934 wedding of Prince George to Princess Marina of Greece, broadcast across the empire, would show how such ideas took hold, referring to how 'The whole Nation – nay, the whole Empire – are the wedding guests; and more than guests, members of the family.' Owens, The Family Firm, p. 83.

447. Strachan, The Politics of the British Army, p. 71.

448. Ibid.

449. Prochaska, The Republic of Britain, p. 167.

5   The Monarchy and the Armistice: Ritualising Victory, Channelling War Grief

1. On victory celebrations, see Victor Demiaux, 'La construction rituelle de la victoire dans les capitales européennes après la Grande Guerre (Bruxelles, Bucarest, Londres, Paris, Rome)' (PhD thesis, Ecole des hautes études en sciences sociales, Paris, 2013) and Victor Demiaux, 'Inter-Allied Community? Rituals and Transnational Narratives of the Great War' in Marco Mondini and Massimo Rospocher, eds., *Narrating War: Early Modern and Contemporary Perspectives* (Berlin, Bologna, 2013), pp. 189–204.

2. On how historical pageants commemorated the war, see Angela Bartie, Linda Fleming, Mark Freeman, Tom Hulme, Paul Readman and Charlotte Tupman, '"And Those Who Live, How Shall I Tell Their Fame?": Historical Pageants, Collective Remembrance and the First World War, 1919–39', *Historical Research*, 90, 249 (2017), 636–61.

3. Bryant, *George V*, p. 107.

4. IWM Documents 12767, Box 04/1/1, Letter from Patricia Wilson to Commander H. M. Wilson, n.d., pp. 1–3.

5. Ibid.

6. Fitzroy, *Memoirs*, Vol. 2, p. 686.

7. Nicolson, *King George the Fifth*, p. 326.

8. RA GV/PRIV/GVD/1918: 11 November.

9. Ibid.

10. RA QM/PRIV/QMD/1914–1918/1918: 11 November.

11. RA QM/PRIV/QMD/1914–1918/1918: 12 and 13 November.

12. Thomson, *The Scene Changes*, p. 382.

13. Gallagher, *Ireland and the Great War*, pp. 168–9.

14. LPL, Papers of Dr Randall T. Davidson, Archbishop of Canterbury, private papers, Vol. 13, f. 348, Memorandum, 3/11/1918.

15. Ibid.

16. Ibid.

17. Nicolson, *King George the Fifth*, p. 326.

18. 'The King and Queen Drive through the Streets', *Daily Mail*, 12/11/1918, p. 3, cited in Jon Lawrence, 'Public Space, Political Space' in Jay Winter and Jean-Louis Robert, eds., *Capital Cities at War: Paris, London, Berlin*, Vol. 2: *A Cultural History* (Cambridge, 2007), pp. 308–9.

19. Nicolson, *King George the Fifth*, p. 327.

20. Prochaska, *The Republic of Britain*, p. 173.

21. LPL, Papers of Dr Randall T. Davidson, Archbishop of Canterbury, private papers, Vol. 13, ff. 363–4, Memorandum, 17/11/1918, p. 10.

22. Ibid.

23. Ibid.

24. Churchill College Archives, DANL 3, Naval Signal, Commander in Chief, 21/11/1918.

25. RA QM/PRIV/QMD/1918: 16 November and 17 November.

26. 'Rendering God Thanks', *The Scotsman*, 22/11/1918, p. 4.

27. Ibid.

28. Ibid.

29. Ibid.

30. Ibid.
31. Kuhn, *Democratic Royalism*, pp. 6–7.
32. LPL, Papers of Dr Randall T. Davidson, Archbishop of Canterbury, private papers, Vol. 13, f. 348, f. 350, Memorandum, 3/11/1918.
33. Hansard, HC Debate, 18/11/1918, Vol. 110, cc. 3204–39, c. 3204.
34. Ibid.
35. Ibid.
36. Ibid., c. 3237.
37. 'The Late Sir Henry Wilson', *Berks and Oxon Advertiser*, 30/6/1922, p. 6.
38. Hansard, HC Debate, 18/11/1918, Vol. 110, cc. 3204–39, c. 3238.
39. RA QM/PRIV/QMD/1914–1918/1918: 19 November.
40. Asquith, *Memories and Reflections*, Vol. 2, p. 164.
41. LPL, Papers of Dr Randall T. Davidson, Archbishop of Canterbury, private papers, Vol. 13, f. 359, Memorandum, 17/11/1918.
42. LPL, Papers of Dr Randall T. Davidson, Archbishop of Canterbury, private papers, Vol. 13, ff. 387–8, Memorandum, 2/3/1919.
43. TNA, CO 323/807, f. 395, Letter from B. B. Cubitt, 25/6/1919.
44. RA GV/PRIV/GVD/1919: 28 June.
45. RA PS/PSO/GV/PS/WAR/QQ22/07603, Folder A, 'Proclamation of Peace July 2nd'.
46. 'Peace Proclamation', *Sheffield Daily Telegraph*, 3/7/1919, p. 7.
47. RA PS/PSO/GV/PS/WAR/QQ22/07603, Folder A, 'Proclamation of Peace July 2nd'.
48. 'Peace Proclamation', *Sheffield Daily Telegraph*, 3/7/1919, p. 7.
49. Ibid.
50. RA PS/PSO/GV/PS/WAR/QQ22/07603, Folder C, Celebrations and Peace Procession, 19 July [1919], Memo by Lord Stamfordham 30/6/1919 of telephone conversation with Lord Curzon.
51. RA PS/PSO/GV/PS/WAR/QQ22/07603, Folder B, Thanksgiving Service at St Paul's on 6 July 1919, note from Stamfordham, 2/7/1919.
52. Ibid., Service Sheet, St Paul's Cathedral, Sunday 6/7/1919.
53. Ibid., Folder C, Celebrations and Peace Procession, 19 July, Memorandum from Stamfordham, 19/7/1919.
54. RA GV/PRIV/GVD/1919: 6 July.
55. Fitzroy, *Memoirs*, Vol. 2, p. 705.
56. RA PS/PSO/GV/PS/WAR/QQ22/07603, Folder B, Thanksgiving Service at St Paul's on 6 July 1919, Lord Mayor Horace Marshall to Stamfordham, 19/9/1920.
57. Frank O. Salisbury, 'National Peace Thanksgiving Service on the Steps of St Paul's Cathedral, 6 July 1919', Royal Exchange, London, mural.
58. Ibid.
59. Frank Salisbury's autobiography, cited at www.rct.uk/collection/404459/king-george-v-and-queen-mary-leaving-st-pauls-cathedral-after-the-national, accessed 17/8/2020. For a photograph of the service, see Alamy Images, G8H8R9.
60. RA PS/PSO/GV/PS/WAR/QQ22/07603, Folder C, Celebrations and Peace Procession, 19 July, Memo by Stamfordham, 15/5/19.
61. Ibid., Extract from Lord Curzon's letter of 24/6/1919.
62. Ibid., Memo by Stamfordham, 15/5/19.
63. Ibid., Stamfordham to Earl Curzon of Kedleston, 22/6/19, with the king's comments on the plans and also letter from Stamfordam to Evans, 10 Downing St, 30/6/19. On the barge event, see 'River Pageant from Tower to Chelsea', *Globe*, 22/7/1919, p. 8.

64. 'River Pageant from Tower to Chelsea', *Globe*, 22/7/1919, p. 8 and 'In the King's Barge' by Philip Gibbs, *Hull Daily Mail*, 5/8/1919, p. 3.

65. 'The King's Barge', *Daily Herald*, 31/7/1919, p. 3.

66. RA PS/PSO/GV/PS/WAR/QQ22/07603, Folder C, Celebrations and Peace Procession, 19 July, Stamfordham to Earl Curzon of Kedleston, 22/6/19, with the king's comments on the plans, and also letter from Stamfordham to Evans, 10 Downing St, 30/6/19.

67. Ibid., Stamfordham to Earl Curzon of Kedleston, 22/6/19, with the king's comments on the plans.

68. Ibid.

69. Ibid., Memorandum by Lord Stamfordham, 30/6/1919.

70. 'At the Palace', *The Times*, 21/7/1919, p. 15.

71. 'With the Wounded', *The Times*, 21/7/1919, p. 15.

72. Fitzroy, *Memoirs*, Vol. 2, p. 706.

73. 'Rejoicings in the Parks', *The Times*, 21/7/1919, p. 16.

74. RA MRH/MISC/048/1, cited in Churchill, *In the Eye of the Storm*, pp. 338–9.

75. 'Peace Day', *Devon and Exeter Gazette*, 19/7/1919, p. 6.

76. *Western Daily Press*, 23/7/1919: www.tytheringtonroots.co.uk/peace_day_celebra tions_1919.htm, accessed 14/2/2018.

77. https://firstworldwar.gwentheritage.org.uk/content/catalogue_item/ebbw-vale -district-peace-celebrations-19-26-july-1919, accessed 14/7/2020.

78. Mary Evans Picture Library, 10636770, 1918 postcard, C. W. Faulkner and Co.

79. Ibid.

80. Ibid.

81. Brad Beavan, 'Challenges to Civic Governance in Post-War England: The Peace Day Disturbances of 1919', *Urban History*, 33, 3 (2006), 382–3.

82. Bartie et al., 'And Those Who Live, How Shall I Tell Their Fame?', 643.

83. David William Lloyd, *Battlefield Tourism: Pilgrimage and the Commemoration of the Great War in Britain, Australia and Canada, 1919–39* (London, Oxford, New York, Toronto, 1998), p. 52.

84. Winter, *Sites of Memory, Sites of Mourning*.

85. Jessica Meyer, *Men of War: Masculinity and the First World War in Britain* (Basingstoke, 2009), p. 74.

86. The Church of England was the only other institution involved to such a degree, but did not lead and symbolise the form of commemorations at both international and national level in the way that the monarchy did.

87. Churchill, *In the Eye of the Storm*, p. 71.

88. Ibid., p. 50.

89. Mark Connelly and Stefan Goebel, 'The Imperial War Graves Commission, the War Dead and the Burial of a Royal Body, 1914–32', *Historical Research*, 93, 262 (2020), 734–53.

90. Sara, *The Life and Times of Princess Beatrice*, p. 133.

91. Connelly and Goebel, 'The Imperial War Graves Commission', 748.

92. RA PS/PSO/GV/PS/MAIN/30880, Armistice Day 1920, Memo by Wigram, 19/10/ 1920.

93. RA LC/LCO/Special/Unknown Warrior, Unveiling of the Cenotaph; Burial of Unknown Warrior, 1920, Royal Family, Letter from Miss Cochrane to Sir Douglas Dawson, n.d.

94. RA LC/LCO/Special/Unknown Warrior, Unveiling of the Cenotaph; Burial of Unknown Warrior, 1920, Royal Family, Letter from Douglas Dawson to Victor Corkran, 4/11/1920, and letter from Douglas Dawson to Miss Cochrane, 8/11/1920.

95. RA PS/PSO/GV/PS/MAIN/30880, Armistice Day, 1920, Wigram to Dawson, 24/10/1920.

96. RA LC/LCO/Special/Unknown Warrior, Unveiling of the Cenotaph; Burial of Unknown Warrior, 1920, Letter from Douglas Dawson to Lord Milford Haven, 4/11/1920 and letter to Capt A. W. Mackintosh from Douglas Dawson, 9/11/1920. 'King Unveils the Cenotaph', *Dundee Courier*, 12/11/1920, p. 5.

97. Emden, *Behind the Throne*, pp. 195–7. 'Death of Prince Henry of Battenberg', *Derby Daily Telegraph*, 22/1/1896, p. 3. The *Berkshire Chronicle* noted that Wantage parish church flew its flag at half mast and tolled its bell to mark the funeral of Prince Henry of Battenberg, 'Wantage', *Berkshire Chronicle*, 8/2/1896, p. 5. 'Death of Prince Christian Victor', *Gloucester Journal*, 3/11/1900, p. 5.

98. Royal Archives, Flickr Album: Album Prince Alexander of Battenberg, Letter from Prince Alexander of Battenberg to Princess Beatrice, 16/9/1914, www.flickr.com/photos/britishmonarchy/albums/72157646469135840, accessed 4/6/2018.

99. Ibid., Alexander of Battenburg to Princess Beatrice, 29/8/1914.

100. RA EDW/PRIV/DIARY/1914: 18 September.

101. RA GV/PRIV/GVD/1914: 31 October. Also Gore, *George V*, p. 293.

102. RA GV/AA59/318, George V to Prince Albert, 8/11/1914 and RA GV/PRIV/GVD/1914: 13 November, both cited in Pennell, *A Kingdom United?*, p. 140.

103. Churchill, *In the Eye of the Storm*, p. 161.

104. Ibid.

105. Ibid., p. 165.

106. Mary Evans Picture Library, 10015640, *Simplicissimus*, 27/6/1916.

107. Pope-Hennessy, *Queen Mary*, p. 504.

108. See for example Rose, *King George V*; Rappaport, *The Race to Save the Romanovs*.

109. Marie Louise of Schleswig-Holstein, *My Memories of Six Reigns*, p. 186.

110. Pope-Hennessy, *Queen Mary*, p. 507.

111. Marie Louise of Schleswig-Holstein, *My Memories of Six Reigns*, p. 187.

112. Ibid., pp. 187–8.

113. Churchill, *In the Eye of the Storm*, p. 123.

114. PA BL/50/3/49, Letter from Stamfordham, 26/5/1915.

115. LPL, Papers of Dr Randall T. Davidson, Archbishop of Canterbury, private papers, Vol. 6, f. 5, Stamfordham to Randall Davidson, 24/5/1915.

116. M. Asquith, *Margot Asquith's Great War Diary*, p. 157.

117. Essex Record Office, ACC.A13528 Diaries of the Right Rev. J. E. Watts-Ditchfield, Bishop of Chelmsford, 30/4/1916, ff. 317–18.

118. Ibid.

119. Ibid., f. 321.

120. Ibid., f. 323.

121. Borden, *Robert Laird Borden: His Memoirs*, Vol. 1, p. 499.

122. Churchill, *In the Eye of the Storm*, p. 123. See also p. 50.

123. Pope-Hennessy, *Queen Mary*, p. 495.

124. Fortescue, *Author and Curator*, p. 225.

125. www.rct.uk/collection/themes/trails/king-george-vs-war-museum/memorial-plaques, accessed 12/2/2019.
126. Ibid.
127. Destroyed in the 1992 fire at Windsor Castle, the memorial has since been restored.
128. The recruitment and amalgamation of the Sandringham Company is discussed in Chapter 1.
129. McCrery, *All the King's Men*, p. 48.
130. 'A Slender Hope', *Yorkshire Evening Post*, 10/1/1916, p. 5.
131. McCrery, *All the King's Men*, pp. 88–9; Churchill, *In the Eye of the Storm*, p. 126.
132. McCrery, *All the King's Men*, p. 91.
133. Ibid., p. 98; also Churchill, *In the Eye of the Storm*, p. 172.
134. 'A Slender Hope', *Yorkshire Evening Post*, 10/1/1916, p. 5.
135. Churchill, *In the Eye of the Storm*, p. 126.
136. McCrery, *All the King's Men*, p. 99.
137. Churchill, *In the Eye of the Storm*, p. 143; p. 193.
138. McCrery, *All the King's Men*, pp. 95–6.
139. Ibid., p. 96.
140. Ibid., p. 98.
141. Battiscombe, *Queen Alexandra*, p. 287.
142. McCrery, *All the King's Men*, p. 104; p. 107.
143. Ibid., p. 121.
144. 'Erected by the King and Queen: A War Memorial at Sandringham', *Illustrated London News*, 21/8/1920, p. 14; McCrery, *All the King's Men*, p. 122.
145. 'Sandringham Memorials Unveiled', *The Scotsman*, 18/10/1920, p. 6.
146. See the discussion regarding the plans for the Cenotaph unveiling discussed in Chapter 6.
147. 'Sandringham Says Farewell "Our Friend"', *Hartlepool Northern Daily Mail*, 22/1/1936, p. 5.
148. 'Death of Prince John', *Runcorn Guardian*, 21/1/1919, p. 3. See similar text in 'Public Sympathy for the King and Queen', *The Scotsman*, 20/1/1919, p. 4.
149. Churchill, *In the Eye of the Storm*, p. 332.
150. Ibid.
151. Ibid., pp. 333–4.
152. Ibid., p. 334.
153. www.cwgc.org/who-we-are/our-history/, accessed 12/4/2021.
154. Churchill, *In the Eye of the Storm*, p. 239.
155. RA EDW/PRIV/DIARY/1914: 5 and 6 November. Edward mentions attending three memorial services on these two days, one for his cousin, Prince Maurice of Battenberg, and the other two for four friends.
156. 'Queen's Tribute to Heroes', *Hartlepool Northern Daily Mail*, 11/8/1916, p. 1.
157. Ibid.
158. 'The Queen in Hackney', *The Sphere*, 19/8/1916, p. 4.
159. 'Queen Visits Hackney', *Yorkshire Evening Post*, 11/8/1916, p. 4.
160. Nottinghamshire Archives, DD/873/35, Telegram from Keeper of the Privy Purse to J. J. Morris, 4/10/1917.
161. East Riding of Yorkshire Archives and Local Studies Service, zDDX952/8, Telegram from the Keeper of the Privy Purse to William England, 7/10/1917.

162. NAM, 2002-02-1337 FOL, Letter of condolence from King George V to Richard Cotter Esq., 2 Barton Cottages, Wilberforce Road, Sandgate, Kent, 1/2/1917.

163. Omissi, ed., *Indian Voices*, p. 289, Extract no. 514, retired Dafadar Iman Khan to Wali Mohamed Khan, 25/4/1917.

164. 'King's Sympathy with Dundee Family', *Dundee Courier*, 14/5/1915, p. 6. For another example with the same wording, see 'King and Queen's Sympathy', *Sheffield Daily Telegraph*, 18/5/1915, p. 4.

165. 'King's Sympathy', *Sussex Agricultural Express*, 16/4/1915, p. 4.

166. 'The King's Sympathy', *Sheffield Daily Telegraph*, 17/12/1915, p. 3.

167. Ibid.

168. 'Three Fallen Sons; The King's Sympathy', *Daily Mail*, 18/8/1915, p. 3.

169. Ibid.

170. 'The Late Capt. D. Henderson, The King's Sympathy', *Hartlepool Northern Daily Mail*, 25/9/16, p. 3.

171. Ponsonby, *Recollections of Three Reigns*, p. 285.

172. 'The Late Capt. D. Henderson, The King's Sympathy', *Hartlepool Northern Daily Mail*, 25/9/1916, p. 3 and 'The King's Sympathy', *Newcastle Journal*, 7/3/1918, p. 6.

173. NLI, Papers of Captain Henry Telford Maffett, 2nd Battalion Leinster Regiment and his sister Emilie Harmsworth (nee Maffett), 1907–42, MS 46536/3/4, Letter from Emilie Harmsworth to Lord Stamfordham, 27/10/1914.

174. Cook, 'The Monarchy Is More than the Monarch', p. 69.

175. See Fig. 38.

176. Ibid.

177. Contemporary report in the *Hertfordshire Countryside*, cited in Berkhamsted Local History and Museum Society, *Men of Berkhamsted: Lest We Forget* (Berkhamsted, 2017), p. 158.

178. Ibid.

179. RA PS/PSO/GV/PS/WAR/6182, Lord Derby to Lord Stamfordham, 4/12/1917.

180. Ibid.

181. Ibid.

182. Ibid., Lord Derby to Rudyard Kipling, 21/11/1917.

183. Ibid.

184. Ibid., Lord Derby to Lord Stamfordham, 4/12/1917.

185. TNA, CO 323/807, f. 166, Letter from B. B. Cubitt, War Office, 14/3/1919.

186. Ibid., Letter from the Controller, Casualty Branch to the Admiralty, RAF, India Office, Colonial Office, 14/7/1920, f. 163.

187. Ibid.

188. Ibid.

189. Richards, *Imperialism and Music*, p. 152.

190. Ibid.

6 The Monarchy's Role in Sacralising Post-War Commemoration

1. Mark Connelly, *The Great War, Memory and Ritual: Commemoration in the City and East London, 1916–39* (Woodbridge, 2002); Winter, *Sites of Memory, Sites of*

Mourning; Adrian Gregory, *The Silence of Memory: Armistice Day 1919–1946* (London, 2014).

2. For an excellent overview of this historiographical discussion on 'collective memory', see Emmanuel Sivan and Jay Winter, 'Setting the Framework' in Emmauel Sivan and Jay Winter, eds., *War and Remembrance in the Twentieth Century* (Cambridge, 1999), pp. 6–39.

3. Dominic Bryan, 'Ritual, Identity and Nation: When the Historian Becomes the High Priest of Commemoration' in Richard S. Grayson and Fearghal McGarry, eds., *Remembering 1916: The Easter Rising, the Somme and the Politics of Memory in Ireland* (Cambridge, 2016), p. 24.

4. Ibid., p. 25.

5. Jon Lawrence, 'Forging a Peaceable Kingdom: War, Violence, and Fear of Brutalization in Post-First World War Britain', *The Journal of Modern History*, 75, 3 (2003), 557–89.

6. Mort, 'Safe for Democracy', 111.

7. Ibid., 112.

8. TNA, CO 323/807, f. 376, B. B. Cubitt, War Office to W. Johnson, 20/6/1919 and TNA CO 323/807, f. 375, Press Communiqué.

9. TNA, CO 323/807, f. 375, Press Communiqué.

10. TNA, CO 323/807, f. 374, B. B. Cubitt, War Office to Undersecretary of State, Colonial Office, 19/6/1919.

11. Ibid.

12. Mary Evans Picture Library, 10729779, Sergeant Charles Edward Brown.

13. Winter, 'Beyond Glory?', pp. 134–44.

14. Ceadel, 'The "King and Country" Debate'.

15. Ibid., 403.

16. Among many press examples: 'Ex-Servicemen and the Jubilee', *Dundee Evening Telegraph*, 23/4/1935, p. 3; 'Ex-Servicemen', *Sheffield Independent*, 11/5/1935, p. 1.

17. Midland Railway Company, *For King and Country* (Derby, 1921); for another example, see University of St Andrews, *Roll of Honour and Roll of Service, 1914–1919 For King and Country* (Edinburgh, 1920).

18. Website of the Scottish National War Memorial, www.snwm.org/gallery/bronze-metal/, accessed 20/12/2015.

19. Richards, *Imperialism and Music*, p. 154.

20. www.findagrave.com/memorial/122609422/albert-ward_spencer-molineaux, accessed 31/3/2019.

21. Noted by the author during a visit to St Edmundsbury Cathedral on 23/3/2019.

22. Noted by the author during visits to both locations: Pevensey, 24/12/2018 and Dagnall, 15/2/2019.

23. See the excellent Irish war memorial website, www.irishwarmemorials.ie /Memorials-Detail?memoId=84, accessed 20/12/2015 and 31/3/2019.

24. Gavin Stamp, *The Memorial to the Missing of the Somme* (London, 2006), p. 142.

25. Ibid., p. 87.

26. Commonwealth War Graves Commission Archive (hereafter CWGC), CWGC 1/1/9/B/27, Menin Gate, Letter from Lord Stamfordham to Fabian Ware, 12/1/1927.

27. 'Sandringham Memorials Unveiled', *The Scotsman*, 18/10/1920, p. 6.

28. 'Queen at Waterloo Station', *Sheffield Daily Telegraph*, 22/3/1922, p. 4.

29. Connelly, *The Great War, Memory and Ritual*, p. 89.

30. 'The R.A. Memorial', *Sheffield Daily Telegraph*, 24/8/1925, p. 4; 'Duke of Connaught at Amiens', *The Scotsman*, 11/7/1923, p. 9.

31. Associate Newspapers Limited, *His Majesty the King*.

32. *Western Daily Press*, 26/10/1923, no title, p. 8; *Derby Daily Telegraph*, 30/7/1924, no title, p. 3; 'Prince in Paris', *Belfast News-Letter*, 8/7/1924, p. 7.

33. 'Royal Visitor', *Bury Free Press*, 12/5/1928, p. 2.

34. CWGC 1/1/9/E/21, Mercantile Marine Memorial – London – Unveiling, 20/N28/2/V, King George's Fund for Sailors, Captain Bosanquet to Fabian Ware, 19/12/1928.

35. 'Queen Unveils War Memorial', *Birmingham Daily Gazette*, 13/12/1928, p. 7.

36. Ibid.

37. CWGC 1/1/9/E/21, Mercantile Marine Memorial – London – Unveiling, 13/N28/1/V, Letter from Fabian Ware to Harry Verney KCVO, 17/12/1928.

38. 'Who, When and Where', *The Bystander*, 26/12/1928, p. 5.

39. Ibid.

40. CWGC 1/1/9/B/42, Thiepval Memorial Unveiling, 'Order of Ceremonial at the Unveiling of the Somme Memorial by His Royal Highness The Prince of Wales K. G. in the Presence of the President of the French Republic on Monday May 16th 1932 at 3pm', p. 4.

41. CWGC 1/1/9/B/42, Thiepval Memorial Unveiling, 'Sir Fabian Ware's Invitation to HRH to Unveil the Memorial'.

42. CWGC 1/1/9/B/42, Final version of Prince of Wales's speech, p. 2, enclosed in letter from Fabian Ware to Godfrey Thomas, 20/7/1932.

43. Ibid., Letter from Fabian Ware to Godfrey Thomas, 20/7/1932 and final version of Prince of Wales's speech enclosed, p. 2.

44. Ibid., Final version of Prince of Wales's speech, enclosed in letter from Fabian Ware to Godfrey Thomas, 20/7/1932 and letter from Fabian Ware to Godfrey Thomas, 23/6/1932.

45. CWGC 1/1/9/B/42, Final version of Prince of Wales's speech, p. 2, enclosed in letter from Fabian Ware to Godfrey Thomas, 20/7/1932; CWGC 1/1/9/B/42, Text of French President's speech, p. 5.

46. Albrecht Mendelssohn Bartholdy, *The War and German Society: The Testament of a Liberal* (New Haven, 1937), p. 5.

47. Stamp, *Memorial to the Missing*, p. 152.

48. CWGC 1/1/9/F/52, Tablets in Cathedrals, UK, Westminster Abbey unveiling.

49. Ibid., Order of Ceremonial for the unveiling of the tablet, 19/10/1926; Letter from Fabian Ware to Geoffrey Dawson, 14/10/1926.

50. Ibid., Fabian Ware to the Dean of Westminster, 30/9/1926.

51. Ibid.

52. Winter, *Sites of Memory, Sites of Mourning*.

53. On the King's initial dislike of the idea, see Goebel, *The Great War and Medieval Memory*, p. 86.

54. Hobsbawm and Ranger eds., *The Invention of Tradition*.

55. RA PS/PSO/GV/PS/MAIN/30880, Armistice Day 1920, Stamfordham to Lionel Earle, Office of Works, 28/9/1920.

56. RA PS/PSO/GV/PS/MAIN/30880, Armistice Day 1920, Letter from Mrs Cazalet to Stamfordham, 11/6/1920.

57. RA PS/PSO/GV/PS/MAIN/30880, Armistice Day 1920, Letter from Stamfordham to Mrs Cazalet, 13/6/1920.

58. RA PS/PSO/GV/PS/MAIN/30880, Armistice Day 1920, Letter from Mrs Cazalet to Stamfordham, 16/6/1920.
59. RA PS/PSO/GV/PS/MAIN/30880, Armistice Day 1920, Prime Minister's office to Stamfordham, 25/9/1920.
60. PA LG/F/29/4/29, Stamfordham to J. T. Davies, 26/9/1920.
61. RA PS/PSO/GV/PS/MAIN/30880, Armistice Day 1920, Telegram from editor of the *Daily Mail* to Stamfordham, n.d.; Telegram from Stamfordham to *Daily Mirror*, 19/9/1920.
62. RA PS/PSO/GV/PS/MAIN/30880, Armistice Day 1920, Letter from Rear Admiral Donald Hopwood to Stamfordham, 1/10/1920.
63. Ibid.
64. RA PS/PSO/GV/PS/MAIN/30880, Armistice Day 1920, Stamfordham memo to Clive Wigram, 3/10/1920.
65. RA PS/PSO/GV/PS/MAIN/30880, Armistice Day 1920, Letter from Randall Davidson to Stamfordham, 6/10/1920.
66. Ibid.
67. Ibid.
68. RA PS/PSO/GV/PS/MAIN/30880, Armistice Day 1920, Stamfordham to Archbishop of Canterbury Randall Davidson, 7/10/1920.
69. Ibid.
70. Ibid.
71. 'At the Cenotaph' and 'Within the Abbey' reports, *The Scotsman,* 12/11/1920, p. 7.
72. Laura Wittman, *The Tomb of the Unknown Soldier: Modern Mourning and the Reinvention of the Mystical Body* (Stanford, 2011), p. 327.
73. Goebel, *The Great War and Medieval Memory*, p. 45.
74. Connelly and Goebel, 'The Imperial War Graves Commission', 749.
75. RA GV/PRIV/GVD/1920: 11 November.
76. Goebel, *The Great War and Medieval Memory*, p. 44.
77. RA PS/PSO/GV/PS/MAIN/30880, Armistice Day 1920, Press release, n.d.
78. 'The Unknown Warrior: A Nation's Tribute', *The Scotsman,* 12/11/1920, p. 7.
79. Mary Evans Picture Library, 11044819, Fortunino Matania sketch; Parliamentary Art Collection, Frank O. Salisbury, 'The Burial of the Unknown Warrior, Westminster Abbey, 1920'.
80. 'At the Cenotaph', *The Scotsman,* 12/11/1920, p. 7.
81. Ibid.
82. 'For Remembrance: Flowers from Princess Mary Placed on the Cenotaph by Regimental Sergeant-Major Barwick during the Drive from Westminster Abbey', *Illustrated London News,* 4/3/1922, p. 36; 'In Westminster Abbey', *Sheffield Daily Telegraph,* 4/3/1922, p. 8.
83. 'Favours to Come', *Yorkshire Post and Leeds Intelligencer,* 27/1/1922, p. 4.
84. 'In Westminster Abbey', *Sheffield Daily Telegraph,* 4/3/1922, p. 8.
85. Andrew Richards, *The Flag: The Story of Revd David Railton MC and the Tomb of the Unknown Warrior* (Oxford, Philadelphia, 2017), p. xiv.
86. Juliet Nicolson, *The Great Silence, 1918–20: Living in the Shadow of the Great War* (London, 2010), p. 342.
87. 'Within the Abbey', *The Scotsman,* 12/11/1920, p. 7.
88. Nicolson, *The Great Silence*, p. 335.

89. RA LC/LCO/Special/Unknown Warrior, Unveiling of the Cenotaph; Burial of Unknown Warrior, 1920; Inscriptions: Letter from Rev. Alex MacKay-Clarke to King George V, 12/11/1920.

90. Ibid., Letter from Douglas Dawson to Rev. Alex MacKay-Clarke, 16/11/1920.

91. Nicolson, *The Great Silence*, p. 336.

92. 'The King's Sword', *Sheffield Daily Telegraph*, 11/11/1920, p. 7; Goebel, *The Great War and Medieval Memory*, pp. 86–7.

93. 'The Unknown Warrior: A Nation's Tribute', *The Scotsman*, 12/11/1920, p. 7; also *Illustrated London News*, 20/11/1920, p. 7.

94. Cannadine, 'The Context, Performance and Meaning of Ritual'.

95. 'Within the Abbey', *The Scotsman*, 12/11/1920, p. 7.

96. Ibid.

97. RA LC/LCO/Special/Unknown Warrior, Unveiling of the Cenotaph; Burial of Unknown Solider, 1920; Applications for seats: Letter from Douglas Dawson, State Chamberlain, to Mrs Chalk, 4/11/1920.

98. Ibid., Letter from Joseph Kaye to King George V, 29/10/1920.

99. Ibid.

100. Ibid.

101. RA LC/LCO/Special/Unknown Warrior, Unveiling of the Cenotaph; Burial of Unknown Soldier, 1920; Applications for seats: Letter from Sydney Turner to King George V, 28/10/1920.

102. Ibid.

103. RA LC/LCO/Special/Unknown Warrior, Unveiling of the Cenotaph; Burial of Unknown Soldier, 1920; Applications for seats: Letter from Mrs Newbold to King George V, 9/11/1920.

104. Ibid.

105. RA LC/LCO/Special/Unknown Warrior, Unveiling of the Cenotaph; Burial of Unknown Warrior, 1920; Inscriptions: H. C. Bayldon to King George V, 11/11/1920.

106. RA LC/LCO/Special/Unknown Warrior, Unveiling of the Cenotaph; Burial of Unknown Warrior, 1920; Inscriptions: Letter from J. R. Griffin, General Secretary, National Federation of Discharged and Demobilised Sailors and Soldiers, to Lord Stamfordham, 26/10/1920.

107. RA LC/LCO/Special/Unknown Warrior, Unveiling of the Cenotaph; Burial of Unknown Warrior, 1920; Inscriptions: Letter from E. B. B. Towse, Chairman, Empire Grand Council, Comrades of the Great War, to Sir Douglas Dawson, 29/10/1920.

108. RA PS/PSO/GV/PS/MAIN/30880, Armistice Day 1920, Memo from Clive Wigram to Douglas Dawson, 25/10/1920.

109. RA PS/PSO/GV/PS/MAIN/30880, Armistice Day 1920, Memo from Clive Wigram to Douglas Dawson, 27/10/1920.

110. RA LC/LCO/Special/Unknown Warrior, Unveiling of the Cenotaph; Burial of Unknown Soldier, 1920; Letters of congratulations: Letter from National Federation of Discharged and Demobilised Sailors and Soldiers to Sir Douglas Dawson, 17/11/1920.

111. RA LC/LCO/Special/Unknown Warrior, Unveiling of the Cenotaph; Burial of Unknown Soldier, 1920; Applications for seats: Letter from M. Nathan to King George V, 8/11/1920.

112. RA LC/LCO/Special/Unknown Warrior, Unveiling of the Cenotaph; Burial of Unknown Soldier, 1920; Applications for seats: Letter from Rose Else to King George V, n.d.

113. TNA, ADM 116/1683, VCs Garden Party at Buckingham Palace 1 January 1914–31 December 1920.

114. Ibid., Mrs F. Spain to Admiralty, 20/6/1920.

115. Ibid., Mrs E. G. Sandford to the Admiralty, 16/6/1920.

116. *Daily Telegraph*, 24/5/1919, cited in Churchill, *In the Eye of the Storm*, p. 327.

117. Churchill, *In the Eye of the Storm*, p. 327.

118. IWM, www.iwm.org.uk/history/voices-of-the-first-world-war-armistice, accessed 26/8/2018.

119. RA PS/PSO/GVI/C/019/441–3, Florence Corkran Norfolk to Edward VIII, 12/12/1936.

120. http://thelincolnshireregiment.org/beechey.shtml, accessed 13/11/2017; also BBC news story, www.bbc.co.uk/news/uk-england-lincolnshire-41920834, accessed 13/11/2017; 'Case of Wartime Letters That Unravel a Tragedy', *Western Morning News*, 13/7/2006, p. 12; Michael Walsh, *Brothers in War* (London, 2011); www.bbc.co.uk/news/uk-england-25497900, accessed 19/9/2018; 'Death at Lincoln of Mrs Amy Beechey', *Lincolnshire Echo*, 26/12/1936, p. 6.

121. Anthony Seldon, 'First World War: Losing One Child in War is a Terrible Thing, So Just Imagine Losing Five', *Daily Telegraph,* 21/2/2014, p. 20.

122. Gregory, *The Silence of Memory.*

123. Ponsonby, *Recollections of Three Reigns*, p. 346.

124. CWGC 1/1/16/8, HM The King visit to France and Belgium, 1/E22/306/V, Letter to Lord Burnham, 2/5/1922.

125. CWGC 1/1/16/8, HM The King visit to France and Belgium, Editor of the Topical Budget, W. H. White, to Arthur Brown, Principal Assistant Secretary, Imperial War Graves Commission, 4/5/1922. On Topical Budget, see McKernan, '"The Finest Cinema Performers That We Possess"', 64.

126. CWGC 1/1/16/8, HM The King visit to France and Belgium, Editor of the Topical Budget, W. H. White, to Fabian Ware, 5/5/1922.

127. CWGC 1/1/16/8, HM The King visit to France and Belgium, 1/E22/306/V, Letter to Lord Burnham, 2/5/1922. See also ibid., Letter to Rudyard Kipling, 7/4/1922.

128. CWGC 1/1/16/8, HM The King visit to France and Belgium, Frederick Ponsonby to Ferdinand Foch, 22/4/1922. Ponsonby, *Recollections of Three Reigns*, p. 342.

129. On battlefield tourism, see Delphine Lauwers, 'Le Saillant d'Ypres entre reconstruction et construction d'un lieu de mémoire: un long processus de négociations mémorielles de 1914 à nos jours', (PhD thesis, European University Institute, 2014) and Lloyd, *Battlefield Tourism.*

130. CWGC 1/1/16/8, HM The King visit to France and Belgium, 1/E22/306/V, Letter to Lord Burnham, 2/5/1922.

131. Anon., *The King's Pilgrimage*, no page numbers.

132. CWGC 1/1/16/9, HM The King visit to France and Belgium, W18/26, Copy of cablegram from Prime Minister of Canada sent to Fabian Ware by W. Griffith, 29/5/1922.

133. CWCG/1/1/16/9, HM The King visit to France and Belgium, Meerut Cemetery, IWGC, 22/5/1922.

134. CWGC 1/1/16/9, HM The King visit to France and Belgium, Notes on the Royal Visit to Etaples Military Cemetery, at 9.20 am of [sic] Saturday May 13th 1922 and Letter to Colonel James Allen, 8/E/303/V, 8/5/1922.

135. CWGC 1/1/16/8, HM The King visit to France and Belgium, Gertrude Drayton, Victoria League to Fabian Ware, Imperial War Graves Commission, 5/5/1922.

136. Ibid.

137. CWGC 1/1/16/8, HM The King visit to France and Belgium, Letter to Fabian Ware, 4/5/1922.

138. CWGC 1/1/16/9, HM The King visit to France and Belgium, Notes on the Royal Visit to Etaples Military Cemetery, at 9.20 am of [sic] Saturday May 13th 1922.

139. CWGC 1/1/16/9, HM The King visit to France and Belgium, 'King's Visit to the Cemeteries', Stoppard, IWGC to Fabian Ware, 19/5/1922.

140. CWGC 1/1/16/9, HM The King visit to France and Belgium, 19/E/320/V, Letter from Fabian Ware to Sir Frederick Ponsonby quoting extract from letter from Captain Parker, 19/5/1922.

141. CWGC 1/1/16/9, HM The King visit to France and Belgium, 19/E22/316/V, Memo cover for letter from Sir Fabian Ware to Sir Frederick Ponsonby, 19/5/1922.

142. CWGC 1/1/16/9, HM The King visit to France and Belgium, Letter to Colonel H. T. Goodland, 30/5/1922.

143. CWGC 1/1/16/9, HM The King visit to France and Belgium, Head Office, IWGC France and Flanders to Fabian Ware, Vice-Chairman, IWGC, 6/2/1923.

144. CWGC 1/1/16/9, HM The King visit to France and Belgium, Fabian Ware to Frederick Ponsonby, 11/8/1927.

145. CWGC 1/1/16/8, HM The King visit to France and Belgium, Lord Stamfordham to Fabian Ware, 7/4/1922.

146. CWGC 1/1/16/8, HM The King visit to France and Belgium, Frederick Ponsonby to Ferdinand Foch, 22/4/1922.

147. Anon., *The King's Pilgrimage*, no page numbers.

148. Ibid.

149. Anon., *The King's Pilgrimage*. Fabian Ware helped draft the King's speech: CWGC 1/1/17/7, King's Pilgrimage.

150. Ibid.

151. CWGC 1/1/16/9, HM The King visit to France and Belgium, Henry Benson to Arthur Browne, IWGC, 16/5/1922.

152. CWGC 1/1/16/9, HM The King visit to France and Belgium, Clive Wigram to Fabian Ware, 17/5/1922.

153. Anon., *The King's Pilgrimage*.

154. CWGC 1/1/16/9, HM The King visit to France and Belgium, Notes for publication.

155. CWGC 1/1/17/7, King's Pilgrimage, Letter from Frederick Ponsonby to Fabian Ware, 6/6/1922.

156. Anon., *The King's Pilgrimage*, no page numbers.

157. Ibid.

158. Ibid.

159. CWGC 1/1/16/9, HM The King visit to France and Belgium, Letter from S. A. Heald to Fabian Ware, 26/5/1922.

160. Anon., *The King's Pilgrimage*, no page numbers.

161. Ibid.

162. CWGC 1/1/16/9, HM The King visit to France and Belgium, Stoppard to Fabian Ware, IWGC, 19/5/1922.

163. CWGC 1/1/16/9, HM The King visit to France and Belgium, 26-E22-507-E, Message to Fabian Ware, 26/5/1922.

164. Anon., *The King's Pilgrimage*, no page numbers.

165. CWGC 1/1/16/9, HM The King visit to France and Belgium, Notes on the royal visit to Etaples Military Cemetery, at 9.20 am of [sic] Saturday May 13th 1922.

166. Anon., *The King's Pilgrimage*, no page numbers.

167. CWGC 1/1/16/15, HM The King's visit to Italy, Mr Chutter to Fabian Ware, IWGC, 15/5/1923.

168. CWGC 1/1/16/15, HM The King's visit to Italy, Colin Coote, *Times* correspondent to Fabian Ware, 5/5/1923.

169. Ina Zweiniger-Bargielowska, 'Royal Death and Living Memorials: The Funerals and Commemoration of George V and George VI, 1936–52', *Historical Research*, 89, 243 (2016) 166.

170. Ibid., 163–4.

171. Gibbs, *George the Faithful*, p. 6.

172. The official biography of Edward covers his war service but does not analyse its formative influence: Ziegler, *King Edward VIII*.

173. TNA, MEPO 2/1980, Records of the Metropolitan Police Office, Police Charities, War Memorial Hospital and New Schools at the Police Orphanage, Twickenham, opening by HRH the Prince of Wales, on 29/6/1923.

174. Churchill, *In the Eye of the Storm*, p. 336.

175. PA LG/F/29/5/9, Prince of Wales Christmas card to Lloyd George, 1920.

176. Edward, Duke of Windsor, *A King's Story*, p. 125.

177. Philip Ziegler, 'Edward VIII: The Modern Monarch?', *The Court Historian*, 8, 1 (2003), 75.

178. Ibid.

179. Edward, Duke of Windsor, *A King's Story*, p. 125.

180. 'Menin Gate: Great Pilgrimage for Memorial Service. Prince at the Head', *Sheffield Daily Telegraph*, 3/8/1928, p. 5.

181. Ziegler, 'Edward VIII: The Modern Monarch?', 74.

182. Ibid.

183. Ibid.

184. 'Speech by HRH the Prince of Wales on Armistice Night, November 11th 1927, Recorded at the "Daily Express" Remembrance Festival, Royal Albert Hall, London': transcribed from YouTube, www.youtube.com/watch?v=wrGN3AIo OSA, accessed 21/09/2017.

185. Ibid.

186. Ibid.

187. Ibid.

188. Cook, 'The Monarchy Is More than the Monarch', p. 20.

189. 'Earl Haig's Fund: Prince at Inauguration of Warrior's Day', *Sheffield Daily Telegraph*, 19/1/1921.

190. 'Men Who Helped to Keep King on Throne', *Derry Journal*, 3/4/1935, p. 4.

191. Karina Urbach, *Go-Betweens for Hitler* (Oxford, 2015), p. 186, p. 188.

192. Cannadine, 'Kaiser Wilhelm and the British Monarchy', p. 200.

193. Ibid.

194. Bundesarchiv-Berlin Lichterfelde, BA R 72/1188: Stahlhelm Bund der Frontsoldaten: Deutsch-britisches 'Frontkämpfer' Treffen.
195. 'Ex-Servicemen Support Prince's Gesture', *Western Mail*, 12/6/1935, p. 8.
196. Adrian Phillips, *The King Who Had to Go: Edward VIII, Mrs Simpson and the Hidden Politics of the Abdication Crisis* (London, 2018), p. 11.
197. Ibid., p. 12.
198. Ibid.
199. Urbach, *Go-Betweens*, p. 188.
200. Ivan Mikhailovich Maisky, *The Maisky Diaries: Red Ambassador to the Court of St James, 1932–1943*, ed. Gabriel Gorodetsky (New Haven, London, 2015), p. 64.
201. Ziegler, 'Edward VIII: The Modern Monarch?', 73. Ziegler provides no source for this quotation.
202. 'Imperial War Museum', *Daily Herald*, 10/6/1920, p. 3.
203. CUL, MS Baldwin, Vol. 176, f. 13, Frederick Maurice to Major Hardinge, 19/11/1936.
204. In fact, although they claimed to have the mass support of veterans, the reality was more limited. In Germany, only the right-wing Stahlhelm veterans' movement really supported the Nazis; in Italy, the National Associations of Mutilated and War Invalids remained independent of the Fascists before the march on Rome. Angel Alcalde, *War Veterans and Fascism in Interwar Europe* (Cambridge, 2017).
205. CUL, MS Baldwin, Vol. 176, f. 13, Frederick Maurice to Major Hardinge, 19/11/1936.
206. Bradford, *King George VI*, p. 265.
207. Owens, *The Family Firm*, p. 225.
208. Ibid., p. 226.
209. Ibid., p. 228.
210. Queen Mary in a letter to the Duke of Windsor, July 1938, *Oxford Dictionary of Modern Quotations*, 3rd edition, ed. Elizabeth Knowles (Oxford, 2007), p. 216.
211. CUL, Baldwin MS, Vol. 176, f. 18, Queen Mary to Stanley Baldwin, 11/12/1936.
212. CUL, Baldwin MS, Vol. 177, ff. 89–90, Earl of Athlone to Stanley Baldwin, 12/12/1936.
213. 'The King: Going Direct to Cannes from Vimy Ridge', *Yorkshire Evening Post*, 13/7/1936, p. 7.
214. 'Inspiring Scene at Vimy Ridge', *Western Daily Press*, 27/7/1936, p. 12.
215. Cook, 'The Monarchy Is More than the Monarch', p. 200. On the *Nahlin* cruise, see Phillips, *The King Who Had to Go*, p. 53.
216. CWGC 1/1/16/17, HM King Edward's visit to Gallipoli, Letter from Duff Cooper to Fabian Ware, 3/9/1936.
217. Press cuttings in CWGC 1/1/16/17, HM King Edward's visit to Gallipoli.
218. 'Royal Holiday', *The Sphere*, 19/9/1936, p. 18.
219. CWGC 1/1/16/17, HM King Edward's visit to Gallipoli, Letter from Fabian Ware to A. H. L. Hardinge, Buckingham Palace, 14/9/1936.
220. BBC Archives, LP20246, recorded at Verdun for NBC, United States.
221. Ibid.
222. T. A. Jenkins, 'The Funding of the Liberal Unionist Party and the Honours System', *The English Historical Review*, 105, 417 (1990), 920–38.
223. PA LG/F/29/4/103, King George to Lloyd George, 3/7/1922.
224. Rose, *King George V*, pp. 246–52.
225. Beckett, 'George V and His Generals'.
226. Stevenson, *Lloyd George: A Diary*, 10/5/1935, p. 309.

Conclusion

1. Owens, *The Family Firm*, p. 23; p. 69. In 1923 the king also attended a Wembley FA Cup final for the first time and presented the trophy, ibid., p. 3.
2. LPL, Papers of Dr Randall T. Davidson, Archbishop of Canterbury, private papers, Vol. 13, f. 387, Memorandum, 2/3/1919.
3. Mort, 'Accessible Sovereignty', 333.
4. On concerns about George VI's wartime popularity, see Olechnowicz, 'A Jealous Hatred', p. 290.
5. Owens, *The Family Firm*, p. 215.
6. Ibid., p. 221.
7. Ibid., p. 269.
8. Ibid.
9. Olechnowicz, 'A Jealous Hatred', p. 290.
10. Owens, *The Family Firm*, p. 263.

BIBLIOGRAPHY

Primary Sources

Archives

Oxford, Bodleian Libraries

Asquith Correspondence 1891–1928, A.1, Royal Correspondence 1907–16
BD MS Asquith, A.1, Vol. 3
BD MS Asquith, A.1, Vol. 4

Asquith Correspondence 1891–1928, A.2, Cabinet Letters: Copies of Asquith's Cabinet Letters to the King, 1908–16
BD MS Asquith, A.2, Vol. 7
BD MS Asquith, A.2, Vol. 8

Asquith: Miscellaneous Letters and Correspondence Arranged by Subject, 1892–1926, Miscellaneous Letters and Memoranda 1914–15
BD MS Asquith, B.26

The British Library, London

Add MSS 46722 1890–1918, Boyd-Carpenter papers, Vol. 6 (ff. 74), unpublished letters from and on behalf of members of the English Royal Family, 1890–1918
Add MS 49686, Correspondence and papers of Sir Arthur Balfour, Balfour Papers, Vol. 4 (ff. 202), 1, ff. 1–150, George V
Add MS 63012, Correspondence and papers of Francis Levenson Bertie, 1st Viscount Bertie, Vol. 2 (ff. 205), 1908–18, ff. 47–205, George V of England: Correspondence with Lord Bertie: 1910–18
MSS EUR E224/37/6, India Office
MSS EUR F112/579, Letters to Curzon from Edward VIII as Prince of Wales, Feb. 1918–Mar. 1921
MSS EUR F112/580, Letters to Curzon from Elisabeth, Queen of the Belgians; Sep. 1914–Jun. 1922

MSS EUR F116/44, Papers of Sir Harcourt Butler, Indian Civil Service, 1890-1928, Governor of United Provinces 1918-22, Governor of Burma 1923-7

MSS EUR F118/83/1/TO/16, Reading (Private) Collection, Letters dated 1909-29 to Lord Reading

MSS EUR F143/64, Papers of Sir Walter Lawrence, Indian Civil Service, Punjab, 1879-95

Add MS 54192 A, Parliamentary Recruiting Committee, Vol. 1 A (ff. viii + 56); Minutes 27 Aug. 1914-29 Nov. 1915

Add MS 54192 B, Parliamentary Recruiting Committee, Vol. 1 B (ff. iv + 73); Minutes, etc., 11 Oct. 1915-6 Jan. 1917. England; Parliament: Army; England: Minutes, etc., of the Parliamentary Recruiting Committee: 1914-17: Typewritten: 11 Oct. 1915-6 Jan. 1917

Add MS 62155, Correspondence of Alfred Charles William Harmsworth, Viscount Northcliffe Papers, Vol. 3 (ff. 219); 1. ff. 1-72, Arthur John Bigge, Baron Stamfordham, 1913-21; 2. ff. 73-120

Cambridge University Library, Cambridge University

The Papers of Stanley Baldwin
Vols 143, 144, 150, 176, 177, 178

The Churchill Archives Centre, Churchill College, Cambridge

Viscount Esher Papers
ESHR 6, August 1878–March 1923:
CHURCHILL/ESHR 6/6 Correspondence with King George V
CHURCHILL/ESHR 6/8 Correspondence with Queen Mary
CHURCHILL/ESHR 6/9 Correspondence with Edward, Prince of Wales
CHURCHILL/ESHR 4/7
CHURCHILL/ESHR 5/VOL. 50
CHURCHILL/ESHR 5/VOL. 51

Papers of Reginald McKenna
CHURCHILL/MCKN 6/7
CHURCHILL/MCKN 6/12

Admiral Sir Charles Daniel Papers
CHURCHILL/DANL 3

Papers of Sir Bryan Godfrey Faussett
CHURCHILL/BGGF 2/5, PT 1 AND 2
CHURCHILL/BGGF 2/6, PT 1 AND 2
CHURCHILL/BGGF 3/5

Amery Papers
AMEL 6/3/32 Jan. 1914–Dec. 1914

The Commonwealth War Graves Commission Archive, Maidenhead

CWGC 1/1/9/B/16, Memorials to Missing, Menin Gate Unveiling
CWGC 1/1/9/B/25, Menin Gate Memorial
CWGC 1/1/9/B/27, Menin Gate
CWGC 1/1/9/B/42, Thiepval Memorial Unveiling
CWGC 1/1/9/F/52, Tablets in Cathedrals, UK, Westminster Abbey unveiling
CWGC 1/1/12/26, Rudyard Kipling correspondence (A) and (B)
CWGC 1/1/12/48, Lutyens E.L.
CWGC 1/1/16/8, HM The King visit to France and Belgium
CWGC 1/1/16/9, HM The King visit to France and Belgium
CWGC 1/1/16/14, The King's visit to France; Sir Herbert Ellissen's correspondence
CWGC 1/1/16/17, HM King Edward's visit to Gallipoli
CWGC 1/1/16/20, HRH The Prince of Wales visit with British Legion
CWGC 1/1/17/7, King's Pilgrimage
CWGC 2/2/1/135, Commission Meeting no. 135
CWGC 2/2/1/136, Commission Meeting no. 136

Dublin City Library and Archive

The Monica Roberts Collection
RDFA 099 Brierley
RDFA 109 Mansfield
RDFA 111 Fay

Essex Record Office, Chelmsford

ACC.AI3528 Diaries of the Right Rev. J. E. Watts-Ditchfield, Bishop of Chelmsford

The Department of Documents, Imperial War Museum

IWM Documents 249, Box 88/52/1, A. J. Jamieson
IWM Documents 251, Box 88/52/1, Memoirs of Frederick Hunt
IWM Documents 312, Box Misc. 147 item 2303, King George V's speech to the Irish Guards, March 1916
IWM Documents 315, Box 90/17/1, Capt. Arthur Guy Osborn, 1st Birmingham Battalion Royal Warwickshire Regiment
IWM Documents 6481, Box 97/18/1, P. Botting

IWM Documents 7218, Box 97/37/1, E. Silas

IWM Documents 7315, Box 76/122/1, Private Papers of Brigadier General Earl of Athlone

IWM Documents 7490, Box 75/78/1, L/Cpl later 2/Lt K. M. Gaunt, 1/16 Battalion London Regiment and 4 Battalion Royal Warwickshire Regiment

IWM Documents 7783, Box 98/2/1, W. Haines

IWM Documents 8035, Box 98/34/1, Brigadier General M. G. Wilkinson

IWM Documents 8061, Box 99/15/1, Diary of Percival Charles Cobb

IWM Documents 8749, Box Misc. 120 item 1851, Royal letter of appreciation of one family's contribution to the Armed Forces, April 1915

IWM Documents 10201, Box Misc. 58, item 866, Address of Loyalty to King George V from Somali Sheiks 1916

IWM Documents 10311, Box Misc. 1840, 118/1 and 118/2, The Chilwell Munitions Factory

IWM Documents 10350, Box Misc. 82 item 1249, The King's Message to the RAF, November 1918

IWM Documents 10507, Box PP/MCR/118, The Papers of Lieutenant-Colonel B. Fitzgerald

IWM Documents 10750, Box Misc. 105 item 1670, Royal letter of appreciation for a disabled serviceman, November 1918

IWM Documents 11289, Box 01/21/1, H. T. Madders, 2/1st Battalion Royal Fusiliers, Diary, 3/4/1918

IWM Documents 11783, Box 01/59/1, W. H. Loosley

IWM Documents 11943, Box 02/12/1, Papers of H. Empson

IWM Documents 12003, Box PP/MCR/82, The 1915–16 letters of Lieutenant J. W. Gamble

IWM Documents 12139, Box PP/MCR/173, The First World War Memoirs of Lt D. C. Burn

IWM Documents 12383, Box 02/29/1, J. Anderson Johnston

IWM Documents 12538, Box 02/55/1, Private papers of F. L. Stone

IWM Documents 12767, Box 04/1/1, Commander H. M. Wilson RN

IWM Documents 13120, Box 06/1/1, Papers of Brigadier General Sir Charles Delmé-Radcliffe

IWM Documents 13253, Box 05/8/1, Papers of Ellis Alban Newton

IWM Documents 14169, Box 67/7/1, Major General V. G. Tofts

IWM Documents 14178, Box 09/57/1, Private papers of Lieut. C. G. Bonner VC

IWM Documents 15403, Box 06/120/1, Dan Joiner

IWM Documents 16149, Box 08/42/1, Captain A. St J. Blunt

IWM Documents 16518, Box 08/100/1, Major E. Lyall

IWM Documents 17029, Box 09/34/1, Captain A. J. Lord

IWM Documents 17596, [no box number], Papers of Captain N. G. Chavasse

IWM Documents 17992, Box 14/18/1, Captain N. J. Ainsworth

IWM Documents 18542, Box 66/160/1, Papers of A. Wells

IWM Documents 18918, Box 15/37/1, G. Harding

IWM Documents 18927, Box 16/30/1, Major F. St J. Steadman
IWM Documents 22414, Box P150, Private papers of Brigadier E. Foster Hall

IWM Sound Archive
IWM Sound Archive, Reginald Haine VC (Oral History), 1973, Catalogue no. 33, reel 5
IWM Sound Archive, Pte Thomas McIndoe (Oral History), 1975, Catalogue no. 568, reel 3
IWM Sound Archive, Eleanora B. Pemberton (Oral History), 1978, Catalogue no. 3188, reel 4
IWM Sound Archive, Colonel Stewart Montagu Cleeve (Oral History), 1983, Catalogue no. 7310, reels 8, 15–16
IWM Sound Archive, Raynor Taylor (Oral History), 1990–2, Catalogue no. 11113, reels 12, 13

Lambeth Palace Library

Papers of Dr Randall T. Davidson, Archbishop of Canterbury
DAVIDSON Private Papers, Vol. 6, 1914–27
DAVIDSON Private Papers, Vol. 13, Diaries and Memoranda, 1914–19
DAVIDSON Private Papers, Vol. 20, Royal Family
DAVIDSON Official Letters, Vol. 195, 1915 and 1916
DAVIDSON Official Letters, Vol. 196, 1917 and 1918

The Liddell Hart Centre for Military Archives, King's College London

Papers of General Sir Ian Hamilton
Hamilton 11/1/1
Hamilton 11/1/3

The Liddle Collection, Leeds University Library

Alfred Edward Burdfield, Liddle/WW1/GS/0222 (2/3 Bn Royal Fusiliers).

The Lincolnshire Archives, Lincoln

Sir Charles L. Cust Papers
BNLW 4/4/8/2, Visit to Army in the Field (N. France), Oct. 1915, Report on the visit
BNLW 4/4/8/3, 'Diary of my trip to France, October 1916'
BNLW 4/4/8/5, 'A short account of my visit to France in Sept. 1917'
BNLW 4/4/8/8, Visit to France, Sept. 1918, Report

The Parliamentary Archives

The Papers of David Lloyd George
Volumes:
PA LG/C/5/1–7
PA LG/E/2/16–24
PA LG/F/3/1–3
PA LG/F/3/4–5
PA LG/F/7/1–3
PA LG/F/12/1–2
PA LG/F/12/3
PA LG/F/29/1–3
PA LG/F/29/4–6
PA LG/F/43/1/5
PA LG/F/59/3–13
PA LG/G/10/16

The National Archives, Kew

TNA, ADM 1/8521/111, Royal Visit to Immingham 10 April 1918

TNA, ADM 116/1683, VCs Garden Party at Buckingham Palace 1 January 1914–31 December 1920

TNA, ASSI 81 Series, Assizes: Midland, Northern, Oxford, Wales and Chester, and Western Circuits, Royal Pardons, 1866–1974, ASSI 81/63 and ASSI 81/66

TNA, CAB 21/247, Irish Settlement: Oath of Allegiance to the Crown, 1922

TNA, CAB 23/2/54, War Cabinet: Minutes of Meetings, 1 March 1917–31 May 1917; HM the King's visit to the Northern Industrial Areas, May 1917

TNA, CAB 24/128, War Cabinet and Cabinet: Memoranda (GT, CP and G War Series) 1921

TNA, CO 323/693, Miscellaneous correspondence, Secretary of State, Oct.–Dec. 1915

TNA, CO 323/720/443, King's Christmas Message to Soldiers and Sick and Wounded 23 December 1916

TNA CO 323/807, Colonies, General: Original Correspondence, Original – Secretary of State. Offices: War, 1919

TNA, CO 323/875/36, Oath of Allegiance in the Colonies and Protectorates, 1921

TNA, CO 762 Series, Irish Distress Committee and Irish Grants Committee, Loyalist Relief Claims, [1922–37] CO 762/1 and CO 762/3

TNA, CO 904/209/12, Michael McEvoy telegram to King George V, 1918

TNA, CO 904/214/10, file 389, A Letter to His Majesty the King from Mrs Alice Russell, 1918

TNA, DO 117/81, Dominions Office: Claims of Irish Loyalists, 1927

TNA, FO 141/781/4, Letters between King George V and King Husein [sic] 1918–25

TNA, FO 383/375, Foreign Office Prisoners of War and Aliens Department: General Correspondence from 1906, Belgium, 1918

TNA, FO 383/502, Letter, 5 August 1919 from German prisoners of war to King George V

TNA, FO 800/199, Earl of Balfour correspondence with HM the King, 1917–18

TNA, HO 45/10743/263275, War: Anti-recruiting and peace propaganda, meetings, marches and speeches 1917–1918

TNA, HO 190/854, Visit of HM King George V and Queen Mary to Carlisle, 18 May 1917

TNA, MEPO 2/1980, Records of the Metropolitan Police Office, Police Charities, War Memorial Hospital and New Schools at the Police Orphanage, Twickenham, opening by HRH the Prince of Wales, on 29 June 1923

TNA, MUN 4/6520, Royal Tour of inspection of textile industry in West Riding of Yorkshire: Press Cuttings, May–June 1918

TNA, PC 2/427, George V Privy Council Register, 1 April–30 June 1916

TNA, PC 12/20, British Nationality and Status of Aliens Acts 1914 and 1918, Privy Counsellors

TNA, PC 12/20, Exclusion of Sir E. Speyer from the Privy Council, 1915–21

TNA, RAIL 1014/10, Great Western Rail Collection, Royal Journeys

TNA, T 172/396, Payment of £100,000 to the Exchequer by King George V

TNA, WO 106/297, 1914–18, King and Queen's visits to the Armies in the Field, Diaries

TNA, WO 141/9, Formation of 'Irish Brigade' among prisoners of war in Germany

TNA, WO 158/12, Visit of His Majesty the King to the Expeditionary Force, 1914

TNA, WO 339/7854, M.V.D. Maurice Victor Donald Battenburg [sic], The King's Royal Rifles

Mass Observation Archive, The Keep, Sussex University Library

Topic Collections, Children and Education, 1937–1952

59-4-A, Miscellaneous Essays by School Children, 'The Royal Family'

59-4-F, Miscellaneous Essays by School Children, 'The Finest Person Who Ever Lived'

59-4-H, Miscellaneous Essays by School Children, 'The Finest Person Who Ever Lived'

The National Library of Ireland, Dublin

The Papers of Captain Henry Telford Maffett and His Sister Emilie Harmsworth (née Maffett)
NLI TELFORD MAFFETT, MS 46536/3/4

The Papers of John Redmond
NLI REDMOND, MS 15188/1

NLI REDMOND, MS 15188/5
NLI REDMOND, MS 15188/14
NLI REDMOND, MS 15259
NLI REDMOND, MS 15519
NLI REDMOND, MS 22187

The Royal Archives, Windsor Castle

RA AEC/GG/027, Letter sent on behalf of the Queen to Mrs Basil Ellis from Eva
    Dugdale on 22 Nov. 1914
RA EDW/PRIV/DIARY: Aug. 1913–Jul. 1917
RA GV/PRIV/AA48/130, 174, Letters from the Archbishop of Canterbury, Randall
    Davidson, to King George V
RA GV/PRIV/AA48/149, 178, Letters from Herbert H. Asquith to King George V
RA GV/PRIV/GVD, Diaries of King George, Vols 1914–22
RA LC/LCO/SPECIAL/UNKNOWN WARRIOR, 1920
RA PS/PSO/GV/C/F/930/2, Herbert H. Asquith to Lord Stamfordham re: appoint-
    ment of Sir A. Hunter to Field Marshal
RA PS/PSO/GV/C/F/973/6, 7, 8, Letters from Lord Stamfordham to Herbert
    H. Asquith, Oct. 1916
RA PS/PSO/GV/C/F/983/1, 2, Letters between Lord Stamfordham and Herbert
    H. Asquith re: appointment of Sir Douglas Haig to Field Marshal
RA PS/PSO/GV/C/I/802/2, Letter from Lord Stamfordham to the Archbishop of
    Canterbury, 5/8/1915
RA PS/PSO/GV/C/I/1075/5, Lord Stamfordham to the Archbishop of Canterbury
    re: appointments to the Deanery of Carlisle and Canonry of Canterbury,
    14 April 1917
RA PS/PSO/GV/C/I/1078/9, Lord Stamfordham to Archbishop of Canterbury,
    27 November 1917
RA PS/PSO/GV/C/I/1171/12, 36, Letters between Lord Stamfordham and the
    Archbishop of Canterbury, 1917
RA PS/PSO/GV/C/I/1240/2, 7, Letters between Lord Stamfordham and the
    Archbishop of Canterbury, October, December 1917
RA PS/PSO/GV/C/I/1368/6, 14, Letters from Lord Stamfordham to the
    Archbishop of Canterbury, 1918
RA PS/PSO/GV/C/J/1072/8, Letter from Lord Stamfordham to David Lloyd
    George, 14 Dec. 1916
RA PS/PSO/GV/C/J/1081/6, Letter from David Lloyd George to Lord
    Stamfordham, 17 Feb. 1917
RA PS/PSO/GV/C/J/1504/2, List of War Honours proposed by King, 15 Nov. 1918
RA PS/PSO/GV/C/K/951/10, 12, 13, Letters between Herbert H. Asquith and Lord
    Stamfordham, 1916
RA PS/PSO/GV/C/K/985/1, Letter from Lord Stamfordham to David Lloyd
    George, 6 May 1917

RA PS/PSO/GV/C/K/1048A/22, Letter from Herbert H. Asquith thanking King for his kind letter on Asquith's resignation, 7 Dec. 1916

RA PS/PSO/GV/C/K/1080/3, Letter from Lord Stamfordham to David Lloyd George, 4 March 1917

RA PS/PSO/GV/C/K/1303/3, Letter from Lord Stamfordham to J. T. Davies

RA PS/PSO/GV/C/K/1348/6, 7, Letters between Lord Stamfordham and David Lloyd George and Randall Davidson, Archbishop of Canterbury, re: John Watts-Ditchfield, Bishop of Chelmsford

RA PS/PSO/GV/C/M/969/1, Letter from Lord Stamfordham to David Lloyd George, 16 April 1917

RA PS/PSO/GV/C/O/1106/1–11, 13, 15–61, 64–6, 68, 'Unrest in the Country'

RA PS/PSO/GV/C/O/1637/1–21, Burial of the Unknown Soldier correspondence

RA PS/PSO/GV/C/O/1735/5–6, 10–11, 83, 86–90, 101–5, US bestowal of Congressional Medal on the Unknown Soldier

RA PS/PSO/GV/C/Q/694/1; RA PS/PSO/GV/C/Q/723A/5; PS/PSO/GV/C/Q/939/1–3, Miscellaneous correspondence between Stamfordham and Kitchener and Stamfordham and Bonham Carter, 1914–16

RA PS/PSO/GV/C/Q/762/40, Letter from David Lloyd George to Lord Stamfordham, 12 April 1915

RA PS/PSO/GV/C/Q/762/62, Archbishop of Canterbury to Lord Stamfordham, 2 Dec. 1915

RA PS/PSO/GV/C/Q/838/26, Letter from Lord Stamfordham to Herbert H. Asquith, 23 Nov. 1915

RA PS/PSO/GV/C/Q/832/111, 113–24, 126–8, 130, 132, 133, 135, 137–41, Letters from Sir Douglas Haig to King George V

RA PS/PSO/GV/C/Q/2520/1–4, Munitions crisis, 1915, correspondence with Clive Wigram

RA PS/PSO/GV/PS/MAIN/30880, Armistice Day 1920

RA PS/PSO/GV/PS/WAR/QQ7/4745, King's visit to the front, 1914

RA PS/PSO/GV/PS/WAR/QQ18/05707, War, Visit of King and Queen to France, 1917

RA PS/PSO/GV/PS/WAR/QQ22/07603, War: Peace celebrations. Messages from the King on the signing of the Peace Treaty

RA PS/PSO/GVI/C/019/441–3, Letters to the Duke of Windsor during the Abdication, 1936

RA QM/PRIV/QMD, Diaries of Queen Mary, Vols 1914–22

Special Collections, Southampton University Library

The Broadlands Archive, The Papers of Louis, Earl Mountbatten of Burma
MB 1/A8, Early life 1910–1916, RNC Darthmouth and Keyham, 1915–16

MB 1/A9, First World War: HMS *Lion* and HMS *Queen Elizabeth* 1916–18

MB 1/A15, Prince of Wales' tour to Australia and New Zealand 1920, correspondence 1974–9

St Bartholomew's Hospital Museum and Archives, London

RLHCI/3/16, framed colour print of Edith Cavell with inscription
RLHINV/551, Royal Visit to Whipps Cross War Hospital Brass Plaque
RLHLH/N/7/15, Letter from matron, The London Hospital Whitechapel, to Mrs Bright, 8 Feb. 1917
RLHLH/N/7/20, Letter, no addressee, n.d. from matron, The London Hospital Whitechapel, describing a wartime Christmas at the hospital
RLHPP/BAX/6/1, Christmas message from Queen Alexandra to all QAIMNS serving in France, December 1914

The Templer Study Centre, The National Army Museum, London

NAM 1981-09-26, First World War recruiting poster
NAM 1987-03-27, Prisoner of war poem
NAM 1989-08-154, Oral history: Alan Maciver's memories of the First World War, 2nd Lancashire Fusiliers, Western Front 1915–18
NAM 1999-11-149-1, Princess Mary Gift Box card
NAM 2002-02-516, FOL Royal portraits and officer commission document
NAM 2002-02-516-3, Photo of King George and Queen Mary
NAM 2002-02-924, War letters from the Prince of Wales, later Edward VIII
NAM 2002-02-1337, FOL Letter of condolence from King George V to Richard Cotter Esq., 2 Barton Cottages, Wilberforce Road, Sandgate, Kent, 1 February 1917
NAM Kitchener Memorial Fund press cuttings, Vol. 1
NAM Kitchener Memorial Fund minutes, Vol. 1

Printed Primary Sources

Albert I, King of the Belgians, *The War Diaries of Albert I, King of the Belgians* (London, 1954)
Alice, Princess of Great Britain, *For My Grandchildren: Some Reminiscences of Her Royal Highness Princess Alice, Countess of Athlone* (London, 1966)
Princess Alice, Duchess of Gloucester, *The Memoirs of Princess Alice, Duchess of Gloucester* (London, 1983)
Princess Alice, Duchess of Gloucester, *Memories of Ninety Years* (London, 1991)
Airlie, Mabell, *Thatched with Gold: The Memoirs of Mabell, Countess of Airlie*, edited and arranged by Jennifer Ellis (London, 1962)
Anand, Mulk Raj, *Across the Black Waters: A Novel* (London, 1940)
Anonymous, *The Civilian War Sufferer: Compiled from the Records of the Civilian War Claimants Association* (London, n.d.).
Anonymous, *The King to His People, 1911–35* (London, 1935)
Anonymous, *The King's Pilgrimage* (London, 1922)

Anonymous, *The Life and Reign of King George V: A Book for Boys and Girls* (Cambridge, 1936)

Anonymous, *Our Noble King: A Pageant of Twenty-Five Years* (London, New York, Toronto, c. 1935)

Anonymous, *The Real Crown Prince: A Record and an Indictment* (London, 1915)

Anonymous, *The Real Kaiser* (London, 1914)

Anonymous, *The Undaunted Seaman Who Resolved to Fight for His King and Country* (London, c. 1690)

Arnander, Christopher, *Private Lord Crawford's Great War Diaries: From Medical Orderly to Cabinet Minister* (Barnsley, 2013)

Arthur, George, *King George V: A Sketch of a Great Ruler* (London, Toronto, 1929)

Asquith, Cynthia, *Lady Cynthia Asquith: Diaries 1915–1918* (London, 1968)

Asquith, Herbert H., *H. H. Asquith, Letters to Venetia Stanley*, eds. Michael and Eleanor Brock (Oxford, 1982)

Asquith, Herbert H., *Memories and Reflections, 1852–1927*, Vol. 2 (London, 1928)

Asquith, Margot, *The Autobiography of Margot Asquith* (London, 1995)

Asquith, Margot, *Margot Asquith's Great War Diary, 1914–1916: The View from Downing Street*, eds. Michael and Eleanor Brock with the assistance of Mark Pottle (Oxford, 2014)

Associated Newspapers Limited, *His Majesty the King, 1910–1935: Twenty Five Years of a Glorious Reign Told in Pictures*, with an introduction by H. W. Wilson (London, n.d.)

Aston, George Grey and Evelyn Graham, *His Royal Highness, the Duke of Connaught and Strathearn: A Life and Intimate Study* (London, 1929)

Baden-Powell, Robert, *Scouting for Boys: The Original 1908 Edition* (New York, 2007 [1908])

Baldwin Papers, *A Conservative Statesman, 1908–47*, ed. Philip Williamson and E. Baldwin (Cambridge, 2004)

Balfour, Michael, *The Kaiser and His Times* (London, 1964)

Barnes, James, *For King or Country: A Story of the American Revolution* (New York, 1896)

Lord Beaverbrook, *Politicians and the War 1914–1916* (London, 1928)

Bernard, John Henry, *In War Time* (London, 1917)

Bibikoff, Massia, *Our Indians at Marseilles* (London, 1915)

Blake, Robert, ed., *The Private Papers of Douglas Haig, 1914–1919* (London, 1952)

Borden, Robert Laird, *Robert Laird Borden: His Memoirs*, Vols 1 and 2 (Toronto, 1938)

Braithwaite, G. H., *Society of Friends and War: To Fight for King and Country Is Not Anti-Christian* (London, 1917)

Bridges, Tom, *Alarms and Excursions: Reminiscences of a Soldier* (London, 1938)

Brimble, E. Lilian, *In the Eyrie of the Hohenzollern Eagle* (London, 1916)

Brittain, Vera, *Testament of Youth: An Autobiographical Study of the Years 1900–1925* (London, 1978 [1933])

Bryant, Arthur, *George V* (London, 1936)

Buchan, John, *The King's Grace, 1910–1935* (London, 1935)

Carey, Mabel C., *Princess Mary: A Biography* (London, 1922)

Carlyle, Thomas, *On Heroes, Hero-Worship and the Heroic in History* (London, 1841)

Cartmell, Harry, *For Remembrance: An Account of Some Fateful Years* (Preston, 1919)

Cassirer, Ernst, *The Myth of the State* (London, 1946)

Catling, A. H., *The Kaiser under the Searchlight* (London, 1914)

Churchill, Winston, *Great Contemporaries* (London, 1941)

Churchill, Winston, *The World Crisis*, 6 vols (London, 1923–31)

Cook, Theodore A., *The Mask of the Beast* (London, 1917)

Cosens, Monica, *Lloyd George's Munition Girls* (London, 1916)

The Marchioness Curzon of Kedleston, *Reminiscences* (London, 1955)

Daily Mail, *The King at the Front: Official Photographs in Colours* (London, n.d.)

Daily Mirror, *King George V, 1910–1936: 'The Father of His People'; 'They Loved Him as a Man'* (London, 1936)

Dooner, Mildred G., *The 'Last Post': A Roll of All Officers (Naval, Military or Colonial) Who Gave Their Lives for Their Queen, King and Country in the South African War 1899–1902* (London, 1903)

Elton, Oliver, ed., *C. E. Montague: A Memoir* (London, 1929)

Emden, Paul, *Behind the Throne* (London, 1934)

Esher, Viscount, *After the War* (London, 1918)

Filon, Augustin, *Recollections of the Empress Eugénie* (New York, Toronto, London, Melbourne, 1920)

Fitzroy, Sir Almeric, *Memoirs*, 2 vols (London, 1925)

For King and Country, Uplifting and Heartening Messages, trench pamphlet (London, 1916)

For King and Country, Uplifting Messages, trench pamphlet (London, 1915)

Fortescue, John William, *Author and Curator: An Autobiography* (Edinburgh, London, 1933)

Foxwell, A. K., *Munition Lasses: Six Months as Principal Overlooker in Danger Buildings* (London, 1917)

Gallacher, William, *Revolt on the Clyde: An Autobiography* (London 1949 [1936])

Garbett, Rev. Cyril F., *The Challenge of the King and Other Addresses* (London, 1915)

Gardiner, Alfred G., *The War Lords* (London, Toronto, 1915)

Gauss, Christian, *The German Emperor as Shown in His Public Utterances* (London, 1915)

Gibbs, Philip, *England Speaks* (London, 1935)

Gibbs, Philip, ed., *George the Faithful: The Life and Times of George 'The People's King' 1865–1936* (London, [1936])

Gibbs, Philip, *Realities of War* (London, 1920)

Gilbert, Martin, ed., *Winston S. Churchill*, Vol. 3: *The Challenge of War 1914–1916* (London, 1990)

Gilbert, Martin, ed., *Winston S. Churchill*, Vol. 4: *World in Torment 1916–1922* (London, 1990)

Gildea, James, *For King and Country: A Record of Funds and Philanthropic Work in Connection with the South African War, 1899–1902* (London, 1902)

Glasier, John Bruce, *Militarism* (Manchester, 1915)

Godfrey, Rupert, ed., *Letters from a Prince, March 1918–January 1921* (London, 1998)

Gore, John, *King George V: A Personal Memoir* (London, 1941)

Gorman, James T., *George VI: King and Emperor* (London, 1937)

Gorman, James T., *Honour the King: A Royal Jubilee Book* (London, 1935)

Grigg, Edward, *The Faith of an Englishman* (London, 1936)

Hamilton, Peggy, *Three Years or the Duration: The Memoirs of a Munition Worker, 1914–1918* (London, 1978)

Hammerton, John Alexander and Herbert Wrigley Wilson, eds., *The Great War: The Standard History of the All-Europe Conflict*, 13 vols (London, 1914–19)

Hankey, Maurice, *The Supreme Command, 1914–1918* (London, 1961)

Harmsworth, Alfred, Viscount Northcliffe, *At the War* (London, 1916)

Harrison, Austin, *The Kaiser's War* (London, 1914)

Hart-Davies, Duff, ed., *End of an Era: Letters and Journals of Sir Alan Lascelles from 1887 to 1920* (London, 1986)

Haselden, W. K., *The Sad Adventures of Big and Little Willie during the First Six Months of the Great War as Portrayed by W. K. Haselden in 'The Daily Mirror'* (London, 1915)

Henderson, Arthur, *The Aims of Labour* (London, 1917)

Henderson, Arthur, *A People's Peace* (London, 1917)

HMSO, *The King's Regulations and Orders for the Army* (London, 1912)

HMSO, *Letter of July 31, 1914, from the President of the French Republic to the King Respecting the European Crisis: and His Majesty's Reply of August 1, 1914* (London, 1915)

HMSO, *A Record of the King's Ceremonies (Public and Private) from the Outbreak of War to the Ratification of the Peace Treaty with Germany, 4th August, 1914– 10th January, 1920* (London, 1920)

Hodge, John, *Workman's Cottage to Windsor Castle* (London, 1931)

Houghton, Henry D., *Is the Kaiser 'Luzifer'?* (London, 1917)

Hudson, Robert, *The People's King* (London, 1929)

Hughes, William Morris, *Crusts and Crusades: Tales of Bygone Days* (Sydney, London, 1947)

Hughes, William Morris, *The Splendid Adventure: A Review of Empire Relations within and without the Commonwealth of Britainnic Nations* (London, 1929)

Hutchinson, Michael, ed., *The Last Days of Dublin Castle: The Mark Sturgis Diaries* (Dublin, 1999)

Iconoclast (pseud.), *Is the Kaiser 'The Beast' Referred to in the Book of Revelation and by the Prophets Isaiah and Ezekiel?* (London, 1914)

Illustrated London News, *The King-Emperor's Activities in War-Time* (London, n.d.)

Irvine, Alexander, *A Yankee with the Soldiers of the King* (New York, 1923)

Jingoes, Stimela Jason, *A Chief Is a Chief by the People: The Autobiography of Stimela Jason Jingoes*, recorded and compiled by John and Cassandra Perry (New York, London, Cape Town, 1975)

Jones, Thomas, *Whitehall Diary*, Vol. 1: *1916–1925* (Oxford, 1969)

Jones, Thomas, *Whitehall Diary*, Vol. 3: *Ireland 1918–1925* (London, 1971)

Keen, Edith, *Seven Years at the Prussian Court* (London, 1916)

Knight, W. S. M., *A History of Britain during the Great War: A Study of a Democracy at War. The Anarchy before the Outbreak* (London, 1915)

Lane, Franklin K., *The Nation in Arms by Franklin K. Lane, Secretary of the Interior, and Newton D. Baker, Secretary of War* (Washington, DC, 1917)

Lascelles, Alan, *King's Counsellor: Abdication and War. The Diaries of Sir Alan Lascelles*, ed. Duff Hart-Davis (London, 2006)

Legge, Edward, *King Edward, the Kaiser and the War* (London, 1917)

Legge, Edward, *The Public and Private Life of the Kaiser Wilhelm II* (London, 1915)

Lichnowsky, Prince Karl Max von, *Heading for the Abyss: Reminiscences* (London, 1928)

Lloyd George, David, *Honour and Dishonour: A Speech* (London, 1914)

Lloyd George, David, *The Truth about the Peace Treaties* (London, 1938)

Lloyd George, David, *The War Memoirs of David Lloyd George*, 2 vols (London, 1938)

Ludendorff, Erich, *My War Memories, 1914–1918*, 2 vols (London, 1940)

Lynn, Escott, *In Khaki for the King: A Tale of the Great War* (London, Edinburgh, 1915)

MacCabe, Joseph, *The Kaiser, His Personality and His Career* (London, 1915)

MacDonald, James Ramsay, *War and the Workers: A Plea for Democratic Control* (London, 1915)

Maine, Basil, *Our Ambassador King: His Majesty King Edward VIII's Life of Devotion and Service as Prince of Wales* (London, c. 1936)

Marston, Louise, *The Call of the King: An Indian Story of the Great War* (London, Madras, Calcutta, Rangoon, Colombo, 1915)

Martin, Kingsley, *The Magic of Monarchy* (London, 1937)

McGovern, John, *Neither Fear Nor Favour* (London, 1960)

McGuire, James K., *The King, the Kaiser and Irish Freedom* (New York, 1915)

McKenzie, Frederick A., *Serving the King's Men: How the Salvation Army Is Helping the Nation* (London, 1918)

Meleady, Dermot, ed., *John Redmond: Selected Letters and Memoranda, 1880–1918* (Dublin, 2018)

Mendelssohn Bartholdy, Albrecht, *The War and German Society: The Testament of a Liberal* (New Haven, 1937)

Menzies, John et al., *Roll of Honour 1914–1919: For King and Country* (Edinburgh, 1921)

Maisky, Ivan Mikhailovich, *The Maisky Diaries: Red Ambassador to the Court of St James, 1932–1943*, ed. Gabriel Gorodetsky (New Haven, London, 2015)

Middleton, Edgar, ed., *H.R.H.: A Pictorial Biography* (London, 1933)

Midland Railway Company, *For King and Country* (Derby, 1921)

Montague, C. E., *Disenchantment* (London, 1922)

Munro, Robert, *From Darwinism to Kaiserism: The Origin, Effects and Collapse of Germany's Attempt at World Dominion* (Glasgow, 1918)

National Institute for the Blind, *Un message de sa Majesté le Roi George V aux soldats aveugles dans les Armées des Alliés* (London, c. 1917)

Oliphant, Ernest Henry Clark, *Germany and Good Faith: A Study of the History of the Prussian Royal Family* (Melbourne, 1914)

O'Malley, Ernie, *On Another Man's Wound* (London, 1961)

O'Malley, Kate, *Ireland, India and Empire: Indo-Irish Radical Connections, 1919–1964* (Manchester, 2008)

Ormanthwaite, Lord, Master of Ceremonies to King Edward VI and George V, *When I Was at Court* (London, 1937)

Pearson, John J., *The Nemesis of Germany and Austria* (London, 1916)

Ponsonby, Sir Frederick, *Recollections of Three Reigns* (London, 1951)

Powell, George H., *The Crown Prince's First Lesson Book or Nursery Rhymes for the Times* (London, 1914)

Prince, Morton, *The Psychology of the Kaiser: A Study of His Sentiments and His Obsessions* (London, 1915)

Punch Cartoons, *George V, 1910–1936: Part Three of the Punch Cartoon History of Modern Britain* (London, n.d.)

Raleigh, Walter, *England and the War: Being Sundry Addresses Delivered during the War and Now First Collected* (Oxford, 1918)

Reich, Emil, *Germany's Swelled Head* (London, 1914)

Reid, Michaela, *Ask Sir James: The Life of Sir James Reid, Personal Physician to Queen Victoria* (London, 1987)

Riddell, George, *Lord Riddell's Intimate Diary of the Peace Conference and After, 1918–1923* (London, 1933)

Riddell, George, *Lord Riddell's War Diary, 1914–1918* (London, 1933)

Rowe, John G., *Queen Alexandra the Beloved* (London, 1925)

Rufli, Bertrand, *All for a King's Shilling a Day* (S.I., 1980)

Sara, M. E., *The Life and Times of HRH Princess Beatrice* (London, 1945)

Schleswig-Holstein, Marie Louise of, *My Memories of Six Reigns* (London, 1956)

Schmitt, Carl, *Constitutional Theory* (Durham, NC, 2008 [1928])

Schmitt, Carl, *Political Theology: Four Chapters on the Concept of Sovereignty* (Cambridge, MA, 1985 [1922])

Scotland, Alexander, *The London Cage* (London, 1957)

Sheffield, Gary and John Bourne, eds., *Douglas Haig: War Diaries and Letters, 1914–1918* (London, 2006)

Smith, Charles, *William of Liverpool, 'The Primal-Root Causes of the Decline of the British Empire 1876–1911: An Appeal to His Majesty King George V'* (London, 1911)

Snowden, Philip, *Autobiography*, Vol. 1: *1864–1919* (London, 1934)

Snowden, Philip, *Labour in Chains* (Manchester, 1917)

Snowden, Philip, *Why the Governments Cannot Make Peace: Address Delivered at the I.L.P. Conference, Leicester, 1918 by Philip Snowden* (Manchester, 1918)

Stephenson, John, ed., *A Royal Correspondence: Letters of King Edward VII and George V to Admiral Sir Henry F. Stephenson* (London, 1938)

Stevenson, Frances, *Lloyd George: A Diary by Frances Stevenson*, ed. A. J. P. Taylor (London, 1971)

Sunday School Union, *In Touch with God: For Soldiers and Sailors on Active Service for Their King and Country* (London, 1915)

Tenison, E. M., *A Character Sketch of Lieutenant-Commander Julian Tenison. Born June 22 1885. Died for his King and Country, August 15, 1916* (S.I., c. 1920)

Thomson, Basil, *The Scene Changes* (London, 1939)

Thomson, Basil, *The Story of Scotland Yard* (London, 1935)

Thorne, Will, *My Life's Battles* (London, 1989 [1925])

Thurtle, Ernest, *Time's Winged Chariot: Memories and Comments* (London, 1945)

The Times, *Hail and Farewell: The Passing of King George V* (London, 1936)

Tschumi, Gabriel, *Royal Chef: Recollections of a Life in Royal Households from Queen Victoria to Queen Mary* (London, 1954)

Turley, Charles [pseud. Charles Smith], *With the Prince round the Empire* (London, 1926)

University of St Andrews, *Roll of Honour and Roll of Service, 1914–1919 for King and Country* (Edinburgh, 1920)

Veer, W. de, *An Emperor in the Dock* (London, 1915)

Viereck, Sylvester George, *The Kaiser on Trial* (New York, 1937)

HRH Viktoria Luise, *The Kaiser's Daughter: Memoirs of HRH Viktoria Luise, Duchess of Brunswick and Lüneberg, Princess of Prussia* (London, 1977)

Vincent, John, ed., *The Crawford Papers: The Journals of David Lindsay Twenty-Seventh Earl of Crawford and Tenth Earl of Balcarres 1871–1940* (Manchester, 1984)

Vischer, A. L., *The Barbed Wire Disease: A Psychological Study of the Prisoner of War* (London, 1919)

Waddington, Mary, *My War Diary* (London, 1918)

War Office, *Manual of Military Law, 1914* (London, 1914)

War Office, *Statistics of the Military Effort of the British Empire during the Great War 1914–1920* (London, 1922)

War Office, *With the Colours for God, King and Country: Psalms and Hymns for Soldiers in the Field* (Edinburgh, 1914)

Watson, Francis, *Dawson of Penn* (London, 1950)

Wells, H. G., *In the Fourth Year: Anticipations of a World Peace* (London, 1918)

Weston, Agnes, *For King and Country* (London, 1911)

Wharton, Edith, *Fighting France: From Dunkerque to Belfort* (New York, 1915)

Wheeler, Harold, *The Story of Seventy Momentous Years: The Life and Times of King George V (1865–1936)* (London, 1937)

Crown Prince Wilhelm of Germany, *My War Experiences* (London, 1922)

Williamson, David, *Twenty-Five Years Reign: The Life Story of the King and Queen* (London, 1935)

Windsor, Edward, Duke of, *A King's Story: The Memoirs of HRH the Duke of Windsor* (London, 1951)

Windsor, Edward, Prince of Wales, *Report to His Majesty the King of the War Pensions Committee* (London, 1917)

Woodward, David, ed., *The Military Correspondence of Field Marshal Sir William Robertson, CIGS, 1915–1918* (London, 1989)

Yardley, John, *Parergon or Eddies in Equatoria* (London, Toronto, 1931)

Secondary Sources

Adelman, Paul, *The Decline of the Liberal Party, 1910–1931* (London, 1981)

Afflerbach, Holger, 'Wilhelm II as Supreme Warlord in the First World War', *War in History*, 5, 4 (1998), 427–49

Alcalde, Angel, *War Veterans and Fascism in Interwar Europe* (Cambridge, 2017)

Aldrich, Robert and Cindy McCreery, eds., *Crowns and Colonies: European Monarchies and Overseas Empires* (Manchester, 2016)

Aldrich, Robert and Cindy McCreery, 'European Sovereigns and Their Empires "beyond the Seas"' in Robert Aldrich and Cindy McCreery, eds., *Crowns and Colonies: European Monarchies and Overseas Empires* (Manchester, 2016), pp. 1–26

Anderson, Benedict, *Imagined Communities: Reflections on the Origin and Spread of Nationalism* (London, 2006)

Anderson, Julie, *War, Disability and Rehabilitation in Britain: 'Soul of a Nation'* (Manchester, 2011)

Appiah, Kwame Anthony, *The Honor Code: How Moral Revolutions Happen* (New York, 2010)

Armstrong Brown, Nancy, 'Monarchy in the Age of Mechanical Reproduction', *Nineteenth Century Contexts: An Interdisciplinary Journal*, 22, 4 (2001), 495–536

Aronson, Theo, *Crowns in Conflict: The Triumph of the Tragedy of European Monarchy* (London, 1986)

Aronson, Theo, *Princess Alice: Countess of Athlone* (London, 1981)

Aronson, Theo, *The Royal Family at War* (London, 1994)

Aronson, Theo, *Royal Subjects: A Biographer's Encounters* (London, 2000)

Ashton, Nigel and Duco Hellema, 'Anglo-Dutch Relations and the Kaiser Question, 1918–1920' in Nigel Ashton and Duco Hellema, eds., *Unspoken Allies: Anglo-Dutch Relations since 1780* (Amsterdam, 2001), pp. 85–100

Ashworth, Tony, *Trench Warfare, 1914–1918: The Live and Let Live System* (London, 1980)

Astor, Johnny and Alexandra Campbell, *Esmond the Lost Idol, 1895–1917* (Solihull, West Midlands, 2017)

Audoin-Rouzeau, Stéphane, 'An Artifact of War Carved in 1917: The Trench Cane of Soldier/Peasant Claude Burloux', *South Central Review*, 34, 3 (2017), 103–14

Audoin-Rouzeau, Stéphane, *L'enfant de l'ennemi, 1914–1918: viol, avortement, infanticide pendant la Grande Guerre* (Paris, 1995)

Audoin-Rouzeau, Stéphane and Annette Becker, *14–18: Understanding the Great War* (New York, 2002)

Baeten, Elizabeth M., *The Magic Mirror: Myth's Abiding Power* (Albany, NY, 1996)

Bagehot, Walter, *The English Constitution*, ed. Miley Taylor (Oxford, 2001 [1867])

Baker, Keith Michael and Dan Edelstein, eds., *Scripting Revolution: A Historical Approach to the Comparative Study of Revolutions* (Stanford, 2015)

Baker, Paul, *King and Country Call: New Zealanders, Conscription and the Great War* (Auckland, 1988)

Bakhtin, Mikhail, *Rabelais and His World* (Bloomington, 1984)

Bamji, Andrew, 'Sir Harold Gillies: Surgical Pioneer', *Trauma*, 8 (2006), 143–56

Banerjee, Milinda, Charlotte Backerra and Cathleen Sarti, eds., *Transnational Histories of the 'Royal Nation'* (Basingstoke, 2017)

Bardgett, Suzanne, 'A Mutual Fascination: Indians in Brighton', *History Today* (March, 2015), 41–7

Barr, Niall, *The Lion and the Poppy: British Veterans, Politics and Society, 1921–1939* (Westport, CT, 2005)

Barrett, John, 'Historical Reconsiderations VII. No Straw Man: C. E. W. Bean and Some Critics', *Australian Historical Studies*, 23, 89 (1988), 102–14

Barthes, Roland, *Mythologies* (Paris, 1957)

Bartie, Angela, Linda Fleming, Mark Freeman, Tom Hulme, Paul Readman and Charlotte Tupman, '"And Those Who Live, How Shall I Tell Their Fame?" Historical Pageants, Collective Remembrance and the First World War, 1919–39', *Historical Research*, 90, 249 (2017), 636–61

Bartlett, Roger and Karen Schönwälder, eds., *The German Lands and Eastern Europe: Essays on the History of Their Social, Cultural and Political Relations* (London, 1999)

Basford, Elisabeth, *Princess Mary: The First Modern Princess* (Cheltenham, 2021)

Battiscombe, Georgina, *Queen Alexandra* (London, 1969)

Beaken, Robert, *The Church of England and the Home Front, 1914–1918: Civilians, Soldiers and Religion in Wartime Colchester* (Woodbridge, 2015)

Beavan, Brad, 'Challenges to Civic Governance in Post-War England: The Peace Day Disturbances of 1919', *Urban History*, 33 (2006), 369–92

Becker, Frank, 'Begriff und Bedeutung des politischen Mythos' in Barbara Stollberg-Rilinger, ed., *Was heißt Kulturgeschichte des Politischen?* (Berlin, 2005), pp. 129–48

Beckett, Ian F. W., 'George V and His Generals' in Matthew Hughes and Matthew Seligmann, eds., *Leadership in Conflict: 1914–1918* (London, 2000), pp. 247–64

Beckett, Ian F. W., 'Royalty and the Army in the Twentieth Century' in Matthew Glencross, Judith Rowbotham and Michael D. Kandiah, eds., *The Windsor Dynasty 1910 to the Present: 'Long to Reign over Us?'* (London, 2016), pp. 109–33

Beem, Charles and Miles Taylor, eds., *The Man behind the Queen: Male Consorts in History* (New York, NY, 2014)

Beiner, Guy, *Forgetful Remembrance: Social Forgetting and Vernacular Historiography of a Rebellion in Ulster* (Oxford, 2018)

Bergen, Leo van, *Before My Helpless Sight: Suffering, Dying and Military Medicine on the Western Front, 1914–1918* (Farnham, Surrey, 2009)

Berger, Peter, Brigitte Berger and Hansfried Kellner, 'On the Obsolescence of the Concept of Honor' in Peter Berger, Brigitte Berger and Hansfried Kellner, eds., *The Homeless Mind: Modernization and Consciousness* (New York, 1973), pp. 83–96

Berger, Stefan, 'On the Role of Myths and History in the Construction of National Identity in Modern Europe', *European History Quarterly*, 39, 3 (2009), 490–502

Berkhamsted Local History and Museum Society, *Men of Berkhamsted: Lest We Forget* (Berkhamsted, 2017)

Bessel, Richard, 'Revolution' in Jay Winter, ed., *The Cambridge History of the First World War*, Vol. 2: *The State* (Cambridge, 2014), pp. 126–44

Biernoff, Suzannah, 'The Rhetoric of Disfigurement in First World War Britain', *Social History of Medicine*, 24, 3 (2011), 666–85

Billig, Michael, *Talking of the Royal Family* (London, 1992)

Bingham, Adrian and Martin Conboy, *Tabloid Century: The Popular Press in Britain, 1896 to the Present* (Oxford, 2015)

Black, Donald, *Moral Time* (New York, Oxford, 2011)

Blackbourn, David, *Marpingen: Apparitions of the Virgin Mary in Nineteenth Century Germany* (London, 1993)

Blackbourn, David and Geoff Eley, *The Peculiarities of German History: Bourgeois Society and Politics in Nineteenth-Century Germany* (Oxford, 1984)

Blackstock, Allan, *Loyalism and the Formation of the British World, 1775–1914* (Woodbridge, 2014)

Bloch, Marc, *The Royal Touch: Sacred Monarchy and Scrofula in England and France* (London, 1973)

Boff, Jonathan, *Haig's Enemy: Crown Prince Rupprecht and Germany's War on the Western Front* (Oxford, 2017)

Bogdanor, Vernon, *The Monarchy and the Constitution* (Oxford, 1995)

Bogdanor, Vernon, ed., *The British Constitution in the Twentieth Century* (Oxford, 2003)

Bonney, Norman, *Monarchy, Religion and the State: Civil Religion in the United Kingdom, Canada, Australia and the Commonwealth* (Manchester, 2013)

Borgonovo, John, *The Dynamics of War and Revolution: Cork City, 1916–1918* (Cork, 2013)

Bottomore, Stephen, '"She's Just Like My Granny! Where's Her Crown?" Monarchs and Movies, 1896–1916' in John Fullerton, ed., *Celebrating 1895: The Centenary of Cinema* (London, 1998), pp. 172–81

Bourke, Joanna, *Dismembering the Male: Men's Bodies, Britain and the Great War* (London, 1996)

Bourke, Joanna, 'Gender Roles in Killing Zones' in Jay Winter, ed., *The Cambridge History of the First World War*, Vol. 3: *Civil Society* (Cambridge, 2014), pp. 153–78

Bowman, Kent, 'Echoes of Shot and Shell: Songs of the Great War', *Studies in Popular Culture*, 10, 1 (1987), 27–41

Boyce, D. G., '"That Party Politics Should Divide Our Tents": Nationalism, Unionism and the First World War' in Adrian Gregory and Senia Pašeta, eds., *Ireland and the Great War: 'A War to Unite Us All'?* (Manchester, 2002), pp. 190–216

Bradford, Sarah, *King George VI: The Dutiful King* (London, 1989)

Bradley, Ian, *God Save the Queen: The Spiritual Dimension of Monarchy* (New York, London, 2002)

Brazier, Rodney, 'The Monarchy' in Vernon Bogdanor, ed., *The British Constitution in the Twentieth Century* (Oxford, 2003), pp. 83–8

Brennan, Patrick, 'The Other Battle: Imperialist versus Nationalist Sympathies within the Officer Corps of the Canadian Expeditionary Force, 1914–1919' in Philip Buckner and R. Douglas Francis, eds., *Rediscovering the British World* (Calgary, 2005), pp. 251–65

Breuilly, John 'Max Weber, Charisma and Nationalist Leadership', *Nations and Nationalism*, 17, 3 (2011), 477–99

Brown, Callum G., *The Death of Christian Britain: Understanding Secularisation 1800–2000* (London, 2009)

Bryan, Dominic, 'Ritual, Identity and Nation: When the Historian Becomes the High Priest of Commemoration' in Richard S. Grayson and Fearghal McGarry, eds., *Remembering 1916: The Easter Rising, the Somme and the Politics of Memory in Ireland* (Cambridge, 2016), pp. 24–42

Buckner, Phillip, 'Casting Daylight upon Magic: Deconstructing the Royal Tour of 1901 to Canada' in Carl Bridge and Kent Fedorowich, eds., *The British World: Diaspora, Culture and Identity* (London, 2003), pp. 158–89

Buckner, Phillip, 'The Royal Tour of 1901 and the Construction of an Imperial Identity in South Africa', *South African Historical Journal*, 41 (1999), 326–48

Burke, Peter, *Eyewitnessing: The Uses of Images as Historical Evidence* (London, 2001)

Burke, Peter, *What Is Cultural History?* (Cambridge, 2004)

Bush, Barbara, *Imperialism, Race and Resistance: Africa and Britain, 1919–1945* (London, 1999)

Cabanes, Bruno, *The Great War and the Origins of Humanitarianism, 1918–1924* (Cambridge, 2014)

Caiani, Ambrogio, 'Re-Inventing the Ancien Régime in Post-Napoleonic Europe', *European History Quarterly*, 47, 3 (2017), 437–60

Campbell, Myles and William Derham, *Making Majesty: The Throne Room at Dublin Castle* (Dublin, 2017)

Cannadine, David, 'Churchill and the British Monarchy', *Transactions of the Royal Historical Society*, 11 (2001), 249–72

Cannadine, David, 'The Context, Performance and Meaning of Ritual: The British Monarchy and the "Invention of Tradition", c. 1820–1977' in Eric Hobsbawm and Terence Ranger, eds., *The Invention of Tradition* (Cambridge, 1983), pp. 101–64

Cannadine, David, 'From Biography to History: Writing the Modern British Monarchy', *Historical Research*, 77, 197 (2004), 289–312

Cannadine, David, *George V: The Unexpected King* (London, 2014)

Cannadine, David, 'Introduction' in David Cannadine and Simon Price, eds., *Rituals of Royalty: Power and Ceremonial in Traditional Societies* (Cambridge, 1992), pp. 1–19

Cannadine, David, 'Kaiser Wilhelm and the British Monarchy' in T. C. W. Blanning and David Cannadine, eds., *History and Biography: Essays in Honour of Derek Beales* (Cambridge 1996), pp. 188–202

Cannadine, David, *Ornamentalism: How the British Saw Their Empire* (London, 2001)

Cannadine, David, 'Rose's Rex', *London Review of Books*, 5, 17 (15 September 1983), 3–5

Cannadine, David and Simon Price, eds., *Rituals of Royalty: Power and Ceremonial in Traditional Societies* (Cambridge, 1987)

Cannon, John, *The Modern British Monarchy: A Study in Adaptation* (Reading, 1987)

Cannon, John, 'The Survival of the British Monarchy', *Transactions of the Royal Historical Society*, 5th ser., 36 (1986), 143–64

Carden-Coyne, Ana, 'Masculinity and the Wounds of the First World War: A Centenary Reflection', *Revue Française de Civilisation Britannique* [Online], 20, 1 (2015), accessed 4/12/2018

Carden-Coyne, Ana, *The Politics of Wounds: Military Patients and Medical Power in the First World War* (Oxford, 2014)

Carden-Coyne, Ana, *Reconstructing the Body: Classicism, Modernism, and the First World War* (Oxford, 2009)

Carkeek, Rikihana, *Home Little Maori Home: A Memoir of the Maori Contingent 1914–1916* (Wellington, 2003)

Carlton, Charles, *Royal Warriors: A Military History of the British Monarchy* (Harlow, 2003)

Carter, Miranda, 'How to Keep Your Crown', *History Today*, 59, 10 (October 2009), 5–6

Carter, Miranda, *The Three Emperors: Three Cousins, Three Empires and the Road to World War One* (New York, London, 2009)

Cassar, George H., *Kitchener: Architect of Victory* (London, 1977)

Ceadel, Martin, 'The King and Country Debate, 1933: Student Politics, Pacifism, and the Dictators', *Historical Journal*, 22 (1979), 297–422

Chartier, Roger, 'Text, Symbols and Frenchness', *The Journal of Modern History*, 57, 4 (1985), 682–95

Chenevix Trench, Charles, *The Indian Army and the King's Enemies* (London, 1988)

Chickering, Roger and Stig Förster, eds., *Great War, Total War: Combat and Mobilization on the Western Front* (Cambridge, 2000)

Churchill, Alexandra, *In the Eye of the Storm: George V at War* (Warwick, 2018)

Clark, Christopher, *Kaiser Wilhelm II* (Harlow, 2000)

Clark, Gemma, *Everyday Violence in the Irish Civil War* (Cambridge, 2014)

Clay, Catrine, *King, Kaiser, Tsar: Three Royal Cousins Who Led the World to War* (London, 2006)

Cochrane, Peter, *Best We Forget: The War for White Australia 1914–1918* (Melbourne, 2018)

Cohen, Deborah, *The War Come Home: Disabled Veterans in Britain and Germany, 1914–1939* (Berkeley, 2001).

Cole, Laurence and Daniel L. Unowsky, eds., *The Limits of Loyalty: Imperial Symbolism, Popular Allegiances, and State Patriotism in the Late Habsburg Monarchy* (Oxford, 2007)

Collingham, Elizabeth M., *Imperial Bodies: The Physical Experience of the Raj* (Cambridge, 2001)

Condell, Diana, 'A Gift for Christmas: The Story of Princess Mary's Gift Fund, 1914', *Imperial War Museum Review*, 4 (1989), 69–77

Connelly, Mark, *The Great War, Memory and Ritual: Commemoration in the City and East London, 1916–39* (Woodbridge, 2002)

Connelly, Mark and Stefan Goebel, 'The Imperial War Graves Commission, the War Dead and the Burial of a Royal Body, 1914–32', *Historical Research*, 93, 262 (2020), 734–53

Connolly, James, 'Mauvaise Conduite: Complicity and Respectability in the Occupied Nord, 1914–1918', *First World War Studies*, 4, 1 (2013), 7–21

Conway, Stephen, 'Transnational and Cosmopolitan Aspects of Eighteenth-Century European Wars' in Dina Gusejnova, ed., *Cosmopolitanism in Conflict: Imperial Encounters from the Seven Years' War to the Cold War* (London, 2017), pp. 29–54

Cook, Chris, *A Short History of the Liberal Party: The Road Back to Power* (Basingstoke, 2010)

Cook, Tim, 'Fighting Words: Canadian Soldiers' Slang and Swearing in the Great War', *War in History*, 20, 3 (2015), 323–44

Cooney, Mark, *Warriors and Peacemakers: How Third Parties Shape Violence* (New York, 1998)

Copland, Ian, *The Princes of India in the Endgame of Empire, 1917–1947* (Cambridge, 1997)

Corbin, Alain, *Time, Desire and Horror: Towards a History of the Senses* (Cambridge, 1995)

Corbin, Alain, *La fraîcheur de l'herbe: histoire d'une gamme d'émotions de l'antiquité à nos jours* (Paris, 2018)

Cornwall, Mark, 'Traitors and the Meaning of Treason in Austria-Hungary's Great War', *Transactions of the Royal Historical Society*, 6th ser., 25 (2015), 113–34

Cornwall, Mark, 'Treason in an Era of Regime Change: The Case of the Habsburg Monarchy', *Austrian History Yearbook*, 50, (2019), 124–49

Courcy, Anna de, *Margot at War* (London, 2014)

Cox, Reginald H. W., *Military Badges of the British Empire, 1914–1918: The Great War* (London, 1982)

Craig, David M., 'Historiographical Reviews: The Crowned Republic? Monarchy and Anti-Monarchy in Britain, 1760–1901', *Historical Journal*, 46, 1 (2003), 167–85

Crawford, John and Ian McGibbon, eds., *One Flag, One Queen, One Tongue: New Zealand, the British Empire and the South African War, 1899–1902* (Auckland, 2003)

Dale, Johanna, *Inauguration and Liturgical Kingship in the Long Twelfth Century: Male and Female Accession Rituals in England, France and the Empire* (Suffolk, 2019)

D'Alton, Ian, 'No Country? Protestant "Belongings" in Independent Ireland, 1922–49' in Ian d'Alton and Ida Milne, eds., *Protestant and Irish: The Minority's Search for Place in Independent Ireland* (Cork, 2019), pp. 27–31

Darnton, Robert, *The Great Cat Massacre and Other Episodes in French Cultural History* (London, 1984)

Darwin, John, 'A Third British Empire? The Dominion Idea in Imperial Politics' in Judith M. Brown and William Roger Louis, eds., *The Oxford History of the British Empire*, Vol. 4: *The Twentieth Century* (Oxford, 1999), pp. 64–87

Das, Santanu, '"The Impotence of Sympathy": Touch and Trauma in the Memoirs of the First World War Nurses', *Textual Practice* 19, 2 (2005), 239–62

Das, Santanu, *India, Empire, and First World War Culture: Writings, Images, and Songs* (Cambridge, 2018)

Das, Santanu, *Touch and Intimacy in First World War Literature* (Cambridge, 2005)

Dawson, Graham, *Soldier Heroes: British Adventure, Empire and the Imagining of Masculinities* (London, 1994)

Delaney, Douglas, *The Imperial Army Project: Britain and the Land Forces of the Dominions and India, 1902–1945* (Oxford, 2018)

Demiaux, Victor, 'Inter-Allied Community? Rituals and Transnational Narratives of the Great War' in Marco Mondini and Massimo Rospocher, eds., *Narrating War: Early Modern and Contemporary Perspectives* (Berlin, Bologna, 2013), pp. 189–204

Dempsey, James, *Aboriginal Soldiers and the First World War* (Ottawa, 2006)

Dempsey, James, *Warriors of the King: Prairie Indians in World War I* (Regina, 1999)

Dennison, Matthew, *The Last Princess: The Devoted Life of Queen Victoria's Youngest Daughter* (London, 2019)

Deploige, Jeroen and Gita Deneckere, eds., *Mystifying the Monarch: Studies on Discourse, Power and History* (Amsterdam, 2006)

Dixon, Thomas, *Weeping Britannia: Portrait of a Nation in Tears* (Oxford, 2015)

Donaldson, Frances, *Edward VIII* (London, 1974)

Dorney, John, 'Republican Representations of the Treaty: "A Usurpation Pure and Simple"' in Liam Weeks and Mícheál Ó Fathartaigh, eds., *The Treaty: Debating and Establishing the Irish State* (Newbridge, 2018)

Douglas, Mary, *Purity and Danger: An Analysis of the Concepts of Pollution and Taboo* (London, 2002 [1966])

Douglas, Roy, 'Voluntary Enlistment in the First World War and the Work of the Parliamentary Recruiting Committee', *The Journal of Modern History*, 42, 4 (1970), 564–85

Douglas-Home, Charles and Saul Kelly, *Dignified and Efficient: The British Monarchy in the Twentieth Century* (London, 2001)

Doyle, Peter, *British Postcards of the First World War* (London, 2011)

Duff, David, *The Shy Princess: The Life of Her Royal Highness Princess Beatrice* (London, 1958)

Duffett, Rachel, 'The War in Miniature: Queen Mary's Dolls' House and the Legacies of the First World War', *Cultural and Social History*, 16, 4 (2019), 431–49

Durham, Helen and Cyril Pearce, 'Patterns of Dissent in Britain during the First World War', *War and Society*, 34 (2015), 140–59

Dutton, Philip, 'Moving Images? The Parliamentary Recruiting Committee's Poster Campaign, 1914–1916', *Imperial War Museum Review*, 4 (1989), 43–58

Edgerton, David, *The Rise and Fall of the British Nation: A Twentieth-Century History* (London, 2018)

Edgerton, David, *Warfare State: Britain 1920–1970* (Cambridge, 2006)

Edwards, Anne, *Matriarch: Queen Mary and the House of Windsor* (London, 1984)

Eley, Geoff and Keith Nield, *The Future of Class in History: What's Left of the Social?* (Ann Arbor, 2007)

Elias, Norbert, *The Civilizing Process: The History of Manners* (Oxford, 1978)

Elias, Norbert, *The Court Society* (Oxford, 1983)

Ellis, John S., 'Reconciling the Celt: British National Identity, Empire and the 1911 Investiture of the Prince of Wales', *Journal of British Studies*, 37, 4 (1998), 391–418

English, Jim, 'Empire Day in Britain 1904–58', *Historical Journal*, 49 (2006), 247–76

Farrell, Mel, '"Stepping Stones to Freedom": Pro-Treaty Rhetoric and Strategy during the Dáil Treaty Debates' in Liam Weeks and Mícheál Ó Fathartaigh, eds., *The Treaty: Debating and Establishing the Irish State* (Dublin, 2018), pp. 14–41

Febb, John, *Royal Tours of the British Empire, 1860–1927* (London, 1989)

Feldman, David, 'The King's Peace, the Royal Prerogative and Public Order: The Roots and Early Development of Binding Over Powers', *Cambridge Law Journal*, 47, 1 (1988), 101–28

Fewster, Kevin, 'Politics, Pagentry and Purpose: The 1920 Tour of Australia by the Prince of Wales', *Labour History*, 38 (1980), 59–66

Fitzpatrick, David, 'The Logic of Collective Sacrifice: Ireland and the British Army, 1914–1918', *Historical Journal*, 38, 4 (1995), 1017–30

Förster, Birte, *Der Königin Luise-Mythos: Mediengeschichte des Idealbilds deutscher 'Weiblichkeit', 1860–1960* (Göttingen, 2011)

'Forum: History of Emotions', *German History*, 28, 1 (2010), 67–80

Foster, Roy and Alvin Jackson, 'Men for All Seasons? Carson, Parnell and the Limits of Heroism in Modern Ireland', *European History Quarterly*, 39, 3 (2009), 414–38

Foucault, Michel, *Discipline and Punish: The Birth of the Prison* (London, 2019 [1977])

Francis, Martin, 'The Domesticisation of the Male? Recent Research on Nineteenth- and Twentieth-Century British Masculinity', *Historical Journal*, 45 (2002), 637–52

Frankland, Noble, *Prince Henry: Duke of Gloucester* (London 1980)

Frankland, Noble, *Witness of a Century: The Life and Times of Prince Arthur, Duke of Connaught, 1850–1942* (London, 1993)

Frevert, Ute, 'Honor, Gender, and Power: The Politics of Satisfaction in Pre-War Europe' in Holger Afflerbach and David Stevenson, eds., *An Improbable War? The Outbreak of World War I and European Political Culture before 1914* (New York, Oxford, 2007), pp. 233–55

Fujitani, Takashi, *Splendid Monarchy: Power and Pagentry in Modern Japan* (Berkeley, 1996)

Fulbrook, Mary and Ulinka Rublack, 'In Relation: The "Social Self" and Ego-Documents', *German History*, 28, 3 (2010), 263–72

Fuller, William, *The Foe Within: Fantasies of Treason and the End of Imperial Russia* (Ithaca, NY, 2006)

Fussell, Paul, *The Great War and Modern Memory* (Oxford, 1975)

Gallagher, Niamh, *Ireland and the Great War: A Social and Political History* (London, 2020)

Galloway, Peter J., *The Order of St Michael and St George* (London, 2000)

Galloway, Peter J., *The Order of the British Empire* (Bromsgrove, 2017)

Geisthövel, Alexa, 'Den Monarchen im Blick: Wilhelm I in der illustrierten Familienpresse' in Habbo Knoch and Daniel Morat, eds., *Kommunikation als Beobachtung: Medienwandel und Gesellschaftsbilder 1880–1960* (Munich, 2003), pp. 59–80

Gellner, Ernest, *Nations and Nationalism* (Oxford, 1983)

The German Historical Institute, *Many Faces of the Kaiser: Wilhelm II's Public Image in Britain and Germany* (London, 2002)

Gerwarth, Robert, *The Bismarck Myth: Weimar Germany and the Legacy of the Iron Chancellor* (Oxford, 2005)

Gerwarth, Robert, 'Introduction', *Hero Cults and the Politics of the Past: Comparative European Perspectives, European History Quarterly*, special edition, 39, 3 (2009), 381–7

Gerwarth, Robert, *The Vanquished: Why the First World War Failed to End, 1917–1923* (London, 2016)

Gerwarth, Robert and John Horne, 'Bolshevism as Fantasy: Fear of Revolution and Counter-Revolutionary Violence, 1917–1923' in Robert Gerwarth and John Horne, eds., *War in Peace: Paramilitary Violence in Europe after the Great War* (Oxford, 2012), pp. 40–51

Gerwarth, Robert and John Horne, eds., *War in Peace: Paramilitary Violence in Europe after the Great War* (Oxford, 2012)

Gerwarth, Robert and Erez Manela, eds., *Empires at War, 1911–1923* (Oxford, 2014)

Gerwarth, Robert and Lucy Riall, 'Fathers of the Nation? Bismarck, Garibaldi and the Cult of Memory in Germany and Italy', *European History Quarterly*, 39, 3 (2009), 388–413

Geyser, O., 'Irish Independence: Jan Smuts and Eamon de Valera', *The Round Table*, 348 (1998), 473–84

Gilbert, Sandra and Susan Gubar, *No Man's Land: The Place of the Woman Writer in the Twentieth Century*, 3 vols (London, New Haven, 1988–9)

Gildea, Robert and Anna von der Goltz, 'Flawed Saviours: The Myths of Hindenburg and Pétain', *European History Quarterly*, 39, 3 (2009), 439–64

Giloi, Eva, 'Durch die Kornblume gesagt: Reliquien Geschenke als Indikator für die öffentliche Rolle Kaiser Wilhelms I.' in Thomas Biskup and Martin Kohlrausch, eds., *Das Erbe der Monarchie: Nachwirkungen einer deutschen Institution seit 1918* (Frankfurt am Main, 2008)

Giloi, Eva, *Monarchy, Myth, and Material Culture in Germany, 1750–1950* (Cambridge, 2011)

Girouard, Mark, *The Return to Camelot: Chivalry and the English Gentleman* (New Haven, London, 1981)

Glassford, Sarah and Amy Shaw, eds., *A Sisterhood of Suffering and Service: Women and Girls of Canada and Newfoundland during the First World War* (Vancouver, 2012)

Glencross, Matthew, 'A Cause of Tension? The Leadership of King George V: Visiting the Western Front' in Matthew Glencross and Judith Rowbotham, eds., *Monarchies and the Great War* (London, 2018), pp. 153–89

Glencross, Matthew, 'George V and the New Royal House' in Matthew Glencross, Judith Rowbotham and Michael D. Kandiah, eds., *The Windsor Dynasty 1910 to the Present: 'Long to Reign over Us?'* (London, 2016), pp. 33–56

Glencross, Matthew, *The State Visits of Edward VII: Reinventing Royal Diplomacy for the Twentieth Century* (London, 2016)

Glencross, Matthew and Judith Rowbotham, eds., *Monarchies and the Great War* (London, 2018)

Glencross, Matthew, Judith Rowbotham and Michael D. Kandiah, eds., *The Windsor Dynasty 1910 to the Present: 'Long to Reign over Us?'* (London, 2016)

Goebel, Stefan, *The Great War and Medieval Memory: War, Remembrance and Medievalism in Britain and Germany, 1914–1940* (Cambridge, 2007)

Golby, John M and A. William Perdue, *The Monarchy and the British People, 1760 to the Present* (London, 1988)

Goltz, Anna von der, *Hindenburg: Power, Myth and the Rise of the Nazis* (Oxford, 2009)

Gordon, Peter and Denis Lawton, *Royal Education: Past, Present and Future* (London, 1999; 2003)

Grayzel, Susan, *At Home and under Fire: Air Raids and Culture in Britain from the Great War to the Blitz* (Cambridge, 2012)

Grayzel, Susan and Tammy Proctor, eds., *Gender and the Great War* (Oxford, 2017)

Greenhalgh, Elizabeth, *Foch in Command: The Forging of a First World War General* (Cambridge, 2011)

Gregory, Adrian, 'British "War Enthusiasm" in 1914: A Reassessment' in Gail Braybon, ed., *Evidence, History and the Great War: Historians and the Impact of 1914–18* (Oxford, 2003), pp. 67–85

Gregory, Adrian, *The Last Great War: British Society and the First World War* (Cambridge, 2008)

Gregory, Adrian, *The Silence of Memory: Armistice Day 1919–1946* (London, 2014)

Gregory, Adrian and Senia Pašeta, eds., *Ireland and the Great War: 'A War to Unite Us All?'* (Manchester, 2002)

Greig, Geordie, *Louis and the Prince: A Story of Politics, Intrigue and Royal Friendship* (London, 1999)

Grieves, Keith, 'C. E. Montague and the Making of "Disenchantment", 1914–1921', *War in History*, 4, 1 (1997), 35–59

Grigg, John, *Lloyd George: War Leader 1916–1918* (London, 2003)

Grimley, Matthew, 'The Religion of Englishness: Puritanism, Providentialism, and "National Character", 1918–1945', *Journal of British Studies*, 46 (2007), 884–906

Grossman, N. J., 'Republicanism in 19th-Century England', *International Review of Social History*, 7 (1962), 47–60

Grundlingh, Albert, 'Mutating Memories and the Making of a Myth: Remembering the SS *Mendi* Disaster, 1917–2007', *South African Historical Journal*, 63, 1 (2011), 20–37

Grundlingh, Albert, *War and Society: Participation and Remembrance. South African Black and Coloured Troops in the First World War 1914–1918* (Stellenbosch, 2014)

Gullace, Nicoletta, *'The Blood of our Sons': Men, Women and the Renegotiation of British Citizenship during the Great War* (Basingstoke, 2002)

Gullace, Nicoletta, 'Sexual Violence and Family Honor: British Propaganda and International Law during the First World War', *American Historical Review*, 102, 3 (1997), 714–47

Gumz, Jonathan *The Resurrection and Collapse of Empire in Habsburg Serbia, 1914–1918* (Cambridge, 2009)

Hackett, Helen, 'Dreams or Designs, Cults or Constructions? The Study of Images of Monarchs', *Historical Journal*, 44, 3 (2001), 811–24

Hadad, Galit, 'La Guerre de 1914–1918, matrice du pacifisme féminin au XXe siècle' in Nicolas Beaupré, Heather Jones and Anne Rasmussen, eds., *Dans la Guerre 1914–1918: accepter, endurer, refuser* (Paris, 2015), pp. 329–53

Hagemann, Karen, 'The Military and Masculinity: Gendering the History of the Revolutionary and Napoleonic Wars, 1792–1815' in Roger Chickering and Stig Förster, eds., *War in an Age of Revolution, 1775–1815* (Cambridge, 2010), pp. 331–52

Hajkowski, Thomas, 'The BBC and the Making of a Multi-National Monarchy' in Thomas Hajkowski, *The BBC and National Identity in Britain, 1922–53* (Manchester, 2013)

Hall, Margaret, *The Imperial Aircraft Flotilla: The Worldwide Fundraising Campaign for the British Flying Services in the First World War* (Lancaster, 2017)

Hansen, Randall, 'The Politics of Citizenship in 1940s Britain: The British Nationality Act', *Twentieth Century British History*, 10, 1 (1999), 67–95

Hardie, Frank, *The Political Influence of the British Monarchy, 1868–1952* (London, 1970)

Harris, *Long to Reign Over Us? The Status of the Royal Family in the Sixties (Mass Observation)* (London, 1966)

Harrison, Mark, *The Medical War: British Military Medicine in the First World War* (Oxford, 2010)

Harvey, Karen, 'What Have Historians Done with Masculinity? Reflections on Five Centuries of British History, circa 1500–1950', introduction to a Special Feature on Masculinities in *The Journal of British Studies* (with Alexandra Shepard), 44, 2 (2005), 274–80

Hayman, Mark, 'Labour and the Monarchy: Patriotism and Republicanism during the Great War', *Journal of First World War Studies*, 5, 2 (2014), 163–79

Hazlehurst, Cameron, *Politicians at War, July 1914 to May 1915: A Prologue to the Triumph of Lloyd George* (London, 1971)

Heinzen, Jasper, 'Monarchical State-Building through Self-Destruction: Hohenzollern Self-Legitimation at the Expense of Deposed Dynasties in the Kaiserreich', *German History* 35, 4 (2017), 525–50

Hennessey, Thomas, 'Ulster Unionism and Loyalty to the Crown of the United Kingdom 1912–74' in Richard English and Graham Walker, eds., *Unionism in Modern Ireland: New Perspectives on Politics and Culture* (London, 1996), pp. 115–29

Hennessy, Peter, *The Hidden Wiring: Unearthing the British Constitution* (London, 1996)

Henry, Wade A., 'Imagining the Great White Mother and the Great King: Aboriginal Tradition and Royal Representation at the "Great Pow-Wow" of 1901', *Journal of the Canadian Historical Association*, new ser., 9 (2000), 87–108

Hiley, Nicholas, 'The Candid Camera of the Edwardian Tabloids', *History Today*, 43 (1993), 16–22

Hill, Robert A. and Carol Rudisell, eds., *The Marcus Garvey and Universal Negro Improvement Association Papers*, Vol. 1: *1826–August 1919* (Berkeley, 1983)

Hobsbawm, Eric, 'Mass-Producing Traditions: Europe 1870–1914' in Eric Hobsbawm and Terence Ranger, eds., *The Invention of Tradition* (Cambridge, 1983), pp. 263–308

Hobsbawm, Eric and Terence Ranger, eds., *The Invention of Tradition* (Cambridge, 1983)

Hofmann, Arne, '*Wir sind das alte Deutschland, Das Deutschland wie es war . . .*': *Der 'Bund der Aufrechten' und der Monarchismus in der Weimarer Republik* (Berlin, 1998)

Horne, John, 'End of a Paradigm? The Cultural History of the Great War', *Past and Present*, 242, (2019), 155–92

Horne, John, ed., *Our War: Ireland and the Great War* (Dublin, 2008)

Horne, John, ed., *State, Society and Mobilization in Europe during the First World War* (Cambridge, 1997)

Horne, John and Alan Kramer, *German Atrocities, 1914: A History of Denial* (New Haven, 2001)

Hough, Richard, *Louis and Victoria: The First Mountbattens* (London, 1974)

Howard, Philip, *The British Monarchy in the Twentieth Century* (London, 1977)

Hughes, Brian, 'Defining Loyalty: Southern Irish Protestants and the Irish Grants Committee, 1926–30' in Ian d'Alton and Ida Milne, eds., *Protestant and Irish: The Minority's Search for Place in Independent Ireland* (Cork, 2019), pp. 34–50

Hughes, Brian, *Defying the IRA: Intimidation, Coercion and Communities during the Irish Revolution* (Liverpool, 2016)

Hughes, Brian and Conor Morrissey, eds., *Southern Irish Loyalism, 1912–1949* (Liverpool, 2020)

Hughes, Matthew and Matthew Seligmann, eds., *Leadership in Conflict: 1914–1918* (London, 2000)

Hull, Isabel V., *The Entourage of Kaiser Wilhelm II: 1888–1918* (Cambridge, 1982)

Hull, Isabel V., *A Scrap of Paper: Breaking and Making International Law during the Great War* (Ithaca, NY, London, 2014)

Hunt, Cathy, *Righting the Wrong: Mary Macarthur 1880–1921: The Working Woman's Champion* (Alcester, 2019)

Hunt, Lynn, 'French History in the Last Twenty Years: The Rise and Fall of the Annales Paradigm', *Journal of Contemporary History*, 21, 2 (1986), 209–24

Hunt, Lynn, ed., *The New Cultural History* (Berkeley, 1989)

Huss, Marie-Monique, *Histoires de famille 1914–1918: cartes postales et culture de guerre* (Paris, 2000)

Hynes, Samuel, *A War Imagined: The First World War and English Culture* (London, 1992)

Jackson, Alvin, 'Unionists' Myths, 1912–1985', *Past and Present*, 136 (1992), 164–85

Jackson, Alvin, 'Widening the Fight for Ireland's Freedom: Revolutionary Nationalism in Its Global Contexts', *Victorian Studies*, 54, 1 (2011), 95–112

Jarboe, Andrew Tait, 'Healing the Empire: Indian Hospitals in Britain and France during the First World War', *Twentieth Century British History*, 26, 3 (2015), 347–69

Jarboe, Andrew Tait and Richard Fogarty, eds., *Empires in World War I: Shifting Frontiers and Imperial Dynamics in a Global Conflict* (New York, London, 2014)

Jeffery, Keith, 'Crown, Communication and the Colonial Past: Stamps, the Monarchy and the British Empire', *Journal of Imperial and Commonwealth History*, 34 (2006), 45–70

Jenkins, Roy, *Asquith* (London, 1986)

Jenkins, T. A., 'The Funding of the Liberal Unionist Party and the Honours System', *The English Historical Review*, 105, 417 (1990), 920–38

Jenkinson, Jacqueline, *Black 1919: Riots, Racism and Resistance in Imperial Britain* (Liverpool, 2009)

Joll, James, *1914: The Unspoken Assumptions* (London, 1968)

Jones, Heather, 'As the Centenary Approaches: The Regeneration of First World War Historiography', *Historical Journal*, 56, 3 (2013), 857–78

Jones, Heather, 'International or Transnational? Humanitarian Action during the First World War', *European Review of History*, 16, 5 (2009), 697–713

Jones, Heather, 'The Nature of Kingship in First World War Britain' in Matthew Glencross, Judith Rowbotham and Michael Kandiah, eds., *The Windsor Dynasty, 1910 to the Present: 'Long to Reign over Us'?* (London, 2016), 195–216

Jones, Heather, 'A Prince in the Trenches? Edward VIII and the First World War' in Heidi Merkhens and Frank Lorenz Müller, eds., *Sons and Heirs: Succession and Political Culture in 19th Century Europe* (London, 2015)

Jones, Heather, *Violence against Prisoners of War, Britain, France and Germany, 1914–1920* (Cambridge, 2011)

Jones, Mark, *Founding Weimar: Violence and the German Revolution of 1918–1919* (Cambridge, 2016)

Jones, Valerie, *Rebel Prods: The Forgotten Story of Protestant Radical Nationalists and the 1916 Rising* (Dublin, 2016)

Jordanova, Ludmilla, *History in Practice* (London, 2016)

Judd, Denis, *The Life and Times of George V* (London, 1973)

Julien, Elise, *Paris, Berlin: la mémoire de la guerre 1914–1933* (Rennes, 2010)

Kantorowicz, Ernst, *The King's Two Bodies: A Study in Mediaeval Political Theology* (Princeton, 1957)

Kaul, Chandrika, 'Monarchical Display and the Politics of Empire: Princes of Wales and India, 1870–1920s', *Twentieth Century British History*, 17, 4 (2006), 464–88

Kearney, Hugh, 'The Importance of Being British', *Political Quarterly*, 71 (2000), 15–25

Keay, Anna, *The Crown Jewels* (London, 2011)

Kelly, Matthew, *The Fenian Ideal and Irish Nationalism, 1882–1916* (Woodbridge, 2006)

Kenny, Mary, *Crown and Shamrock: Love and Hate between Ireland and the British Monarchy* (Dublin, 2009)

Kent, Susan K., *Queen Victoria: Gender and Empire* (Oxford, 2016)

Kernahan, Coulson, *Experiences of a Recruiting Officer* (London, 1915)

Kertzer, David, *Ritual, Politics and Power* (New Haven, 1988)

King, Alex, *Memorials of the Great War in Britain: The Symbolism and Politics of Remembrance* (London, 2014)

King, Laura, *Family Men: Fatherhood and Masculinity in Britain, 1914–1960* (Oxford, 2015)

Knirck, Jason, *Imagining Ireland's Independence: The Debates over the Anglo-Irish Treaty of 1921* (Plymouth, 2006)

Kohlrausch, Martin, 'The Unmanly Emperor: Wilhelm II and the Fragility of the Royal Individual' in Regina Schulte, Pernille Arenfeldt, Martin Kohlrausch and Xenia von Tippelskirch, eds., *The Body of the Queen: Gender and Rule in the Courtly World, 1500–2000* (New York, Oxford, 2006), pp. 254–80

Kollander, Patricia, *Frederick III: Germany's Liberal Emperor* (Wespoint, CT, London, 1995)

Kolonitskii, Boris and Orlando Figes, *Interpreting the Russian Revolution: The Language and Symbols of 1917* (New Haven, London, 1999)

Koselleck, Reinhart, Javiér Fernández Sebastián and Juan Francisco Fuentes, 'Conceptual History, Memory, and Identity: An Interview with Reinhart Koselleck', *Contributions to the History of Concepts*, 2, 1 (March, 2006), 99–127

Koven, Seth, 'Remembering and Dismemberment: Crippled Children, Wounded Soldiers, and the Great War in Great Britain', *American Historical Review*, 99, 4 (1994), 1167–202

Koven, Seth, *Slumming: Sexual and Social Politics in Victorian London* (Princeton, 2006)

Kowalsky, Meaghan, '"This Honourable Obligation": The King's National Roll Scheme for Disabled Ex-Servicemen 1915–1944', *European Review of History/ Revue européenne d'histoire*, 14, 4 (2007), 567–84

Kroll, Frank-Lothar and Martin Munke, eds., *Hannover – Coburg – Windsor: Probleme und Perspektiven einer vergleichenden deutsch-britischen Dynastiegeschichte vom 18. bis in das 20. Jahrhundert* (Berlin, 2015)

Kroll, Frank-Lothar and Dieter J. Weiß, eds., *Inszenierung oder Legitimation? / Monarchy and the Art of Representation: die Monarchie in Europa im 19. und 20. Jahrhundert. Ein deutsch-englischer Vergleich* (Berlin, 2015)

Kuhn, William M., 'Ceremony and Politics: The British Monarchy, 1871–1872', *Journal of British Studies*, 26 (1987), 133–62

Kuhn, William M., *Democratic Royalism: The Transformation of the British Monarchy, 1861–1914* (London, 1996)

Kumar, Krishan, *The Making of English National Identity* (Cambridge, 2003)

Kumarasingham, Harshan, 'A New Monarchy for a New Commonwealth? Monarchy and the Consequences of Republican India' in Robert Aldrich and Cindy McCreery, eds., *Crowns and Colonies: European Monarchies and Overseas Empires* (Manchester, 2016), pp. 283–308

Kumarasingham, Harshan, 'Rhetoric of the Realm: Monarchy in New Zealand, Political Rhetoric and Adjusting to the End of Empire' in Martin Thomas and Richard Toye, eds., *Rhetorics of Empire: Languages of Colonial Conflict after 1900* (Manchester, 2017), pp. 228–48

Kumarasingham, Harshan and Ruth Craggs, 'Losing an Empire, Building a Role: The Queen, Geopolitics and the Construction of the Commonwealth Headship at the Lusaka Commonwealth Heads of Government Meeting, 1979', *Journal of Imperial and Commonwealth History*, 43, 1 (2015), 80–98

Langewiesche, Dieter, *Die Monarchie im Jahrhundert Europas: Selbsbehauptung durch Wandel im 19. Jahrhundert* (Heidelberg, 2013)

Langewiesche, Dieter, 'Monarchy-Global: Monarchical Self-Assertion in a Republican World', *Journal of Modern European History*, 15, 2 (2017), 280–308

Laqueur, Thomas, 'Bodies, Details and the Humanitarian Narrative' in Lynn Hunt, ed., *The New Cultural History* (Berkeley, 1989), pp. 176–205

Lawrence, Jon, 'Forging a Peaceable Kingdom: War, Violence, and Fear of Brutalization in Post-First World War Britain', *The Journal of Modern History*, 75, 3 (2003), 557–89

Lawrence, Jon, 'Public Space, Political Space' in Jay Winter and Jean-Louis Robert, eds., *Capital Cities at War: Paris, London, Berlin*, Vol. 2: *A Cultural History* (Cambridge, 2007), pp. 280–312

Lawrence, Jon, 'The Transformation of British Public Politics after the First World War', *Past and Present*, 190 (2006), 185–216

Le Roy Ladurie, Emmanuel, *Montaillou: Cathars and Catholics in a French Village, 1294–1324* (London, 2013 [1980])

Leerssen, Joep, 'Englishness, Ethnicity and Matthew Arnold', *European Journal of English Studies*, 10, 1 (2006), 63–79

Lees-Milne, James, *The Enigmatic Edwardian: The Life of Reginald, 2nd Viscount Esher* (London, 1986)

Lees-Milne, James, *Harold Nicolson: A Biography*, Vol. 2: *1930–1968* (London, 1981)

Lefebvre, Georges, *The Great Fear of 1789: Rural Panic in Revolutionary France* (London, 1976 [1932])

Lerman, Katharine, 'Wilhelm's War: A Hohenzollern in Conflict, 1914–1918' in Frank Müller and Heidi Mehrkens, eds., *Sons and Heirs: Succession and Political Culture in 19th Century Europe* (London, 2015), 247–62

Levine, Philippa, *Gender and Empire* (Oxford, 2004)

Lieven, Dominic, *Nicholas II: Emperor of all the Russias* (London, 1993)

Lloyd, David William, *Battlefield Tourism: Pilgrimage and the Commemoration of the Great War in Britain, Australia and Canada, 1919–39* (London, Oxford, New York, Toronto, 1998)

Lockhart, J. G., *Cosmo Gordon Lang* (London, 1949)

Loughlin, James, *The British Monarchy and Ireland, 1800 to the Present* (Cambridge, 2007)

Lovejoy Edwards, Carol, *Mansfield in the Great War* (Barnsley, 2015)

Lynch, Robert, *The Partition of Ireland, 1918–1925* (Cambridge, 2019)

Lysaght, D. R. O'Connor, 'The Irish Citizen Army, 1913–1916: White, Larkin and Connolly', *History Ireland*, 2, 14 (March/April 2006), www.historyireland.com /20th-century-contemporary-history/the-irish-citizen-army-1913-16-white-larkin -and-connolly/, accessed: 15/4/2021

Macdonald, Lyn, *1914: The Days of Hope* (London, 2014)

Macdonald, Lyn, *Somme* (London, 2013)

Mack Smith, Denis, *Italy and Its Monarchy* (New Haven, London, 1989)

Mackenzie, Norman and Jeanne Mackenzie, *H. G. Wells: A Biography* (New York, 1973)

Macleod, Jenny, 'Britishness and Commemoration: National Memorials to the First World War in Britain and Ireland', *Journal of Contemporary History*, 48 (2013), 647–65

Macleod, Jenny, *Reconsidering Gallipoli* (Manchester, 2004)

Macmillan, James, *The Honours Game* (London, 1969)

Madigan, Edward, *Faith under Fire: Anglican Army Chaplains and the Great War* (Basingstoke, 2011)

Manela, Erez, *The Wilsonian Moment: Self-Determination and the International Origins of Anti-Colonial Nationalism* (Oxford, 2007)

Marti, Steve, *For Home and Empire: Voluntary Mobilization in Australia, Canada and New Zealand during the First World War* (Vancouver, 2019)

März, Stefan, *Das Haus Wittelsbach im Ersten Weltkrieg: Chance und Zusammenbruch monarchischer Herrschaft* (Regensburg, 2013)

Mayer, Arno, *The Persistence of the Old Regime: Europe to the Great War* (London, 1981)

Mayhall, Laura E. Nym, 'The Prince of Wales *versus* Clark Gable: Anglophone Celebrity and Citizenship between the Wars', *Cultural and Social History*, 4 (2007), 529–43

McCarthy, Helen, 'Whose Democracy? Historians of British Political Culture between the Wars', *Historical Journal*, 55 (2012), 221–38

McConnel, James, '"Apres la guerre": John Redmond, The Irish Volunteers, and Armed Constitutionalism, 1913–1915', *English Historical Review*, 131, 553 (2016), 1445–70

McConnel, James, 'The Children of the Irish Parliamentary Party', *Irish Historical Studies*, 42, 161 (2018), 87–114

McConnel, James, 'The Franchise Factor in the Defeat of the Irish Parliamentary Party, 1885–1918', *Historical Journal*, 47, 2 (2004), 355–77

McConnel, James, *The Irish Parliamentary Party and the Third Home Rule Crisis* (Dublin, 2013)

McConnel, James, '"Jobbing with Tory and Liberal": Irish Nationalist MPs and the Politics of Patronage, 1880–1914', *Past and Present*, 188 (2005), 105–31

McConnel, James, 'John Redmond and Irish Catholic Loyalism', *The English Historical Review*, 125, 512 (2010), 83–111

McConnel, James, 'Recruiting Sergeants for John Bull? Irish Nationalist MPs and Enlistment during the Early Months of the Great War', *War in History*, 14, 4 (2007), 408–28

McCoole, Sinéad, 'Debating Not Negotiating: The Female TDs of the Second Dáil' in Liam Weeks and Mícheál Ó Fathartaigh, eds., *The Treaty: Debating and Establishing the Irish State* (Dublin, 2018), pp. 136–59

McCrery, Nigel, *All the King's Men: One of the Greatest Mysteries of the First World War Finally Solved* (London, 1999)

McGarry, Fearghal, '1916 and Irish Republicanism: Between Myth and History' in John Horne and Edward Madigan, eds., *Towards Commemoration: Ireland in War and Revolution* (Dublin, 2012), pp. 46–53

McGarry, Fearghal, 'Violence and the Easter Rising' in David Fitzpatrick, ed., *Terror in Ireland, 1916–1923* (Dublin, 2012), pp. 39–57

McGarry, Fearghal and James McConnel, eds., *The Black Hand of Republicanism: Fenianism in Modern Ireland* (Dublin, 2009)

McGaughey, Jane, *Ulster's Men: Protestant Unionist Masculinities and Militarization in the North of Ireland, 1912–1923* (Montreal, 2012)

McKernan, Luke, '"The Finest Cinema Performers That We Possess": British Royalty and the Newsreels, 1910–37', *The Court Historian*, 8, 1 (2003) 59–71

McKernan, Luke, '"The Modern Elixir of Life": Kinemacolor, Royalty and the Delhi Durbar', *Film History*, 21 (2009), 122–36

McKibbin, Ross, *Classes and Cultures: England, 1918–1951* (Oxford, 2000)

McLean, Roderick, 'Kaiser Wilhelm II and the British Royal Family: Anglo-German Dynastic Relations in Political Context, 1890–1914', *History*, 86 (2001), 478–502

McLean, Roderick, *Royalty and Diplomacy in Europe, 1890–1914* (Cambridge, 2000)

McNamara, Conor, *Liam Mellowes: Soldier of the Irish Republic. Selected Writings 1914–1922* (Dublin, 2019)

McNamara, Conor, *War and Revolution in the West of Ireland, 1913–1922* (Dublin, 2018)

Meleady, Dermot, *John Redmond: The National Leader* (Dublin, 2018)

Merck, Mandy, ed., *The British Monarchy on Screen* (Manchester, 2016)

Merkhens, Heidi and Frank Lorenz Müller, eds., *Sons and Heirs: Succession and Political Culture in 19th Century Europe* (London, 2015)

Meyer, Jessica, *Men of War: Masculinity and the First World War in Britain* (Basingstoke, 2009)

Middlebrook, Martin, *The First Day on the Somme* (London, 1976)

Millman, Brock, *Managing Domestic Dissent in First World War Britain* (Oxford, 2000)

Mombauer, Annika and Wilhelm Deist, eds., *The Kaiser: New Research on Wilhelm II's Role in Imperial Germany* (Cambridge, 2004)

Moore, Cormac, *The Birth of the Border: The Impact of Partition on Ireland* (Dublin, 2019)

Mort, Frank, 'Accessible Sovereignty: Popular Attitudes to British Royalty during the Great War', *Social History*, 45, 3 (2020), 328–59

Mort, Frank, 'Love in a Cold Climate: Letters, Public Opinion and Monarchy in the 1936 Abdication Crisis', *Twentieth Century British History*, 25, 1 (2014), 30–62

Mort, Frank, 'On Tour with the Prince: Monarchy, Imperial Politics and Publicity in the Prince of Wales's Dominion Tours 1919–20', *Twentieth Century British History*, 29, 1 (2018), 25–57

Mort, Frank, 'Safe for Democracy: Constitutional Politics, Popular Spectacle, and the British Monarchy, 1910–1914', *Journal of British Studies*, 58, 1 (2019), 109–41

Morton-Jack, George, *The Indian Empire at War. From Jihad to Victory: The Untold Story of the Indian Army in the First World War* (London, 2018)

Mosse, George, *Fallen Soldiers: Reshaping the Memory of the World Wars* (Oxford, 1991)

Moyd, Michelle, *Violent Intermediaries: African Soldiers, Conquest and Everyday Colonialism in German East Africa* (Athens, OH, 2014)

Mullen, John, *The Show Must Go On! Popular Song in Britain during the First World War* (London, 2016)

Müller, Frank and Heidi Mehrkens, eds., *Royal Heirs and the Uses of Soft Power in Nineteenth-Century Europe* (London, 2016)

Mulligan, William, *The Origins of the First World War* (Cambridge, 2010)

Munro, Kenneth, 'Canada as Reflected in Her Participation in the Coronation of Her Monarchs in the 20th Century', *Journal of Historical Sociology*, 14 (2001), 21–46

Murphy, James H., *Abject Loyalty: Nationalism and Monarchy during the Reign of Queen Victoria* (Washington, DC, 2001)

Murphy, Philip, *Monarchy and the End of Empire: The House of Windsor, the British Government, and the Postwar Commonwealth* (Oxford, 2015)

Myerly, Scott Hughes, '"The Eye Must Entrap the Mind": Army Spectacle and Paradigm in Nineteenth-Century Britain', *Journal of Social History*, 26, 1 (1992), 105–31

Nairn, Tom, *The Enchanted Glass: Britain and Its Monarchy* (London, 1988)

Nairn, Tom, *The Break-Up of Britain: Crisis and Neo-Nationalism* (London, 1977)

Nash, David and Antony Taylor, eds., *Republicanism in Victorian Society* (Stroud, 2000)

Nettelbeck, Amanda, *Indigenous Rights and Colonial Subjecthood: Protection and Reform in the Nineteenth-Century British Empire* (Cambridge, 2019)

Newbury, Colin, *Patrons, Clients and Empire: Chieftaincy and Over-Rule in Asia, Africa and the Pacific* (Oxford, 2003)

Newman, John Paul, ed., *Cultures of Victory and Victorious Societies in the Twentieth Century*, special edition of the *Journal of Contemporary History*, 54, 3 (2019)

Nicolson, Harold, *King George the Fifth: His Life and Reign* (London, 1952)

Nicolson, Harold, *Harold Nicolson: Diaries and Letters 1930–1964*, ed. Stanley Olsen (London, 1980)

Nicolson, Harold, *Harold Nicolson: Diaries and Letters, 1945–62*, ed. Nigel Nicolson (London, 1968)

Nicolson, Juliet, *The Great Silence, 1918–20: Living in the Shadow of the Great War* (London, 2010)

Nora, Pierre, ed., *Les Lieux de Mémoire*, 3 vols (Paris, 1984–92)

Novick, Ben, *Conceiving Revolution: Irish Nationalist Propaganda during the First World War* (Dublin, 2001)

Offer, Avner, 'Going to War in 1914: A Matter of Honour?', *Politics and Society*, 23, 2 (1995), 213–41

Olechnowicz, Andrzej, 'Historians and the Modern British Monarchy' in Andrzej Olechnowicz, ed., *The Monarchy and the British Nation 1780 to the Present* (Cambridge, 2007), pp. 6–44

Olechnowicz, Andrzej, '"A Jealous Hatred": Royal Popularity and Social Inequality' in Andrzej Olechnowicz, ed., *The Monarchy and the British Nation 1780 to the Present* (Cambridge, 2007), pp. 280–314

Olechnowicz, Andrzej, ed., *The Monarchy and the British Nation 1780 to the Present* (Cambridge, 2007)

Oliver, Terry, *For King, Country and Caddington 1914–1918* (Caddington, 2014)

Olusoga, David, *The World's War* (London, 2014)

Omissi, David, ed., *Indian Voices of the Great War: Soldiers' Letters, 1914–1918* (Basingstoke, 1999)

Oram, Gerard, '"The Administration of Discipline by the English is Very Rigid": British Military Law and the Death Penalty (1868–1918)', *Crime, Histoire et Sociétés*, 5, 1 (2001), 93–110

Otnes, Cele and Pauline Maclaren, *Royal Fever: The British Monarchy in Consumer Culture* (Berkeley, 2015)

Otte, Thomas, *July Crisis: The World's Descent into War, Summer 1914* (New York, Cambridge, 2014)

Owens, Edward, 'All the World Loves a Lover: Monarchy, Mass Media and the 1934 Royal Wedding of Prince George and Princess Marina', *English Historical Review*, 133, 562 (2018), 597–633

Owens, Edward, *The Family Firm: Monarchy, Mass Media and the British Public, 1932–53* (London, 2019)

Ozseker, Okan, *Forging the Border: Donegal and Derry in Times of Revolution, 1911–1925* (Dublin, 2019)

Packer, Ian, *Liberal Government and Politics 1905–1915* (Basingstoke, 2006)

Palmer, Alan W., *Twilight of the Habsburgs: The Life and Times of Emperor Francis Joseph* (New York, 1995)

Pankratz, Anette and Claus-Ulrich Viol, eds., *(Un)Making the Monarchy* (Heidelberg, 2017)

Parasecoli, Fabio and Peter Scholliers, eds., *A Cultural History of Food*, 6 vols (London, 2016)

Paris, Michael, *Warrior Nation: Images of War in British Popular Culture 1850–2000* (London, 2000)

Parker, Peter, *The Old Lie: The Great War and the Public School Ethos* (London, 1987)

Pašeta, Senia, *Before the Revolution: Nationalism, Social Change, and Ireland's Catholic Elite, 1879–1922* (Cork, 1999)

Pašeta, Senia, 'Nationalist Responses to Two Royal Visits to Ireland, 1900 and 1903', *Irish Historical Studies*, 31, 124 (1999), 488–504

Paul, Kathleen, *Whitewashing Britain: Race and Citizenship in the Postwar Era* (Ithaca, NY, 1997)

Paulmann, Johannes, '"Dearest Nicky": Monarchical Relations between Prussia, the German Empire and Russia during the Nineteenth Century' in Roger Bartlett and Karen Schönwälder, eds., *The German Lands and Eastern Europe: Essays on the History of Their Social, Cultural and Political Relations* (London, 1999), pp. 157–81

Paulmann, Johannes, *Pomp und Politik: Monarchenbegegnungen zwischen Ancien Régime und Erstem Weltkrieg* (Paderborn, 2000)

Paulmann, Johannes, 'Searching for a "Royal International": The Mechanics of Monarchical Relations in Nineteenth-Century Europe' in Martin Geyer and Johannes Paulmann, eds., *The Mechanics of Internationalism: Culture, Society and Politics from the 1840s to the First World War* (Oxford, 2001), 145–76

Pedersen, Susan, *After the Victorians: Private Conscience and Public Duty in Modern Britain* (London, 1994)

Pennell, Catriona, *A Kingdom United? Popular Responses to the Outbreak of the First World War in Britain and Ireland* (Oxford, 2012)

Peristiany, John G., ed., *Honour and Shame: The Values of Mediterranean Society* (Chicago, 1966)

Perry, Heather, *Recycling the Disabled: Army, Medicine, and Modernity in WWI Germany* (Manchester, 2014)

Peukert, Detlev, *The Weimar Republic. The Crisis of Classical Modernity* (London, 1991)

Phillips, Adrian, *The King Who Had to Go: Edward VIII, Mrs Simpson and the Hidden Politics of the Abdication Crisis* (London, 2018)

Plunkett, John, 'A Media Monarchy? Queen Victoria and the Radical Press, 1837–1901', *Media History*, 9 (2003), 3–18

Plunkett, John, *Queen Victoria: First Media Monarch* (Oxford, 2003)

Pocock, J. G. A., 'The Concept of Language and the *métier d'historien*: Some Considerations on Practice' in Anthony Pagden, *The Language of Political Theory in Early Modern Europe* (Cambridge, 1987), pp. 19–38

Polland, Imke, 'How to Fashion the Popularity of the British Monarchy: Alexandra, Princess of Wales and the Attractions of Attire' in Frank Lorenz Müller and Heidi Mehrkens, eds., *Royal Heirs and the Uses of Soft Power in Nineteenth-Century Europe* (London, 2016), pp. 201–21

Pope-Hennessy, James, *Queen Mary, 1867–1953* (London, 1959)

Pope-Hennessy, James, *The Quest for Queen Mary*, ed. Hugo Vickers (London, 2018)

Porter, Bernard, *The Absent-Minded Imperialists: Empire, Society and Culture in Britain* (Oxford, 2004)

Potter, Simon, *Broadcasting Empire: The BBC and the British World, 1922–1970* (Oxford, 2012)

Potter, Simon, 'Empire, Cultures and Identities in Nineteenth- and Twentieth-Century Britain', *History Compass*, 5, 1 (2007), 51–71

Prochaska, Frank, 'The Crowned Republic and the Rise of the Welfare Monarchy' in Frank-Lothar Kroll, and Dieter J. Weiß, eds., *Inszenierung oder Legitimation? / Monarchy and the Art of Representation: die Monarchie in Europa im 19. und 20. Jahrhundert. Ein deutsch-englischer Vergleich* (Berlin, 2015), pp. 141–50

Prochaska, Frank, 'George V and Republicanism 1917–1919', *Twentieth Century British History*, 10, 1 (1999), 27–51

Prochaska, Frank, *The Republic of Britain, 1760–2000* (London, 2000)

Prochaska, Frank, *Royal Bounty: The Making of a Welfare Monarchy* (New Haven, 1995)

Prochaska, Frank, *Royal Lives: Portraits of Past Royals by Those in the Know* (Oxford, 2002)

Prutsch, Markus J., *Making Sense of Constitutional Monarchism in Post-Napoleonic France and Germany* (Basingstoke, 2013)

Pryke, Sam, 'The Popularity of Nationalism in the Early British Boy Scout Movement', *Social History*, 23, 3 (1998), 309–24

Rappaport, Helen, *The Race to Save the Romanovs: The Truth behind the Secret Plans to Rescue Russia's Imperial Family* (London, 2018)

Readman, Paul, 'The Place of the Past in English Culture c. 1890–1914', *Past and Present*, 186 (2005) 147–99

Readman, Paul, *Storied Ground: Landscape and the Shaping of English National Identity* (Cambridge, 2018)

Rebentisch, Jost, *Die vielen Gesichter des Kaisers: Wilhelm II. in der deutschen und der britischen Karikatur (1888–1918)* (Berlin, 2000)

Reed, Charles, *Royal Tourists, Colonial Subjects and the Making of a British World, 1860–1911* (Manchester, 2016)

Reed, David, 'What a Lovely Frock: Royal Weddings and the Illustrated Press in the Pre-Television Age', *Court Historian*, 8 (2003), 41–50

Reimann, Aribert, *Der große Krieg der Sprachen: Untersuchungen zur historischen Semantik in Deutschland und England zur Zeit des Ersten Weltkriegs* (Essen, 2000)

Reinermann, Lothar, *Der Kaiser in England: Wilhelm II. und sein Bild in der britschen Öffentlichkeit* (Paderborn, 2001)

Reinermann, Lothar, 'Fleet Street and the Kaiser: British Public Opinion and Wilhelm II', *German History*, 26, 4 (2008), 469–85

Rey, Matthieu, 'The British, the Hashemites and Monarchies in the Middle East' in Robert Aldrich and Cindy McCreery, eds., *Crowns and Colonies: European Monarchies and Overseas Empires* (Manchester, 2016), pp. 227–44

Reznick, Jeffery S., *Healing the Nation: Soldiers and the Culture of Caregiving in Britain during the Great War* (Manchester, 2004)

Riall, Lucy, *Garibaldi: Invention of a Hero* (New Haven, London, 2007)

Richards, Andrew, *The Flag: The Story of Revd David Railton MC and the Tomb of the Unknown Warrior* (Oxford, Philadelphia, 2017)

Richards, Jeffery, 'Imperial Messages: The British Empire and Monarchy on Film', *Cultures*, 2 (1974), 79–114

Richards, Jeffery, *Imperialism and Music: Britain 1876–1953* (Manchester, 2001)

Richards, Jeffery, 'The Monarchy and Film, 1900–2006' in Andrzej Olechnowicz, ed., *The Monarchy and the British Nation 1780 to the Present* (Cambridge, 2007), pp. 258–79

Richardson, Neil, *According to Their Lights: Stories of Irishmen in the British Army, Easter 1916* (Cork, 2015)

Rieger, Bernhard and Martin Daunton, 'Introduction' in Bernhard Rieger and Martin Daunton, eds., *Meanings of Modernity: Britain from the Late Victorian Era to World War II* (Oxford, 2001), pp. 1–21

Robinson, Anna and Tara Hamilton Stubber, *Princess Mary: The Princess Royal, Countess of Harewood*, ed. David Lascelles (Harewood, Leeds, 2014)

Roby, Kinley, *The King, the Press and the People: A Study of Edward VII* (London, 1975)

Röhl, John C. G., 'Goodbye to All That (Again)? The Fischer Thesis, the New Revisionism and the Meaning of the First World War', *International Affairs*, 91, 1 (2015), 153–66

Röhl, John C. G., *The Kaiser and His Court: Wilhelm II and the Government of Germany* (Cambridge, 1995)

Röhl, John C. G., *Wilhelm II: der Weg in den Abgrund, 1900–1941* (Munich, 2008)

Röhl, John C. G., *Wilhelm II: die Jugend des Kaisers, 1859–1888* (Munich, 1993)

Röhl, John C. G., *Wilhelm II: Into the Abyss of War and Exile, 1900–1941*, transl. Sheila de Bellaigue and Roy Porter (Cambridge, 2015)

Röhl, John C. G., *Wilhelm II: The Kaiser's Personal Monarchy, 1888–1900* (Cambridge, 2004)

Röhl, John C. G. and Nicolaus Sombart, eds., *Kaiser Wilhelm II: New Interpretations. The Corfu Papers* (Cambridge, 1982)

Roper, Lyndal, 'Martin Luther's Body: The "Stout Doctor" and His Biographers', *American Historical Review*, 115, 2 (2010), 351–84

Roper, Michael, *The Secret Battle: Emotional Survival in the Great War* (Manchester, 2009)

Roper, Michael, 'Slipping out of View: Subjectivity and Emotion in Gender History', *History Workshop Journal*, 59 (2005), 57–72

Rose, Andrew, *The Prince, the Princess and the Perfect Murder* (London, 2013)

Rose, Kenneth, *George V* (London, 1983)

Rose, Kenneth, *Kings, Queens and Courtiers* (London, 1985)

Rosenthal, Michael, 'Knights and Retainers: The Earliest Version of Baden-Powell's Boy Scout Scheme', *Journal of Contemporary History*, 15, 4 (1980), 603–17

Rosenwein, Barbara H., 'Problems and Methods in the History of Emotions', *Passions in Context*, 1 (2010), 1–32

Rowbotham, Judith, '"How to Be Useful in War Time": Queen Mary's Leadership in the War Effort, 1914–1918' in Matthew Glencross and Judith Rowbotham, eds., *Monarchies and the Great War* (London, 2018), pp. 191–223

Roy, Franziska, Heike Liebau and Ravi Ahuja, eds., *'When the War Began, We Heard of Several Kings': South Asian Prisoners in World War I Germany* (Delhi, 2011)

Rubin, G. R., 'Parliament, Prerogative and Military Law: Who Had Legal Authority over the Army in the Late Nineteenth Century?', *The Journal of Legal History*, 18, 1 (1997), 45–84

Rubinstein, William D., 'Henry Page Croft and the National Party, 1917–22', *Journal of Contemporary History*, 9, 1 (1974), 129–48

Rüger, Jan, *The Great Naval Game: Britain and Germany in the Age of Empire* (Cambridge, 2009)

Ryu, Jiyi, 'The Queen's Dolls' House within the British Empire Exhibition: Encapsulating the British Imperial World', *Contemporary British History*, 33, 4 (2019), 464–82

Sanborn, Joshua, *Imperial Apocalypse: The Great War and the Destruction of the Russian Empire* (Oxford, 2014)

Sanborn, Joshua, 'The Mobilization of 1914 and the Question of the Russian Nation: A Re-Examination', *Slavic Review*, 59, 2 (2000), 267–89

Sapire, Hilary, 'Ambiguities of Loyalism: The Prince of Wales in India and Africa, 1921–22 and 25', *History Workshop Journal*, 73 (2012), 37–65

Saunders, Nicholas, ed., *Matters of Conflict: Material Culture, Memory and the First World War* (New York, London, 2004)

Saunders, Nicholas, *Trench Art: A Brief History and Guide, 1914–1939* (Barnsley, 2001)

Saunders, Nicholas, *Trench Art: Materialities and Memories of War* (London, 2003)

Saunders, Nicholas and Paul Cornish, eds., *Bodies in Conflict: Corporeality, Materiality and Transformation* (London, 2014)

Schabas, William, *The Trial of the Kaiser* (Oxford, 2018)

Schama, Simon, 'The Domestication of Majesty: Royal Family Portraiture 1500–1850', *The Journal of Interdisciplinary History*, 17, 1, (1986), 155–83

Schiera, Pierangelo, 'Europäisches Verfassungsdenken 1815–1847: die Zentralität der Legislativgewalt zwischen monarchischem Prinzip und Legitimität' in W. Daum, ed., with P. Brandt, M. Kirsch and A. Schlegelmilch, *Handbuch der europäischen Verfassungsgeschichte im 19. Jahrhundert, Institutionen und Rechtspraxis im gesellschaftlichen Wandel*, Vol. 2: *1815–1847* (Bonn, 2012), pp. 165–207

Schönpflug, Daniel, *Die Heiraten der Hohenzollern: Verwandtschaft, Politik und Ritual in Europa, 1640–1918* (Göttingen, 2013)

Schönpflug, Daniel, *Luise von Preußen: Königin der Herzen* (Munich, 2010)

Schulte, Regina, Pernille Arenfeldt, Martin Kohlrausch and Xenia von Tippelskirch, eds., *The Body of the Queen: Gender and Rule in the Courtly World, 1500–2000* (New York, Oxford, 2006)

Schwarz, Bill, *The White Man's World* (Oxford, 2013)

Schwarzenbach, Alexis, *Königliche Träume: eine Kulturgeschichte der Monarchie, 1789–1997* (Zurich, 2009)

Schwarzenbach, Alexis, 'Love, Marriage and Divorce: American and European Reactions to the Abdication of Edward' in Luisa Passerini, Liliana Ellena and Alexander C. T. Geppert, eds., *New Dangerous Liaisons: Discourses on Europe and Love in the Twentieth Century* (New York, 2010), pp. 137–57

Schwarzenbach, Alexis, 'Royal Photographs: Emotions for the People', *Contemporary European History*, 13 (2004), 255–80

Scott, Joan Wallach, 'Gender: A Useful Category of Historical Analysis', *American Historical Review*, 91, 5 (1986), 1053–75

Scott, Joan Wallach, *Gender and the Politics of History* (New York, 1999)

Scott, Joan Wallach in AHR Forum, 'Revisiting "Gender: A Useful Category of Historical Analysis"', *American Historical Review*, 113, 5 (2008), 1344–1430

Sellin, Volker, *Gewalt und Legitimität: die europäische Monarchie im Zeitalter der Revolutionen* (Munich, 2011)

Sellin, Volker, *European Monarchies from 1814 to 1906: A Century of Restoration* (Oldenbourg, 2017)

Shawcross, William, *Queen Elizabeth, the Queen Mother: The Official Biography* (Basingstoke, 2009)

Sheffield, Gary, *The Chief: Douglas Haig and the British Army* (London, 2012)

Sheffield, Gary, *Douglas Haig: From the Somme to Victory* (London, 2016)

Shils, Edward and Michael Young, 'The Meaning of the Coronation', *The Sociological Review*, 1, 2 (1953), 63–81

Signori, Elisa, 'La monarchia italiana e la Grande Guerra: il mito del "re soldato"' in Marina Tesoro, ed., *Monarchia, tradizione, identità nazionale: Germania, Giappone e Italia tra ottocento e novecento* (Milan, 2004), pp. 183–213

Simkins, Peter, *Kitchener's Army: The Raising of the New Armies, 1914–1916* (Manchester, 1988)

Singh, Gajendra, *The Testimonies of Indian Soldiers and the Two World Wars: Between Self and Sepoy* (London, 2014)

Sinha, Mrinalini, *Colonial Masculinity: The 'Manly Englishman' and the 'Effeminate Bengali' in the Late Nineteenth Century* (Manchester, 1995)

Skinner, Quentin, 'The Idea of a Cultural Lexicon', *Essays in Criticism*, 29, 3 (1979), 205–24

Smallwood, Stephanie, 'The Politics of the Archive and History's Accountability to the Enslaved', *History of the Present*, 6, 2 (2016), 117–32

Smith, Anthony D., *Theories of Nationalism* (London, 1971)

Smith, Anthony D., *The Ethnic Origins of Nations* (Oxford, 1986)

Smith, Bonnie G., *The Gender of History: Men, Women and Historical Practice* (Cambridge, MA, 2000)

Smith, Leonard V., *Sovereignty at the Paris Peace Conference of 1919* (Oxford, 2018)

Smith, Nicola, *The Royal Image and the English People* (Aldershot, 2001)

Smith, Richard, *Jamaican Volunteers in the First World War: Race, Masculinity and the Development of National Consciousness* (New York, Manchester, 2004)

Snape, Michael, *God and the British Army: Religion and the British Army in the First and Second World Wars* (London, 2005)

Sombart, Nicolaus, 'The Kaiser in His Epoch: Some Reflections on Wilhelmine Society, Sexuality and Culture' in Nicolaus Sombart and John Röhl, eds., *Kaiser Wilhelm II: New Interpretations. The Corfu Papers* (Cambridge, 1982), pp. 287–312

Sorg, Moritz, 'From Equilibrium to Predominance: Foreign Princes and Great Power Politics in the Nineteenth Century', *Journal of Modern European History*, 16, 1 (2018) 81–104

Stamp, Gavin, *The Memorial to the Missing of the Somme* (London, 2006)

Stedman Jones, Gareth, 'The "Cockney" and the Nation' in David Feldman and Gareth Stedman Jones, eds., *Metropolis: Histories and Representations since 1800* (London, 1989), pp. 272–324

Stevenson, David, *1917: War, Peace and Revolution* (London, 2017)

Stewart, Frank, *Honor* (Chicago, 1994)

Stewart-Wilson, Mary, *Queen Mary's Doll's House* (London, 1988)

Stibbe, Matthew, 'Kaiser Wilhelm II: The Hohenzollerns at War' in Matthew Hughes and Matthew Seligmann, eds., *Leadership in Conflict: 1914–1918* (London, 2000)

Stock, Paul 'Towards a Language of "Europe": History, Rhetoric, Community', *The European Legacy: Towards New Paradigms*, 20, 6 (2017), 647–66

Strachan, Hew, *The Politics of the British Army* (Oxford, 1997)

Strasdin, Kate, 'Empire Dressing: The Design and Realization of Queen Alexandra's Coronation Gown', *Journal of Design History*, 25 (2012), 155–70

Streets, Heather, *Martial Races: The Military, Race and Masculinity in British Imperial Culture, 1857–1914* (Manchester, 2004)

Szreter, Simon and Kate Fisher, *Sex before the Sexual Revolution: Intimate Life in England, 1918–1963* (Cambridge, 2010)

Taylor, Antony, *'Down with the Crown': British Anti-Monarchism and Debates about Royalty since 1790* (London, 1999)

Taylor, Antony, '"Pig-Sticking Princes": Royal Hunting, Moral Outrage and the Republican Opposition to Animal Abuse in 19th- and early 20th-Century Britain', *History*, 89, 293 (2004), 30–48

Taylor, Antony and Luke Trainor, 'Monarchism and Anti-Monarchism: Anglo-Australian Comparisons, c. 1870–1901', *Social History*, 24 (1999), 158–73

Taylor, Miles, 'The British Royal Family and the Colonial Empire from the Georgians to Prince George' in Robert Aldrich and Cindy McCreery, eds., *Crowns and Colonies: European Monarchies and Overseas Empires* (Manchester, 2016), pp. 27–50

Thane, Pat, *Divided Kingdom: A History of Britain 1900 to the Present* (London, 2019)

Thompson, Francis M. L., ed., *Cambridge Social History of Britain 1750–1950*, 3 vols (Cambridge, 1990)

Thompson, Francis M. L., *English Landed Society in the Nineteenth Century* (London, 1963)

Thompson, James, *British Political Culture and the Idea of 'Public Opinion', 1867–1914* (Cambridge, 2013)

Thompson, Mathew, 'Psychology and the "Consciousness of Modernity" in Early Twentieth-Century Britain' in Bernhard Rieger and Martin Daunton, eds., *Meanings of Modernity: Britain from the Late Victorian Era to World War II* (Oxford, 2001), pp. 97–115

Tinniswood, Adrian, *Behind the Throne: A Domestic History of the Royal Household* (London, 2018)

Tonkin, Elizabeth and Dominic Bryan, 'Political Ritual: Temporality and Tradition' in Asa Boholm, ed., *Political Ritual* (Gothenburg, 1996), pp. 14–36

Tosh, John, *Manliness and Masculinities in Nineteenth-Century Britain: Essays on Gender, Family and Empire* (London, 2016)

Tosh, John, 'What Should Historians Do with Masculinity? Reflections on Nineteenth-Century Britain', *History Workshop Journal*, 38, 1 (1994), 179–202

Trentmann, Frank, 'Materiality in the Future of History: Things, Practices and Politics', *Journal of British Studies*, 47 (2009), 283–307

Trethewey, Rachel, *Before Wallis: Edward VIII's Other Women* (Stroud, 2018)

Trethewey, Rachel, *Pearls before Poppies: The Story of the Red Cross Appeal* (Stroud, 2018)

Tumblin, Jesse, *The Quest for Security: Sovereignty, Race and the Defense of the British Empire, 1898–1931* (Cambridge, 2019)

Turner, Frank M., 'Rainfall, Plagues and the Prince of Wales', *Journal of British Studies*, 13 (1974) 46–65

Turner, John, *British Politics and the Great War: Coalition and Conflict, 1915–1918* (London, New Haven, 1992)

Tynan, Jane, *British Army Uniform and the First World War: Men in Khaki* (London, 2013)

Ugolini, Laura, 'War-Stained: British Combatants and Uniforms, 1914–1918', *War and Society*, 33, 3 (2014) 155–71

Ungari, Andrea, *La guerra del re: monarchia, sistema politico e forze armate nella Grande Guerra* (Milan, 2018)

Urbach, Karina, *Go-Betweens for Hitler* (Oxford, 2015)

Van Ginderachter, Maarten, 'Public Transcripts of Royalism: Pauper Letters to the Belgian Royal Family (1880–1940)' in Gita Deneckere and Joeren Deploige, eds., *Mystifying the Monarch: Studies on Discourse, Power and History* (Amsterdam, 2006), pp. 223–34

Van Ypersele, Laurence, *Le roi Albert: histoire d'un mythe* (Ottignies, 1995)

Vickers, Hugo 'Monarchy in Wartime: King George V and King George VI' in Peter Liddle, John Bourne and Ian Whitehead, eds., *The Great World War, 1914–1945*, Vol. 1: *Lightning Strikes Twice* (London, 2000), pp. 369–82

Villa, Valentina, 'The Victorious King: The Role of Victor Emmanuel III in the Great War' in Matthew Glencross and Judith Rowbotham, eds., *Monarchies and the Great War* (London, 2018), pp. 225–49

Virgili, Fabrice, *La France virile: des femmes tondues à la Libération* (Paris, 2000)

Waites, Bernard, *A Class Society at War: Britain 1914–1918* (Leamington Spa, 1987)

Wake, Jehanne, *Princess Louise: Queen Victoria's Unconventional Daughter* (London, 1988)

Walsh, Maurice, *Bitter Freedom: Ireland in a Revolutionary World, 1918–1923* (London, 2015)

Walsh, Michael, *Brothers in War* (London, 2011)

Ward, Paul, *Britishness Since 1870* (London, 2004)

Warren, Allen, 'Sir Robert Baden-Powell, the Scout Movement and Citizen Training in Great Britain, 1900–1920', *The English Historical Review*, 101, 399 (1986), 376–98

Watson, Alexander, *Enduring the Great War: Combat, Morale and Collapse in the German and British Armies, 1914–1918* (Cambridge, 2008)

Watson, Francis 'The Death of George V', *History Today*, 36, 12 (December 1986), 21–30

Weeks, Liam and Mícheál Ó Fathartaigh, eds., *The Treaty: Debating and Establishing the Irish State* (Dublin, 2018)

Wehler, Hans-Ulrich, *Das deutsche Kaiserreich, 1871–1918* (Göttingen, 1973)

Wehler, Hans-Ulrich, *Deutsche Gesellschaftsgeschichte*, 5 vols (Munich, 1987–2008)

Wellington, Jennifer, *Exhibiting War: The Great War, Museums and Memory in Britain, Canada and Australia* (Cambridge, 2017)

Whelan, Kevin, *The Tree of Liberty: Radicalism, Catholicism and the Construction of Irish Identity, 1760–1830* (Cork, 1996)

Wilkinson, Alan, *The Church of England and the First World War* (London, 1996)

Willan, B. P., 'The South African Native Labour Contingent, 1916–1918', *The Journal of African History*, 19, 1 (1978), 61–86

Williams, Richard, *The Contentious Crown: Public Discussion of the British Monarchy in the Reign of Queen Victoria* (Aldershot, 1997)

Williamson, Philip, 'The Monarchy and Public Values, 1910–1953' in Andrzej Olechnowicz, ed., *The Monarchy and the British Nation, 1780 to the Present* (Cambridge, 2007), pp. 223–57

Williamson, Philip, *National Crisis and National Government: British Politics, the Economy and Empire 1926–1932* (Cambridge, 1992)

Williamson, Philip, 'National Days of Prayer: The Churches, the State and Public Worship in Britain, 1899–1957', *English Historical Review* 128, 531 (2013), 323–66

Williamson, Philip, 'State Prayers, Fasts and Thanksgivings: Public Worship in Britain 1830–1897', *Past and Present*, 200 (2008), 121–74

Winegard, Timothy C., *For King and Kanata: Canadian Indians and the First World War* (Winnipeg, 2012)

Winegard, Timothy C., *Indigenous Peoples of the British Dominions and the First World War* (New York, 2011)

Winter, Jay, 'Beyond Glory? Cultural Divergences in Remembering the Great War in Ireland, Britain and France' in John Horne and Edward Madigan, eds., *Towards Comemmoration: Ireland in War and Revolution* (Dublin, 2012), pp. 134–44

Winter, Jay, 'British National Identity and the First World War' in Simon J. D. Green and R. C. Whiting, *The Boundaries of the State in Modern Britain* (Cambridge, 1996), pp. 261–77

Winter, Jay, ed., *The Cambridge History of the First World War*, 3 vols (Cambridge, 2014)

Winter, Jay, *Sites of Memory, Sites of Mourning: The Great War in European Cultural History* (Cambridge, 1995)

Winter, Jay, *Socialism and the Challenge of War: Ideas and Politics in Britain 1912–18* (London, 1974)

Winter, Jay, *War beyond Words: Languages of Remembrance from the Great War to the Present* (Cambridge, 2017)

Winter, Jay and Emmanuel Sivan, 'Setting the Framework' in Jay Winter and Emmanuel Sivan, eds., *War and Remembrance in the Twentieth Century* (Cambridge, 2009), pp. 6–39

Wittman, Laura, *The Tomb of the Unknown Soldier: Modern Mourning and the Reinvention of the Mystical Body* (Stanford, 2011)

Wolffe, John, *God and Greater Britain: Religion and National Life in Britain and Ireland, 1843–1945* (London, 1994)

Wolffe, John, *Great Deaths: Grieving, Religion and Nationhood in Victorian and Edwardian Britain* (Oxford, 2000)

Wolffe, John, 'The People's King: The Crowd and the Media at the Funeral of Edward VII, May 1910', *Court Historian*, 8 (2003), 23–30

Wolffe, John, 'Protestantism, Monarchy and the Defence of Christian Britain, 1837–2005' in Callum Brown and Michael Snape, eds., *Secularisation in the Christian World* (Aldershot, 2010), pp. 57–74

Wolffe, John, 'The Religions of the Silent Majority' in Gerald Parsons, ed., *The Growth of Religious Diversity: Britain from 1945*, Vol. 1: *Traditions* (London 1993), pp. 305–46

Woodcare, Elena, Lucinda H. S. Dean, Chris Jones, Zita Rohr and Russell Martin, *The Routledge History of Monarchy* (London, 2019)

Woods, Judith, 'Edward, Prince of Wales's Tour of India, October 1921–March 1922', *Court Historian*, 5 (2000), 217–21

Wortman, Richard S., *Scenarios of Power: Myth and Ceremony in Russian Monarchy*, 2 vols (Princeton, 1995–2000)

Yeomans, Henry, *Alcohol and Moral Regulation: Public Attitudes, Spirited Measures and Victorian Hangovers* (Bristol, 2014)

Ziegler, Philip, 'Edward VIII: The Modern Monarch?', *The Court Historian*, 8, 1 (2003), 73–83

Ziegler, Philip, *King Edward VIII: The Official Biography* (London, 1990)

Zweiniger-Bargielowska, Ina, 'Keep Fit and Play the Game: George VI, Outdoor Recreation and Social Cohesion in Interwar Britain', *Cultural and Social History*, 11, 1 (2014), 111–29

Zweiniger-Bargielowska, Ina, 'Royal Death and Living Memorials: The Funerals and Commemoration of George V and George VI, 1936–52', *Historical Research*, 89, 243 (2016), 158–75

Zweiniger-Bargielowska, Ina, 'Royal Rations', *History Today*, 43 (1993), 13–15

Unpublished Theses, Manuscripts and Papers

Beatty, Aidan, 'Royalism in Republicanism: The Political Vocabulary of Irish National Sovereignty, 1912–1924', Unpublished paper, open access work-in-progress: www.academia.edu/38553631/Royalism_in_Republicanism_The_Political_Vocabulary_of_Irish_Sovereignty_1912-1924_Work_in_Progress,_accessed 7/12/2019

Cook, Kathryn, 'The Monarchy Is More than the Monarch: Australian Perceptions of the Public Life of Edward, Prince of Wales, 1916–1936' (Unpublished DPhil thesis, Australian National University, 2017), https://openresearch-repository.anu.edu.au/bitstream/1885/117268/1/Cook%20Thesis%202017.pdf, accessed 13/4/2021

Curtis, Jonathan, 'Methodism and Abstinence: A History of the Methodist Church and Teetotalism' (Unpublished PhD thesis, University of Exeter, 2018)

Demiaux, Victor, 'La construction rituelle de la victoire dans les capitales européennes après la Grande Guerre (Bruxelles, Bucarest, Londres, Paris, Rome)' (PhD thesis, Ecole des hautes études en sciences sociales, Paris, 2013)

Glencross, Matthew, 'The Influence of Royal Tours on the Conduct of British Diplomacy 1901–1918' (Unpublished PhD thesis, King's College, London, 2014)

Lauwers, Delphine, 'Le Saillant d'Ypres entre reconstruction et construction d'un lieu de mémoire: un long processus de négociations mémorielles de 1914 à nos jours' (PhD thesis, European University Institute, 2014)

Lewis, Jonathan, 'Jewish Chaplaincy in the British Armed Forces, from Its Inception in 1892 until the Present Day' (Unpublished PhD thesis, UCL, 2020)

Naylor, Stanley, 'Remembrance "Lest We Forget": To the Memory of the Gallant Sons of Kirton Who Unstintingly Gave Their Lives for King and Country in Two Great Wars; 1914–1918; 1939–1945' (Unpublished history, Boston, 2008)

INDEX